Social Work Research and Evaluation

Quantitative and Qualitative Approaches

Sixth Edition

Richard M. Grinnell, Jr.
Illinois State University

Contents in Brief

Contents in Detail

PART III   MEASUREMENT IN SOCIAL WORK RESEARCH

PART V   DATA COLLECTION METHODS

Preface

WITH THE INPUT from hundreds of students and instructors who used the previous five editions of *Social Work Research and Evaluation: Quantitative and Qualitative Approaches*, we have refined this edition with their comments in mind. Nevertheless, the audience of this edition remains the same as the previous ones—advanced undergraduate and beginning graduate social work students who are taking a one-semester (or quarter) research methods course. The book is particularly useful for MSW foundation research courses.

THE GOAL OF THE BOOK

As before, our emphasis continues to be on how the goals of social work are furthered by the research process. Our belief is that research endeavors underlie and support our profession. Thus, research in social work is presented as more than just a way to solve human problems, or to add to our knowledge base, or to guide practice—though it is all of these. For over two decades, this book has symbolized tradition and change; it has applied timeless issues of research design and measurement to changing methodologies and social concerns. It has broken some traditions and has taught readers to try new research methods without losing sight of the old.

Many research instructors first cover basic research methodology and then apply this course content to more advanced research courses that specialize in single-system designs (case-level evaluation) or program evaluations. Accordingly, we have designed this book to give students the basic methodological foundation they need in order to obtain the advanced knowledge and skills presented in these two specialized research courses.

EXPERTISE OF CONTRIBUTORS

Collaborative efforts are certainly not uncommon in academia. In fact, most of the success this book has enjoyed can be attributed to its collaborative nature. We have once again secured an excellent and diverse group of social work research educators. The thirty-one contributors know firsthand, from their own extensive teaching and practice experiences, what social work students need to know in relation to research. They have subjected themselves to a discipline totally uncommon in compendia—that is, writing in terms of what is most needed for an integrated basic research methods book, rather than writing in line with their own predilections. To further our efforts to produce a book that is consistent across chapters, the content has been revised and annotated extensively to maintain a common editorial approach and writing style.

STUDENT LEARNING FEATURES

We have made an extraordinary effort to make this edition less expensive, more esthetically pleasing, and much more useful for students than ever before. In addition, we have incorporated a number of learning features social work students will find useful:

- Numerous boxes are inserted throughout the book to complement and expand on the chapters; these boxes present interesting research examples, provide additional aids to learning, and offer historical, social, and political contexts of social work research.
- The book's content is explained in terms of social work examples that students can easily understand. In recognition of the need for us to be knowledgeable of their needs and concerns, many of our examples center around women and minorities. Special consideration has been given to the application of research methods concerning these groups.

- Numerous tables and figures have been used to provide visual representations of the concepts presented in the book.
- A comprehensive student glossary has been added to this edition.
- An integrated *Student Study Guide* (by Yvonne A. Unrau, Judy L. Krysik, and Richard M. Grinnell, Jr.) is available with this edition.

NEW CONTENT

A tremendous amount of new content has been added to this edition in an effort to keep current, while retaining material that has stood the test of time. Some research instructors have expressed disappointment that several of the chapters in the earlier editions have been deleted. In general, chapters were dropped because they were not being assigned as required reading in a majority of research courses, and it was necessary to make room for new ideas and development while retaining a manageable and accessible size for this revision. The work of former contributors is still readily available in many copies of the preceding editions, however.

What's New in This Edition?

Compared to the fifth edition, this one contains seven new chapters (in addition to a glossary):

- Chapter 2, "Science, Society, and Research"
- Chapter 3, "Research Contexts"
- Chapter 4, "Research Ethics"
- Chapter 7, "Utilization of Research Approaches"
- Chapter 20, "Writing Research Proposals"
- Chapter 21, "Writing Research Reports"
- Chapter 22, "Evaluating Research Reports"
- "Glossary"

Four of the chapters that appeared in the fifth edition now have new authors in the sixth:

- Chapter 5, "Formulating Research Questions"
- Chapter 6, "Research Approaches"
- Chapter 23, "Single-System Designs"
- Chapter 24, "Program-Level Evaluation"

With slight editing, fourteen chapters in the sixth edition have remained essentially the same as in the fifth:

- Chapter 1, "Introduction to Research"
- Chapter 8, "Measuring Variables"
- Chapter 9, "Measuring Instruments"
- Chapter 10, "Designing Measuring Instruments"
- Chapter 11, "Sampling"
- Chapter 12, "Group Research Designs"
- Chapter 13, "Case Research Designs"
- Chapter 14, "Participant Observation"
- Chapter 15, "Survey Research"
- Chapter 16, "Secondary Analysis"
- Chapter 17, "Utilizing Existing Statistics"
- Chapter 18, "Content Analysis"
- Chapter 19, "Selecting a Data Collection Method and Data Source"
- Chapter 25, "Evaluation in Action"

In a nutshell, over one-third of this edition contains new chapters compared to the previous one; 15 percent of the chapters in the previous edition have been totally rewritten by new authors; and about half of the chapters from the last edition have essentially stayed the same in the sixth.

CONTENT TAILORED TO THE CSWE'S REQUIREMENTS

As with the previous editions, we have written this one to comply with the Council on Social Work Education's (Council's) research requirements for accredited schools and departments of social work at the undergraduate and graduate levels.

NEW ORGANIZATION

Over the years, we have received hundreds of comments from users of the first five editions. With these comments, and with the Council's research requirements in mind, we determined the specific topics to cover, the depth of the topics covered, and the sequencing of chapters within the book.

As in the preceding five editions, this one is neither a brief primer in social work research nor a book intended for use as a reference manual. With a tremendous amount of instructor and student input, this edition has been reorganized into seven parts and 25 chapters. The new organization is an attempt to make the book more functional, realistic, and manageable for students and instructors alike.

LOGICAL AND FLEXIBLE TEACHING PLAN

The book is organized in a way that makes good sense in teaching fundamental research methods. Many other sequences that could be followed would make just as much sense, however. The chapters (and parts) in this book were consciously planned to be independent of one another. They can be read out of the order in which they are presented, or they can be selectively omitted. However, they will probably make the most sense to students if they are read in the sequence as presented, because each builds upon the preceding one.

In general, this edition is organized to help students master eight basic learning objectives:

Objective 1: Understand the Place of Research in Social Work
— Chapter 1

Objective 2: Understand Social Work Research Contexts and Ethics
— Chapters 2, 3, and 4

Objective 3: Understand How to Formulate Research Questions
— Chapters 5, 6, and 7

Objective 4: Understand How Measurement Is Used in Social Work
— Chapters 8 through 10

Objective 5: Understand the Logic of Research Designs
— Chapters 11 through 13

Objective 6: Understand How to Collect Data
— Chapters 14 through 19

Objective 7: Understand How to Write and Evaluate Proposals/Reports
— Chapters 20 through 22

Objective 8: Understand How to Evaluate Practices and Programs
— Chapters 23 through 25

INSTRUCTOR'S MANUAL AND TEST BANK IS AVAILABLE

A complementary copy of the *Instructor's Manual and Test Bank* is available with this edition. It was written by Christopher B. Aviles, Ph.D. The 375-page *Instructor's Manual and Test Bank* (including a computer disk) contains over 40 true-false and 40 multiple-choice questions for a majority of the chapters in the book. It was written on a mastery learning model where each question has its parallel version (i.e., parallel forms). Thus, research instructors can test two different research sections of the same course without constructing two different exams.

Research instructors who use this book in the classroom can receive a hard copy and computer disk that contains the *Instructor's Manual and Test Bank* by faxing a request on letterhead stationery to Richard M. Grinnell, Jr. (309) 438-5880, or by calling (309) 438-5913. Please state the platform (e.g., IBM, Mac, ASCII) and the word processing language (e.g., WordPerfect, Word) you desire. You can also e-mail your request to: rgrinn@ilstu.edu. Please allow three days for shipping. The *Instructor's Manual and Test Bank* can also be sent to you via e-mail as an attachment.

ACKNOWLEDGMENTS

Many individuals, in addition to the over 100 contributors since the book's conception, have seriously augmented the continual development and preparation of this text. For individual chapters, a number of people aided in the production by critiquing and reacting to chapter drafts, suggesting text and/or chapter content, and encouraging others to contribute.

These include: Susan Anderson-Ray, David Austin, Mike Austin, Don Beless, Martin Bloom, Floyd Bolitho, Ed Borgatta, Ed Brown, Harry Butler, Harris Chaiklin, Heather Coleman, Don Collins, Kayla Conrad, Jill Crowell, Rick Dangel, Inger Davis, Liane Davis, Wayne Duehn, Eugene Durman, Paul Ephross, Irwin Epstein, Roland Etcheverry, Michale Fabricant, Phil Fellin, Joel Fischer, Chuck Garvin, Neil Gilbert, Lewayne Gilchrist, Tom Givler, Harvey Gochros, Richard Gorsuch, Don Granvold, Tony Grasso, Ernest Greenwood, Jim Gripton, Charles Grosser, Lynda Hacker, Bud Hansen, Diane Harrison, Joseph Heffernan, George Hoshino, Walt Hudson, Jackie Ismael, Ittleson Foundation, Inc., Siri Jayaratne, Anne Kincaid, Mike Kolevzon, Mike Lauderdale, Alice Lieberman, E.E. LeMasters, Charles Levy, Rona Levy, Duncan Lindsey, Mary Ann Lynch, Mary Martin Lynch, Tony Maluccio, Rachel Marks, Bob Mayer, John McAdoo, Clyde McDaniel, Grant McDonald, Lynn McDonald, Tom McDonald, Robert Morris, Ed Mullen, Judy Nelson, and Kim Ng.

Others include: Dan O'Brien, Don Pilcher, Norman Polansky, Alan Press, Paul Raffoul, Reyes Ramos, Frank Raymond, Rick Reamer, Bill Reid, Joan Robertson, Peggy Rodway, Sheldon Rose, Marti Royer, Mary Russell, Beatrice

Saunders, Steve Schinke, Dick Schoeck, John Schuerman, Jim Seaberg, Judith Sears, Fred Seidl, Larry Shulman, Deb Siegel, Max Siporin, Norm Smith, Harry Specht, Dick Stuart, Paul Stuart, Jim Taylor, Eli Teram, Ed Thomas, Ron Toseland, Tony Tripodi, John Tropman, Barbara Turman, Lynn Vogal, Tom Watts, Margaret Whelan, Stan Witkin, Sidney Zimbalist, and Lou Zurcher.

Within the limits of time frames and resources, we have tried to follow the suggestions offered by these colleagues. However, they should not be held responsible for our sins of omission or commission. Special thanks go to the contributors for their hard work and individual participation. This book is a product of their experiences and their desire to introduce others to social work research, which they have found so challenging and stimulating.

As usual, the excellent staff at F.E. Peacock Publishers has been more than helpful in seeing this project through to completion.

A FINAL WORD

The field of research in our profession is continuing to grow and develop. We believe this edition will contribute to that growth. A seventh edition is anticipated, and suggestions for it are more than welcome. Please send your comments directly to:

Richard M. Grinnell, Jr.
Professor and Director
School of Social Work
Illinois State University
Normal, Illinois 61790 - 4650
rgrinn@ilstu.edu

Richard M. Grinnell, Jr.

Contributors

Gerald J. Bostwick, Jr., Ph.D., is an associate professor within the School of Social Work at the University of Cincinnati, Cincinnati, Ohio 54221.

Elaine Bouey, M.ED., is a Librarian at The University of Calgary, Calgary, Alberta T2N 1N4, Canada.

Kevin Corcoran, Ph.D., is a professor within the Graduate School of Social Work at Portland State University, Portland, Oregon 97207.

David E. Cournoyer, Ph.D., is an associate professor within the School of Social Work at the University of Connecticut, West Hartford, Connecticut 06117.

Irwin Epstein, Ph.D., is a professor within the Hunter College School of Social Work, New York, New York 10021.

Joel Fischer, DSW, is a professor within the School of Social Work at the University of Hawaii at Manoa, Honolulu, Hawaii 96822

Cynthia Franklin, Ph.D., is a professor within the School of Social Work at The University of Texas at Austin, Austin, Texas 78712.

Peter A. Gabor, Ph.D., is a professor within the Faculty of Social Work at The University of Calgary, Calgary, Alberta T2N 1N4, Canada.

Lewayne D. Gilchrist, Ph.D., is a professor within the School of Social Work at the University of Washington, Seattle, Washington 98105.

Jane F. Gilgun, Ph.D., is a professor within the School of Social Work at the University of Minnesota at Minneapolis, Minneapolis, Minnesota 55455.

Richard M. Grinnell, Jr., Ph.D., is a professor within the School of Social Work at Illinois State University, Normal, Illinois 61790.

Carol Ing, MS., is an instructor within the Child and Youth Care Program at Lethbridge Community College, Lethbridge, Alberta P1K 1L6, Canada.

Catheleen Jordan, Ph.D., is a professor within the School of Social Work at the University of Texas at Arlington, Arlington, Texas 76019.

Waldo C. Klein, Ph.D., is an associate professor within the School of Social Work at the University of Connecticut, West Hart-ford, Connecticut 06117.

Judy L. Krysik, Ph.D., is an assistant professor with the Graduate School of Social Work at The University of Denver, Denver, Colorado 80208.

Nancy S. Kyte, M.S.W., is a social worker within the Department of Behavioral Medicine at Clermont Mercy Hospital, Batavia, Ohio 54221.

Craig W. LeCroy, Ph.D., is a professor within the School of Social Work at Arizona State University, Tempe, Arizona 85287.

Robert W. McClelland, Ph.D., is an associate professor within the Faculty of Social Work at the University of Calgary, Calgary, Alberta T2N 1N4, Canada.

Steven L. McMurtry, Ph.D., is a professor within the School of Social Welfare at the University of Wisconsin at Milwaukee, Milwaukee, Wisconsin 53201.

Charles H. Mindel, Ph.D., is a professor within the School of Social Work at the University of Texas at Arlington, Arlington, Texas 76019.

Kathryn E. Moss, Ph.D., is a senior research fellow, Jordan Institute for Families, School of Social Work, University of North Carolina at Chapel Hill, Chapel Hill, North Carolina 27599.

William J. Reid, DSW, is a professor within the School of Social Welfare at the State University of New York at Albany, Albany New York 12222.

Gayla Rogers, Ph.D., is a professor within the Faculty of Social Work at the University of Calgary, Calgary, Alberta T2N 1N4, Canada.

Russel K. Schutt, Ph.D., is a professor within the Department of Sociology at the University of Massachusetts, Boston, Massachusetts 02215.

Jackie D. Sieppert, Ph.D., is an associate professor within the Faculty of Social Work at the University of Calgary, Calgary, Alberta T2N 1N4, Canada.

Steven P. Schinke, Ph.D., is a professor within the School of Social Work at Columbia University, New York, New York 10025.

Gary Solomon, M.S.W., currently resides in Portland Oregon 97207.

Bruce A. Thyer, Ph.D., is a professor within the School of Social Work at the University of Georgia, Athens, Georgia 30602.

Yvonne A. Unrau, Ph.D., is an assistant professor within the School of Social Work at Illinois State University, Normal, Illinois 61790.

Robert W. Weinbach, Ph.D., is a distinguished emeritus professor within the College of Social Work at the University of South Carolina, Columbia, South Carolina 29208.

Margaret Williams, Ph.D., is an associate professor within the Faculty of Social Work at the University of Calgary, Calgary, Alberta T2N 1N4, Canada.

Part I

The Contexts of
Knowledge Generation

Richard M. Grinnell, Jr.

C h a p t e r 1

Introduction to Research

WHAT IS THE ROLE that research plays in contemporary social work
education and practice? In one word—*significant!* That is the position
of both the Council on Social Work Education (CSWE) and the
National Association of Social Workers (NASW). The CSWE is the official
"educational organization" that sets minimum curriculum standards for BSW
and MSW programs throughout North America. The NASW is a parallel
"practice organization" that works to enhance the professional growth and
development of practicing social workers. In a nutshell, both organizations
firmly believe in the relevance of research and evaluation to social work
education (Box 1.1) and social work practice (Box 1.2).

With Boxes 1.1 and 1.2 in mind, this book provides the beginning research
and evaluation content that must be taught in all accredited BSW and MSW
social work programs. Unlike card and palm readers as illustrated in Box 1.3,
contemporary social work practitioners are expected to have a substantial
research and evaluation knowledge base to guide and support their interventions. This knowledge base is generally derived from a social work research
and evaluation course such as the one that has required you to buy this book.

Box 1.1_____

Council on Social Work Education's
BSW and MSW Curriculum Research Content

B6.0—BSW Curriculum Content

- The research curriculum must provide an understanding and appreciation of a scientific, analytic approach to building knowledge for practice and to evaluating service delivery in all areas of practice. Ethical standards of scientific inquiry must be included in the research content.
- The research content must include quantitative and qualitative research methodologies; analysis of data, including statistical procedures; systematic evaluation of practice; analysis and evaluation of theoretical bases, research questions, methodologies, statistical procedures, and conclusions of research reports; and relevant technological advances.
- Each program must identify how the research curriculum contributes to the student's use of scientific knowledge for practice.

M6.0—MSW Curriculum Content

- The foundation research curriculum must provide an understanding and appreciation of a scientific, analytic approach to building knowledge for practice and for evaluating service delivery in all areas of practice. Ethical standards of scientific inquiry must be included in the research content.
- The research content must include qualitative and quantitative research methodologies; analysis of data, including statistical procedures; systematic evaluation of practice; analysis and evaluation of theoretical bases, research questions, methodologies, statistical procedures, and conclusions of research reports; and relevant technological advances.
- Each program must identify how the research curriculum contributes to the student's use of scientific knowledge for practice.

_____

Source: Council on Social
Work Education (2000)

HOW DO WE OBTAIN OUR KNOWLEDGE BASE?

Each of us already has a great deal of knowledge about various things. Some of the things we know stem from tradition because they are commonly thought of as "true" by everyone in our culture. We now "know" that the Earth is round; although, if we had been born a few centuries earlier, we would have "known" that it was flat. Some things we know because someone in authority told us about them: We may have been told that smoking causes cancer, or that when one spouse batters the other it results in a helpless response rather than flight.

Other things we know because we have personally experienced them or believe them to be true: We may have found out through experience that knives are sharp the first time we came into contact with one, or that we intuitively believe that the world would be a better place to live if there were

Box 1.2_____

NASW's *Code of Ethics for Research*

- Social workers should monitor and evaluate policies, and the implementation of programs, and practice interventions.
- Social workers should promote and facilitate evaluation and research to contribute to the development of knowledge.
- Social workers should critically examine and keep current with emerging knowledge relevant to social work and fully use evaluation and research evidence in their professional practice.
- Social workers engaged in evaluation or research should carefully consider possible consequences and should follow guidelines developed for the protection of evaluation and research participants. Appropriate institutional review boards should be consulted.
- Social workers engaged in evaluation or research should obtain voluntary and written informed consent from participants, when appropriate, without any implied or actual deprivation or penalty for refusal to participate; without undue inducement to participate; and with due regard for participants' well-being, privacy, and dignity. Informed consent should include information about the nature, extent, and duration of the participation requested and disclosure of the risks and benefits of participation in the research.
- When evaluation or research participants are incapable of giving informed consent, social workers should provide an appropriate explanation to the participants, obtain the participants' assent to the extent they are able, and obtain written consent from an appropriate proxy.
- Social workers should never design or conduct evaluation or research that does not use consent procedures, such as certain forms of naturalistic observation and archival research, unless rigorous and responsible review of the research has found it to be justified because of its prospective scientific, educational, or applied value and unless equally effective alternative procedures that do not involve waiver of consent are not feasible.
- Social workers should inform participants of their right to withdraw from evaluation and research at any time without penalty.
- Social workers should take appropriate steps to ensure that research participants have access to supportive services.
- Social workers engaged in evaluation or research should protect participants from unwarranted physical or mental distress, harm, danger, or deprivation.
- Social workers engaged in the evaluation of services should discuss collected information only for professional purposes and only with people professionally concerned with this information.
- Social workers engaged in evaluation or research should ensure the anonymity or confidentiality of participants and of the data obtained from them.
- Social workers should inform participants of any limits of confidentiality, the measures that will be taken to ensure confidentiality, and when any records containing research data will be destroyed.
- Social workers who report evaluation and research results should protect participants' confidentiality by omitting identifying information unless proper consent has been obtained authorizing disclosure.
- Social workers should report evaluation findings accurately. They should not fabricate results and should take steps to correct any errors later found in published data using standard publication methods.
- Social workers engaged in evaluation or research should be alert to and avoid conflicts of interest and dual relationships with participants, should inform participants when a real or potential conflict of interest arises, and should take steps to resolve the issue in a manner that makes participants' interests primary.
- Social workers should educate themselves, their students, and their colleagues about responsible research practices.

_____
Source: National Association of Social Workers (1999)

Box 1.3_____

Can A Psychic Card and Palm Reader Solve Human Problems?

Madame X is a psychic card and palm reader. She has practiced in our local community for several years and has gained the highest admiration of many people. She advertises in the local newspaper, claiming:

> With my advice and insight, I will guide and help you to a more successful life. I can help you with such things as love, business, health, and marriage. One visit will convince you that I can solve any of your problems—big or small.

A number of questions should immediately come to mind upon reading Madame X's self-proclaimed expertise: Can she really solve human problems? How does she do it? Is she effective in her problem solving? Is she more (or less) effective than others who also claim to solve such problems? A cynical social worker might even ask: What is the future of my social work practice if Madame X were to establish her practice in my community?

While it is doubtful that any of us would be threatened by Madame X's claims, her advertisement does serve to illustrate how the process and objectives of helping people can mistakenly be reduced to simplicity or, in this case, mysticism. A person who is a true believer in psychic card and palm reading would probably ask very few questions of Madame X. Most of us, however, would want to know much more about her knowledge base. We would want to ascertain why she feels she can take the complex process of human problem solving and claim to "solve any of your problems—big or small" by reading cards or palms.

It is less likely that similar questions would be addressed to social workers. Society generally makes certain assumptions regarding the extent of our knowledge base, the competency of our practice skills, and the effectiveness of our social service programs. Society is more discriminating about Madame X than it is about social workers because it has greater expectations for the way we develop our knowledge base and practice skills. Social workers—like all professionals (e.g., lawyers, physicians, nurses, architects, police officers)—are expected to have a good knowledge base to guide their interventions.

_____

Source: Grinnell, Rothery, and Thomlison (1993)

---

no war. Or, we know things are "true" because we heard "facts" via the media. The previous five example of ways of obtaining knowledge—tradition, authority, experience, intuition, and media—combined with the research method (the focus of this book)—form six ways of developing our knowledge base. These six ways are highly interactive with one another, but for the sake of simplicity, each one is discussed separately. Let us now turn our attention to the first way of obtaining knowledge—tradition.

Tradition

Most people tend to accept traditional cultural beliefs without much question. They may doubt some of them and test others for themselves, but, for the most part, they behave and believe as tradition demands. Such conformity has its uses, however. Society could not function if each custom and belief were

reexamined by each individual in every generation. On the other hand, unquestioning acceptance of traditional dictates can lead to stagnation and to the perpetuation of wrongs. It would be unfortunate if women had never been allowed to vote because "women had never traditionally voted," or if racial segregation were perpetuated because that was the "way things were done."

Authority

The reliance on authority figures is the second way we can "know" something. When Galileo looked through his telescope in the year 1610, for example, he saw four satellites circling the planet Jupiter. His discovery presented a problem, as it was truly believed that there were seven heavenly bodies: the Sun, the Moon, and five planets. Seven was a sacred number proclaimed by previous authority figures, but the addition of Jupiter's satellites brought the number to eleven.

And there was nothing mystic about the number eleven! It was partly for this reason that professors of philosophy denounced the telescope and refused to believe in the existence of Jupiter's satellites.

In the twentieth century, we may find it incredible that educated people would behave in this way. After all, the doubting professors in Galileo's time had only to look through the telescope in order to see Jupiter's satellites for themselves. Today's "see for yourself" philosophy is based on the belief that "true" knowledge can best be gained through research, which begins with "objective data" about the real world.

In the seventeenth century, obtaining knowledge through the research method was considered a less valid source of knowledge development than tradition and authority (in addition to experience and intuition, to be discussed shortly). Hence, the professors may not have accepted the "objective data" (in this case, their own personal observations) of their eyes as "*the* truth" if this "new truth" conflicted with traditional beliefs and the established authority of the state or church.

Questioning the Accuracy of Data

The same dilemma exists with authority as with tradition—the question of the accuracy of the data obtained. Students have a right to expect that data, or information, given to them by their teachers are current and accurate. They will not learn very much if they decide it is essential to verify everything the instructor says. In the same way, the general public trusts that statements made by "experts" will be true. This trust is necessary, since lay people usually have neither the time nor the energy to conduct or evaluate the specialized research studies leading to scientific discoveries.

Advertisers both use and misuse this necessary reliance on authority figures. Cat foods are promoted by veterinarians, since veterinarians are assumed to be experts on the nutritional needs of cats and it is expected that cat owners will heed their pronouncements. On the other hand, all kinds of products are promoted by movie stars, rock stars, and athletes, whose authority lies not in their specialized knowledge but only in their personal charisma and status in the public eye.

As might be expected, it is advisable to place most trust in experts speaking within their field of expertise and less trust in those who lack expert knowledge. Even experts can be wrong, however, and the consequences can sometimes be disastrous. A social work treatment intervention that was developed several decades ago provides a good example. The intervention focused on families in which one member suffered from schizophrenia, and primary treatment intervention was an attempt to change the family system.

At the time, authority figures in psychoanalysis and family therapy believed that schizophrenia was caused by faulty parenting, so emphasis was placed on such factors as parental discord, excessive familial interdependency, and mothers whose overprotective and domineering behaviors did not allow their children to develop individual identities.

Following this theory, some social workers assumed that all families with a schizophrenic member must be dysfunctional. Because they focused their interventions on changing the family system, they often inadvertently instilled guilt into the parents and increased tensions rather than helping the parents to cope with their child who had been diagnosed as schizophrenic.

Recent research studies have shown that schizophrenia is caused largely by genetic and other biological factors, not by bad parenting. Furthermore, one of the most effective social work interventions is to support the family in providing a nonstressful environment. It is not surprising that, previously, social workers acted on the beliefs of experts in schizophrenia without personally evaluating the research studies that had led to those beliefs. Had they investigated for themselves, and had they been trained in research techniques, they may have found that there was little real objective data to support the bad-parenting theory. Consequently, they may have been more supportive of parents and thus more effective helpers.

While we are in school, our learning is largely structured for us. It is likely that we will spend far more time as practicing social workers than we will in school; and there is an old saying that learning does not really begin until formal education has ended. Out in the field, we will still be required to attend workshops, conferences, and staff training sessions, but most of our learning will come from what we read and from what people tell us. Our reading material is likely to consist mostly of books and journal articles related to our specific field of practice—whether it be senior citizens, children who have been abused, adolescent offenders, or some other special group. Most of the articles that we read will deal with research studies; many of the books we come across will interpret, synthesize, and comment upon research studies. None of them

will explain how research studies ought to be conducted, because it is assumed we learned that in school. With this in mind, we now turn our attention to sorting out good advice.

Sorting Out "Advice" from "Good Advice"

When we first enter a social work agency, as either practicum students or a graduate social workers, our supervisors and colleagues will start to show us how the agencies run. We may be given a manual detailing agency policies and procedures: everything from staff holidays, to locking up client files at night, to standard techniques for interviewing children who have been physically and emotionally abused. Informally, we will be told other things: how much it costs to join the coffee club, whom to ask when we want a favor, whom to phone for certain kinds of information, and what form to complete to be put on the waiting list for a parking space.

In addition to this practical information, we may also receive advice about how to help clients. Colleagues may offer opinions about the most effective treatment intervention strategies. If we work in a child sexual abuse treatment agency, for example, it may be suggested to us that the nonoffending mother of a child who has been sexually abused does not need to address her own history of abuse in therapy in order to empathize with and protect her daughter. Such a view would support the belief that the best interventive approach is a behavioral/learning one, perhaps helping the mother learn better communication skills in her relationship with her daughter. Conversely, the suggestion may be that the mother's personal exploration is essential and that, therefore, the intervention should be of a psychodynamic nature.

Whatever the suggestion, it is likely that we, as beginning social workers, will accept it, along with the information about the coffee club and the parking space. We will want to fit in, to be a member of the team. If this is the first client for whom we have really been responsible, we may also be privately relieved that the intervention decision has been made for us. We may rightfully believe that colleagues, after all, have more experience than we and they should surely know best.

Perhaps they do know best. At the same time, it is important to remember that they also were once beginning social workers and they formed their opinions in the same way as we are presently forming ours. They too once trusted in their supervisors' knowledge bases and the experiences of their colleagues. Much of what we will initially be told is based upon tradition and authority. Like all knowledge derived from these two sources, the practice recommendations offered by our colleagues allow us to learn from the achievements and mistakes of those who have tried to do our job before us. We do not have to "reinvent the wheel." We are being given a head start.

On the other hand, knowledge derived from tradition and authority has the disadvantage that it can become too comfortable. We know that the traditional approaches to client problems practiced in our agency are effective because everyone says they are; we know that certain intervention strategies work because they have worked for years. And armed with this comfortable and certain knowledge, we may not look for better ways of helping our clients.

In addition, we may not wish to test the intervention methods presently employed to see if they work as well as our colleagues say. We may even be inclined to reject out-of-hand evidence that our present interventions are ineffective or that there is a better way. And if we do happen to seek and find new interventions, we may discover that our colleagues are unreceptive or even hostile. Tradition dies hard, and authority is not so easily relinquished.

In summary, authority is one of the many ways of knowing, and it sometimes gets confused with the use of personal practice experience and intuition as additional ways of knowing. We now turn our attention to how experience and intuition are used in the generation of social work knowledge.

Professional Experiences and Personal Intuition

The third and fourth ways of obtaining knowledge are through professional experience and personal intuition. Learning from professional experience is great—no one will ever deny this. Relying solely on personal intuition, sometimes referred to as *common sense,* however, is another matter. There are many reasons why we should not rely solely on personal intuitions when working with clients. Box 1.4 illustrates this point further by using a simple example we all can relate to—our own personal intuition.

Media Myths

The fifth way of obtaining knowledge is by watching television shows and movies in addition to reading newspapers and magazine articles. These four forms of communication provide rich information (right and wrong) about the social life of individuals and society in general. Most people, for example, who have had no contact with criminals learn about crime by these forms of communication. However, as we know too well, the media can easily perpetuate the myths of any given culture (Neuman, 1997):

> . . . The media show that most people who receive welfare are African American (most are actually non-African American), that most people who are mentally ill are violent and dangerous (only a small percentage actually are), and that most people who are elderly are senile and in nursing homes (a tiny minority are).
>
> Also, a selected emphasis on an issue by the media can change public thinking about it. For example, television repeatedly shows low-income, inner-city African-American youth using illegal drugs. Eventually, most people "know" that

urban African Americans use illegal drugs at a much higher rate than other groups in the United States, even though this notion is false. (p. 4)

The Research Method

This sixth method of obtaining knowledge is sometimes called the problem-solving method and contains two complementary research approaches to generating knowledge in our profession—the quantitative approach and the qualitative approach (Chapter 6).

We will highlight these throughout this book, as they are today's primary two approaches to obtaining knowledge in contemporary social work research. However, we emphasize that the other four forms of knowledge development are also of some importance in the knowledge-building enterprise.

On a very general level, and in the simplest of terms, the two research approaches have four highly interrelated generic phases:

Phase 1   Observing (or measuring) a person, an object, or an event
Phase 2   Making an assumption on the basis of the observation (or measurement)
Phase 3   Testing the assumption to see to what extent it is true
Phase 4   Revising the assumption on the basis of the test

Suppose, for example, we observe that the hairy males of our acquaintance seem more intelligent than males endowed with a lesser amount of body hair. It has, in fact, been suggested—though by no means "proven"—that body hair is related to intelligence, since the skin and brain develop from the same embryonic tissues. Therefore, we might make the assumption that, if males in general are placed on a continuum from the most hairy to the least hairy, those on the hairy end will be significantly more intelligent than those on the other end.

We might test this assumption by selecting a number of males, measuring their intelligence, and devising a means of measuring their body hair that is both accurate and socially acceptable. If we find that pronounced hairiness is positively associated with high intelligence in a significant number of cases, we can be reasonably certain that our original assumption was correct. If we find no such association, our assumption was probably wrong.

Whatever we find, our conclusions will be suspect until someone else has undertaken a similar study and confirmed our results. Utilizing the research method to obtain knowledge is a *public method of knowing*. It relies not on private avenues to knowledge—such as inspiration or visions—but rather on a careful sequence of activities that can be duplicated (as much as possible) by other people. We will be more certain of the relationship between hairiness

Box 1.4_____

Jane and Her Physician

Suppose one day Jane goes to a physician for a medical checkup because she has been feeling tired and depressed. After talking with her for a few minutes, the physician concludes that she has high blood pressure and gives her hypertension medication. Following the physician's advice, Jane takes the medication for a few months and begins to feel better. Since she is now feeling better, she phones the physician and asks if it is all right to stop taking the medication. The physician says yes.

At no time did the physician take her blood pressure, either to confirm the initial diagnostic hunch or to determine the effects of the medication. Hence, it was entirely possible that she was taking a drug for which she had no need, or a drug that could actually harm her, or that she stopped taking the medication that was helping her. The point here is that the physician made crucial decisions to begin and end intervention (treatment) without gathering all the necessary data.

Ethical social workers do *not* do what the physician did in the preceding two paragraphs. Just as the wrong medication has the potential to harm, so does the wrong social work intervention. In the past, some studies have shown that the recipients of social work services fare worse, or no better, than people who do not receive our services. Thus, we have a responsibility always to evaluate the impact of our interventions.

We must fully realize that we have no business intervening in other peoples' lives simply on the assumption that our *good* intentions lead to *good* client outcomes. Although we may mean well, our good intentions alone do not ensure that we really "help" our clients. Research and evaluation must be integrated within our practice so we can measure the effects of our helping efforts. We have a moral obligation to do this—even more so when clients have not asked for our services. Truly professional social workers never rely solely on their good intentions, intuitions, subjective judgments, and practice wisdoms. They use the research process to *guide* their interventions and assess their effectiveness.

Despite the compelling ethical reason for using research and evaluation in social work practice, a few social workers still continue to rely only on their intuitions, informed judgments, and practice wisdoms to assess, monitor, and "evaluate" their practice activities. These workers usually argue that they simply lack the expertise, time, money, and inclination to gather the data needed to determine whether their clients have improved at all. These workers believe that trying to measure the effects of their practices is like trying to catch a sunbeam. They maintain that what social workers do is an art that cannot be measured and guided by the research method. Additionally, they *feel* that important changes in their clients' lives are not measurable in the first place.

These social workers are making a serious mistake. They are ignoring four important problems inherent in their sole reliance on intuition: (1) intuition and reality do not always mesh, (2) intuitive judgments may lead to superstitious behavior and complacency, (3) intuitive judgments vary dramatically from person to person, and (4) intuition is susceptible to bias.

Intuition and Reality
Do Not Always Mesh

The first problem that is inherent when we use *only* intuition in assessing, monitoring, and evaluating our practices is that intuition and reality do not always mesh. It is deceptively easy to underestimate the impact of our practice efforts on our clients. For example, if we fail to recognize our clients' growth and change when growth and change have in fact occurred, several unfortunate consequences are possible. The clients may be deprived of the reinforcement that strengthens their future efforts and encourages further movement.

In addition, we may suffer unnecessary feelings of defeat and impotence. Such feelings may contribute to burnout or simply diminish our effectiveness, since effective helpers must have faith in their own abilities as change agents and belief in their clients' ability to self-actualize. Further, our profession is deprived of knowledge about the effective-

Box 1.4 Continued_____

ness of a particular intervention with a particular client system.

On the other hand, we may overestimate the extent of our client's growth and change. Such overestimation may result in loss of opportunity for the client to progress in further problem resolution; reinforcement of the client's ineffective coping efforts; misapplication by the worker of similarly ineffective interventions in future cases; and wasted time and money for the client, the worker, and the agency.

Intuitive Judgments May Lead to Superstitious Behavior

A second limitation of intuition is that an erroneous intuited judgment may lead to a superstitious behavior and complacency. A social worker may, for example, use certain interventions assuming that they are effective when they are in fact useless. This is akin to the people who wear a rabbit's foot around their necks in order to keep vampires away. They are certain that the charm works because vampires have never appeared. A knowledge-based social worker knows that this same fallacious kind of logic can lead to equally superstitious behaviors in our profession.

Intuitive Judgments Vary Dramatically

A third limitation of intuition is that intuitive subjective judgments vary dramatically from person to person. Obviously, one social worker's intuition is not necessarily the same as another's. Two people who observe the same phenomenon can easily come to very different conclusions about what was seen. So, for example, in the absence of valid and reliable data documenting client change over the course of an intervention, there is no basis to support the assertions of either the worker who maintains that "little change" has occurred or the worker who asserts that "much change" has occurred.

Intuition Is Susceptible to Bias

Finally, intuition is notoriously susceptible to bias. Workers who believe it is important to uncover early childhood experiences in order to unleash pent-up rage and grief, for example, may consider the client's newfound tears as indicators of forward "movement." The client, on the other hand, may be horrified at falling apart. Is the client growing or decompensating? This is a question that intuition alone cannot answer.

Or, consider a director of residential institutions for juveniles who have committed violent crimes. The director may view a child whose only offense is truancy to be less in need of help than other children because he or she compares the child with the other youths at the institution. Health planners who come from a mental health background may see mental illness as the most compelling community health problem to be addressed simply because, in their own work, they are confronted by it daily, even when other public health issues may in fact be more widespread or intense. In short, our individual biases color our intuitions and thus our intuitions are not necessarily valid indicators of reality.

_____

Source: Grinnell and Siegel (1988)

---

and intelligence if someone else has found the same relationship. The more people who find it, the more certain we will become.

Nevertheless, we cannot be *certain* that a thing exists, no matter how many people have found it. We cannot be certain that there is a relationship between two or more things no matter how many people have found one. Nothing is certain; nothing is absolute. It is a matter of slowly acquiring knowledge by making observations, via qualitative and quantitative research approaches, deriving theories from those observations, and testing the theories by making further observations. Even the best-tested theory is held to be true only until something comes along to disprove it. Nothing is forever.

Besides the comfortable certainty of tradition and authority, the research method of obtaining knowledge is a prickly bedfellow. But, of all the possible ways of knowing, we have discovered that it has brought us farthest in terms of food, clothing, shelter, and freedom from diseases. Mystic numbers have not successfully predicted the end of the world; authoritative statements have often proved to be inaccurate; and ill-conceptualized efforts at helpfulness, no matter how well intended, may not provide assistance to some of our clients. Social workers must know *how* to help—for our own sakes, and for the sake of our profession and the clients we serve.

Approaches to the Research Method

As we have established, the research method of knowing contains two complementary research approaches, the quantitative approach and the qualitative approach. Quantitative research studies rely on quantification in collecting and analyzing data and sometimes use statistics to test hypotheses established at the outset of the study. On the other hand, qualitative studies rely on qualitative and descriptive methods of data collection and generate hypotheses and generalizations as a part of the research process.

Their unique characteristics and contributions to the knowledge base of social work are examined in Chapters 6 and 7. Which approach is to be taken is determined by the research question or hypothesis, or by the philosophical inclination of the researcher. The quantitative and qualitative research approaches complement each other and are equally important in the generation and testing of social work knowledge.

The Quantitative Approach   A quantitative research study follows the general steps of the generic research process in a more-or-less straightforward manner. First, a problem area is chosen and a relevant researchable question (or specific hypothesis) is specified. Second, relevant variables within the research question (or hypothesis) are delineated. Third, a plan is developed for measuring the variables within the research question (or hypothesis). Fourth, relevant data are gathered for each variable and then analyzed to determine what they mean. Fifth, on the basis of the data generated, conclusions are drawn regarding the research question (or hypothesis). Finally, a report is written giving the study's findings, conclusions, and recommendations.

The study may then be evaluated by others and perhaps replicated (or repeated) to support or repudiate the application of the study's findings. Chapter 6 presents in more detail how to do a quantitative research study.

The Qualitative Approach   Qualitative research studies are also driven by meaningful problem areas. However, their direct relationship to the research process is somewhat different. In a quantitative study, conceptual clarity about the research question (or hypothesis) usually precedes the collection and analysis of data. In contrast to the quantitative approach, researchers doing qualitative studies do not use the data collection and analysis process simply to answer questions (or to test hypotheses). It is used first to discover what the most important questions are, and then to refine and answer questions (or test hypotheses) that are increasingly more specific. The process is one of moving back and forth between facts and their interpretation, between answers to questions and the development of social work theory. We will discuss in more detail how to do a qualitative research study in Chapter 6.

Steps Within the Research Method

As we now know, there are four highly interrelated phases of the research method. With these generic phases in mind, we will now turn our attention to the steps (and the chapters within this book that discuss each step) that the research method follows in order to obtain knowledge that is as "error free" and "objective" as possible. Thus, when you do any research study, you will need to:

Step 1   Understand the Place of Research in Social Work
— This step is discussed in this chapter

Step 2   Understand Social Work Research Contexts and Ethics
— This step is discussed in Chapters 2, 3, and 4

Step 3   Understand How to Formulate Research Questions and Hypotheses
— This step is discussed in Chapters 5, 6, and 7

Step 4   Understand How Measurement, Sampling, and Research Designs Help Answer Research Questions and Test Hypotheses
— This step is discussed in Chapters 8 through 13

Step 5   Understand How to Collect Data and Select a Data Collection Method
— This step is discussed in Chapters 14 through 19

Step 6   Understand How to Analyze and Interpret the Data Gathered by the Data Collection Method
— This step is not discussed in this book

Step 7   Understand How to Write and Evaluate Research Reports and Proposals
— This step will be discussed in Chapters 20 through 22

Step 8   Understand How to Evaluate Practices and Programs
— This step will be discussed in Chapters 23 through 25

Now that we know the four generic phases of doing a research study and the specific chapters in this book that will assist you, via the research method, it is important to see how they are translated into doing a cross-cultural research study, as illustrated in Box 1.5.

The Research Attitude

The steps of the research method, or "scientific method" if you will, described above refer to the many ideas, rules, techniques, and approaches that we—the research community—use. The research attitude, on the other hand is simply a way that we view the world. It is an attitude that highly values craftsmanship, with pride in creativity, high-quality standards, and hard work. These traits must be incorporated into each one of the six steps within the research method in order for the findings generated from research studies to be appropriately utilized within our profession's knowledge base. As Grinnell (1987) states:

> Most people learn about the "scientific method" rather than about the scientific attitude. While the "scientific method" is an ideal construct, the scientific attitude is the way people have of looking at the world. Doing science includes many methods: what makes them scientific is their acceptance by the scientific collective. (p. 125)

DEFINITION OF RESEARCH

So far, we have discussed the six ways of obtaining knowledge and looked at the characteristics of the research method. Armed with this knowledge, we now need a definition of *research*, which is composed of two syllables, *re* and *search*. Dictionaries define the former syllable as a prefix meaning again, anew, or over again, and the latter as a verb meaning to examine closely and carefully, to test and try, or to probe (Duehn, 1985).

Together, these syllables form a noun describing a careful and systematic study in some field of knowledge, undertaken to establish facts or principles. Social work research therefore can be defined as:

> a structured inquiry that utilizes acceptable methodology (i.e., quantitative and qualitative) to solve human problems and creates new knowledge that is generally applicable.

Box 1.5_____

Steps in Conducting a Cross-Cultural Research Study

Step 1: Defining the Research Participants

1a Use labels such as race, nationality, ethnicity, religion correctly.
1b Be familiar with the cultural labels used to describe the group of interest.
1c Determine whether the group of interest has shown a preference for or resentment of any particular label.
1d Ask research participants to indicate national origin or ancestry.

Step 2: Avoiding Previous Pitfalls

2a Consider multiculturalism versus social deficit or pathology framework to guide cross-cultural research.
2b Review P. Pedersen's (1988, 1991) ten assumptions that can contribute to cultural encapsulation.
2c Explore reasonable opposites to biased assumptions.
2d Use cultural relativity to conceptualize behavior.
2e Use concepts that are culturally relevant with the group of interest.
2f If feasible, become immersed in the target group's culture.
2g Procure cultural data through consultation with the group of interest.
2h Attend to between- and within-group differences and similarities such as race, gender, class, nationality, historical background, and language.
2i Factor in relevant variables to reduce confusion about whether differences are cultural or socioeconomic.

Step 3: Knowing Cultural Variables

3a *Collectivism Versus Individualism.* If the group of interest demonstrates collectivistic tendencies, consider a personal rather than impersonal approach. For example, send a personal invitation to participate, conduct interviews, do case studies.
3b *Communication Styles.* If the group of interest uses a nonverbal and indirect communication style, consider personal contact, development of rapport and trust with research participants, mutual respect, and the use of culturally similar research aides.
3c *Time Orientation.* If the group of interest is present-oriented, understand and accept differences in time orientation and be flexible with respect to time lines and scheduling.

Step 4: Using Measuring Instruments

4a Make sure the the cultural concepts are relevant.
4b Use a measuring instrument that employs the same language, that is, one that takes into account language, dialect, fluency, and socioeconomic variables, of the group of interest.
4c Use a simple translation process that includes minority cultural information gained through consultation or collaboration and testing.

Step 5: Gathering Data

5a Find out about the culture of interest through consultation or collaboration.
5b Use the personal rather than the impersonal approach to gather data.
5c Use culturally similar research assistants.
5d Engender trust.
5e Speak the language and know the culture of the research participant.

Step 6: Becoming a Good Researcher

6a Become familiar with cultural sensitivity and white racial and minority identity development models.
6b Know your own developmental stage.
6c Participate in activities that can promote movement toward the integration stage in which diversity is recognized, valued, and respected.

_____
Source: Wilkinson and McNeil (1997)

While we obtain much of our knowledge base from the findings derived from research studies, all research studies have built-in biases and limitations that create errors and keep us from being absolutely certain about the studies' outcomes.

This text helps us to understand these limitations and to take them into account in the interpretation of our research findings, and it helps us avoid making errors or obtaining wrong answers. One of the principal products of a research study is obtaining "objective" data—via the research method—about reality as it is, "unbiased" and "error-free."

Pure and Applied Research Studies

The goals of social work research studies differ according to whether the study can be described as pure or applied. The goal of pure research studies is to develop theory and expand the social work knowledge base. The goal of applied studies is to develop solutions for problems and applications in practice. The distinction between theoretical results and practical results marks the principal difference between pure and applied research studies. Much more will be said about this in the following chapter.

THE SOCIAL WORKER'S ROLES IN RESEARCH

Armed with the knowledge of how our profession's knowledge base is obtained—especially through the use of the research method—we will now explore how we can perform three complementary research-related roles (Garvin, 1981): (1) the research consumer, (2) the creator and disseminator of knowledge, and (3) the contributing partner.

The Research Consumer

The first research role that social workers can perform is that of research consumer. As we have said, social workers deal with people's lives. We have a responsibility to evaluate the effectiveness of our interventions before we use them with clients; and we must also ensure that the interventions we select are the best possible ones, given the limits of social work knowledge. In other words, we must keep up with advances in our field, as doctors, lawyers, and other professionals do. We must acquaint ourselves with the findings from the latest research studies and decide which findings are important, which might possibly be useful, and which should be ignored.

Sometimes, social workers want to conduct their own research studies, particularly when they have read about findings that come into the "possibly useful" category. Nevertheless, every new intervention must be tried once for the first time, and a social worker who wants to build a repertoire of interventions will experience a number of "first times." It is particularly important to understand how others have implemented the intervention—if others have—and to monitor the client's progress carefully.

Social workers contemplating larger research studies will obviously need to be well acquainted with previous studies. However, it is a mistake to believe that only those who "do research" read research studies. The purpose of a research study is to collect objective data, which are combined with other objective data to generate knowledge. The purpose of generating knowledge, in social work, is to pass the knowledge to social workers, who will accomplish the primary purpose of the profession—helping clients to help themselves.

Consuming research findings—reading with understanding in order to utilize the findings—is the most important research role a social worker can play.

The Creator and Disseminator of Knowledge

The second research role that social workers can undertake is that of knowledge creator and disseminator. Social workers who conduct their own research studies, for example, are helping to create knowledge—provided that they inform others about their findings. Many social workers try something new from time to time. However, comparatively few social workers use the research method of testing their new interventions in an effort to gather evidence about how well these interventions work with different clients in various situations. Even fewer share their findings—or even their interventions—with their colleagues; and fewer still disseminate the information to the profession as a whole by writing manuscripts to submit to journals for possible publication.

The consequence, as previously mentioned, is that most of the best work accomplished by social work professionals is never recorded and never used by anyone but its creator. Clients who could be helped derive no benefit, because a social worker in Chicago does not know that the problem has already been solved by a colleague in Boston.

The Contributing Partner

The third research role that social workers undertake is that of contributing partner. We have said that researchers conducting a large study are often dependent on agency staff for help and advice, and many studies can succeed only if staff and researchers form a team. Different staff members can contribute their own various talents to the team effort. One member may be particularly acute and accurate when it comes to observing client behavior; another may have practical and innovative ideas about how to solve a problem; a third may act as a liaison between researcher and client, or between one agency and another. All may be asked to help in testing and designing measuring instruments and gathering or providing data.

It is a rare social worker who is not involved in one research study or another. Some social workers are cooperative, some less so, depending on their attitudes toward research. The ones who know most about research methods tend to be the most cooperative, and also the most useful. Hence, the greater the number of social workers who understand research principles, the more likely it is that relevant studies will be successfully completed and social work knowledge will be increased.

Integrating the Three Research Roles

The three research roles are not independent of one another. They must be integrated if research is to accomplish its goals of increasing our profession's knowledge base and improving the effectiveness of our interventions with clients (Garvin, 1981).

The issue is not whether social workers should consume research findings, produce and disseminate research results, or become contributing partners in research studies. Rather it is whether they can engage the full spectrum of available knowledge and skills in the continual improvement of their practices. Social workers who adopt only one or two research roles are shortchanging themselves and their clients (Reid & Smith, 1989):

> . . . If research is to be used to full advantage to advance the goals of social work, the profession needs to develop a climate in which both doing and consuming research are normal professional activities. By this we do not mean that all social workers should necessarily do research or that all practice should be based on the results of research, but rather that an ability to carry out studies at some level and the facility in using scientifically based knowledge should be an integral part of the skills that social workers have and use. (p. ix)

There are economic as well as ethical reasons for our profession's commitment to research and evaluation. It was once believed that perhaps throwing money at social problems would solve them. Today, funding sources demand evidence that social service agencies are accomplishing their intended goals and objectives.

Anecdotal case studies alone are lame when unaccompanied by valid and reliable data of the agency's effectiveness. In the competitive scramble of social service agencies for limited funds, the agencies that can demonstrate their

effectiveness and efficiency will prevail. Hence, learning how to integrate practice activities with the research process is a matter of survival in our profession.

Expanding our research/practice base is also a way of enabling our profession to assert its place in the community of human service professionals. It is a way of carving out a niche of respectability, of challenging the insidious stereotype that, although social workers have their hearts in the right place, they are uninformed and ineffective.

Any profession (and especially ours) that bases its credibility on faith or ideology alone will have a hard time surviving. Although a research base to our profession will not guarantee us public acceptance, the absence of such a base and the lack of vigorous research efforts to expand it will—in the long run—undoubtedly erode our credibility.

SUMMARY

Knowledge is essential to human survival. Over the course of history, there have been many ways of knowing, from divine revelation to tradition and the authority of elders. By the beginning of the seventeenth century, people began to rely on a different way of knowing—the research method, more commonly referred to as the problem-solving method.

Social workers derive their knowledge from tradition, authority, experience, intuition, and through the media as well as from findings derived from research studies—which differ in important ways from the other methods.

There are two basic complementary research approaches—quantitative and qualitative. They obtain and use data differently, and each approach has utility in the generation of relevant social work knowledge.

There are two main goals of social work research—pure and applied. The purpose of a pure research study is to develop theory and expand the social work knowledge base. The purpose of an applied study is to develop solutions for problems and relevant applications for social work practice. Both goals complement each other.

Social workers engage in three research roles. They can consume research findings by using the findings of others in their day-to-day practices, they can produce and disseminate research results for others to use, and they can participate in research studies in a variety of ways.

This chapter has briefly explored the place of research in social work. The following the three chapters will discuss the contexts in which it takes place.

C h a p t e r   2

Science, Society, and Research

THE WINTER OF **1997** was not a good season for persons living on the street. In Boston, police found Jack Olson frozen to death on New Year's morning (Kahn, 1997). It had been 4 degrees Fahrenheit that New Year's Eve, and Mr. Olson had celebrated with an all-day vodka binge, followed by a night of drinking Listerine after the liquor stores closed. He had been panhandling and sleeping in shelters or on the streets. He had hoped to bring his two sons to Boston; he had gotten engaged to a woman two weeks previously; he had promised his fiancee that he would get sober. But on the morning of December 31 he started drinking and didn't stop.

Jack Olson was not the only homeless person to die on the streets of Boston that winter. But his death attracted more attention than most, perhaps because he had befriended so many others: "a beautiful person," his fiancee said. "He was a fun-loving, caring person if he was sober," a homeless friend recalled. Perhaps the attention had something to do with Mr. Olson's efforts to change. He had spent many weeks in detox, talked about finding a restaurant job, about making a home for himself and his sons.

Perhaps it was because his death seemed so senseless: If only his friends had not left him curled up on a heating grate that night. Perhaps it was just an appealing human interest story for the holidays. In any case, Jack Olson's story

soon disappeared from the newspapers. He had become, so to speak, just another statistic.

Does the Jack Olson story sound familiar? Such newspaper stories proliferate when the holiday season approaches, but what do they really tell us about homelessness? Why do people live on the streets? In the rest of this chapter, you will learn how social science research methods go beyond stories in the popular media to help us answer questions like these.

REASONING ABOUT THE SOCIAL WORLD

The story of just one homeless person, like Jack Olson, raises many questions. Take a few minutes to read each of the following questions and jot down your answers. Do not ruminate about the questions or worry about your responses: This is *not a test;* there are no "wrong" answers.

- How would you describe Jack Olson?
- Why do you think Jack Olson died?
- Was Jack Olson typical of the homeless population?
- In general, why do people become homeless?
- How have you learned about homelessness?

Let us now consider for a moment the possible answers to some of these questions. The information we have to describe Jack Olson is scant (Kahn, 1997). He had come to Boston from Arizona five years before he died, leaving a cook's job and a broken marriage. He wanted to make a new home for his two sons, but calls back to them in Arizona often ended in disappointment. He was a heavy drinker but also was being treated for manic-depressive illness, according to friends. A staff member of the church where Mr. Olson ate his free meals noted that "Jack had a hard life out there."

Do you have enough information now to understand why Jack Olson died? His fiancee sounded bitter about the possibility that people might have stepped over his body while on their way to New Year's celebrations: "Nobody should be allowed to go out and freeze to death." Should we attribute his death in part to a lack of concern by others? What about the apparent disappointments he suffered when he made calls to Arizona to talk to his sons? Was a feeling of failure in his role as a father a factor in his death? Was the cause of his death all "the sauce" he imbibed? "Alcohol is killing a lot of people out there," a social service worker noted. Or is inadequate treatment for mental illness the issue?

Now can you construct an adequate description of Jack Olson? Can you explain the reason for his death? Or do you feel you need to know more about Mr. Olson, about his friends and the family he grew up in? And how about his

experiences with treatment for alcoholism and an apparent manic-depressive disorder? We've attempted to investigate just one person's experiences, and already our investigation is spawning more and more questions.

Questions and Answers About the Social World

When the questions concern not just one person but many people or general social processes, the possible questions and the alternative answers multiply. For example, consider the question of why people become homeless. Responses to a 1987 survey of Nashville residents illustrate the diverse answers that people have (Lee, Jones, & Lewis, 1990):

- Changes in Society   58.6%
- Mental Illness   53.1%
- Bad Luck   51.0%
- Work Aversion   45.2%
- Alcoholism   44.5%
- Personal Choice   36.6%

Compare the above answers with the opinion you recorded earlier. Was your idea about the causes of homelessness one of the more popular ones?

We cannot avoid asking questions about the actions and attitudes of others. We all try to make sense of the social world, which is a very complex place, and to make sense of our position in it, in which we have quite a personal stake. In fact, the more that you begin to "think like a social scientist," the more questions will come to mind.

But why does each question have so many possible answers? Surely, our unique perspective plays a role. One person may see a homeless individual as a victim of circumstance, and another person may see the same individual as a shiftless bum. When confronted with a homeless individual, one observer may stop to listen, another may recall a news story on street crime, and another may be reminded of her grandfather. Their different orientations will result in different answers to the questions prompted by the same individual or event.

Answers to questions about the social world also vary because what people have "seen" varies. The Nashville survey—by Barrett Lee, Sue Hinze Jones, and David Lewis (1990)—gives some idea of the basis for people's opinions about homelessness: Individuals who had less education and more conservative political beliefs were more likely than others to think that homelessness is a matter of personal choice. Personal contact also made a difference: People who had been panhandled by a homeless person were more likely to think that homelessness is a matter of personal choice.

But those who had had an informal conversation with a homeless person about something other than money were less likely to believe that homelessness is a matter of personal choice. Do these bases for opinions inspire your confidence? Is your opinion about why people become homeless based on direct experience, or is it based on what other people have said or written?

ERRORS IN REASONING

People give different answers to questions about the social world for yet another reason: It's simply too easy to make errors in logic, particularly when we are analyzing the social world in which we ourselves are conscious participants. We can call some of these "everyday errors" because they occur so frequently in the nonscientific, unreflective discourse about the social world that we hear on a daily basis.

A clear example of everyday errors in reasoning comes from a letter to Ann Landers. The letter was written by someone who had just moved with her two cats from the city to a house in the country. In the city she had not let her cats outside and felt guilty about confining them. When they arrived in the country, she threw her back door open. Her two cats cautiously went to the door and looked outside for a while, then returned to the living room and lay down. Her conclusion was that people shouldn't feel guilty about keeping their cats indoors—that even when they have the chance, cats don't really want to play outside.

Do you see this person's errors in reasoning?

- **Overgeneralization** — She observed only two cats, both of which previously were confined indoors.
- **Selective observation or inaccurate observation** — She observed the cats at the outside door only once.
- **Illogical reasoning** — She assumed that others feel guilty about keeping their cats indoors and that cats are motivated by emotions.
- **Resistance to change** — She was quick to conclude that she had no need to change her approach to the cats.

You do not have to be a scientist or use sophisticated research techniques to avoid these four errors in reasoning. If you recognize these errors for what they are and make a conscious effort to avoid them, you can improve your own reasoning. In the process, you will also be implementing the admonishments of your parents (or minister, teacher, or other adviser) to not stereotype people; to avoid jumping to conclusions; to look at the big picture. These are the same errors that research methods are designed to help us avoid.

Overgeneralization

Overgeneralization is an error in reasoning. It occurs when we conclude that what we have observed or what we know to be true for some cases is true for all cases. We are always drawing conclusions about people and social processes from our own interactions with them but sometimes forget that our experiences are limited. The social (and natural) world is, after all, a complex place. We have the ability (and inclination) to interact with just a small fraction of the individuals who inhabit our world, especially in a limited span of time.

Selective or Inaccurate Observation

We also have to avoid selective observation—choosing to look only at things that are in line with our preferences or beliefs. When we are inclined to criticize individuals or institutions, it is all too easy to notice their every failing. For example, if we are convinced in advance that all homeless persons are substance abusers, we can find many confirming instances. But what about such homeless people as Debbie Allen, who ran away from a home she shared with an alcoholic father and psychotic mother; Charlotte Gentile, a teacher with a bachelor's degree living with two daughters in a shelter after losing her job; and Faith Brinton, who walked out of her rented home with her two daughters to escape an alcoholic and physically abusive husband and ended up in a shelter after her husband stopped paying child support? If we acknowledge only the instances that confirm our predispositions, we are victims of our own selective observation.

Recent research on cognitive functioning (how the brain works) helps to explain why our feelings so readily shape our perceptions (Seidman, 1997). Emotional responses to external stimuli travel a shorter circuit in the brain than reasoned responses do. The result, according to some cognitive scientists, is that "what something reminds us of can be far more important than what it 'is'" (Goleman, 1995:294-295). Our emotions can influence us even before we begin to reason about what we have observed.

Our observations can also be simply inaccurate. If a woman says she is "hungry" and we think she said she is "hunted," we have made an inaccurate observation. If we think five persons are standing on a street corner when seven actually are, we have made an inaccurate observation.

Such errors occur often in casual conversation and in everyday observation of the world around us. In fact, our perceptions do not provide a direct window onto the world around us, for what we think we have sensed is not necessarily what we have seen (or heard, smelled, felt, or tasted). Even when our senses are functioning fully, our minds have to interpret what we have sensed (Humphrey, 1992).

Illogical Reasoning

When we prematurely jump to conclusions or argue on the basis of invalid assumptions, we are using illogical reasoning. It is not reasonable, for example, to propose that homeless individuals do not want to work if evidence indicates that the reason many are unemployed is a shortage of jobs or a tendency for the unemployed to have mental or physical disabilities. On the other hand, an unquestioned assumption that everyone who can work will work is also likely to be misplaced. Of course, logic that seems impeccable to one person can seem twisted to another—the problem usually is reasoning from different assumptions rather than just failing to "think straight."

Resistance to Change

Resistance to change, the reluctance to change our ideas in light of new information, may occur for several reasons:

- **Ego-Based Commitments** — We all learn to greet with some skepticism the claims by leaders of companies, schools, agencies, and so on that people in their organization are happy, that revenues are growing, that services are being delivered in the best possible way. We know how tempting it is to make statements about the social world that conform to our own needs rather than to the observable facts. It can also be difficult to admit that we were wrong once we have staked out a position on an issue. For example, we may want our experiences while volunteering in a shelter for homeless persons to confirm our political stance on homeless people and therefore resist changing our beliefs in response to new experiences.

- **Excessive Devotion to Tradition** — Some degree of devotion to tradition is necessary for the predictable functioning of society. Social life can be richer and more meaningful if it is allowed to flow along the paths charted by those who have preceded us. But too much devotion to tradition can stifle adaptation to changing circumstances. When we distort our observations or alter our reasoning so that we can maintain beliefs that "were good enough for my grandfather, so they're good enough for me," we hinder our ability to accept new findings and develop new knowledge. The consequences can be deadly, as residents of Hamburg, Germany, might have realized in 1892 (Freedman, 1991). Until the last part of the nineteenth century, people believed that cholera, a potentially lethal disease, was due to minute, inanimate, airborne poison particles.

    In 1850, English researcher John Snow demonstrated that cholera was, in fact, spread by contaminated water. When a cholera epidemic hit Hamburg in 1892, the authorities did what tradition deemed appropriate:

digging up and carting away animal carcasses to prevent the generation of more miasmas. Despite their efforts, thousands died. New York City adopted a new approach based on Snow's discovery, which included boiling drinking water and disinfecting sewage. As a result, the death rate in New York City dropped to a tenth of what the death rate had been in a previous epidemic.

- **Uncritical Agreement with Authority** — If we do not have the courage to evaluate critically the ideas of those in positions of authority, we will have little basis for complaint if they exercise their authority over us in ways we don't like. And if we do not allow new discoveries to call our beliefs into question, our understanding of the social world will remain limited. An extreme example of this problem was the refusal of leaders in formerly communist countries to acknowledge the decaying social and environmental fabric of their societies while they encouraged their followers to pay homage to the wisdom of Comrades Mao, Lenin, and Stalin. But we do not have to go so far afield to recognize that people often accept the beliefs of those in positions of authority without question.

Reexamining Your Beliefs

Now take just a minute to reexamine the beliefs about homelessness that you recorded earlier. Did you grasp at a simple explanation even though reality is far more complex? Were your beliefs influenced by your own ego and feelings about your similarities to or differences from homeless persons? Are your beliefs perhaps based on stories you have heard about the "hobos" of an earlier era? Did you weigh carefully the opinions of political authorities or just accept or reject those opinions out of hand? Could knowledge of research methods help to improve your own understanding of your social world? Do you see some of the challenges faced by our profession?

THE RESEARCH APPROACH

As we saw in the last chapter, the research method of knowing (the scientific approach) is designed to reduce greatly these potential sources of error in everyday reasoning. As we now know, science relies on logical and systematic methods to answer questions, and it does so in a way that allows others to inspect and evaluate its methods. In the realm of social work research, these methods are not so unusual. After all, they involve asking questions, observing social groups, and counting people, which we often do in our everyday lives. However, social work researchers develop, refine, apply, and report their understanding of the social world more systematically, or "scientifically," than John and Joanna Q. Public do:

- Research methods can reduce the likelihood of overgeneralization by using systematic procedures for selecting individuals or groups to study that are representative of the individuals or groups to which we wish to generalize.

- To avoid illogical reasoning, researchers use explicit criteria for identifying causes and for determining whether these criteria are met in a particular instance.

- Research methods can reduce the risk of selective or inaccurate observation by requiring that we measure and sample phenomena systematically.

- Because they require that we base our beliefs on evidence that can be examined and critiqued by others, research methods lessen the tendency to develop answers about the social world from ego-based commitments, excessive devotion to tradition, and/or unquestioning respect for authority.

MOTIVES FOR DOING RESEARCH

Like you, researchers read stories about individuals, observe homeless persons in their everyday lives, and try to make sense of what they see. For most, that is the end of it. But for some, the problem of homelessness has become a major research focus. The motivations for selecting this particular research focus, as with any topic, can be any of the following or some combination: (1) policy motivations, (2) academic motivations, and (3) personal motivations.

Policy Motivations

Many social service agencies and elected officials seek better descriptions of the homeless population so they can identify needs and allocate responsibility among agencies that could meet these needs. For example, federal agencies want to identify the scope of health problems among the homeless, and many state and local officials use research methods to guide development of their social service budgets. Shelters for homeless persons often use research to learn more about the needs of their clientele. These policy-guidance and program-management needs have resulted in numerous research projects.

Academic Motivations

The homeless population has been a logical focus for research on issues ranging from influences on physical health to consequences of poverty. For example, sociologists have long been concerned with the impact of different types and levels of social ties on individual behavior and attitudes. Homeless persons, cut off from community-based and other traditional social networks, provide an opportunity to study the effects of social isolation. For psychologists, social workers, and psychiatrists, the homeless population provides a test case for evaluating the impact of residential and social instability on mental health. Those who study social policy also have sought to determine whether the "deinstitutionalization" of psychiatric patients in the 1960s and 1970s was actually a cause of homelessness in the 1980s and 1990s.

Personal Motivations

Many of those who conduct research on homelessness feel that by doing so they can help to ameliorate the conditions that produce homelessness and thus reduce the suffering of homeless persons. Some researchers first volunteered in shelters or soup kitchens and only later began to develop a research agenda based on their experiences. Community groups have sought help from researchers to determine whether shelters for the homeless lower property values or influence the crime rate.

TYPES OF RESEARCH STUDIES

Of course, homelessness did not first appear in the United States in the 1980s. Social historians have described homelessness as far back as colonial times, and the first survey of homeless persons was reported in 1899. But homeless persons became markedly more numerous and visible in the 1980s than they had been at any time since the Great Depression. Researchers began studying contemporary homelessness in the early 1980s, amassing a substantial body of research findings that have refined knowledge about the problem and shaped social policy (Schutt & Garrett, 1992). These studies fall into the four broad categories: (1) descriptive, (2) exploratory, (3) explanatory, and (4) evaluatiive.

Descriptive Studies

Defining and describing social phenomena of interest is a part of almost any research investigation, but descriptive research was the primary focus of the early studies of homelessness. Some of the central questions were "Who is homeless?" and "What are the needs of homeless persons?" and "How many people are homeless?" Measurement (the topic of Part III) and sampling (Chapter 11) are central concerns in descriptive research.

Exploratory Studies

Exploratory research seeks to find out how people get along in the setting under question, what meanings they give to their actions, and what issues concern them. The goal is to learn "What is going on here?" and to investigate social phenomena without expectations. This purpose is associated with the use of methods that capture large amounts of relatively unstructured information. For example, researchers investigating homelessness in the 1980s were encountering a phenomenon with which they had no direct experience. Thus, an early goal was to find out what it was like to be homeless and how homeless persons made sense of their situation. Exploratory research like this frequently involves qualitative methods, which are discussed in Chapters 6, 7, 13, and 14.

Explanatory Studies

Many consider explanation the premier goal of any science. Explanatory research studies seek to identify causes and effects of social phenomena, to predict how one phenomenon will change or vary in response to variation in some other phenomenon. Homelessness researchers adopted explanation as a goal when they began to ask such questions as "Why do people become homeless?" and "Does the unemployment rate influence the frequency of homelessness?" Methods with which to identify causes and effects are the focus of Chapters 12 and 13.

Evaluative Studies

Seeking to determine the effects of a social service program or other type of intervention is a type of explanatory research, because it deals with cause and effect. However, evaluation research differs from other forms of explanatory research because evaluation research considers the implementation and effects of social policies and programs. These issues may not be relevant in other types of explanatory research. The problem of homelessness spawned many new government programs and, with them, evaluation research to assess the impact of these programs. Much more will be said about evaluation in Part VII of this book.

EXAMPLES OF RESEARCH STUDIES

Given the four types of research studies mentioned above, we will now summarize a research study in each of these four areas to give you a feel for the projects motivated by these different concerns.

A Descriptive Study: Who Are the Homeless?

In the 1980s Dee Roth was chief of the Ohio Department of Mental Health's Office of Program Evaluation and Research. Her study of homelessness in Ohio, one of the most ambitious descriptive studies, was funded by the National Institute of Mental Health (Roth, Bean, Lust, & Saveanu, 1985). A general purpose of the study was to learn who the homeless are and how they relate to family, friends, and mental health agencies.

Because homeless people do not have regular addresses or phone numbers, Roth could not simply select individuals from a list of currently occupied residences or phone numbers in use; instead, she designed a more complex study. The study's first element was a "key informant survey." Roth asked personnel in service agencies and shelters who worked with the homeless where homeless persons could be found in their local area and what the characteristics of these persons were. Then she surveyed state psychiatric hospital and community mental health agency staff and asked them to identify homeless persons who had used their facilities. Finally, her staff interviewed 979 homeless persons in 20 counties selected to represent urban, mixed, and rural areas throughout Ohio.

Responses in the key informant survey reinforce the importance of research methods. These key informants were all employed in work with homeless persons, and yet their responses were not at all consistent. Their descriptions of the homeless population tended to focus only on the characteristics of homeless persons they interacted with in their own work, and almost none of the informants were able to estimate accurately the size of the homeless population in their county. Direct experience itself was an insufficient basis for developing a generalizable description.

Before we go on to tell you the results of the survey of psychiatric hospitals and community mental health centers, let us try a little experiment. You probably have heard or read statements that give you an idea about the proportion of homeless persons served by such facilities. What is your guesstimate? Less than 10 percent, about one-third, more than half, or some other proportion? The answers: 7 percent of new hospital patients were homeless at the time they were admitted, and 4 percent of the discharged hospital patients were said by community mental health center staff to have become homeless at some time after they were discharged. Are you surprised or reassured?

Roth's homeless person survey revealed a diverse population not unlike that reported in other studies of the time. About 80 percent of the homeless were men, 66 percent were white, 50 percent were high school graduates (just over 10 percent had some college experience), only 10 percent were married, and almost 33 percent were veterans. Health problems were common. Almost one-third had been in a psychiatric hospital, and a similar proportion reported some psychiatric impairment; almost one-third reported physical health problems; one-fifth reported problem drinking.

An Exploratory Study: What Is It Like to Be Homeless?

By the mid-1980s, in spite of a spate of descriptive studies, sociologists David A. Snow and Leon Anderson (1987) felt that they still did not understand life on the streets and how people adapted to it. Snow and Anderson helped to close this research gap by conducting an exploratory field study of homeless persons in Austin, Texas. For one year, they (primarily Anderson) hung out with homeless persons, followed them through their daily routines, and asked them about their lives. Six homeless persons were studied more intensively with taped, in-depth life-history interviews. At the end of the year, Snow and Anderson had spent 405 hours in 24 different settings, from soup kitchens to hospitals, and had interacted, on average, three times each with 168 homeless persons.

One research focus was how homeless individuals try to justify to themselves their homelessness. This "identity work," Snow and Anderson found, took three different verbal forms, which are illustrated in the following quotes:

- Distancing — *"They have gotten used to living on the streets and are satisfied with it. But not me!" (p. 1349).*
- Embracement — *"His talk was peppered with references to himself as a tramp. He indicated, for example, that he had appeared on a television show in St. Louis as a tramp and that he had 'tramped' his way across the country" (p. 1355).*
- Fictive Storytelling — *"I am going to catch a plane to Pittsburgh and tomorrow night I'll take a hot bath, have a dinner of linguini and red wine in my own restaurant . . . and have a woman hanging on my arm" (p. 1362).*

The prevalence of such identity talk suggested to Snow and Anderson that homeless persons share with the rest of the population a concern with their social standing. Before this study, researchers had assumed that the homeless were preoccupied with basic survival. At the same time, Snow and Anderson caution us to avoid concluding that many homeless persons "want" to be homeless because they have embraced in their conversation the identity of being homeless; instead, Snow and Anderson point out, it is likely that the experience of being homeless causes people to adjust their identities.

An Explanatory Study: Why Do People Become Homeless?

Sociologist Peter H. Rossi secured funding from two private charitable found-ations and the Illinois Department of Public Aid for a survey of homeless persons in Chicago in the fall and winter of 1986. His comparison of these persons with other extremely poor Chicagoans allowed him to address this explanatory research question: Why do people become homeless? Rossi's book on this study, *Down and Out in America: The Origins of Homelessness* (1989), has already become a classic.

Rossi surveyed a sample of homeless persons in shelters and all those he and his assistants could find on the streets. The street sample was something of a challenge. Rossi consulted with local experts to identify on which of Chicago's 19,400 blocks he would be most likely to find homeless persons at night. Then he drew samples of blocks from each of the three resulting categories: blocks with a high, medium, and low probability of having homeless persons at night. Finally, Rossi's interviewers visited these blocks on several nights between 1 am and 6 am and briefly interviewed people who seemed to be homeless.

After extensive analysis of the data, Rossi developed a straightforward explanation of homelessness: Homeless persons are extremely poor, and all extremely poor persons are vulnerable to being displaced because of the high cost of housing in urban areas. Those who are most vulnerable to losing their homes are individuals with problems of substance abuse or mental illness, which leave them unable to contribute to their own support. Extremely poor individuals who have these characteristics and are priced out of cheap lodging by urban renewal and rising housing prices often end up living with relatives or friends. However, the financial and emotional burdens created by this arrangement eventually strain social ties to the breaking point, and a portion of these persons therefore end up homeless.

Rossi made a series of recommendations to reduce homelessness based on his analysis of why people become homeless. Some recommendations are:

- Implement aggressive outreach programs to extend welfare coverage to the many eligible poor persons and families who do not now receive it.
- Subsidize housing for younger unattached persons; stop the release of chronically mentally ill persons from hospitals until supportive living arrangements are arranged.
- Furnish support to families who subsidize their destitute, unattached members.

An Evaluative Study: What Services Help The Homeless?

What should supportive housing of the type recommended by Rossi and others consist of? Psychiatrist Stephen M. Goldfinger, psychologist Barbara Dickey, social worker Sondra Hellman, and several other investigators (1997)—including psychologists Walter Penk and Larry Seidman, social worker Martha O'Bryan, and me—designed a study of homeless mentally ill persons in Boston to evaluate the effectiveness of different types of housing for this population. With funding from the National Institute of Mental Health, we recruited 118 mental health agency clients who were homeless and who were not judged to be a risk to themselves or others if they lived on their own.

We randomly assigned half of those who agreed to participate in the study to their own small efficiency apartments; the rest were assigned to one of eight group homes that were opened specifically for the study. We assigned people randomly to the two types of housing so we could be more confident that any differences found between the groups at the study's end had arisen after the research participants were assigned to the housing. We assigned case managers to all study participants in both housing types to ensure that medical and social services were provided.

The group homes were not the type of group living arrangements traditionally used by mental health authorities, with staffing around the clock and decision making firmly in the hands of the staff. Instead, the group homes were designed to assist residents to take control of their own affairs. Although the group homes began with full staffing, residents were encouraged to meet together to set rules for the household and eventually to terminate staff as they felt able to manage on their own. We termed this housing model "evolving consumer households."

Most the study's participants—80 percent in fact—were still in their housing after one year in the study, and in most respects the two types of housing produced the same results. However, more of those living in the independent apartments left their housing at some point and returned to the streets or shelters. Paradoxically, though, those who were assigned to independent apartments were more satisfied with their housing (Schutt, Goldfinger, & Penk, 1997). Another difference, reported by the project's anthropologists, was the gradual emergence of collegial decision making in some of the group homes. And our neuropsychological tests identified an increase in mental flexibility among group home residents.

STRENGTHS AND LIMITATIONS OF THE RESEARCH METHOD

The above are only four of the dozens of large studies of homelessness since 1980, but they illustrate some of the questions researchers can address, several different methods social scientists can use, and ways social science research can inform public policy. Notice how each one of the four studies was designed to reduce the errors common in everyday reasoning:

- The clear definition of the population of interest in each study and the selection of a broad, representative sample of that population in two studies (Roth's and Rossi's) increased the researchers' ability to draw conclusions without overgeneralizing findings to groups to which they did not apply.
- The use of surveys in which each respondent was asked the same set of questions reduced the risk of selective or inaccurate observation, as did careful and regular note-taking by the field researchers observing homeless persons on the streets of Austin and in the evolving consumer households in Boston.
- The risk of illogical reasoning was reduced by carefully describing each stage of the research, clearly presenting the findings, and carefully testing the basis for cause-and-effect conclusions.
- Resistance to change was reduced by designing an innovative type of housing and making an explicit commitment to evaluate it fairly.

Nevertheless, it would be less than honest if we implied that we enter the realm of beauty, truth, and light when we engage in social research or when we base our opinions only on the best available research methods. Research studies always have some limitations and some flaws (as does any human endeavor), and the findings derived from them are always subject to differing interpretations. As we have seen from the last chapter, the research approach permits us to see more, to observe with fewer distortions, and to describe more clearly to others what our opinions are based on, but it will not settle all arguments.

Others will always have differing opinions, and some of those others will be researchers who have conducted their own studies and drawn different conclusions. Are people encouraged to get off welfare by requirements that they get a job? Some research studies suggests that they are, other studies find no effect caused by work incentives, and one major study found positive but short-lived effects. More convincing answers must await better research methodologies, more thoughtful analyses, or wider agreement on the value of welfare and work.

But even in topic areas that are fraught with controversy, where social scientists differ in their interpretations of the evidence, the quest for new and more sophisticated research has value. What is most important for improving understanding of the social world is not the result of any particular study but the accumulation of evidence from different studies of related issues. By designing new studies that focus on the weak points or controversial conclusions of prior research studies, researchers contribute to a body of findings that gradually expands our knowledge about the social world and resolves some of the disagreements about it.

Researchers will always disagree somewhat because of their differing research opportunities, methodological approaches, and policy preferences. For example, many research studies indicate that low levels of social support increase the risk of psychological depression. But are these answers incorrect in some circumstances? One study of homeless persons suggested that social support was not associated with less depression, perhaps because of the extremely stressful circumstances homeless persons face (La Gory, Ferris, & Mullis, 1990). But then another study using a different indicator found social support to be as beneficial for homeless persons as it is for others (Schutt, Meschede, & Rierdan,1994). Additional studies using a variety of research methods may resolve this discrepancy.

VALIDITY: THE RESEARCH METHOD'S GOAL

A social work researcher seeks to develop an accurate understanding of empirical reality, the reality we encounter firsthand, by conducting research studies that lead to valid knowledge about the world. And when is knowledge valid? We have reached the goal of validity when our statements or conclusions about empirical reality are correct.

For example, you can look out your window and observe that it is raining—a valid observation, if your eyes and ears are to be trusted. You can pick up the newspaper and read that Russian people have turned against political and economic reform. This conclusion is of questionable validity, based as it is on an interpretation of the meaning of votes cast by presumably only a portion of the Russian population.

If validity sounds desirable to you, you are a good candidate for becoming a researcher. If the goal of validity sounds a bit far-fetched—after all, how can we really be sure our understandings of empirical phenomena are correct when we can perceive the world only through the filter of our own senses?—you need not worry. Such skepticism will help you to remember the tenuousness of all knowledge and keep you properly skeptical about new discoveries.

This book is about validity more than anything else, about how to conduct studies that lead to valid interpretations of the social world. The goal of research studies is not to come up with conclusions that people will like or conclusions that suit our own personal preferences. The goal is to figure out how and why the social world—some aspect of it, that is—operates as it does.

We must always be concerned with three aspects of validity:

- **Measurement validity** — Measurement validity exists when a measure measures what we think it measures.
- **Generalizability** — Generalizability exists when a conclusion holds true for the population, group, setting, or event that we say it does, given the conditions that we specify.

- Causal validity — Causal validity exists when a conclusion that A leads to or results in B is correct. Causal validity is also called internal validity.

Each of these three aspects of validity is essential: Conclusions based on invalid measures, invalid generalizations, or invalid causal inferences will themselves be invalid. Imagine for a moment that we survey a sample of 250 Seattle residents and ask them two questions:

- Do you have someone to depend on in times of need? (the social support measure)
- During the past week, how often have you felt depressed? (the depression measure)

We then compare the frequency of depression between people with high and low levels of social support. We find that Seattle residents with less social support are more likely to say that they are depressed, and we conclude that the depression we found among some of Seattle's residents resulted, in part, from their lower level of social support.

- But did our questions indeed tell us how depressed our respondents were and how high or low their level of social support was? If they did, we achieved *measurement validity*.
- Do our results hold true for the larger Seattle population to which our conclusion referred? If so, our conclusion would satisfy the criterion for *generalizability*.
- Did respondents' levels of depression tend to rise because of a reduction in their level of social support? If so, our conclusion is *causally valid*.

As we know from the preceding chapter, the goal in the research method is to achieve valid understandings of the social world by coming to conclusions that rest on valid measures and valid causal assertions and that are generalizable to the population of interest. Once we have learned how to develop studies that give us reasonably valid results and how to evaluate studies according to how well they meet this criterion, we will be well along on the road to becoming expert researchers.

Measurement Validity

Measurement validity should be the first concern in establishing the validity of the results from a research study. Without having measured what we think we measured, we really do not know what we are talking about. Measurement validity is covered in detail in Part III in this book.

To see how important measurement validity is, let us look at the case of the researchers who have found a high level of serious and persistent mental illness among homeless persons, based on interviews with samples of homeless persons at one point in time. The researchers have been charged with using invalid measures. Mental illness has typically been measured by individuals' responses to a series of questions that ask if they are feeling depressed, anxious, paranoid, and so on. Homeless persons more commonly say yes to these questions than do other persons, even other extremely poor persons who have homes.

But for these responses to be considered indicators of mental illness, the responses must indicate relatively enduring states of mind. Critics of these studies note that the living conditions of homeless persons are likely to make them feel depressed, anxious, and even paranoid. Feeling depressed may be a normal reaction to homelessness, not an indication of mental illness. Thus, the argument goes, typical survey questions may not provide valid measures of mental illness among the homeless.

One careful research study suggests that this criticism is not correct, that homelessness is not in itself a cause of depression. Paul Kogel and M. Audrey Burnam (1992) found that the symptoms of depression most likely to result from the living conditions of some homeless people in Los Angeles, such as having trouble with sleeping or concentrating, were not particularly more common among those studied than among those with homes.

Suffice it to say at this point that we must be very careful in designing our measures and in subsequently evaluating how well they have performed. We cannot just assume that the measurements used in any research study are valid or invalid.

Generalizability

The generalizability of a research or evaluation study is the extent to which it can be used to inform us about persons, places, or events that were not studied. Generalizability is the focus of Part IV in this book.

Although most American cities have many shelters for homeless persons and some homeless persons sleep on the streets to avoid shelters, many studies of "the homeless" are based on surveys of individuals found in just one shelter. When these studies are reported, the authors state that their results are based on homeless persons in one shelter. But then they go on to talk about "the homeless this" and "the homeless that," as if their study results represented all homeless persons in the city or even in the nation.

People may be especially quick to make this mistake in discussing these studies because it is very difficult to track down homeless persons outside of shelters and because some shelter directors do not allow researchers to survey individuals at their shelters. Yet social work researchers (and most everyone else, for that matter) are eager to draw conclusions about homeless persons in general. Generalizations make their work (and opinions) sound more important.

If every homeless person were like every other one, generalizations based on observations of one homeless person would be valid. But of course that is simply not the case. In fact, homeless persons who avoid shelters tend to be different from those who use shelters, and different types of shelters may attract different types of homeless persons. We are on solid ground if we question the generalizability of statements about homeless persons based on the results of a survey in just one shelter.

Generalizability has two aspects:

- Sample Generalizability — This exists when a conclusion based on a sample drawn from a larger population holds true for the population from which the sample was drawn. Sample generalizability is a key concern in survey research (see Chapter 15). Political pollsters may study a sample of likely voters, for example, and then generalize their findings to the entire population of likely voters. No one would be interested in the results of political polls if they represented only the tiny sample that actually was surveyed rather than the entire population.
- Cross-Population Generalizability — This refers to the ability to generalize from findings about one group or population or setting to other groups or populations or settings. Cross-population generalizability occurs to the extent that the results of a study hold true for multiple populations; these populations may not all have been sampled, or they may be represented as subgroups within the results to the population from which the sample was studied.

Consider the debate over whether social support reduces psychological distress among homeless persons as it does among housed persons (Schutt et al., 1994). A study based on a sample of only homeless persons could not in itself resolve this debate. But in a heterogeneous sample of both homeless and housed persons, the effect of social support on distress among both groups could be tested.

As we will see in Part IV in this book, generalizability is a key concern in research design. We rarely have the resources to study the entire population that is of interest to us, so we have to select cases to study that will allow our findings to be generalized to the population of interest. We can never be sure that our propositions will hold under all conditions, so we should be cautious in generalizing to populations that we did not actually sample.

Causal Validity

Causal validity, also known as internal validity, refers to the truthfulness of an assertion that A causes B. It is the focus of Chapters 12 and 13.

Most research studies seek to determine what causes what, so we must frequently must be concerned with causal validity. Imagine that we are searching for ways to improve high school programs. We start by searching for what seem to be particularly effective programs in area schools. We find a program at a local high school, Brockton Academy, that a lot of people have talked about, and we decide to compare the standardized achievement test scores of tenth graders in that school with those of tenth graders in another school, Hilltop School, that does not offer the special program. We find that students in the school with the special program have higher scores, and we decide that the special program caused the better scores. Are you confident about the causal validity of our conclusion? Probably not. Perhaps the students in the school with the special program performed better even before the special program began, even before they started school.

This is the sort of problem that such randomized experiments as the Goldfinger et al. (1997) study of housing for the homeless are designed to resolve. By randomly assigning research participants to the two housing types, we made it very unlikely that persons who were older, substance abusers, lacking in social supports, and so on were disproportionately in one housing type rather than the other. We compared participants in our housing groups in terms of hundreds of characteristics and found almost no differences at the start of the experiment.

On the other hand, causal conclusions also can be mistaken because of some factor that was not recognized during planning for the study, even in randomized experiments. Perhaps the school with the special program also had a better library, which is what led to the higher scores. If the independent apartments in the homeless housing study had been in neighborhoods with more drug pushers than the group homes had been in, residents in the independent apartments could have done more poorly for reasons quite apart from their housing type.

Establishing causal validity can be quite difficult. You will learn in more detail in subsequent chapters how experimental designs and statistics can help us evaluate causal propositions, but the solutions are neither easy nor perfect: We always have to consider critically the validity of causal statements that we hear or read.

SUMMARY

We hope this chapter and the preceding one have given you an idea of what to expect in the rest of the book. Our aim is to introduce you to research methods by describing what social work researchers have learned about the social world, as well as how they learned it. The substance of our profession inevitably is more interesting than its research methods, but the methods also become more interesting when they are not taught as isolated techniques.

The theme of validity ties the entire book's chapters together. In a nutshell, you must learn to evaluate how each research technique presented in this book helps us obtain more valid conclusions. Each technique must be evaluated in terms of its ability to help us with measurement validity, generalizability, and causal validity. In addition, you must ask a critical question of each research project you examine: How valid are its conclusions?

We have focused attention here on research studies of the homelessness; in subsequent chapters, we will introduce examples from other areas.

Robert W. Weinbach

C h a p t e r 3

Research Contexts

IN ORDER TO CONDUCT any quantitative or qualitative research study, as presented in the previous two chapters, we need to understand the problem-solving paradigm that is used to formulate practice and research problems. In addition to understanding and knowing how to use the paradigm, we need to face the fact that it is impossible to conduct any research study in a social work setting without an appreciation for the *contexts* in which the study will take place.

If we desire to do a research study in an agency and ignore the special characteristics of conducting our study within the agency, then we are destined for a catastrophe. Social work research is unique because social work practice settings are unique. There are unparalleled opportunities to execute research studies in applied settings, but there are also constraints inherent within these same settings. Thus, only understanding and knowing how to use to formulate practice and research problems are not enough. We must also be aware of, and appreciate, the "special factors" that we must take into account when we want to do a social work research study—the focus of this chapter.

FACTORS AFFECTING SOCIAL WORK RESEARCH

There are three major factors that shape social work research, and it is senseless to view them separately. They always interact, as do components in any system, to create a research environment whose potential for support of research endeavors ranges all the way from complete enthusiasm and sanction to virtual sabotage. This interaction is compounded by the individual personalities, values, and needs of the people who work within the agencies.

The three contextual factors that serve as major shaping forces for all social work research studies are: (1) the social service agency, (2) the social work profession, and (3) the social workers themselves.

The Social Service Agency

The first factor that affects social work research is the agency where the research study actually takes place. The majority of social workers are employed by social service agencies. Some agencies, particularly in the private sector, have demonstrated over the years a strong commitment toward research. As voluntary financial support has decreased in a time of economic problems for many citizens, traditional research roles and responsibilities of social workers employed within the agencies are being examined.

We cannot yet ascertain whether research in private social service agencies will move in the direction of the "luxury" status that it currently enjoys in many public agencies. The future of agency-generated (and agency-supported) research remains at best tenuous for the foreseeable future. But what happens to those of us who may merely be seeking to conduct a simple research study within an agency without requesting extensive agency or financial support? What climate exists within agencies that will affect the potential for at least a minimal support of our research interests?

Generalizations regarding agencies (which range from public social service settings employing thousands to two- or three-person counseling offices) are always dangerous and rarely apply perfectly to any one setting. However, there are six general characteristics that are appropriate to the majority of agencies. These six characteristics are: (1) agencies have accountability concerns, (2) all research has evaluative potential, (3) accountability pressures create a market for research, (4) agencies exist in hostile environments, (5) agencies have scarce financial resources, and (6) agencies have client files.

Accountability Concerns

As discussed in the previous two chapters, accountability is the need for us to demonstrate our effectiveness and efficiency to those who pay the bills. However, accountability has resulted in a mixed blessing for social work research. As we will see in Part VII in this book, evaluative research, or program evaluation, is a logical response to demands that an agency demonstrate that it is doing what it claims to be doing—and doing it relatively inexpensively. At the same time, agency administrators are acutely aware of the threat of unfavorable program evaluations and are fearful that such evaluations may provide justification for funding cutbacks or termination of inefficient, but needed, social service programs. These programs may seem inefficient, and a real fear may be that program evaluations will overemphasize inefficiency without paying adequate attention to the necessity for the services upon which our clients depend.

Evaluative Potential

Like all people, social workers tend to be suspicious of any research study that is evaluative in nature. We rightfully fear that the results of the study will have negative consequences for us and our clients, for many of the same reasons that agency administrators fear it. These fears within agencies are not limited to program evaluations, however. Despite widespread agreements regarding the need for meaningful research studies, particularly in the evaluation of social service programs, our attitude toward research remains typically one of anxiety, distrust, and apathy. A generalized fear of research is not totally unfounded.

Even simple research designs, which seek only to describe or to identify a relationship between two variables, have the potential to embarrass individual social workers, their supervisors, and management. If data are incorrectly (or correctly but tactlessly) interpreted or made available to an audience hostile to the agency or one or more of its staff members, research studies of *any type* can be a legitimate threat.

An agency's administrator "once burned" can be expected to be extremely wary of a proposed research study, no matter what assurances are made and what controls are included in the study's design. Only after past negative experiences are explored and the appropriate assurances made can any reasonable level of approval and support be anticipated from an agency.

It must be emphasized that social work "researchers" may have far different perspectives and needs from those of the agency practitioner and administrators. The questions that interest researchers and comprise the most important issues for them may not interest the staff of the agencies where they wish to conduct their studies. Agency administrators may prefer (and need) to see requests for research studies in terms of cost/benefit ratios.

They are especially concerned with what and how agency resources will be diverted from normal client service to support the proposed study. They may have difficulty in justifying such a reallocation of funds and staff, especially if previous research studies within their agencies resulted in a promised research report that was never delivered. Or worse, they may have received a report that was written in such an esoteric form that it had little potential for utilization by anyone but the researchers themselves.

Many agency administrators have had at least one negative experience with a research study that has embarrassed either the agency, its programs, or the very administrators who risked their reputations to support the research study. Sometimes all of these negative experiences have occurred to the point that the next, well-meaning, potential social work researcher has an especially difficult sales task. Occasionally it is not the past negative experiences, but a genuine fear that threatens support for a research study within an agency.

While accountability pressures have successfully eliminated some agencies that were ineffective and/or inefficient, a few such agencies still remain because they have been able to cover up their shortcomings. If we seek to do a research study in such an agency, we must recognize that any meaningful support from the agency is potentially nil and special diplomacy and determination will be required. Good program evaluations will always pose a serious threat to poorly administered programs and their administrators.

Market for Research

On the positive side, pressures for accountability and resultant fears regarding it in social service agencies have created an environment of interest in program evaluation. Since we are trying to demonstrate our accountability, we are now searching for evaluative methods that will be fair to the agencies, while at the same time providing useful feedback for the improvement of their services to clients.

At first there was a tendency to try to apply systems-oriented evaluation methods developed for use in business (i.e., profit-making) to agencies. This seemed logical, placed a renewed emphasis on efficiency, and was supported and even imposed by people in funding organizations. Advocates of these methods had little understanding of the unique nature of social service agencies committed to public service rather than to private profit.

Use of such evaluative techniques as planning, programming, budget systems (PPBS); program evaluation review techniques (PERT); and other systems analysis–oriented methods provided proof to us that "evaluation" was legitimately to be feared. The specter of cost efficiency used as a criterion for evaluation of social services was threatening and was resisted unless mandated. Agencies that knowingly offered services (e.g., counseling for people who have addictions) that were "inefficient" on a unit basis and had a relatively low success rate (effectiveness) were especially fearful.

Obviously, the use of only profit-oriented measurements of success within social service agencies is totally inappropriate. A renewed interest in different types of program evaluation methods that take into account such factors as the need for services (*despite* inefficiency) is becoming more apparent. There now are many books and articles written by social workers proposing program evaluation methods that we feel are infinitely more fair and reasonable than those utilized in business (e.g., Gabor, Unrau, & Grinnell, 1998; Unrau, Gabor, & Grinnell, 2001).

A positive changing attitude toward program evaluation within social service agencies is now being observed. Agency administrators, faced with the need for evaluation, have turned to people in our own profession to provide it. Social workers, who are more familiar with both the strengths and limitations of day-to-day social work practice, provide evaluations that are not excessively rigid or critical. We also generate more meaningful recommendations that have greater utility for improving services to clients than do researchers' outside our field who may be utilizing criteria inappropriate for a social service agency.

Unlike researchers in other fields, social work researchers understand the limits of knowledge that exist within our profession. We will not mistakenly assume that cause-effect knowledge exists and that this type of knowledge can be applied in a given situation in which our own professional judgment is really the only measurement instrument currently available.

The development of program evaluation methods and the increased interest among us in doing program evaluation have contributed to the fact that agency administrators seem less fearful of evaluation now than in the late 1970s. Some even welcome it as an important skill by which to upgrade the delivery of services to the clients they serve. There is now an increasing acceptance of the importance of evaluation and research activities for the future development of our profession.

As we will see in Chapter 23, we have also begun to look critically at the effectiveness and efficiency of our individual practices. With encouragement from the professional literature, we have shown an increased interest in both group- and single-subject research as vehicles to evaluate our daily work and to generate suggestions for improving it.

Hostile Environments

Although most agencies are readily valued and accepted within their communities, unfortunately, some are not. Public, tax-supported agencies, such as public assistance and criminal justice facilities, are nearly always misunderstood and frequently resented. They may be perceived by the general public as giving away the public's tax dollars to undeserving and undesirable clients. Letters to the editor columns in local newspapers illustrate the low regard and even outright hostility reserved for these agencies and the clients they serve.

Research, which has the potential to dispel commonly believed negative mythology about agencies, may be especially useful, particularly in the agency's ongoing public relations struggle. Any data that can improve the credibility and the overall image of an agency are useful.

Scarce Financial Resources

Some social service agencies that suffer from a public image problem as noted in the previous section could benefit from research studies that would result in a more accurate portrayal of themselves to the general public. However the financial resources that are needed for such projects are often simply not available. Research related to advancing practice theory must often compete with other activities that appear more politically desirable (e.g., policing of clients, fraud investigation) within the critical spotlight of the community.

Resources that are available for a research study may be committed almost entirely to the tasks of data compilation, storage, and retrieval—a tremendous undertaking in a large public agency. Overall experience seems to demonstrate that the agencies in which we work are rarely able to provide the continuity of financing and the staff required by research studies designed to advance practice theory.

As we have seen in Chapter 1, social service agencies usually cannot afford to do "pure research." For obvious reasons they are much more receptive to doing "applied research." We may find them even more receptive to research suggestions, provided we are willing to conduct our study with minimal resource support. Agency administrators would often like to improve the agency's image by showing a commitment to greater accountability, but cannot because they lack the personnel to conduct the needed research studies.

If we are interested in an area that may potentially improve the agency's image, we may be permitted access to data otherwise inaccessible for "pure research" purposes. Research activities that suggest an interest in improving quality of services and a commitment to more efficient use of funds are a valuable tool for an administrator seeking to improve community relations, to deal with suspicious board members, or to negotiate next year's budget.

Client Files

The bureaucratic nature of social service agencies provides a desirable resource for social work research. As presented in Part V in this book, there is often a tendency for us to think in terms of collecting original data. However a wealth of existing data in the form of case records (client files) and regularly gathered statistics often goes untapped. Data may be gathered within agencies because of federal or state mandate or because administrators feel they need to have sufficient records in case of legal actions. Social workers themselves are accustomed to making voluminous notes, whether out of habit or because the notes may actually serve some need, such as "jogging the memory" about a client seen only occasionally.

For legal and other reasons, client files are not and should not be readily available. However, since research has many advantages for agencies in the present environment, client files can usually be obtained. An agency administrator is charged with both safeguarding the confidentiality of client information and creating a good public image for the agency. Research that threatens either of these will result in denial of access to the data residing in client files. Thus, it is essential that tact be used and all necessary assurances be given when proposing a research study to an agency administrator.

Agency administrators are aware that research involving agency data will usually require the time of agency staff. To safeguard confidentiality, a staff member will probably need to be present when client files and other databases are utilized in a research study. If data are computerized, agency personnel may be required simply to obtain the desired data in a form usable to the researcher. Agency records are a relatively economical data source, but various limitations in the use of such databases need to be noted:

- First, generalizations of the study's findings to the clientele of other agencies may not be possible. Every social service agency is unique. While some phenomena (e.g., certain human problems and behavioral characteristics) transcend the boundaries of a given agency, factors such as catchment areas (i.e., geographical areas served) and eligibility criteria (e. g., unemployed youths) of individual agencies may result in a research sample unlike any other. As we will see in Chapter 11, we must be attuned to any biasing effects that arise from the samples we eventually use.

- Second, client files often lack standardization. Data in some agencies are abundant, but not in a sufficiently standardized format to be readily accessible or analyzed. Data within client files tend to change as federal and state requirements are modified. Sometimes it is more economical to collect original data in the usual standardized format than it is to use already existing data from somewhere within the agency.

- Third, client files may be biased. The sources for most agency records and client files are the individual social workers, whose effectiveness is sometimes evaluated in part by what is reflected in their clients' files. As with most human beings, few of us are sufficiently honest (or masochistic) as to record our failures and errors of judgment in agency records. Certain data that result in the evaluation of our own effectiveness are especially suspect.

Even if every effort has been made to record data in client files as accurately as possible, it must be remembered that the social work researcher who uses client files still has no firsthand knowledge of the client. The data ultimately used for a research study may easily become distorted in the necessary chain of translations from the actual behaviors of the client to the practitioner's perceptions of these behaviors (case files) to the researcher's measurement instruments (categorizations) to the data analyses.

- Fourth, client files may contain deliberate omissions. Sensitive client data that may be subject to court subpoena may never appear in clients' files. Sometimes, data (variables) that would be most valuable (e.g., assignment of clients to diagnostic categories) are deleted as a matter of agency policy or worker discretion. In short, client files—for reasons of political and client interest—must be assumed to be inconsistently incomplete data sources.

Increase in computerization of client files and legal concerns regarding the safeguarding of client data may not portend well for social work researchers' using agency records. Every time an agency must defend itself in court either for refusing to release data (client and/or agency) or for releasing data with questionable authorization, the climate for the storage of accessible client information worsens. Issues of confidentiality have led to questions of whether written client files have become a dangerous anachronism now that these necessary data can be stored in coded form accessible by only a few selected staff members. Although this is not yet a common practice, if it were to become widespread it would have a limiting effect on social work research in agency settings.

The Social Work Profession

The second factor that affects social work research is our profession. What is possible and desirable in social work research is shaped by professional values, standards, and definitions that differ from those in any other discipline. There are three characteristics inherent in our profession which shape social work research: (1) the profession's values and ethics, (2) the profession's beliefs and practices, and (3) the rewards for doing research. Membership in our profession carries certain responsibilities, and these responsibilities, combined with professional objectives, constitute both supports and obstacles for those of us who seek to advance social work practice-relevant knowledge through research.

Values and Ethics

Physical scientists need not concern themselves with the rights of their research subjects. Nonorganic matter may be manipulated in a way that will minimize the researcher's three enemies, which are investigator bias, intervening variables, and chance (Weinbach & Grinnell, 2001). The following chapter presents many of the ethical issues that must be addressed in the use of human subjects as research participants. Our profession reflects special concerns relating to the protection of clients whom we are committed to help—not to harm. Some of these concerns are quite legitimate; others are somewhat less so. Nevertheless, our profession, with its protectiveness toward our clients, tends to set limits on research studies that exceed a generalized concern for protecting the rights of human research participants.

Specifically, there are research situations that our profession generally will not (and should not) tolerate, despite the apparent potential for building knowledge for practice theory. As we will see in Chapter 12, research studies involving the random assignment of clients to different practice methods in order to compare the relative effectiveness of the methods are usually opposed.

Probably the most dramatic example of a conflict between professional values and responsibilities and research requirements relates to the issue of the denial of services. In evaluating the effectiveness of a social work treatment intervention, for example, it would be highly desirable, from a research perspective, to randomly form a group of people who are seeking help but are denied it (control group) so that a direct comparison can later be made with those who received help (experimental group). As we will see in the next chapter, such a decision would be a violation of professional social work ethics.

Beliefs and Practices

Some characteristics of our profession are not written down so easily or so easily identified as its values and ethics. Certain beliefs, traditions, and professional definitions, while elusive, nevertheless have their effect on the shaping of research investigations in our profession. Whether they are based on a verifiable *fact* or have their basis in mythology is really unimportant.

Social work practice, particularly at the direct practice level, is believed to be highly dependent on the social worker–client relationship. Not surprisingly, any action (even in the interest of knowledge building) that might be perceived as threatening or in any way changing this relationship will be opposed.

While it may be easy for us to build a logical case for evaluation of practice methods, or for describing the nature of social work practice through direct observation of social worker–client interaction, requests for permission for us to do this are usually not well received. Students in their field practicum courses may observe a similar resistance when they make what appears to be a perfectly reasonable request to learn treatment techniques (e.g., active listening) of a particular intervention (e.g., nondirective therapy) by observing their field instructors in an interview.

The rationale most frequently given for not permitting onsite observation of direct treatment, even in the interest of research, is that it would jeopardize the treatment relationship. While the cynic might see this as an effort to avoid exposing the errors that even a very experienced social worker inevitably makes, it is more likely a sincere belief, based in part on professional tradition and folklore. Despite the fact that skilled observers are rarely an impediment to any treatment relationship (they are soon ignored), the belief persists. This belief presents an obstacle to research studies where firsthand observation of an intervention would be the best means to collect data for the study.

While accountability pressures have recently tended to prod our profession to examine and evaluate our treatment interventions, the nature of our practice is such that effective practice remains difficult to conceptualize and operationalize. Such vague outcome measures as progress and growth—when applied to client problem areas equally as vague, such as communication, self-esteem, and social functioning—become especially elusive. As presented in Chapters 8 through 10, a tremendous amount of progress has been made in the measurement of these and many other concepts. However, our profession has a certain folklore that remains somewhat distrustful of measurement packages that do not take into consideration the professional judgment of the social worker.

Some social workers may prefer to perceive improvement in client functioning subjectively rather than objectively. Research methods that rely heavily on objective measures are likely to be suspect; thus, the utilization potential of quantitative research findings may be readily dismissed because the findings are solely based on quantitative data sources.

Research Rewards

Research has not always been synonymous with status in our profession, as it has in many other fields. Rewards in the form of promotions and recognition have more often gone to skilled practitioners, especially to those of us who have evolved a new intervention (e.g., primal scream, trust fall, trust walk) or pioneered practice methods with a newly discovered client group (e.g., people with AIDS).

Professional social work journals publish fewer reports of quantitatively based research studies than qualitatively based studies. Whether this phenomenon occurs because of editorial preference or the unavailability of high-standard qualitative research reports for publication is not precisely the issue. What is important is that there has been a message within the profession that tends to say that published reports of research findings are of secondary importance to other forms of communication.   A constant pressure for more and better research endeavors has come from ongoing efforts to further professionalize social work. No matter which of several available lists of professional attributes are applied, social work appears especially vulnerable to accusations of nonprofessional status because of its heavy reliance on knowledge derived from other fields, such as psychology and sociology.

The lack of a clear-cut body of knowledge unique to social work practice, and hence the concern about this shortcoming, will continue to foster practice-relevant research. Current emphasis on single-subject research methodologies for use by the individual social worker is but one example of this trend. The popularity of program evaluation is another example. As more of us become involved in doing research, we will see its value to professionalization and, thus, to practice.

Our profession can be expected to become even more supportive of research efforts as professionalization takes hold, because professionals need to do research and use research findings in their practices for reasons previously discussed. Those of us seeking to conduct research studies might well make use of this point to gain acceptance and support for our research aspirations.

The Social Work Practitioners

The final factor that affects social work research is the social workers themselves. As in the case of the agencies and the profession, generalizations about the characteristics of social work practitioners are dangerous. Of course there are always exceptions, but social workers, as a group, seem to have three characteristics that are useful in understanding their role as it affects social work research. These three characteristics are: (1) social workers are people oriented; (2) social workers have a vested interest in practice, and (3) social workers need research.

People Orientation

A certain selection process takes place when any career is chosen. People committing themselves to our profession have done more than choose an academic field or a knowledge area in which to work. They have made statements about themselves in regard to the personal needs and values they possess. In general, we choose our profession because we feel a need and a responsibility to help other people help themselves.

We believe that we are capable of interacting meaningfully with others, either on a one-to-one basis (e.g., direct practice) or on a more indirect level of helping (e.g., research, administration). Furthermore, we desire this type of interaction and probably believe that the helping process and the interaction will provide gratification for us. The selection of our profession is, in part, an acknowledgment of our desire to work with the real and the human, rather than with the abstract or the inanimate. As we saw from Chapter 1, social work research usually involves working with social workers—either as research participants, as research collaborators, or as researchers themselves.

The people orientation of social workers is an important point for us to remember when we wish to gain entry into an agency to conduct a research study. Because of this orientation, relatively few students in social work programs would elect to concentrate on a study of social work research. We can only speculate as to how many social work students would choose to take even a single research course if it were not a degree requirement.

Social workers have a certain amount of disinterest in, or even terror of, research. They have not generally exhibited either the reliance on, or the interest in, research that would be reasonable to expect among those seeking professionalization by attempting to move toward a more knowledge-based practice. Rather than using research-based practice knowledge, we often prefer to rely on what we describe as a combination of humanitarian impulse, occupational folklore, and common sense.

These phenomena should not be viewed as "anti-research" so much as "pro-people." To many of us, research is abstract, dry, theoretical, and totally unrelated to practice. This impression is not without its basis in reality. Until recently, much of social work research has lacked relevance to practice and has had little potential for utilization. The combination of researchers not always in tune with social work practitioners' practice needs and practitioners disinterested in, and uninformed about, research has resulted in attitudes of apathy and even antagonism toward research. However, this attitude has begun to change in recent years as social work graduates have come to a better understanding of research and a knowledge of more practice-relevant methodologies; the people orientation of social workers can be expected to continue.

More often than not, we have a tendency to be advocates for our clients and coworkers alike; we usually reflect optimism and hope that our clients' situations are improving and will continue to improve. Although this positive characteristic is necessary and desirable for social work *practitioners,* it can often drive social work *researchers* to frustration because of the potential biasing effects that this tendency can have. As presented in Chapters 1 and 2, we are notoriously poor resources for the measurement of our clients' success. We sometimes tend to subjectively view clients in a positive light, which interferes with our ability to objectively evaluate our clients' success.

In evaluating the functioning level of clients, objectivity seems to be compromised even further by our need to somehow reward past client growth or even client effort by unrealistically favorable current measurements. Research measurements involving the "subjective" perceptions of our clients' functioning must always be viewed as suspect and in need of "objective" corroboration. The characteristics of emphasizing strengths and the good in people, absolutely essential to good social work *practice,* may be almost diametrically opposed to what is necessary for valid and reliable success measures in social work research.

Vested Interest in Practice

We not only believe in people; we also believe in the treatment interventions that we use to help people help themselves. This results in a confidence that is as desirable for practice as are optimistic evaluations of clients. Unfortunately, the confidence that we have in our interventions may give rise to a resistance both to certain types of research and to our acceptance of research findings that are not supportive of the interventions. It can result in an unwillingness or even an inability on our part to question and, hence, to revise our interventions and treatment techniques on the basis of emerging research findings.

Some social workers employ favorite treatment interventions and have done so for many years. They have become skilled at them through repetition and experience. Some of us have gone even further by writing papers and books about the interventions and their corresponding techniques.

Some of us have also been acknowledged by peers as experts in our specializations. Some social workers have sought to become more proficient at what they do and have made personal and financial sacrifices to receive advanced training in specialized interventions. If we wish to evaluate whether an intervention is truly effective, we will likely meet a wall of resistance based upon one or a combination of these investments.

Research studies that evaluate an intervention and/or its corresponding techniques must be totally objective. Its findings can challenge accepted practices and, in some cases, threaten the reputation and status of those people most associated with its theory (if a theory exists). While this type of research may be what is most needed in our profession, we must anticipate that some of us will be reluctant to participate in research studies and will be reluctant to utilize the findings if they are not an endorsement of our favorite intervention.

Need for Research

It would be erroneous to suggest that the characteristics of social workers present the only barrier to research in our profession. There is another side, based in part on the same attributes, which can provide support for those of us who wish to build a social work knowledge base for practice theory. Generally, we welcome research that is clearly aimed toward improving client services. Having been convinced that a proposed research study has this goal, we will more than likely support the study and participate in it. Until quite recently, there were few research studies that represented methodologically sound evaluations of treatment interventions.

The paucity of these evaluations and the need for them represent an excellent opportunity for research activity. Positions taken by our professional organizations such as the National Association of Social Workers on the need to evaluate social work interventions may be having an effect on the attitudes of practitioners. The entire theme of this book is that our profession needs to incorporate into agency operations, and the daily routine of practice, the developing means for continuously monitoring and assessing the results of our efforts. Research will help us in our difficult task of explaining to others what we are doing, with what success, and its importance.

As a group, we are more humble than arrogant, more open to learning from others than smug about our own knowledge. We are generally realistic about the effectiveness of our helping skills, particularly in working with client groups and problems where experience in the problem area is limited. The nature of our profession is such that a large percentage of those who practice in it are forced to make decisions and to intervene without the assistance of a vast body of sound knowledge. We will welcome research findings that assist us in functioning less on our instinct and good intention and more on a sound knowledge base that was generated through quantitative and qualitative research studies.

SUMMARY

In order to conduct a research study, we need to take into account not only the design of the study itself but the environment in which it will be conducted. The three contextual forces that shape all social work research studies are: the agency, the profession, and the individual social workers involved in the research studies.

This chapter presented the three contexts in which research studies are conducted. The next chapter builds upon this one by discussing the major ethical issues that must be addressed before any research study can take place in any agency setting.

Lewayne D. Gilchrist
Steven P. Schinke

C h a p t e r   4

Research Ethics

SOCIAL WORKERS should always abide by clearly defined ethical principles in both their practice and research activities. Since social work practice and research focus on actual people, real problems, and identifiable social service settings, we are always privy to a great deal of personal and private information. Ethical principles and guidelines for social work practice and research help us to protect our clients, delineate our professional responsibilities, direct our data gathering, and guide our change efforts toward acceptable and worthwhile goals. This chapter presents a few ethical issues that we must be aware of when we do any type of research study.

ENFORCING ETHICAL PRACTICES

Past gross misjudgments in research with human research participants caused the United States Congress, in 1974, to create the National Commission for the Protection of Human Research Subjects of Biomedical and Behavioral Research. The Commission examined documentation on the treatment of research participants, held hearings and conferences on related issues, and developed detailed safeguards for research studies that involved human beings. Although formally dissolved in 1978, the Commission's activities were taken over by other federal agencies (Maloney, 1984). A variety of professional organizations and interested lay groups have also focused on ensuring the physical safety and emotional well-being of research participants taking part in biomedical, behavioral, and social research.

Government regulations allow many institutions engaging in frequent research with human research participants—for example, universities, clinics, and hospitals—to set up their own boards to review and monitor research studies supported by their own funds. The mission of these institutional review boards (IRBs) is both to protect research participants and to ensure that we recognize and respond to the ethical issues that may be embedded in our research studies.

At least two-thirds of all IRB members must be people from the community, with institutionally affiliated persons and outside consultants comprising the remaining third. All meetings held by IRBs are open to the public and all boards must keep five-year records of their deliberations. Thus, the community at large has some control over many research studies involving human research participants.

Professional associations such as the American Psychological Association (APA) and the National Association of Social Workers (NASW) match government moves toward awareness, attention, and positive action to prevent ethical transgressions in research studies that involve human research participants. Associations whose members serve in multiple human services capacities—service, administration, research, teaching, consultation—have carefully established separate ethical codes for various professional roles.

The APA has three sets of ethical guidelines to help direct the work of its members. These guidelines cover three domains: (1) those areas in which all psychologists share responsibilities; (2) those areas of responsibility shared by clinicians, supervisors, and administrators in community and institutional service programs; and (3) those areas relevant to laboratory and field investigations (American Psychological Association, 1977). As we will see latter in this chapter, the NASW devotes one section of its *Code of Ethics* to research and evaluation.

Despite added vigor in government and professional association standards for ethics in social work research studies, the ultimate burden on infusing ethical practices throughout the practice and research processes rests with the individual social worker. NASW refines and disseminates ethical codes and guidelines appropriate for its members. But neither NASW nor the government can continuously monitor how these ethical codes and guidelines are translated into the *actual* conduct of social work research and evaluation.

NASW RESEARCH GUIDELINES

As we saw in Chapter 1, a comprehensive ethical code by the NASW addresses the multiple aspects of our professional roles, which encompass workers' responsibilities and obligations to our clients, colleagues, employers, our profession, and society (see Box 1.2 on Page 3). These guidelines express our profession's concern for clients' rights to confidentiality, privacy, protection, and self-determination. Recognition of the special ethical problems encountered in the research process is an important advancement for the *Code*.

Given the highly interrelated ethical guidelines contained in Box 1.2 that must be followed for all research and evaluation studies that use human research participants, the remainder of this chapter will discuss how some of the more consequential guidelines for research participants can easily be followed without much fuss.

Consequences for Human Beings

It is possible that the very nature of some social work research questions—apart from implementation—may violate a research participant's rights. Evaluating the ethical aspects of a research question is always difficult. As we will see in the next chapter, we must always put a great deal of time and effort into reviewing available literature, lay and professional. In addition we should consult with professional colleagues, clients, and any person who may be affected both by attempts to answer the research question and by the answers these attempts might yield.

The kind of ethical breach that is possible when the consequences of a social work research study are not carefully considered is illustrated in the following case example.

Example

A social worker employed by the Children's Service Division to help evaluate a family therapy program has been asked to study the direction of future planning for client services. These services are based on the belief that placement in foster care of referred children from lower socioeconomic homes would break the cycle of poverty and would thus allow social workers more time for intensive services to children without parental interference. The social worker is asked to test relevant hypotheses in practice situations.

After careful consideration, the social worker decides that such a study is unethical. The worker based this conclusion on values and codes questioning the removal of children from their parents without substantial evidence of abuse or neglect *solely* for research purposes. To investigate whether separating children and parents from lower socioeconomic homes will break the poverty cycle and permit better social work services is unethical.

The social worker suggested conducting a longitudinal study to examine differences between the socioeconomic status of abused or neglected children placed in foster care and those remaining in their own homes. The two groups could then be compared with respect to the children's functioning and the quality of social work services. Such a design allows the research question to be answered without violating ethical standards.

Voluntary and Informed Consent

We must always acquaint our research participants with every aspect of the study. Full permission for involvement is always obtained via informed consent procedures prior to initiation of any research study. Informed consent ensures protection not only for the research participants but also for the social workers who are carrying out the study.

The U.S. Department of Health and Human Services codes provide lengthy and detailed operational definitions of informed consent (Maloney, 1984). Essentially, informed consent requires that research participants fully understand what their participation entails, and that they freely agree to participate. Informed consent is obtained prior to the initiation of any research procedure, and it is documented by signed statements from research participants indicating that they have read or heard a complete description of the research study (American Association on Mental Deficiency, 1977).

Since review boards develop standards appropriate to their individual needs, the organization and wording of specific informed consent statements vary among institutions and agencies. Research participants' signatures usually follow a written summary of intended research procedures, including the social worker's name and telephone number for further information. Box 4.1 provides a brief discussion of the importance of informed consent.

The National Commission for the Protection of Human Research Subjects requires all informed consent procedures to meet three criteria: (1) participants must be competent to consent; (2) sufficient information must be provided to allow for a balanced decision; and (3) consent must be voluntary and uncoerced.

Participants Must Be Competent to Consent

The first criterion, competency to consent, encompasses the legal and mental capabilities of research participants to give permission for activities

Box 4.1_____

Obtaining Informed Consent

The most important consideration in any research study is to obtain the participants' *informed* consent. The word "informed" means that each participant fully understands what is going to happen in the course of the study, why it is going to happen, and what its effect will be on him or her. If the participant is psychiatrically challenged, mentally delayed, or in any other way incapable of full understanding, our study must be fully and adequately explained to someone else—perhaps a parent, guardian, social worker, or spouse, or someone to whom the participant's welfare is important.

It is clear that no research participant may be bribed, threatened, deceived, or in any way coerced into participating. Questions must be encouraged, both initially and throughout the course of the study. People who believe they understand may have misinterpreted our explanation or understood it only in part. They may say they understand, when they do not, in an effort to avoid appearing foolish. They may even sign documents they do not understand to confirm their supposed understanding, and it is our responsibility to ensure that their understanding is real and complete.

It is particularly important for participants to know that they are not signing away their rights when they sign a consent form. They may decide at any time to withdraw from the study *without penalty*, without so much as a reproachful glance. The results of the study will be made available to them as soon as the study has been completed. No promise will be made to them that cannot be fulfilled.

A promise that is of particular concern to many research participants is that of anonymity. A drug offender, for example, may be very afraid of being identified; a person on welfare may be concerned whether anyone else might learn that he or she is on welfare. Also, there is often some confusion between the terms "anonymity" and "confidentiality."

Some studies are designed so that no one, not even the person doing the study, knows which research participant gave what response. An example is a mailed survey form, bearing no identifying mark and asking the respondent not to give a name. In a study like this, the respondent is *anonymous*. It is more often the case, however, that we do know how a particular participant responded and have agreed not to divulge the information to anyone else. In such cases, the information is *confidential*. Part of our explanation to a potential research participant must include a clear statement of what information will be shared with whom.

All this seems reasonable in theory, but ethical obligations are often difficult to fulfill in practice. There are times when it is very difficult to remove coercive influences because these influences are inherent in the situation. A woman awaiting an abortion may agree to provide private data about herself and her partner because she believes that, if she does not, she will be denied the abortion. It is of no use to tell her that this is not true: She feels she is not in a position to take any chances.

There are captive populations of people in prisons, schools, or institutions who may agree out of sheer boredom to take part in a research study. Or, they may participate in return for certain privileges, or because they fear some penalty or reprisal. There may be people who agree because they are pressured into it by family members, or they want to please the social worker, or they need some service or payment that they believe depends on their cooperation. Often, situations like this cannot be changed, but at least we can be aware of them and try to deal with them in an ethical manner.

A written consent form should be only part of the process of informing research participants of their roles in the study and their rights as volunteers. It should give participants a basic description of the purpose of the study, the study's procedures, and their rights as voluntary participants. All information should be provided in plain and simple language, without jargon.

A consent form should be no longer than two pages of single-spaced copy, and it should be given to all research participants. Survey questionnaires may have a simple introductory letter containing the required information, with the written statement that the completion of the questionnaire is the person's agreement to participate. In telephone surveys, the information will need to

Box 4.1 Continued

be given verbally and must be standardized across all calls. A written consent form should contain the following items, recognizing that the relevancy of this information and the amount required will vary with each research project:

1. A brief description of the purpose of the research study, as well as the value of the study to the general/scientific social work community (probability and nature of direct and indirect benefits) and to the participants and/or others.

2. An explanation as to how and/or why participants were selected and a statement that participation is completely voluntary.

3. A description of experimental conditions and/or procedures. Some points that should be covered are:

   a The frequency with which the participants will be contacted.

   b The time commitment required by the participants.

   c The physical effort required and/or protection from overexertion.

   d Emotionally sensitive issues that might be exposed and/or follow-up resources that are available if required.

   e Location of participation (e.g., need for travel/commuting).

   f Information that will be recorded and how it will be recorded (e.g., on paper, by photographs, by videotape, by audiotape).

4. Description of the likelihood of any discomforts and inconveniences associated with participation, and of known or suspected short- and long-term risks.

5. Explanation of who will have access to the collected data and to the identity of the participants (i.e., level of anonymity or confidentiality of each person's participation and information) and how long the data will be stored.

6. Description of how the data will be made public (e.g., scholarly presentation, printed publication). An additional consent is required for publication of photographs, audiotapes, and/or videotapes.

7. Description of other projects or other people who may use the data.

8. Explanation of the participants' rights:

   a That they may terminate or withdraw from the study at any point.

   b That they may ask for clarification or more information throughout the study.

   c That they may contact the appropriate administrative body if they have any questions about the conduct of the people doing the study or the study's procedures.

Source: Adapted and modified from:
Williams, Unrau, and Grinnell (1998);
Williams, Tutty, and Grinnell (1995); and
Grinnell and Williams (1990)

---

affecting their rights and welfare. Minors, for instance, are not legally capable of signing or entering into such agreements.

Children cannot be expected to understand the research study sufficiently to give legally binding permission for their own participation. Their parents or legal guardians must provide such permission for them. Ethically, however, children may reasonably be expected to want some voice in what happens to them. They may or may not agree with the permission to participate that has been given for them. If they do agree, this agreement process is referred to as *assent* rather than *consent*. Whenever possible, we should always involve *both* parents (or guardians) *and* children in consent and assent processes.

Informed consent procedures become more difficult for minors whose legal guardianship is not clear. Research in the area of delinquency provides an example. The following excerpt is from a researcher at a social work agency:

It was not uncommon for doubt to exist, because of unavailability of records, or inaccuracies in various documents, regarding just who (i.e., parent, relative, agency, court) was the legal guardian of a youth in such cases. Therefore, it was deemed advisable to obtain informed consent or agreement from every party possible. While occasionally quite frustrating and time-consuming, such a conservative approach avoids misunderstanding later if various parties find that their memories of verbal agreements differ. Agreements which are entirely verbal do not seem prudent in most situations. (Maloney, 1984)

Assessing the mental competency of older potential research participants can also become a complex problem, particularly if our research study engages clients who are in treatment for temporary or chronic psychological problems or mental disorders. Changing laws concerning these groups' legal rights increase the difficulty of competency assessment. Thus, we should gain informed written consent from at least one significant person in such research participants' lives—a parent, guardian, court-appointed social worker, or spouse, for example.

People who are mentally handicapped are highly vulnerable to abuse of their welfare, rights, and privacy. In response to this, significant changes in federal regulations protect them when they participate in social work research efforts. One measure aimed at safeguarding institutionalized, mentally handicapped persons requires advocates to audit the protection given research participants during any research procedure. To ensure objective assessment of risk, regulations set explicit criteria for electing advocates; no one may serve as an advocate who has an interest in, or association with, the agency conducting or sponsoring the research study. Where the research participant is a ward of a state or of another social service agency, institution, or entity, the advocate may not have an interest in that entity. Advocates must also be familiar with the physical, psychological, and social needs, and the legal status of individuals under study.

Adequate Information Must Be Given

The second informed consent criterion, that participants receive adequate information about the research study before consenting, also entails specific standards. Differences among formats required by individual review boards are determined by whether the sponsoring institution is a university, medical school, hospital, public school system, or social service agency.

Operationally, adequate information means detailing what the research study will demand in terms of time, activities, and disclosure of private facts and attributes, as well as the risks and benefits. Research participants must be guaranteed opportunities before signing and during the research study to ask questions about any facet of the study. They must be assured that they can decline involvement in any or all aspects of the research study and, further, they must be assured that personally identifiable information about them will be destroyed at their request. Should individuals decline to participate or choose to withdraw from the study, guarantees prohibit any loss to them of benefits, services, or funds available to the usual clientele of the sponsoring organization.

Participation Must Be Voluntary

The third informed consent criterion of voluntary participation prohibits us from coercing, deceiving, or fraudulently recruiting research participants. This requirement may be more difficult than it first appears, since involvement in a research study often brings explicit or implicit rewards. Research participants may be offered cash payments for their time, or they may be promised less immediate but equally tangible benefits such as special social work services, differential treatment in a health care facility, or enriched educational curricula. Despite our good intentions, extra payoffs for a research participant to participate can easily represent powerful inducements for volunteering. When our target groups are from lower socioeconomic levels or other deprived populations, for example, even small inducements may be too great for them to refuse. Further, children may have difficulty refusing anything that an adult asks of them.

The line between voluntary and involuntary participation is even fuzzier when potential research participants are institutionalized or have their freedom restricted. Captive populations such as schoolchildren, mental hospital patients, treatment center residents, and prisoners may volunteer for unpleasant research tasks to escape institutional tedium. The timing of a request to participate in a study can also result in extra pressure to volunteer. A couple just ready to enter a hearing on termination of parental rights because of child abuse may have difficulty turning down a request to examine their case file for research purposes. Or, women waiting for an abortion may not feel free to reject a request for private nonmedical information about themselves, their families, or their past sexual partners.

Social workers should also consider the potential coerciveness of the context and setting in which consent is to be obtained. The presence of such influential people in our research participant's life such as parents, spouse, social worker, teacher, or physician is likely to make the voluntary participation less objective. Admittedly, we cannot control all the factors that could possibly influence voluntary consent procedures. Agency settings especially limit our ability to orchestrate environmental influences. But these complexities should never deter us from removing as many coercive influences as possible and giving potential research participants maximum freedom to accept or refuse participation.

The case material from a proposed social work research study that follows depicts major precautions we must always be aware of when working with research participants.

Example   Two social work graduate students were satisfying their field placement requirements at a Community Action Commission. The agency primarily served single-parent families in a federal housing project. Part of the students' responsibilities was facilitating monthly tenant meetings. The students received an assignment to design and implement a field research study. The Community Action Commission meetings appeared to be a logical site for the study, and the students planned procedures to collect observational data on various interactional patterns: who attended the meetings, who spoke, who assumed leadership roles, and so forth.

One of the students asserted that telling meeting members about the study in advance would alter the members' interactional patterns and suggested that the purpose of the study should not be revealed until after all the necessary data were collected. The other student opposed such deception and advocated informed consent procedures from all members who went to the monthly meetings before beginning the study. Unable to agree, the two students deferred to their instructor.

The instructor listened to both sides of the argument and agreed that awareness of the research study would change the interactional patterns of the potential research participants. Nevertheless, the instructor maintained that informed consent was absolutely necessary and noted that the interaction patterns of the participants could be ethically examined by collecting data in two different formats: in front of the consenting participants and out of their sight. Comparing data collected under both conditions would show how the level of awareness affected interactions, at no cost to research ethics.

Protection from Physical and Mental Harm

Sound ethical choices go beyond analysis of research questions, research participant recruitments, and informed consent procedures. The actual implementation of social work research also entails risks. During implementation, we must scrutinize the effects of our research designs, procedures for intervention, data collection and analyses, and the reporting of the research study in professional journals and books.

Research designs can also violate ethical standards in several respects. For example, the use of control groups allows us greater confidence in our study's findings. A group of individuals exposed to an experimental treatment intervention can easily be contrasted with a group of individuals not receiving the treatment. If the two groups are equivalent in every way except exposure to the intervention, our findings may conclude that differences between the two groups may be due to the intervention. However, the omission or variation of treatment may violate the rights of the research participants in the control group. For example, the people in the control group may be denied essential social work services, funds, or such adjunctive resources as food stamps. The research design, therefore, must be evaluated for its negative potential consequences for research participants in the control group.

Data collection demands attention to ethical issues in selecting and using collection instruments and in analyzing and presenting data. Data collection instruments such as those mentioned in Part III of this book must accurately measure the relevant concepts we are studying. In addition, our measuring instruments must be unbiased. Literature on similar research and pilot projects is invaluable in helping us to choose precise measuring instruments. Investigations with psychological and social data collection instruments have stimulated critical assessment of measures for bias against racial, cultural, and handicapped groups. Such concerns suggest care at this stage of the research process so that special populations are not misrepresented.

We must always be sure that all data collection instruments selected for our study follow administrative protocol as much as possible. Research integrity and respect for research participants' rights rest on cautious data collection procedures.

As we will see in Chapter 23, the analysis and presentation of our data also demand extra attention. Specific data that we provide individuals on their own or others' results need to be carefully couched to obviate negative interpretations. We should keep our feedback to agency coworkers and auxiliary personnel to an aggregated, or nonspecific, level. Revealing the substance of specific results or detailed feedback risks damaging research participant and worker confidentiality which could launch unfortunate comparisons among individuals and collaborating sites. The case that follows highlights key issues in implementation.

Example

A school social worker has earned a reputation as being knowledgeable and effective in helping teachers use various behavior management techniques. One of the kindergarten teachers seeks the social worker's assistance in controlling an unruly afternoon class and asks advice on maintaining an orderly classroom.

The social worker agrees to help the teacher develop and implement an improved learning environment but explains that careful assessment is necessary first, since the intervention finally selected would reflect these assessment data and conventional procedures. However, the teacher wants a quick response and opposes an assessment procedure because it will delay classroom intervention. Knowing the harm that a poorly planned intervention might cause, the social worker agrees to become involved only if they jointly devise a plan to assess the problem, develop an appropriate intervention program, and evaluate its efficacy.

The social worker explains to the teacher that unless they systematically follow each phase, they may base their decisions on insufficient or erroneous assumptions. They also will not be able to pinpoint exactly what worked and what did not, and other teachers with similar problems will not be able to benefit from their experience.

Confidentiality

Social workers receive a tremendous amount of privileged communications. Temptations to share personal reactions and evaluations of interesting cases can cause those of us who are unprepared to informally and inappropriately disclose sensitive and privileged information. We must be careful never to discuss research details informally with family, friends, colleagues, or representatives from the media. Outside the formal professional social work context, such careless disclosures are unethical and may harm not only the client or research participant, but the indiscreet social worker and, by extension, our profession as a whole. Issues of appropriate professional disclosure are closely linked with concern for client and research participant confidentiality. Protection of privacy is a *basic right* guaranteed to all social work practice clients and research participants. Protection of privacy is not a *privilege*—it's a right!

Discussions may easily result in inappropriate identification of the research participants. We must always realize that research settings, client or research participant identification, and occasionally geographic locale must be masked to meet guidelines for confidentiality in reporting. We should also destroy our data and research records at the conclusion of the study in accordance with promises we made to our research participants.

In many social service settings, however, those people who handle the data are usually asked to sign confidentiality pledges in which they formally agree not to discuss any aspect of the research study or the data with anyone other than the research staff.

Ethical issues will become more complex when third parties outside the researcher/research participant relationship express interest in our study's findings. Parents, for example, sometimes ask us how their child responded to given questions; teachers may ask us the responses given by a particular student. We must always follow through on our guarantees to our research participant where we promised confidentiality of individual responses.

Occasionally—especially in research studies that focus on the use of illegal substances—questions may arise regarding the ethics and the legality of withholding data from law enforcement agencies. Although never put to legal tests, the government has recognized the primacy of research interests in these conflicts. Many federal agencies and institutes issue special protections so that federally funded researchers may not be compelled by any federal, state, or local, civil, criminal, administrative, legislative, or other proceedings to reveal names or identifying characteristics of their research participants. The right of social work researchers to withhold such information in nonfederally sponsored research projects is less clear. Professional disclosure and confidentiality issues are illustrated in the following example.

Example

A young social work graduate was employed in a large social service clinic that served children who were mentally handicapped. On the bus home one night, a friendly neighbor complimented her in reference to helping children who had such handicaps. Enthusiastically, but without mentioning names or other specific identifiers, the young social worker outlined the kind of problems encountered by several typical children she was working with. The next morning, in a hastily called meeting, the young worker's supervisor stated that the director of the clinic had received an angry call withdrawing one of the worker's children from the clinic. A relative of one of the worker's clients had been sitting in a seat close by on the bus and recognized the details of the worker's comments The child's family, angered by the apparent breach of confidentiality, withdrew their child from the clinic.

Credit in Scholarly and Research Endeavors

Multiple collaborative relationships are numerous in social work research. We soon learn—planning fully or by trial and error—how and when to delegate responsibilities and tasks to peers, research assistants, and adjunctive support staff. Judging how much to rely on others, assessing in advance individual expertise, and tactfully but quickly terminating unworkable relationships will usually mean the difference between successful and less than successful research projects.

Ethical concerns we face in collaborative relationships in a research study are not unlike those in any professional contact. Still, we are often faced with special considerations. For example we can use collegial consultations in selecting an appropriate research problem, study population, and research method. We can also use the advice and counsel from colleagues who have different racial, sexual, and cultural perspectives. In what manner and to what extent these contributions are credited should be carefully considered. Such credit becomes a formal issue when final reports are written for publication.

As presented in Chapter 20, regardless of individual agency requirements, a social worker's professional responsibility remains unmet until the study's findings have been written and reproduced in retrievable form. New theory and new practice methods are useless if such developments perish with their creators. As was seen in the previous chapters, accumulation of knowledge is not a private effort. Thus, a professional ethic demands that such accretions become a part of the public domain.

Government policy has given added weight to the need for us to disseminate our research findings. The Federal Council of Science and Technology, for example, states that the publication of research results is an essential part of the research process. This has been recognized with authorization to pay publication costs from federal research grants and contract funds.

Sharing authorship and research credit with collaborators may become an ethical issue. Research activities can enhance professional reputations and are often associated with such tangible recognitions as merit pay increases and promotions. Research findings become the bases for grant applications and peer reviewed publications. Ambiguous guidelines for determining authorship complicate this delicate matter even further.

A general rule in determining authorship is to determine the amount, or effort, of the contribution made by each participant in the research study. However the amount of the contribution one makes is often difficult to determine. Whenever possible, potential coauthors should meet together, review their relative contributions, and jointly decide on how the authorship is to be stated. All contributors are contacted before being listed on a document to authorize proper use and placement of names—in footnotes, title, or text—and to demonstrate how their contributions will be acknowledged. Correct spellings, credentials, and institutional affiliations can easily be verified at this time. Evaluation and dissemination activities that operationalize ethics are evident in the following case example.

Example

A social work supervisor at a Department of Social Service (DSS) staff development center was responsible for training social workers in three regional offices. To evaluate a specific training program, the supervisor and DSS administrators designated that social workers in each office were to be trained in sequence, with one month between phases. This interval allowed training to be measured. Measurement included knowledge questionnaires, attitudinal scales, and skill performance tests. Results of the study showed that the staff in each office improved only after they had been trained. In short, training was deemed successful. The findings also revealed differences among the three offices, with social workers at two offices improving more than those at the third. Further, workers in the same office increased their skills at varying rates; some improved a great deal, others very little.

The supervisor wanted to share the findings with each office on the basis that the workers, supervisors, and agency administrators involved would appreciate seeing how research and evaluation methods were applied in their agencies. However, showing and explaining research findings can easily have negative effects by highlighting differences among the participating workers and agencies. Thus, the supervisor compromised by collating all data into composite results across staff and agencies. This procedure greatly reduced the likelihood of generating between-worker or between-staff competition between workers or staff, yet provided everyone an objective glimpse at the training program.

The DSS director strongly encouraged the supervisor to submit a report of the project for possible publication. Authorship for the written report was determined in the following way. The supervisor, as the designer and implementor of the study, wrote up the methods and procedures sections of the report and was designated first author. The director, a far more experienced writer, wrote the report's introduction and conclusion sections and a section on policy implications and edited the entire manuscript to conform with publication guidelines. The director was designated second author. An acknowledgments section on the paper's title page thanked all involved DSS administrators, the two social work graduate students who were involved in the data collection and coding, and the secretary who typed the manuscript.

SUMMARY

Future social work research studies will become more and more occupied with ethical questions, issues, and procedures. Proposed legislation, federal regulations, and modified professional codes suggest that research studies with humans as research participants will require us to be more careful with ethical safeguards for all of our research participants. Some fear that social work research will become so encumbered by externally imposed constraints that only unimaginative, simple, and irrelevant studies can be launched.

Indeed, evidence indicates that people are highly suggestible and that information alone changes attitudes, moods, feelings, and perceptions. Thus, efforts to obtain informed consent may have negative effects if research participants adversely react to information. If protection of the research participant is the reason for obtaining informed consent, the possibility of harm as a direct result of the consent process must then be considered. Criticisms from the professional community will surely intensify as government agencies and professional associations require additional ethical safeguards.

The federal government continues to release regulations on social research. For example, recent guidelines direct all institutions receiving U.S. Department of Health and Human Services (formerly Department of Health, Education, and Welfare) funds to inform research participants not only of study risks but of medical treatment and financial compensation available should any harm take place (Department of Health, Education, and Welfare, 1978). Social work research ethics address concerns and questions raised throughout the social work research process. We should be mindful that we alone can apply and monitor ethical standards. Those of us who conduct a

research study within this conceptual framework will limit the risk of harming clients, ourselves, or the lay, professional, and scientific communities to which we are accountable.

Ethics are not merely derived from etiquette. They express beliefs and guide professionals in achieving those beliefs. As an integral part of our profession, they foster practice and research endeavors that are compatible with our profession's goals and values. Social workers committed to ethical practice and research look for the most valid and reliable data possible without deceiving others, causing harm, or being dishonest in any way.

This is the final chapter in our discussion of the contexts of social work research. In Part II, we shall begin to look at ways we can formulate research questions and hypotheses and how quantitative and qualitative research approaches are used to generate knowledge for our profession.

Problem Formulation and Research Approaches

David E. Cournoyer
Waldo C. Klein

C h a p t e r 5

Formulating Research Questions

A PROMINENT EXPERIMENTAL SOCIAL SCIENTIST visiting a small college campus asked a gathering of students what they found the most difficult about their research methods courses. One surprising answer was "Finding a question to study!" This is a common complaint among students in social work research classes. Many instructors require students to design and/or conduct a research study as part of their training. Students frequently report spending an inordinate amount of time in the selection of a topic to study. In addition to the usual case of procrastination, this difficulty arises from two related problems:

- First, many students arrive in social work classes without a clear idea of what is scientific thinking, and lack the skills to formulate a researchable social work question.

- Second, the tendency to emphasize the rational aspects of science misleads students concerning the origins of research questions. Although this whole book is about scientific thinking, this chapter provides special emphasis on the identification of researchable questions.

Understanding the nature and origins of researchable ideas is important in your role as a future social work practitioner as well as your role as a student. Evaluation of practice is an ethical requirement for social workers, as is the ability to use and contribute to the empirical knowledge base of our profession. This chapter will help you get off to a good start by describing the characteristics of researchable questions and explaining how to translate everyday practice interests into researchable questions. Learning to ask researchable questions will also add value to the hours you spend studying the empirical basis of interventions in your social work classes, because researchable questions are excellent devices for anchoring ideas more firmly in the mind.

Finally, this chapter will help you to understand some of the sociocultural hurdles you need to leap in order to obtain the resources you need in the pursuit of new knowledge. For those of you who become active scholars, the ability to ask researchable questions will become so automatic that you will find a world with many more researchable questions than time and resources allow you to answer. Understanding the sociopolitical side of social science research is a great help in the quest for expanded research resources to answer emerging questions.

RESEARCHABLE (EMPIRICAL) AND NONEMPIRICAL QUESTIONS

Much of science can be reduced to the design and testing of mental models (theories) that are expected to account for regularities in the empirical world. Although that world is knowable to us only in an indirect and human way, the methods of science help us untangle some of the logical fallacies associated with human thought and perception and come to consensus about states and relationships in the empirical world. It must seem logical, therefore, that the kinds of questions of interest to people when using their scientific reasoning are questions that reference people, things, and events in the empirical world.

Questions that ask about the state of the empirical world, the pattern of forces that may account for current states in the world, or how consistent a set of observations is with a theory designed to explain, predict, or control empirical events are all researchable questions. The use of both logic and references to observables are two characteristics that make scientific propositions and questions different from other types of questions. In sum, researchable questions are usually logical propositions about observable things, events, or people.

It seems possible that the definition of researchable questions proposed earlier is so broad that very little would appear not to qualify. Can you imagine questions that do not test ideas about the empirical world or do not involve logical propositions? Yes, in fact it is quite easy. Many kinds of questions tend to be argued on purely philosophical, religious, political, or mystical grounds.

Ideas about right and wrong, good and evil, and the ultimate meaning of life all have researchable aspects, such as determining what the beliefs of a group of individuals are, but many questions in these areas are formed in ways that do not reference empirical events. Individuals who believe as a matter of faith in the Book of Genesis as a literal accounting of the origins of the universe are little affected either by the logical difficulties this account contains or the strong observational data inconsistent with the biblical account. Likewise, anything that comes under the rubric of taste or preference is likely to be unresolvable through empirical observation. What is the best clothing style, the best society, the best religious organization? What criteria are optimal for making judgments of "best" in any of these contexts? These are not researchable questions as stated.

Having said that questions of value, belief, or taste are not researchable, we can state that science may have something to contribute to these areas also, but only if we start from a place other than determining what is "good," "right," or "moral." To the extent that discussions of values and beliefs include assumptions about empirical events, science can enter into the process to test those assumptions. We can conduct surveys, for example, to determine the proportion of people who hold certain beliefs. Exploratory research methods can be used to identify the meaning systems in which values are embedded. We can even look at the behavior consequences of holding certain beliefs. However, science is not likely to resolve questions about the ultimate "right or wrong" of a value or belief.

Many questions include both empirical and nonempirical aspects. Consider the question concerning corporal punishment. Is it good to use physical punishment to discipline children? Western social scientists have long been suspicious that corporal punishment does more harm to children and families than good. Family sociologist Murray A. Straus is one of the strongest opponents of corporal punishment. Straus titled his book on the subject *Beating the Devil out of Them: Corporal Punishment in American Families* (1991). The main thesis of the book is that corporal punishment is not an effective form of discipline and, in fact, is hurtful and likely to be the precursor of more child misbehavior, family violence, and violence outside of the family. Straus provides evidence from his own studies of thousands of families and the results of hundreds of other studies that clearly document negative consequences of corporal punishment.

The paradox here is that the assumed beneficial or at least benign effects of corporal punishment are not the sole criteria for making decisions about such behaviors. The Bible contains language that has been interpreted as requiring parents to provide physical punishment as a matter of moral necessity. What is a person to do when moral teachings command behaviors that scientists suggest may lead to negative consequences for families? How should scientific findings and belief systems enter into public policy decisions and definitions of concepts such as child abuse? The answers are not clear.

Table 5.1   Examples of Researchable Questions

✓ Do parents with major depression who receive a standard therapeutic intervention show decreased depression after treatment?

✓ Do youth who are teamed up with mentors demonstrate fewer problem behaviors when compared to youth who do not have mentors?

✓ Do frail elders who receive in-home support services report higher quality of life than frail elders who do not receive such services?

✓ Are rates of alcoholism higher among Japanese Americans than other ethnic groups in the United States?

✓ What do parents and children in the Czech Republic believe about women's roles?

✓ How do African American women make moral judgments?

✓ What are the precursors to youth joining a gang?

✓ What do community organizers do?

✓ How depressed is my client?

✓ Is my intervention working?

Straus was successful in describing and explaining the antecedents and consequences of corporal punishment in the United States. However, persons who regard corporal punishment as a biblically sanctioned essential form of parenting are not likely to be influenced by his treatment of the subject. All the evidence of the harmful effects does not mitigate the moral imperative to "beat the devil out of them." These are examples of questions that are important, but not satisfactorily resolved exclusively within the context of scientific study.

Although scientific study is not designed to answer moral questions in absolute terms, that does not mean that scientific study is not relevant to moral debates. For instance, science is unlikely to ever rule on the moral rightness of taking retribution on some criminals through capital punishment. However, science is well equipped to determine whether capital punishment is an effective deterrent to crime (in persons other than the executed). Likewise, if one can define "holy" or "moral" in terms of actions of people in the real world, it is possible to ask whether corporal punishment results in people who are more "holy" or "moral."

Often, rules for human conduct are based on beliefs about the consequences of that conduct. Because those beliefs are expressed in terms of observables, they are amenable to test. See the point? "Is TV violence bad?" is a moral question not amenable to a scientific study. However, when translated into "Does TV violence produce increased violence in children?" it is a researchable question. Table 5.1 above offers some researchable questions that span many social work interests. Although finding answers to these questions would involve many different research techniques, they are all amenable to scientific exploration.

Some of the questions listed in Table 5.1 are paraphrased from studies in scholarly journals. Others reflect questions that social workers have asked us. Some of these questions are general and exploratory, whereas some are very precise predictions about empirical events called hypotheses. The questions cover very different topics. However, there is a pattern—do you see it? All the questions ask about aspects of the empirical world—that is, things that we could all experience. The other chapters that follow in this book discuss how to turn questions like these into procedures for getting answers.

CHARACTERISTICS OF USEFUL QUESTIONS

There are five simple rules that can be used to construct questions that could usefully guide scientific inquiry in social work:

1. The question must be posed in terms of observables.
2. The question must be expressed in terms for which nominal definitions are available.
3. The scope of possible answers should not be arbitrarily limited.
4. The question should be testable in principle.
5. The answer should be important—it should matter to someone.

Questions Should Be Posed in Terms of Observables

The requirement that researchable questions be referenced in terms of observables simply means that it contains a proposition or inquiry about the state of the empirical world under some conditions. Identifying referents for things that have a physical existence—such as age, gender, and income—is fairly easy. However, when our questions concern such mental constructs as loneliness or oppression, finding referents can be a bit more challenging. Referents are the real-world things; they are observables that allow us to accurately infer that the quality indicated by a mental construct is present.

The topic of conceptualization—that is, working out meaning systems—will be taken up in more detail in the following chapter. For now, it is enough to remember that researchable questions make reference to observables or ideas that can be defined unambiguously in terms of observables. For example:

Initial Unresearchable Question:
• Is it just to refuse education to children of undocumented workers?

The above example is not researchable in its present form. "Just" does not have an empirical referent. (It reflects a value.) Resolving this question would be primarily a matter of political, religious, or philosophical discourse. Three researchable alternatives to the question above might include:

Three Possible Researchable Questions:

- What proportion of the population thinks that refusing education to children of undocumented workers is a desirable social policy?
- What are the costs of educating children of undocumented workers?
- What are the ways that the presence of children of undocumented workers influences communities?

Many other possibilities exist, and providing answers would help us understand the phenomenon of children of undocumented workers, but none of the three possible researchable questions listed above would answer the initial question, which is phrased in terms of values.

Questions Should Contain Nominal Definitions

Nominal definitions are social conventions about the classes of experiences that are associated with a particular word or symbol. Ideas that are so subjective and personal as to be impossible to define in ways recognizable by others are seldom researchable. If you cannot explain the question in ways that are meaningful to others, you probably do not have a researchable question. In fact, many areas of research emerge only after some enterprising social scientist resolves definition and measurement problems to the satisfaction of most of her or his peers. In order for a question to be researchable, it must be expressed in terms that are understandable to other persons who have an interest in the answer. This does not mean that unconventional questions are not researchable, just that researchable questions tend to be consciously phrased in words that have conventional meanings to persons interested in the question.

The requirement that the elements of a research question reflect shared definitions and meanings is not meant to suggest that there are "real" definitions for ideas that are the absolute standards of meaning. In fact, consensus around meanings in any cultural context tends to be incomplete and evolving. What is needed here is enough shared meaning that the domains to be tapped by the question can be approximately identified. For example, pollsters have found that asking questions about "welfare" has produced unexpected results, in part because of the negative stereotyping associated with the word, but also because of its ambiguity.

Different patterns of response result when a more precise label, such as AFDC (Aid to Families with Dependent Children), is referenced in the question. In areas of interest where many ideas are not yet worked out at a conceptual level, expressing the question clearly may include some explanation and definition. For example, research questions involving concepts such as homelessness, underemployment, or at-risk clients usually require some explanation of what is meant by these terms as part of the research question.

The requirement that research questions use terms for which nominal definitions exist or potentially exist plays out similarly in research activities designed to uncover meaning systems of clients or populations. "How do the people in this community think about crime?" is a perfectly valid ethnographic question. So is "What do fights with her spouse mean to my client?"

In this type of research, however, the definitions of terms such as *crime* and *fights* that are assumed by the social worker asking the question are only starting points. Activities designed to answer such questions would most likely involve the social worker's looking for differences and similarities between conventional uses of the terms and the way they are used by the community members or clients germane to the study.

Possible Answers for Questions Should Not Be Limited

The third criterion proposed is that research questions must be phrased in such a way that answers other than the one favored by the researcher are permissible. This is actually a difficult criterion to meet because the very act of asking questions tends to limit the range of acceptable answers. One operating rule is that a question that permits only one acceptable answer is too restrictive to ever be useful. A research question cannot be phrased as a statement (Proving the value of treatment *X*) but rather as an interrogatory concerning classes of alternatives (Whether or not treatment *X* works under specified conditions). Beyond the criterion that a question that permits only one answer is too restrictive, any question that eliminates classes of plausible answers by rhetoric and definition is problematic.

For example, consider the question, Do children of the poor learn the successful coping strategies of successful families or do they remain stuck in the maladaptive strategies of the culture of poverty? This question, as stated, unnecessarily restricts the answers to it as it assumes that strategies of successful families are adaptive and those of poor families are maladaptive. This particular example also gets close to the issue of values implicit in questions. The tendency to assume that behaviors of the poor are necessarily maladaptive arises from a value base that sees the poor as personally responsible for their fate. We will return to the issue of values implicit in questions shortly. The point here is that values tend to narrow the range of answers that are logically possible. This is also true of exploratory questions if the structure of the question leads the investigator to overlook the unexpected.

Questions Should Be Answerable

Even if the first three conditions (i.e., posed in terms of observables, nominal definitions available, not arbitrarily limited) are met, the question may still not be scientifically useful if it is not answerable in principle. This criterion requires that the questioner be able to specify the conditions under which an answer may be obtained. If it is possible to envision conditions under which a credible answer to the question can be obtained, then the question is probably researchable.

This criterion is tricky, because technical, ethical, and resource concerns may make some questions very difficult to pursue and thus blur the boundary between answerable and nonanswerable questions. For example, ethical considerations may make an experiment involving comparing emerging therapies infeasible, or lack of cultural contact may make it difficult to test some propositions in cross-cultural settings. However, if there exist some conditions under which it is possible to address the otherwise sound question, then it probably meets our definition of a researchable question.

Question Should Be Important

Finally, the question must be important and the answer to it should matter. As an aspiring member of a helping profession, you recognize that empirical studies often compete with direct services for time and resources. Therefore, your research study should put something back into the system for the good of clients. Even if the study requires very little beyond your own time and energy, you should be able to justify its value to the profession and to the clients we serve—for your time and energy are valuable resources that should not be squandered on trivial research studies. Of course, the degree of importance of a question is, once again, not purely an objective matter. The question of who gets to define the criteria for "important" is a sociocultural concern.

To some individuals, a very narrow experimental hypothesis that tests a critical implication of a theory is very important; to others, this may seem trivial. Research questions that focus on the unique viewpoints of individuals or nondominant groups sometimes have been unenthusiastically received by the scientific community and power elite, reflecting a bias toward generalizing statements. The requirement that a researchable social work question be nontrivial includes implicitly the view that importance is the result of social consensus, not the application of fixed criteria.

SOCIOCULTURAL ORIGINS OF RESEARCH QUESTIONS

Fashion and Fads

The kinds of questions that are addressed by scientists and the way those questions are expressed tend to reflect the preoccupation of the individuals conducting the research and their culturally learned assumptions about the world. Numerous scholars have made this point, perhaps none better than Thomas S. Kuhn in his landmark history of science (1970). Despite the assumed existence of an empirical world filled with objects and energy, people do not experience these directly, but rather experience a process in which the senses interpret environmental information (i.e., visual, auditory, tactile, olfactory, taste) through cultural lenses.

Which sensation is important enough to attend to and how that sensation is classified and attached to meanings are the result of the various processes of socialization and enculturation. We learn what is what, and what is nothing, by watching others, by having experiences, and through formal education. Thus, as social workers, we have inherited a cultural preoccupation with particular classes of events, culturally determined ways of structuring experience, and also a capacity for our own personal experience to allow us to dissent, but not disconnect, from those cultural influences.

What are some examples of the scientific and sociocultural fads that might influence social work research questions? Preoccupation with integration of human services during the Nixon presidency led to many studies of linkages between social service agencies, a line of research that received little attention before that time. This macro focus was related to national legislation, the Allied Health Services Act. Long-standing cultural beliefs that raising children is women's work led to a large body of socialization research that ignored caregivers other than mothers and other female relatives.

Only recently has the role of fathers in children's adjustment and maladjustment become the focus of broad scholarly interest. Expanded research interest in gerontology has accompanied the aging of the front wave of the "baby boom" generation. Current national preoccupation with law enforcement and drug abuse has led to an interesting combination of research and social experiments in these areas.

Because money and related resources tend to follow cultural preoccupation, these are likely to influence what questions seem worthy of study and how those questions will be phrased. Even the ability of individual social workers to challenge existing ways of thinking about social events is influenced by this flow of resources, because your ability as a social worker to have certain classes of experiences (and thus be prompted to ask certain questions) is shaped by the availability of work contexts.

Preferred Research Paradigms

Although the interplay between the scientific and social work communities and the rest of society tends to shape both the topics and form of questions, preferences for certain kinds of research methods also tend to influence questions. Modern sociology of science identifies the tendency for researchers to express strong preferences for various research methods. Some researchers prefer predominantly laboratory research, others prefer field experiments, and still others prefer exploratory studies. Some prefer designs that use extensive mathematics, whereas others prefer data expressed in words, pictures, artifacts, and the like.

These preferences are important because many of the research methods are designed to address only a limited set of research questions. For example, methods such as ethnography are primarily involved with inductive processes, that is, answering questions about the nature of meaning systems. Other methods, such as laboratory experiments, require that meaning systems be worked out in advance and are associated largely with testing one or a few specific hypotheses.

A preference for surveys over interviews is likely to influence the degree of openness or preconceptions in questions. Surveys tend to feature simple questions with simple answers, often in precoded categories. Persons who favor this kind of research tend to phrase questions in very focused formats. Conversely, interviews tend to provide many more opportunities to spontaneously follow leads and seek clarification.

Although many interviews are highly structured, the potential flexibility allows questions to be phrased in ways that are more open and allows adjustment of response categories and questions as needed. These are only a few examples out of many different approaches to research methods. They will be discussed in more detail in the chapters contained in Part V of this book.

The social worker who is attempting to turn a vague concern into a researchable question is likely to try to shoehorn the concern into a form that fits the research methods that he or she knows or prefers. The relationship between preferred methods and the kinds of questions asked is likely to occur at an unconscious level. When faced with a task such as doing a program evaluation, the ethnographically oriented evaluator is likely to ask how the program works, and the experimentally oriented evaluator is more likely to ask whether it produces measurable outcomes. The emphasis on process does not necessarily exclude interest in outcome, any more than interest in outcome precludes interest in process. However, in practice, the tendency to think about research questions in terms of the tools at hand is pervasive.

Identification of the Value Base of Questions

It is hoped that the foregoing has convinced you that useful social work research questions arise from cultural processes and personal interest. Because all cultural processes are linked to implicit values, all researchable questions thus reflect personal and cultural values and beliefs. These values and beliefs define the domain within which allowable answers can be found. Answers that do not fall within this domain will not be allowed. Therefore, in considering the adequacy of a social work research question, it is appropriate to ask about the value base of the question in order to determine what is likely to be included and excluded in the set of possible answers. That is, is the diverse range of values around this question adequately integrated or are certain viewpoints arbitrarily excluded?

The existence of a value base is not necessarily a deficiency. In fact, it is necessary if a research question is to meet the criterion for importance. However, given the diversity of values across various cultures and classes, it would be foolish not to inquire how the values implicit in a particular question limit the range of applicability of the question. Furthermore, a divergence of basic values between the persons studied and the persons doing the studying, and perhaps the ultimate consumers of the study findings, is likely to result in miscommunication and error.

After all, the choice of whose values determine the question is a matter of power and potentially an avenue of oppression. It is important to be clear that:

1 a particular set of values underlies every research question,
2. those values limit the range of possible answers allowed, and
3. the interpretation of the results of a study of a research question is influenced by the values of both the persons doing the study and those interpreting the findings.

Decoding values implicit in a research question or any text is not a simple matter. Aside from looking for obviously biased language that would signal belief and value systems, there are few rules that always work. Often, the values are reflected in the tone of the question in a holistic sense. A research question on parenting such as "Is parental use of corporal punishment predictive of acting out behavior of children?" may reflect a perspective on parents as sources of children's maladjustment. "Does the presence of a warm, supportive caregiver help children in disadvantaged families to cope with school failure?" sounds like an inherently parent-friendly question and may reflect the value that parents be viewed as potential, positive coping resources for a maladapted child.

A question about the effectiveness of couple therapy may reflect a perspective that maintaining a marital union is a high goal, whereas phrased another way, the underlying value may be on personal self-actualization. Can you see how the values that underlie the question limit the range of answers that may be found and the context in which the answers may be applied?

The Role of Stakeholders in Question Formulation

One way to limit problems related to unexamined and conflicting values is to involve stakeholders in question formulation. Social work researchers, like many modern social scientists, are acutely aware that in research involving people as research participants, these participants have a stake in the outcome of that research and thus deserve a share of the power to influence both the question and the methods through which it is answered. This position is probably easier for persons trained in ethnographic methods to accept but valid across the continuum of research methods.

Just how to involve stakeholders in the question formulation process varies from one situation to another. As discussed in Chapter 23 on single-subject research designs, problem identification, goal setting, and research questions are negotiated jointly between the practitioner/researcher and the client. And, as will be seen in Chapter 24, standards for large-scale program evaluation activities include stakeholder involvement in the conceptualization of research questions as an ethical standard (Sanders, 1994). Typical techniques for stakeholder involvement in research questions involve formal negotiations with clients or key informants, focus groups, interviews, or surveys. We must always be aware of the unexamined values and beliefs implicit in our research questions that may inappropriately narrow the ranges of the questions we ask or the answers we allow.

QUESTION FORMULATION FOR STUDENT PROJECTS

Students often are in a unique position regarding the selection of a research question in conjunction with their academic work. As we discussed earlier, most researchable questions arise from substantive interests of social scientists and other professionals. They arise from the work we all do and have a history and context. The student role is unique in that the student assigned to select a research question may be lacking this context or perhaps thrust into an unfamiliar context (by being assigned a topic). This may be complicated by a lack of understanding of the implications of the form of the question for research design.

Now that you have some idea what a researchable question looks like, you are on your way to being able to find one. In general, we see two sources of research questions.

- First, the question may arise deductively from theories you have been studying. Although it is a myth to think that research questions arise exclusively as a logical extension of existing theory, the questions underlying much student research, especially experimental theses and dissertations, often do arise deductively from existing theory.

- Second, research questions may arise from the experience of the student. A student intern placed in a shelter for battered women, for example, may develop research questions concerning socialization for violence. Excellent questions concerning the lifeways of persons in the United States who are from nondominant groups have been raised by persons who themselves are from nondominant groups (Matsumoto, 1994).

More than likely, the applied researcher often starts with some personal interest in an area or with an opportunity to study a particular situation, rather than starting from a theoretical basis. The empirically oriented social worker is then likely to search the literature, find theories that bear on the topic of interest, and generate a researchable question that makes sense in the light of existing theory. Thus, it is often some personal or professional concern that initiates the process, rather than some kind of insightful and researchable question that emerges from focused attention to some theory. If the research study primarily tests a theory, so much the better, but theory testing is often secondary to some other preoccupation.

What this means for you as a student is that you need to develop the ability to connect your interests with the empirical database of the profession. This usually means asking, "How do social scientists talk about the constructs of interest to me?" "What theories seem to account for the areas of interest to me?" "Has anyone developed and tested a model of causes and effects that includes the constructs of interest?" It is helpful to employ a two-step process:

- First, try to be specific about what your interest or question is and write it down. Writing is a great way of determining if you have a clear idea. Be mindful of the criteria for good social work research questions described earlier.
- Second, hit the books and journals looking for nominal definitions of terms and the specialized vocabulary that the authors use to discuss the topic of interest to you. It may take some time to find the scientific synonyms for the everyday words you use. A recent journal article that attempts to review everything known about your topic often can be found.

Use your reading to accomplish three tasks:

- First, find out how other persons conceptualize the important ideas in your question. (More about conceptualization is presented in the following chapter.) The main point here is to recognize the meaning systems that other people are using to understand the phenomenon of interest to you so that you can benefit from the head start that prior work might provide.

- Second, try to identify populations or settings in which the phenomenon of interest is likely to be found. Those settings are the places where answers to your question will be found also.
- Third, try to find a causal model of the forces that seem to influence the phenomenon you wish to study. This might seem most relevant to largely deductive questions, such as the probability that increasing the amount of social support will improve adjustment. However, this is equally applicable to inductive questions in which models of socialization forces, economic process, or political process will help guide meaning identification. Use all this information to fine-tune your research question.

You are probably starting to see why some beginning students find such difficulty in choosing a question. At the beginning of your career, locating a researchable question is in part requiring you to develop the art of empirical thinking, perhaps before you know what that is. The student with little training in the social sciences, and particularly in empirical reasoning, may have had insufficient time and opportunity to develop this list of personal interests. It seems artificial to us to force the issue by requiring beginners to invent questions. A better strategy is to ask students to learn what empirical thinking is, read in their areas of interest, and let the questions flow! Ultimately, the topics you study will come from personal experience, social concerns and conflicts, or as an extension of some theory of interest to you.

However, in order for such questions to flow effortlessly, it is necessary to first cultivate the habits of critical thinking. The mental habits involved with critical thinking give you a whole new perspective through which to view your professional practice and cause those researchable questions to flow faster than time allows you to answer them. Helping you to develop those habits is part of what this book is about. As your scientific thinking skills and education progress, you will have no difficulty finding researchable questions without getting hung up on the artificiality of producing questions on demand.

When you are seriously considering investigating a research question, you should determine whether your question fits into the priorities of persons and organizations that control resources needed to conduct your study. One of the most hotly debated aspects of science these days is its sociocultural origins. To be sure, the way that scientists conceptualize the things they study, the questions that are asked, and the resources dedicated to finding answers form a thoroughly cultural and political process.

The kinds of information in the scientific literature suggest that a rather whimsical collection of initiatives arising from direct experience, personal beliefs, and social and political forces is emerging, along with valuable information about our strongest theories. What does this mean? It means that social scientists study what is of interest to their cultures and themselves.

As the people who do empirical social science research have become more diverse, the research questions that are pursed have changed to reflect this diversity. This is a very positive change in the culture of social research. For example, fewer researchers study mothers as an exclusive source of socialization, preferring to define socialization as the result of caregiver systems. The plight of the poor is seldom conceptualized as "the culture of poverty," but is more likely to be studied as complex adaptive systems in response to power distribution. Very limited views of women and non-Europeans that characterized earlier work have yielded to more refined explorations, due in no small part to greater diversity among scientists.

Occasionally, one encounters tracts written under the banner "postmodernism" that view these sociocultural origins of social science ideas as evidence for the fundamental futility of the science enterprise. If all knowledge is cultural and political, so the argument goes, and there are no absolute grounds for choosing one belief over another, then knowledge based on scientifically tested questions is no better than any other political or faith statements.

Propositions about empirical states and events that are tested by scientific methods are logically superior to all forms of conjecture without evidence if the criteria for superiority are prediction, control, and replicability. Although empirical tests of questions are potentially vulnerable to many kinds of distortions related to who is asking and observing, the very nature of the scientific method is designed to limit the sources of such bias and allow the questioner to transcend, even a little, the limits of his or her sensory and cultural limitations.

SUMMARY

Researchable questions are those that: are posed in terms of observables, are expressed in nominal and operational definitions of variables, do not arbitrarily limit the range of possible answers, are answerable in principle, and are important. Some of the sociocultural forces that influence question formulation include fashion and fad, preferred research paradigms, and values. Although all questions are cultural and personal in origin, involvement of relevant stakeholders can help forge a consensus and allow meaningful work to proceed.

Margaret Williams
Yvonne A. Unrau
Richard M. Grinnell, Jr.

C h a p t e r   6

Research Approaches

THERE ARE TWO RESEARCH APPROACHES we can use in social work research—quantitative and qualitative. As we have stressed in the previous five chapters, they both complement one another. The quantitative research approach has typically been associated with research studies in disciplines such as medicine, education, psychology, and sociology, while the qualitative research approach has been associated with disciplines such as anthropology and ethology. Social work's long historical ties to the medical model and its reliance on psychology and sociology for theories of human behavior can explain, in part, why quantitative research studies have had such a commanding role in the social work profession—until now, that is.

As the years go by, our profession is becoming more appreciative of the qualitative research approach and how it can be used in actual social work research situations. The research methods associated with qualitative "ways of knowing" have filled a much-needed research gap within our profession. With both quantitative and qualitative research approaches at our disposal, we are now better equipped to learn more about complex social problems through their use.

PHILOSOPHICAL DIFFERENCES

It is important to note at this point that the quantitative and qualitative research approaches have different philosophical underpinnings. Let us briefly compare the differences between the two approaches in relation to how each one perceives reality, how it relates to the ways of knowing, how it uses its value base, and how it is applied (Jordan & Franklin, 1995):

- Perceptions of Reality
    - Quantitative   One reality exists and it can be separated and studied only in parts; the reality is "objective."
    - Qualitative   Multiple realities exist and they are studied holistically; the reality is "subjective."

- Ways of "Knowing"
    - Quantitative   Knowledge is generated through a process of strict logic and reason; knowledge is generated primarily through a deductive process.
    - Qualitative   Knowledge is personally constructed and contextually bound; knowledge is generated primarily through an inductive process.

- Value Bases
    - Quantitative   The research process is "value-free" and "unbiased." The researcher is separate and independent from the research participants and data analyses.
    - Qualitative   The research process is "value-bound." The researcher and research participant mutually enter a "research partnership" to produce data.

- Applications
    - Quantitative   Research results are generalized across time, people, places, and contexts. Data exist separate and apart from the research participants who provided them.
    - Qualitative   Research results provide a richer understanding of a particular person, problem, or event. Data are "expressions" of the participants who provide them.

By comparing these four features and the philosophical underpinnings of quantitative and qualitative research approaches, we can more fully appreciate their important differences. Each approach offers us a unique method for studying a social work–related problem; and *any research problem* can be studied using either approach. Suppose, for example, we are interested in a broad social problem such as racial discrimination. In particular, let us say we are interested in studying the social problem of racial discrimination within public social service agencies. Let us revisit the differences between quantitative and qualitative research approaches and see how our research problem, racial discrimination, could be studied under both approaches.

- Perceptions of Reality
  - Quantitative   Ethnic minorities share similar experiences within the public social service system. These experiences can be described objectively; that is, reality exists outside any one person.
  - Qualitative   Individual and ethnic group experiences within the public social service system are unique. Their experiences can only be described subjectively; that is, reality exists within each person.

- Ways of "Knowing"
  - Quantitative   The experience of ethnic minorities within public social services is made known by closely examining specific parts of their experiences. Scientific principles, rules, and tests of sound reasoning are used to guide the research process.
  - Qualitative   The experience of ethnic minorities within public social services is made known by capturing the whole experiences of a few cases. Parts of their experiences are considered only in relation to the whole of it. Sources of knowledge are illustrated through stories, diagrams, and pictures that are shared by the people with their unique life experiences.

- Value Bases
  - Quantitative   The researchers suspend all their values related to ethnic minorities and social services from the steps taken within the research study. The research participant "deposits" data, which are screened, organized, and analyzed by the researchers, who do not attribute any personal meaning to the research participants or to the data they provide.
  - Qualitative   The researcher *is* the research process, and any personal values, beliefs, and experiences of the researcher will influence the research process. The researcher learns from the research participants, and their interaction is mutual.

- Applications
  - Quantitative   Research results are generalized to the population from which the sample was drawn (e.g., other minority groups, other social services agencies). The research findings tell us, on the average, the experience that ethnic minorities have within the social service system.
  - Qualitative   Research results tell a story of one individual's or one group's experience within the public social service system. The research findings give us an in-depth understanding of a few people. The life context of each research participant is key to understanding the stories he or she tells.

SIMILAR FEATURES

So far we have been focusing on the differences between the quantitative and qualitative research approaches. They also have many similarities. First, they both use careful and diligent research processes in an effort to discover and interpret knowledge. They both are guided by systematic procedures and orderly plans.

Second, both approaches can be used to study any particular social problem. The quantitative approach is more effective than the qualitative approach in reaching a specific and precise understanding of one aspect (or part) of an already well-defined social problem. The quantitative approach seeks to answer research questions that ask about quantity, such as:

1. Are women more depressed than men?
2. Does low income predict one's level of self-concept?
3. Do child sexual abuse investigation teams reduce the number of times an alleged victim is questioned by professionals?
4. Is degree of aggression related to severity of crimes committed among inmates?

A qualitative research approach, on the other hand, aims to answer research questions that provide us with a more comprehensive understanding of a social problem from an intensive study of a few people. This approach is usually conducted within the context of the research participants' natural environments (Rubin & Babbie, 1997b). Research questions that would be relevant to the qualitative research approach might include:

1. How do women experience depression as compared to men?
2. How do individuals with low income define their self-concept?

3. How do professionals on child sexual abuse investigation teams work together to make decisions?

4. How do federal inmates describe their own aggression in relation to the crimes they have committed?

Not only can both approaches be used to study the same social problem, they both can be used to study the same research question. Whether a quantitative or qualitative research approach is used clearly has impact on the type of findings produced to answer a research question (or to test a research hypothesis).

Regardless of the research approach we use to answer any given research question, we now know from the previous chapters in this book that there are six generic and highly overlapping steps that are common to both approaches:

1. Choosing a general research topic
2. Focusing the topic into a research question
3. Designing the research study
4. Collecting the data
5. Analyzing and interpreting the data
6. Writing the report

As we will see, each research approach is played out a bit differently in relation to each of the above research steps.

THE QUANTITATIVE RESEARCH APPROACH

The quantitative research approach, a "tried and tested" method of scientific inquiry, has been used for centuries. It is front-end loaded; that is, all of the critical decisions to be made in a quantitative study (e.g., conceptualization, sample selection, operationalization of variables, data collection procedures, data analysis procedures) occur *before* the study is ever started.

This means that the researcher is well aware of all the study's limitations before a single speck of datum is ever collected. It is possible, therefore, for a researcher to decide that a quantitative study has simply too many limitations and eventually decides not to carry it out. Regardless of whether a proposed quantitative study is ever carried out or not, the process always begins with choosing a research topic and focusing the research question.

Steps 1 and 2: Choosing a General Research Topic and Focusing the Topic into a Research Question

Box 6.1 presents some useful hints in choosing research questions. Quantitative research studies are usually deductive processes; that is, they usually begin with a broad and general query about a social problem and then pare it down to a specific research question. For instance, our general research problem previously introduced may have started out as a result of a general curiosity about racial discrimination within the public social service agencies.

We may have noticed through our professional practices, for example, that many of our clients who are from ethnic minorities have high unemployment rates, have a large proportion of their members living under the poverty level, and have low levels of educational attainment—three conditions that may increase the likelihood of their using public social services.

Yet, at the same time, we may have also observed that our clients who are Caucasian far outnumber our clients who come from ethnic minorities. Our personal observations may then lead us to question whether discrimination of ethic minorities exists within the public social service system. We can easily test the possibility of such a relationship between the two concepts by using the quantitative research approach.

The next step in focusing our research question would be to visit the library and review the literature related to our two concepts:

- Discrimination within social service agencies (Concept 1)
- Access to social service (Concept 2)

We would want to read theoretical and empirical literature related to the two main concepts within our research question—racial discrimination within social service agencies, and access to social services. We would want to learn about how various theories explain both of our main concepts in order to arrive at a meaningful research question. It may be, for example, that many ethnic minority cultures are unlikely to ask "strangers" for help with life's personal difficulties.

Furthermore, we may learn that most social service agencies are organized using bureaucratic structures, which require new clients to talk to several strangers (e.g., telephone receptionist, waiting-room clerk, intake worker) before they are able to access social services. Given that we know that ethnic minorities do not like talking with strangers about their personal problems, and that social services is set up for clients to deal with a series of strangers, we could ask a very simple quantitative research question:

Research Question:
Do clients who come from an ethnic minority have difficulty in accessing social services?

Box 6.1_____

Hints for Selecting a Research Area

Perhaps your research teacher is requiring you to conduct a research project for this course. Here are some hints, in case you're having trouble coming up with a good idea. Your problem probably will become selecting one idea from many possibilities, rather than locating a single idea.

1. Pick a social work theory that interests you. Your introductory social work textbook may be a good source to remind you of a variety of social work theories. Find a few research studies that have been done to test this theory. Perhaps you can replicate or modify one of them. Design your own study to test the accuracy of this theory or to demonstrate its applicability to some issue.

2. Think of some familiar phrase, such as "A stitch in time saves nine" or "Absence makes the heart grow fonder." Consider stereotypes. Do women actually talk more than men? Are children's cartoons really violent? Perhaps you could design a simple research study to analyze the accuracy of one of these stereotypes.

3. Don't be afraid to test your own intuition. Perhaps you've always believed that attractive people are more popular than unattractive people or that teachers give higher grades to typed papers than to handwritten papers. You could design a study to test your intuitive conclusions.

4. Spend some time in a public place observing people. What do you see? How do you explain it? Can you test your theory? For example, you might notice that people tend to face the door in elevators. Maybe you can develop and test a theory that explains this behavior.

5. Scan some journals and read a few articles that interest you. Perhaps you could replicate one of the studies described, or part of it. Do the articles end with suggestions for further research or a discussion of limitations that you could explore?

6. Pick an issue that is important to you. Are you interested in affirmative action, AIDS, study skills, or alcoholism? Do some reading to find out what is already known about this area, and design a study that replicates previous research studies or that makes use of procedures or materials that have already been developed.

7. Ask a practical question and design a study to answer it. For example, you might be interested in how students can learn to study better, and you might decide to conduct an exploratory study contrasting students with high grades and students with low grades.

8. Don't lose track of the purpose of this assignment. The goal of this assignment is for you to practice conducting a study. You are not expected to invent a new theory that applies to all human behaviors. Keep your study simple. You will discover that even simple studies involve a series of tough decisions.

_____
Source: Allen (1995)

Our simple straightforward research question has become more specific as a result of our literature review. Our literature review also played a key role in determining which concepts we are going to include in our study. In our research question, for example, we have identified client ethnicity and access to social services as our two concepts of interest. We must always remember the four characteristics of the quantitative research approach while formulating our research question in addition to defining our concepts and variables, as outlined in Box 6.2.

Box 6.2_____

Characteristics of the
Quantitative Research Approach

The quantitative research approach strives for: (1) measurability, (2) objectivity, (3) reducing uncertainty, (4) duplication, and (5) standardized procedures.

Striving Toward Measurability

The quantitative research approach tries to study only those variables that can be objectively measured. That is, knowledge gained through this research approach is based on "objective measurements" of the real world, not on someone's opinions, beliefs, or past experiences. Conversely, knowledge gained through tradition or authority *depends* on people's opinions and beliefs. Entities that cannot be measured, or even seen, such as id, ego, or superego, are not amenable to a quantitative study but rather rely on tradition and authority.

In short, the phenomena we believe to exist must be measurable. However, at this point in our discussion, it is useful to remember that quantitative researchers believe that practically everything in life is measurable.

Striving Toward Objectivity

The second characteristic of the quantitative research approach is that it strives to be as *objective* as possible. The direct measurements of the real world that comprise *empirical data* must not be affected in any way by the person doing the observing, or measuring. Physical scientists have observed inanimate matter for centuries, confident in the belief that objects do not change as a result of being observed. In the subworld of the atom, however, physicists are beginning to learn what social workers have always known. Things *do* change when they are observed. People think, feel, and behave very differently as a result of being observed. Not only do they change, they change in different ways depending on who is doing the observing.

There is yet another problem. Observed behavior is open to interpretation by the observer. To illustrate this point, let us take a simple example of a client we are seeing, named Ron, who is severely withdrawn. He may behave in one way in our office in individual treatment sessions, and in quite another way when his mother joins the interviews. We may think that Ron is unduly silent, while his mother remarks on how much he is talking. If his mother *wants* him to talk, perhaps as a sign that he is emerging from his withdrawal, she may perceive him to be talking more than he really is.

Researchers go to great lengths to ensure that their own hopes, fears, beliefs, and biases do not affect their research results, and that the biases of others do not affect them either. Nevertheless, as discussed in later chapters, complete objectivity is rarely possible in social work despite the many strategies we have developed in our efforts to achieve it.

Suppose, for example, that a social worker is trying to help a mother interact more positively with her child. The worker, together with a colleague, may first observe the child and mother in a playroom setting, recording how many times the mother makes eye contact with the child, hugs the child, criticizes the child, makes encouraging comments, and so forth on a three-point scale (i.e., -1 = discouraging, 0 = neutral, 1 = encouraging). The social worker may perceive a remark that the mother has made to the child as "neutral," while the colleague thinks it was "encouraging."

In such a situation, it is impossible to resolve the disagreement. If there were six objective observers, however, five opting for "neutral" and only one for "encouraging," the one observer is more likely to be wrong than the five, and it is very likely that the mother's remark was "neutral." As more people agree on what they have observed, the less likely it becomes that the observation was distorted by bias, and the more likely it is that the agreement reached is "objectively true."

As should be obvious by now, objectivity is largely a matter of agreement. There are some things—usually physical phenomena—about which most people agree. Most people agree, for example, that objects fall when dropped, water turns to steam at a

Box 6.2 Continued

certain temperature, sea water contains salt, and so forth. However, there are other things—mostly to do with values, attitudes, and feelings—about which agreement is far more rare.

An argument about whether Beethoven is a better composer than Bach, for example, cannot be "objectively" resolved. Neither can a dispute about the rightness of capital punishment, euthanasia, or abortion. It is not surprising, therefore, that physical researchers, who work with physical phenomena, are able to be more "objective" than social work researchers, who work with human beings.

Striving Toward Reducing Uncertainty

The quantitative research approach tries to rule out uncertainty. Since all observations in both the physical and social sciences are made by human beings, personal bias cannot be entirely eliminated, and there is always the possibility that an observation is in error, no matter how many people agree about what they saw. There is also the possibility that the conclusions drawn from even an accurate observation will be wrong.

A number of people may agree that an object in the sky is a UFO when in fact it is a meteor. Even if they agree that it is a meteor, they may come to the conclusion—probably erroneously—that the meteor is a warning from an angry extraterrestrial person.

In the twentieth century, most people do not believe that natural phenomena have anything to do with extraterrestrial people. They prefer the explanations that modern researchers have proposed. Nevertheless, no researcher would say—or at least be quoted as saying—that meteors and extraterrestrial beings are not related for certain. When utilizing the research method of knowledge development, nothing is certain. Even the best-tested theory is only tentative, accepted as true until newly discovered evidence shows it to be untrue or only partly true. All knowledge gained through the research method (whether quantitative or qualitative) is thus provisional. Everything presently accepted as true is true only with varying degrees of probability.

Let us suppose we have lived all alone in the middle of a large forest. We have never ventured as much as a hundred yards from our cabin and have had no access to the outside world. We have observed for our entire life that all of the ducks that flew over our land were white. We have never seen a different-colored duck. Thus, we theorize, and rightfully so, that all ducks are white. We would only have to see one nonwhite duck fly over our land to disprove our theory: Nothing is certain no matter how long we "objectively observed" it.

Striving Toward Duplication

The quantitative research approach tries to do research studies in such a way that they can be duplicated. Unlike qualitative studies, if quantitative studies cannot be duplicated, they are not really quantitative endeavors. As we have said before, the quantitative research approach, and to some extent, the qualitative approach as well, is a public method of knowing.

Evidence for the relationship between students' grade point average and their future abilities as good social workers must be open to public inspection if it is to be believed. Furthermore, belief is more likely if a second researcher can produce the same findings by using the same research methods.

In scientific laboratories, the word "replication" refers to the same experiment conducted more than once in the same way, at approximately the same time, by the same person. A person testing a city's water supply for pollutants, for example, will take several samples of the water and test them simultaneously under identical conditions, expecting to obtain close to identical results.

If the water needs to be retested for some reason, further samples will be taken and the same procedures followed, but now another person may do the work and the test conditions may be very slightly different: A recent downpour of rain may have flushed some of the pollutants out of the reservoir, for example. The second set of tests are then said to be *duplicates* of the first. Social workers are not able to replicate research studies, because no person, situation, or event is identical to any other.

Box 6.2 Continued

Example of Duplication Suppose we are running a 12-week intervention program to help fathers who have abused their children to manage their anger without resorting to physical violence.

We have put a great deal of effort into designing this program, and believe that our intervention (the program) is more effective than other interventions currently used in other anger-management programs. We develop a method of measuring the degree to which the fathers in our group have learned to dissipate their anger in nondamaging ways and we find that, indeed, the group shows marked improvement.

Improvement shown by one group of fathers is not convincing evidence for the effectiveness of our program. Perhaps our measurements were in error and the improvement was not as great as we hoped for.

Perhaps the improvement was a coincidence, and the fathers' behavior changed because they had joined a health club and each had vented his fury on a punching bag. In order to be more certain, we duplicate our program and measuring procedures with a second group of fathers: In other words, we duplicate our study.

After we have used the same procedures with a number of groups and obtained similar results each time, we might expect that other social workers will eagerly adopt our methods. As presented in Chapter 1, tradition dies hard. Other social workers have a vested interest in *their* interventions, and they may suggest that we found the results we did only because we *wanted* to find them.

In order to counter any suggestion of bias, we ask another, independent social worker to use the same anger-management program and measuring methods with other groups of fathers. If the results are the same as before, our colleagues in the field of anger management may choose to adopt our intervention method (the program).

Tradition does not merely die hard, however. It dies with enormous difficulty, and we should not be surprised if our colleagues choose, instead, to continue using the familiar interventions they have always used.

Whatever our colleagues decide, we are excited about our newfound program. We wonder if our methods would work as well with women as they do with men, with adolescents as well as with adults, with Native Americans, Asians, or African Americans as well as with Caucasians, with mixed groups, larger groups, or groups in different settings. In fact, we have identified a lifetime project, since we will have to apply our program and measuring procedures repeatedly to all these different groups.

Striving Toward the Use of Standardized Procedures

Finally, the quantitative research approach tries to use, if at all possible, well-accepted standardized procedures. For quantitative research studies to be creditable, and before others can accept our results, they must be satisfied that our study was conducted according to accepted scientific standardized procedures. The allegation that our work lacks "objectivity" is only one of the criticisms they might bring.

In addition, they might suggest that the group of fathers we worked with was not typical of abusive fathers in general, and that our results are not therefore applicable to other groups of abusive fathers. It might be alleged that we did not make proper measurements, or we measured the wrong thing, or we did not take enough measurements, or we did not analyze our data correctly, and so on.

In order to negate these kinds of criticisms, social work researchers have agreed on a set of standard procedures and techniques that are thought most likely to produce "true and unbiased" knowledge—which is what this book is all about. Certain steps must be performed in a certain order. Foreseeable errors must be guarded against.

Ethical behavior with research participants and colleagues must be maintained. These procedures must be followed if our study is both to generate usable results and to be accepted as useful by others.

Source: Adapted from: Williams, Tutty, and Grinnell (1995)

Our next step in the quantitative research process is to redefine our concepts into variables. To make a very long story short, the main difference between a concept and a variable is that a variable can be measured and a concept cannot. That is, the two variables within our research question are operationalized so we can determine if they exist or not.

Take our concept of client ethnicity, for example. Suppose we develop the following conceptual definition of client ethnicity:

Conceptual Definition of Client Ethnicity:
Racial groups of people who can be differentiated by common customs, traits, and language

In order to measure our conceptual definition above, we need to operationalize it by creating a variable (called *client ethnicity*), which we operationally define by using existing meaningful "ethnicity categories," such as:

What is your ethnicity (check one category below)?
• Aboriginal
• African American
• Asian
• British
• Dutch
• German
• Hispanic
• Italian
• Native American
• Other_____

We can be as specific—or broad—as would be meaningful to our research question. We could, for example, operationally define our ethnicity variable by using only two "ethnicity categories," such as:

What is your ethnicity (check one category below)?
_____ Ethnic minority
_____ Non–ethnic minority

We defined the two broad categories above by "collapsing" our nine more specific categories. That is, we may have assigned our Aboriginal, African American, Asian, Hispanic, and Native American categories to a single category called "ethnic minority." Likewise, we could group our British, Dutch,

German, and Italian categories into a single category called "non–ethnic minority." We would simply ask all of our clients to check off one of the two categories that they felt pertained to them.

Our second variable, difficulty in assessing social services, also has to be measured. Like our oversimplified two-category ethnicity variable above, we could also operationalize this variable in a variety of ways. We have chosen to operationalize it once again in a simple "yes-no" format. We could ask all of our clients, for example:

Did you have difficulty in accessing any form of social services over the last 12-month period (check one category below)?

_____ Yes

_____ No

So far in our quantitative research study we have refined both variables so that each one can be easily measured. Both variables are two-category variables in that a client can only be in one category for each variable. For example, a client can only be:

- An ethnic minority **and had difficulty** in accessing social services
- An ethnic minority **and did not have difficulty** in accessing social service

- - -

- A non–ethnic minority **and had difficulty** in accessing social services
- A non–ethnic minority **and did not have difficulty** in accessing social services

Research Hypotheses

We can focus our research question even further by formulating a research hypothesis, in which we make an educated guess about the relationship between our two variables. Box 6.3 presents a few criteria for evaluating research hypotheses, of which there are two types: (1) nondirectional, and (2) directional.

Nondirectional Research Hypotheses   A very basic nondirectional research hypothesis (also called a two-tailed hypothesis), is simply a statement that says we expect to find a relationship between our two variables. We are not willing, however, to "stick our necks out" as to the specific relationship between them. A nondirectional hypothesis for our research question could be, for example:

Box 6.3_____

Evaluating a Research Hypothesis

As we know by now, a hypothesis is derived from the research question, which is derived from the research problem area.

There are four criteria that can used to differentiate a good, useful hypothesis from one that is not so good or useful. They are: (1) relevance, (2) completeness, (3) specificity, and (4) potential for testing.

Relevance

It is hardly necessary to stress that a useful hypothesis is one that contributes to our knowledge base. Nevertheless, some social work problem areas are enormously complex, and it is common for people to get so sidetracked in reading the professional literature that they develop very interesting hypotheses totally unrelated to the original problem area they wanted to investigate.

The relevancy criterion is a reminder that, to repeat, the research hypothesis must be directly related to the research question, which in turn must be directly related to the general research problem area.

Completeness

A hypothesis should be a complete statement that expresses our intended meaning in its entirety. The reader should not be left with the impression that some word or phrase is missing. "Moral values are declining" is one example of an incomplete hypothesis.

Other examples include a whole range of comparative statements without a reference point. The statement, "Males are more aggressive," for example, may be assumed to mean "Men are more aggressive than women," but someone investigating the social life of animals may have meant, "Male humans are more aggressive than male gorillas."

Specificity

A hypothesis must be unambiguous. The reader should be able to understand what each variable contained in the hypothesis means and what relationship, if any, is hypothesized to exist between them. Consider, for example, the hypothesis, "Badly timed family therapy affects success." Badly timed family therapy may refer to therapy offered too soon or too late for the family to benefit; or to the social worker or family being late for therapy sessions; or to sessions that are too long or too short to be effective.

Similarly, "success" may mean resolution of the family's problems as determined by objective measurement, or it may mean the family's—or the social worker's—degree of satisfaction with therapy, or any combination of these.

With regard to the relationship between the two variables, the reader may assume that we are hypothesizing a negative correlation: That is, the more badly timed the therapy, the less success will be achieved. On the other hand, perhaps we are only hypothesizing an association: Bad timing will invariably coexist with lack of success.

Be that as it may, the reader should not be left to guess at what we mean by a hypothesis. If we are trying to be both complete and specific, we may hypothesize, for example:

Family therapy that is undertaken after the male perpetrator has accepted responsibility for the sexual abuse of his child is more likely to succeed in reuniting the family than family therapy undertaken before the male perpetrator has accepted responsibility for the sexual abuse.

This hypothesis is complete and specific. It leaves the reader in no doubt as to what we mean, but it is also somewhat wordy and clumsy. One of the difficulties in writing a good hypothesis is that specific statements need more words than inspecific, or ambiguous statements.

Potential For Testing

The last criterion for judging whether a hypothesis is good and useful is the ease with which the truth of the hypothesis can be verified. Some statements cannot be verified at all with presently available measurement

Box 6.3 Continued_____

techniques. "Telepathic communication exists between identical twins," is one such statement. Moreover, much of Emile Durkheim's work on suicide was formulated in such a way that it was not testable by the data gathering techniques available in the 1960s.

A hypothesis of sufficient importance will often generate new data gathering techniques,

which will enable it to be eventually tested. Nevertheless, as a general rule, it is best to limit hypotheses to statements that can be tested immediately by available measurement methods in current use.

_____

Source: Adapted from: Williams, Tutty, and Grinnell (1995)

Nondirectional Research Hypothesis:
Ethnic minorities have different levels of difficulty in accessing social services, compared to non–ethnic minorities.

Notice that the above nondirectional research hypothesis does not propose that ethnic minorities have any more (or less) difficulty in accessing social services than non–ethnic minorities.

Directional Research Hypotheses   A directional research hypothesis (also called a one-tailed hypothesis) specifically indicates the "predicted" direction of the relationship between the two variables. The direction stated is based on an existing body of knowledge related to our research question. Let us return to what we learned from our literature review. We may find out, for example, that clients who are from ethnic minorities may be less likely to seek help from strangers than clients who do not come from ethnic minorities. And, since social service agencies are full of strangers, we might develop the following directional research hypothesis:

Directional Research Hypothesis:
Ethnic minorities have more difficulty in accessing social services than non–ethnic minorities.

Rival Hypotheses

Another kind of hypothesis to be aware of is the rival hypothesis. This hypothesis states that there is something that exists apart from our research hypothesis (i.e., nondirectional, directional); it takes into consideration other variables that are not a part of our nondirectional or directional research hypothesis. Take another look at the directional research hypothesis above. It identifies only ethnicity (independent variable) as a variable that affects access to social services (dependent variable). There are many other variables that could also affect our dependent variable but are not a part of our research study. Variables such as available transportation, amount of family support, and location of residence are a few of the many examples that might explain why clients have difficulties in accessing social services—regardless of their ethnicity.

These other variables are known as competing variables, or rival variables, and could be formulated into a statement that "rivals" our nondirectional or directional research hypothesis. Rival hypotheses are not statistically tested and no data are usually collected in relation to them. Rather, they are simply statements that demonstrate the thought we have given to the variables that are extraneous to our research hypothesis.

Step 3: Designing the Research Study

Having focused our research question, and if appropriate, developed a research hypothesis, we enter into the next phase—designing the study. We begin with a word about sampling. One of the major objectives of the quantitative research approach is to generate knowledge that can be generalized beyond our study's sample. For now, it is useful to know that the "ideal" sample for a quantitative study is one that has been randomly selected from a carefully defined population. The topic of sampling will be discussed much more fully in Chapter 11.

As we know, most research questions have at least one independent variable and one dependent variable. As indicated above, the independent variable in our study is client ethnicity (i.e., ethnic minority, non–ethnic minority) and the dependent variable is difficulty in accessing social services (i.e., yes, no). We organize our variables in this way because we are expecting that our clients' ethnicity is somehow related to their difficulty in accessing social services. It would be absurd to say the opposite—that the degree of difficulty that potential clients have in accessing social services influences their ethnicity.

Having set out our hypothesis in this way, we can plainly see that our research design will compare two groups (i.e., ethnic minorities, non–ethnic minorities) in terms of whether or not (i.e., yes, no) each group had difficulty accessing a social service of some kind. Our research design is the "blueprint" for our study. It is a basic guide to deciding how, where, and when data will be collected. How data are collected and where they are collected from are determined by the data collection method we choose (Chapter 19). *When* data are collected is dictated by the specific research design we select (Chapters 12 and 13). Clearly, there are many things for us to consider when developing our research design.

All quantitative research designs are not created equal. Chapter 12 discusses three groups of research designs (i.e., exploratory, descriptive, explanatory) and how each varies in terms of the knowledge it produces. Exploratory type research designs are the most simple. These research designs are useful for describing variables but do not have anything to say about the relationships (that may or may not exist) between and among them. An exploratory design can answer questions such as:

1. How many smokers have cancer?
2. What is the amount of study time logged by students with high grades?
3. How many clients who are ethnic minorities have experienced difficulty in accessing social services?

Descriptive research designs establish whether or not two or more variables are related to one another. They tell us whether a change in the first variable predictably varies with a change in the second variable. We could ask, for example:

1. Are people who smoke more likely to be diagnosed with cancer, compared to people who do not smoke?
2. Is studying related to achieving higher grades for students?
3. Are clients who are ethnic minorities more or less likely to experience difficulty accessing social services than clients who are not ethnic minorities?

"Cause-effect" type quantitative research designs are at the explanatory level. They can help us determine whether a causal relationship existed between the two variables within our research hypothesis:

1. Does smoking *cause* cancer?
2. Does studying *cause* good grades?
3. Does being a client from an ethnic minority *cause* people to experience more difficulty in accessing social services?

Establishing causal relationships between variables, however, requires sophisticated research designs that are usually not feasible in social work.

Step 4: Collecting the Data

As we know, data collection is one phase within any research design. Data collection is the step in which we truly test out the operational definitions of our study's variables. There are three features of data collection that are key to all quantitative research studies:

1. All of our variables must be measurable — This means that we must precisely record the variable's frequency, its duration, or its magnitude (intensity). Think about our ethnic minority independent variable for a minute. As noted earlier, we simply operationalized this variable into two categories: ethnic minority and non–ethnic minority. Here we are simply measuring the presence (ethnic minority) or absence (non–ethnic minority) of a trait for each participant within our study.

    We also needed to operationalize our dependent variable, difficulty in accessing social services. Once again, we could have operationalized this variable in a number of ways. We chose, however, to operationalize it in such a way that each client could produce a simple response to a simple question: Did you have difficulty (i.e., yes, no) in accessing any form of social services over the last 12-month period?

2. All of our data collection procedures must be objective — That is, the data are meant to reflect a condition in the *real* world and should not be biased by the person collecting the data in any way. In our study, the clients produced the data—not the researcher. That is, the researcher only recorded the data that each client individually provided for both variables:

    • "Ethnic Minority" *or* "Non–Ethnic Minority" for the independent variable
    • "Yes" *or* "No" for the dependent variable

3. All of our data collection procedures must be able to be duplicated — In other words, our data collection procedures that we used to measure our independent and dependent variables must be clear and straightforward enough that other researchers could use them in their research studies.

The three features of measurability, objectivity, and duplication within a quantitative research study are accomplished by using a series of standardized uniform steps that are applied consistently throughout a study's implementation. We want to ensure that all of our research participants are measured the same way—in reference to their ethnicity and whether they had any difficulty in accessing social services within the last 12 months, that is.

Step 5: Analyzing and Interpreting the Data

There are two major types of quantitative data analyses: (1) descriptive statistics, and (2) inferential statistics.

Descriptive Statistics

Descriptive statistics describe our study's sample or population. Consider our ethnicity variable for a moment. We can easily describe our research participants in relation to their ethnicity by stating how many of them fell into each category of the variable. Suppose, for example, that 50 percent of our sample were in the ethnic minority category and the remaining 50 percent were in the non–ethnic minority category as illustrated below:

Variable Categories:
• Ethnic minority.............. 50%
• Non–ethnic minority..... 50%

The two percentages above give us a "picture" of what our sample looked like in relation to their ethnicity. A different picture could be produced in which 10 percent of our sample are ethnic minorities and 90 percent are not, as illustrated below:

Variable Categories:
• Ethnic minority.............. 10%
• Non–ethnic minority..... 90%

The above describes only one variable—client ethnicity, or our independent variable. A more detailed picture is given when data about an independent variable and a dependent variable are displayed at the same time. Suppose, for example, that 60 percent of our clients who are ethnic minorities reported that they had difficulty in accessing social services, compared to 20 percent of our clients who are non–ethnic minorities:

	Dependent Variable	
Independent Variable	Yes	No
• Ethnic minority	60%	40%
• Non–ethnic minority	20%	80%

Other descriptive information about our research participants could include variables such as average age, percentages of males and females, average income, and so on.

Inferential Statistics

Inferential statistics determine the probability that a relationship between the two variables within our sample also exists within the population from which it was drawn. Suppose in our study, for example, we find a statistically significant relationship between our clients' ethnicity and whether they successfully accessed social services. The use of inferential statistics permits us to say whether or not the relationship detected in our sample exists in the larger population (i.e., the population from which our sample was drawn) and the exact probability that our finding is in error.

Clearly, a basic understanding of mathematics is needed to analyze quantitative data. With advances in computerized software packages, however, we also need to be sure that we understand the functions performed by the computer so that we can accurately interpret any computer output.

Interpreting the Findings

Interpreting quantitative findings is not as straightforward as it first may appear. We must be careful in our interpretations at two levels. First, we must be aware that expert interpretation of data is required at the level of statistical analysis. Second, interpretation of findings is greatly influenced by the case or group design selected.

Step 6: Writing the Report

Quantitative research findings are easily summarized in tables, figures, and graphs. When data are disseminated to lay people, we usually rely on straightforward graphs and charts to illustrate our findings.

THE QUALITATIVE RESEARCH APPROACH

The qualitative research approach is akin to exploring a "social problem maze" that has multiple entry points and paths. We have no way of knowing whether the maze will lead us to a place of importance or not, but we enter into it out of our own curiosity and, perhaps, even conviction. We enter the maze without a map or a guide; we have only ourselves to rely on and a notebook to record important events, observations, conversations, and impressions along the way.

We begin our journey of qualitative inquiry by stepping into one entrance and forging ahead. We move cautiously forward, using all of our senses in an

---

Van Maanen's Taxonomy of Tales

John Van Maanen has classified qualitative research reports into three types, which he describes as different categories of tales. Each uses a distinctive type of literary exposition.

Realist Tales   A single author narrates the outcome of the study in a dispassionate, third-person voice. According to Van Maanen, "Perhaps the most striking characteristic of ethnographic realism is the almost complete absence of the author from most segments of the finished text. Only what members of the studied culture say and do and, presumably, think are visible."

Confessional Tales   The author attempts to demystify fieldwork or participant observation by showing how the technique is practiced in the field. Such accounts are in the first person, seldom are dispassionate, and unfold over time. Fieldwork is narrated as a series of events leading to certain conclusions or results. The narrator-hero is typically beset along the way by troubles, uncertainty, and doubt.

Impressionist Tales   The author provides vivid, memorable stories, reconstructing in dramatic detail the "facts" of an episode or life. Such yarns are often incorporated into "realist" writing.

Figure 6.1   Types of Qualitative Reports

effort to pinpoint our location and what surrounds us at any one time. We may enter into dead-end rooms within the maze and have to backtrack. We may also encounter paths that we did not think possible.

Steps 1 and 2: Choosing a General Research Topic and Focusing the Topic into a Research Question

Qualitative studies are generally inductive and can be categorized into three types as illustrated in Figure 6.1 above. They require us to reason in such a way that we move from a part to a whole or from a particular instance to a general conclusion. Box 6.4 illustrates the similarities among all qualitative studies.

Let us return to our research problem introduced at the beginning of this chapter—discrimination within the social services. We begin the qualitative research process, once again, from our observations—ethnic minorities are among the highest groups for unemployment, poverty, and low education; Caucasian clients outnumber ethnic minority clients within agencies.

We can focus our qualitative research question by identifying the key concepts in our question. These key concepts set the parameters of our research study—they are the "outside" boundaries of our maze. As in the quantitative research approach, we would want to visit the library and review the literature related to our key concepts. Our literature review, however, takes

Box 6.4_____

What Do Qualitative Research Studies Look Like?

Below are a few characteristics that most qualitative research studies have in common:

- Research studies that are conducted primarily in the natural settings where the research participants carry out their daily business in a "nonresearch" atmosphere.

- Research studies where variables cannot be controlled and experimentally manipulated (though changes in variables and their effect on other variables can certainly be observed).

- Research studies in which the questions to be asked are not always completely conceptualized and operationally defined at the outset (though they can be).

- Research studies in which the data collected are heavily influenced by the experiences and priorities of the research participants, rather than being collected by predetermined and/or highly structured and/or standardized measurement instruments.

- Research studies in which meanings are drawn from the data (and presented to others) using processes that are more natural and familiar than those used in the quantitative method. The data need not be reduced to numbers and statistically analyzed (though counting and statistics can be employed if they are thought useful).

_____

Source: Rothery, Tutty, and Grinnell (1996)

---

on a very different purpose. Rather than pinpointing "exact" variables to study, we review the literature to see how our key concepts are generally described and defined by previous researchers.

Going with the maze example for the moment, we might learn whether our maze will have rounded or perpendicular corners, or whether it will have multiple levels. The knowledge we glean from the literature assists us with ways of thinking that we hope will help us move through the maze in a way that we will arrive at a meaningful understanding of the problem it represents. Because we may never have been in the maze before, we must also be prepared to abandon what we "think we know" and accept new experiences presented to us along the way.

Let us revisit our research question presented earlier—*Do clients who come from an ethnic minority have difficulty in accessing social services?* In our literature review, we would want to focus on definitions and theories related to discrimination within the social services. In the quantitative research approach, we reviewed the literature to search for meaningful variables that could be measured. We do not want, however, to rely on the literature to define key variables in our study. Rather, we will rely upon the qualitative research process itself to identify key variables and how they relate to one another.

Hypotheses can also be used in a qualitative study. They can focus our research question even further. A hypothesis in a qualitative study is less likely to be "accepted" or "rejected" outright, as is the case in a quantitative study.

Rather, the hypothesis is refined over time as new data are collected. Our hypothesis is changed throughout the qualitative research process based on the reasoning of the researcher—not on a statistical test.

Step 3: Designing the Research Study

We can enter into a qualitative research study with general research questions or specific hypotheses but we are far less concerned about honing-in on specific variables. Because qualitative research studies are inductive processes, we do not want to constrain ourselves with preconceived ideas about how concepts or variables will relate. Thus, while we will have a list of key concepts, and perhaps variables, we want to remain open to the possibilities of how they are defined by our research participants and any relationships that our research participants may draw. Box 6.5 lists the common characteristics of what researchers actually do when they design qualitative research studies.

A qualitative study is aimed at an in-depth understanding of a few cases, rather than a general understanding of many cases, or people. In other words, the number of research participants in a qualitative study is much smaller than in a quantitative one. Sampling, therefore, is a process of selecting the "best-fitting" people to provide data for our study. Nonprobability sampling strategies are designed for this task because they purposely seek out potential research participants. More will be discussed about nonprobability sampling strategies in Chapter 11.

The qualitative research approach is about studying a social phenomenon within its natural context. As such, the case study is a major qualitative research design. A case can be a person, a group, a community, an organization, or an event.

It is possible to ask exploratory, descriptive, or explanatory level research questions within a case. In the quantitative research approach, each level of research question is accompanied by a particular case or group design. This is not true for the qualitative research approach. Instead, the level of question being pursued guides the continued focusing of the research question and helps us to know when our study should end.

Let us revisit our research problem related to discrimination within the public social service system. At an exploratory level, we may ask questions to see whether other people have noted the same observations as we. We could identify various colleagues who work in social services and ask them about their observations of the clients who are from an ethnic minority. Our questions can reach a descriptive level if we begin to ask our research participant to describe any relationship between clients who are from an ethnic minority and their access to social services. At the explanatory level, our questions are even more specific. Are clients who are from an ethnic minority more likely to experience barriers to accessing social services?

Box 6.5_____

What Do Qualitative Researchers Do?

Now that we know what qualitative research studies look like (from Box 6.4), we can describe what some of our roles and responsibilities would be if we actually carried out a qualitative research study. Below is a helpful summary of what would be required to do a qualitative investigation. In sum, the qualitative researcher:

• Observes ordinary events and activities as they happen in natural settings, in addition to any unusual occurrences.

• Is directly involved with the people being studied and personally experiences the process of daily social life in the field.

• Acquires an insider's point of view while maintaining the analytic perspective or distance of an outsider.

• Uses a variety of techniques and social skills in a flexible manner as the situation demands.

• Produces data in the form of extensive written notes, as well as diagrams, maps, or pictures to provide detailed descriptions.

• Sees events holistically (e.g., as a whole unit, not in pieces) and individually in their social context.

• Understands and develops empathy for members in a field setting, and does not just record "cold" objective facts.

• Notices both explicit and tacit aspects of culture.

• Observes ongoing social processes without upsetting, disrupting, or imposing an outside point of view.

• Is capable of coping with high levels of personal stress, uncertainty, ethical dilemmas, and ambiguity.

Many of the above roles and activities are not only carried out in qualitative research studies but are required for good social work practice as well.

_____

Source: Neuman (1997)

Any case study design can be guided by different qualitative research methods. Grounded theory is a method that guides us in a "back and forth" process between the literature and the data we collect. Using grounded theory, we can look to the literature for new ideas and linkages between ideas that can bring meaning to our data. In turn, our data may nudge us to read in areas that we might not have previously considered.

Ethnography is a branch of qualitative research that emphasizes the study of a culture from the perspective of the people who live the culture. With our research example, we would be interested in studying the culture of social services, particularly with respect to how ethnic minorities experience it.

Phenomenology is another branch of qualitative research. "It is used to emphasize a focus on people's subjective experiences and interpretations of the world" (Rubin & Babbie, 1993). These subjective experiences include those of the researcher, as well as of the research participants. As researchers in our discrimination study, we would want to keep a careful account of our reactions and questions to the events we observe and the stories we hear. Our task is to search for meaningful patterns within the volumes of data (e.g., text, drawings, pictures, video recordings).

Step 4: Collecting the Data

"Qualitative researchers are the principal instruments of data collection." (Franklin & Jordan, 1997). This means that data collected are somehow "processed" through the person collecting them. Interviewing, for example, is a common data collection method that produces text data. Data collection in the interview is interactive, whereby we can check out our understanding and interpretation as researchers through dialogue with our research participants.

To collect meaningful data, we want to be immersed into the context or setting of the study. We want to have some understanding, for example, of what it is like to be a client of social services before we launch into a dialogue with clients about their experiences of discrimination, if any, within the social services. If we do not have a grasp of the setting in which we are about to participate, then we run the risk of misinterpreting what is told to us.

Given that our general research question or specific hypothesis evolves in a qualitative study, the data collection process is particularly vulnerable to biases of the data collector. There are several principles to guide us in data collection. First, we want to make every effort to be aware of our own biases. In fact, our own notes on reactions and biases to what we are studying are used as sources of data later on, when we interpret the data.

Second, data collection is a two-way street. The research participants tell their stories to the researcher and, in turn, the researcher tells the research participant his or her understanding or interpretation of the stories. It is a process of check and balance. Third, qualitative data collection typically involves multiple data sources and multiple data collection methods. In our study, we may see clients, workers, and supervisors as potential data sources. We may collect data from each of these groups using interviews, observation, and existing documentation.

Step 5: Analyzing and Interpreting the Data

Collecting, analyzing, and interpreting qualitative data are intermingled. Let us say that, in our first round of data collection, we interview a number of clients who come from ethnic minorities about discrimination in social services. Suppose they consistently tell us that, to be a client of social services, they must give up many of their cultural values. We could then develop more specific research questions for a second round of interviews in an effort to gain more of an in-depth understanding of the relationship between cultural values and being a social service client.

Overall, the process of analyzing data is an iterative one. This means that we must read and reread the volumes of data that we collected. We simply look for patterns and themes that help to capture how our research participants are experiencing the social problem we are studying.

Box 6.6_____

Is Qualitative Research Good Research?

There are a few general criticisms leveled against the qualitative research approach when it is directly compared to the quantitative approach. Some people claim that it is too subjective, its procedures are so vague they cannot be replicated, sweeping conclusions are made on the basis of too few cases, and often there is no way to tell if the conclusions are really supported by the data.

There is also confusion between the terms "empiricist" and "empirical." Empiricist refers to the teaching of the twentieth-century philosophy of science known as logical empiricism or logical positivism. The qualitative research approach does not follow this school, so qualitative research is nonempiricist. Empirical, on the other hand, refers to data or knowledge derived from observation, experience, or experiment. All science therefore is empirical, and qualitative research is about as empirical as anything.

Confusion also arises because some qualitative research studies are not intended to be "science." The aim of science is to produce robust generalizations (capable of standing up to further research) about the real world. Some qualitative studies aim instead to broaden awareness of the human condition and perhaps to move the reader to empathy, indignation, or action. Such studies, which are not much different from good journalism or investigative reporting, are usually described as ideographic. Their aims are worthy, but they are not the aims of science.

What should be asked of any research approach that claims to be "objective"? Four requirements apply:

1. If someone else examines the data a researcher has collected and applies the same analytic procedures, the exact same results should be obtained.
2. If a second researcher collects data from the same kinds of sources, under similar circumstances, and using comparable methods of data elicitation and coding, then similar results should be obtained. If the second researcher's findings differ, the data were probably not much good in the first place.

3. The conclusions drawn from the data should be clearly supported by those data. Data that seem contradictory to the conclusions should be fully reported, and it must be demonstrated that the data do not negate the conclusions.
4. If researchers generalize their findings and claim that the results they have obtained from X_1 will also hold for X_2, X_3.... X_n, their claims should be clearly supported by the data, and the rationale for the conclusions should be clear.

These four requirements are no more than common sense. They are also the general standards of science. In traditional research terms, the first requirement speaks to the reliability of measurement methods, the second to the replicability of findings, the third to the internal validity of conclusions, and the fourth to the external validity of results.

These concepts are discussed later on in this text. There is no inherent reason why qualitative studies cannot meet all four requirements, although practical realities sometimes stand in the way.

Simple checks on the reliability of coding procedures take care of the first requirement, but the second requirement is not so cut and dried. Many qualitative studies cannot be replicated even in part: the cost is too high, the interest too low, or the setting too difficult. Cultures and groups change; today's observations are tomorrow's history.

However, a researcher can often test the replicability of findings using several methods. In Hanson's (1989) study of families with chronic mental patients, for example, he used his interview findings as the basis for a brief mailback questionnaire and obtained comparable results from this larger sample.

The third requirement—that any conclusion should be in accord with the empirical findings—has to do with the care with which the analysis has been done. Has the researcher systematically examined all relevant data to support the conclusions, or simply picked some convenient piece of text to illustrate them, without searching for counter-

Box 6.6 Continued

examples? Are counterexamples adequately explained? Does any other evidence bear on the conclusions? And beyond the data is the argument itself; useful data can be nullified by shoddy thinking. Does the researcher make a good case for the conclusions? Are the concepts clear and well enough defined so that another person could judge their fit to the data, or are "weasel words" used that sound *profound* but have unclear *referents?* Is the reasoning straightforward?

The fourth requirement, concerning generalization to other groups, places, or times, also rests primarily on logic. Hanson,

for example, found that the families all described similar issues, whether they were old or young, in a rural or urban community, poor or rich.

Nor did the findings vary for different institutions and centers. He had chosen his informants by purposive sampling in order to maximize diversity. Since, nevertheless, the informants agreed, then other informants *probably would also. By this logic, the con-* clusions could be generalized.

_____

Source: Adapted from: Taylor (1993); Franklin and Jordan (1997)

The ultimate goal is to interpret data in such a way that the true expressions of research participants are revealed. We want to explain meaning according to the beliefs and experiences of those who provided the data. The aim is to "walk the walk" and "talk the talk" of research participants and not to impose "outside" meaning to the data they provided. Box 6.6 illustrates how qualitative research studies, when the text data have been analyzed correctly, can add to our profession's knowledge base.

Step 6: Writing the Report

Qualitative research reports are lengthier than quantitative ones. It is not possible to strip the context of a qualitative study and present only the study's findings. The knowledge gained from a qualitative endeavor is nested within the context from which it was derived. Furthermore, text data are more awkward and clumsy to summarize. We cannot rely on a simple figure to indicate a finding. Instead, we display text usually in the form of quotes or summary notes to support our conclusions.

USING BOTH APPROACHES IN ONE STUDY

Given the seemingly contradictory philosophical beliefs associated with quantitative and qualitative research studies, it is difficult to imagine how they could exist together in one research study. As is stands, most research studies incorporate only one approach. The reason may, relate, in part, to philosophy, but practical considerations of cost, time, and resources are also factors.

It is not unusual, however, to see numerical data in a qualitative study or text data in a quantitative study. Just think that, if we were to use a quantitative approach, there is no reason why we could not ask research participants a few open-ended questions to more fully explain their experience. In this instance, our quantitative research report would contain some pieces of text data to help bring meaning to the study's findings.

Let us say we want to proceed with a qualitative research study to examine our research question about discrimination within the public social service system. Surely, we would want to identify how many research participants were included, as well as important defining characteristics such as their average age, the number who had difficulty accessing social services, or the number who were satisfied with the services they received.

While it is possible to incorporate qualitative research activity into a quantitative study (and quantitative research activity into a qualitative study), the approach we use is guided by our purpose for conducting the study. Ultimately, research—quantitative or qualitative—is about the pursuit of knowledge. Just what kind of knowledge we are after is up to us.

SUMMARY

This chapter briefly discussed the differences and similarities between the quantitative and qualitative research approaches. These two complementary and respected research approaches are divergent in terms of their philosophical principles. Yet, they share six common steps: choosing a general research topic, focusing the topic into a research question, designing the research study, collecting the data, analyzing and interpreting the data, and writing the report. The following chapter expands upon this one by going into detail how quantitative and qualitative research approaches are used in our profession in order to expand its knowledge base.

Irwin Epstein

C h a p t e r   7

Utilization of Research Approaches

THIS CHAPTER IS A CONTINUATION of the previous one. As we now know from the previous six chapters in this book, a fundamental distinction in social work research is that between the use of quantitative and qualitative research approaches. We use quantitative approaches to count and correlate social and psychological phenomena. Likewise, we use qualitative research approaches to seek the essential character of these social and psychological phenomena. Both approaches attempt to describe and explain reality. The two approaches have been available for our use throughout the history of our profession. There is little agreement among us, however, on the exact differences and commonalities between them.

However, in reaction to the high status given the use of the quantitative approach to research in our profession, some social workers are beginning to advocate more use of the qualitative approaches and are focusing on the conflicting aspects of the two approaches (Geismar & Wood, 1982). In doing so, they create an erroneous impression that the choice between the two is political and that social workers must decide and declare which side they are on (DeMaria, 1981). In arguing their case, they have characterized quantitative research approaches as archaic, politically conservative, and ill-suited to the social action and social change traditions of our profession.

EPISTEMOLOGICAL ORIGINS

Broadly speaking, epistemology refers to the theory of knowledge. Quantitative approaches have epistemological roots in logical positivism. Logical positivism refers to a theory of meaning in which a proposition is acceptable only if there are data derived from a quantitative research study that determines whether or not the proposition is true. The theory requires that all meaningful propositions have to be tested by "objective" observation and experiment. Common to these philosophical orientations is the application of the logic and principles of measurement from the physical sciences to the social world, with the goal of prediction and validation of these predictions. In this spirit, the ultimate purpose of such research studies is to generate universal "laws" of social behavior analogous to the laws of the physical sciences.

Qualitative research approaches assume that the subjective dimensions of human experience are continuously changing and cannot be studied using the principles of quantitative research methodologies. Instead, emphasis is placed on fully describing and comprehending the subjective meanings of events to individuals and groups caught up in them.

The two research approaches have existed side by side since the beginnings of contemporary social science. Thus, in discussing the epistemological roots of psychoanalysis, Bettleheim (1982) remarks:

> In the German culture within which Freud lived, and which permeated his work, there existed and still exists a definite and important division between two approaches to knowledge. Both disciplines are called Wissenschaften (sciences), and they are accepted as equally legitimate. These two are the Naturwissenschaften (natural sciences) and Geisteswissenschaften (which defies translation into English; its literal meaning is sciences of spirit) and the concept is deeply rooted in German idealist philosophy. These disciplines represent entirely different approaches to understanding the world.

Attempting to explain some of the distortions that occurred when Freudian theory was translated into English, Bettleheim (1982) notes a division of knowledge between a hermeneutic-spiritual way of knowing and a positivistic-pragmatic way of knowing:

> In much of the German world, and particularly in Vienna before and during Freud's life, psychology clearly fell into the realm of the former (Geisteswissenschaften); in much of the English-speaking world, on the other hand, psychology clearly belonged to the Naturwissenschaften.

Despite these philosophical differences and the theoretical distortions that may have occurred, psychology and psychoanalysis have flourished, with significant contributions based on both of the epistemological approaches. Similarly, in describing the origins of organizational theory, Gouldner (1970) contrasts the perspectives of the early French social philosophers Saint-Simon and Comte. Saint-Simon was the first person to recognize the significance of organizations for the modern state; organizational expertise and the "authority of the administrators would rest upon their possession of scientific skills and 'positive' knowledge."

For Comte, on the other hand, organizations and, indeed, all social institutions were best maintained by subjective and spontaneous forms of knowledge and interventions that were indigenous to particular organizations and institutions. Saint-Simon's approach gradually evolved into the "rational model" of organizational analysis, Comte's into the "natural systems" model.

Saint-Simon's approach relies heavily on quantitative measurement and empirical testing of existing theory. In direct contrast, Comte's approach relies heavily on qualitative case studies of single organizations and emphasizes conceptual and theory development. Without both approaches—and their cross-fertilization—our current understanding of organizations would be greatly diminished.

PATTERNS OF UTILIZATION

Given the divergent philosophical underpinnings of the quantitative and qualitative research approaches, how have they been utilized by the social sciences in the study of social reality? To answer this question, let us briefly consider the differences between the quantitative and qualitative approaches in terms of their ultimate purpose, their logic, their point of view, the language they use, the research designs they employ, and their theoretical bases. In emphasizing differences, however, our discussion is not meant to imply that the quantitative and qualitative approaches are incompatible within any given research study or that no exceptions exist in the patterns described.

Ultimate Purpose

In general, we use quantitative research approaches in the testing and validation of predictive, cause-effect hypotheses about social reality. By employing qualitative approaches, on the other hand, we can assemble detailed descriptions of social reality. These descriptions can serve as ends-in-themselves, or they may be useful in generating hypotheses that we can test at a later date by using quantitative approaches.

Logic

As we saw in the last chapter, in order to achieve their individual ultimate purposes, each research approach emphasizes a different form of logic. In short, quantitative approaches tend to rely on deductive logic (i.e., applying social science theory to the social reality under investigation). On the other hand, qualitative approaches are used inductively (i.e., deriving concepts and theory from the social reality being studied). This inductive strategy for theory development has been referred to as *grounded theory* and is more suited to the study of relatively uncharted social terrain. The quantitative approach is best suited to studying phenomena that have previously had a high degree of conceptual development, theory construction, and hypothesis testing.

Point of View

Quantitatively oriented research studies attempt to describe social reality from an "objective" standpoint. The adjective (objective) is in quotes because we can never totally eliminate subjectivity from the social judgments that are inevitably involved in all aspects of social science. Still, quantitative approaches place an emphasis on the perceptions that *outside* observers bring to the study of social systems.

Qualitative approaches, on the other hand, are employed most often to describe social reality from the points of view of the research participants within the systems studied. This is based on the assumption that actors in a social situation can tell us most about what they are doing and why.

Language

Another indication of the differences in the two research approaches is the language through which the study's findings are ultimately expressed. Thus, quantitatively oriented studies translate constructs and concepts into operational definitions and finally into numerical indices. Hypotheses are tested and predictions validated through the use of statistical procedures and inferences drawn from them (Weinbach & Grinnell, 2001). Qualitative studies, on the other hand, employ the research participants' natural language, and intense attention is given to the argot of system members. Concepts and theories are validated by logical induction and through detailed observation of events and discussion of their meanings with system members.

Research Designs

Quantitative research studies tend to utilize social surveys, structured interviews, self-administered questionnaires, census data, existing statistics, and the like. These approaches, while efficient and systematic, have the disadvantage of being imposed on the systems studied. As presented in the chapters contained in Part V, the data collection approaches themselves may influence and distort the reality that we wish to describe through the measurement process itself. The result may be gross inconsistencies between what system members *tell* us and what they *actually do.*

Qualitative research studies usually rely heavily on participant observation and related methods such as purposeful conversation. Although qualitative approaches create their own problems of inference, they come close to being "unobtrusive." In other words, this research approach has a minimal effect, compared to the quantitative approach, on the people and events being studied.

As presented in the last chapters in this book, quantitative research approaches usually implement descriptive and/or explanatory research designs. Such designs are best suited to testing the causality between two or more variables. Their major disadvantage has been described as design intrusiveness. So, for example, the implementation of a single-subject experimental design in a social service agency may necessitate incomplete, delayed, or denied service; may impose extraneous requirements on the helping situation; and may result in adverse client reactions. Qualitative research methodologies, on the other hand, more often than not use exploratory research designs. As we will see in Chapter 12, these types of research designs make definite cause-effect knowledge difficult to derive and are indeed less intrusive than quantitative ones.

Theoretical Basis

Finally, we can contrast the type of theory used and/or generated by these two divergent research approaches. Although there is no inherent relationship between the theoretical discipline and the approach employed, qualitative studies have been more likely to remain within the disciplinary boundaries of psychology and sociology. Qualitative studies, on the other hand, have generally been social-psychological. It should be stressed that such divisions are historical and arbitrary. They may undergo change in the future as our profession assumes a more scientific base through all types of research studies.

Differences and Similarities

In this discussion we have described and emphasized major differences in the application of the quantitative and qualitative research approaches, ignoring many exceptions to the generalizations. Thus, for example, qualitative studies are sometimes used for purely descriptive purposes. Alternatively, qualitative studies are sometimes searching for causal explanations. Similar exceptions could be stated for most of the differentiating dimensions listed. Nevertheless, the discussion captures trends or emphases in the actual application of these two research approaches.

Despite their differences, however, both research approaches are planful, systematic, and empirical. By empirical (often incorrectly used as a synonym for quantitative), we refer to a reliance on practical experience and observation as a source of knowledge verification. In short, both approaches are equally valid methods to social work knowledge generation.

CRITIQUES OF QUANTITATIVE APPROACHES

Despite the legitimacy of the two research approaches, the quantitative approach has dominated social work research. This is in part a response to the requisites of the professionalization of our profession. Neo-Marxist critics have alleged that quantitative research approaches are conservative instruments of the social science establishment.

Within social work research, quantitative approaches tend to enjoy greater respectability. And, in a response to this quantitative "emphasis," a few social work researchers have recently begun to question the use of quantitative research approaches in our profession. They are calling for a broader application of qualitative approaches, claiming that the total commitment to measurement and quantitative analyses seems now to have been premature in a field of inquiry still lacking a clear description of how things really happen in the real world.

Taking a similar position, Taylor (1977) suggests that the qualitative research approach, as compared with the quantitative one, is often more in keeping with the internal logic of our profession and more relevant to the problems of day-to-day social work practice. He cites the significant contributions that many qualitative researchers have made to social work knowledge development. He maintains that there is a real conflict between the "proof-oriented," quantitative research approaches and the "discovery-oriented" work that social work practitioners do in their day-to-day practices.

Similarly, DeMaria (1981) argues that quantitative research methodology in particular, and empiricism in general, represent an "impoverished" research paradigm for social work because they fail to question the social structure and dominant values of our society. In other words, quantitative research approaches maintain the institutional status quo. Moreover, DeMaria contends that empirically oriented research studies are incompatible with the reform tradition of social work. Finally, Heineman (1981) goes so far as to declare that the quantitative research approach are obsolete, outmoded, and overly restrictive.

This critical orientation toward quantitative approaches has expressed itself recently in challenges to particular practice research methodologies. For example, it has been suggested that single-subject methodology in social work practice is scientifically simplistic and overly restricts the mode of treatment interventions. It has also been suggested that a great deal of quantitative research studies are not useful and the types of problems social workers deal with, whether they are working with groups or individuals, often require knowledge that, to date, can be developed only through the qualitative approaches.

MYTHS SURROUNDING THE RESEARCH APPROACHES

The anti-quantitative ideology that runs through the preceding critiques has been responsible for the creation of four major misconceptions about the quantitative and qualitative research approaches. These four myths are: (1) quantitative approaches are inherently politically conservative and therefore unsuited to the reform tradition of our profession, (2) qualitative approaches are inherently politically progressive and therefore ideally suited to social work, (3) qualitative approaches are more likely to be utilized by practitioners than are quantitative ones, and (4) quantitative and qualitative approaches are inherently incompatible with one another.

Conservatism

The first myth is that quantitative approaches are inherently conservative. This myth is easily dispelled by considering quantitative social work research studies that have had critical consciousness and that have been change oriented. Consider, for example, Piven and Cloward's book, *Regulating the Poor: The Functions of Public Welfare* (1971). Their book is a quantitative study of relief policies in the United States and the authors used extensive quantitative data to link relief policies to social control and the muting of potential civil disorder. The authors, perhaps the most significant radical theoreticians in social work today and two of the architects of the welfare rights movement, apparently see no incompatibility between the requisites of social action and quantitative research methodologies.

Progressiveness

The second myth is that qualitative approaches are inherently politically progressive. Much could be written concerning the trivial preoccupations of many of the qualitative research studies that have been conducted and on the scant attention given to social and political influences in much of this literature. Instead, however, let us consider a qualitative research study by a single author well known to social workers. It has been contended that Oscar Lewis's (1966) anthropological-oriented, qualitative research study has been largely responsible for promoting the concept of a "culture of poverty" that separates the poor from other social classes and contributes to the poors' own lack of social mobility. Based on participant observation and lengthy in-depth open-ended interviews, Lewis's work has been utilized to indict the poor rather than the social structure that creates and maintains poverty.

In a criticism of Lewis's research approach, data analysis, and interpretation of the data, Valentine (1971) comments:

> The scientific status of the culture of poverty remains essentially a series of undemonstrated hypotheses. With respect to many or most of these hypotheses, alternative propositions are theoretically more convincing and are supported by more available evidence. The complex of conceptions, attitudes, and activities that has grown up around the "culture of poverty" has had a predominantly pernicious effect on American society. This complex has been a keystone in the crumbling arch of official policy toward the poor.

Valentine goes on to show how Lewis's central idea has been used to blame poverty on the poor themselves and to justify programs designed to inculcate middle-class values and virtues among the poor and especially their children, rather than changing the conditions of their existence. Hence, Lewis's qualitative methodology did not ensure against the conservative practice of "blaming the victim."

Utilization

The third myth is that qualitative research approaches are more likely to be utilized by social worker practitioners than quantitative ones. Although this has not been true historically, it is difficult to say what the future will bring. In a paper concerning the incorporation of various research approaches into social work practice, Tripodi and Epstein (1978) hypothesize that the utilization of research approaches by social workers will depend on the following four conditions: (1) the availability of research approaches, (2) the compatibility of research approaches to the informational requirements of social workers, (3) the extent to which those approaches can be implemented, and (4) their costs.

Availability

It could be said that the quantitative research approaches are more readily available to social work practitioners than qualitative ones. It could also be argued that the social-psychological perspective that is characteristic of much of contemporary qualitative research is more compatible with the "person-in-environment" perspective of social work practice than the quantitative approaches. Nevertheless, with the advent and development of single-subject designs (see Chapter 23), practice research methodology requires knowledge of quantitative principles as well.

Informational Requirements

Compatibility is the extent to which the knowledge and values necessary to employ the research approaches are compatible with the knowledge and value structures of the social work practitioners themselves. On this dimension, qualitative approaches probably are superior to quantitative ones. Thus, the descriptive, inductive, subjective, and unobtrusive approach to information gathering associated with qualitative approaches is much closer to traditional social work practice than quantitative ones. In addition, social workers are more likely to accept an approach based on natural language than one based on numbers and statistical manipulation. Nevertheless, the implicit logic, specificity, and rigor of quantitative research can still make a significant contribution to social work data gathering and knowledge, even if quantitative approaches, per se, are rejected.

Implementation

Implementation is the degree to which a research approach can be used directly or indirectly. A research approach is directly useful when it can be employed without any modification in format or procedures. In contrast, a research approach that is indirectly useful is one that requires change so that it can be adapted to actual social work practice situations. As we know, the emphasis within the qualitative approaches is on the use of exploratory, or descriptive, unobtrusive research designs and suggests that they would offer fewer problems of direct implementation than would explanatory research designs. Nonetheless an exploratory, or formative, research design can be used at the program level (see Chapter 24) and at the single-subject level (see Chapter 23). These designs offer greater flexibility for those of us who are interested in the direct implementation of quantitative approaches in social work practice.

As for indirect uses, it could be argued that effective social work practice is based on the extent to which social workers think systematically, test their intuitions with observations, and analyze information through a disciplined use of logic. These elements are part of *both* quantitative and qualitative research approaches.

Costs

Cost considerations are difficult to assess. Doing a qualitative research study is frequently time-consuming and therefore often expensive. These difficulties may render it inaccessible, especially to social workers whose employing agencies expect them to be engaged in client service delivery and in research studies *only* as it relates immediately to client service delivery.

Compatibility

The fourth myth is that the two research approaches are inherently incompatible with one another because they rest on different epistemological assumptions. Although it is true that there are epistemological differences between these two research approaches, some of the most practical and innovative research to be published in recent years makes use of both quantitative and qualitative data. Thus, Maluccio's book, *Learning from Clients (1979)*, makes use of quantitative and qualitative data collected from clients and social workers to generate ideas about the treatment process and the impact of environmental factors on service delivery in a family service agency.

In a study of classroom structure and teaching style on student compliance, Bossert (1979) skillfully integrated quantitative data concerning teacher and student behavior with narrative descriptions, verbatim accounts of conversation between pupils and teachers, interviews, and so on. A final example is Fabricant's (1982) work on juveniles in the family court stysem. Here again, we find an effective interplay of quantitative and qualitative research methodologies in a critique of the institutional processing of young offenders. Thus, to imply that we, as professional social workers, must make a choice between one or the other research approach is senseless. Both approaches make meaningful contributions to our understanding of the social world and, when used *together,* can obviously augment it.

UTILIZATION GUIDELINES

Thus far we have maintained that quantitative and qualitative approaches each have their special uses—it is only the uneducated person who states that one approach is unequivocally better than the other. As a result, rather than asking which is best, it makes more sense for us to ask under what conditions each approach is better than the other in order to answer a particular research question.

Quantitative approaches are probably most useful when we have extensive prior knowledge of the culture and environment in which our study will take place. Qualitative approaches, on the other hand, are more suitable when we are entering a relatively unfamiliar social system. Quantitative studies often require ease of access and a high level of legitimation because they are generally more intrusive than qualitative approaches. Alternatively, qualitative researchers have given considerable attention to ways of securing access and legitimation in systems that have not as yet been studied. Ease of access is facilitated by the employment of their relatively unobtrusive methods of data gathering as well.

Quantitative approaches are probably preferable in those contexts in which we have a high degree of control and authority. If these conditions are not present, the research design, data collection methods, and other essential components of the research process are likely to be subverted. In situations in which we have relatively little control and formal authority, qualitative approaches recommend themselves.

In areas of inquiry in which there has been a considerable amount of conceptual development, theory construction, and testing, quantitative approaches are usually preferable. On the other hand, qualitative approaches are most suitable when there has been a relatively low level of conceptualization and theory building. Here qualitative approaches are appropriately exploratory.

Finally, quantitative approaches are best suited in trying to establish cause-effect relationships between or among variables or to describe relatively straightforward characteristics such as demographic variables. Qualitative approaches lend themselves to the description of complex social processes and the rendering of the subjective implications of these processes by people involved in them. As a result, qualitative approaches are ideal for identifying new concepts and for hypothesis formulation.

This is not to say that occasional departures from these generalizations would not have a positive effect on knowledge development. For example, the literature on social work professionalization is dominated by quantitative research findings. However it would be interesting to explore the subjective meanings social workers attribute to "professionalization." Alternatively, labeling theory, which is firmly rooted in qualitative methodology, has been uncritically welcomed by social workers despite the paucity of quantitative evidence to support its validity.

Overall, neither quantitative nor qualitative methodology is in any ultimate sense superior to the other. The two approaches exist along a continuum on which neither pole is more "scientific" nor more suited to social work knowledge development. As Geismar and Wood (1982) state:

> *Each research model is needed. But needed also is a more sophisticated awareness of what the questions are that are being posed, and the suitability of each type of research for particular practice problems. To attempt to decide the direction for social work research on any other ground such as those based on emotional faith in any model, subverts the principles of scientific inquiry on which research is based, and on which practice should be based.*

SUMMARY

Quantitative and qualitative research approaches have existed side by side since the beginning of contemporary social science. They both attempt to describe and explain social reality. Their main difference lies in the way they do it. Quantitative approaches are based on deductive logic; that is, they proceed from a general theory to a particular instance. Qualitative approaches, on the other hand, are based on inductive logic; that is, they proceed from a particular social reality to a general social theory. Despite their differences, however, both approaches are planful, systematic, and empirical. They are equally valid approaches to social work knowledge generation.

This book contends that neither research approach is clearly more suitable for social work utilization. Instead, we need to consider the context in which our research study is taking place and the question we are attempting to answer.

In the next section of this book we look at measurement issues that must be addressed in all quantitative and qualitative research studies.

Part III

Measurement in Social Work Research

Nancy S. Kyte
Gerald J. Bostwick, Jr.

C h a p t e r   8

Measuring Variables

THIS IS THE FIRST chapter of this text that deals with the measurement of variables. At this point, it is assumed the reader will have read the previous chapters and has an appreciation of how both research approaches can be used to develop knowledge for our profession. As we have seen, both research approaches require measuring something or another, usually referred to as variables. Thus, this chapter will provide a brief discussion of how variables can be measured, in addition to discussing the validity and reliability of the measurements used.

Measurement is a pervasive part of daily living. Our morning routine, for example, may include stepping on a scale, adjusting the water for a shower, and making breakfast. Not much thought needs to be given to these activities, but measurements are being taken of weight, water temperature, and food portions. The scale, a heat-sensitive finger, and a measuring cup or spoon are all measuring instruments.

What distinguishes this type of measurement from that engaged in by social workers is the nature of the measuring procedures used. For us, measurement is a systematic process involving the assignment of symbols to properties of objects, according to specified rules. As we have seen in Chapter 6, these rules are designed to increase the probability that the world of concepts corresponds accurately to the world of reality. The development of measurement procedures is an intricate process in the physical sciences, but it is even more complex in the social sciences. In physics, for example, measurement is concerned largely with such fundamental variables as weight, length, time, density, volume, and velocity. In social work, our interest is primarily in psychosocial variables such as racial conflict, social status, aggression, and group cohesion. We focus on the properties of individuals, families, groups, communities, and institutions, for which accurate measurement is always problematic.

DEFINITIONS AND FUNCTIONS OF MEASUREMENT

This chapter adopts a broad definition of measurement as the assignment of numerals to the properties or attributes of objects or events, according to rules. Another way to understand measurement is in terms of the functions it serves.

Because the assignment of numerals carries a quantitative meaning, the terms *measurement* and *quantification* have often been used as if they were interchangeable. Recent efforts to develop a less restrictive view of measurement have produced broader definitions with less emphasis on quantification. These definitions have included the assignment of symbols to observations, the assignment of quantitative or qualitative values to attributes, and the assignment of numerals to either quantitative or qualitative response categories.

Common Characteristics of Measurement Definitions

Whether or not qualitative as well as quantitative components are included in these definitions, they all have in common three interrelated characteristics. First is the assignment of numerals (e.g., 1, 2, 3) or symbols (e.g., A, B, C), which are basically synonymous. When a numeral is used to identify something it has no intrinsic quantitative meaning and is nothing more than a label. Thus the numeral 1 is simply a symbol of a special kind, like a + is used to refer to addition or a $ used to refer to money. The letter A could be used just as easily. Measurement, however, has traditionally used numerals, which become numbers after they are assigned a quantitative meaning.

The second common characteristic of measurement definitions is that numerals or symbols are assigned to properties of objects rather than to the objects themselves. Put another way, objects are not measured *per se*; rather, their properties or characteristics are measured. To be even more precise, indicants of these properties are measured. This is important when measuring a complex concept where direct observation is impossible. Hostility, depression, and intelligence, for example, are concepts that cannot be directly observed. These properties must always be inferred from observations of their presumed variables (or indicants), such as fighting or crying.

The third characteristic is that numerals or symbols are assigned to (indicants of) properties of objects according to specified rules. The importance of these rules, often referred to as rules of correspondence or assignment, cannot be overemphasized (Kaplan, 1964). Measurement is a game played with objects and numerals. Games have rules, and rules can be good or bad. Other things being equal, good rules lead to good measurement, and bad rules lead to bad measurement. At its most basic level, then, a rule is a guide, method, or command that says what to do (Kerlinger, 1986).

Suppose a client is asked to identify five possible solutions to a problem and then rank-order them according to some criterion, such as probable effectiveness. A rule may be formulated that states that the range of numerals (1–5) should be assigned in such a manner that the highest (5) represents the solution the client judges to be the most effective and the lowest (1) represents the least effective solution. This rule clearly tells how to assign the range of numerals to the domain of problem-solving options that the client has identified.

While a definition of measurement stipulates the formulation of and adherence to rules, it does not restrict the kind of rules that can be used. Rules may be developed deductively, be based on previous experience, stem from common sense, or be pure hunches. Whatever the origin of the rules, the utility of any measure is contingent on its ability to explain adequately the variable being studied. Therefore, no measurement procedure is any better than its rules.

In summary, any endeavor attempting to assign numerals or symbols to (indicants of) properties of objects according to specified rules qualifies as measurement, and measurement of anything is theoretically possible if rules can be set up on some rational or empirical basis. Whether that measurement is good or bad will depend on the formulation of clear, unambiguous rules of correspondence that can themselves be empirically tested.

Functions of Measurement

Measurement is not an end in itself. We can appreciate its usefulness only if we know what it is intended to do and what role and function it has in our profession. Its functions include correspondence, objectivity and standardization, quantification on different levels, and replication and communication.

Correspondence

Measurement theory calls for the application of rules and procedures to increase the correspondence between the real world and the world of concepts. The real world provides us with empirical evidence; the world of concepts provides us with a theoretical model for making sense out of that segment of the real world that we are trying to explain or predict. It is through measurement's rules of correspondence that this theoretical model can be connected with the world of reality.

Objectivity and Standardization

Measurement helps take some of the guesswork out of scientific observation; the observations are considerably more objective than, for example, personal judgments. The scientific principle that any statement of fact made by one person should be independently verifiable by another is violated if there is room for disagreement about observations of empirical events.

In the absence of a standardized measurement of narcissism, for instance, two social workers may disagree strongly about how narcissistic a particular client is. Obviously, then, we would find it impossible to make any empirical test of hypotheses derived from theories of narcissism. This, unfortunately, is frequently the case. We have a myriad of theories at our disposal, but because these theories often involve variables that cannot be adequately measured, the hypotheses they generate must remain untested. Thus, additions to our knowledge base depend on the extent to which it becomes possible to measure certain variables and theoretical constructs accurately.

Quantification

By allowing for the quantification of data, measurement increases not only the objectivity of our observations but also the ability for us to describe them precisely. Different types or levels of measurement result in different types of data. Classification, for example, makes it possible to categorize variables such as gender and religion into subclasses such as male-female and Protestant-Catholic-Jewish.

A second, higher level of measurement makes it possible not only to define differences between and among variable subclasses but also to determine greater-than and less-than relationships. Thus, a particular variable might be classified not only as occurring or not occurring but also as never, rarely, sometimes, often, or always occurring.

An even higher level makes it possible to rank-order certain variable characteristics and specify the exact distances between the variable subclasses. This makes it possible to say that a family with an income of $13,000 has $5,000 more than a family with an income of $8,000, or a social service agency employing 20 social workers has a professional staff that is twice as large as that of an agency employing 10 social workers.

Each type of measurement provides important data that enable us to describe physical, psychological, or social phenomena empirically. The precision of the measurement increases as it moves from the lower (less sophisticated and refined) to the higher levels.

A related advantage of measurement is that it permits the use of powerful methods of statistical analysis. Once numbers are assigned, information can be analyzed with statistical techniques (Weinbach & Grinnell, 2001). Suppose we are conducting a study to determine what characteristics differentiate clients who continue in family therapy from those who drop out. We collect data from a variety of sources, such as clients, social workers, and independent judges, using questionnaires, in-person interviews, case records, and tape recordings of family therapy sessions. We must then be able to make some sense out of all these data, in order to explain what is going on and why. The variables studied must be quantified, or reduced to numerical form, so that our data can be analyzed with statistical techniques and the formulated hypotheses can be tested.

As seen throughout this text, when a hypothesis is supported in social work practice or research, the theory or theories from which it was derived are also supported, at least tentatively. Supporting a theory is tantamount to endorsing the explanations it provides for why certain events occur as they do. Measurement, therefore, facilitates the ability to discover and establish relationships among variables. When numbers are properly applied, the full range of mathematics can be used in constructing and testing theories aimed at explaining or predicting the phenomena of the real world.

Replication and Communication

The research process is concerned not only with conducting tests of theories but also with replicating and communicating the results. The more objective and precise the measurement procedures used in a particular study, the easier it will be for others to replicate the study and thereby to confirm or refute the results obtained. And the more rigorously measurement procedures have been specified, the greater will be the potential for increasing the effective communication of the study's findings.

MEASUREMENT VALIDITY AND RELIABILITY

The two most important considerations in choosing a measuring instrument are the validity and reliability of the instrument and, as a consequence, the validity and reliability of the data it generates. Where these two concepts have been referred to in preceding chapters, they have been identified only briefly and in simple terms. Validity has been described as the degree to which an instrument measures what it is supposed to, and reliability has been described as the degree of accuracy or precision of a measuring instrument.

The next three sections explore the meanings of validity and reliability in measurement more precisely. If we do not know how valid and reliable our measures are, we can put little faith in the results they obtain or the conclusions that are drawn from those results. In short, we cannot be sure of what we have measured.

VALIDITY OF MEASURING INSTRUMENTS

A measuring instrument is valid when it does what it is intended to do (Cronbach, 1970). To put it another way, valid measuring instruments measure what they are supposed to measure and yield scores whose differences reflect the true differences of the variable they are measuring.

An instrument such as a self-administered questionnaire, achievement test, personality inventory, or problem checklist is valid to the extent that it actually measures what it is meant to measure. An instrument that measures a variable such as dominance is valid only to the degree that it truly measures this trait—dominance. If the instrument actually measures some other variable, such as sociability, it is not a valid measure of dominance, but it may be a valid measure of sociability.

The definition of measurement validity has two parts: the extent to which an instrument actually measures the variable in question, and the extent to which it measures that variable accurately. While it is possible to have the first without the second, the second cannot exist without the first. That is, a variable cannot be measured accurately if some other variable is being measured instead.

To establish the validity of a measuring instrument, therefore, we must think in terms not of its validity but rather of its validities. Validity refers broadly to the degree to which an instrument is doing what it is intended to do—and an instrument may have several purposes that vary in number, kind, and scope.

The various kinds of validity—content, criterion, and construct—relate to the different purposes of measurement. Each type has a specific purpose that dictates the type of evidence (logical or statistical) that is needed to demonstrate that the instrument is valid. The three types of validity (and face validity, a subtype) are listed in Table 8.1, along with the questions of validity each one can address.

Table 8.1   Types of Measurement Validity
               and Questions Addressed by Each

Type	Question Addressed
Content Validity	Does the measuring instrument adequately measure the major dimensions of the variable under consideration?
(Face Validity)	Does the measuring instrument appear to measure the subject matter under consideration?
Criterion Validity	Does the individual's measuring instrument score predict the probable behavior on a second variable (criterion-related measure)?
Construct Validity	Does the measuring instrument appear to measure the general construct (element) it purports to measure?

Content Validity

Content validity is concerned with the representativeness or sampling adequacy of the content of the measuring instrument, such as the items or questions it contains. The instrument must provide an adequate sample of items (or questions) that represent the variables of interest, and it must measure the variable it is assumed to be measuring.

All variables being measured, therefore, must produce operational definitions (Nunnally, 1975). Moreover, the data gathered to measure the variables must be directly relevant and meaningful to these variables. If the properties of the measured variables are not all equally represented in the measuring instrument, a biased sample of responses will result, and the data will be meaningless and therefore useless.

Suppose, for example, we want to construct an instrument to measure students' general social work knowledge. The variable of general social work knowledge is operationally defined as including the following properties: knowledge about social welfare policy, social work research, casework, group work, and community organization. Before administering the instrument, several colleagues who are experts in these fields are asked to evaluate the instrument's contents—that is, to determine its content validity.

The community organization expert points out that no mention is made of several important functions of community organization, and the group work expert advises that there are no questions dealing with group cohesion and the normal phases of group development. Does the instrument have content validity? No, because its intended purpose—to measure general social work knowledge— will not be achieved.

Assuming that the other areas of the instrument are judged to be adequate, could the obtained data be used to validly determine a student's knowledge about casework, social work research, and social welfare policy? Here the answer is yes. Although there would be no justification for using the instrument to determine general social work knowledge, it could be used to assess knowledge about these three areas. Thus the instrument is content valid for one purpose but not for another.

Content validation is, by and large, a judgmental process; the colleagues asked to assess the instrument were also being asked to use their judgments to establish content validity. It may be assessed in the same instrument as high by one person but low by another. But if we had not asked for the judgments of colleagues or consulted with experts in each of the major areas of social work, the questions on the instrument might not have been representative of general social work knowledge. The resultant interpretations would have been open to question, to say the least.

Content validity also requires (at least in principle) specification of the universe of questions from which the instrument's questions are to be drawn. That is, the instrument must contain a logical sampling of questions from the entire universe of questions that are presumed to reflect the variable being measured. Further, the sampling of questions must correspond with the universe of questions in some consistent fashion. This is no easy task. There may be no consensus about the definition of the variable to be measured, and it may be difficult to identify the universe of questions. The potential number of representative questions to be included in the measuring instrument could approach infinity, particularly in measuring variables that are complex and multidimensional in nature.

The personal judgment of the person constructing the instrument determines how a variable is to be defined, how the universe of questions is to be identified, and how the sample of representative questions from that universe is to be drawn. Thus the general content validity of any instrument rests to a large extent on the skill and judgment of the person who constructs it. If poor judgment has been used—and this is always a possibility—the instrument is likely to have little, or no, content validity.

Face Validity

The terms *face validity* and *content validity* are often used interchangeably in the professional literature, but they are incorrectly thought of as synonymous. Technically, face validity is not a form of validation because it refers to what an instrument "appears to" measure rather than what it "actually" measures (that is, it appears relevant to those who will complete or administer it). Nevertheless, face validity is a desirable characteristic for a measuring instrument. Without it, there may be resistance on the part of respondents, and this can adversely affect the results obtained. Consequently, it is important to structure an instrument so that it not only accurately measures the variables under consideration (content validity) but also appears to be a relevant measure of those variables (face validity).

To assess the effects of a communication skills training course offered at a school of social work, for example, an assessment form is to be administered to each student at the beginning and end of the course. A search of the literature locates a standardized instrument that measures the types of skills the course is designed to teach.

This instrument, however, was originally developed for use with upper- and middle-management personnel. If our students were presented with items reflecting the business world, they might well question how their responses could tell anything about how they work with clients. The items should be rephrased to reflect social work situations in order to increase the face validity of the instrument.

Criterion Validity

Criterion validity, which involves multiple measurement, is established by comparing scores of the measuring instrument with an external criterion known (or believed) to measure the variable being measured. Thus there must be one or more external, or independent, criteria with which to compare the scores of the instrument.

In order to validate an instrument that has been constructed to predict our students' success in a BSW program, for example, the measuring instrument is administered to students entering their first semester. These test scores are then compared with their subsequent grade point averages. Here, the external criterion (or dependent variable) is grade point average. Other potential external criteria might be individual or combined ratings of academic and field practicum performance and graduation from the program.

The external criterion used, of course, should itself be reasonably valid and reliable. If a criterion that is inaccurate or undependable is chosen, the instrument itself will not be validated adequately. Unfortunately, valid and reliable criteria may not exist or may not have been thoroughly tested. In such a case, the one that seems most adequate (keeping in mind its limitations) should be chosen, supplemented, if possible, with other relevant criteria. The nature of the predictions and the techniques available for checking out criteria generally determine which ones are relevant.

Concurrent and Predictive Validity

Criterion validity may be classified as concurrent or predictive. Concurrent validity refers to the ability of a measuring instrument to predict accurately an individual's current status. An example of an instrument with concurrent validity is a psychopathology scale that is capable of distinguishing between adolescents who are *currently* in need of psychiatric treatment and those who are not.

Predictive validity denotes an instrument's ability to predict future performance or status from present performance or status. An instrument has predictive validity if it can distinguish between individuals who will *differ at some point in the future.* A psychopathology scale with predictive validity would be capable of differentiating not only those adolescents who need psychiatric treatment but those who will need it one year from now.

Both concurrent and predictive validity are concerned with prediction, and both make use of some external criterion that is purportedly a valid and reliable measure of the variable being studied. What differentiates the two is time. Concurrent validity predicts current performance or status, while predictive validity predicts future performance or status. Moreover, concurrent validity involves administering an instrument and comparing its scores with an external criterion at approximately the same time, or concurrently. In contrast, predictive validity entails comparative measurement at two different (present and future) points in time.

The major concern of criterion validity, however, is not whether an instrument is valid for concurrent or future discriminations. Rather, the concern is with the use of a second measure as an independent criterion to check the validity of the first measure.

Construct Validity

What sets construct validity apart from content and criterion validity is its preoccupation with theory, explanatory constructs, and the testing of hypothesized relationships between and among variables. Construct validity is difficult to understand because it involves determining the degree to which an instrument successfully measures a theoretical concept. The difficulty derives in part from the abstract nature of concepts.

A concept is a characteristic or trait that does not exist as an isolated, observable dimension of behavior. It cannot be seen, felt, or heard, and it cannot be measured directly—its existence must be inferred from the evidence at hand. Thus the concept, hostility, may be inferred from observations of presumably hostile or aggressive acts; the concept, anxiety, may be inferred from test scores, galvanic skin responses, observations of anxious behaviors, and so on. Other typical concepts of concern to us are motivation, social class, delinquency, prejudice, and organizational conflict.

Construct validity is evaluated by determining the degree to which certain explanatory concepts account for variance, or individual differences, in the scores of an instrument. Put another way, it is concerned with the meaning of the instrument—that is, what it is measuring and how and why it operates the way it does. To assess the construct validity of the Rorschach inkblot test, for example, we would try to determine the factors, or concepts, that account for differences in responses on the test. Attempts might be made to determine if the test measures emotional stability, sociability, or self-control and whether it also measures aggressiveness. The question would be: What proportion of the total test variance is accounted for by the concepts of emotional stability, sociability, self-control, and aggressiveness?

With construct validity, there is usually more interest in the property, or concept, being measured than in the instrument itself. Thus it involves validation not only of the instrument but also of the theory underlying it. To establish construct validity, the meaning of the concept must be understood, and the propositions the theory makes about the relationships between this and other concepts must be identified. We try to discover what predictions can be made on the basis of these propositions and whether the measurements obtained from the instrument will be consistent with those predictions. If the predictions are not supported, there is no clear-cut guide as to whether the shortcoming is in the instrument or in the theory.

Suppose a study is conducted to test the hypothesis that self-referred clients are more likely to have favorable attitudes toward treatment than those who come to the agency on some other basis. If the findings do not support the predicted relationship between self-referral and attitude toward treatment, should it be concluded that the measure is not valid or that the hypothesis is incorrect? In such a situation the concept of attitude toward treatment and the network of propositions that led to this prediction should be reexamined. Then the concept might be refined with more detailed hypotheses about its relationship to other concepts, and changes might be made in the instrument.

Construct validation makes use of data from a variety of sources. It is a painstaking building process much like theory construction—an attempt to ferret out the dimensions that an instrument is tapping and thereby to validate the theory underlying the instrument. This can be accomplished through a three-step process: (1) suggesting what concepts might account for performance on an instrument, (2) deriving hypotheses from the theory surrounding the concepts, and (3) testing these hypotheses empirically (Cronbach, 1970). The testing of the hypotheses can involve many procedures, including convergent-discriminant validation and factor analysis.

Convergent-Discriminant Validation

Convergent validity means that different measures of a concept yield similar results (i.e., they converge). Put another way, evidence gathered from different sources and in different ways leads to the same (or a similar) measure of the concept. If two different instruments, each alleging to measure the same concept, are administered to a group of people, similar responses or scores should be found on both instruments. And if one instrument is administered to groups of people in two different states, it should yield similar results in both groups. If it does not, the theory underlying the concept being measured should be able to explain why.

Discriminant validity means that a concept can be empirically differentiated (i.e., discriminated) from other concepts. The test is to see if an instrument is (or is not) related to other concepts from which, according to theory, it should differ. If it can be shown that an instrument measures a concept in the same way other instruments measure it, and that it is not related to any other concepts from which it should theoretically differ, it has both convergent and discriminant validity.

Factor Analysis

Another powerful method for determining construct validity is factor analysis, a statistical procedure in which a large number of questions or instruments (called factors) is reduced to a smaller number. The procedure is used to discover which factors go together (i.e., measure the same or similar things) and to determine what relationships exist between these clusters of factors.

Suppose we develop a measuring instrument and administer it, along with seven other different instruments, to a group of clients. Factor analysis would allow us to identify the concepts that are being measured by these eight instruments and to determine which instruments, if any, are essentially measuring the same concepts. The relationships of the new instrument to the other seven could be examined to determine which concept(s) it actually measures. Our understanding of that concept is improved by knowledge of the degree to which the other concepts are or are not related to the one measured in the new instrument.

Choosing the Best Approach

Content, criterion, and construct validity are three interrelated approaches to instrument validation. They are all relevant to any research situation. Because each type of validation functions in a different capacity, it is difficult to make any blanket generalizations about which is the best approach.

Three questions can be asked to discover how valid an instrument is (Thorndike & Hagen, 1969). They are:

1. How well does this instrument measure what it should measure?
2. How well does this instrument compare with one or more external criteria purporting to measure the same thing?
3. What does this instrument mean—what is it in fact measuring, and how and why does it operate the way it does?

The questions we choose to answer dictate which types of validation are of primary concern. The first would require content validity, the second criterion validity, and the third, construct validity. Our objectives and planned use of the instrument determine what kind of validity evidence is needed the most. When an instrument is employed for different purposes, it should be validated in different ways. If it is used for any purpose other than that for which it was intended—or if it is used with a different client population or in a different setting—we have the responsibility to revalidate it accordingly.

RELIABILITY OF MEASURING INSTRUMENTS

The degree of accuracy, or precision, in the measurements an instrument provides is called reliability. Dependability, stability, consistency, predictability, reproducibility, and generalizability are all synonyms for reliability. A measuring instrument is reliable to the extent that independent administrations of the same instrument (or a comparable instrument) consistently yield similar results.

In its broadest sense, an instrument's reliability indicates the degree to which individual differences in scores are attributable to "true" differences in the property being measured or to errors of measurement. As will be discussed in a later section of this chapter, errors of measurement involving reliability are random, rather than constant. They are the product of causes and conditions, such as fatigue and fluctuations of memory or mood, which are essentially irrelevant to the purpose of the instrument. Scores on an instrument therefore tend to lean now this way, now that.

Since random errors are present in all measurement, no instrument is 100 percent reliable. The data yielded by an instrument will be dependable only to the extent that the instrument is relatively free from errors of measurement. Consequently, every instrument should be tested for reliability before it is formally administered, rather than after.

The term *reliability* is frequently used to refer to three different but interrelated concepts: (1) stability, (2) equivalence, and (3) homogeneity. Underlying each of these is the notion of consistency.

- Stability, also called temporal stability, refers to an individual's responses from one administration of an instrument to another. It is determined by the test-retest method, which compares the results of repeated measurements.
- Equivalence concerns an individual's responses on different instruments intended to measure the same thing. It can be established using alternate, or parallel, forms.
- Homogeneity focuses on the internal consistency of an instrument and can be determined with the split-half method.

Table 8.2   Types of Measurement Reliability
and Questions Addressed by Each

Type	Question Addressed
Test-Retest Method	Does an individual respond to a measuring instrument in the same general way when the instrument is administered twice?
Alternate-Forms Method	When two forms of an instrument that are equivalent in their degree of validity are given to the same individual, is there a strong convergence in how that person responds?
Split-Half Method	Are the scores on one half of the measuring instrument similar to those obtained on the other half?

All three concepts and procedures essentially involve establishing the degree of consistency or agreement between two or more independently derived sets of scores. The three general methods for establishing the reliability of a measuring instrument are listed in Table 8.2, along with the measurement reliability question addressed in each.

The Test-Retest Method

A common approach to establishing reliability is through repeated measurement. The same instrument is administered to the same group of individuals on two or more separate occasions. Then the results are compared by correlating the sets of scores and calculating what is known as a reliability coefficient, which indicates the extent of the relationship between the scores. If this coefficient is high, it can be concluded that the instrument has good test-retest reliability.

Test-retest reliability thus estimates the stability of an instrument by permitting it to be compared with itself and by showing the extent to which its scores are consistent over time. The higher the reliability, the less susceptible the scores are to random daily changes in the condition of the individual (e.g., fatigue, emotional strain, worry) or the testing environment (e.g., noise, room temperature). And the less susceptible the instrument is to such extraneous influences, the more reliable it is.

Effects of Retesting

To determine if a difference between measurements of the same measuring instrument is due to extraneous factors or to a genuine change in the variable being measured, the first consideration is the possibility that the first testing has influenced the second. The very process of remeasuring may have increased the influence of extraneous factors. Individuals may be less interested, less motivated, and less anxious during the second testing because they are already familiar with the instrument, for example. If the time interval between retests is fairly short, they may remember their answers and simply repeat many of the responses they provided the first time.

Another possibility is that the first testing has actually changed the variable being measured. For instance, a self-administered questionnaire assessing attitudes toward the elderly may raise questions people have never thought about before, so their interest in the issue is heightened and they form definite opinions. Thus a "do not know" response on the first testing may be replaced by a "definitely agree" or "definitely disagree" response on the second. It is also possible that a genuine change due to influences unrelated to the testing has occurred.

Because test-retest reliability is subject to a number of biases due to the effects of recall, practice, or repetition, measuring instruments that are appreciably affected by memory or repetition do not lend themselves to this method. If the measures obtained on an instrument will not be appreciably affected by a repeat testing, the test-retest method can be used, but careful consideration must be given to the time interval between tests. The shorter this interval, the more likely it is that the first testing will have an effect on the second one; the longer the interval, the more likely it is that real change will have occurred. A shorter interval increases the likelihood of erring in the direction of overestimating reliability, and a longer interval may result in underestimating reliability.

There are no hard and fast rules for judging the optimal time interval between tests. A two- or four-week interval is generally considered suitable for most psychological measures, and the waiting period should rarely exceed six months. On a general level, wait long enough for the effects of the first testing to wear off, but not long enough for a significant amount of real change to occur. If an IQ test is administered to a group of children on two separate occasions, approximately one month apart, for example, changes in scores would not be anticipated, but an interval of five years could be expected to produce significant changes.

An example of the use of the test-retest method in social work practice involves a series of instruments to assess the extent of clients' problems and to obtain evaluative feedback on therapeutic progress (Nurius & Hudson, 1993). Clients complete them every week or two weeks, and we can use their scores to monitor and guide the course of our treatment. The test-retest reliability of these scales was established by asking a group of clients to complete them at one sitting, wait a minimum of two hours and a maximum of 24 hours, and complete them again. The resultant reliability coefficients were high. In clinical applications, the reliability of these measures has not appeared to change markedly as a result of repeated administrations.

The Alternate-Forms Method

One way to avoid some of the problems encountered with test-retest reliability is to use alternate (or parallel) forms. The alternate-forms method involves administering, in either immediate or delayed succession, supposedly equivalent forms of the same instrument to the same group of individuals. The reliability coefficient obtained indicates the strength of the relationship between the two alternate forms.

Alternate forms can be thought of as instruments with equivalent content that are constructed according to the same specifications. The forms contain questions that are different (thus eliminating exact recall) but are intended to measure the same variable equally. Form A and Form B of a reading comprehension test, for example, should contain passages of equal difficulty and should ask similar types of questions. If Form A uses a passage from a novel and Form B uses an excerpt from a research text, the levels of difficulty can be expected to be quite different. Any observed differences, then, could be explained as a result of the test's content, not differing levels of reading comprehension.

Use of the alternate-forms method requires both appropriate time intervals and equivalent sets of questions. Each alternate form must contain a sampling of questions that is truly representative. Questions must be randomly drawn from the universal pool of potential questions in such a way that if the same procedure were followed a second or even a third time, essentially equivalent sets of questions would result each time. Each set would then qualify as an alternate form of the instrument. In addition to content-equivalent questions, alternate forms should contain the same number of questions, questions expressed in a similar form, and questions of equal difficulty, and they should have comparable instructions, formats, illustrative examples, and time limits.

Considerable time and effort are needed to develop and administer truly equivalent forms. All the problems of measuring social and psychological phenomena are compounded by the need to construct two instruments.

The Split-Half Method

The split-half method of establishing reliability involves administering an instrument to a group of people, with the questions divided into comparable halves and the scores on the two parts compared to determine the extent to which they are equivalent. This is in many ways analogous to alternate-forms reliability because each half is treated as if it were a parallel form of the same instrument.

If the two halves are not equivalent, the instrument may not have a representative sampling of questions, and an individual's score may be influenced more by the questions than by the variable being measured. If the scores obtained from the two halves are similar, it can be assumed that the individual's performance is not appreciably affected by the sampling of questions in either half of the instrument.

One of the main problems with split-half reliability is how to divide the instrument into equivalent halves. The first thought might be to divide the instrument in half by counting the total number of questions and dividing by two; a 30-question instrument would be split so that Questions 1 through 15 would make up the first half and Questions 16 through 30 the second half. But what happens if the nature or level of difficulty of the questions is different at the beginning and end of the instrument? And how can such extraneous factors as fatigue and boredom, which may influence responses at the beginning and end of the instrument differently, be controlled for?

One answer is the odd-even procedure, whereby all the even-numbered questions are assigned to one group and all the odd-numbered questions to the other group. Then the scores from the two groups are compared.

THE VALIDITY-RELIABILITY RELATIONSHIP

Although validity and reliability have been treated as separate properties of a measuring instrument, they are clearly related. There cannot be validity without reliability, but there can be reliability without validity. Put simply, high reliability does not guarantee validity. Reliability can only show that something is being measured consistently, but that "something" may or may not be the variable that is to be measured. Thus an instrument that is reliable may not be valid. However, it is not possible to have an instrument that is valid but not reliable. If an instrument measures what it says it measures, then by definition it must be reliable.

The relationship between validity and reliability can be illustrated with an analogy. Suppose a new rifle is used in a sharpshooter contest, but first the new sight and overall accuracy of the weapon must be checked out. A target is set up and five rounds are fired. As Figure 8.1a shows, the shots are scattered all over; not one has hit the target, let alone the bull's-eye.

Luckily, another shooter notices that the rifle is jerked when fired, which could account for the scattering of shots. The rifle is then put on a stand to minimize this effect, and on the next try five rounds are fired. As Figure 8.1b illustrates, all five shots are grouped together in a pattern, which seems to indicate that the inconsistency on the first attempt was due to the jerking of the rifle and not to a problem with the rifle itself. However, the shots are still off target.

The problem must be the new rifle sight; the target is not being hit where the rifle is aimed. After realigning the sight, another five rounds are fired, and this time they hit the bull's-eye every time (Figure 8.1c). This analogy shows that it is possible to have an instrument that is both unreliable and invalid

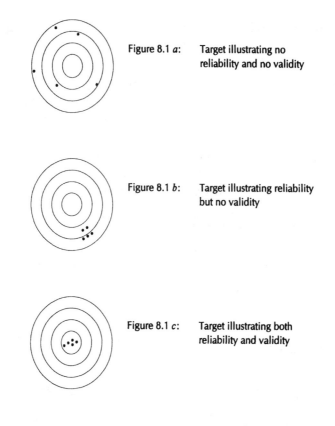

Figure 8.1 *a*:   Target illustrating no
reliability and no validity

Figure 8.1 *b*:   Target illustrating reliability
but no validity

Figure 8.1 *c*:   Target illustrating both
reliability and validity

Figure 8.1   Validity and Reliability
Relationship

(Figure 8.1a), that has high reliability and no validity (Figure 8.1b), or that has high reliability and high validity (Figure 8.1c).

SOURCES OF MEASUREMENT ERROR

Measurement error is any variation in responses on a measuring instrument—such as answers on a questionnaire or ratings made by an independent observer—that cannot be attributed to the variable being measured. Thus measurement error is inversely related to the validity and reliability of an instrument. The greater the variation due to extraneous factors, the lower will be the validity and reliability of the measurements taken.

Our goal, therefore, is to develop or locate a measuring instrument that is as free as possible from outside, unwanted influences. However, most measurement occurs in more-or-less complex situations in which numerous factors may affect both the variable being measured and the process of measurement. As a result, it is virtually impossible to construct a perfectly valid and reliable instrument.

Because measurements are never totally free of error, we must identify potential sources of error and then control or lessen their impact. Put simply, the aim is to minimize error and maximize accuracy. Of the myriad of extraneous influences that could be operating in any measurement situation as sources of error, only the most common will be reviewed in this section. There are basically two categories of the factors that may have unwanted influence on a measurement so that they obscure the "true" differences in the variable being measured—either constant (systematic) or random (variable) sources of error.

Constant Error

Constant, or systematic, error refers to those factors that consistently or systematically affect the variable being measured. By their nature, these factors are concerned with relatively stable qualities of the respondents to the measuring instruments. Demographic characteristics and personal style are the two most common sources of constant error.

Demographic variables that could influence an individual's responses include intelligence, education, socioeconomic status, race, culture, and religion. Suppose an assessment is to be made of the job satisfaction of a group of young people who dropped out of high school and enrolled in a job training program. The measuring instrument (a self-administered job satisfaction questionnaire) requires an ability to read at the eighth-grade level.

If the measuring instrument is administered to the trainees without determining their reading levels in advance, it is likely to produce a set of confounded scores. That is, the scores will reflect not their job satisfaction, either before or after completing the program, but rather their ability to read and understand the questions. It cannot be assumed that the respondents represent a homogeneous group with respect to demographic characteristics or that these characteristics exert little influence on the measurements. In this example, there would be no justification for assuming that since all of the trainees had dropped out of high school, they can all read at the eighth-grade level.

Personal Styles or Response Sets

Test constructors and research methodologists have devoted most attention to the personal styles of the respondents as a source of error. This is partly because different personal styles, or response sets, have come to be viewed as indicants of personality traits. Some of the common personal styles that can consistently affect the responses of individuals or the reactions of observers are listed in Figure 8.2.

Response-Set Sources of Error

- Errors Due to Personal Styles of Respondents:

  Social Desirability — A tendency to try to give a favorable impression of oneself in one's responses.

  Acquiescence — A tendency to agree with statements regardless of their content.

  Deviation — A tendency to give unusual or uncommon responses.

- Errors Due to Reactions of Observers:

  Contrast Error — A tendency to rate others as opposite to oneself in regard to a particular trait or characteristic.

  Halo Effect — A tendency to be unduly influenced by a single favorable trait or to let one's general impression affect one's ratings of a single trait or characteristic.

  Error of Leniency — A tendency to rate too high or to always give favorable reports.

  Error of Severity — A tendency to rate too low or to always give unfavorable reports.

  Error of Central Tendency — A tendency to rate in the middle, thus avoiding any extreme positions.

Figure 8.2   Constant Errors in Measurement Attributable to Respondents' Personal Style or Observers' Reactions

There is some controversy about the actual biasing or error effects of response sets. Some maintain that they explain only a small portion of the variance in measurement and do not apply to all types of instruments. Ideally, however, every measurement situation would be examined for such sources of error and appropriate steps would be taken to reduce their confounding effects. Control procedures for errors due to personal styles of respondents include development of subtle or socially neutral questions and items, incorporation of various response-set or "faking" indicators, and concealment of the instrument's true purpose. Control efforts to minimize observers' reactions include careful training of observers and use of multiple observers.

Random Error

Random error (or variable error), refers to unknown or uncontrolled factors that affect the variable being measured and the process of measurement in an inconsistent (variable) fashion. Unlike constant error, random error effects have no uniform trend or direction. Measurements are affected in such a way that both overestimates and underestimates of the "true" differences in the variable being measured may result.

These errors therefore are self-compensating; that is, they tend to cancel each other out, especially where there is a relatively large sample of respondents. Nevertheless, it is advisable to try to minimize their potential effects. The ideal situation is one in which the respondent's physical or emotional state, the testing environment, and the procedures used to administer the instrument all exert little or no influence on the measurement process.

The types of random errors reflect three criteria: (1) the transient qualities of the respondent, (2) situational factors in the measurement, and (3) factors related to the administration of the instrument. The transient qualities of respondents to a measuring instrument are those that can vary from day to day—indeed, from moment to moment. These include physical or mental health, mood, motivation, and degree of alertness, boredom, or fatigue. We must consider each quality separately and make a judgment as to how germane or influential it may be in a particular measurement situation.

External, or situational, factors also can introduce unwanted sources of variation into the measures. These include factors in the physical setting, such as seating arrangements, work space, noise, lighting, or the presence of a tape recorder, as well as factors in the social setting, such as the degree of anonymity afforded respondents and the presence or absence of peers. It would not be surprising, for example, to find that adolescents provide different responses to questions about gang behavior when interviewed on the street or at a police station, as a group or individually, or in the presence or absence of family members.

Random error attributable to the administration of the measuring instrument often stems from a lack of uniformity in applications. For instance, interviewers without adequate training might add or omit material or change the wording of questions; group administrators might improvise their own instructions; observers might use different criteria or types of information to classify behaviors. Standardization helps minimize the amount of subjectivity influencing the measurement process and maximize the comparability and objectivity of measurements.

The administrator of the instrument also can be a source of error. It has been found, for example, that an administrator's demeanor and physical appearance, as well as such characteristics as race, gender, age, and socioeconomic status, can affect how an individual will respond. Administrators of measuring instruments must be aware of the image they present and try to minimize the effects of demographic dissimilarities between themselves and respondents.

Administrative factors have a good deal to do with controlling or reducing all three types of random errors. One way is for the administrator to foster rapport with the respondents by arousing interest in the instrument, eliciting cooperation, spending time getting acquainted, increasing motivation, reducing anxiety, and making sure the respondents are capable of completing the tasks required. Another is to select a setting that is conducive to the types of responses needed, such as separate interviews for husbands and wives to determine their attitudes toward their marriages. The use of clear, standardized instructions and the advance preparation of interviewers, observers, and administrators with rehearsals or trial runs will further reduce administrative errors.

SUMMARY

Measurement is a necessary part of social work research that facilitates the correspondence between the world of concepts and the world of observations. It has a meaningful role not only in the selection of appropriate methods of data collection but also in the operationalization of variables and the testing of hypotheses. Through its rules of correspondence, measurement serves to increase the objectivity of observations, the potential duplication of research studies, and the effective communication of findings.

Validity and reliability are the most important characteristics to be considered in selecting a measuring instrument. Validity refers to the degree to which an instrument measures what it is supposed to measure. An instrument may have several purposes that vary in number, kind, and scope, for each of which validity must be established. There are three types of validity: content, criterion, and construct. Measurement reliability refers to the accuracy or precision of an instrument. There are three general methods for establishing reliability: the test-retest, alternate-forms, and split-half methods. Reliability and validity are highly interrelated.

Measurement error refers to variations in instrument scores that cannot be attributed to changes in the variable being measured. Basically, all measurement errors can be categorized as constant (systematic) error or random (variable) error. While measurement errors can never be completely eliminated, all possible steps must be taken to minimize their impact, since the validity and reliability of the instrument decrease as the measurement error increases.

The next two chapters deal with the basic types of measuring instruments. A thorough treatment of standardized instruments, describing how they are constructed and used, is given in Chapter 9, and instruments designed by a social worker for a specific purpose are discussed in Chapter 10. The choice between these two types is usually moot; if a standardized measuring instrument is available that will provide valid and reliable measures of the variables under consideration, it is almost always used.

Catheleen Jordan
Cynthia Franklin
Kevin Corcoran

Chapter   9

Measuring Instruments

A **GREAT VARIETY** of standardized measuring instruments is available to cover most of our research needs. The selection of an appropriate instrument(s) for a specific measurement purpose requires a thorough understanding of how standardized instruments are constructed and used. Only with this knowledge can we evaluate competing instruments and choose the one(s) that will provide the most valid and reliable data for a particular purpose. A measuring instrument is standardized through rigorous research procedures aimed at empirically verifying its characteristics, results, and applicability. The level of their development varies from minimal to extensive. A well-developed instrument is better than a less-developed instrument.

ADVANTAGES OF STANDARDIZED MEASURING INSTRUMENTS

Every person to whom a particular standardized measuring instrument is administered should be treated in exactly the same way. In theory, the only reason individuals should score differently on the instrument is because they differ on the variable that is being measured. By providing uniform administration and scoring procedures and normative data that can be used as a basis for comparison, standardized measuring instruments help ensure that the data collected will be valid and reliable measures.

Uniform Administration and Scoring

In standardized measuring instruments, measurement conditions and outcomes are clearly specified to assure comparability across respondents and across research situations. Detailed instructions about how the instrument is to be administered, to whom it is to be administered, and the exact meaning of the results usually are included in a technical manual that accompanies the instrument. Specifications include the materials to be used, the oral instructions to be given while administering the instrument, preliminary demonstrations, scoring methods, and the meaning of the scores produced.

These directions must be followed explicitly in order to reduce the sources of measurement error. With any instrument, care must be taken that constant errors, such as personal style and demographic characteristics, and random errors, such as changeable qualities of the respondents and situational and administrative factors, do not affect the measurements taken (see Chapter 8).

Generation of Normative Data

Normalization, or the establishment of normative data (norms), is essential to the scoring and interpretation of a standardized instrument. Norms are group standards, usually based on a group's average or mean score on a measuring instrument. By giving information on the typical (or average) performance of a particular group, norms provide a point of comparison that can be used to interpret individual scores (Sattler, 1988; Graham & Lilly, 1984). Norms also empirically define the limits and applicability of the measuring instrument by establishing data such as the means and standard deviations of the measures and identifying types of groups for which the instrument is appropriate.

Norms are developed by administering the instrument to a large representative sample (the normalization or norm group) whose demographic characteristics are known. Descriptive statistics are computed for the sample, and an individual's score on an instrument can then be compared to the norms established by the representative sample group.

The raw score of a respondent also can be converted into a derived score, which can be directly compared to the average score achieved by the sample to determine the respondent's standing in relation to the normalization group. Examples of derived scores used in normative measurement include clinical cutting points (such as "A score of 30 or above is considered clinically significant") and age-grade equivalents. Statistical concepts such as standard scores (for example, a *T*-score with a mean of 50 and a standard deviation of 10) and percentile ranks are also derived scores. Jerome Sattler (1988) provides three guidelines for evaluating the norms of a standardized instrument:

1. The norm group (the sample) should have the same characteristics as the potential respondents. For example, if Asian students are to be assessed to determine why they consistently score high in academic programs, an instrument for which few or no Asians had been included in the sample should not be used.
2. The larger and more representative the norm group, the better. As a general rule, the sample should consist of at least 100 individuals with similar characteristics.
3. The relevance of a particular norm group to the population to be studied must be determined. Many standardized measuring instruments provide several different norm groups ranked by characteristics, from which the group that best characterizes the one to be measured can be chosen.

VALIDITY OF STANDARDIZED INSTRUMENTS

It is through standardization that the validity of the measuring instrument is established. This concept has been defined as the extent to which the instrument actually measures what it is intended to measure. The scores on a measuring instrument should reflect the true differences of the variable they are measuring. The definition therefore includes not only the extent to which an instrument actually measures the variable in question, but also the extent to which it measures that variable accurately.

Three types of validity for measuring instruments were identified in the previous chapter: content, criterion, and construct. Some guidelines for establishing each of these validities in evaluating standardized instruments are briefly discussed in this section. Each type of validity is related to a different purpose of measurement, and no one type is appropriate for every measurement situation. Validity, therefore, must be verified with reference to the intended use of a particular standardized instrument. In other words, potential users of an instrument must ask what it is valid for and for whom it is valid. Let us now turn to the three types of validity.

Content Validity

To ensure content validity, a measuring instrument must include an adequate sample of the universe of questions or items that represent the variable under consideration. This type of validity represents the extent to which the content of a measuring instrument reflects the variable that is being measured and in fact measures that variable and not another. Eight general guidelines have been proposed for the establishment of content validity in a standardized measuring instrument. Many of these points are discussed further in Chapter 10 in relation to the design and construction of a measuring instrument for specific purposes. We need to consider the following points when it comes to adopting a standardized measuring instrument:

1. Each question or item must represent an aspect of the variable being measured. (*Question* is the term used to designate the item to be rated or responded to, although it could be in the form of a statement.)
2. Questions should be empirically related to the construct being measured.
3. Questions must differentiate among individuals at different points in the dimension being measured. In other words, the instrument should discriminate between individuals at low and high extremes and in the middle.
4. Double-barreled questions or otherwise ambiguous interpretations should be avoided (see Chapter 10).
5. Some questions should be worded positively and others negatively so the variable being measured can be indicated by a yes or agree response approximately half the time and by a no or disagree response half the time. Alternating positive and negative wording for questions breaks up the social desirability response set (see Chapter 10).
6. Short questions should be used when possible.
7. Negative questions should be avoided.
8. Biased questions should be avoided, including derogatory statements, slang terms, and prejudicial or leading questions.

The two principal methods used in selecting questions for a measuring instrument so as to ensure content validity—the rational-intutitive and empirical methods—are discussed later in this chapter.

Criterion Validity

Criterion validity has been defined as a process of comparing scores on a measuring instrument with an external criterion. Some criteria that can be used to establish criterion validity for standardized measuring instruments are described in this section (Anastasi, 1988).

One criterion is performance in school or training programs. Independent criteria against which instrument scores can be compared include grades, commendations, and credits earned. This method is used for all types of achievement and diagnostic measuring instruments.

Another criterion involves contrast groups. The scores of one group may be compared with those of another that is assumed to be different, such as the scores of salespersons and accountants, or the scores of an individual may be compared with those of a group. This method is used in the development of personality, interest, and aptitude inventories.

Psychiatric diagnoses also can be used as an external criterion. This involves comparing an individual's performance on a measuring instrument with the psychiatric diagnosis of the person. As a basis of test validity, a psychiatric diagnosis is often used to validate personality instruments and other diagnostic measuring instruments. The validity of a psychiatric diagnosis should be checked before it is used as an indicator or predictor in this way, however.

Other measuring instruments for which criterion validity has been established are often used to establish an instrument's validity. Comparing scores on these instruments with those of the instrument under consideration is a validation method that can be used with all types of measuring instruments.

Other criteria are provided through ratings by observers. Ratings of children's behavior by teachers, parents, or peers and ratings of employees' attitudes by supervisors, coworkers, or others are frequently used in the development of personality measuring instruments.

Construct Validity

Construct validity has been defined as the degree to which an instrument successfully measures a theoretical construct, or an unobservable characteristic or trait. There is more interest in the construct being measured than in the measuring instrument or the scores it generates. The ability to predict developmental changes in children, for example, is a traditional criterion for the construct of IQ scores, which should increase as children get older (Anastasi, 1988). Developmental changes reflected in test scores may be taken as evidence of the measuring instrument's construct validity.

Another way to establish construct validity suggested by Anastasi is to use other measuring instruments with proven construct validity to validate new instruments for measuring related constructs. Scores on the new instrument should correlate highly with those on the other one, but not too highly. There might not be a good reason for developing the new measuring instrument if it does not improve on already available instruments in some way.

Statistical techniques and hypothesis testing procedures such as factor analysis and the establishment of convergent-discriminant validation (see Chapter 8) also can be used to establish construct validity. Factor analysis is particularly relevant because it identifies underlying dimensions of traits or behaviors, as well as the common factors existing in or between measuring instruments. Convergent-discriminant validation concerns the extent to which measures of a construct from different instruments yield similar results, or converge, and the extent to which constructs tested can be empirically discriminated, or differentiated, from other constructs.

The constructs of a measuring instrument also can be validated with experimental interventions, as in the one-group pretest-posttest research design described in Chapter 12. For example, we might be given a pretest in the form of an anxiety-measuring instrument, be subjected to some type of anxiety-raising stimulus such as having to meet higher productivity levels, and then be retested to see if our anxiety scores had risen. In this case, a rise in scores could be taken as evidence of the measuring instrument's ability to reflect our current anxiety levels.

CONSTRUCTION OF STANDARDIZED INSTRUMENTS

A standardized measuring instrument that lacks both validity and reliability would not be a good candidate for selection. Constructors of standardized instruments, therefore, seek to develop instruments that are as valid and reliable as possible. After questions have been selected to maximize content validity, the principal concerns are with the response categories for each question and the length of the instrument.

Question Selection

Two basic methods of selecting questions so as to enhance the content validity of a measuring instrument are the rational-intuitive and empirical methods (Fairweather & Tornatsky, 1977).

The rational-intuitive method involves choosing questions in a logical manner. A group of experts such as clinical social workers, for example, might be asked to suggest questions for determining the presence of a high-risk suicidal behavior. Similar questions suggested might be included, while dissimilar questions would be excluded. Questions selected would then be arranged in groups that logically appear to measure the same variable. Questions related to level of impulse control, such as drug usage and temper tantrums, might be grouped together, and questions related to the immediate danger of suicidal action, such as having a clear plan of doing the act and the means to do it, might form another group.

In the empirical method of establishing content validity, statistical techniques are used to select questions. In the development of a service-satisfaction measuring instrument for a social work agency, for example, we might conduct a simple exploratory study and sample the agency's records to determine all the different services offered by the agency. The various types of services offered would then guide the types of questions to be included on the satisfaction questionnaire. A combination of the rational-intuitive and the empirical methods is often used in the development of measuring instruments. Questions are generated utilizing experts (rational-intuitive method) and later tested using factor analysis techniques (empirical method).

Response Category Selection

Once the questions have been developed for a standardized instrument, the possible responses for each question are assigned. This provides some notion of the magnitude of the variable being measured for an individual respondent. One logical way is to assign a value for each response, with a low value indicating a low level of the variable being measured and a larger value indicating a higher level.

Values can be thought of as being situated on a continuum of degree, intensity, or magnitude. An example of a question with five responses (i.e., never, rarely, occasionally, frequently, very frequently) and their respective values (i.e., 1, 2, 3, 4, 5) is:

I often get angry at my spouse. (Circle one number below.)

1. Never
2. Rarely
3. Occasionally
4. Frequently
5. Very frequently

Number of Categories

The next decision concerns the number of response categories for a particular variable. Should five responses be included, as in the example above, or should as many as 10 or 20 be used?

As a general rule, the number of response categories should be large enough to allow for some variance in responses but small enough so that appropriate discriminations can be made between the levels. If there are too many response categories, the difference between one level and the next may not be clear. The Subjective Units of Disturbance Scale has 100 possible deviations, and respondents rate their anxiety along a 100-point continuum (Barlow, Hayes, & Nelson, 1984). The problem is to determine the meaningfulness of a score of, say, 85, compared to a score of 90. The opposite is true if an instrument uses only three or four response categories; not enough latitude is allowed to determine the true differences in responding. Including between five and nine response categories is generally the most appropriate and reliable method for standardized instruments.

A choice also must be made between using an odd or an even number of categories. If an odd number is chosen, respondents may choose the middle-of-the-road responses to avoid revealing their true feelings. An example of a question with an odd number of response categories is:

The bus service in this city is adequate. (Circle one number below.)
1. Strongly disagree
2. Disagree
3. Neither agree nor disagree
4. Agree
5. Strongly agree

If an even number of categories is chosen, however, there is no middle road, so respondents are forced to respond one way or the other. Then the problem is that they may develop a response set favoring one side or the other, or refuse to answer questions at all. An example of a question with an even number of response categories is:

The bus service in this city is adequate. (Circle one number below.)
1. Strongly disagree
2. Disagree
3. Agree
4. Strongly agree

Unfortunately, there are no guidelines for determining the ideal number of response categories or the advantages of an odd or an even number of categories. The choice is left to the discretion of the instrument's developer.

The Response-Value Continuum

Defining the response-value continuum involves decisions about how respondents should be rated—according to frequencies or to agree-disagree, true-false, or yes-no dichotomies. Hudson (1981) suggests that in rating human or social problems, an appropriate approach is to first write questions so that a yes-no or true-false answer indicates that the problem is either present or absent and then scale the responses to get some idea of their magnitude.

Determination of Instrument Length

Ordinarily, the longer the measuring instrument, the greater its reliability. However, lengthy instruments are cumbersome to use and difficult to administer and score. The general rule is that the instrument should include as many questions as necessary to establish its content validity. A minimum of five questions is usually needed.

TYPES OF STANDARDIZED INSTRUMENTS

There are three basic types of standardized measuring instruments: (1) rating scales, (2) questionnaire-type scales, and (3) modified scales. All three aim to measure variables; the difference lies in the scaling techniques they use. Rating scales use judgments by self or others to assign an individual a single score (or value) in relation to the variable being measured. Questionnaire-type scales combine the responses of all the questions within an instrument to form a single overall score for the variable being measured. Modified scales do not fit into either of these classifications.

Rating Scales

The common feature in the various types of rating scales is the rating of individuals, objects, or events on various traits or characteristics at a point on a continuum or a position in an ordered set of response categories. In order to rate the person or thing, numerical values are assigned to each category.

Rating scales for individuals may be completed by the person being evaluated (self-rating) or by some significant other, such as a parent, supervisor, spouse, or social worker. Sometimes a client and a significant other are asked to complete the same rating scale in order to provide us with two different views. A wife and her husband might each rate the latter's openness to communication and other characteristics, for example. Self-ratings are helpful because individuals can evaluate their own thoughts, feelings, and behaviors accurately, provided they are self-aware and willing to be truthful.

Four types of rating scales—graphic rating, itemized rating, comparative rating, and self-anchored scales—are discussed in this section.

Graphic Rating Scales

In graphic rating scales, a variable is described on a continuum from one extreme to the other, such as low to high or most to least. The points of the continuum are ordered in equal intervals and are assigned numbers. Most points have descriptions to help respondents locate their correct positions on the scale. The example below is a "feeling thermometer" on which children are asked to rate, via a check mark, their level of anxiety from very anxious to very calm:

___ 100 Very anxious
___ 90
___ 80
___ 70
___ 60
___ 50 Neither anxious nor calm
___ 40
___ 30
___ 20
___ 10
___ 0 Very calm

Another example is a scale on which clients are asked to rate their individual therapy sessions from not productive to very productive:

Please circle the number that comes closest to describing your feelings about the session you just completed.

1	2	3	4	5
Not productive		Moderately productive		Very productive

The major advantage of graphic rating scales is that they are easy to use, though care should be taken in the development of appropriate descriptive statements. End statements that are excessive, such as "extremely hot" or "extremely cold," should not be used.

Itemized Rating Scales

Itemized rating scales offer a series of statements designed to rank different positions on the variable being measured. Respondents may be asked to check all the statements with which they agree, or only the one statement that is closest to their own position. On the itemized rating scale below, for example, clients are asked to prioritize questions related to self-image (Warwick & Lininger, 1975):

If someone asked you to describe yourself, and you could tell only one thing about yourself, which of the following answers would you be most likely to give? (Put a 1 in the space to the left of that question.)

___ I come from (home state)

___ I work for (employer)

___ I am a (my occupation or type of work)

___ I am a (my church membership or preference)

___ I am a graduate of (my school)

Itemized rating scales vary according to the number of statements given and the specificity of the descriptive statements. Higher scale reliability is associated with clear definitions of categories. Even the use of precise categories, however, cannot obviate the fact that clients respond differentially, due to their individual frames of reference. The less homogeneous the group of respondents, the less suitable is an itemized rating scale.

Comparative Rating Scales

In comparative rating scales, respondents are asked to compare an individual (or object) being rated with others. An often-cited example is the ratings that professors are asked to give for students applying to enter graduate school. They may be asked to compare a student with others they have known and then to rate the individual in the top 10 or 20 percent of students.

A variation of the comparative rating scale is the rank-order scale, in which the rater is asked to rank individuals (or objects or events) in relation to one another on some characteristic. Below is an example of a rank-order scale on which a social work supervisor is asked to rank-order four workers who have been recommended for promotion:

Below are the four individuals that your department has recommended for promotion. Please rank-order these individuals from highest to lowest.

___ Mary Smith

___ Mike Jones

___ Jane Johnson

___ Jim Jackson

The assumption underlying comparative rating scales is that the rater has some knowledge of the comparison groups. If a small, select group such as the one above is being ranked, the scale would have little usefulness in other settings or with other groups.

Self-Anchored Rating Scales

Self-anchored rating scales are similar to others in that respondents are asked to rate themselves on a continuum, usually a seven- or nine-point scale from low to high. However, the specific referents for each point on the continuum are defined by the respondent. This type of scale is often used to measure such attributes as intensity of feeling or pain. Clients who have difficulty in being honest in group therapy sessions, for example, could complete the following question, which is intended to measure their own perceptions of their honesty. The advantage is that they do not have to attempt to compare themselves with any external group.

Extent to which you feel you can be honest in the group:

       1   2   3   4   5   6   7   8   9

   Can never   Can sometimes   Can always be
   be honest   be honest   completely honest

Questionnaire-Type Scales

Whereas rating scales require judgments on the part of a respondent who is asked to make a single judgment about the topic of interest, questionnaire-type scales include multiple questions that the respondent is asked to answer. Then a total composite score of all the questions is obtained to indicate the individual's position on the variable of interest. The most useful questionnaire-type scale is the summated scale.

Summated Scales

Summated scales are widely used in assessing individual or family problems, for needs assessment, and for other types of program evaluation. In the summated scale, respondents indicate the degree of their agreement or disagreement with each question. Response categories may include strongly agree, agree, neutral, disagree, or strongly disagree. Two examples of summative scales are presented in Figures 9.1 and 9.2.

Modified Scales

Modified scales such as the semantic differential scale and the Goal Attainment Scale have been developed to elicit responses that are not ordinarily included in a rating scale or questionnaire-type scale.

Semantic Differential Scales

The semantic differential scale rates the respondent's perception of three dimensions of the concept under study: evaluation (bad-good), potency (weak-strong), and activity (slow-fast). Each dimension includes several questions scored on a 7- or 11-point continuum on which only the extreme positions are identified. Below are a few questions taken from a scale designed to measure patients' feelings toward the nursing home in which they live (Atherton & Klemmack, 1982):

Below are 29 pairs of words that can be used to describe nursing homes in general. For each pair of words, we would like you to circle the number that comes closest to your feelings about nursing homes. For example, if you feel that nursing homes are more good than bad, circle a number closer to good. The closer the number you circle is to good, the more good and less bad you feel nursing homes in general to be. Continue with each pair.

Good	1	2	3	4	5	6	7 Bad
Beautiful	1	2	3	4	5	6	7 Ugly
Rigid	1	2	3	4	5	6	7 Flexible
Dirty	1	2	3	4	5	6	7 Clean
Happy	1	2	3	4	5	6	7 Sad

The semantic differential scale correlates well with, and appears more direct than, some other scales. However, the scale is not completely comparable across variables. Much depends on the variable being measured and whether or not the three dimensions—evaluation, potency, and activity—are the best ways to measure a particular variable.

INDEX OF SELF-ESTEEM

Name: _____ Today's Date:_____

Context: _____

This questionnaire is designed to measure how you see yourself. It is not a test, so there are no right or wrong answers. Please answer each item as carefully and as accurately as you can by placing a number beside each one as follows:

1 = None of the time
2 = Very rarely
3 = A little of the time
4 = Some of the time
5 = A good part of the time
6 = Most of the time
7 = All of the time

1. _____ I feel that people would not like me if they really knew me well.
2. _____ I feel that others get along much better than I do.
3. _____ I feel that I am a beautiful person.
4. _____ When I am with others I feel they are glad I am with them.
5. _____ I feel that people really like to talk with me.
6. _____ I feel that I am a very competent person.
7. _____ I think I make a good impression on others.
8. _____ I feel that I need more self-confidence.
9. _____ When I am with strangers I am very nervous.
10. _____ I think that I am a dull person.
11. _____ I feel ugly.
12. _____ I feel that others have more fun than I do.
13. _____ I feel that I bore people.
14. _____ I think my friends find me interesting.
15. _____ I think I have a good sense of humor.
16. _____ I feel very self-conscious when I am with strangers.
17. _____ I feel that if I could be more like other people I would have it made.
18. _____ I feel that people have a good time when they are with me.
19. _____ I feel like a wallflower when I go out.
20. _____ I feel I get pushed around more than others.
21. _____ I think I am a rather nice person.
22. _____ I feel that people really like me very much.
23. _____ I feel that I am a likeable person.
24. _____ I am afraid I will appear foolish to others.
25. _____ My friends think very highly of me.

3, 4, 5, 6, 7, 14, 15, 18, 21, 22, 23, 25.

Figure 9.1   Hudson's Index of Self-Esteem

Using the scale from one to five described below, please indicate on the line to the left of each item the number that comes closest to how you feel.

    1   Strongly agree
    2   Agree
    3   Undecided
    4   Disagree
    5   Strongly disagree

_____ 1   The social worker took my problems very seriously.
_____ 2   If I had been the social worker, I would have dealt with my problems in just the same way.
_____ 3   The worker I had could never understand anyone like me.
_____ 4   Overall the agency has been very helpful to me.
_____ 5   If friends of mine had similar problems I would tell them to go to the agency.
_____ 6   The social worker asks a lot of embarrassing questions.
_____ 7   I can always count on the worker to help if I'm in trouble.
_____ 8   The agency will help me as much as it can.
_____ 9   I don't think the agency has the power to really help me.
_____ 10   The social worker tries hard but usually isn't too helpful.
_____ 11   The problem the agency tried to help me with is one of the most important in my life.
_____ 12   Things have gotten better since I've been going to the agency.
_____ 13   Since I've been using the agency my life is more messed up than ever.
_____ 14   The agency is always available when I need it.
_____ 15   I got from the agency exactly what I wanted.
_____ 16   The social worker loves to talk but won't really do anything for me.
_____ 17   Sometimes I just tell the social worker what I think she wants to hear.
_____ 18   The social worker is usually in a hurry when I see her.
_____ 19   No one should have any trouble getting some help from this agency.
_____ 20   The worker sometimes says things I don't understand.
_____ 21   The social worker is always explaining things carefully.
_____ 22   I never looked forward to my visits to the agency.
_____ 23   I hope I'll never have to go back to the agency for help.
_____ 24   Every time I talk to my worker I feel relieved.
_____ 25   I can tell the social worker the truth without worrying.
_____ 26   I usually feel nervous when I talk to my worker.
_____ 27   The social worker is always looking for lies in what I tell her.
_____ 28   It takes a lot of courage to go to the agency.
_____ 29   When I enter the agency I feel very small and insignificant.
_____ 30   The agency is very demanding.
_____ 31   The social worker will sometimes lie to me.
_____ 32   Generally the social worker is an honest person.
_____ 33   I have the feeling that the worker talks to other people about me.
_____ 34   I always feel well treated when I leave the agency.

Figure 9.2   Reid-Gundlach Social Service Satisfaction Scale

Goal Attainment Scales

Goal Attainment Scaling (GAS) is used widely to evaluate client or program outcomes. Specific areas of change are described and the range of possible outcomes, which usually consists of most unfavorable to best anticipated or most favorable outcomes, is identified. These scales can be completed by clients, independent judges, social workers, or other interested persons. Figure 9.3 is an example of a GAS for a nine-year-old boy with three problem areas: being overweight, spending too much time alone, and behavior problems in school (Siegel, 1988).

SELECTION OF A STANDARDIZED INSTRUMENT

The selection of a standardized measuring instrument for a particular social work research study is dependent on how the research question has been conceptualized and operationalized. It is through operational definitions of the variables being measured that the independent and dependent variables in a research hypothesis are quantified. If it is asserted in a single-system research design, for example, that a particular intervention (independent variable) causes a particular change in a client's target problem (dependent variable), both the intervention and the client's problem must be operationalized in such a way that they can be objectively measured. The operational definitions of the variables determine the field of available standardized measuring instruments that are capable of measuring them.

There are three general considerations in the selection of a measuring instrument: determining measurement need (why, what, who, which type, where, and when), locating measuring instruments capable of measuring the variables, and evaluating the alternatives among the instruments that are available.

Determining Measurement Need

The first consideration in selecting an appropriate standardized measuring instrument is to determine measurement need as specifically as possible. In order to do this, we need to know precisely why we want to measure a particular variable, who would complete the instrument, which type of measurement format is acceptable, which type should be used in a specific setting or environment, and how often the instrument is to be administered. The six critical questions listed below are guides that can be used to determine measurement need:

1. *Why will the measurement occur?*
    a. Research
    b. Assessment/diagnosis
    c. Evaluation
2. *What will be measured?*
    Specify_____
3. *Who is appropriate for making the most direct observations?*
    a. Research participant/client
    b. Practitioner or researcher
    c. Relevant other
4. *Which type of format is acceptable?*
    a. Inventories and surveys
    b. Indexes
    c. Scales
    d. Checklists and rating systems
5. *Where will the measurement occur?*
    a. General setting
    b. Situation-specific environment
6. *When will the measurement occur?*
    a. Random
    b. Posttest only
    c. Repeated over time

Why Is the Measurement Needed?

Standardized measuring instruments are used for three general purposes, each with different measurement requirements. Some measuring instruments are more appropriate than others, depending on the purpose of the research study: applied research, assessment and diagnosis, or evaluation of practice effectiveness (Sunberg, 1977). In an applied research study where participation is involuntary, for example, participants may have little investment in completing an instrument, so shorter instruments are preferable. In single-system research designs, both the social worker and the client often are more interested in treating feelings, behaviors, or cognitions than in measuring them, so short instruments that can measure specific presenting problems or treatment goals are needed (Barlow & Hersen, 1984).

The purpose of a research study also has an influence on how stringent the psychometric properties (mental measurement techniques) of the instrument must be. Requirements for validity and reliability may be less rigid if the purpose is applied or theoretical research, where the resulting theory will be

Outcomes	Scale 1 Overweight	Scale 2 Spending Time Alone	Scale 3 Behavior Problems in School
Most unfavorable outcome thought likely (Score −2)	Gain of 3 lbs.	Spends 12 hours or more in own room	School contract indicates fighting and time in isolation
Less favorable outcome (Score −1)	Loss of 1 lb.	Spends 10 hours in own room	School contract indicates fighting
Expected outcome (Score 0)	Loss of 5 lbs.	Goes to activity room on staff suggestion	School contract shows point loss for behavior modification
More favorable outcome (Score +1)	Loss of 7 lbs.	Spends time in activity room on own initiative	School contract shows no point loss
Most favorable outcome thought likely (Score +2)	Loss of 10 lbs.	Participates in some activities	School contract gives points for cooperation

Figure 9.3   Example of a Goal Attainment Scale

tentative. These requirements are more rigid in testing a hypothesis or if the results will impact on a person's life. The most rigid requirements apply to measuring instruments used for assessment and diagnostic purposes and to those used in single-system studies where the results can affect termination, referral, or third-party reimbursement.

What Is to Be Measured?

The second question is what is to be measured. Many measuring instruments are used to collect data about a variable such as thoughts, feelings, or behaviors. The variable may be covert and known only to the research participants, or it may be overt and observable. The guiding principle in determining what to measure is the degree of specificity required, which is less when there is an interest in a broad trait or characteristic and greater when an explicitly defined variable is being measured. Measurement instruments for global, or broad, variables, which are called wideband instruments, assess variables in a general sense but lack specificity. Measures for more narrowly focused variables, which are called narrowband instruments, provide more precision in measuring the variable but little meaningful overall data.

Who Could Make Direct Observations?

Measurement need also depends on who could make the most reliable direct observations to complete the instrument. There are three sources of observers: outside observers, usually professionals; indigenous observers, including relevant others (such as family members or peers) and collaterals (such as staff members); and self-observers, the research participants themselves. The instrument chosen must allow use of the type of observer that we consider most effective.

A school social worker, for example, may want to evaluate how an interpersonal skills training program affects the quality of the social relationships among students and teachers. An instrument that can be used for self-reports by students or teachers or one that calls for students and teachers to rate one another might be selected. Since both of these sources may be biased, however, the observations could be made by some other relevant person such as a school principal (Hops & Greenwood, 1981).

The decision about which source to use must always be made on the basis of who will provide the most accurate and objective assessment. If at all possible, more than one source of observations should be used in order to increase the reliability of the observations.

Which Type of Format Is Most Acceptable?

The fourth question concerns the format of the measuring instrument to be used. The choice among inventories, surveys, indexes, scales, checklists, or rating systems is based on consideration of the variable being measured and who is to complete the instrument.

In general, inventories and surveys are multidimensional, wideband instruments. The questions may take on a variety of formats, such as true-false or ratings of intensity or frequency. Traditionally, inventories and surveys have been fairly lengthy; an example is the Minnesota Multiphasic Personality Inventory. Scales and indexes generally are unidimensional and fairly short, with no more than 50 questions. Scales and indexes can be defined as narrowband measuring instruments that assess a particular variable at an interval or ratio level of measurement (Weinbach & Grinnell, 2001).

These distinctions among formats are fairly arbitrary. Inventories, surveys, indexes, and scales are similar in that they can be used when the variable is observable only to the respondent. When a relevant other can observe the variable, an option is to use a rating system or checklist. These instruments also have a variety of formats; in fact, some self-report types may be checklists, such as the Symptom Checklist (Derogates, Rickles, & Rock, 1976). Examples of rating systems include the Discharge Readiness Inventory, which is multidimensional (Hogerty & Ulrich, 1972), and the Behavior Rating Scale, which is unidimensional (Cowen et al., 1970). In sum, there are many formats from which to choose. The choice should always be on which format will collect the most valid and reliable data.

Where Will the Measurement Be Done?

Measurement can be done in various settings and can reflect behaviors or feelings that are specific to an environment (Wicker, 1981). Moreover, observations in one situation may not necessarily generalize to others (Bellack & Hersen, 1977; Mischel, 1968). Determination of measurement need therefore depends on the setting where the measuring instrument is to be completed and the environment the observations represent.

Many variables of interest to us are situation-specific; that is, the variable may be observable only in certain environments and under certain circumstances or with particular people. When a measuring instrument is needed for a situation-specific variable, it is best to choose one that can be completed in that environment (Nelson & Barlow, 1981). It is more valuable to have a parent complete a checklist of a child's problems at home where the trouble occurs than in a social worker's office, for example (Goldman, Stein, & Guerry, 1983). If the variable is not situation-specific (that is, it is assumed to be a trait manifested in a variety of settings), an instrument can be chosen that can be completed in any environment that does not influence the respondent's observations (Anastasi, 1988).

When Will the Measurements Be Taken?

The final question to be considered in determining measurement need is the time frame for administering the instrument. Ideally, the instrument chosen would allow the measurement to be made after the independent variable has been introduced, so the change to be measured (the dependent variable) has occurred. In many single-system research designs, for example, target problems are measured both before and after the intervention has been introduced. The instrument should also allow for the instrument to be administered as closely as possible to the occurrence of a change in behavior or feeling. Observing these two principles increases the accuracy and reliability of the observations.

An additional consideration is how often the measurement will be taken. A single-case design such as the ABAB design requires two administrations of the instrument over a period of time, whereas group designs such as the one-group posttest-only design require only one administration. When a measuring instrument is to be administered more than once, the internal validity of the results may be threatened by the effects of retesting (see Chapter 12). Respondents' answers on a posttest may be affected by their ability to recall questions or responses on a pretest, or they may be less interested, less motivated, or less anxious during the second testing.

Locating Standardized Instruments

Once the measurement need has been established, the next consideration is locating appropriate standardized measuring instruments from which to choose. The two general sources for locating such instruments are commercial or professional publishers and the professional literature.

Publishers

Numerous commercial and professional publishing companies specialize in the production and sale of standardized measuring instruments for use in social work research and practice. The cost of instruments purchased from a publisher varies considerably, depending on the instrument, the number of copies needed, and the publisher. The instruments generally are well developed and their psychometric properties are supported by the results of several research studies. Often they are accompanied by normative data.

Publishers are expected to comply with professional standards such as those established by the American Psychological Association. These standards address the claims made about the instrument's rationale, development, psychometric properties, administration, and interpretation of results.

Standards for the use of some instruments have been developed to protect the integrity of research participants, clients, respondents, and the social work profession. Consequently, purchasers of instruments may be required to have certain qualifications, such as a college course in testing and measurement or an advanced degree in a relevant field. A few publishers require membership in particular professional organizations. Most publishers will accept an order from a student if it is cosigned by a qualified person, such as an instructor, who will supervise the use of the instrument. A selected list of publishers of measuring instruments can be found in Jordan, Franklin, and Corcoran (1993).

Journals and Books

Standardized measuring instruments are most commonly reproduced in professional research journals; in fact, most commercially marketed instruments appear first in one of these publications. The instruments usually are supported by evidence of their validity and reliability, although they often require cross-validation and normative data from more representative samples.

Locating instruments in journals or books is not easy. Of the two methods used most often, computer searches of data banks and manual searches of the literature, the former is faster, unbelievably more thorough, and easier to use. This is especially true when the research question combines several important variables, such as the effects of poverty on the self-esteem of minority youth from rural and urban areas. Moreover, the data banks used in computer searches are updated regularly.

Financial support for the development of comprehensive data banks has been limited and intermittent, however. Another disadvantage is that many articles on instruments are not referenced with the appropriate indicators for computer retrieval. These limitations are being overcome by the changing technology of computers and information retrieval systems. Several services allow for a complex breakdown of measurement need. Data banks that include references from over 1300 journals, updated monthly, are now available from a division of Psychological Abstracts Information Services, and Bibliographic Retrieval Services offers the entire eighth edition of O. K. Buros's Mental Measurements Yearbook (1978).

Nevertheless, in the absence of means for making thorough and inexpensive computer searches for measuring instruments, most social workers will probably rely on manual searches of references such as Psychological Abstracts. While the reference indices will be the same as those in the data banks accessible by computer, the literature search can be supplemented with appropriate seminal (original) reference volumes.

Evaluating Standardized Instruments

A literature search should produce several standardized instruments that would be suitable for use in measuring a particular variable. The choice of one instrument over others depends on the strength of the quantitative data the instrument provides and its practicality in application. These two dimensions can be evaluated by finding answers to a number of questions that focus on the population or sample to be used, the validity and reliability of the instrument, and the practicality of administering the instrument:

1. *The Sample from Which Data Were Drawn:*
   a. Are the samples representative of pertinent populations?
   b. Are the sample sizes sufficiently large?
   c. Are the samples homogeneous?
   d. Are the subsamples pertinent to respondents' demographics?
   e. Are the data obtained from the samples up to date?

2. *The Validity of the Instrument:*
   a. Is the content domain clearly and specifically defined?
   b. Was there a logical procedure for including the items?
   c. Is the criterion measure relevant to the instrument?
   d. Was the criterion measure reliable and valid?
   e. Is the theoretical construct clearly and correctly stated?
   f. Do the scores converge with other relevant measures?
   g. Do the scores discriminate from irrelevant variables?
   h. Are there cross-validation studies that conform to the above concerns?
3. *The Reliability of the Instrument:*
   a. Is there sufficient evidence of internal consistency?
   b. Is there equivalence between various forms?
   c. Is there stability over a relevant time interval?
4. *The Practicality of Application:*
   a. Is the instrument an appropriate length?
   b. Is the content socially acceptable to respondents?
   c. Is the instrument feasible to complete?
   d. Is the instrument relatively direct?
   e. Does the instrument have utility?
   f. Is the instrument relatively nonreactive?
   g. Is the instrument sensitive to measuring change?
   h. Is the instrument feasible to score?

The questions related to the validity and reliability of both the instrument and the data collected with it are concerned with issues discussed in Chapter 8. These issues are the most crucial concerns in evaluating any standardized measuring instrument.

Representativeness of the Sample

Another major concern in the evaluation of standardized instruments is the extent to which the data collected in setting the norms for the instrument represent the population from which the sample is to be drawn for the proposed study (see Chapter 11). If the instrument being considered, for example, was formulated and tested on a sample drawn from a population of white Anglo-Saxon males, it might give perfectly valid results when administered to white Anglo-Saxons males but not if it is to be administered to Native Americans, African Americans, or females.

In general terms, the samples used in setting the norms for an instrument must reflect a population that is pertinent to the respondents who will complete the instrument. Subsamples of demographic characteristics such as age, gender, race, and socioeconomic status must be considered. Thus if the sample on which the norms were established consisted of middle-class African Americans, its applicability to a sample of inner-city African Americans would be suspect.

Another consideration is the size of the sample, which affects sampling error. As pointed out in Chapter 11, sampling error is reduced to the extent that the sample is sufficiently large and homogeneous. The larger the sample, and the less variance there is in the population from which the sample has been drawn, the smaller the standard error will be.

When the data were collected from the sample is another concern. Data based on samples gathered 20 years ago may not be an adequate basis for accepting the instrument as psychometrically sound for today's use. One popular measure of social desirability developed over 30 years ago, for example, includes questions pertaining to the social status derived from owning an automobile (Crowne & Marlowe, 1960). Predicted responses would be substantially different today.

Practicality of Application

Consideration of the practicality of application in social work research and practice involves implementation of the instrument and analysis of the data it generates. The first three practicality questions (i.e., 4a–c) concern the likelihood that research participants will complete the instrument. Even the most valid and reliable instrument has no practical utility if it is left unanswered because it is too long, it is not socially acceptable to the respondent, or the respondent does not understand the instructions or questions.

While a longer instrument is usually more reliable than a shorter one (Allen & Yen, 1979), it is also more time-consuming and may not be completed. This is especially important in single-case research designs where multiple measures are needed and in survey research where the response rate is critical.

The social acceptability of a measuring instrument concerns the respondent's evaluation of the appropriateness of the content (Haynes, 1983). The perceived appropriateness of the content as a measure of the variable of interest—not what the instrument measures but what it appears to measure—is referred to as face validity (see Chapter 8). An instrument that is offensive or insulting to respondents will not be completed. Instruments also should be easy for respondents to complete, with content and instructions that are neither above nor below their typical functioning level and questions that can be answered easily.

The other five practicality questions (i.e., 4d–h) concern the meaning or interpretation of the results provided by the instrument. Interpretation is easiest and most practical when the instrument provides direct measurements, has utility, is nonreactive, is sensitive to small changes, and is easy to score.

Variables that can be measured directly include physical ones such as height, weight, and age. Other variables, such as self-esteem or depression, can only be measured indirectly. An instrument is considered to have utility if the results provide some practical advantage or useful data. The results of an instrument are influenced by whether the instrument is obtrusive, or reactive, or it is unobtrusive. An instrument is said to be reactive if administration of it can affect the respondent or alter the variable being measured. The self-monitoring of cigarette smoking, for example, actually influences this behavior. The degree of internal and external validity depends on minimizing the reactive effects that completing an instrument can have by selecting instruments that are unobtrusive, or nonreactive.

The instrument also has to be sensitive enough to pick up small changes in the variable being measured. If the research purpose is assessing client change, for example, the instrument must be sensitive to changes in the dependent variable that could occur from one administration to the next.

What is done with the instrument after it has been completed is also a practicality consideration. It may seem self-evident that if an instrument is to provide meaningful information it must be possible to score it. However, many instruments have scoring procedures that are too complicated and time-consuming to be practical in social work research and practice situations. Even though they are psychometrically sound, they should be eliminated in favor of others that can be scored more easily.

NONSTANDARDIZED MEASURING INSTRUMENTS

Wherever possible, we should select a standardized measuring instrument, not only because it has been developed and tested by someone else—which saves us an inestimable amount of time and trouble—but also because of the advantages it has with regard to uniformity of content, administration, and scoring. There will be occasions, however, when no standardized instrument seems to be right for our particular purpose. Some standardized instruments are excessively long, complicated, and difficult to score and interpret: That is, they do not meet the criteria for practicality previously mentioned.

Let us take an example from a practice perspective on how to use nonstandardized instruments. No standardized instrument may enable us to discover how Ms. Yen feels about her daughter's marriage. The only way to get this information is to ask Ms. Yen; and if we want to keep on asking Ms. Yen—if the object of our intervention, say, is to help her accept her daughter's marriage—it will be best to ask the questions in the same way every time, so that we can compare the answers and assess her progress with some degree of certainty.

In other words, we will have to develop our own measuring instrument. Perhaps we might begin by asking Ms. Yen to list the things that bother her about her daughter's marriage; that is, we might ask her to develop an inventory. Or, if we do not think Ms. Yen is up to making a list, we might develop our own checklist of possibly relevant factors and ask her to check off all that apply.

Once we know what the factors are, we might be interested in knowing to what degree each one bothers Ms. Yen. Perhaps her daughter's marriage will involve moving to a distant town with her new husband, and it is this that is most important to Ms. Yen. Or perhaps her daughter's prospective husband has characteristics that Ms. Yen perceives as undesirable: He may be non-Asian, while Ms. Yen is Asian, or he may hold unacceptable religious or political views, or come from the "wrong" social or occupational class, and so on.

With Ms. Yen's help, we might develop a simple scale, running from "very bothersome" to "not at all bothersome." Perhaps, we might settle on something like the following:

Here are a number of statements about your daughter's marriage. Please show how bothersome you find each statement to be by writing the appropriate number in the space to the left of each statement.

1 = Not at all bothersome
2 = A little bothersome
3 = Quite bothersome
4 = Very bothersome

_____ My daughter will move away after her marriage.
_____ My daughter's husband is non-Asian.
_____ My daughter's husband has been married before.
_____ I don't like my daughter's husband's family.
_____ My daughter's husband is unemployed.
_____ ...

We then assess Ms. Yen's total botherment by adding up her scores on the individual items.

Sometimes we will stumble across an existing instrument that has not been standardized. Figure 9.4 presents a checklist of some questions to ask when trying to determine if a specific nonstandardized instrument should be used.

	YES	NO
1. Will the responses to the questionnaire provide the data needed to answer the research question?	____	____
2. Does the questionnaire address the same types of variables that are to be studied (i.e., value, attitude, personality traits, behavior, knowledge, skill, perception, judgment)?	____	____
3. Is the level of measurement appropriate for the intended statistical analyses?	____	____
4. Is the format of the items appropriate to the level of inquiry?	____	____
5. Does the questionnaire have known reliability? Are the circumstances in which reliability was established known?	____	____
6. Does the questionnaire have known validity?	____	____
7. Have there been other applications of the instrument? Or has the instrument been reviewed by other professionals in journals, books, or other publications?	____	____
8. Is the language of the questionnaire appropriate for the sample or population?	____	____
9. Are the instructions clear and easy to follow?	____	____
10. Do the items meet standards for item construction (i.e., clear, precise, not double-barreled, or biased)?	____	____
11. Is the flow of the questionnaire logical and easy to follow?	____	____
12. Is the questionnaire the appropriate length for the time available for data collection, the attention span of intended respondents, and other circumstances related to the design?	____	____

Figure 9.4   Checklist for Assessing Existing
                   Nonstandardized Measuring Instruments

Advantages

The major advantage of a nonstandardized instrument is that it is customized: That is, it is totally pertinent and appropriate to a particular client because it was designed with the client in view; possibly it was even designed by the client or at least with the client's help. We are not worried, as we would be with a standardized instrument, that the instrument was developed with a population different from the client's, or that the sample used for development and testing was not representative of the population from which it was drawn.

This advantage is more likely to apply if we have developed our own instrument than if we have borrowed one from a colleague who happened to have a similar client in a similar situation. Our colleague's client is not our client, and so we do not really know how appropriate the instrument will be. Neither can we be sure that we are administering or scoring the instrument in the same way as did our colleagues, since the administration and scoring instructions are unlikely to be written down.

If we develop our own instrument, it will probably be simple to administer and score because we knew when we designed it that we would personally have to administer and score it. Most of the previous questions about an instrument's practicality will have been answered in the affirmative. We know that the instrument provides useful information, and that it is relatively direct, of an appropriate length, feasible to complete, and acceptable to the client. We do not know, however, whether it is sensitive to real, small changes and to what degree it is nonreactive.

The main advantage, then, of using nonstandardized measures is that they can be constructed for an individual measurement purpose. We could use an instrument like the one displayed in Figure 9.5, however. Here, we are interested in ascertaining the perceptions of people who live in a specific community.

Disadvantages

Because the instrument is nonstandardized, we do not know to what degree it is valid and reliable. With respect to reliability, we do not know whether a difference in score from one administration to the next means that Ms. Yen's attitudes toward her daughter's marriage have really changed, or whether the difference is due to the instrument's instability over time or measurement error. With respect to validity, we do not know to what degree the instrument is content valid: that is, to what degree the items on our instrument include every aspect of Ms. Yen's feelings about the marriage. Perhaps what is really bothering her is that she believes her daughter suffers from an emotional disorder and is in no fit state to marry anyone. She has not mentioned this, there is no item on the instrument that would reveal it, and so we will never be able to discuss the matter with her.

In other words, we are not sure to what degree our instrument is providing a reliable and valid measure of Ms. Yen's attitudes toward her daughter's marriage. Perhaps the instrument focuses too much on the prospective husband, and it is really Ms. Yen's attitudes toward the husband that we are measuring, not her attitudes toward the marriage.

Unless we have a real interest in the development of measuring instruments, however, we are unlikely to run validity and reliability checks on instruments we have developed ourselves. Our nonstandardized instruments may therefore be somewhat lacking with respect to validity and reliability. We will not be able to use them to evaluate our own practice, nor to compare our client's scores with the scores of other similar people in similar situations. We

This part of the survey is to learn more about your perceptions of these problems in the community. Listed below are a number of problems some residents of Northside have reported having.

Please place a number from 1 to 3 on the line to the right of the question that represents how much of a problem they have been to you within the last year:

1. No problem (or not applicable to you)
2. Moderate problem
3. Severe problem

	Questions	*Responses*			
1.	Finding the product I need	1	2	3	_____
2.	Impolite salespeople	1	2	3	_____
3.	Finding clean stores	1	2	3	_____
4.	Prices that are too high	1	2	3	_____
5.	Not enough Spanish-speaking salespeople	1	2	3	_____
6.	Public transportation	1	3	3	_____
7.	Getting credit	1	2	3	_____
8.	Lack of certain types of stores in Northside	1	2	3	_____
9.	Lack of an employment assistance program	1	2	3	_____
10.	Finding a city park that is secure	1	2	3	_____
11.	Finding a good house	1	2	3	_____

Figure 9.5   Example of a Nonstandardized Survey Measuring Instrument

will, however, be able to use them both to help determine the problem and to assess the client's progress in solving the problem. And a nonstandardized instrument is sometimes better than no instrument at all.

SUMMARY

Standardized measuring instruments are designed to quantify the variables being measured. They have the advantages of uniform administration and scoring and the generation of normative data. Constructors of standardized measures seek to develop instruments that are as valid and reliable as possible. The major considerations are the selection of questions that will maximize content validity, the number of response categories, and the length of the instrument. The difference between the three major types of measuring instruments (i.e., rating scales, questionnaire-type scales, and modified scales), is the scaling techniques used. Rating scales use judgments by self or others to assign an individual a single score (or value) in relation to the variable being measured. Questionnaire-type scales combine the responses on several questions to form a single overall score on the variable of interest for each respondent. Modified scales do not fit either of these classifications.

The selection of a standardized measuring instrument for a particular research study depends on how the research question has been conceptualized and the variables represented in it have been operationally defined. The three general considerations are determination of measurement need, locating a number of measuring instruments capable of measuring the variables, and evaluating the alternatives among the instruments available. Measurement need is related to our purpose, the research question, and the circumstances in which the instrument is to be administered.

Instruments that satisfy these needs can be selected from the two principal sources: publishing houses and the professional literature. They can be evaluated by considering questions that focus on the sample used in developing each instrument, the instrument's validity and reliability, and practicality issues such as the likelihood that respondents will complete the instrument and interpretation of the results.

The following chapter completes the discussion of measurement by describing how we can design and construct a measuring instrument to fit a particular research need in the event that a suitable standardized instrument cannot be located.

Charles H. Mindel

C h a p t e r   10

Designing Measuring Instruments

IF AN APPROPRIATE standardized measuring instrument is not available for a particular research purpose, we need to know how to design and construct one. While, as noted in Chapter 9, a standardized measuring instrument is rarely unavailable, knowledge of how valid and reliable instruments are designed not only is useful in certain research situations, it also improves understanding of measurement principles.

The type of measuring instrument used as an example in this chapter is primarily applicable to survey research (Chapter 15), one of the data collection methods discussed in Part V of this text. The principles of design and construction described in this chapter, therefore, are most appropriate to survey instruments, but they generally also apply to most other types of measuring instruments as well.

In our discussion of how we can design and construct measuring instruments, our two guiding principles are based on sampling procedures (described in Chapter 11) and measurement validity and reliability (described in Chapters 8 and 9).

- First, the design and construction of our instrument should attempt to maximize the response rate of individuals in our sample or population.

- Second, our instrument should minimize the amount of measurement error in the responses of individuals.

An instrument that embodies these two principles is well constructed. The product of the research process, particularly in quantitative research studies, is data that have been gathered with some type of measuring instrument so they can be quantified and analyzed. In survey research, the instrument utilized to collect data is called a self-administered questionnaire. When data are collected by means of face-to-face interviews or telephone surveys, the data collection instrument is referred to as an interview schedule. In this text, a measuring instrument is considered to be any type of data collection device or procedure designed to gather data in any research study.

SOCIAL WORKERS' USE OF SURVEY RESEARCH

The survey is a popular form of data collection because it provides a useful and convenient way to acquire large amounts of data about individuals, organizations, or communities. It can be used to determine what people know, believe, or expect about a research question. It also can provide data on how they feel, what they want, what they intend to do, what they have done, and why.

One of the most important uses of survey research is to determine certain kinds of facts about individuals or other units of analysis. Social service agencies, for example, undertake surveys to collect facts about people in order to gather such data as the number and characteristics of individuals who request our services.

Survey research also is useful for gathering reports about people's behavior, both past and present. These kinds of data are often needed in our profession, particularly in service utilization studies. Clients might be asked how many times they had visited a physician in the past year or the past month, for example. The potential problem with these types of data is their accuracy. The instrument must not require individuals to reconstruct events from so far in the past that they cannot remember them accurately. It is much better to ask specific questions about events within a reasonable time frame than to ask global, general questions ranging over a long period.

Determining Beliefs, Feelings, and Ethical Standards

Surveys are particularly useful in helping to investigate unobservable variables such as attitudes, beliefs, feelings, and ethical standards. The distinction between what the facts are and what people believe them to be is often important. A social service agency, for example, might want to investigate why it is having difficulty recruiting staff or serving an intended population. A study might show that the beliefs of individuals in the community about that agency (whether or not they are based on fact) are quite negative.

In program planning, the existence of a certain social problem may or may not coincide with the attitudes in the community toward the existence of that problem. At one time, for example, African American families were considered dysfunctional by outside observers, but many African Americans disputed this evaluation and maintained that their family form worked well for them. Difficulties are inevitable if an agency attempts to organize a program to address a social problem that the community does not recognize. An important part of a community needs assessment therefore is to determine the beliefs of individuals and constituencies about it.

Measuring instruments also explore individuals' feelings and desires. We often need to measure our clients on a variety of feelings or states, such as anxiety or marital satisfaction. Many well-established, standardized instruments that explore feelings are available. Instruments also can probe individuals' ethical standards, or their attitudes toward what should be done or what can feasibly be done with respect to certain social policies. Many instruments have examined attitudes toward abortion, women's rights, and education, for example. Ethical standards are also represented in questions that explore what individuals would do in certain situations. Questions that explore what people should or would do do not necessarily indicate what they actually do, however. Attitudes are not the same as behavior (LaPiere, 1934).

We can also use survey research to try to ascertain why people behave, believe, or feel the way they do. Instruments often contain questions exploring this. In a research study on elderly parents who live with their adult children, for example, one question asked why and under what circumstances this family arrangement had been formed. The history of the event, the types of reactions individuals felt at the time this event occurred, and the process at work were all relevant.

VALIDITY FACTORS IN INSTRUMENT DESIGN

The most crucial considerations in the construction of a measuring instrument by a social worker are the same as those in the development of a standardized instrument—validity and reliability. Applications of these concepts to measurement and the evaluation of standardized measuring instruments were examined in the two preceding chapters. Chapter 8 defines reliability as the accuracy or precision of the results the instrument produces, and validity in terms of content, criterion, and construct validities.

This chapter adopts the external and internal validity terms used in Chapter 12 on group research designs. Internal validity refers to the degree to which the instrument actually measures the concept being studied and, moreover, measures that concept accurately. External validity goes a step further to consider the degree to which the answers to the questions given by the individuals in the sample can be generalized to a larger population or a different research setting. Some methods we can use to improve the external and internal validities of the instruments we construct are reviewed in the following sections.

Maximizing External Validity

There are several reasons why an instrument will fail to achieve an adequate response rate, thus affecting the degree to which responses to the questions can be generalized to a larger population or a different population or setting. Following the suggestions below for design and construction of the instrument, including the choice and wording of questions and their format and layout, can help to achieve external validity and ensure generalizability. The external validity of an instrument we construct may be compromised, however, by the fact that there are no normative data to compare scores against and uniform administration procedures are not specified, as in standardized instruments.

Clearly State the Purpose of the Study

One way to assure an adequate response rate is to be explicit in explaining to potential respondents why a study is being undertaken. If they feel it is being used for purposes other than those stated, or if they have other misgivings about the study or the person conducting the study, their responses may be inhibited or inaccurate. One way to offer this explanation is with a cover letter to respondents or research participants describing the study, written under the official letterhead of the sponsoring organization (see Figure 10.1). Public knowledge that the study is to take place also helps.

Feelings of being exploited by research studies are most common among minority group members. One way to counter this attitude is to demonstrate that there is something of value to the group or individuals that justifies their participation. This might involve meetings with community members to discuss the purposes of the study and its value to them or hiring minority group members as staff.

Keep Sensitive Questions to a Minimum

Some individuals may feel that a particular research study would invade their privacy. The instrument may include personal questions in sensitive areas,

---

[Agency Letterhead]

Dear _____ :

    Our agency recognizes research as a basic method for evaluating old ways and developing new ways of providing more effective services for couples adopting children. The State Division of Child Welfare, in cooperation with this and other Twin City adoption agencies, is currently conducting a study of the supervisory period in adoption.

    Because you have recently adopted a child through this agency, your experiences and opinions would be of much value. We are therefore asking your cooperation in this study. Your participation will involve an interview between each of you and a researcher from the State Division of Child Welfare.

    We wish to emphatically assure you that the information requested in your interview will be treated confidentially by the researcher. Your observations and comments will in no way be identified with your name to this agency. Your information will be known only to the researcher who is conducting this study and will be incorporated anonymously, with that of many other adoptive parents, into the final research report.

    Within the next few weeks you will be called by Mr. Smith to arrange an appointment with you. We hope you will be able to participate in this most important study. Thank you for your anticipated cooperation.

                                  Sincerely,

                                  Executive Director

Figure 10.1   Example of a Simple Cover Letter

and respondents often believe that participants can be identified. These fears can be alleviated by omitting or reducing personal or sensitive questions and by assuring anonymity or confidentiality. On many mailed questionnaires, however, some form of identification of participants is necessary so a follow-up can be sent in order to ensure an adequate response.

    Sensitive questions will also be disregarded if their content or wording causes them to be perceived by respondents as insulting or offensive. As pointed out in Chapter 8, the face validity of an instrument (not what it does but what it appears to do) often determines whether or not it will be completed.

Avoid Socially Desirable Responses

The tendency of respondents to adopt the social desirability response set and answer in a way they think will make them look good is another threat to achieving a valid and reliable response. With direct-service questionnaires, particularly, respondents are apt to be unsophisticated and unfamiliar with the types or format of questions used. University students may be used to taking tests and filling out answer sheets, but others will be at a loss as to how to complete an instrument. If they answer as they think they should, the possibility of measurement error is increased and the generalizability of the results is reduced. The constructor of the instrument therefore must word questions sensitively and assure respondents that there are no right or wrong answers.

Ask Only Relevant Questions

The relevancy of questions is particularly important in social work policy studies, where the population being studied often consists of professionals facing time constraints who may not feel justified in responding to numerous or lengthy questions. The importance of the research question under study and of their responses should be emphasized, and the instrument must not be too long or vague. No item should be included that is not relevant to the study's research question. Sending professionals a questionnaire that is too long or too general would demonstrate that the person doing the study is unsophisticated in using the research process, and potential respondents would be apt to ignore the instrument.

Maximizing Internal Validity

Internal validity is basically concerned with reducing or eliminating measurement error in the content of the instrument. The paragraphs that follow comprise a checklist of procedures to be used in selecting and presenting effective questions. As in the preceding chapter, *question* is the general term used to refer to the items, statements, or questions that, together with the accompanying response categories, comprise the instrument.

Make Questions Clear

Aside from the fact that all questions on an instrument must be relevant to the research question being investigated, the most important factor in wording questions to avoid measurement error is clarity. The words used must not mean different things to different individuals; this applies to ambiguous or vague words as well as to slang terms or colloquial expressions that may be familiar to certain groups but not to others. Meanings can vary across age levels, ethnic groups, social classes, and regions. We can become so close to the studies we are doing that questions that are perfectly clear to us are not clear at all to others. Consider the following example:

What is your marital status? (Circle one number below.)

1. Married
2. Divorced
3. Separated
4. Widowed
5. Never Married

It is not clear whether "marital status" refers to present status or whether the respondents are being asked if they were ever married, divorced, separated, or widowed. The way the question is stated, a person might in fact fit into the first four of the five categories. This question is more accurately stated: What is your present marital status?

Other problems with ambiguity are apt to occur when we are not familiar with the population being studied, such as elderly people, a racial or ethnic minority group, or professionals. Questions with little or no meaning to respondents can result.

Use Simple Language

The language used in questions may also be much too complicated for a respondent. The wording must be simple enough for the least educated person, while at the same time it must not insult the intelligence of anyone who could be presented with the instrument. If we were interested in the types of health care services utilized by individuals, for example, we might provide a checklist that would include such medical specialties as ophthalmology, otolaryngology, and dermatology. A list more likely to be understood by all respondents would call these specialists eye doctors, ear, nose, and throat doctors, and doctors for skin diseases.

Ask Questions That Respondents Are Qualified to Answer

Some measuring instruments ask individuals to respond to questions to which they have not given much thought or which they may not be competent to answer. In a public opinion poll, for example, an unknowledgeable research sample might be asked to provide opinions about psychotherapeutic techniques or needs tests in social welfare. We run the risk of being misled by the responses if the respondents are not qualified to answer such a question.

Avoid Double-Barreled and Negative Questions

Double-barreled questions contain two questions in one. A simple example of such a question is:

Do you feel that the federal government should make abortion or birth control available to women in households that receive welfare?

The problem with this question is that some respondents might agree to tax support for birth control but not for abortion, or for abortion but not birth control. The way the question is worded, we would never know which position the respondents are taking. The solution, of course, is to present the two questions separately. A clue to double-barreled questions is the presence of an *and* or an *or*. Such questions should be reexamined to see whether they include two questions.

Another type of question to be avoided is negative questions, such as asking whether respondents agree or disagree with a negative statement. An example is:

Federal funds should not be used to pay for abortions for women receiving welfare benefits.

The word *not* is often overlooked in these kinds of questions, and the error that is therefore introduced can be considerable. This question should be rephrased in one of these two ways:

The federal government should pay for abortions for women receiving welfare benefits.

— or —

Abortions for women receiving welfare benefits should only be paid for by nongovernmental sources.

Keep Questions Short

Questions that are kept short get to the point quickly, so respondents will be more likely to read them and complete them. Keeping questions short and to the point helps maintain the relevance, clarity, and precision of the instrument.

Pretest the Instrument

The traditional way in which the clarity of questions (and consequent internal validity) is examined is by pretesting the instrument on a sample of individuals who will not take part in our final study. Our pretest is concerned not with the answers to the questions per se but rather with the difficulties respondents may have in answering the questions. Are the questions clear and unambiguous, and do respondents understand what our instrument is trying to accomplish?

The pretest should be followed by a debriefing to uncover any difficulties. Pretesting is discussed further in the last section of this chapter.

OPEN- AND CLOSED-ENDED QUESTIONS

When constructing a measuring instrument, we must take into account differences not only in the wording of questions but in the kinds of responses asked for. There are two general categories: open-ended questions, in which the response categories are not specified in detail and are left unstructured, and closed-ended or fixed-alternative questions, in which respondents are asked to select one (or more) of several response categories provided in the instrument. Each of these methods for responding has particular purposes, as well as certain strengths and disadvantages.

Open-Ended Questions

Open-ended questions are designed to permit free responses; they do not incorporate any particular structure for replies. An example is:

We would like to know some of your feelings about your job as an employee of the Department of Social Services:

1. What types of duties are most satisfying to you?
2. What types of duties are most dissatisfying to you?

The above open-ended questions ask for much information and considerable thought, since they deal with a complex issue that could involve several dimensions of feeling.

If we are unaware of the various sources of satisfaction and dissatisfaction in the department, answers to the two open-ended questions will produce some clues. Open-ended questions are often used when all of the possible issues (and responses) involved in a question are not known or when we are interested in exploring basic issues and processes in a situation. Such questions are usually used in a preliminary phase of the study. Responses to open-ended questions, however, may be used in constructing questions for use in a later phase. An important function of open-ended questions, in fact, is their use in the development of closed-ended questions.

An additional advantage of open-ended questions is that they put few constraints on individuals' statements of their feelings. A closed-ended question might list various sources of satisfaction and ask individuals to check how they feel about them. Open-ended questions allow respondents to go into detail and to express greater depth in their answers. They are not forced to choose among alternatives we developed but can express their feelings on a matter more precisely. If an interviewer administers the instrument, it is possible to probe responses and elicit them by using appropriate attending behaviors. These techniques encourage respondents to provide fuller, more thoughtful answers.

There are also some distinct disadvantages; open-ended questions may lead to a lower response rate and decrease external validity. A measuring instrument with many open-ended questions takes considerable time to complete, and a long questionnaire can discourage potential respondents. Some people may be discouraged from replying to an instrument composed of open-ended questions because they are not articulate enough to provide their own responses, particularly if they must express themselves in writing. Only those with high levels of education may respond to such questions. In a study with a population that is homogeneous with respect to education, this is less of a problem. With a well-educated population, it may even be advisable to take advantage of the respondents' expertise by using open-ended questions.

Internal validity can also be a consideration with respect to open-ended questions, which introduce an element of subjectivity to the responses. Suppose 100 social workers on the staff of a department of social services complete a measuring instrument that asks for a paragraph describing why they are satisfied with the agency. In order to analyze the data, we need to code these individual replies into meaningful categories.

From answers to the question, "Are you satisfied working in the department?" a list of different sources of satisfaction could be deduced. The problem is that different individuals may state the same kind of satisfaction in different ways. One respondent, for example, may say: "I like the personal autonomy that is provided by this agency," and another might say, "They leave me alone here, and the supervisor does not bother me very much." It is our responsibility to decide whether or not such answers fall in the same category. The potential for error is the miscoding of responses, or lack of interrater reliability.

Interrater reliability can be achieved by having more than one person (usually called a rater) code the responses. When several raters code the same responses and develop their own sets of categories, a measure of interrater reliability, such as the percentage of responses for which the raters agree on an appropriate code, can be calculated. When low interrater reliability is found for the response to a particular question, we should try to ascertain the reasons why. If it is impossible to solve this problem, serious consideration should be given to eliminating the question, because it is useless to include a question that different respondents will interpret in different ways.

Closed-Ended Questions

In closed-ended questions, responses can be selected from a number of specified choices: expressing a simple yes or no, selecting degrees of agreement, or choosing one or more of a list of response categories. Two examples of closed-ended questions are:

1. *If the abused child is out of the home, which situation best describes your current plan of action? (Circle one number below.)*
   1. Return child to intact family
   2. Return child if abuser remains out of home
   3. Continue foster care
   4. Seek adoptive placement
   5. None of the above
   8. Not applicable
   9. Do not know

2. *Did the mother deny having knowledge of sexual abuse? (Circle one number below.)*
   1. Yes
   2. No
   8. Not applicable
   9. Do not know

The advantages of fixed-alternative questions are fairly obvious. These kinds of questions can be presented in such a way as to attract and maintain reliable responses from individuals. Answers are easily compared from person to person, and there is no need for time-consuming coding procedures such as those involved with open-ended questions. Because choices are provided, respondents are less apt to leave certain questions blank or to choose a "do not know" response. Missing data can be a serious problem when analyzing the data collected for a study, particularly if the response rate is low.

Closed-ended questions can elicit data on topics that would be difficult to obtain by other methods. It is difficult to get responses to an open-ended question on sexual behavior, for example. A series of short, closed-ended questions inquiring whether respondents agree or disagree with a statement or whether they participate in a certain behavior to a greater or lesser extent is much more likely to be answered. Moreover, a variable such as income level, for example, can be difficult to measure when asked as an open-ended question, such as:

- What is your present income?
- How much money did you make last year?

It is much more effective to ask individuals to place themselves in a set of categories containing a range of income levels, such as $10,000–$20,000.

Respondents may also be reluctant to answer questions about their age; this may or may not be a sensitive topic, depending on the study's population. As a rule, however, data on variables such as age, which are primarily measured at the interval or ratio level (such as years of education, income level, number of children in the home, or number of years married), should be gathered with open-ended questions. Thus, a more precise answer will be provided by an open-ended question on age that uses the following form:

What was your age at your last birthday? (Place number on line below.)

_____

Less usable data will be provided by a closed-ended question with a range of responses, such as:

What is your age? (Circle one number below.)
1. 1 to 5 years
2. 6 to 10 years
3. 11 to 15 years
4. 16 to 20 years
5. More than 20 years

Only when questions about these kinds of variables are sensitive and there is reason to believe there will be a low or mistaken response to them should the responses be grouped into categories. By grouping, we are throwing away important data; putting a child who is 10 years old into the same category as one who is 6 years old, for example, is needlessly inexact.

There are other problems with closed-ended questions. Respondents may not feel that the alternatives provided are appropriate to their answers. They also may be tempted to give an opinion on something they have never thought about before; the tendency to simply circle a fixed alternative is much greater than to answer an open-ended question where it is necessary to write something down. In respect to closed-ended questions used in interview situations, respondents who do not want to appear ignorant or who want to give socially desirable answers may say they do not know.

Comparison of the Two Types of Questions

As the preceding sections have shown, both open- and closed-ended questions have advantages and disadvantages, and each serves purposes that make it most appropriate for certain usages. One type of question therefore cannot be said to be better than the other. Open-ended questions are appropriate in exploratory studies with complex research questions, especially when all the alternative choices are not known. Closed-ended questions are preferable when the choices are all known or limited in number or when respondents have clear opinions on specific issues and feelings.

An important consideration in the choice of open- or closed-ended questions is the time required to measure the responses. Open-ended questions are time-consuming to code, introduce error, and require more personnel for data processing. Closed-ended questions can be designed so they do not require extensive coding and can go to the data processing stage quickly.

The type of question to be used is not necessarily an either/or choice; a measuring instrument can easily include both open- and closed-ended questions. It is possible to analyze the responses to open-ended questions individually and to have the responses to a series of closed-ended questions processed and analyzed by a computer.

INSTRUMENT CONSTRUCTION AND APPEARANCE

A list of questions is not a measuring instrument. How an instrument is constructed and what it looks or sounds like also determine whether or not those to whom it is sent or administered will respond. Those who receive a measuring instrument in the mail or in person or who interact with an interviewer face-to- face or on the telephone must be given the impression that completing the questionnaire or being interviewed is worthwhile and will not be too difficult or time-consuming. This is particularly the case with a mailed instrument, which can easily be discarded. To assure an adequate response rate, a written instrument should be designed to provide immediate positive impressions about its importance, difficulty, and length. Each of these factors can be manipulated by careful attention to detail.

To some extent it is possible to indicate the importance of an instrument by a professional appearance, and the difficulty can be indicated by how the questions are ordered. The length can be controlled by structuring the questions to save space or by including only those questions that are absolutely necessary for studying the research question.

Somewhat different methods are necessary when the instrument is to be used in interviewing respondents face-to-face or on the telephone. Procedures for developing an interview schedule for use in these cases are described in Chapter 15.

General Impression

Appearance, or how the instrument looks to potential respondents, often is affected by cost constraints. If these considerations can be overlooked, we can think in terms of the best way to present the instrument to make a good appearance.

The brief description of the design of a printed measuring instrument in this section is based on Donald Dillman's (1978) total design method for survey instruments. This is an expensive design to execute, but it illustrates the preferred method. The instrument is printed as a booklet. It consists of 8¼" by 12¼" sheets of paper folded in the middle and, if more than one sheet is used, stapled to form a booklet with the dimensions of 8¼" by 6⅛".

No questions are included on the front or back pages, which should stimulate the interest of recipients of the instrument. Pages are typed on a word processor using 12-point (Elite) type in a 7" by 9½" space on regular 8½" by 11" paper. To fit the booklet format, the pages are photographically reduced to 70 percent of the original size. They are reproduced on white or off-white paper by a printing method that produces quality work.

This format has several advantages. Photographically reducing the size of the page makes the questionnaire appear shorter and uses less paper; it also lowers postage costs if a mailed questionnaire is used. The booklet format and the use of a cover page give the appearance of a professionally produced document, which lends the impression that considerable thought has gone into the process. In contrast, instruments that are typed, photocopied, and held together with a single staple in the upper-left corner present an uneven and unprofessional appearance. Particularly to be avoided is a form that consists of several 8½" by 14" sheets of legal-size paper, folded several times to fit into a business envelope. Though this design probably saves money, the larger size and unattractive appearance are likely to discourage respondents.

Page Layout

In addition to how the questions in an instrument are presented in type, the design format determines how they are laid out on the page. This is an important consideration in producing a professional-appearing instrument that will encourage a high response rate. The instrument must be constructed so that respondents decide to complete it and do not overlook any question or section.

To keep sections of questions together and separated from other sections, various levels of spacing are used. If possible, questions and response categories should not start on one page and continue on another. Questions in a series, particularly, should be kept together or clearly follow one another. Confusion and mistakes often result when parts of questions or questions and responses become separated. Nevertheless, large blank spaces should be avoided when possible, for economy as well as appearance.

Typographical considerations in the layout of the instrument also can facilitate data processing by making answers easier to locate and to score. Careful design and planning with respect to how the instrument is to be processed once the questions have been answered can save much time, energy, and money.

Question Order

The ordering of questions in measuring instruments has been a topic of debate, but there appears to be some consensus on certain aspects. It is generally agreed, for example, that instruments should begin with questions that are interesting to the respondent and relevant to the purpose of the study, as stated in either the cover letter accompanying the mailed instrument or the introductory statement delivered by an interviewer.

To begin by asking for demographic data such as gender, age, or educational level can irritate respondents, who may regard the instrument as an application or evaluation form of some kind. Questions should be ordered along a descending gradient of social usefulness or importance. That is, questions that are judged to be the most important to the research question should be stated first. Demographic data should appear at the end of the instrument.

Potentially sensitive or objectionable questions also should be positioned later. It would not be wise, for example, to begin by asking how many times respondents had engaged in sexual intercourse in the previous week.

Another principle of ordering is that questions should be arranged by content area. Respondents should not be forced to constantly switch their train of thought by having to consider a question on one topic, followed by another on a totally different topic. Some of us maintain that forcing respondents to switch from one topic to another reduces their tendency to try to structure answers so they appear consistent. In fact, however, respondents are apt to give more thought to their answers if the instrument presents consecutive questions on a single general topic. Much less mental effort is required in responding to an instrument if the questions are organized by topic or content area.

Within the content areas, questions should be grouped by type of question (closed- versus open-ended). This means that questions requiring a simple yes or no answer or those in which responses are asked on a range of agreement to disagreement should appear together. Not only does this ease the mental effort required in responding to the questions, but it makes the instrument appear more logically constructed.

At times, of course, compromises must be made in question ordering; it is not always possible to follow all these principles. For example, we may not be able to sort the questions by content area and then sort them again by type of question in such a way as to give the appearance of a well-thought-out instrument. The goal always is to try to strike a satisfactory balance.

Presentation of Questions and Responses

One of the most common reasons for mistakes in constructing questionnaires is the mistaken assumption that the average person will know how to complete the instrument. Procedures that we take for granted can be mysteries to respondents, and detailed directions on how to answer the questions often are needed. In face-to-face or telephone interviews, explanations can be given verbally. But in a mailed questionnaire, or one that respondents are to complete on their own, questions that are not understood can be a source of serious error.

Figure 10.2 shows both unacceptable and acceptable ways of asking five typical questions in a survey instrument. In a question where the appropriate answer is to be circled, for example, unless this is explicitly stated in the instructions, respondents may circle more than one. For each question, directions such as "Circle one number below" must be given (see Questions 1–5 in Section B).

Response categories should not appear on the same line as the question but should be placed on the line below, and questions should not be squeezed onto a page with little room between items or between a question and its response categories. This not only produces a very cluttered and unsightly appearance, it increases the likelihood that respondents will overlook questions or make mistakes in answering.

A. Unacceptable Question Forms

1. Sex: M _____   F _____

2. Number of children at home
   0-1 _____   2-3 _____   4-5 _____   6 or more _____

3. Do you own your own home?   Y _____   N _____

4. Religious preference:
   Protestant _____
   Catholic _____
   Jewish _____

5. Health: Good _____   Fair _____   Poor _____

B. Acceptable Question Forms

1. What is your gender? (Circle one number below.)
   0. Male
   1. Female

2. How many of your children live at home with you? (Place number on line below.)

   _____

3. Do you own your own home? (Circle one number below.)
   0. No
   1. Yes
   8. Not applicable
   9. Do not know

4. What is your religious preference? (Circle one number below.)
   1. Protestant
   2. Catholic
   3. Jewish
   4. None
   5. Other (please specify) _____

5. How would you describe your physical health? (Circle one number below.)
   1. Poor
   2. Fair
   3. Good
   9. Do not know

Figure 10.2   Unacceptable and Acceptable Survey Questions

Precoding Responses

There are several ways to provide for questions to be answered, such as blank lines to be filled in or boxes to be checked. A better technique is precoding, or numbering the categories on the left and asking respondents to circle the appropriate number. This technique aids in data analysis because a number is preassigned to each alternative or response, as in Section B of Figure 10.2. Having respondents circle the number when they answer the question eliminates an additional step in data processing and another potential source of error. The number for each response should be placed at the left of the answer rather than at the right or anywhere else because responses could have different lengths (see Question 4 in Section B in Figure 10.2).

As an aid to both respondents and coders, it is helpful if certain numerical values are always used for the same types of responses. If there are numerous questions asking for yes or no responses, for example, the same value should be used for all the yes answers and another value for all the no answers. Thus, a value of 0 might be used for "no" and a value or 1 for "yes," throughout the instrument. A single value can also be used for the "missing data" category, so that all "Do not know," "No opinion," or "Not applicable" answers would have the same value. Thus, in Section B, 9 is the value for the "Do not know" answers in Questions 3 and 5, and 8 is the value for the "Not applicable" response in Question 3.

Precoded questions should be arranged one below the other, and response categories also should be in vertical order rather than side by side. If there are several choices of response categories on the same line, respondents may circle the wrong number or overlook some responses.

Edge-Coding Responses

In edge coding, another technique that aids in data processing, a series of blanks is added at the right side of the instrument (see Figures 9.5 and 10.3). Respondents are instructed not to write on these lines; they are utilized by us to transfer the response number circled by the respondent over to the blank line allocated for each question. This simple procedure eliminates the preparation of coding sheets, onto which responses otherwise are transferred after being converted into numbers. The inclusion of edge-coding lines may be distracting on the page, but the lines need not be obtrusive. Considering the savings of time and effort they provide, the possible disadvantages are minimal.

Organization of Content

In the two principal ways of organizing the contents of a questionnaire, respondents are asked to respond to a series of questions or to rank-order their responses. With a series of questions, respondents may be asked, for example, to choose whether they strongly agree, disagree, or strongly disagree on several questions. If the guidelines given above for question and response presentation were all followed, this type of scale would likely take up a large amount of space, as well as being needlessly repetitive. There are special ways to handle a series of questions in a small amount of space so the instrument appears less cluttered and easier to follow.

Figure 10.3, for example, is an example of a needs assessment in a specific community. Rather than asking 11 separate questions regarding the severity of problems in the community, the questions have been set up in a multiquestion format. First there is an opening statement briefly describing the purpose of the questionnaire and providing directions for answering the series of questions. Respondents are requested to circle the number that represents how they feel, and the three choices are given with their appropriate values (e.g., 1, 2, 3). The questions are listed consecutively on the left side of the page. The values appear in columns at the right of the 11 statements, and at the far right are the edge-coding lines.

Other techniques can be used when the same data are needed about a number of different people, such as collapsing questions into a single matrix. In the example presented in Figure 10.3, respondents are requested to state the occupational categories of their fathers and mothers. Rather than presenting the list of occupational categories twice, it is given once, and the same series of values is repeated for father and for mother in separate columns. The values must appear in both columns, and clear instructions must be given to circle only one number in each column.

An alternative way of presenting questions is the use of rank-ordering. Respondents might be asked to consider the 11 problems listed in Figure 10.3, for example, and rank them in terms of the severity each problem represents for them.

This form of question is not recommended, for several reasons. It is very difficult to consider more than three or four different concepts at once for rank-ordering purposes. If the list consists of 11 or more problems (as in Figure 10.3), it would be virtually impossible to give adequate thought to the severity of each problem. In addition, rank-ordering usually takes more time than if each question is considered on an individual basis. And, for data analysis purposes, rank-ordering restricts the type of analyses that can be carried out with the question.

If a series of questions is used, we can rank-order the responses and carry out other analyses as well. By calculating the mean score for each of the 11 questions listed in Figure 10.3 and then rank-ordering these means, for example, the same result can be achieved as if we had been asked to rank-order the questions themselves. In addition, using a series of questions makes it possible to create an index or scale and calculate its reliability, which could not be done if rank-orders were used.

Into which occupational category do your father and mother presently fall? (Circle one number in each column below.)

Relationship

Occupational Category	Father	Mother	
Professional	1	1	
Manager	2	2	____
Sales worker	3	3	____
Clerical worker	4	4	____
Craftsperson	5	5	____
Equipment operator	6	6	____
Laborer	7	7	____
Farmer	8	8	____
Service	9	9	____
Unemployed	10	10	____
Do not know	88	88	____
Deceased (not applicable)	99	99	____
Other (specify)	13	13	____

Figure 10.3   Single Questionnaire Format for Dual Responses

Transition Statements

Transition statements are used for several purposes. One is that by speaking directly to the respondents, they lend informality to the instrument and reduce monotony. This type of statement helps respondents answer the questions and become involved in the task. An example is:

In this section of our survey we would like to develop a sort of thumbnail sketch of your everyday life, the things you do, the things that worry or concern you, and the things that make you happy.

Transition statements are also used when the instrument introduces a new line of questioning. They tell people that they will be changing directions and forewarn them not to be surprised when they get to the next section. An example is:

Now I would like to ask you a few questions concerning recreational activities.

A third type of transition statement occurs toward the end of the questionnaire. The section asking for demographic data should be introduced with a statement such as the following:

Finally, we would like to ask you a few questions about yourself for statistical purposes.

This kind of statement indicates the approaching end of the instrument. Transition statements are important, but they can be overdone. Overly long statements and those that may inadvertently bias the response by pressuring the respondent toward a certain kind of answer should be avoided. Moreover, the approach should not be so didactic that it alienates respondents or makes them appear ignorant or foolish.

EVALUATING AND PRETESTING THE INSTRUMENT

A measuring instrument should be evaluated before it is administered. This can be done by providing answers to the questions presented in Chapter 9. The instrument also should be pretested to determine whether individuals responding understand the questions and have a favorable impression of the appearance and utility of the instrument. Beginning researchers often conduct pretests as an afterthought, as something that must be done as part of the research process. This does not fulfill the real purposes of a pretest, which, according to Dillman (1978), should provide answers to eight specific questions about the measuring instrument:

1. Is each question measuring what it is intended to measure?
2. Are all the words understood?
3. Are questions interpreted similarly by all individuals?
4. Does each closed-ended question have a response category that applies to each person?
5. Does the questionnaire create a positive impression, one that motivates people to answer it?
6. Can the questions be answered correctly?
7. Are some questions missed? Do some questions elicit uninterpretable answers?
8. Does any aspect of the instrument suggest bias on the part of the investigator?

Answers can be found for some of these questions by mailing out the questionnaire to a sample of individuals who are similar to the study's sample or population. What we are really concerned with, however, is feedback from these individuals, and this can best be gathered by direct interaction with them.

Essentially, a sample of respondents from three types of groups is preferable for use in a pretest of a measuring instrument: colleagues, the potential users of the data, or individuals drawn from the population to be surveyed. Each of these groups can provide a different type of feedback to the instrument designer. Colleagues may be fellow students, instructors, or associates. All should have specialized experience and understand the study's purpose. Potential users of the data—agency personnel, policy makers, clients, professionals—can indicate whether any of the questions are irrelevant to their purposes or reveal a lack of knowledge on our part. People who might be the focus of the study can provide information as to the clarity and difficulty of the questions, the appropriateness of the response categories, and so on.

To gather this feedback, perhaps the best method is to administer the instrument to representatives of one of these types of groups, individually or together, and follow with a debriefing session. This gives the pretest respondents an opportunity to discuss with us what they did and did not like about the instrument, what kinds of problems they had with it, and how they felt about the experience.

SUMMARY

We can construct measuring instruments when standardized instruments are simply not available. We can use them to determine and quantify facts about people and their behaviors, beliefs, feelings, and ethical standards.

The validity and reliability of the instrument are the most crucial concerns in the design and construction of a measuring instrument. External validity can be maximized by assuring an adequate response rate. This can be done by clearly stating the purpose of the study, avoiding sensitive questions and socially desirable answers, and asking only relevant questions. Internal validity can be maximized by reducing or eliminating measurement error in the content of the instrument. The principal concern in achieving internal validity is to make the questions clear and understandable.

The constructor of an instrument must take into account not only the content of the questions but the kinds of responses asked for. The two principal types of questions and response categories are open-ended questions, for which respondents supply their own responses, and closed-ended questions, for which they can select responses from a number of specified choices.

A measuring instrument should give an immediate positive impression to potential respondents. This can be achieved by attention to the appearance of the instrument, the order of questions, the manner of presenting questions and responses, the organization of questions in a series or rank-ordering format, and the use of transition statements.

The principles of measurement set forth in Chapter 8, the help given in Chapter 9 for understanding and evaluating measuring instruments, and the concrete suggestions for constructing instruments given in this chapter have laid a solid foundation for the next phase of the research process—selecting an appropriate sample and a corresponding research design.

Part IV

The Logic of Research Design

Peter A. Gabor
Carol Ing

C h a p t e r 11

Sampling

AFTER WE HAVE CHOSEN an instrument to measure the dependent variable(s) in our quantitative research study—or after we have chosen our research question for a qualitative study—we need to start thinking about how we are going to select a sample of research participants (or events or objects) that will provide data to answer our research question or test our hypothesis. Ideally, we should collect data from or about each and every person (or event or object) in a given population, or set. The resulting data would then be descriptive of the entire set. In practice, however, it is rarely possible (or feasible) to obtain data about every single unit in a population; such a process would be way too time-consuming and costly.

The common practice therefore is to gather data from some units and use these data to describe the entire set from which they came. Thus, sampling is defined as the selection of some units to represent the entire population (or set) from which the units were drawn. If the selection is carried out in accordance with the requirements of sampling theory, the data obtained from the sample should quite accurately pertain to the entire population from which the sample was taken.

SAMPLING THEORY

To illustrate the logic of sampling theory, consider the example of a research project in Kansas City that seeks to assess the extent of drug dependence among people who are elderly and chronically ill. As we know, the total set of people is referred to as a population—in this case, the entire group of people who have the following three characteristics: (1) they are chronically ill, (2) they are older, and (3) they live in Kansas City. Because it would not feasible to study the drug dependence of each and every individual in this specific population, some of these people are selected for a sample. Data are then collected about the sample's drug dependency.

The findings from the sample are then generalized to the population from which the sample was drawn. This procedure can only be justified if our sample is representative of the population—that is, if the relevant characteristics of the sample are similar to the characteristics of the population from which the sample was drawn. To ensure that a sample and population will be similar in all relevant characteristics, the sample must be chosen with a procedure that provides each member of the population with the same probability of being selected. If we study drug dependency of an appropriately drawn sample of people—who are chronically ill, who are older, and who live in Kansas City—we are in a position to describe drug dependency for the entire group of these people.

The use of sampling techniques is not limited to the study of people, however. Any population can be described with considerable accuracy through the selection of an appropriate sample. A population, for example, can be composed of objects such as client files. Through the selection of a sample of files, questions relating to all the files in the agency could be answered. Similarly, events and processes such as decision making about foster home placement in a particular county can be the objective of a research study. An appropriately selected sample would yield data about placement decision making in that county.

There are two major categories of sampling procedures, probability and nonprobability. In probability sampling, every member within a population has a known probability of being selected for the sample, so it can be established that the sample is representative of the population from which it was drawn. In nonprobability sampling, the probability of selection cannot be estimated, and it is difficult to determine the representativeness of the sample.

The Sampling Frame

In selecting a probability sample, our first step is to compile a sampling frame. The sampling frame is that collection of units (e.g., people, objects, or events) having a possibility of being selected. In short, it is simply the list from which our sample is actually selected. Ideally, it would be best to use the entire population as the sampling frame; however, this is seldom feasible because complete lists of populations rarely exist.

An example could be a research project that tries to ascertain the experiences social workers in Phoenix have had with their supervision. The population of interest in this study is defined as all social workers in Phoenix on January 1, 2001. Ideally, the procedure would begin with drawing a sample from this population. There is no definitive list containing the names of all social workers in Phoenix, however, so our first task is to create a list of social workers from which the sample can be drawn. This list is called a sampling frame.

A number of strategies can be employed in compiling a sampling frame in our example. One strategy is to obtain lists of social workers from all social service agencies and organizations that are known to employ them. Social workers in private practice who are listed in the telephone book could then be added to this list. If the task is executed with care, a reasonably complete list of social workers in Phoenix would result.

For a number of reasons, however, it is not likely that our sampling frame would be identical to the population. The lists of workers provided by agencies and organizations may not be up to date; some workers may have been hired since the agency lists were compiled, others might have resigned or found positions in other agencies. Social workers who have recently entered private practice may not be listed in the telephone book, while others who are listed may have left private practice. Some organizations that employ social workers may have been missed entirely.

In short, the sampling frame and the population are not identical, although it is desirable that the sampling frame approximate the population as closely as possible. Because in practice it is from our sampling frame that our sample is actually drawn, the representativeness of our sample is limited by how closely our sampling frame approximates the population of interest.

PROBABILITY SAMPLING

In probability sampling, because every member of a designated population has a known probability of being selected for a sample, it is possible to calculate the degree to which the sample is representative of the population from which it was drawn. Probability sampling strategies may have one or several stages.

One-Stage Probability Sampling

In one-stage probability sampling, the strategies or procedures can be classified as simple, systematic, or stratified random sampling. In each case, the selection of the sample is completed in one process or one stage.

Simple Random Sampling

In simple random sampling, members of a population are selected, one at a time, until the desired sample size is obtained. Once an individual unit (e.g., person, object, event) has been selected, it is removed from the population and has no chance of being selected again. This procedure is often used in selecting winning lottery numbers.

The objective of a particular lottery, for example, may be to guess 6 of 50 numbers. The winning numbers are selected by placing 50 balls, numbered 01–50, in a bowl and asking a blindfolded person to select, one at a time, six balls from the bowl. Each time a ball is selected, it is set aside and becomes one of the winning numbers; the end result is that six different numbers are selected by chance.

In practice, it is necessary to assign a unique number to each member within the population. As an example, consider a situation where our population consists of 500 full-time students in a school of social work. We decide that a sample of 100 (a sampling fraction of 1/5, or 20 percent, of the population) is required. First, each student is assigned a number from 001 to 500. Next, 100 numbers in the range 001–500 are randomly selected. The students who had been assigned the 100 selected numbers constitute our sample. The selection of numbers can be carried out with the assistance of a computer or by using a published table of random numbers.

A variety of computer programs that generate random numbers is available. Typically, all that is required is entering into the computer the range from within which selections are to be made, as well as the quantity of random numbers required. The computer then generates a list of the required quantity of numbers.

Alternatively, a published table of random numbers can be used to select the sample manually. Part of such a table is shown in Table 11.1. The selection process begins with the random selection of a single number anywhere in the table. Suppose the numeral zero in the number 63028 (third column from left, eighth row) is selected in this manner. Actually, three-digit numbers are required for our example, because the possible range of selection is from 001 to 500. Accordingly, the two digits to the right of the selected number (in this case 2 and 8) will also be used, making the first entry 028. (We also could have decided to use the two digits to the left, in which case the first entry would be 630—too large to fit the 001–500 range.)

Table 11.1   Partial Table of
Random Numbers

68184	44863	98829	87654	98712	08417
90103	90103	61257	56521	74090	09650
90103	89378	11410	45871	80932	15798
39883	87129	51877	25803	12597	35799
59342	89532	92446	68743	69876	12120
91041	76320	90940	12987	23099	43787
15685	56009	14001	35988	11435	56545
90159	76010	63028	56279	43450	09714
40814	09125	31846	09213	53074	27651
09299	09135	13441	98723	09123	76500
16920	78327	38334	38945	12345	89743
70083	90438	26713	23854	09457	67412
95826	67409	70856	76321	32198	69829
95791	81209	65385	45097	38764	90543
30403	40981	39854	76093	76328	40999
16036	76109	04720	76512	21232	09816
21652	89613	71900	50091	98541	89036
06990	90231	17209	78451	57690	90846

The student who had been assigned the number 028 is the first person selected for our sample. Because we have planned to move down the table, immediately under 028 the next three-digit number would be 846. This number is out of range, so it is skipped. The next number is 441; the student who had been assigned that number is selected.

Our selection then continues with student number 334, and so on. At the bottom of the column we move either right or left to the next column, according to a preset plan. When all 100 numbers have been selected, our random sample is complete.

Systematic Random Sampling

Conceptually, the selection of a simple random sample is a relatively simple and straightforward process. In practice, however, such a procedure is rarely used, particularly when the population from which a sample is to be selected is fairly large and the random numbers are to be selected one-by-one, by hand. The procedure can be quite tedious and time-consuming. A more practical alternative is systematic random sampling.

In this procedure, we determine the total number of units in the sampling frame and decide on the size of the sample. Assume that our sampling frame is again comprised of 500 students and the desired size of our sample is 100. Dividing the former by the latter (500/100 = 5) provides the size of the sampling interval, which in this case is five.

Thus, every fifth student on the list will be selected to constitute the sample. The selection process begins by randomly selecting a number from 1 to 5. The number selected designates the first student, and every fifth student is subsequently chosen. Suppose the number selected is 2. In such a case, students who had been assigned 002, 007, 012, 017, 022, and so forth will be chosen; student number 497 will complete the sample.

In most cases, a systematic random sample is equivalent to a simple random sample. However, it is possible that the sampling frame on which the selection is based has a recurring pattern that can bias the sample. For example, professional staff members in a social service agency may be listed on a unit-by-unit basis, with each unit having nine line-level social workers and one supervisor. The supervisor is listed as the tenth person in the unit. A systematic sample drawn from such a listing would almost certainly contain a bias.

In a sampling plan that calls for names to be selected at intervals of five, the first number chosen would determine if supervisors would be either over-represented or underrepresented in the sample. If the first number selected were 1, 2, 3, or 4, no supervisors at all would be included in the sample, even though they comprise 10 percent of the population. If the first number selected is 5, every second person selected for the sample would be a supervisor, and supervisors would be grossly overrepresented.

With systematic random sampling, it is essential to closely study the sampling frame from which the selections are to be made to ensure that no underlying patterns that could bias the sample are present. If it can be confirmed that the list is free of recurring patterns, systematic random sampling is an efficient and effective way of selecting a sample from a population.

Stratified Random Sampling

Stratified random sampling is a procedure that can help reduce chance variation between a sample and the population it represents. This procedure may be used when a population can be divided into two or more distinct groups, called strata. The strata are then sampled separately, using simple random-sampling or systematic random-sampling techniques.

In our example above, the population of professional staff members in the social service agency is constituted of 90 percent social workers and 10 percent supervisors. Of the professional staff complement of 500, therefore, 450 are social workers and 50 hold supervisory positions. Theoretically, a 20 percent simple random sample of the professional staff should yield 90 social workers and 10 supervisors. However, this will not always happen because although a random sample may be representative of the population, it is not necessarily identical to it. Chance (or normal sampling error) may result in a sample that is composed of 92 social workers and 8 supervisors, or 87 social workers and 13 supervisors, or some other combination.

But this population of agency professionals is composed of two groups, or strata: line-level social workers and supervisors. A separate sample therefore can be drawn from each group, using simple random-sampling or systematic random-sampling techniques. A 20 percent sample can be drawn from each group, resulting in a total sample of 100 people, 90 social workers and 10 supervisors.

Because the same sampling fraction is used for each stratum, the approach is known as proportional stratified sampling. One of the advantages of such a sample is that it perfectly represents the characteristics of the population from which it was drawn in regard to the variable, or variables, on which the stratification was based. Some sampling error would normally be expected if either simple random sampling or systematic random sampling had been used. Using stratified random sampling can eliminate this source of sampling error.

It is also possible to draw a disproportional sample from the strata. In this procedure, different sampling fractions are used for some or all of the strata. We might use a 1/5 sampling fraction (a 20 percent sample), for example, when selecting line-level social workers but a 3/5 sampling fraction (a 60 percent sample) in the selection of supervisors. This procedure would yield 90 line-level social workers and 30 supervisors.

It would make sense to proceed in this manner if one of the objectives of the study were to examine closely some characteristic of the supervisors. Using proportional sampling, only 10 supervisors would be available for study. If the subsequent analysis required further division of this group (for example, according to educational level, age, or gender), only a small number of supervisors would be left in each group, making such analysis difficult. By sampling disproportionally, the total number of supervisors in the sample is increased, which makes it possible to conduct further detailed analyses.

When strata that have been disproportionately sampled are combined in order to make estimates about the total population, it is necessary to weight each stratum that was sampled at a higher rate to compensate for the higher rate of selection. If supervisors were selected at three times the rate of line-level social workers, an adjustment factor of 1/3 (the inverse of 3 to 1) is used to adjust for the disproportional selection of supervisors. The numbers and percentages of line-level workers and supervisors in the sample then would accurately represent those in the population. Table 11.2 provides a brief summary of disproportional sampling and the adjustment process in relation to our hypothetical example in this section.

Multistage Probability Sampling

The single-stage probability sampling procedures described above depend on the availability of a sampling frame from which the sample is to be selected. It is not always possible to compile a sampling frame for the population of

Table 11.2   Data for Disproportional
                    Stratified Sampling for a
                    Population of Line-Level
                    Workers and Supervisors

	Line-Level Workers	Supervisors
Number in population	450	50
Percent of population	90	10
Sampling fraction	1/5	3/5
Number in sample	90	30
Percent of unweighted sample	75	25
Weighting factor	1	1/3
Number in weighted sample	90	10
Percent of weighted sample	90	10

interest, however; this is likely to be the case when a population from a city, county, or state is to be sampled. Multistage-sampling procedures provide a strategy through which a population can be sampled when a comprehensive list does not exist and it is not possible to construct one. The most commonly used procedure is cluster sampling.

Cluster Sampling

Cluster sampling is more complicated than the single-stage sampling strategies; essentially, each stage of multistage sampling is in itself a simple random sample or a systematic random sample. The stages are combined to build on one another and arrive at a final sample.

Suppose we are conducting a community needs assessment, for example, and want to determine the types of community support that single parents need. Many of the agencies and social workers providing help to single parents undoubtedly have opinions about this, but suppose very little is known about what single parents themselves perceive their needs to be. In fact, it is not even known how many single parents there are in the community. Since no comprehensive list of single parents can be compiled, it is not possible to proceed with a one- stage probability sampling strategy.

A form of cluster sampling, known as area probability sampling, provides the means to carry out such a study. Stage 1 of this strategy involves listing all the residential blocks, known as clusters, within the community and then drawing a sample from these clusters. Suppose there are 300 residential blocks and we decide that a sample of 50 (a sampling fraction of about 1/6) will constitute an adequate sample.

Fifty blocks are selected, using simple random sampling. In the next stage, the residential units located on those blocks are to be sampled.

We then decide that in Stage 2, 20 percent of the residential units located on the blocks selected in Stage 1 will provide an appropriate sample. All 2000 units on the 50 blocks are listed, and 20 percent are randomly selected. Interviewers are assigned to contact the residents in these 400 units to determine if any resident is a single parent.

When the number of single parents in the sample has been determined, the incidence of single parenthood in the community can be estimated. Moreover, we now have a list of single parents, which is required for Stage 3.

In Stage 3, a sample is drawn of the single parents listed. We may decide, for example, that about 25 percent of the single parents should be interviewed. A random list of the names of the 100 single parents who were located in Stage 2 is compiled, and, using a systematic random sample strategy, every fourth name is selected for the final sample. A final sample of 25 single parents is thus obtained. In-depth interviews are then conducted with the single parents in the sample to determine the types of community support that single parents generally would like.

NONPROBABILITY SAMPLING

With nonprobability sampling, the probability of selection cannot be estimated, so there is little or no support for the claim that the sample is representative of the population from which it was drawn. Nevertheless, there are many situations where it is unfeasible or impossible to draw a probability sample, and nonprobability sampling is the only alternative. Four types of nonprobability sampling—convenience, purposive, quota, and snowball sampling—are described in this section. Box 11.1 presents a graphic summary of these sampling strategies.

Convenience Sampling

Convenience sampling, sometimes called availability sampling, relies on the closest and most available subjects to constitute the sample. This procedure is used extensively in social work research.

Let us say, for example, we are interested in the various therapeutic techniques social workers use with clients who are depressed. We could use this specific group of people being treated at a specific social service agency within the past six months as our sample. Our findings could yield data on the various techniques social workers use with this group of people in general.

It would be very difficult, however, to determine to what degree the clients in our sample are representative of all people who are depressed and receiving treatment in other geographical locations. It is possible that clients receiving

Box 11.1_____

Nonprobability Sampling Strategies

Convenience Sampling: Sample is composed of nearest and most available participants.

Purposive Sampling: Research participants who are known or judged to be good sources of information are specifically sought out and selected for the sample.

Quota Sampling:
1. Variables relevant to the study are identified (e.g., gender and age).
2. Variables are combined into discrete categories (e.g., younger female, younger male, older female, older male).
3. The percentage of each of these categories in the population is determined (e.g., 35% younger female, 25% younger male, 30% older female, 10% older male).
4. The total sample size is established (e.g., $N = 200$).

5. Quotas are calculated (younger females = 35% of 200 = 70; younger males = 25% of 200 = 50; older females = 30% of 200 = 60; older males = 10% of 200 = 20).
6. The first available participants possessing the required characteristics are selected to fill the quotas.

Snowball Sampling:
1. A small number of participants are located in the population of interest.
2. Data are obtained from these participants and they are also asked to identify others in the population.
3. The newly identified participants are contacted, data are obtained, and this group is also asked to identify others in the population.
4. The process continues until the desired sample size is obtained.

---

services from our particular agency are different, in important ways, from people who are depressed and receiving services elsewhere. These differences may well affect the nature of the services provided. For this reason, the opportunity to generalize the findings from our study is limited.

Purposive Sampling

In purposive sampling, also known as judgmental or theoretical sampling, we use our own judgment in selecting a sample. The basis for selecting such a sample is that it can yield considerable data particularly when used within qualitative research studies, as pointed out in Chapters 6 and 7.

Let us say, for example, the objective of our exploratory research study is to examine the workings of new legislation regarding young offenders. It might make sense to interview a small number of social workers, probation officers, lawyers, judges, and directors of detention facilities who have worked extensively under this legislation. The people in this sample could be used as key informants in an attempt to construct a picture of how the legislation has been implemented.

The selection might also be made with a view of choosing information-rich cases. One approach to studying the reasons for breakdown in foster care placement for preschool children, for example, would be to select a sample of

Box 11.2_____

Sample Size and Errors in Research Studies

Sample Size

To illustrate the concept of sample size, we will take an example of Antonia, a school social worker at Wilson Elementary School, who wants to teach second-grade students how to protect themselves from being physically abused by their parents. In a nutshell, she wants to institute a school-based program that will teach these children how to defend themselves from being abused. Before Antonia institutes the program, however, she wants to make sure the parents approve of their children learning such material.

Let us say that Antonia wants to conduct a very simple study with mothers who have at least one child attending her school. She wants to ascertain their opinions of her idea—that is, teaching their children about the prevention of child abuse. In order to gather data—the parents' opinions, that is—to help her decide if the content should be taught to second-grade children, Antonia wants to survey the mothers of 100 children in grade two.

Before her sample can be selected, it is obviously necessary to decide how large the sample needs to be. The correct sample size for any particular study depends on how confident we need to be about the results. If Antonia wants to be completely (100 percent) confident about the mothers' opinions on child abuse prevention education being taught to second-grade children, she needs to survey every mother.

That is, she must not draw a sample at all. Generally speaking, the more mothers she surveys, the more confident she can be that the results of her survey reflect the opinions of the population of mothers at Wilson.

The sample size also depends on how homogeneous, or how alike, the population is. If Antonia's population of mothers were all identical robots, she would need only to survey one to be completely confident of the opinions of the rest.

If they were all middle-aged, middle-income Caucasian Catholics, she would need to survey fewer than if they comprised a wide range of ethnic and religious groups of varying ages and incomes.

Sample size must also be considered in relation to the number of categories required. If Antonia had wanted to look at mothers of 5 to 9 year old children and mothers of 10 to 14 year old children, she would have needed two mothers—one from each category—even if all the mothers are identical robots.

The more dissimilar the mothers are, the more she will need to survey in each of the categories she wants to consider. In addition, if there are very few mothers in one category, she may need to survey all the mothers in that category, or at least a large proportion of them, while surveying smaller proportions of parents in the other categories.

Generally speaking, the larger the sample the better, taking into account restrictions of time and cost. With respect to the minimum sample size required, experts differ. Some say that a sample of 30 is large enough to perform basic statistical procedures, while others advise a minimum sample size of 100. There are formulas available for calculating sample size but they are somewhat complicated.

Usually, a sample size of one-tenth of the population (with a minimum of 30) is considered sufficient to provide reasonable control over sampling error. The same one-tenth convention also applies to categories of the population: One-tenth of each category can be included in the sample.

Errors

Errors in research findings may result either from the sampling procedure, in which case they are called sampling errors, or from other errors arising in the research study, called nonsampling errors. Both types of errors must be assessed within a research study.

Sampling Errors

Sampling errors have to do with the fact that a representative sample—a sample that exactly represents the population from which it was drawn—almost never exists in reality. When Antonia surveys a random sample of mothers, she will not obtain exactly the same results from the sample as she would have

Box 11.2 Continued_____

obtained had she surveyed the entire population of mothers. The difference between the results she did obtain (actuality) and the results she would have obtained (theoretical) comprises the sampling error.

In order to better understand the concept of representativeness, suppose that two variables are particularly important in determining whether mothers will approve of child abuse prevention education taught to their second-grade children: the mothers' degree of belief that their own children are at risk of abuse (Figure 11.1, page 221); and the mothers' degree of fear that child abuse prevention education may somehow psychologically harm their children (Figure 11.2, page 222).

Suppose further that these two variables can be measured, both for a random sample of 100 mothers and for the entire population 1,000 mothers. All the mothers in the school may be asked to rate the degree to which they feel their own children are at risk of abuse, on a scale of 1 to 10, from "no risk at all" to "very high risk." A graph may then be drawn of the number of mothers on the vertical axis against rating of risk on the horizontal axis, as illustrated in Figure 11.1.

As Figure 11.1a shows, a few of the mothers in the population feel that their children are at high risk (rating the risk as 10 on the scale), a few feel that there is very little risk (a rating of 1), and most believe that there is moderate risk. If a random sample of mothers is then selected from the population of mothers and the same procedure is carried out, almost identical results may be obtained, as shown in Figure 11.1b. The degree of similarity between graphs 11.1a and 11.1b is the degree to which the sample is representative of the population, with respect to the belief that their children are at risk.

Now suppose that the population of mothers and the sample of mothers are separately asked to rate the degree to which they fear that child abuse prevention education may somehow harm their children. The results for the population and the sample are shown in Figure 11.2.

As Figure 11.2a shows, the majority of the population of mothers have very little fear that their children will be harmed by child abuse prevention being taught in schools. A few have extreme fear, a few have moderate fear, and a few have no fear at all.

Conversely, the majority of the sample display moderate fear that their children will be harmed; the hump of the graph, which is skewed to the left in Figure 11.2a, is essentially centered in Figure 11.2b. If these graphs were placed one on top of another, they would not coincide. Thus, the sample does not very adequately represent the population of mothers, with respect to fear that their children will be harmed.

In sum, while no sample will perfectly represent the population from which it was drawn, it is quite probable that a randomly drawn sample will represent the population adequately with respect to one variable. It is less probable that the sample will represent the population adequately with respect to two variables, and, the more variables there are, the less probable adequate representation becomes.

A member of congress, for example, may represent his or her constituents' views on state-funded abortions exactly, but it is unlikely that their views on Medicare will also be reflected, as well as their views on capital punishment and their views on national health care.

Nonsampling Errors

In addition to reducing sampling error to a minimum, efforts must also be made to reduce nonsampling sources of error. One source of nonsampling error is an inadequate sampling frame, which has already been mentioned. Because the sample is drawn from the sampling frame, if the list does not correspond well to the population of interest, it will be difficult to infer anything about the population from the sample.

Other nonsampling errors include nonresponse from research participants, field errors, response errors, and coding and data entry errors. While these are not sampling errors, they also affect our ability to estimate the precision of the sample.

Effects of Nonresponse

In making estimates from probability samples, it is assumed that we have collected data from every unit designated for our sam-

Box 11.2 Continued

ple. In this sense, however, a sample is only a theoretical entity, for seldom can a complete set of data be collected. The sample always includes some individuals who cannot be reached or refuse to respond. A high rate of nonresponse offers a distinct possibility that the sample obtained will be biased, since those who do respond may be in some way different from those who do not. Nonresponse is particularly a problem when data are collected by mail surveys.

In a study to examine the frequency of evaluation activities in children's group-care programs in a large state, for example, data are collected by mailing questionnaires to the executive directors of a sample of agencies offering such programs. Completed questionnaires are returned by 55 percent of the directors sampled. Does the 45 percent non-response rate result in a biased sample?

There is no simple answer to such a question, and, unless further data are collected from nonrespondents, it is not possible to answer it with any degree of certainty. Suppose (as is likely the case) that the directors who respond are more interested in evaluation because there is a high level of such activities in their agencies.

Under such circumstances, the sample would be biased, resulting in an overestimation of evaluation activities. The sample would not be biased if the reasons for the lack of response are not related to the variables under study. Clearly, every effort should be made to incorporate into the research design strategies that will ensure a high response rate.

Field Errors and Response Errors

Other nonsampling errors occur in the field or in participants' responses to interviews or questionnaires. Ideally, the research design would not allow the field staff much discretion in selecting the sample. If given

latitude they might select for the sample only those files that are well organized and neatly written, those individuals who are easily accessible and nonthreatening, or those housing units that are well maintained and easy to reach.

Interviewers can almost always exercise some discretion in conducting complex interviews, providing prompts, or recording the data. When the data collection method is observation, observers can decide what to observe and how to record it. Field errors resulting from such circumstances can be minimized by ensuring that field staff are well trained and supervised and that the procedures they are to follow have been explicitly stated in detail.

Skillfully designed questionnaires and well-trained interviewers also can minimize the impact of response errors. The quality of the data collected will suffer if large numbers of respondents misunderstand questions or are not qualified to answer but provide answers nevertheless. Respondents also may attempt to present themselves (or their opinions) in a socially desirable manner. They may profess views they do not actually hold or deny behaviors or feelings that they believe might be met with disapproval.

Coding and Data Entry Errors

In the final analysis, the best sampling design and the most meticulous data collection will be to no avail if the resulting data are inaccurately coded or entered. Training and supervision of the clerical staff responsible for these functions and judicious use of standard double-coding and double-entry procedures lessen the possibility of coding and data entry errors.

Source: Grinnell and Williams (1990); Williams, Tutty, and Grinnell (1995); and Gabor and Ing (1997)

cases where five or more placement changes have taken place. While these cases would (it is hoped) not be representative of foster care cases generally, they could provide clues to the factors involved in placement breakdown.

Table 11.3   Quota Sampling Matrix: Percentages
                    and Quotas of Gender and Age Among
                    Social Workers

	Age					
	Younger (n = 120)		Older (n = 80)		Total (N = 200)	
Gender	Number	Percent	Number	Percent	Number	Percent
Female	70	35	60	30	130	65
Male	50	25	20	10	70	35
Totals ...	120	60	80	40	200	100

Quota Sampling

Quota sampling is somewhat analogous to stratified random sampling. Essentially, the strategy consists of identifying variables or characteristics of the sample that are relevant to the study, determining the proportion (quota) of these characteristics in the population, and then selecting participants in each category until the quota is achieved.

Let us take an example of a research study that examines the skills social workers use to establish working relationships with their clients. We have a hunch that there are differences in the various approaches taken by female and male social workers (Variable 1) and by older and younger social workers (Variable 2). These two variables are displayed in Table 11.3 (i.e., gender, age) and are combined into four discrete groups: younger female social workers, younger male social workers, older female social workers, and older male social workers.

Then the percentage of workers in each of the four categories within the population of interest is determined. Suppose we determine that the percentages are 35, 25, 30, and 10 percent, respectively, as indicated in Table 11.3. If a total sample of 200 is required, 70 younger females (35 percent of 200), 50 younger males, 60 older females, and 20 older males will constitute the sample. The final step in selecting a quota sample is to find a sufficient number of social workers to fit each of these characteristics.

The main limitation of quota sampling is that considerable discretion is exercised in selecting individuals to fill each quota. In our example, we might go to two large agencies and find sufficient numbers of social workers to draw the entire sample. While this would be convenient, the representativeness of such a sample would be questionable. It could be argued, for example, that social workers in smaller agencies relate to clients differently than those in larger agencies.

A second problem with quota sampling is that to establish the quotas, reasonable knowledge of the characteristics of the population under study is

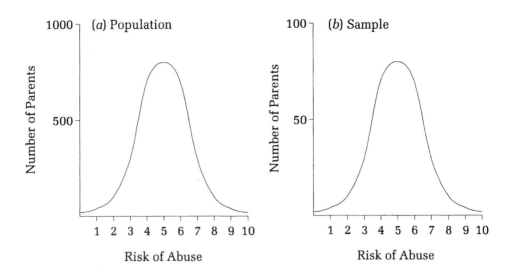

Figure 11.1   Theoretical Distributions of Mothers' Risk of Abuse
                   Ratings from a Population of 1,000 (*a*) and a Random
                   Sample of 100 (*b*)

required. Where precise data about the variables relevant to quota setting are
not available, the quotas may not accurately represent the population.

Snowball Sampling

Snowball sampling is particularly useful when members of a population are
difficult to identify and locate. This is often the case when studying people
whose behavior is regarded as deviant or illegal or is otherwise received with
social disapproval. It is often difficult to identify members of such populations
as prostitutes, homeless people, or intravenous drug users, for example.

The strategy of snowball sampling is to locate a few individuals in the
population of interest and ask them to identify other people in the same group.
These people, in turn, are asked to identify still other respondents. The cycle
continues until an adequate sample size has been achieved. Although this
strategy may be the only one through which a sample can be drawn from
certain populations, it has the evident drawback that the sample depends
entirely on the individuals who are first contacted. If the sampling were
initiated with a different set of individuals, the entire sample might be
differently constituted. Consequently, the degree to which a snowball sample
is representative of any population cannot be determined.

Snowball sampling may also be used to locate people with divergent views
on a topic to ensure that the sample represents all segments of a population.
This is important in a population where minority opinions might otherwise be
disregarded. It is particularly useful in qualitative research studies.

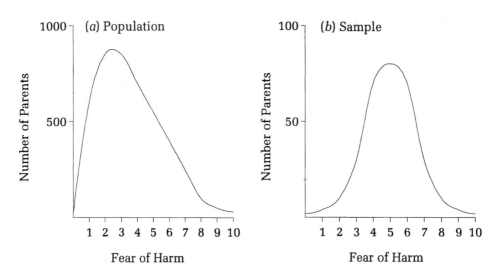

Figure 11.2   Theoretical Distributions of Mothers' Fear of Harm Ratings from a Population of 1,000 (*a*) and a Random Sample of 100 (*b*)

SAMPLE SIZE AND ERRORS

Box 11.2, presented on pages 217-219, illustrates how the size of a sample in a research study can affect the results of the study. In addition, it presents the different types of sampling and nonsampling errors that have to be controlled for in the study.

SUMMARY

Because it is usually not feasible to obtain data from an entire population (of people, things, or events) in which we are interested, sampling procedures are used to select some individuals (or other units) as representative of the entire population. The two main types of sampling procedures are probability and nonprobability sampling.

The first step in probability sampling is to construct a sampling frame, a list of units from which the sample is to be selected. The sample is then drawn, using either one-stage sampling (with simple random, systematic random, or stratified random sample strategies) or multistage (cluster) sampling. In all forms of probability sampling, random selection procedures are used, all units in the sampling frame have the same known probability of selection, and it is possible to make an estimate of the precision of the sample.

In some situations where probability sampling is not possible, a non-probability sample may be drawn. The four kinds of nonprobability samples described in this chapter are convenience, purposive, quota, and snowball sampling. Such samples may provide data that would otherwise be inaccessible, but these approaches are less powerful than probability sampling because various selection biases in them cannot be ruled out. In addition, it is not possible to estimate the precision of the sample.

If probability sampling is used, sampling errors can be estimated. Such errors can be controlled by using a sample of sufficient size or by employing a sampling design that incorporates stratification. Nonsampling errors also contribute to the overall possibility of error in the research project. Care should be taken in the design to minimize nonresponse, an inadequate sampling frame, field and response errors, and coding and data entry errors.

Now that we know something about how to obtain a sample for a research study, let us turn our attention to the selection of an appropriate research design that will help us obtain the most "objective" data possible that will help us answer our research question or test our research hypothesis.

Richard M. Grinnell, Jr.
Yvonne A. Unrau

C h a p t e r   12

Group Research Designs

NOW THAT WE KNOW how to draw samples for qualitative and quantitative research studies, we turn our attention to the various designs that research studies can take. The two most important factors in determining what design to use in a specific study are: (1) what the research question is, and (2) how much knowledge about the problem area is available. If there is already a substantial knowledge base in the area, we will be in a position to address very specific research questions, the answers to which could add to the explanation of previously gathered data. If less is known about the problem area, our research questions will have to be of a more general, descriptive nature. If very little is known about the problem area, our questions will have to be even more general, at an exploratory level. Portions of this chapter have been adapted and modified from Grinnell and Williams (1990), Grinnell and Stothers (1988), Grinnell (1993a), Williams, Tutty and Grinnell (1995), Grinnell and Unrau (1997), Williams, Unrau, and Grinnell (1998), Gabor and Grinnell (1994), Gabor, Unrau, and Grinnell (1998), Unrau, Gabor, and Grinnell (2001).

Research knowledge levels are arrayed along a continuum, from exploratory at the lowest end to explanatory at the highest. Because research knowledge levels are viewed this way, the assignment of the level of knowledge accumulated in a problem area prior to a research study, as well as the level that might be attained by the research study, is totally arbitrary. There are, however, specific designs that can be used to provide us with knowledge at a certain level.

At the highest level are the explanatory designs, also called experimental designs or "ideal" experiments. These designs have the largest number of requirements (examined in the following section). They are best used in confirmatory research studies where the area under study is well developed, theories abound, and testable hypotheses can be formulated on the basis of previous work or existing theory. These designs seek to establish causal relationships between the independent and dependent variables.

In the middle range are the descriptive designs, sometimes referred to as quasi-experimental. A quasi-experiment resembles an "ideal" experiment in some aspects but lacks at least one of the necessary requirements.

At the lowest level are the exploratory designs, also called preexperimental or nonexperimental, which explore only the research question or problem area. These designs do not produce statistically sound data or conclusive results; they are not intended to. Their purpose is to build a foundation of general ideas and tentative theories, which can be explored later with more precise and hence more complex research designs, and their corresponding data gathering techniques.

The research designs that allow us to acquire knowledge at each of the three levels are described in a later section of this chapter. Before considering them, however, it is necessary to establish the characteristics that differentiate an "ideal" experiment, which leads to explanatory knowledge, from other studies that lead to lower levels of knowledge.

CHARACTERISTICS OF "IDEAL" EXPERIMENTS

An "ideal" experiment is one in which a research study most closely approaches certainty about the relationship between the independent and dependent variables. The purpose of doing an "ideal" experiment is to ascertain whether it can be concluded from the study's findings that the independent variable is, or is not, the only cause of change in the dependent variable. As pointed out in previous chapters, some social work research studies have no independent variable—for example, those studies that just want to find out how many people in a certain community wish to establish a community-based halfway house for people who are addicted to drugs.

The concept of an "ideal" experiment is introduced with the word "ideal" in quotes because such an experiment is rarely achieved in social work research situations. On a general level, in order to achieve this high degree of certainty and qualify as an "ideal" experiment, an explanatory research design must meet six conditions:

1. The time order of the independent variable must be established.
2. The independent variable must be manipulated.
3. The relationship between the independent and dependent variables must be established.
4. The research design must control for rival hypotheses.
5. At least one control group should be used.
6. Random assignment procedures (and if possible, random sampling from a population) must be employed in assigning research participants (or objects) to groups.

Controlling the Time Order of Variables

In an "ideal" experiment, the independent variable must precede the dependent variable in time. Time order is crucial if our research study is to show that one variable causes another, because something that occurs later cannot be the cause of something that occurred earlier.

Suppose we want to study the relationship between adolescent substance abuse and gang-related behavior. The following hypothesis is formulated after some thought:

Adolescent substance abuse causes gang-related behavior.

In the hypothesis, the independent variable is adolescent drug use, and the dependent variable is gang-related behavior. The substance abuse must come *before* gang-related behavior because the hypothesis states that adolescent drug use causes gang-related behavior. We could also come up with the following hypothesis, however:

Adolescent gang-related behavior causes substance abuse.

In this hypothesis, adolescent gang-related behavior is the independent variable, and substance abuse is the dependent variable. According to this hypothesis, gang-related behavior must come *before* the substance abuse.

Manipulating the Independent Variable

Manipulation of the independent variable means that we must do something with the independent variable in terms of at least one of the research participants in the study. In the general form of the hypothesis, if X occurs then Y will result, the independent variable (X) must be manipulated in order to effect a variation in the dependent variable (Y). There are essentially three ways in which independent variables can be manipulated:

1. *X present versus X absent.* If the effectiveness of a specific treatment intervention is being evaluated, an experimental group and a control group could be used. The experimental group would be given the intervention, the control group would not.
2. *A small amount of X versus a larger amount of X.* If the effect of treatment time on client's outcomes is being studied, two experimental groups could be used, one of which would be treated for a longer period of time.
3. *X versus something else.* If the effectiveness of two different treatment interventions is being studied, Intervention X_1 could be used with Experimental Group 1 and Intervention X_2 with Experimental Group 2.

There are certain variables, such as the gender or race of our research participants, that obviously cannot be manipulated because they are fixed. They do not vary, so they are called constants, not variables, as was pointed out in Chapter 6. Other constants, such as socioeconomic status or IQ, may vary for research participants over their life spans, but they are fixed quantities at the beginning of the study, probably will not change during the study, and are not subject to alteration by the one doing the study.

Any variable we can alter (e.g., treatment time) can be considered an independent variable. At least one independent variable must be manipulated in a research study if it is to be considered an "ideal" experiment.

Establishing Relationships Between Variables

The relationship between the independent and dependent variables must be established in order to infer a cause-effect relationship at the explanatory knowledge level. If the independent variable is considered to be the cause of the dependent variable, there must be some pattern in the relationship between these two variables. An example is the hypothesis: The more time clients spend in treatment (independent variable), the better their progress (dependent variable).

Controlling Rival Hypotheses

Rival hypotheses must be identified and eliminated in an "ideal" experiment. The logic of this requirement is extremely important, because this is what makes a cause-effect statement possible.

The prime question to ask when trying to identify a rival hypothesis is, "What other extraneous variables might affect the dependent variable?" (What else might affect the client's outcome besides treatment time?) At the risk of sounding redundant, "What else besides X might affect Y?" Perhaps the client's motivation for treatment, in addition to the time spent in treatment, might affect the client's outcome. If so, motivation for treatment is an extraneous variable that could be used as the independent variable in the rival hypothesis, "The higher the clients' motivation for treatment, the better their progress."

Perhaps the social worker's attitude toward the client might have an effect on the client's outcome, or the client might win the state lottery and ascend abruptly from depression to ecstasy. These extraneous variables could potentially be independent variables in other rival hypotheses. They must all be considered and eliminated before it can be said with reasonable certainty that a client's outcome resulted from the length of treatment time and not from any other extraneous variables.

Control over rival hypotheses refers to efforts on our part to identify and, if at all possible, to eliminate the extraneous variables in these alternative hypotheses. Of the many ways to deal with rival hypotheses, three of the most frequently used are to keep the extraneous variables constant, use correlated variation, or use analysis of covariance.

Keeping Extraneous Variables Constant

The most direct way to deal with rival hypotheses is to keep constant the critical extraneous variables that might affect the dependent variable. As we know, a constant cannot affect or be affected by any other variable. If an extraneous variable can be made into a constant, then it cannot affect either the study's real independent variable or the dependent variable.

Let us take an example to illustrate the above point. Suppose, for example, that a social worker who is providing counseling to anxious clients wants to relate client outcome to length of treatment time, but most of the clients are also being treated by a consulting psychiatrist with antidepressant medication. Because medication may also affect the clients' outcomes, it is a potential independent variable that could be used in a rival hypothesis. However, if the study included only clients who have been taking medication for some time before the treatment intervention began, and who continue to take the same medicine in the same way throughout treatment, then medication can be considered a constant (in this study, anyway).

Any change in the clients' anxiety levels after the intervention will, therefore, be due to the intervention with the help of the medication. The extraneous variable of medication, which might form a rival hypothesis, has been eliminated by holding it constant. In short, this study started out with one independent variable, the intervention, then added the variable of medication to it, so the final independent variable is the intervention plus the medication.

This is all very well in theory. In reality, however, a client's drug regime is usually controlled by the psychiatrist and may well be altered at any time. Even if the regime is not altered, the effects of the drugs might not become apparent until the study is under way. In addition, the client's level of anxiety might be affected by a host of other extraneous variables over which the social worker has no control at all: for example, living arrangements, relationships with other people, the condition of the stock market, or an unexpected visit from an IRS agent. These kinds of pragmatic difficulties tend to occur frequently in social work practice and research. It is often impossible to identify all rival hypotheses, let alone eliminate them by keeping them constant.

Using Correlated Variation

Rival hypotheses can also be controlled with correlated variation of the independent variables. Suppose, for example, that we are concerned that income has an effect on a client's compulsive behavior. The client's income, which in this case is subject to variation due to seasonal employment, is identified as an independent variable. The client's living conditions—in a hotel room rented by the week—are then identified as the second independent variable that might well affect the client's level of compulsive behavior. These two variables, however, are correlated since living conditions are highly dependent on income.

Correlated variation exists if one potential independent variable can be correlated with another. Then only one of them has to be dealt with in the research study.

Using Analysis of Covariance

In conducting an "ideal" experiment, we must always aim to use two or more groups that are as equivalent as possible on all important variables. Sometimes this goal is not feasible, however. Perhaps we are obliged to use existing groups that are not as equivalent as we would like. Or, perhaps during the course of the study we discover inequivalencies between the groups that were not apparent at the beginning.

A statistical method called *analysis of covariance* can be used to compensate for these differences. The mathematics of the method is far beyond the scope of this text, but an explanation can be found in most advanced statistics texts.

Using a Control Group

An "ideal" experiment should use at least one control group in addition to the experimental group. The experimental group may receive an intervention that is withheld from the control group, or equivalent groups may receive different interventions or no interventions at all.

A social worker who initiates a treatment intervention is often interested in knowing what would have happened if the intervention had not been used or had some different intervention been substituted. Would members of a support group for alcoholics have recovered anyway, without the social worker's efforts? Would they have recovered faster or more completely had family counseling been used instead of the support group approach?

The answer to these questions will never be known if only the support group is studied. But, what if another group of alcoholics is included in the research design? In a typical design with a control group, two equivalent groups, 1 and 2, would be formed, and both would be administered the same pretest to determine the initial level of the dependent variable (e.g., degree of alcoholism). Then an intervention would be initiated with Group 1 but not with Group 2. The group treated—Group 1 or the experimental group—would receive the independent variable (the intervention). The group not treated—Group 2 or the control group—would not receive it.

At the conclusion of the intervention, both groups would be given a posttest (the same measure as the pretest). The pretest and posttest consist of the use of some sort of data gathering procedure, such as a survey or self-report measure, to measure the dependent variable before and after the introduction of the independent variable. There are many types of group research designs and there are many ways to graphically display them. In general, group designs can be written in symbols as follows:

$$
\begin{array}{llll}
\text{Experimental Group:} & R & O_1 \; X \; O_2 \\
\text{Control Group:} & R & O_1 \quad\;\; O_2
\end{array}
$$

Where:

R = Random assignment to group

O_1 = First measurement of the dependent variable

X = Independent variable

O_2 = Second measurement of the dependent variable

The two Rs in this design indicate that the research participants were randomly assigned to each group. The symbol X, which, as usual, stands for the independent variable, indicates that an intervention is to be given to the experimental group after the pretest (O_1) and before the posttest (O_2). The absence of X for the control group indicates that the intervention is not to be given to the control group. This design is called a classical experimental design because it comes closest to having all the characteristics necessary for an "ideal" experiment.

Table 12.1 displays results from a research study of this type. If the experimental group is equivalent to the control group, the pretest results should be approximately the same for both groups. Within an acceptable margin of error, 24 is approximately the same as 26. Since the control group has not received the intervention, the posttest results for this group would not be expected to differ appreciably from the pretest results.

In fact, the posttest score, 27, differs little from the pretest score, 26, for the control group. Because the experimental and control groups may be considered equivalent, any rival hypotheses that affected the experimental group would have affected the control group in the same way. No rival hypothesis affected the control group, as indicated by the fact that without the intervention, the pretest and posttest scores did not differ. Therefore, it can be assumed that no rival hypothesis affected the experimental group, either, and the difference between pretest and posttest scores (–44) for the experimental group was probably due to the intervention and not to any other factor.

Randomly Assigning Research Participants to Groups

Once a sample has been selected (see previous chapter), the individuals (or objects or events) in it are randomly assigned to either an experimental or a control group in such a way that the two groups are equivalent. This procedure is known as random assignment or randomization. In random assignment, the word *equivalent* means equal in terms of the variables that are important to the study, such as the clients' motivation for treatment, or problem severity.

If the effect of treatment time on clients' outcomes is being studied, for example, the research design might use one experimental group that is treated for a comparatively longer time, a second experimental group that is treated for a shorter time, and a control group that is not treated at all. If we are concerned that the clients' motivation for treatment might also affect their outcomes, the

Table 12.1   Clients' Outcomes
by Group

Group	Pretest	Posttest	Difference
Experimental	24	68	– 44
Control	26	27	– 1

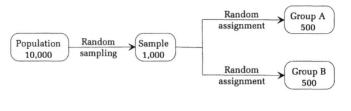

Figure 12.1   Random Sampling and
                     Random Assignment
                     Procedures

research participants can be assigned so that all the groups are equivalent (on the average) in terms of their motivation for treatment.

The process of random sampling from a population followed by random assignment of the sample to groups is illustrated in Figure 12.1. Let us say that the research design calls for a sample size of one-tenth of the population. From a population of 10,000, therefore, a random sampling procedure is used to select a sample of 1,000 individuals.

Then random assignment procedures are used to place the sample of 1,000 into two equivalent groups of 500 individuals each. In theory, Group A will be equivalent to Group B, which will be equivalent to the random sample, which will be equivalent to the population in respect to all important variables contained within the research study.

Matched Pairs

Besides randomization, another, more deliberate method of assigning people or other units to groups involves matching. The matched pairs method is suitable when the composition of each group consists of variables with a range of characteristics. One of the disadvantages of matching is that some individuals cannot be matched and so cannot participate in the study.

Suppose a new training program for teaching parenting skills to foster mothers is being evaluated, and it is important that the experimental and control groups have an equal number of highly skilled and less skilled foster parents before the training program is introduced. The women chosen for the sample would be matched in pairs according to their parenting skill level; the two most skilled foster mothers are matched, then the next two, and so on. One person in each pair of approximately equally skilled foster parents is then randomly assigned to the experimental group and the other is placed in the control group.

Let us suppose that in order to compare the foster mothers exposed to the new training program with women who were not, a standardized measuring instrument that measures parenting skill level (the dependent variable) is administered to a sample of ten women. The scores can range from 100 (excellent parenting skills) to zero (poor parenting skills). Then their scores are rank-ordered from the highest to the lowest, and out of the foster mothers with the two highest scores, one is selected to be assigned to either the experimental group or the control group. It does not make any difference which group our first research participant is randomly assigned to, as long as there is an equal chance that she will go to either the control group or the experimental group. In this example the first person is randomly chosen to go to the experimental group, as illustrated below:

Rank Order of Parenting Skills Scores (in parentheses)
   First Pair:
   — (99) Randomly assigned to the experimental group
   — (98) Assigned to the control group

   Second Pair:
   — (97) Assigned to the control group
   — (96) Assigned to the experimental group

   Third Pair:
   — (95) Assigned to the experimental group
   — (94) Assigned to the control group

   Fourth Pair:
   — (93) Assigned to the control group
   — (92) Assigned to the experimental group

   Fifth Pair:
   — (91) Assigned to the experimental group
   — (90) Assigned to the control group

The foster parent with the highest score (99) is randomly assigned to the experimental group, and this person's "match," with a score of 98, is assigned to the control group. This process is reversed with the next matched pair, where the first person is assigned to the control group and the match is assigned to the experimental group. If the assignment of research participants according to scores is not reversed for every other pair, one group will be higher than the other on the variable being matched.

To illustrate this point, suppose the first participant (highest score) in each match is always assigned to the experimental group. The experimental group's average score would be 95 (99 + 97 + 95 + 93 + 91 = 475/5 = 95), and the control group's average score would be 94 (98 + 96 + 94 + 92 + 90 = 470/5 = 94). If every other matched pair is reversed, however, as in the example, the average scores of the two groups are closer together; 94.6 for the experimental group (99 + 96 + 95 + 92 + 91 = 473/5 = 94.6) and 94.4 for the control group (98 + 97 + 94 + 93 + 90 = 472/5 = 94.4). In short, 94.6 and 94.4 (difference of 0.2) are closer together than 95 and 94 (difference of 1).

INTERNAL AND EXTERNAL VALIDITY

We must remember that the research design we finally select should always be evaluated on how close it comes to an "ideal" experiment in reference to the six characteristics presented at the beginning of this chapter. As stressed throughout this book, most research designs used in social work do not closely resemble an "ideal" experiment. The research design finally selected needs to be evaluated on how well it meets its primary objective—to adequately answer a research question or to test a hypothesis. In short, a research design will be evaluated on how well it controls for:

- Internal validity (Box 12.1, pages 235-239)—the ways in which the research design ensures that the introduction of the independent variable (if any) can be identified as the *sole cause* of change in the dependent variable.
- External validity (Box 12.2, pages 240-241)—the extent to which the research design allows for generalization of the findings of the study to other groups and other situations.

Both internal and external validity are achieved in a research design by taking into account various threats that are inherent in all research efforts. A design for a study with both types of validity will recognize and attempt to control for potential factors that could affect our study's outcome or findings. An "ideal" experiment tries to control as many threats to internal and external validity as possible.

GROUP RESEARCH DESIGNS

While, in a particular case, a group research design may need to be complex to accomplish the purpose of the study, a design that is unnecessarily complex costs more, takes more time, and probably will not serve its purpose nearly as well as a simpler one. In choosing a research design (whether a single case [see next chapter] or group), therefore, the principle of parsimony must be applied: The simplest and most economical route to the objective is the best choice. The three knowledge levels and the group research designs that are usually associated with each are listed in Table 12.2 on page 242.

Box 12.1_____

Threats to Internal Validity

In any explanatory research study, we should be able to conclude from our findings that the independent variable is, or is not, the only cause of change in the dependent variable. If our study does not have internal validity, such a conclusion is not possible, and the study's findings can be misleading.

Internal validity is concerned with one of the requirements for an "ideal" experiment—the control of rival hypotheses, or alternative explanations for what might bring about a change in the dependent variable. The higher the internal validity of any research study, the greater the extent to which rival hypotheses can be controlled; the lower the internal validity, the less they can be controlled. Thus, we must be prepared to rule out the effects of factors other than the independent variable that could influence the dependent variable.

History

The first threat to internal validity, history, refers to any outside event, either public or private, that may affect the dependent variable and was not taken into account in our research design. Many times, it refers to events occurring between the first and second measurement of the dependent variable (the pretest and the posttest). If events occur that have the potential to alter the second measurement, there would be no way of knowing how much (if any) of the observed change in the dependent variable is a function of the independent variable and how much is attributable to these events.

Suppose, for example, we are investigating the effects of an educational program on racial tolerance. We may decide to measure the dependent variable, racial tolerance in the community, before introducing the independent variable, the educational program.

The educational program is then implemented. Since it is the independent variable, it is represented by X. Finally, racial tolerance is measured again, after the program has run its course. This final measurement yields a posttest score, represented by O_2. The one-group pretest-posttest study design can be written as:

$$O_1 \quad X \quad O_2$$

Where:

O_1 = First measurement, or pretest score, of racial tolerance

X = Educational program (independent variable) (see Box 12.3)

O_2 = Second measurement, or posttest score, of racial tolerance

The difference between the values O_2 and O_1 represent the difference in racial tolerance in the community before and after the educational program. If the study is internally valid, $O_2 - O_1$ will be a crude measure of the effect of the educational program on racial tolerance; and this is what we were trying to discover. Suppose, before the posttest could be administered, an outbreak of racial violence, such as the type that occurred in Los Angeles in the summer of 1992, occurred in the community.

Violence can be expected to have a negative effect on racial tolerance, and the posttest scores may, therefore, show a lower level of tolerance than if the violence had not occurred.

The effect, $O_2 - O_1$, will now be the combined effects of the educational program *and* the violence, not the effect of the program alone, as we intended.

Racial violence is an extraneous variable that we could not have anticipated and did not control for when designing the study. Other examples might include an earthquake, an election, illness, divorce, or marriage—any event, public or private that could affect the dependent variable. Any such variable that is unanticipated and uncontrolled for is an example of history.

Maturation

Maturation, the second threat to internal validity, refers to changes, both physical and psychological, that take place in our research participants over time and can affect the

Box 12.1 Continued

dependent variable. Suppose that we are evaluating an interventive strategy designed to improve the behavior of adolescents who engage in delinquent behavior. Since the behavior of adolescents changes naturally as they mature, the observed changed behavior may have been due as much to their natural development as it was to the intervention strategy.

Maturation refers not only to physical or mental growth, however. Over time, people grow older, more or less anxious, more or less bored, and more or less motivated to take part in a research study. All these factors and many more can affect the way in which people respond when the dependent variable is measured a second or third time.

Testing

The third threat to internal validity, testing, is sometimes referred to as the initial measurement effect. Thus, the pretests that are the starting point for many research designs are another potential threat to internal validity. One of the most utilized research designs involves three steps: measuring some dependent variable, such as learning behavior in school or attitudes toward work; initiating a program to change that variable (the independent variable); then measuring the dependent variable again at the conclusion of the program.

This simple one-group pretest-posttest design can be written as follows:

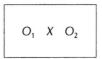

Where:

O_1 = First measurement of the dependent variable, or pretest score

X = Independent variable (see Box 12.3)

O_2 = Second measurement of the dependent variable, or posttest score

The testing effect is the effect that taking a pretest might have on posttest scores. Suppose that Roberto, a research participant, takes a pretest to measure his initial level of racial tolerance before being exposed to a racial tolerance educational program. He might remember some of the questions on the pretest, think about them later, and change his views on racial issues before taking part in the educational program.

After the program, his posttest score will reveal his changed opinions, and we may incorrectly assume that the program was responsible, whereas the true cause was his experience with the pretest.

Sometimes, a pretest induces anxiety in a research participant, so that Roberto receives a worse score on the posttest than he should have; or boredom with the same questions repeated again may be a factor. In order to avoid the testing effect, we may wish to use a design that does not require a pretest.

If a pretest is essential, we then must consider the length of time that elapses between the pretest and posttest measurements. A pretest is far more likely to affect the posttest when the time between the two is short. The nature of the pretest is another factor. Questions dealing with factual matters, such as knowledge levels, may have a larger testing effect because they tend to be more easily recalled.

Instrumentation Error

The fourth threat to internal validity is instrumentation error, which refers to all the troubles that can afflict the measurement process. The instrument may be unreliable or invalid, as presented in Chapter 8. It may be a mechanical instrument, such as an electroencephalogram (EEG), that has malfunctioned. Occasionally, the term *instrumentation error* is used to refer to an observer whose observations are inconsistent; or to measuring instruments, such as the ones presented in Chapter 8, that are reliable in themselves, but not administered properly.

"Administration," with respect to a measuring instrument, means the circumstances under which the measurement is made: where, when, how, and by whom. A mother being asked about her attitudes toward her

Box 12.1 Continued

children, for example, may respond in one way in the social worker's office and in a different way at home when her children are screaming around her feet.

A mother's verbal response may differ from her written response; or she may respond differently in the morning than she would in the evening, or differently alone than she would in a group. These variations in situational responses do not indicate a true change in the feelings, attitudes, or behaviors being measured, but are only examples of instrumentation error.

Statistical Regression

The fifth threat to internal validity, statistical regression, refers to the tendency of extremely low and extremely high scores to regress, or move toward the average score for everyone in the research study. Suppose that a student, named Maryanna, has to take a multiple-choice exam on a subject she knows nothing about. There are many questions, and each question has five possible answers. Since, for each question, Maryanna has a 20 percent (one in five) chance of guessing correctly, she might expect to score 20 percent on the exam just by guessing. If she guesses badly, she will score a lot lower; if well, a lot higher. The other members of the class take the same exam and, since they are all equally uninformed, the average score for the class is 20 percent.

Now suppose that the instructor separates the low scorers from the high scorers and tries to even out the level of the class by giving the low scorers special instruction. In order to determine if the special instruction has been effective, the entire class then takes another multiple-choice exam. The result of the exam is that the low scorers (as a group) do better than they did the first time, and the high scorers (as a group) worse. The instructor believes that this has occurred because the low scorers received special instruction and the high scorers did not.

According to the logic of statistical regression, however, both the average score of the low scorers (as a group) and the average score of the high scorers (as a group) would move toward the total average score for both groups (i.e., high and low).

Even without any special instruction and still in their state of ignorance, the low scorers (as a group) would be expected to have a higher average score than they did before. Likewise, the high scorers (as a group) would be expected to have a lower average score than they did before.

It would be easy for the research instructor to assume that the low scores had increased because of the special instruction and the high scores had decreased because of the lack of it. Not necessarily so, however; the instruction may have had nothing to do with it. It may all be due to statistical regression.

Differential Selection of Research Participants

The sixth threat to internal validity is differential selection of research participants. To some extent, the participants selected for a research study are different from one another to begin with. "Ideal" experiments, however, require random sampling from a population (if at all possible) and random assignment to groups.

This assures that the results of a study will be generalizable to a larger population, thus addressing threats to external validity. In respect to differential selection as a threat to internal validity, "ideal" experiments control for this since equivalency among the groups at pretest is assumed through the randomization process.

This threat is, however, present when we are working with preformed groups or groups that already exist, such as classes of students, self-help groups, or community groups. In terms of the external validity of such designs, because there is no way of knowing whether the preformed groups are representative of any larger population, it is not possible to generalize the study's results beyond the people (or objects or events) that were actually studied. The use of preformed groups also affects the internal validity of a study, though. It is probable that different preformed groups will not be equivalent with respect to relevant variables, and that these initial differences will invalidate the results of the posttest.

A child abuse prevention educational program for children in schools might be evaluated by comparing the prevention skills of one group of children who have experi-

Box 12.1 Continued_____

enced the educational program with the skills of a second group who have not. In order to make a valid comparison, the two groups must be as similar as possible, with respect to age, gender, intelligence, socioeconomic status, and anything else that might affect the acquisition of child abuse prevention skills.

We would have to make every effort to form or select equivalent groups, but the groups are sometimes not as equivalent as might be hoped—especially if we are obliged to work with preformed groups, such as classes of students or community groups. If the two groups are different before the intervention was introduced, there is not much point in comparing them at the end.

Accordingly, preformed groups should be avoided whenever possible. If it is not feasible to do this, rigorous pretesting must be done to determine in what ways the groups are (or are not) equivalent, and differences must be compensated for with the use of statistical methods.

Mortality

The seventh threat to internal validity is mortality, which simply means that individual research participants may drop out before the end of the study. Their absence will probably have a significant effect on the study's findings because people who drop out are likely to be different in some ways from the other participants who stay in the study. People who drop out may be less motivated to participate in the intervention than people who stay in, for example.

Since dropouts often have such characteristics in common, it cannot be assumed that the attrition occurred in a random manner. If considerably more people drop out of one group than out of the other, the result will be two groups that are no longer equivalent and cannot be usefully compared.

We cannot know at the beginning of the study how many people will drop out, but we can watch to see how many do. Mortality is never problematic if dropout rates are 5 percent or less *and* if the dropout rates are similar for the various groups.

Reactive Effects of Research Participants

The eighth threat to internal validity is reactive effects. Changes in the behaviors or feelings of research participants may be caused by their reaction to the novelty of the situation or the knowledge that they are participating in a research study. A mother practicing communication skills with her child, for example, may try especially hard when she knows the social worker is watching. We may wrongly believe that such reactive effects are due to the independent variable.

The classic example of reactive effects was found in a series of studies carried out at the Hawthorne plant of the Western Electric Company in Chicago many years ago. Researchers were investigating the relationship between working conditions and productivity. When they increased the level of lighting in one section of the plant, productivity increased; a further increase in the lighting was followed by an additional increase in productivity.

When the lighting was then decreased, however, production levels did not fall accordingly but continued to rise. The conclusion was that the workers were increasing their productivity not because of the lighting level but because of the attention they were receiving as research participants in the study.

The term *Hawthorne effect* is still used to describe any situation in which the research participants' behaviors are influenced not by the independent variable but by the knowledge that they are taking part in a research project. Another example of such a reactive effect is the placebo given to patients, which produces beneficial results because they believe it is medication.

Reactive effects can be controlled by ensuring that all participants in a research study, in both the experimental and control groups, appear to be treated equally. If one group is to be shown an educational film, for example, the other group should also be shown a film—some film carefully chosen to bear no relationship to the variable being investigated. If the study involves a change in the participants' routine, this in itself may be enough to change behavior, and care must be taken to continue the study until novelty has ceased to be a factor.

Box 12.1 Continued

Interaction Effects

Interaction among the various threats to internal validity can have an effect of its own. Any of the factors already described as threats may interact with one another, but the most common interactive effect involves differential selection and maturation.

Let us say we are studying two groups of clients who are being treated for depression. The intention was for these groups to be equivalent, in terms of both their motivation for treatment and their levels of depression. It turns out that Group A is more generally depressed than Group B, however. Whereas both groups may grow less motivated over time, it is likely that Group A, whose members were more depressed to begin with, will lose motivation more completely and more quickly than Group B. Inequivalent groups thus grow less equivalent over time as a result of the interaction between differential selection and maturation.

Relations Between Experimental and Control Groups

The final group of threats to internal validity has to do with the effects of the use of experimental and control groups that receive different interventions. These effects include: (1) diffusion of treatments, (2) compensatory equalization, (3) compensatory rivalry, and (4) demoralization.

Diffusion of Treatments

Diffusion, or imitation, of treatments may occur when the experimental and control groups talk to each other about the study. Suppose a study is designed that presents a new relaxation exercise to the experimental group and nothing at all to the control group. There is always the possibility that one of the participants in the experimental group will explain the exercise to a friend who happens to be in the control group. The friend explains it to another friend, and so on. This might be beneficial for the control group, but it invalidates the study's findings.

Compensatory Equalization

Compensatory equalization of treatment occurs when the person doing the study and/or the staff member administering the intervention to the experimental group feels sorry for people in the control group who are not receiving it and attempts to compensate them.

A social worker might take a control group member aside and covertly demonstrate the relaxation exercise, for example. On the other hand, if our study has been ethically designed, there should be no need for guilt on the part of the social worker because some people are not being taught to relax. They can be taught to relax when our study is "officially" over.

Compensatory Rivalry

Compensatory rivalry is an effect that occurs when the control group becomes motivated to compete with the experimental group. For example, a control group in a program to encourage parental involvement in school activities might get wind that something is up and make a determined effort to participate too, on the basis that "anything they can do, we can do better." There is no direct communication between groups, as in the diffusion of treatment effect—only rumors and suggestions of rumors. However, rumors are often enough to threaten the internal validity of a study.

Demoralization

In direct contrast with compensatory rivalry, demoralization refers to feelings of deprivation among the control group that may cause them to give up and drop out of the study, in which case this effect would be referred to as mortality. The people in the control group may also get angry.

Source: Grinnell and Stothers (1988); Grinnell and Williams (1990); Grinnell (1993a); Williams, Tutty, and Grinnell (1995); Grinnell and Unrau (1997); and Williams, Unrau, and Grinnell (1998)

Box 12.2

Threats to External Validity

External validity is the degree to which the results of our research study are generalizable to a larger population or to settings outside the research situation or setting.

Pretest-Treatment Interaction

The first threat to external validity, pretest-treatment interaction, is similar to the testing threat to internal validity. The nature of a pretest can alter the way research participants respond to the experimental treatment, as well as to the posttest. Suppose, for example, that an educational program on racial tolerance is being evaluated.

A pretest that measures the level of tolerance could well alert the participants to the fact that they are going to be educated into loving all their neighbors, but many people do not want to be "educated" into anything. They are satisfied with the way they feel and will resist the instruction. This will affect the level of racial tolerance registered on the posttest.

Selection-Treatment Interaction

The second threat to external validity is selection-treatment interaction. This threat commonly occurs when a research design cannot provide for random selection of participants from a population. Suppose we wanted to study the effectiveness of a family service agency staff, for example. If our research proposal was turned down by 50 agencies before it was accepted by the 51st, it is very likely that the accepting agency differs in certain important aspects from the other 50.

It may accept the proposal because its social workers are more highly motivated, more secure, more satisfied with their jobs, or more interested in the practical application of the study than the average agency staff member.

As a result, we would be assessing the research participants on the very factors for which they were unwittingly (and by default) selected—motivation, job satisfaction, and so on. The study may be internally valid, but, since it will not be possible to generalize the results to other family service agencies, it would have little external validity.

Specificity of Variables

Specificity of variables has to do with the fact that a research project conducted with a specific group of people at a specific time and in a specific setting may not always be generalizable to other people at a different time and in a different setting.

For example, a measuring instrument developed to measure the IQ levels of upper-socioeconomic level, Caucasian, suburban children does not provide an equally accurate measure of IQ when it is applied to lower-socioeconomic level children of racial minorities in the inner city.

Reactive Effects

The fourth threat to external validity is reactive effects which, as with internal validity, occur when the attitudes or behaviors of our research participants are affected to some degree by the very act of taking a pretest. Thus, they are no longer exactly equivalent to the population from which they were randomly selected, and it may not be possible to generalize our study's results to that population. Because pretests affect research participants to some degree, our results may be valid only for those who were pretested.

Multiple-Treatment Interference

The fifth threat to external validity, multiple-treatment interference, occurs if a research participant is given two or more interventions in succession, so that the results of the first intervention may affect the results of the second one. A client attending treatment sessions, for example, may not seem to benefit from one therapeutic technique, so another is tried.

In fact, however, the client may have benefitted from the first technique but the benefit does not become apparent until the second technique has been tried. As a result,

Box 12.2 Continued_____

the effects of both techniques become commingled, or the results may be erroneously ascribed to the second technique alone.

Because of this threat, interventions should be given separately if possible. If our research design does not allow this, sufficient time should be allowed to elapse between the two interventions in an effort to minimize the possibility of multiple-treatment interference.

Researcher Bias

The final threat to external validity is researcher bias. Researchers, like people in general, tend to see what they want to see or expect to see. Unconsciously and without any thought of deceit, they may manipulate a study so that the actual results agree with the anticipated results. A practitioner may favor an intervention so strongly that the research study is structured to support it, or the results are interpreted favorably.

If we know which individuals are in the experimental group and which are in the control group, this knowledge alone might affect the study's results. Students who an instructor believes to be bright, for example, often are given higher grades than their performance warrants, while students believed to be dull are given lower grades.

The way to control for such researcher bias is to perform a double-blind experiment in which neither the research participants nor the researcher knows who is in the experimental or control group or who is receiving a specific treatment intervention.

_____

Source: Grinnell and Stothers (1988); Grinnell and Williams (1990); Grinnell (1993a); Williams, Tutty, and Grinnell (1995); Grinnell and Unrau (1997); and Williams, Unrau, and Grinnell (1998)

Exploratory Designs

At the lowest level of the continuum of knowledge that can be derived from research studies are exploratory group research designs. An exploratory study explores a research question about which little is already known, in order to uncover generalizations and develop hypotheses that can be investigated and tested later with more precise and, hence, more complex designs and data gathering techniques.

The four examples of exploratory designs given in this section do not use pretests; they simply measure the dependent variable only after the independent variable has been introduced. Therefore, they cannot be used to determine whether changes took place in the study's research participants; these designs simply describe the state of the research participants after they had received the independent variable (if any—see Box 12.3).

There does not necessarily have to be an independent variable in a study, however; we may just want to measure some variable in a particular population such as the number of people who receive AFDC benefits over a 10-year period. In this situation, there is no independent or dependent variable.

Table 12.2   Knowledge Levels and Corresponding
              Research Designs

Knowledge Levels	Research Designs
1. Exploratory	a: One-group posttest-only b: Multigroup posttest-only c: Longitudinal case study d: Longitudinal survey
2. Descriptive	a: Randomized one-group posttest-only b: Randomized cross-sectional and longitudinal survey c: One-group pretest-posttest d: Comparison group posttest-only e: Comparison group pretest-posttest f: Interrupted time-series
3. Explanatory	a: Classical experimental b: Solomon four-group c: Randomized posttest-only control group

One-Group Posttest-Only Design

The one-group posttest-only design (Design 1a) is sometimes called the one-shot case study or cross-sectional case study design. It is the simplest of all the group research designs.

Suppose in a particular community, Rome, Wisconsin, there are numerous parents who are physically abusive toward their children. The city decides to hire a school social worker, Antonia, to implement a program that is supposed to reduce the number of parents who physically abuse their children. She conceptualizes a 12-week child abuse prevention program (the intervention) and offers it to parents who have children in her school who wish to participate on a voluntary basis. A simple research study is then conducted to answer the question, "Did the parents who completed the program stop physically abusing their children?" The answer to this question will determine the success of the intervention.

There are many different ways in which this program can be evaluated. For now, and to make matters as simple as possible, we are going to evaluate it by simply counting how many parents stopped physically abusing their children after they attended the program.

At the simplest level, the program could be evaluated with a one-group posttest-only design. The basic elements of this design can be written as follows:

$$X \quad O_1$$

Where:

X = Independent variable (Child Abuse Prevention Program, the intervention) (see Box 12.3)

O_1 = First and only measurement of the dependent variable (number of parents who stopped physically abusing their children, the program's outcome, or program objective)

All that this design provides is a single measure (O_1) of what happens when one group of people is subjected to one treatment or experience (X). The program's participants were not randomly selected from any particular population, and, thus, the results of the findings cannot be generalized to any other group or population.

It is safe to assume that all the members within the program had physically abused their children before they enrolled, since people who do not have this problem would not enroll in such a program. But, even if the value of O_1 indicates that some of the parents did stop being violent with their children after the program, it cannot be determined whether they quit because of the intervention (the program) or because of some other rival hypothesis.

Perhaps a law was passed that made it mandatory for the police to arrest anyone who behaves violently toward his or her child, or perhaps the local television station started to report such incidents on the nightly news, complete with pictures of the abusive parent. These other extraneous variables may have been more important in persuading the parents to cease their abusive behavior toward their children than their voluntary participation in the program. In sum, this design does not control for many of the threats to either internal or external validity. In terms of internal validity, the threats that are not controlled for in this design are history, maturation, differential selection, and mortality.

Cross-Sectional Survey Design   Let us take another example of a one-group posttest-only design that *does not* have an independent or dependent variable. In survey research, this kind of a group research design is called a cross-sectional survey design.

Box 12.3_____

Treatment: A Variable or a Constant?

For instructional purposes, group designs are displayed using symbols where X is the independent variable (treatment) and O is the measure of the dependent variable. This presentation is accurate when studies are designed with two or more groups. When one-group designs are used, however, this interpretation does not hold. In one-group designs, the treatment, or program, cannot truly vary because all research participants have experienced the same event; that is, they all have experienced the program. Without a comparison or control group, treatment is considered a constant because it is a quality shared by all members in the research study. In short, *time* is the independent variable.

In doing a cross-sectional survey, we survey *only once* a cross-section of some particular population. In addition to Antonia's child abuse prevention program geared for abusive parents, she may also want to start another program geared for all the children in the school (whether they come from abusive families or not)—a child abuse educational program taught to children in the school.

Before Antonia starts the program geared for the children, however, she wants to know what parents think about the idea. She may send out questionnaires to all the parents or she may decide to personally telephone every second parent, or every fifth or tenth, depending on how much time and money she has. The results of her survey constitute a single measurement, or observation, of the parents' opinions of her second proposed program (the one for the children) and may be written as:

$$\boxed{O_1}$$

The symbol O_1 represents the entire cross-sectional survey design since such a design involves making only a single observation, or measurement, at one time period. Note that there is no X, as there is really no independent variable. Antonia only wants to ascertain the parents' attitudes toward her proposed program—nothing more, nothing less.

Multigroup Posttest-Only Design

The multigroup posttest-only design (Design 1b) is an elaboration of the one-group posttest-only design (Design 1a) in which more than one group is used. To check a bit further into the effectiveness of Antonia's program for parents who have been physically abusive toward their children, for example, she might decide to locate several more groups of parents who had completed her program and see how many of them had stopped abusing their children—and so on, with any number of groups. This design can be written in symbols as follows:

$$
\begin{array}{lll}
\text{Experimental Group 1:} & X & O_1 \\
\text{Experimental Group 2:} & X & O_1 \\
\text{Experimental Group 3:} & X & O_1 \\
\text{Experimental Group 4:} & X & O_1 \\
\end{array}
$$

Where:

> X = Independent variable (Child Abuse Prevention Program, the intervention) (see Box 12.3)
>
> O_1 = First and only measurement of the dependent variable (number of parents who stopped physically abusing their children, the program's outcome, or program objective)

With the multigroup design it cannot be assumed that all four Xs (the independent variables) are equivalent because the four programs might not be exactly the same; one group might have had a different facilitator, the program might have been presented differently, or the material could have varied in important respects.

In addition, nothing is known about whether any of the research participants would have stopped being violent anyway, even without the program. It certainly cannot be assumed that any of the groups were representative of the larger population. Thus, as in the case of the one-group posttest-only design, the same threats to the internal and the external validity of the study might influence the results of the multigroup posttest design.

Longitudinal Case Study Design

The longitudinal case study design (Design 1c) is exactly like the one-group posttest-only design (Design 1a), except that it provides for more measurements of the dependent variable (Os). This design can be written in symbols as follows:

$$X \ \ O_1 \ \ O_2 \ \ O_3 \ldots$$

Where:

> X = Independent variable (Child Abuse Prevention Program, the intervention) (see Box 12.3)
>
> O_1 = First measurement of the dependent variable (number of parents who stopped physically abusing their children, the program's outcome, or program objective)
>
> O_2 = Second measurement of the dependent variable (number of parents who stopped physically abusing their children, the program's outcome, or program objective)

O_3 = Third measurement of the dependent variable (number of parents who stopped physically abusing their children, the program's outcome, or program objective)

Suppose that, in our example, Antonia is interested in the long-term effects of the child abuse prevention program. Perhaps the program was effective in helping some people to stop physically abusing their children, but will they continue to refrain from abusing their children? One way to find out is to measure the number of parents who physically abuse their children at intervals—say at the end of the program, the first three months after the program, then the next three months after that, and every three months for the next two years.

Design 1c can be used to monitor the effectiveness of treatment interventions over time and can be applied not just to groups but also to single-client systems, as described in Chapters 13 and 23. However, all of the same threats to the internal and external validity that were described in relation to the previous two exploratory designs also apply to this design.

Longitudinal Survey Design

Unlike cross-sectional surveys, where the variable of interest (usually the dependent variable) is measured only once, longitudinal surveys (Design 1d) provide data at various points so that changes can be monitored over time. Longitudinal survey designs can be written as:

$$O_1 \quad O_2 \quad O_3$$

Where:

O_1 = First measurement of some variable
O_2 = Second measurement of some variable
O_3 = Third measurement of some variable

Longitudinal survey designs usually have no independent and dependent variables and can be broken down into three types: (1) trend studies, (2) cohort studies, and (3) panel studies.

Trend Studies   A trend study is used to find out how a population, or sample, changes over time. Antonia, the school social worker mentioned previously in this chapter and in the last one, may want to know if parents of young children enrolled in her school are becoming more receptive to the idea of the school teaching their children child abuse prevention education in the second grade (Williams, Tutty, & Grinnell, 1995). She may survey all the parents of Grade 2 children this year, all the parents of the new complement of Grade 2 children next year, and so on until she thinks she has sufficient data.

Each year the parents surveyed will be different, but they will all be parents of Grade 2 children. In this way, Antonia will be able to determine whether parents are becoming more receptive to the idea of introducing child abuse prevention material to their children as early as Grade 2. In other words, she will be able to measure any attitudinal trend that is, or is not, occurring. The research design can still be written:

$$O_1 \quad O_2 \quad O_3$$

Where:

O_1 = First measurement of some variable for a sample

O_2 = Second measurement of some variable for a different sample

O_3 = Third measurement of some variable for yet another different sample

Cohort Studies   Cohort studies are used over time to follow a group of people who have shared a similar experience—for example, AIDS survivors, sexual abuse survivors, or parents of grade-school children. Perhaps Antonia is interested in knowing whether parents' attitudes toward the school offering abuse prevention education to second-grade students change as their children grow older. She may survey a sample of the Grade 2 parents who attend a Parent Night this year, and survey a different sample of parents who attend a similar meeting for the same parents next year, when their children are in Grade 3.

The following year, when the children are in Grade 4, she will take another, different sample of those parents who attend Parent Night. Although different parents are being surveyed every year, they all belong to the same population of parents whose children are progressing through the grades together. The selection of the samples was not random, though, because parents who take the time to attend Parent Night may be different from those who stay at home. The research design may be written:

$$O_1 \quad O_2 \quad O_3$$

Where:

O_1 = First measurement of some variable for a sample drawn from some population

O_2 = Second measurement of some variable for a different sample drawn from the same population one year later

O_3 = Third measurement of some variable for a still different sample, drawn from the same population after two years

Panel Studies   In a panel study, the *same individuals* are followed over a period of time. Antonia might select one particular sample of parents, for example, and measure their attitudes toward child abuse prevention education in successive years. Again, the design can be written:

$$O_1 \quad O_2 \quad O_3$$

Where:

O_1 = First measurement of some variable for a sample of individuals

O_2 = Second measurement of some variable for the same sample of individuals one year later

O_3 = Third measurement of some variable for the same sample of individuals after two years

A trend study is interested in broad trends over time, whereas a cohort study provides data about people who have shared similar experiences. In neither case do we know anything about *individual* contributions to the changes that are being measured. A panel study provides data that we can use to look at change over time as experienced by particular individuals.

Descriptive Designs

At the midpoint of the knowledge continuum are descriptive designs, which have some but not all of the requirements of an "ideal" experiment. They usually require specification of the time order of variables, manipulation of the independent variable, and establishment of the relationship between the independent and dependent variables.

They may also control for rival hypotheses and use a second group as a comparison (not a control). The requirement that descriptive designs lack most frequently is the random assignment of research participants to two or more groups.

We are seldom in a position to randomly assign research participants to either an experimental or control group. Sometimes the groups to be studied are already in existence; sometimes ethical issues are involved. It would be unethical, for example, to assign clients who need immediate help to two random groups, only one of which is to receive the intervention. Since a lack of random assignment will affect the internal and external validities of the study, the descriptive research design must try to compensate for this.

Randomized One-Group Posttest-Only Design

The distinguishing feature of the randomized one-group posttest-only design (Design 2a) is that members of the group are randomly selected for it. Otherwise, this design is identical to the exploratory one-group posttest-only design (Design 1a). The randomized one-group posttest-only design is written as follows:

$$R \quad X \quad O_1$$

Where:

R = Random selection from a population

X = Independent variable (see Box 12.3)

O_1 = First and only measurement of the dependent variable

In the example of the child abuse prevention program, the difference in this design is that the group does not accidentally assemble itself by including anyone who happened to be interested in volunteering for the program. Instead, group members are randomly selected from a population, say, of all the 400 parents who were reported to child welfare authorities for having physically abused a child and who wish to receive voluntary treatment in Rome, Wisconsin, in 1997. These 400 parents comprise the population of all the physically abusive parents who wish to receive treatment in Rome, Wisconsin.

The sampling frame of 400 people is used to select a simple random sample of 40 physically abusive parents who voluntarily wish to receive treatment. The program (X) is administered to these 40 people, and the number of parents who stopped being abusive toward their children after the program is determined (O_1). The design can be written as:

$$R \quad X \quad O_1$$

Where:

R = Random selection of 40 people from the population of physically abusive parents who voluntarily wish to receive treatment in Rome, Wisconsin

X = Child Abuse Prevention Program (see Box 12.3)

O_1 = Number of parents in the program who stopped being physically abusive to their children

Say that the program fails to have the desired effect, and 39 of the 40 people continue to physically harm their children after participating in the program. Because the program was ineffective for the sample and the sample was randomly selected, it can be concluded that it would be ineffective for the physically abusive parent population of Rome, Wisconsin—the other 360 who did not go through the program. In other words, because a representative random sample was selected, it is possible to generalize the program's results to the population from which the sample was drawn.

Since no change in the dependent variable occurred, it is not sensible to consider the control of rival hypotheses. Antonia need not wonder what might have caused the change—X, her program, or an alternative explanation. If her program had been successful, however, it would not be possible to ascribe her success solely to the program.

Randomized Cross-Sectional and Longitudinal Survey Design

As discussed earlier, a cross-sectional survey obtains data only once from a sample of a particular population. If the sample is a random sample—that is, if it represents the population from which it was drawn—then the data obtained from the sample can be generalized to the entire population. A cross-sectional survey design using a random sample can be written:

$$R \quad O_1$$

Where:

R = Random sample drawn from a population

O_1 = First and only measurement of the dependent variable (see Box 12.3)

Explanatory surveys look for associations between variables. Often, the suspected reason for the relationship is that one variable caused the other. In Antonia's case, she has two studies going on: the child abuse prevention program for parents who have physically abused their children, and her survey of parental attitudes toward the school that is teaching second-grade children child abuse prevention strategies. The success of the child abuse prevention program (her program) may have caused parents to adopt more positive attitudes toward the school in teaching their children child abuse prevention (her survey). In this situation, the two variables, the program and survey, become commingled.

Demonstrating causality is a frustrating business at the best of times because it is so difficult to show that nothing apart from the independent variable could have caused the observed change in the dependent variable. Even supposing that this problem is solved, it is impossible to demonstrate causality unless data are obtained from random samples and are generalizable to entire populations.

One-Group Pretest-Posttest Design

The one-group pretest-posttest design (Design 2c) is also referred to as a before-after design because it includes a pretest of the dependent variable, which can be used as a basis of comparison with the posttest results. It is written as:

$$O_1 \ X \ O_2$$

Where:

O_1 = First measurement of the dependent variable

X = Independent variable, the intervention (see Box 12.3)

O_2 = Second measurement of the dependent variable

The one-group pretest-posttest design, in which a pretest precedes the introduction of the independent variable and a posttest follows it, can be used to determine precisely how the independent variable affects a particular group. The design is used often in social work decision making—far too often, in fact, because it does not control for many rival hypotheses. The difference between O_1 and O_2, on which these decisions are based, therefore, could be due to many other factors rather than the independent variable.

Let us take another indicator of how Antonia's child abuse prevention program could be evaluated. Besides counting the number of parents who stopped physically abusing their children as the only indicator of the program's success, she could have a second outcome indicator such as reducing the parents' risk for abusive and neglecting parenting behaviors. This dependent variable could be easily measured by an instrument that measures their attitudes of physical punishment of children.

Let us say that Antonia had the parents complete the instrument *before* the child abuse prevention program (O_1) and *after* it (O_2). In this example, history would be a rival hypothesis or threat to internal validity because all kinds of things could have happened between O_1 and O_2 to affect the participants' behaviors and feelings—such as the television station deciding to publicize the names of parents who are abusive to their children. Testing also could be a problem. Just the experience of taking the pretest could motivate some participants to stop being abusive toward their children. Maturation—in this example, the children becoming more mature with age so that they became less difficult to discipline—would be a further threat.

This design controls for the threat of differential selection, since the participants are the same for both pretest and posttest. Second, mortality would not affect the outcome, because it is the differential drop-out between groups that causes this threat and, in this example, there is only one group (Williams, Tutty, & Grinnell, 1995).

Comparison Group Posttest-Only Design

The comparison group posttest-only design (Design 2d) improves on the exploratory one-group and multigroup posttest-only designs by introducing a comparison group that does not receive the independent variable, but is subject to the same posttest as those who do (the experimental group).

A group used for purposes of comparison is usually referred to as a comparison group in an exploratory or descriptive design and as a control group in an explanatory design. While a control group is always randomly assigned, a comparison group is not. The basic elements of the comparison group posttest-only design are as follows:

```
Experimental Group:  X   O₁
Comparison Group:        O₁
```

Where:

X = Independent variable, the intervention

O_1 = First and only measurement of the dependent variable

In Antonia's child abuse prevention program, if the January, April, and August sections are scheduled but the August sessions are canceled for some reason, those who would have been participants in that section could be used as a comparison group. If the values of O_1 on the measuring instrument were similar for the experimental and comparison groups, it could be concluded that the program was of little use, since those who had experienced it (those receiving X) were not much better or worse off than those who had not.

A problem with drawing this conclusion, however, is that there is no evidence that the groups were equivalent to begin with. Selection, mortality, and the interaction of selection and other threats to internal validity are, thus, the major difficulties with this design. The comparison group does, however, control for such threats as history, testing, instrumentation, and statistical regression.

Comparison Group Pretest-Posttest Design

The comparison group pretest-posttest design (Design 2e) elaborates on the one-group pretest-posttest design (Design 2c) by adding a comparison group. This second group receives both the pretest (O_1) and the posttest (O_2) at the same time as the experimental group, but it does not receive the independent variable. This design is written as follows:

```
Experimental Group:  O₁   X   O₂
Comparison Group:    O₁       O₂
```

Where:

O_1 = First measurement of the dependent variable, the parents' scores on the measuring instrument

X = Independent variable, the intervention

O_2 = Second measurement of the dependent variable, the parents' scores on the measuring instrument

The experimental and comparison groups formed under this design will probably not be equivalent, because members are not randomly assigned to them. The pretest scores, however, will indicate the extent of their differences. If the differences are not statistically significant, but are still large enough to affect the posttest, the statistical technique of analysis of covariance can be used to compensate for this. As long as the groups are equivalent at pretest, then, this design controls for nearly all of the threats to internal validity. But, because random selection and assignment were not used, the external validity threats remain.

Interrupted Time-Series Design

In the interrupted time-series design (Design 2f), a series of pretests and posttests are conducted on a group of research participants over time, both before and after the independent variable is introduced. The basic elements of this design are illustrated as follows:

$$O_1 \; O_2 \; O_3 \; X \; O_4 \; O_5 \; O_6$$

Where:

Os = Measurements of the dependent variable

X = Independent variable (see Box 12.3)

This design takes care of the major weakness in the descriptive one-group pretest-posttest design (Design 2c), which does not control for rival hypotheses. Suppose, for example, that a new policy is to be introduced into an agency whereby all promotions and raises are to be tied to the number of educational credits acquired by social workers. Since there is a strong feeling among some workers that years of experience should count for more than educational credits, the agency's management decides to examine the effect of the new policy on morale.

Because agency morale is affected by many things and varies normally from month to month, it is necessary to ensure that these normal fluctuations are not confused with the results of the new policy. Therefore, a baseline is first established for morale by conducting a number of pretests over, say, a six-month period before the policy is introduced. Then, a similar number of posttests is conducted over the six months following the introduction of the policy. This design would be written as follows:

$$O_1 \ \ O_2 \ \ O_3 \ \ O_4 \ \ O_5 \ \ O_6 \ \ X \ \ O_7 \ \ O_8 \ \ O_9 \ \ O_{10} \ \ O_{11} \ \ O_{12}$$

The same type of time-series design can be used to evaluate the result of a treatment intervention with a client or client system, as in case-level designs described in Chapter 23. Again, without randomization, threats to external validity still could affect the results, but most of the threats to internal validity are addressed.

Explanatory Designs

Explanatory group research designs approach the "ideal" experiment most closely. They are at the highest level of the knowledge continuum, have the most rigid requirements, and are most able to produce results that can be generalized to other people and situations. Explanatory designs, therefore, are most able to provide valid and reliable research results that can serve as additions to our professions' knowledge base.

The purpose of an explanatory design is to establish a causal connection between the independent and dependent variable. The value of the dependent variable could always result from chance rather than from the influence of the independent variable, but there are statistical techniques for calculating the probability that this will occur.

Classical Experimental Design

The classical experimental design (Design 3a) is the basis for all the experimental designs. It involves an experimental group and a control group, both created by a random assignment method (and if possible, random selection from a population). Both groups take a pretest (O_1) at the same time, after which the independent variable (X) is given only to the experimental group, and then both groups take the posttest (O_2). This design is written as follows:

> Experimental Group: R O_1 X O_2
> Control Group: R O_1 O_2

Where:

R = Random selection from a population and random assignment to group

O_1 = First measurement of the dependent variable

X = Independent variable, the intervention

O_2 = Second measurement of the dependent variable

Because the experimental and control groups have been randomly assigned, they are equivalent with respect to all important variables. This group equivalence in the design helps control for rival hypotheses, because both groups would be affected by them in the same way.

Solomon Four-Group Design

The Solomon four-group research design (Design 3b) involves four rather than two randomly assigned groups as in Design 3a. There are two experimental groups and two control groups, but the pretest is taken by only one of each of these groups. Experimental Group 1 takes a pretest, receives the independent variable, and then takes a posttest. Experimental Group 2 also receives the independent variable but takes only the posttest. The same is true for the two control groups; Control Group 1 takes both the pretest and posttest, and Control Group 2 takes only the posttest. This design is written in symbols as follows:

> Experimental Group 1: R O_1 X O_2
> Control Group 1: R O_1 O_2
> Experimental Group 2: R X O_2
> Control Group 2: R O_2

Where:

R = Random assignment to group
O_1 = First measurement of the dependent variable
X = Independent variable, the intervention
O_2 = Second measurement of the dependent variable

The advantage of the Solomon four-group research design is that it allows for the control of testing effects, since one of the experimental groups and one of the control groups do not take the pretest. All of the threats to internal validity are addressed when this design is used. It has the disadvantage that twice as many study participants are required, and it is considerably more work to implement than the classical experimental design.

Randomized Posttest-Only Control Group Design

The randomized posttest-only control group research design (Design 3c) is identical to the descriptive comparison group posttest-only design (Design 2d), except that the research participants are randomly assigned to two groups. This design, therefore, has a control group rather than a comparison group.

The randomized posttest-only control group research design usually involves only two groups, one experimental and one control. There are no pretests. The experimental group receives the independent variable and takes the posttest; the control group only takes the posttest. This design can be written as follows:

Experimental Group: R X O_1
Control Group: R O_1

Where:

R = Random selection from a population and random assignment to group
X = Independent variable, the intervention
O_1 = First and only measurement of the dependent variable

Suppose we want to test the effects of two different treatment interventions, X_1 and X_2. In this case, Design 3c could be elaborated upon to form three randomly assigned groups, two experimental groups (one for each intervention) and one control group. This design would be written as follows:

Experimental Group 1: R X_1 O_1
Experimental Group 2: R X_2 O_1
Control Group: R O_1

Where:

R = Random selection from a population and random assignment to group

X_1 = Different independent variable than X_2

X_2 = Different independent variable than X_1

O_1 = First and only measurement of the dependent variable

In addition to measuring change in a group or groups, a pretest also helps to ensure equivalence between the control and experimental groups. As you know, this design does not have a pretest. The groups have been randomly assigned, however, as indicated by R, and this, in itself, is theoretically enough to ensure equivalence without the need for a confirmatory pretest. This design is useful in situations where it is not possible to conduct a pretest or where a pretest would be expected to strongly influence the results of the posttest due to the effects of testing. This design also controls for many of the threats to internal validity.

SUMMARY

Group research designs are conducted with groups of cases rather than on a case-by-case basis. They cover the entire range of research questions and provide designs that can be used to gain knowledge on the exploratory, descriptive, and explanatory levels.

A group research study is said to be internally valid if any changes in the dependent variable, Y, result only from the introduction of an independent variable, X. In order to demonstrate internal validity, we must first document the time order of events. Next, we must identify and eliminate extraneous variables. Finally, we must control for the factors that threaten internal validity. In summary, threats to the internal validity of a research design address the assumption that changes in the dependent variable are solely because of the independent variable. "Ideal" experimental designs account for virtually all threats to internal validity—a rarity in social work research studies.

External validity is the degree to which the results of a research study are generalizable to a larger population or to settings other than the research setting. If a research study is to be externally valid, we must be able to demonstrate conclusively that the sample we selected was representative of the population from which it was drawn. If two or more groups are used in the study, we must be able to show that the two groups were equivalent at the beginning of the study.

Most importantly, we must be able to demonstrate that nothing happened during the course of the study, except for the introduction of the independent variable, to change either the representativeness of the sample or the equivalence of the groups.

The degree of control we try to exert over threats to internal and external validity varies according to the research design. Threats to internal and external validity may be more or less problematic depending on what particular research design we select. When we design a study, we must be aware of which threats will turn into real problems and what can be done to prevent or at least to minimize them. When doing an exploratory study, for example, we will not be much concerned about threats to external validity because an exploratory study is not expected to have any external validity anyway. Nor do we attempt to control very rigorously for threats to internal validity.

When we use a descriptive research design, we might be trying to determine whether two or more variables are associated. Often, descriptive designs are employed when we are unable, for practical reasons, to use the more rigorous explanatory designs. We do our best to control for threats to internal validity because, unless we can demonstrate internal validity, we cannot show that the variables are associated.

When using explanatory designs, we are attempting to show causation; that is, we are trying to show that changes in one variable cause changes in another. We try hard to control threats to internal validity because, if the study is not internally valid, we cannot demonstrate causation. We would also like the results of the study to be as generally applicable as possible and, to this end, we do our best to control for threats to external validity.

Exploratory designs are used when little is known about the field of study and data are gathered in an effort to find out "what's out there." These ideas are then used to generate hypotheses that can be verified using more rigorous research designs. Descriptive designs are one step closer to determining causality. Explanatory designs are useful when considerable preexisting knowledge is available about the research question under study and a testable hypothesis can be formulated on the basis of previous work. They have more internal and external validity than exploratory and descriptive designs, so they can help establish a causal connection between two variables.

No one group research design is inherently inferior or superior to the others. Each has advantages and disadvantages. Those of us who are familiar with all three categories of group research designs will be equipped to select the one that is most appropriate to a particular research question. In the following chapter we will turn our attention away from group research designs and concentrate on case study designs.

C h a p t e r   13

Case Research Designs

THE PREVIOUS CHAPTER PRESENTED basic content for the understanding of group-level research designs—designs that usually study more than one research participant at a time. As we know, however, group designs can also study a single group of people (or objects or events) such as all four of the exploratory designs (i.e., 1a, b, c, d), and four of the six descriptive designs (i.e., 2a, b, c, f) as illustrated in Table 12.2. This chapter elaborates on the preceding one by describing how any one-group nonrandomized design can be turned into a case study design. Many of the concepts of the previous 12 chapters are utilized in case designs, so it may be a good time to review them.

THE CASE

The case is the basic unit of social work practice, whether it be *an* individual, a couple, *a* family, *an* agency, a community, a county, a state, or a country. Case studies are more useful than traditional group designs when we want to study situations in depth and to understand how our therapeutic processes affect client outcomes. A case study fits naturally with many forms of social work practice, and by definition, it is an intense in-depth study of "one unit." Our profession deals with these "one units," which are always embedded in multiple societal, environmental, financial, and personal contexts.

The "Case" and Social Work Practice

Although case studies have much utility, our profession has had a love-hate relationship with them. Their main shortcoming is that they contain multiple variables that usually are not controllable (either statistically or through the manipulation of variables). We have used case studies for research and teaching for decades, however. The "case" has been the basis for the construction of various theories, such as the theories of human behavior, psychotherapy, family therapy, and cognitive development.

THE CASE STUDY

The recognition of the interaction of the numerous variables within a client system (a unit, or the case) is a defining characteristics of our profession. Thus, a case study considers the multiple variables (e.g., intervening, extraneous, independent) that affect the "unit" of study within its own context. Case study research does not ignore the major contextual variables that affect the course of our treatment—which sometimes happens when doing a group research project that strives to increase its internal and external validity.

Characteristics

As we know from the last chapter, there are a variety of ways to do group research designs. So, too, in case study research. They can be constructed using quantitative approaches and/or qualitative approaches (Chapters 6 and 7). They can be applied or pure; their links to theory can be deductive or inductive, or in some combination.

We can use a wide range of data sources (e.g., individuals, families, groups, organizations, couples) and data collection methods (e.g., surveys, interviews, participant observation, document analysis—all discussed in Part V). A case study routinely uses multiple data sources and data collection methods in order to attain an in-depth understanding of the case being studied. As mentioned, data can be quantitative or qualitative or both. Measurements can be taken at a single time and setting, or over time and multiple settings. Case studies perform many of the tasks that traditional group research designs do and can range from exploratory to explanatory.

Developing Theory and Testing Hypotheses

Case studies are used to develop theory and test hypotheses. These studies can include modified analytic induction, task analysis, and grounded theory (Berlin, Mann, & Grossman, 1991; Bogdan & Biklen, 1992; Gilgun, 1992b, 1995; Glaser & Strauss, 1967). In modified analytic induction and task analysis, our research study begins with a hypothesis that is tested on more than one case. Then, our hypothesis is continuously modified in response to the data generated from case to case (Chapter 6). Case studies can also be used in grounded theory research studies where our main purpose is to develop hypotheses and concepts (Charmaz, 1990; Gilgun, 1994a, 1994c; Glaser & Strauss, 1967; Strauss & Corbin, 1990).

Both modified analytic induction and grounded theory facilitate an in-depth understanding of the phenomena being studied. In addition, they follow many procedures similar to the procedures of direct practice, and we, therefore, already have many of the skills necessary to conduct excellent grounded theory and analytic induction studies (Gilgun, 1992a).

CASE STUDIES AND THE THREE COMPONENTS OF PRACTICE

There are three main types of case studies: (1) case studies that generate knowledge about our clients and their situations [assessment], (2) case studies that evaluate social work intervention, or therapeutic processes [intervention], and (3) case studies that evaluate client outcome [client outcome].

Assessment

Let us take an example of how case study research can contribute to the enhancement of our assessment techniques. In a case study research project, only two research participants (or cases) provided data to demonstrate that pre-verbal children can store their memories of sexual abuse and retrieve and articulate those memories when they are older (Hewitt, 1994). The author presented rich detail on both cases and provided concrete data that these two children were able to articulate experiences they had when they were too young to talk. These findings can be helpful in our assessment and treatment planning.

In another case study research project, 11 perpetrators of child sexual abuse as avengers, conquerors, playmates, and lovers were interviewed (Gilgun, 1994b). Based on intensive interviews, this project presented in detail the subjective accounts by perpetrators of child sexual abuse of their relationships with child victims. Such data help persons who have been victimized understand how much planning, manipulation, and self-deception are involved in the perpetrators' destructive behaviors. Thus, this project provided data to help us understand client situations and to aid in our assessments and treatment plans with this particular group of individuals.

Assessment-related case studies are particularly helpful in presenting our clients' perspectives. This quality is important, since a guiding principle of social work practice is to "start where the client is." In sum, we must grasp, interpret, and understand the perspectives and experiences of our clients if we are to be effective (Denzin, 1989; Goldstein, 1983).

Evaluating the usefulness of assessment-relevant case studies involves appraising whether they depict the subjective experiences of our clients—how they view their world, how they understand their experiences and relationships with other people, and how they account for their own behaviors and the behaviors of others. An in-depth understanding of our clients' perspectives fosters a unique collaboration between us and our clients, provides a firm basis for treatment planning, and, when sufficiently compelling, can lead to major advances in policy and social service delivery programs.

In general, the following guidelines are utilized when evaluating an assessment-related case study. It:

- Focuses on the perspectives of the study's participants
- Provides new insights into causes of clients' conditions
- Provides new insights into the meaning of a participant's life
- Clarifies confusing aspects of a participant's issue(s)
- Helps social work practitioners make new connections
- Conveys the historical and social conditions under which a participant developed (e.g., provides a thick description of context)

Intervention

As social workers, we are immersed in the intervention process. By examining these processes, we can illuminate the micro-steps that lead to good client outcomes. An excellent example of process research is a study where two social workers interviewed 15 of their colleagues who had experienced psychotherapy (Mackey & Mackey, 1994). They simply wanted to know how therapy affected the social workers' practice. Through a detailed analysis of comprehensive interviews, they demonstrated that a social worker's own therapy can have a profound positive effect on the intervention processes of his or her practice.

Process research and client outcome (to be discussed) are important parts of our profession. Simply put, good client outcomes depend on good interventions. The more we can identify the interventive processes that lead to good client outcomes, the more likely we are to replicate effective practice. In this age of managed physical and mental health care, accountability is taking on new and compelling meanings. Some social service delivery programs, for example, may not be funded when they cannot demonstrate their effectiveness. Process-oriented case studies may prove to be central to effective responses to increased demands for accountability. These types of case studies can be evaluated on the following criteria. They:

- Illuminate the "black box" of intervention (e.g., describe patterns, linkages, and interactions)
- Advance our understanding of exactly what happened
- Describe how programs and interventions work and what they do
- Reflect the complexity of implementing treatment interventions
- Show the human, subjective, and reflective side of intervention processes
- Provide new insights that affect client outcomes

Client Outcome

As should be evident by now, the ultimate goal of social work practice is to: assess correctly, intervene appropriately, and have good client outcomes. To achieve that, we must have knowledge of our clients and their situations (assessment), we must pay attention to therapeutic processes (intervention), and we must have evidence that our client outcomes were in fact achieved (client outcome).

A study of a woman being treated for obsessive-compulsive disorders is a good example of an outcome-oriented case study (Cooper, 1990). In a single case, the outcome variable was easily measured—a simple count of her obsessive-compulsive behaviors, which were graphed over time. This process indicated whether there was a reduction of these behaviors over the course of treatment.

Some outcome studies are not so quantifiable, however, and a study's results cannot be put on a graph. Sometimes these studies require the qualitative accounts (words) of clients and our qualitative observations. In the case study discussed earlier on school-aged children's ability to recall sexual abuse before they could talk, the outcome variable was simply their ability to recall their sexual abuse that took place when they were preverbal. This outcome is not quantifiable, per se, but nevertheless, it is a bona fide client outcome. The researcher simply gave a clear and credible account of the outcome instead of providing numbers, statistics, and graphs. How to evaluate the reliability and validity of such client outcomes depends on the nature of the outcome. Some outcomes are qualitative, some quantitative.

Outcome-oriented case studies can be evaluated on the following criteria:

- Statistical conclusion validity (see Chapter 8):
  — Demonstrates that a relationship between two variables exists
  — Conditions under which data are collected are standardized within and across cases
  — Sufficient detail is present so that readers can draw independent conclusions about whether our interventions and client outcomes are related
  — For studies utilizing quantification:
    — Appropriate statistics are used
    — Reliable and valid measuring instruments are used
- Internal validity (see Chapter 12):
  — Rules out alternative hypotheses
  — Points out alternative hypotheses that cannot be ruled out
  — Uses pretests, baselines, and/or participant recall (if possible)
  — Continues measurement after the intervention until trends appear to stabilize (if possible)
  — Uses multiple cases (if possible)
- Construct validity (see Chapter 8)
- External validity (see Chapter 12):
  — The context of the intervention is described in detail
  — The intervention is described in detail
  — Research participants are described in detail
  — Findings are discussed as hypotheses to be tested in other situations

CONSIDERATIONS WHEN DOING CASE STUDIES

Case studies are complex and can be difficult to conceptualize, operationalize, execute, and evaluate. Yet, we must try, since they have a great potential to contribute to our knowledge base. In the final analysis, however, the value of case study research is whether their findings will enhance our assessments, interventions, and client outcomes. This section explores some of the general issues we need to address when doing case study research: (1) generalizability, (2) conceptual issues, (3) contextual detail, (4) causation, (5) construct validity, and (6) presentation of findings.

Generalizability

Findings from a case study are not generalizable to the same extent as research findings generated from a group design that utilized a random sample. Nevertheless, they are generalizable to some degree. As we know from Chapters 11 and 12, research findings generated with random samples can be generalized to populations from which they were drawn. Applying research findings from a group research design or a case study design to an individual case is identical. We cannot, for example, assume that any research finding, whether derived from a survey, a randomized group design, or a case study, will fit a particular case. In a nutshell, each and every research finding must be tested for its fit with an individual case.

The Case Represents Itself

The individual case is unique and represents only itself. In fact, the root meaning of *ideographic* is the study of a unique case. No single case is likely to be identical to any other case. This is not a hard concept for us to understand, since we are trained to view each case as unique and to individualize a client's situation. We also know that even individual and unique cases often have something in common with other cases. Furthermore, working with cases is facilitated by our level of knowledge in the problem area, amount of practice experience, personal experience, use of research findings, and use of theory. Generalizing from one case to another requires at least three skills:

- The ability to draw practice principles from individual cases
- The ability to test whether practice principles derived from previous cases fit the present case
- The willingness to change even cherished practice principles when data from new cases contradict these principles

The type of generalizability associated with case studies is called *analytic generalization*. This means that their research findings are not assumed to fit another case no matter how apparently similar. Instead, research findings are tested to see if they do in fact fit. As discussed earlier, these processes are no different from how findings from any other kind of research study are used. Furthermore, the findings of case study research are not definitive. That is, they are not true for all persons, settings, and times—as often has been the goal in group studies aiming for probabilistic generalizability. Instead, case study findings are open-ended and are subject to revision as new data are discovered.

Let us go back to our example of the school-aged children's ability to recall sexual abuse before they could talk. This case study can illustrate the above principles. As discussed, the study used two children who articulated sexual abuse that occurred years earlier when they were preverbal. This is a practice principle, but it only opens up possibilities. It does not guarantee that all children who have been sexually abused when they were preverbal will later be able to articulate such abuse. As a working hypothesis, however, we can test whether this principle illuminates our practice with our clients who have been sexually abused when very young and whether it will hold up in other similar cases. As our clinical experiences accumulate, we may be able to delineate specific conditions under which this principle holds—and conditions under which it does not.

Analytic Generalizations as Working Hypotheses

Those of us who use analytic generalization view practice principles as working hypotheses, subject to revision when new data emerge. In using analytic generalization, we actively seek to contradict our practice principles in an effort to ensure that we truly are individualizing our practice knowledge and are not imposing our *general* preconceived ideas upon an *individual* client. Since using analytic generalization involves modifying our practice principles to fit individual cases, we do not try to mold our clients to fit our preconceived ideas.

Conceptual Issues

Like other forms of research endeavors, conceptual issues also need to be taken into account in case studies. Conceptual frameworks must be clearly delineated by making a direct statement on the study's purpose and presenting its guiding principles—which usually are hypotheses or research questions. In addition, we must share our reasoning that lead to the hypotheses or research questions and meticulously define all relevant concepts. Literature reviews and practice wisdom are the usual sources of conceptual frameworks for case studies. Below are a few criteria for evaluating the conceptual framework for a case study research project:

- Purpose of the study is clearly stated
- Principles guiding the study are clearly stated—either as hypotheses or as research questions

- Reasoning leading to the hypothesis or research question is clearly stated; this should be based on a literature review and on the reasoning of the researcher(s)
- Concepts are carefully defined

Contextual Detail

The unit of analysis in a case study is embedded in its environment, which deeply affects how the unit functions. To provide a basis for the understanding and interpreting of case studies, therefore, we must provide meaningful contextual detail. Notions of multiple, interactive, and contextual systems contained in the ecosystemic conceptual framework are useful in developing contextual detail.

Specific details of how our case study was conducted, with whom, and under what conditions are important to note. We must give enough information about our research participants, research setting, data collection sources and methods, and data analysis so that readers of our report can make a judgment about the adequacy of our research effort. This will also permit someone else to replicate our study.

This discussion demonstrates the importance of contextual detail in evaluating case studies for internal, construct, and external validity. With adequate detail, those who read our case studies (or hear about them at case conferences) will have enough information to evaluate our conclusions. The readers can make their own independent judgments. When sufficient contextual detail is present in case studies, the case study is interpretable. Another social worker with a similar case using similar intervention methods may obtain very different results, however. Divergent therapeutic processes and client outcomes with apparently similar cases are attributable to many factors.

Causation

As we know, our profession is an applied one whose goal is to understand social processes and, when they are problematic, to change them. If we are to understand change, we must be able to identify both the variables that caused the undesirable social conditions in the first place and the variables that can ameliorate them. Causation, then, is at the heart of social work practice—and social work research for that matter. The interventions we devise are meant to bring about positive change in client systems. In the language of research, we are seeking to identify and then implement the independent variables (Xs) that bring about the occurrence of dependent variables (Ys). We want to know: Does X cause Y? In social work practice, we want to know if the interventions that compose X cause outcomes that compose Y. We want to identify causal variables because, when we do, our interventions will be more effective and more efficient.

Deterministic Versus Probabilistic Causation

There is more than one way to think about cause, however. One definition is deterministic: When a particular effect appeared, the associated cause was always there. No other variables influenced the relationship between cause and effect—there is no effect in the absence of the cause. Another definition is probabilistic: When the presumed cause was present, the associated outcome may or may not have been present. Shooting another person in the eye, for example, deterministically will cause a great deal of physical and psychological harm. Other outcomes are not deterministic. Being sexually abused in childhood does not deterministically cause individuals to be sexually abusive people when they are older. There is a probability that these people will become sexually abusive, but not a certainty. Other variables, or factors, influence whether people who have been previously sexually abused when they were young actually become sexually abusive when they grow older.

Intervening and Extraneous Variables

Intervening and extraneous variables can mediate client outcomes. Competent social work practice identifies them and rules them out as competing alternative causes. The case study earlier in this chapter describing a woman who had obsessive-compulsive disorders illustrates these principles. The author attributed the reduction of her client's symptoms to a behaviorally oriented intervention. Yet, other variables may have affected her client's outcome. In the author's in-depth description of her client's history, she reported that her client had several years of psychodynamic therapy before undergoing behavioral treatment. In addition, the woman was married while in treatment. These and other extra-treatment circumstances (intervening and extraneous variables) might have influenced the client's outcome.

In this case, then, the causal agent (the intervention) was not 100 percent clear. Both within-treatment and extratreatment variables may have been responsible for the outcome. The causal variable, was thus *confounded*. This is a typical kind of client outcome. We often cannot be sure if our treatment intervention was *solely* responsible for our client's outcome when other influences may have facilitated or undermined it.

External conditions are likely to be part of the package of processes leading to client change. Confounding is part and parcel of social work practice because client systems are embedded in many environments that affect their functioning. Interactions between clients and practitioners are sources of other possible confounds. These variables mediate between our interventive efforts and our client outcomes.

Cause, then, rarely is easily identifiable in doing a case study. We, and our clients alike, are contending with too many variables to identify a specific causal variable(s). The best we can do is to rule out plausible rival hypotheses to our original hypothesis. When we cannot rule out plausible alternative hypotheses to client change, then we must delineate all the possible intervening and extraneous variables associated with client change.

Assessing trends in client behaviors or feelings of interest and then noting if the trend changes in response to our intervention can help identify and rule out rival hypotheses. Baselines, pretests, and asking our clients about pertinent issues prior to intervention are all helpful in assessing trends. Graphing trends over the course of treatment also help establish internal validity, although the possibility of rival hypotheses needs to be continually monitored (see Chapter 23).

We can, however, tentatively rule out rival hypotheses and have some confidence that our treatment intervention had a causal relationship to our client outcome. This is done when several cases are conducted at various times, with a number of similar people, with a variety of practitioners, and embedded in variety of settings, and they show similar results (Kazdin, 1981). External conditions vary from one client system to another. Consistency of findings across similar conditions bolsters an argument that a particular form of treatment was the causal variable and is effective for a particular type of client problem.

Thus, replication of causal studies increases their internal validity. To demonstrate the effectiveness of behavioral approaches with persons with obsessive compulsive behaviors, then, Cooper (1990) would have to replicate her study with several other cases—not only one. Then, other practitioners would have to do this as well. Despite this goal of multiple replications, the findings of a single case study can be a rich source for the construction of a working hypothesis.

In addition, replication across persons, settings, and time also bolsters arguments for a general applicability of findings—that is, *external validity*. However, even widely replicated findings must be tested for fit with individual cases.

Construct Validity

Construct validity is explained in detail in Chapter 8. Though concerned with intervening and extraneous variables, as discussed earlier, construct validity has other facets. In general, construct validity directs us to pay careful attention to how and whether we identify and define our treatment interventions and client outcome variables.

Convergence and Divergence

Construct validity is based on the ideas of convergence and divergence, in addition to the idea of multiple data collection methods and data sources. A study of staff/patient communication in a few neonatal units is exemplary in its use of multiple data methods and sources (Bogdan, Brown, & Foster, 1984). The data collection methods included observations and interviews with a range of informants (data sources) over time at four neonatal units. This approach developed a trustworthy understanding of the multiple facets of staff/patient communication in a typical neonatal unit.

Sometimes the purpose, or feasibility, of a case study puts some limits on using multiple data collection methods and sources, however. If our research goal is to understand only our key informant's perspective, or, if the informant is the only source of knowledge about phenomena—such as experiences of near death—then we only need one informant per study.

On the other hand, if our goal is to understand multiple perspectives within a system, such as a couple, a family, or an agency, then multiple persons need to be interviewed. Testing for the generality of findings requires multiple case studies, although the findings of even these replications have to be assessed for their fit with any individual case.

The rationale for the use of multiple data sources is based on the ideas of convergence and replication. As occurrences of a phenomenon increase, we can place more confidence that a finding is reliable. Replication can be difficult to achieve, however. The concepts that we deal with are often embedded in multiple contexts and are contingent upon time. When this is combined with variations in individual client systems and how we practice, replication can be extremely difficult to achieve. Yet, some findings actually do repeat themselves over people, places, and times.

When these multiple data sources do not overlap, we can assume that the variables we are measuring are not the same. When data from different sources converge, then we can assume that the variables we are measuring are indeed similar. As we know from Chapter 6, the use of multiple data sources is called *triangulation*.

The notion of construct validity also guides us to use multiple measures at pretests, during interventions, and at posttests (outcomes). Rarely does any intervention involve one outcome, and rarely is only one part of a client system relevant in assessment and treatment planning. Therefore, in order to understand and identify the variables that are of an interest to us, we must use multiple measures.

Construct validity is also about operational definitions. When we define our constructs of interest, readers of our case studies can evaluate the adequacy of our assessments, interventions, and evaluations. Adequate definitions inform others of how we thought about what they were doing. Readers can then draw their own conclusions about whether we were dealing with what we thought we were dealing with and whether we were doing what we thought we were doing. Careful operational definitions not only increase our understanding but foster replication of case study findings.

Finally, ideas embedded in the notion of construct validity direct us to account for multiple client outcomes, not simply a dominant outcome. Hewitt (1994), for example, could have added a third case to her research study, a case where a child could not recall documented sexual abuse that occurred while she was preverbal. In that way, Hewitt would have had a stronger argument for the construct validity of her study. She could have argued that she presented the dominant finding and another finding that was not consistent with the dominant one. Thus, case studies are strengthened when dominant patterns and exceptions to dominant patterns are reported.

Presentation of Findings

Presentation of a case study's findings is challenging. Accurate accounts of our study's findings require much thought, excellent analytic skills, and data that fit the analysis. Case studies typically generate a great deal of data, and we must identify themes and concepts that organize them—that become the headings of the final report. The various ways to identify themes and concepts is beyond the scope of this chapter, but excellent guidance can be found in Chapter 23.

In presenting a study's findings, we must persuade our readers that the conclusions we drew were based on the data. The usual mode of presenting findings involves general statements about the findings, supported by data derived from the case. Citing findings not supported by data is a common error that harms the study's credibility. Dominant patterns in our findings as well as exceptions to the dominant patterns are presented. Finally, our findings are linked to previous research studies, theory, and practice wisdom. Below are a few criteria for evaluating the clarity and accuracy of findings presented in a final report:

- Findings are well organized and communicated clearly:
  — A general statement is made about each research finding
  — Each general statement is supported by evidence taken from the data
  — Presentation of findings is separate from the categories that organize the findings
  — Multiple dimensions of the findings are clearly presented including:
    — Dominant patterns and exceptions to dominant patterns
    — Descriptions of conditions under which patterns appear
- Findings are based on data as follows:
  — Generalizations are based on the data

- Findings are clearly interpreted in a pattern-matching way and not in a probabilistic way
- More than one person interpreted the data
- Research participants read and comment on the final report
- Other knowledgeable persons read and comment on the final report
- Findings are related to previous research studies and theory
- Clinical and theoretical relevance and programmatic or policy implications are discussed

SUMMARY

The findings from case studies can be a rich source of practice knowledge. To develop them effectively, however, we need to pay attention to the guidelines discussed in this chapter. Case studies must be evaluated for what they are. They cannot do what experiments do, but they can be a major factor in the development of practice guidelines. They are particularly useful for obtaining the perspectives of key informants and for tracking the therapeutic processes that lead to client outcomes.

Case studies fit well with social work practice. Not only do they support the three components of practice—assessment, intervention, and evaluation—but they call upon the skills that trained social workers already have.

Gayla Rogers
Elaine Bouey

C h a p t e r   14

Participant Observation

PARTICIPANT OBSERVATION, like survey research presented in the previous chapter, is both a data collection method and a research approach. Like all the other data collection methods presented in this book, its appropriateness for any particular research study is directly related to the study's research question. This chapter provides a definition and description of participant observation and discusses its practical application to social work research. We both describe various roles that a participant observer, the researcher, can take and present a step-by-step overview of how to do a participant observation study.

DEFINITION

It is difficult to provide an exact definition of participant observation, since there are many different ways of defining it depending on the discipline of the definer and how it has been applied to research situations over the past eighty years. Participant observation as a data collection method began with early anthropological ethnomethodology studies in the 1920s. Since then, it has undergone a radical transformation as a result of an effort to look for new ways to obtain useful, reliable, and valid data from research participants. Currently, participant observation is viewed as more of a mind-set (or an orientation) toward research rather than as a set of specific, applied data collection techniques (Neuman, 1994). Further, the terms *field research, ethnographic research,* and *ethnography* are often used interchangeably with *participant observation.*

Distinguishing Features

Participant observation is an obtrusive data collection method as it requires the one doing the study, the participant observer, to undertake roles that involve establishing and maintaining ongoing relationships with research participants who are often in field settings.

The passage of time is also an integral part of participant observation. We need to consider, for example, the sequences of events (and monitor processes) over time so the relationships and meanings of what our research participants are experiencing can be discovered. We gather data primarily through direct observation, supplemented with other data gathering methods such as, interviewing, using existing documents (Part V), and using our own personal experiences.

Participant observation is an excellent way to gather data for understanding how other people see or interpret their experiences (Spradley, 1980). It represents a unique opportunity to see the world from *other* points of view, often at the sites where the activities or phenomena occur. It is also compatible with the "reflective practitioner" model of social work practice, as a part of the process involves examining our personal insights, feelings, and perspectives in order to understand the situations we are studying (Papell & Skolnik, 1992; Schön, 1983).

A key factor of participant observation is its emphasis on *less structured* data gathering methods, such as observing everyday events in natural settings in an effort to understand how other people see or interpret their experiences, then stepping outside that perspective to add a "more objective" viewpoint (Neuman, 1994). In practice, however, it is often a back and forth (or recursive) process. Through observations and interactions with research participants over time (e.g., weeks, months, years) a great deal can be learned about them—their histories, habits, and hopes; and their cultures, values, and idiosyncrasies as well. These observations and interactions can be fascinating and fun as well as time-consuming, costly, and emotionally draining.

As we know, data derived from a participant observation study can easily be augmented with survey research data. In addition it can be used with both research approaches—quantitative or qualitative. Using different data gathering methods, such as participant observation and survey research, in addition to using different data sources such as existing documents, as well as observing people in different roles, create the potential for a fuller understanding of the phenomena being studied.

Participant observation is an excellent data collection method for exploring a wide variety of social settings, subcultures, and most aspects of social life. It is valuable, for example, in studying deviant behavior (e.g., prostitution, drug use), unusual or traumatic circumstances (e.g., spinal cord injury, rape), and important life events (e.g., birth, divorce, death). It can be used to study entire communities in a range of settings, or relatively small groups who interact with each other on a regular basis in a fixed setting.

Some examples include studies of women's emergency shelters, the workings of social service agencies from the perspective of the members in those settings, or an immigrant group living in a particular neighborhood. Participant observation can also be used to study social experiences that are not fixed in a place but where in-depth interviewing and direct observation are the only ways to gain access to the experience—for example, the feelings of women who have left violent relationships.

Researchers participating in these settings can also occupy other roles including: social worker, volunteer, English as a Second Language tutor, program aide, or administrative assistant. The more roles we assume, the better our understanding of the situation because of different points of view.

When to Use Participant Observation

Participant observation as a data collection method is well suited to situations where we wish to better understand how people see their own experiences, as well as when we want to gain an in-depth perspective on people within the contexts and environments in which these events occur. It is exceptionally useful when it is applied to the study of processes, interrelationships among people and their situations, and events that happen over time and the patterns that have developed, as well as the social and cultural contexts in which human experiences occurred (Jorgensen, 1989).

Participant observation allows for the collection of data about phenomena that are not commonly obvious from the viewpoint of the nonparticipant. It provides an opportunity for a comprehensiveness of understanding of human situations, and richly textured perspectives. Furthermore, when conducted in natural settings, it has the potential to elucidate certain nuances of attitude, or behaviors that may not be included when data are gathered using other data collection methods.

Participant observation is often helpful in identifying problem areas that can be the topics for subsequent studies that use other data collection methodologies. We can then *triangulate*, or compare and contrast, the data gathered via these different methods in order to enhance our study's credibility. We may initially select a role as a volunteer in a women's emergency shelter, for example, find that we would like to learn more about the conditions that led women to the shelter, and subsequently gain permission to both review intake records and conduct structured interviews with a sample of women who enter the shelter. Participant observation is especially appropriate for scholarly problems in the following circumstances (Jorgensen, 1989):

- Little is known about a situation or event (e.g., job satisfaction among workers at a women's emergency shelter).
- There are important differences between the views of one group and another (e.g., perspectives on domestic violence as held by police and medical service professionals versus perspectives of social workers inside a women's emergency shelter).
- The phenomenon is obscured in some way from those outside a setting (e.g., spouse battering within a community of immigrants who do not commonly interact with social service agencies, and who do not speak English).
- The phenomenon is hidden from society in general (e.g., drug abuse treatment of those in higher socioeconomic statuses).

While participant observation is appropriate for gathering data for almost any aspect of human existence, it is, however, not suited to every scholarly research enquiry involving humans and their interactions with one another. It is particularly applicable to exploratory and descriptive studies out of which theoretical interpretations and hypotheses emerge. Its primary contribution allows for the creation of in-depth understandings of situations in an effort to support the development of different theoretical view points.

Minimal Conditions for Participant Observation

In using participant observation as a data collection method, there are minimal conditions that must be present (Jorgensen, 1989):

- The research question is concerned with human meanings and interactions viewed from the insider's perspective.
- The phenomenon is observable within an everyday life setting or situation.
- Gaining access to an appropriate setting is not a problem.
- The phenomenon is sufficiently limited in size and location to be studied as a case (Chapter 13).
- The research question is appropriate for a case study (Chapter 13).

- The research question can be addressed by qualitative data gathered by direct observation and other means pertinent to the field setting (Chapters 6 and 7).

Getting Involved and Observing

Participant observation involves a dual purpose: *getting involved* in activities appropriate to the situation, and *observing* people, the physical site, and the events happening in a particular context or setting. While a regular member experiences events in a direct and personal manner, the participant observer experiences being both an insider (with a "subjective" viewpoint) and an outsider (with a more "objective" viewpoint). Thus, it requires personal preparation and ongoing mindfulness to maintain an objective perspective at the same time as being involved in a field setting as a participant. It means being explicitly aware of our values and assumptions while holding our judgments in abeyance. This is often challenging and proves to be a very intensive experience for the participant observer.

There is little question that the participant observer's involvement in a setting can have an emotional impact of varying degrees. As Neuman (1994) notes:

> *Field research can be fun and exciting, but it can also disrupt one's personal life, physical security, or mental well being. More than other types of social research, it reshapes friendships, family life, self identity, or personal values. (p. 335)*

Since we are the primary instruments through which our data are gathered and interpreted, we may have a potential influence on our study. This is why it is crucial to prepare ourselves as much as possible in advance for this experience, maintain a separate log of personal notes and reflections, as well as make arrangements for regular advisory and debriefing sessions.

It is also important to note that some of us may be very well suited to use participant observation as a data collection method, while others may be advised to use other data collection methodologies. Thus, a team approach is often appropriate, with one person doing participant observation, and another conducting structured interviews and examining existing documentation, for example.

ROLES

This section provides an overview of the various roles for those involved in a participant observation study and describes the tasks associated with each role.

Being a *participant observer* in a field setting is quite different from being a *regular participant* in a field setting. Researchers using participant observation as a data collection method often assume a variety of roles. These roles can be placed on a continuum and are classified into four categories as presented in Figure 14.1: (1) complete participant, (2) observer-participant, (3) participant-observer, and (4) complete observer.

We can sit in on staff meetings, for example, and view other operational activities as a *complete observer* to gather data on how social agency staff function in an office setting; or with varying degrees of involvement as a *participant observer* or *observer participant*, we can be volunteers who come in to help with some aspect of the program's operation on a regular basis to gather data on how a particular program works; or as a *complete participant* we can, at the other end of the continuum, be one of the permanent staff in an agency who also happens to be doing a research study on the day-to-day activities within the program.

Balancing the Roles

In assuming any one of the four roles in doing a participant observation study, we need to be acutely aware of the need to maintain a balance between our participation and our ability to be objective. There may be many temptations to become so totally involved that we can easily lose this balanced perspective. This is often a particular challenge when we are *complete participants* as compared to *complete observers*. Some aids to maintaining this balance include reflective journal writing and regular debriefing sessions with other professionals who are not familiar with our field setting.

When we take on different roles, however, these roles can be overtly revealed, or in some cases they can be undertaken on a covert basis and not revealed. We strongly recommend, whenever possible, that any role played be on an overt or openly explained basis. This helps us with ethical considerations as well as in keeping with the way in which participant observation has evolved and its application to social work settings.

If we are going to be studying a women's emergency shelter with all the appropriate advance clearances for access to that setting, for example, and if we assume a role as a children's playroom assistant so that we can observe the interaction of the children with their mothers and with the shelter's staff, it is absolutely mandatory that we let the parents, the shelter's staff, and the children know why we are there (our dual role) and what we will be doing

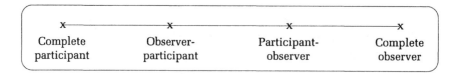

Figure 14.1   Continuum of Participant Observation

with the data collected. These need not be lengthy explanations initially, but they set the stage for trust and acceptance. We should be ready to answer questions as they surface. On the other hand, sharing of the initial analyses of our raw observational data, or our personal recorded reflections, is not appropriate. Yet, it is quite reasonable to provide a summary (or full copy) of our final research report to interested participants.

In assuming roles in a field setting, we should be aware that the social and physical locations are very important influences on the type of data we will be able to collect. As we note *what* occurs at different points in time and space, we may begin to recognize that *when* something occurs is often important. In a women's emergency shelter, for example, the physical locations at which we observe could include the children's playroom, the outside playground, and the dining room. The different roles we could take—such as a social worker or a children's playroom aide—would affect our interactions with those at the shelter and, in turn, would provide us with a rich variety of different perspectives. In some cases it might be difficult to operate in these different roles in one field setting, so we could choose to select one or two roles at one women's shelter, and others at another shelter.

NEEDED STRATEGIES AND SKILLS

As previously mentioned, the participant observation experience is intense and demanding. It is both an art and a science, calling on many aspects of our capabilities. In order to deal with the many situations that come up in a field setting, there are a few strategies we can use to both minimize difficulties and stresses for all those involved, as well as to ensure that a high-quality research study takes place.

- We need to practice observing and making notes that are as detail rich as possible, based on our recall of events (e.g., we could observe people interacting in a busy city recreation center).
- We need to keep a daily personal journal that includes our reflections on events that are occurring in our life; this will help with both the discipline of writing field notes and with enhancing our self-knowledge.
- We need to get help from a knowledgeable advisor in designing, planning, and implementing our research study, as well as setting up a regular schedule of debriefing and advisory sessions throughout the study.
- We need to tap into supporting systems and services regarding our physical, emotional, and spiritual well-being.
- We need to develop a working knowledge of our topic area by reading the literature and talking with people who have done research studies in our particular research area.

- We need to identify, record, and, if possible, let go of our assumptions or preconceptions that might influence the study.

The specific skills needed for using participant observation as a data collection method are:

- The skills of careful looking and listening—paying attention to all possible details.
- The skills of remembering things—including verbatim comments, nonverbal cues, and "climatic" conditions.
- The skills of disciplined, regular writing—describing events and exchanges as well as personal reactions and reflections.
- The skills of tuning into oneself—knowing our vulnerabilities, values, and views; owning our thoughts and feelings, assumptions, and biases.

STEPS IN DOING PARTICIPANT OBSERVATION

Our direct participation in, and observation of, events as they occur in their natural field settings is the cornerstone of using participant observation as a data collection method. Thus, it is essential that we be well organized and prepared, but also flexible and adaptable enough to change with the circumstances. The specific steps of using participant observation as a data collection method cannot be entirely predetermined, however they can serve as a guide to the overall process. We need to recognize and seize opportunities and rapidly adjust to these new situations as they occur in the field. In the beginning of our study, we can expect to have little control over our data and not much focus. Once we are socialized into our field setting, however, we can focus our inquiry and gain some control over the data we finally end up gathering.

Notwithstanding that participant observation is characterized by a back and forth, nonlinear process, there are six fundamental steps that serve as a guide. These steps are: (1) Gaining access and entry to a study site, (2) engaging and forming relationships, (3) gathering the data, (4) recording the data, (5) making sense of the data, and (6) reporting the findings.

Step 1: Gaining Access and Entry to a Study Site

A site is the context in which our study occurs and it need not be a fixed geographic location. A particular group of research participants, for example, may interact across several sites. In addition, our own characteristics may limit access to a site. A white single male, for example, may have a difficult time gaining access to a group of single-parent women of color. Physical access can also be an issue, in that we may find that we are not allowed on a site(s) or there are legal or political barriers to access, such as in public schools, hospitals, and prisons.

Access to such settings depends on *gatekeepers*—those with formal or informal authority to control access to sites. Permission is usually required from a gatekeeper and involves bargaining and negotiating. In some cases, permission from gatekeepers may inhibit the cooperation of people whom we want to study. Juvenile offenders, for example, may not want to participate in a study if they know that the Director of Secure Treatment has authorized us to be there. Gaining access and entering a site depends on our personal attributes, prior connections, and social skills.

Entry and access is more analogous to peeling away the layers of an onion than it is to opening a door. We begin at the outermost layer where access is easy. At this stage, as outsiders, we are most likely looking for data more or less in the public domain. The next layer requires an increased degree of access as we become more of a passive unquestioning observer of events occurring in the field setting. Over time, and as trust develops, we peel off another layer and observe more sensitive interactions or activities and ask for clarification of our personal observations. At yet a deeper layer, we can shape or influence the interaction so that particular data or certain behaviors are revealed. This layer is also necessary in order to access highly sensitive material that requires a deep level of trust.

Step 2: Engaging and Forming Relationships

The process of engaging and developing relationships with our research participants requires sensitivity and well-developed communication and interpersonal skills. We must be prepared to explain what we are doing and why, repeatedly, with each research participant. We should be ready to deal with a degree of hostility, rejection, and resistance. There will be more or less of this depending on who we are and the population we are studying. Gaining entry and access to women with breast cancer, for example, may pose fewer obstacles if the researcher is a woman who has had breast cancer, than if she is trying to enter a poor Hispanic neighborhood and is seen as part of the "white establishment."

The participant observer must establish rapport and build relationships. This is not always easy, as field settings can be very uncomfortable and individuals in these settings can behave in frightening ways. Building trust is a complex matter: It develops over time, and requires continual reaffirmation. We need to learn the language and the meanings constructed by the research participants we are studying—how to think and act from the perspective of the *insiders*. In short, we need to empathize and understand their experiences. Thus, it is crucial to monitor how our actions and appearances affect the members so that the data we gather are as rich and reflective as possible. This requires a degree of sharing and disclosure on our part; we cannot remain neutral or distant and expect to be a participant observer.

Our relationships must be characterized by dialogue and partnership, mutual interest and reciprocity, trust and cooperation, while we are still working within the parameters of professional ethics. This means we must be alert to the dimensions of cultural, ethnic, and other differences while being sensitive to the dynamics of power and privilege in the relationships we are building. The longer (or more often) we are in a field setting, the more we will be regarded as nonthreatening and our presence taken for granted.

As our relationships evolve and deepen over time, we must be careful about not slipping over into roles that may be an aside to being a researcher, which would breach the agreement we made with our research participants. In some circumstances it may be easier to become a therapist, change agent, advocate, or active member (full participant), than it is to remain a participant observer. Should we undertake such roles, however, we will change the nature of our relationships, which will impact and likely thwart the original purpose of our research study.

Some of the first questions that research participants ask are, "Why should I cooperate with your research study?" "What's in it for me/us?" "What's in it for you?" Our direct and candid answers to these questions are important. Research participants need to know that we seek to understand and describe their reality from their point of view, and that ultimately there is value in having their stories told. But they also need to know that we expect to gain such things as publications, expertise, or an academic degree from the study. The data collected will hopefully contribute to existing knowledge and may lead to solutions to their problems. They also need to know, however, that there are no absolute guarantees; nor is it the intent that our study will change their lives in any meaningful way.

Engaging and forming relationships that are sustained over time with insiders in a field setting is imperative to gathering meaningful, valid, and reliable data. Building these relationships is like being socialized into a way of life. We need to "be there," to "hang out," to "watch, listen, and learn the norms, language, and patterns of interaction." The same skills used to make friends are used to connect with the insiders, our research participants, in a field setting so that we have the ability to gather meaningful data that will be used to answer our research question.

Step 3: Gathering the Data

Participant observation data are usually gathered in four nonmutually exclusive ways: (1) observing, (2) interviewing, (3) using existing documents and other materials, and (4) reflecting upon our personal experiences.

Observing

Good observers need to use all of their senses to notice what they saw, heard, touched, smelled, and tasted. Start with the physical surroundings of the settings, for example, and pay particular attention to the details that influence human behavior such as lighting, temperature, colors, odors, and available space.

The next level is observing people and their actions. Begin by noting observable physical characteristics of individuals and the composition of the group in such areas as gender, ethnicity, age, shape/size, and appearance. Notice what people do in relation to each other, such as who talks, who listens, and who sits or stands next to whom. As our observations become more focused, we pay more attention to such issues as the nature of the gathering and discern if this is typical or unusual. At this stage, however, our observations serve the purpose of familiarizing ourselves with the field setting, getting a "feel for the people and the place." These observations allow the widest possible field of vision. We are, however, limited to learning by looking and listening and will soon need to more sharply focus our attention and move away from passive observation to being a more active participant by asking questions through interviewing.

Interviewing

The data collected at the beginning of a participant observation study is in the form of words, including direct quotes and thick descriptions of particular events. There are general guidelines for asking good questions, but the type and style depends on the purpose and nature of the specific research study.

Questions that ask *what, when, where,* and *how* provide good descriptive data. Questions that ask *why* pressure people, put them on the defensive, and should therefore be selectively used. *Compare and contrast* questions illustrate another type of inquiry. By asking how things are similar to and different from one another, we can discern what is included or excluded, what is part of or outside of the phenomena, and start to grasp the multiple meanings and layers involved in understanding the phenomena we are studying.

Data gathered by engaging in dialogue and asking questions may be undertaken in a variety of situations ranging from casual conversations through formal interviews. Data gathered by a structured interview schedule through formal interviews, where specific questions are asked in exactly the same way with different research participants, have the advantage of producing a uniform set of data.

On the other hand, as we know from the previous chapter, unstructured interviews have the advantage of producing richly qualitative data at a more in-depth level of disclosure. Both structured and unstructured interviewing contributes useful and meaningful data. Gayla Rogers and Elaine Bouey (1996) present a clear description of how to collect interview data in qualitatively oriented research studies. Figure 14.2 provides a summary of the main differences between survey and participant observation interviewing (Neuman, 1994).

Using Existing Documents and Other Materials

In the course of a participant observation study, it is not unusual to come across existing documents—files, records, articles, pamphlets, and other materials, such as objects, artwork, videos, clothing—that provide different sources of data. These data are extremely useful in providing support for the findings we derived from our observing and interviewing. They also provide a background, in addition to alternative points of view or explanations. The use of existing documents are unobtrusive data collection methods and are discussed in detail in Part V in this book.

Reflecting Upon Our Personal Experiences

Our feelings, insights, and perceptions are other sources of data and should be treated as just that—duly documented and reported, however. By participating in the world of those we are studying, we generate the experiences of an insider. Reflecting upon our personal experiences in our field setting gives us access to the standpoint of the insider. It provides us with insights and new understandings of particular ways of life. These data can be used as a source of further questions to be asked of our research participants in order to check out our inner responses, hypotheses, and assumptions.

Through these various methods, high-quality data are gathered. This means our data are richly varied, detailed descriptions that emerge from our observations and experiences.

Step 4: Recording the Data

Regardless of the type of data collected, their purpose is lost if we fail to adequately record our observations, impressions, and actual words. In addition to our notes, tapes, and transcriptions, we can use visual aids, such as diagrams, flowcharts, eco-maps and genograms, and photographs. Their type, form, and content depend on a number of factors: the field setting, the available and suitable technologies, the purpose of our study, and our personal preferences.

Survey Interview	Participant Observation Interview
1. It has a clear beginning and conclusion.	1. The beginning and end are not clearly defined. The interview can be picked up later.
2. The same standard questions are asked of all research participants in the same order.	2. The questions and the order in which they are asked are tailored to certain people and situations.
3. The interviewer remains neutral at all times.	3. The interviewer shows interest in responses, encourages elaboration.
4. The interviewer asks questions, and the interviewee answers.	4. It is like a friendly conversational exchange, but with more interview-like questions.
5. It is almost always with a single research participant.	5. It can occur in a group setting or with others in the area, but varies.
6. Professional tone and businesslike focus. Diversions are ignored.	6. It is interspersed with jokes, asides, stories, diversions, and anecdotes, which are recorded.
7. Closed-ended questions are common, with rare probes.	7. Open-ended questions are common, and probes are frequent.
8. The interviewer alone controls the speed and direction of the interview.	8. The interviewer and insider jointly influence the pace and direction of the interview.
9. The social context in which the interview takes place is not considered and is assumed to make little difference.	9. The social context of the interview is noted and seen as essential for interpreting the meaning of responses.
10. The interviewer attempts to shape the communication pattern into a standard framework.	10. The interviewer adjusts to the insider's norms and language usage, following his or her lead.

Figure 14.2   Survey Research Interviews Versus Participant Observation Interviews

There is a great temptation to postpone systematically recording the gathered data. This is a mistake, as data that are not carefully organized and stored after they have been recorded create many challenges in the data analysis stage. Developing a habit of regularly recording what is seen, heard, and experienced is strongly encouraged.

There are many ways to record data when using participant observation as a data collection method. Three of the more common ones are: (1) using field notes, (2) using taping devices, and (3) using visual aids.

Using Field Notes

The majority of gathered data are in the form of field notes. Writing field notes requires self-discipline and a time allocation for the task. We will save a lot of backtracking (not to mention aggravation) if we organize our notes into categories at the outset of the study. Visualize creating separate containers to hold different types of notes. Factual observations, for example, are noted separately from personal feelings, impressions, or speculations; notes about our reactions to an interview or extraneous factors affecting the interview are kept separate from transcriptions or direct quotes from an interview. It may be hard to decide, particularly during the initial stages, what constitutes something worth noting. It may also worry us at later stages that, having made all these notes, we have so much data that it seems impossible to decipher any of them. These concerns can be addressed by following the recommendations noted below for making field notes (Neuman, 1994):

- Make notes as soon as possible after each period in the field.
- Begin a record of each field visit with a new page, and the date and time noted.
- Use jotted notes only as a temporary memory aid—with key words or terms, or the first and last things said.
- Use wide margins and double-space everything to make it easy to add to notes at any time. Add to the notes if you remember something later.
- Type notes and store on disk in separate files so it will be easy to go back to them later.
- Record events in the order in which they occur, and note how long they last (e.g., a 15-minute wait, a one-hour ride).
- Make notes as concrete, specific, complete, and comprehensible as possible.
- Use frequent paragraphs and quotation marks. Exact recall of phrases is best, with double quotes; use single quotes for paraphrasing.
- Record small talk or routines that do not appear to be significant at the time; they may become important later.
- "Let your feelings flow" and write quickly without worrying about spelling or "wild ideas." Assume that no one else will see the notes, but use pseudonyms as a precaution to maintain confidentiality.
- Never substitute tape recordings completely for field notes.
- Include diagrams or maps of the setting, and note your own movements and those of others during the period of observation.
- Include your own words and behavior in the notes. Also record emotional feelings and private thoughts in a separate section.
- Avoid evaluative summarizing words. Use nonjudgmental, descriptive words. Instead of "The sink looked disgusting," say, "The sink was rust-

stained and looked as if it had not been cleaned in a long time. Pieces of food and dirty dishes that looked several days old were piled into it."

- Reread notes periodically and record ideas triggered by the rereading.
- Organize materials neatly into types, or methods of data collected so they can be easily accessed.
- Always make one or more backup copies, keep them in a locked location, and store the copies in different places in case of fire.

There are many different types of field notes. We have chosen to describe four that represent different levels of data: (1) direct observation notes, (2) interpretive notes, (3) thematic notes, and (4) personal journal notes.

Using Direct Observation Notes   The first level of field notes, *direct observation notes*, are usually organized chronologically and contain a detailed description of what was seen and heard. At this level the notes report the facts—such as, who, what, when, and where—and include verbatim statements, paraphrases, and nonverbal communications. These also include summary notes made after an interview.

Using Interpretive Notes   The next level of field notes are *interpretive notes*. Our interpretations of events are kept separate from the record of the facts noted as direct observations, but need to be located in an adjacent column to the direct observations. These notes include our interpretation of the meanings inferred by the words and gestures we observed. We can speculate about the social relationships, the emotions, and the influence of culture and context on what actually took place. By keeping our interpretations separate, we leave room for multiple interpretations (or different interpretations) to arise as our knowledge and experience increase. If we are not vigilant, however, it is quite easy to combine the facts with our interpretation of them, and we run the risk later on of viewing our interpretations as fact, which in turn might narrow our ability to see other versions or meanings emerge.

Using Thematic Notes   The third level of field notes is *thematic notes*. They provide a place to record our emerging ideas, hypotheses, theories, and conjectures. This is the place to speculate and identify themes, make linkages between ideas and events, and articulate our thoughts as they emerge while we are still in the field setting. In these notes, we might expand on some of the ideas that have occurred, and develop our theories as we go, or as we reread our direct observation notes and interpretive notes. This is the place to describe the thoughts that emerge in the "middle of the night" or to elaborate on any "Aha!" connections. Thus, it is critical to have a separate container for these thoughts at this level, even if they are speculative and in early stages of development, because we might lose an important seed for later analysis if it is not recorded.

Using Personal Journal Notes   Keeping a journal of *personal notes* provides an outlet for recording our feelings and emotional reactions, as well as the personal experiences of being the researcher or the participant observer. These are a rich source of data. They give voice to our journey over time and provide a place to consider such things as what is going on at any given time during our involvement in the field. A running record of personal life events, feelings, physical well-being, and our moods, particularly as they relate to events in the field, will facilitate our data analysis. In this way we can capture any particular intrapersonal or interpersonal experiences that might affect the way we make sense of the data. The process has an effect upon the quality of the content gathered, our interpretation of the content, and what next steps we decide to take. Identifying these effects as they are revealed also facilitates our interpretation and reporting of them later.

The four different levels of field notes are shown below using an example of recording a period of observation in a field setting with a woman named Kay (Neuman, 1994):

— **Direct Observation**   *Sunday, October 4, 1997: Kay's Cafe 3:00 p.m. Large white male in mid 40s, overweight, enters. He wears worn brown suit. He is alone sits at booth #2. Kay comes by asks, "what'll it be?" Man says, "Coffee, black for now." She leaves and he lights cigarette and reads menu. 3:15 p.m. Kay turns on radio.*

— **Interpretive**   *Kay seems friendly today, humming. She becomes solemn and watchful. I think she puts on the radio when nervous.*

— **Thematic**   *Women are afraid of men who come in alone since the robbery.*

— **Personal Journal**   *It is raining. I am feeling comfortable with Kay but am distracted today by a headache.*

Using Taping Devices

As we participate more actively and purposefully in the field setting and as our interactions with our research participants become less casual and more planned, we conduct interviews that are recorded and later transcribed. There are three typical approaches to recording the data gathered in qualitative research interviews: (1) taping the interview (either audio or video); (2) taking notes during the interview; and (3) recording immediately following the interview.

Taping the Interview   There are both advantages and disadvantages to *tape-recording* interviews. The presence of a recorder can be intrusive and a barrier to full disclosure, however it may be the only way to capture the richness and subtleties of speech. In the case of video recording, it is the only way to capture the nonverbal language used by our research participants, or to accurately identify each speaker in a group situation. Recording devices may also be a means of self-monitoring and an improvement for the interviewer. The tape recorder may provide us with confidence to focus all our attention on the person being interviewed, knowing we do not have to worry about remembering all of the details or writing notes. At the same time, however, knowing the tape will record everything that is said, we might be tempted to let our minds wander.

Ultimately, the decision about whether to tape depends on what we want to do with the data gathered. If we want to include many direct quotes, for example, then it is useful to have the verbatim account, which can be transcribed and subjected to editing at a later date. If capturing the exact phrasing of all interview responses is not critical to the study, then note-taking may suffice. If time and money are not an issue, it is clearly best to fully transcribe all interviews from the tape. On the other hand, if time and money are limited, we might listen to the tape and use our notes to help decide what parts to transcribe and paraphrase.

Taking Notes During the Interview   Many interviewers advocate *taking notes during the interview* as well as tape-recording them. The notes serve as a backup or safeguard against mechanical difficulties. They also serve as guides to the tape in helping decide what to transcribe and what to leave out. In some cases, where tape recording is not possible, brief notes may be the only way of recording the data. In this case we would try to write down some exact quotations and brief comments, supplemented by notes after the interview.

Recording Immediately Following the Interview   The third approach to recording interview data is to *make a record of the interview soon after it occurs*. This can be done in a variety of ways but it is important to allow sufficient time for this. One hour of interviewing may require four hours to develop the notes afterwards, particularly if this is the only record of the interview. Writing a process recording of the interview as soon as possible after the interview helps. The same four levels used in making field notes can be used in writing up research interviews—that is, to use a four-column format. In the first column we write as close to a verbatim account of the interview as we can recall. This would include our questions, probes and statements as well as the interviewee's responses.

Use the next column to note our interpretations of the meanings, emotions, and relationships inferred from the words and gestures. In the third column, any insights or themes that occur are noted. The fourth column is to reflect on what we were thinking or feeling at the time and to note other things that were occurring that may have caused interference (e.g., room was too warm or too noisy, other distractions).

Using Visual Aids

Data are recorded using a variety of visual aids to supplement and support our field notes and tapes. Diagrams show how ideas are related, and flow charts outline sequences, processes, and events. Eco-maps and genograms present relationships and their various dimensions. Photographs capture the field setting or environment. All of these visual aids contain a great deal of data and depict our specific field setting and the people within it, in a manner that written words simply cannot convey as effectively or as economically. Visual aids add an additional dimension in combination with other data collection methods.

Step 5: Making Sense of the Data

Analyzing qualitative data is presented in depth in Chapter 22. It is important to keep in mind at this point, however, that we need to make some sense of our experiences as participant observers. This involves analyzing the data collected. At some point, notwithstanding some initial prior reviews of the data as they are being gathered and organized, there comes a time when a full-scale intensive analysis occurs as the next step in the research process.

Step 5 is marked by a critical shift in how we have been working so far, and it requires the use of a different set of skills and abilities. It is also a time when we are quite overwhelmed with the prospect of wading through masses of data and making sense of them. It may be a particular challenge to move into this step, particularly if our forte has been the developing of social relationships, taking on various participant observer roles, and being flexible and resourcefully adaptable in our field setting in an effort to ensure that we have good data to analyze.

The analysis step allows our data to be coded, sifted, sorted, and categorized so that themes, theories, and generalizations can be constructed and generated. In this way, meaning can be made of our research endeavor, and our results can be reported.

Step 6: Reporting the Findings

As should be evident by now, participant observation studies allow for the creation of a rich source of data about a situation or phenomenon involving people. The raw data include such items as our written observation notes and correspondence, audiotapes, videotapes, personal journals with reflections, as well as notes made after debriefing and consultation sessions with research advisors. A final report of our study includes an overview of our research question and the methods and techniques used in the study, detailed descriptions of the people and related phenomena, themes or hypotheses emerging from all the different data sources, information about our personal process, biases, and assumptions, and recommendations based upon our findings.

Normally, once the data are gathered and analyzed, they are written up as a case study using quite detailed descriptions about the events or situation being studied. The final report includes themes and theoretical interpretations (or hypotheses) emerging from the data. It includes recommendations for further study or action.

The intended audience of the report impacts what and how it is written. The general public requires a different level of explanation than does an academic audience. The use of jargon is avoided unless the audience is comprised of others working in a similar or related area. Other possible audiences include other researchers or professional practitioners and government departments or agencies. Given the newly emerging view of research participants as having a vital partnership role in the research process, all those having a part in our study should have access to, or otherwise be provided with, a summary or a full copy of the final report.

Writing is facilitated by having blocks of uninterrupted time and perseverance. It involves drafting and editing, and often includes showing early drafts to some or all of the insiders and consulting with research advisors. Eventually, a unique document is produced that is appropriate for the study undertaken and its intended audience.

Robert McClelland and Carol D. Austin (1996) present a very clear description of exactly how to write up a qualitatively oriented final report.

ETHICAL CONSIDERATIONS

Ethical considerations must be taken into account for any research situation. There are additional ethical issues that must be addressed in doing participant observation because of the close and sustained relationships with research participants and the fact that the balance of research activities occurs in a field setting where many other influences may surface and need to be dealt with as the study proceeds. Thus, through proper sponsorship and approvals, plus informed consent of all those involved, it is crucial to attend to what is required to prevent adverse consequences.

Beyond this, there is the issue of the level of information we provide our research participants in reference to the roles we assumed during the study, and the degree to which we disclosed personal information. While there are different views on this, we advise that, wherever possible, our research participants should be included as copartners in our research study in as open and as equal a way as possible. We have to decide how much to reveal about ourselves and the research project itself. Disclosure ranges on a continuum from fully covert (no one in the field setting is aware of the study) to fully disclosed (everyone knows the specifics of the study).

It is unlikely, however, that a social work research project would get approval from an ethics board either in an academic or in a social-work–related setting, unless it was near the fully disclosed end of the spectrum, where our research participants give their informed consent and know how our data will be stored and used. Covert research studies are simply not ethical.

SUMMARY

This chapter presented an overview of participant observation as an obtrusive data collection method. It described its unique characteristics, such as issues of gaining access and entry into a field setting, forming and sustaining relationships (which includes the continuum of roles adopted by the researcher), and data gathering involving the use of less structured data gathering approaches.

We included strategies for recording the data and have attempted to create an awareness of the fine and delicate balance that exists between the participant-observer and the research participants, and of how crucial it is for us to be both attuned to this, as well as to make the necessary adjustments as our study unfolds to assure that the perspective of our research participants comes through clearly, accurately, and in considerable detail.

The following chapter presents how to collect data through surveys.

Chapter   15

Survey Research

ALMOST EVERYONE has been asked to take part in a survey of some form or another—a curbside interview, an exit poll after voting, a mass-mailed marketing survey, a seemingly random telephone opinion poll. To some extent, every research study that uses a survey as the data collection method can be called "survey research."

These studies can be designed to achieve a variety of ends, but they all seek to collect data from many individuals in order to understand something about them as a whole. It is essential, therefore, that survey research procedures produce data that are accurate, reliable, and representative, so findings can be generalized from a sample to the larger population or to different research situations. Survey research thus is a systematic way of collecting data by obtaining opinions or answers from selected respondents who represent the population of interest, or, occasionally, from an entire population.

The major steps in survey research are outlined on the left side of Figure 15.1, and the tasks to be completed in each step are listed on the right side.

Development and application of the sampling plan are essential to ensure the representativeness of the data collected (see Chapter 11). In most surveys, random sampling procedures are used to increase the probability that every person in the population has an equal opportunity of being selected for the

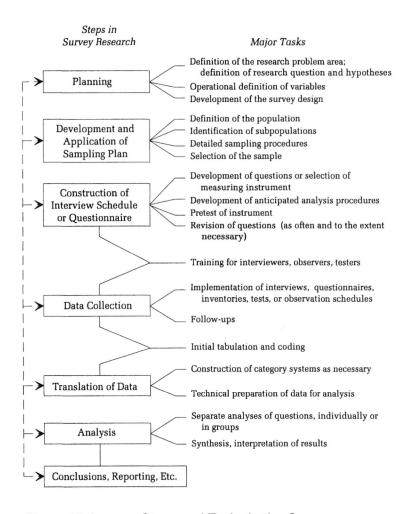

*Steps in
Survey Research*   *Major Tasks*

Figure 15.1   **Steps and Tasks in the Survey
Research Process**

sample. Probability sampling makes it possible to calculate the degree to which the sample is representative of the population from which it was drawn.

The steps in the research process that are unique to the survey method of data collection correspond to the measurement process that is at the center of any research effort. These steps include the construction of the interview schedule (for face-to-face and telephone interviews) or questionnaire (for mail surveys), the procedures for data collection, and to some extent, data coding and analysis.

Survey research was introduced in Chapter 10 as an example for the discussion of the design and construction of measuring instruments. Surveys can be used to collect data on facts about individuals separately and in organizations and communities, as well as data on their behaviors and unobservable variables such as attitudes, beliefs, feelings, and ethical standards.

SURVEY RESEARCH DESIGNS

Because survey research studies social phenomena by collecting data on numerous individuals in order to understand the group or population they represent, the research designs used usually follow the principles of group designs discussed in Chapter 12.

Knowledge Level

As Chapter 12 points out, the knowledge levels at which research studies are conducted are arranged on a three-point continuum from exploratory at the lowest level, to descriptive, to explanatory at the highest level, where "ideal" experiments can be conducted. Data can be collected with surveys at all three levels of design.

In exploratory designs, data are collected in order to form general ideas and tentative theories about the research question. In descriptive designs, the collection of data should result in more specific descriptions of the variables of interest; surveys are used as the data collection method in most descriptive studies to gather data on a sample or population in order to characterize it in terms of the variables under study.

A survey design that serves a descriptive purpose can also be exploratory if the collection of data allows the formulation of hypotheses that can be submitted to further study. One way this can be accomplished is with the use of open-ended questions in the survey instrument; this was the method employed in a study on sources of antiwar sentiment during the Vietnam era (Schuman, 1972).

Explanatory research designs are concerned with developing an understanding of social phenomena on the basis of the relationships among the variables of interest. Surveys are less commonly thought of as tools for explanatory studies, but they can be used effectively in these situations. Consider an executive director in a social work agency who is trying to determine if the agency should adopt a new technique for counseling victims of violent crime. For a number of reasons, it is decided that an experimental study (in which clients would be randomly assigned to the old or new method) is just not feasible. The director, however, reasons that another way to assess the quality of the new counseling approach would be to ask clients how satisfied they were with the outcomes it produced. This is an explanatory research problem, but in this case the only way to address it would be with survey methods such as mailing self-administered questionnaires to former clients of the agency.

The Dimension of Time

The dimension of time also must be taken into account in deciding on a survey research design. Most phenomena are subject to change over time, and many variables that are of interest in social work research, such as attitudes, emotional states, and social service utilization, can change rapidly. The two basic types of survey research designs are defined in terms of whether the variable is to be measured once, with a cross-sectional design, or over time, with a longitudinal design. Examples of these two types of survey designs are discussed in Chapter 12—the randomized cross-sectional survey and the randomized longitudinal survey.

To find out how satisfied an agency's clients are with the quality of services they have received, for example, the simplest and most direct approach would be to survey a sample of former clients about their attitudes toward services at the time they terminated. Even though a few weeks might be needed to survey enough clients to secure a sample of reasonable size, all data would be collected within a narrow time interval to provide data on clients' attitudes toward services at the time of termination. Cross-sectional designs use a "snapshot" method of data collection to provide data that are specific to a particular point in time.

If only the most satisfied clients actually complete the program, however, and many others who are dissatisfied drop out before completion, surveying only those who completed the program could provide a distorted picture of the true level of client satisfaction with the agency. To control for this threat to internal validity, a sample of clients might be followed from the start of services until they have all either dropped out or completed them. During this time, regular measurements would be taken of the clients' satisfaction with their services, and the variation of these measurements across time would be evaluated. Longitudinal designs use this method of data collection to monitor changes in variables of interest over an extended period of time.

Cross-Sectional Designs

Studies based on cross-sectional designs are usually associated with exploratory and descriptive research designs because they do a good job of providing data on the characteristics of a sample or population. A cross-sectional survey can be used to determine whether a particular problem exists within a group of clients and what the level of the problem is. Needs assessments, used by community development workers to identify neighborhood problems and service gaps, are an example. The principal advantage of this approach to survey research is that the necessary data can be collected quickly and inexpensively.

Cross-sectional studies are also used in explanatory designs to test relationships among characteristics of members of a sample or population. The main problem with these studies is that, because of their one-shot nature, they cannot clearly establish the time order of variables (see Chapter 12).

Longitudinal Designs

In longitudinal studies, data collected to indicate characteristics of a sample or population are repeated over two or more time periods, which allows consideration of how the sample characteristics have changed. The three types of longitudinal studies—trend, cohort, and panel studies—all use this repeated-measures approach to data collection.

Trend Studies   Trend studies utilize data from surveys carried out at periodic intervals on samples drawn from a particular population. The U.S. Department of Labor, under contract with the Census Bureau, for example, conducts the Current Population Survey (CPS) every March. Though a new sample is drawn each year, the population of interest remains the same. The data collected by the CPS are used primarily to gauge annual trends in unemployment and labor-force participation, but they also provide valuable data on other changes in the characteristics of the U.S. population. The accuracy of the assessments of trends revealed by these types of surveys depends on their regular use over a considerable period of time.

Cohort Studies   Cohort studies focus on specific groups of people who share certain characteristics. A cohort can be defined as a set of individuals who undergo a particular experience at a certain time, such as all high school graduates entering college in a certain year. Successive random samples are drawn from this group to monitor how the characteristics of members change over time. The baby boom generation is an example of a birth cohort—in this case, all persons born in the period from approximately 1946 to 1962. Studies of random samples of its members have been used to identify trends in American life, from fashion to family structure to political preferences.

A foster care administrator might use a cohort study to evaluate services to children who entered foster homes during a particular year. In each subsequent year a random sample would be drawn from among members of the cohort who remained in care, and data from these samples could be used to distinguish children who had exited quickly from the program from those who had experienced long or repeated stays in out-of-home care.

Panel Studies   Both trend studies and cohort studies monitor changes in a population through use of a series of random samples of the members of the group, with each sample being comprised of a different group of individuals. In contrast, a panel study is designed to follow the same set of individuals over time and to collect data on a regular basis.

Some of the best-known research studies on the effects of public assistance programs have come from the Panel Study on Income Dynamics (PSID), conducted by researchers at the University of Michigan's Survey Research Center. The project began with 5,000 families in 1968 and included more than 20,000 families some 20 years later. The longitudinal nature of this study has enabled researchers to examine transitions into and out of poverty and to study events associated with these transitions through related studies that have produced important results. Mary Jo Bane (1986), for example, studied episodes of poverty among children in the sample, recognizing that most poor children are not always poor but instead live in families that move into and out of poverty as their circumstances change. Her findings showed that many white children made the transition into poverty as a result of becoming part of a female-headed household, but for African American children, poverty more often resulted from being born into a poor family.

Social workers have begun to recognize the advantages offered by longitudinal studies over the cross-sectional approach. The opportunity to monitor the service histories of clients or groups over time is often more valuable than simply determining their average condition at a particular point in time. Still, longitudinal designs are more costly, time-consuming, and complex than cross-sectional studies. In addition, the successful use of longitudinal designs requires careful planning and an orientation toward long-term rather than short-term research goals.

APPROACHES TO DATA COLLECTION FOR SURVEYS

The general classes of survey measuring instruments—self-report questionnaires and interview schedules for face-to-face and telephone interviews—were identified in Chapter 10. This chapter distinguishes among these approaches to data collection for surveys on the basis of the assistance offered to respondents from the researcher.

In the face-to-face interview, the interviewer poses questions directly to each member of the study sample and immediately records the responses on an interview schedule. In self-administered surveys, respondents complete the survey instrument without any direct assistance from an interviewer. This type includes group-administered questionnaires and mail surveys; by far the most frequently used form is the mailed questionnaire, which relies on respondents both to fill out the survey instrument and to mail it back. In telephone interviews, the interviewer poses questions and records data provided by respondents, but there is no face-to-face contact.

The three principal approaches to data collection in surveys are listed in Figure 15.2 along with the advantages and disadvantages of each one.

Technique	Advantages	Disadvantages
Face-to-Face Interview	◦ Highest response rate ◦ Subjects tend to provide more thoughtful answers ◦ Allows for longer, more open-ended responses ◦ Allows recording of nonverbal information ◦ Can reach disabled or illiterate respondents ◦ Interviewer can clarify questions for respondent ◦ Subjects more willing to answer sensitive questions	◦ Highest cost ◦ Highest chance for introduction of experimenter bias ◦ Respondent may react to personality of interviewer rather than content of the interview ◦ Interviewer may mis-record response
Mail Survey	◦ Lowest cost ◦ Subjects can read and respond to questions at their own pace ◦ Visual arrangement of items on written instrument can facilitate comprehension ◦ Provides greatest sense of anonymity/ confidentiality ◦ Lowest chance of introduction of experimenter bias	◦ Lowest response rate ◦ Feasible only with subjects having relatively good reading skills ◦ No opportunity to clarify confusing items ◦ Difficult to get in-depth or open-ended responses ◦ Cannot ensure that intended respondents are the actual respondents
Telephone Survey	◦ Relatively low cost ◦ Can be completed quickly ◦ Interviewer can clarify questions for respondent ◦ Can reach respondents with poor reading/writing skills ◦ Allows direct computer data entry	◦ Not useful for low-income respondents who do not have a tele-phone ◦ High initial vocal inter-action, misses nonverbal responses ◦ Requires simple questions, unless a copy of the survey instrument is mailed in advance

Figure 15.2   Advantages and Disadvantages to Three
                   Principal Approaches to Data Collection
                   in Survey Research

FACE-TO-FACE INTERVIEWS

Face-to-face verbal contact is the most basic and most common form of communication among humans. Survey respondents are usually more willing to participate when questions are posed directly by someone in their presence, so response rates for face-to-face interviews are relatively high. Respondents also are less likely to give distracted or ill-considered answers to questions in the presence of a person who directly asks for their views.

Even the simplest questions in an interview schedule may be confusing to some people or in some circumstances, and an interviewer can explain the meaning each question is intended to convey in a way that is impossible with self-administered written survey instruments. Face-to-face interviews also allow inclusion of respondents who have various disabilities, such as a lack of reading and writing skills, language barriers, or visual or physical impairments.

Within limits, the interview setting also avoids some of the rigid structure that must be imposed on the construction of questions and responses in a written instrument. Not only can the interviewer explain the questions in detail, but, particularly if a tape recorder is used, detailed verbal answers that respondents would be unable or unwilling to put in writing can be recorded. Face-to-face interviews thus can incorporate more open-ended questions than is possible with mailed surveys. Moreover, the presence of the interviewer makes it possible to capture nuances of responses that would otherwise be lost.

Somewhat paradoxically, respondents have been found to be more likely to answer sensitive personal questions when they are posed by face-to-face interviewers rather than telephone interviewers (Groves, 1988). One explanation is that face-to-face interviewers are better able to establish legitimacy by sending cover letters, presenting their credentials, and maintaining a professional demeanor.

Limitations

In spite of these advantages, comparatively few surveys employ face-to-face interviews as the principal data collection method. The main reason is the cost of employing and training interviewers; this is often the major expenditure in survey research, and it is extremely high with face-to-face interviewing. In order to satisfy cost constraints, we may have to abandon plans for such interviews or drastically scale down the scope of our study. This is a problem with longitudinal studies and cross-sectional projects, where time, energy, and expense may be needed to train interviewers to replace those who leave.

The time and cost for interviewers to travel to meet with respondents represent another expense. The Postal Service does the work of delivering mail surveys, and telephone interviewers are connected instantly to respondents, but face-to-face interviewers often must go where the respondents are. Moreover, when respondents are not at home, telephone interviewers can call back later, and mailed questionnaires wait to be retrieved from the mailbox. In studies using face-to-face interviews, respondents who cannot be located or who fail to keep an appointment also add to the expense of follow-up.

While the direct human interaction in face-to-face interviews facilitates respondents' willingness to participate and improves their understanding of the survey instrument, it may also bias their answers in various ways and thus be a source of measurement error. Respondents may answer in a way that they believe will please the interviewer rather than according to their own beliefs, or if they are participating reluctantly or take a dislike to the interviewer, they may deliberately misrepresent their views. Because of their response sets (see Chapter 8), survey participants may give answers that they believe are socially acceptable, agree with statements regardless of their opinion, or try to give unusual or unexpected responses.

Interviewers also can be a source of bias or error. Poorly trained personnel often make clerical errors or are inconsistent in recording data, and even the best-trained interviewers can subtly influence respondents' answers through verbal or nonverbal cues of which they themselves may be unaware.

Preparing for the Interview

When face-to-face interviewing is the data collection method, preparation for the interview is a very lengthy process indeed. Before the interview takes place, we must lay the groundwork by developing the interview schedule, hiring and training interviewers, choosing the sample, obtaining respondents' consent, and making arrangements for the interview.

Developing the Interview Schedule

The interview schedule is the survey instrument used with both face-to-face and telephone interviews. The guidelines presented in Chapter 10 for constructing questionnaires for use as survey instruments are applicable to interview schedules as well. Interview schedules, however, have certain features that distinguish them from other types of questionnaires, particularly those used in mailed surveys.

Figure 15.3 reproduces the opening portion of an interview schedule used with 300 mothers whose children had been placed in foster care (Jenkins & Norman, 1972). The entire interview instrument covered 34 pages and included open- and closed-ended questions, checklists, and scales; the interview lasted about two hours. Figure 15.4 presents the entire interview schedule for a study by Harvey Gochros (1970) on postplacement adoption services, for which he was the sole interviewer. This schedule was used with 114 adoptive parents, and a similar one was used with 18 postplacement social workers. Extensive use of abbreviations (AP = adoptive parent, CW = caseworker, SP = supervisory or postplacement period) contributed to the

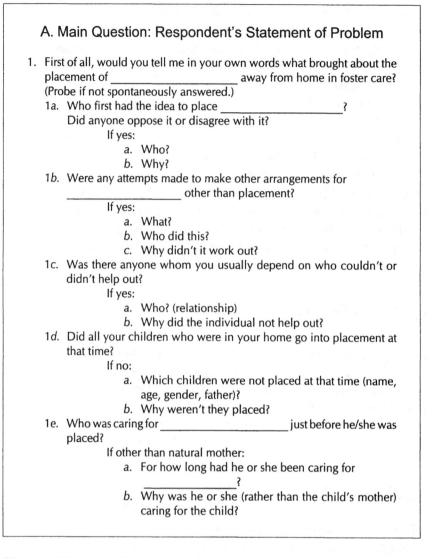

A. Main Question: Respondent's Statement of Problem

1. First of all, would you tell me in your own words what brought about the placement of _____ away from home in foster care? (Probe if not spontaneously answered.)

    1a. Who first had the idea to place _____ ? Did anyone oppose it or disagree with it?
         If yes:
             a. Who?
             b. Why?

    1b. Were any attempts made to make other arrangements for _____ other than placement?
         If yes:
             a. What?
             b. Who did this?
             c. Why didn't it work out?

    1c. Was there anyone whom you usually depend on who couldn't or didn't help out?
         If yes:
             a. Who? (relationship)
             b. Why did the individual not help out?

    1d. Did all your children who were in your home go into placement at that time?
         If no:
             a. Which children were not placed at that time (name, age, gender, father)?
             b. Why weren't they placed?

    1e. Who was caring for _____ just before he/she was placed?
         If other than natural mother:
             a. For how long had he or she been caring for _____ ?
             b. Why was he or she (rather than the child's mother) caring for the child?

Figure 15.3   Portion of an Interview Schedule on Foster Care Placement

brevity of the instrument. Interview schedules do not look like familiar questionnaire forms because they are designed to be completed by the interviewer rather than the respondent.

With self-administered questionnaires, substantial design efforts are necessary to ensure that respondents will be able to understand and complete all questions on the form. Because interview schedules are seen only by the interviewer, design efforts can be directed to maximizing the ease and accuracy of data recording and subsequent coding. Instructions to respondents are also included in interview schedules, but because they are read and, if necessary, explained by the interviewer, they can be more concise.

1. What were you told about the purposes and content of the SP?
2. What did you expect the visits to be like?
3. How were they different from what you expected?
4. Why do you think there is a SP?
5. How many SP visits were there? Average length?
6. How many AP initiated? Why?
7. How many unexpected? Opinion
8. How many were you present:
9. Ever feel left out?
10. What did you talk about?
11. What do you think CW wanted you to bring up or discuss in SP visits?
12. Subsequent contacts.
13. What sort of problems did you run into during the SP?
14. Books recommended? Why? Read? Useful?
15. Did you think of CW more as a friend or caseworker?
16. What did you like most about CW? What did you like least about CW?
17. Did CW create the kind of atmosphere where you felt free to talk over your real feelings about things?
18. Did you ever withhold any information or feelings from CW?
19. How much do you think CW knew about child care and development?
20. What did you think about when you knew a visit was scheduled?
21. What did you think about just after the visit was over?
22. Did your feelings change about the visits during the SP?
23. What did you find the most helpful result of the visits?
24. What did you find to be the least and most unpleasant aspect of the CW?
25. Any way agency could have been more helpful during the SP?
26. How helpful was the SP to you, overall?
27. Will the visits by helpful to you in the future?
28. How did you feel when the decree was finally granted?
29. Do you think there should be a waiting period?
30. If yes, how long?
31. Should there be CW visits? Why?
32. Compulsory? Why?
33. If they had been voluntary, would you have requested any?
34. If you adopt again and if voluntary, would you have requested any?
35. Groups for parents of 5-year-olds, interested?
36. Groups for parents of adolescents, interested?
37. If ran into a problem with a child, contact worker?
38. Second child: planning, applied, placed, not planning?
39. If worker was different from study, was transition difficult?
40. Comments:

Figure 15.4   Interview Schedule Used for Study on Postplacement Adoption Services

A particularly useful characteristic of interview schedules is that they can include prompts, reminders, and explanatory notes for interviewers. In a survey of client satisfaction, for example, clients might be asked to identify the one aspect of an agency's services that they thought was most helpful. The schedule could include instructions for the interviewer on how to help clients who offer more than one answer to select the most appropriate one. Clients might be asked to list all the services they had received at the agency as a way of indicating those that they found memorable. Other prompts could be included for use in stimulating clients' memories, but their selective use by interviewers can introduce problems of response bias.

Some studies supplement the interview schedule with written material to be given to respondents. Lengthy questions, those that are based on prior contingencies (e.g., "If yes,"), and those in which the respondent is asked to choose from a long list of possible responses are often enhanced by written aids, for example.

Hiring and Training Interviewers

In the same way that counseling requires greater verbal ability than simple conversation, face-to-face interviewing requires more skill than everyday communication. Careful selection of interviewers and training to develop their skills are crucial in the use of face-to-face interviews. Competent interviewers are more likely to elicit truthful, comprehensive data from respondents and less likely to make mistakes in administering the interview schedule and recording the data.

Hiring interviewers who are appropriate to the task is the first consideration; there must be a good fit between the interviewer and the respondent. Because people generally relate best to those they perceive as similar to themselves, interviewers should, as far as possible, reflect the characteristics of potential respondents in such variables as age, gender, race or ethnicity, and life experiences (Schuman & Converse, 1971; Singer, Frankel, & Glassman, 1983). For studies that focus on a very narrow sample or involve only a small number of interviewers, the goal should be to select interviewers who could put the respondents at ease and overcome their perceptions of differences between themselves and the interviewer.

The traits to look for in interviewers are similar to those that characterize good social workers—warmth, sincerity, appropriate dress and appearance, and good verbal and nonverbal skills. Interviewers must also possess the skills necessary to read and understand the interview schedule, interpret it for respondents, and express their responses in writing.

The process of training interviewers is devoted to enhancing these basic skills, with the goal of reducing bias or other sources of measurement error. Among the most common sources of error in interviewing are instruction and interrogation error (not reading the instructions or questions exactly as they are written on the interview schedule), response option error (failing to give the exact list of possible responses to a question from which the respondent is to choose), and recording error (inaccurately recording the response). More difficult to monitor is interviewer bias, which occurs when interviewers give cues concerning the responses they expect or favor, or when they interpret and record respondents' answers in a way that fits their own desires or expectations.

Choosing the Population or Sample

The basic sampling principles presented in Chapter 11 apply to any data collection technique. With face-to-face interviews, however, a specific consideration is the use of the smallest possible sample that will allow for acceptable sampling error, due to the expense associated with interviewing each member of the sample. Somewhat smaller samples may be accepted with this data collection method than with mail or telephone surveys, on the premise that the quality of data gathered by the interview will balance the increased likelihood of incorrectly inferring population characteristics due to the smaller sample size.

Research studies based on face-to-face interviews often make use of a form of cluster sampling known as area probability sampling, in which the sample is selected from persons living in selected geographic areas. This not only ensures the geographic representativeness of the sample, it also facilitates efficient transportation arrangements for interviewers.

These studies also use nonprobability sampling techniques such as convenience or snowball sampling to select respondents. In one study, for example, a researcher conducted in-depth interviews with a sample of 20 individuals who had been divorced after reaching the age of 60 (Weingarten, 1988). Members of the sample were selected on the basis of their association with a support group for people who had experienced late-life divorce. Convenience sampling was the only practical means of identifying members of this unique population, and their special needs were perhaps best served by face-to-face interviews.

Obtaining Consent of Respondents

Before data can be collected from respondents in any research study, their written, informed consent must be obtained (see Chapter 4). Informed consent means that respondents have agreed to participate after having been notified of at least the general purpose of the study, the uses to be made of the data, and the means by which confidentiality is to be maintained.

Though agency-based studies such as those used as examples in this chapter may not be subjected to the formal scrutiny of an institutional review board, they are expected to conform to the ethical standards enforced by such boards. We must ensure that our research participants will not be subjected to any unnecessary risks. For example, one risk is that topics covered in the interview schedule might involve sensitive or stressful issues for some respondents. Another is the risk to the privacy of respondents who are asked to provide information that they might otherwise not want to reveal.

To counter such risks, we can contact potential respondents in advance by mail, telephone, or personal communication to explain the type of information to be sought and the safeguards that are to be taken to ensure their confidentiality. Often this notification takes the form of a cover letter that includes a consent form to be signed by respondents who agree to participate. A checklist for developing cover letters can be found in Figure 15.6.

Informed consent may also be obtained through an organization with which potential respondents are affiliated. In this case, obtaining consent is a two-stage process in which we must gain the sanction of the organization before contacting its members. In any case, our task is to explain the merits of our study in such a way that those contacted will be able to make the decision to participate or decline freely and on a factual basis.

Arranging the Interviews

Once enough respondents for the sample have given their consent to take part in our study, we need to perform the logistical tasks involved in arranging the interviews. Advance planning is necessary; arrangements often must be made at the time the respondent is asked to participate. The characteristics of sample members may dictate that interviews must be conducted in the evening or on weekends, for example, and this would affect the hiring of interviewers. It also would restrict the number of interviews that can be completed in a day or a week, so we might have to hire more interviewers or extend the study.

The location of the interview is another consideration. Because people generally are more comfortable in familiar surroundings, the best location often is in the respondent's home, office, or some similar setting. Other options are the interviewer's office or a meeting place that is neutral for both respondent and interviewer. The preferences of the respondent, the cost of transportation, and safety concerns for both the respondent and the interviewer must be taken into account. Some areas are dangerous for both residents and visitors, especially if the interview must be scheduled late in the day.

The location also must be conducive to the interviewing process. Because clients are often more willing to discuss personal issues at home and professional issues at the office, the subject matter of the interview should be considered in determining the location. Potential problems with a location should be anticipated; a home, workplace, or neutral site such as a crowded restaurant may be plagued by high noise levels, lack of privacy, and distractions that can interfere with the success of the interview.

Some cancellations and no-shows by respondents are inevitable, but their frequency and the amount of difficulty they create can be minimized. One of the simplest but most effective precautions is to contact respondents ahead of time, usually the day before the interview, to remind them of the appointment and confirm the time and location. Monetary rewards are another strategy that can improve participation. The payment is usually small, from $5 to $50, but offering it can increase respondents' willingness to take part in the study and likelihood of keeping the interview appointment. If scheduled interviews do

[University Letterhead]

Dear _____ :

As part of my doctoral program in Social Welfare at the University of Washington, I am seeking information about the attitudes and perceptions of mental health agency staff regarding program evaluation and accountability of mental health professionals.

As an employee of one of the mental health agencies in this state, you are being asked to complete two questionnaires regarding the subjects mentioned above. The first questionnaire is attached. The second questionnaire will follow in approximately four months. Each questionnaire will take about 20–30 minutes to complete. Should you complete the first questionnaire, I ask that this be an expression of your intent to complete the second questionnaire, although participation in both cases is entirely voluntary. You are free to withdraw your consent to participate or discontinue participation at any time.

All questionnaires will be kept in a locked file and I am the only person who will have access to this file. All questionnaires will be destroyed 6 months following completion of the study.

I hope you will be willing to help in this project but wish to assure you that your participation is entirely voluntary. You are welcome to ask questions regarding the study and your participation in it. I will be visiting your agency when I distribute the questionnaires or you may contact me at the University. I wish to remind you that your comments will remain strictly confidential. Thank you for your assistance and co-operation.

_____ Investigator   _____ Date
    Joan Avery

I voluntarily agree to complete this questionnaire and have the opportunity to ask questions.

_____ Respondent   _____ Date

Figure 15.5   Example of a Simple Cover Letter

not take place, we must remain extremely polite and very accommodating and try to reschedule.

Interviewing Skills

The basic principles of research interviewing are well established, and a few of the most important skills interviewers should have are identified in this section. These are not traits possessed by certain individuals but abilities that can be learned or improved by any competent person.

Rapport-building involves the interviewer's ability to make personal contacts with respondents beyond just asking them questions. Rapport is the

	YES	NO
1. Does the letter communicate the appeal to respondents?		
2. Does it include a reasonable explanation of the study by anticipating and countering respondents' questions?	___	___
3. Does it set forth the benefits of the study?	___	___
4. Does it describe the importance of the respondent to the study and indicate that no one else can be substituted?		
5. Does it exceed the maximum of one page?	___	___
6. Does it appear under an appropriate letterhead?	___	___
7. Do the individualized name and address and the date appear on the letter?	___	___
8. Is the investigator's individually applied signature included?	___	___
9. Does the letter include a confidentiality statement and explanation of the coding procedures?	___	___
10. Does the attachment to the cover letter include a stamped, self-addressed questionnaire reply envelope?	___	___
11. Does the letter indicate how results will be shared with respondents?	___	___
12. Are there instructions for indicating that a copy of the results is wanted (e.g., placing name and address on back of return envelope)?	___	___
13. Is the letter reproduced on a word processor?	___	___

Figure 15.6   Checklist for Developing a Cover Letter

spirit of affinity with respondents communicated by the interviewer, so they know they are recognized and appreciated as real people, not simply as guinea pigs or faceless sources of information. The level of rapport appropriate to a research interview is much lower than in a counseling interaction, because the interviewer is only collecting data, not offering professional assistance. Still, people are more truthful and open with those who they believe are genuinely interested in them. An interviewer who engages in a brief conversation before the interview will often be rewarded with more accurate and informative responses.

The interviewer must also be willing to answer questions from respondents concerning the purpose of the study, the nature of the interview schedule, and other aspects of the study. We can anticipate such questions and incorporate the answers in written instructions to the interviewer or in a set of standardized responses to be learned by the interviewer. Unanticipated questions do arise, however, and we must learn how to respond to them without biasing responses.

Another concern is the overly talkative respondent. Many studies in which face-to-face interviews are used focus on populations that are difficult to reach by other means, so people sampled from these populations may be isolated and lonely and welcome the opportunity to interact with the interviewer. Difficulties arise when this need for interaction interferes with the interviewer's ability to complete the schedule. Conversational digressions can be controlled by gently but consistently bringing the respondent back to the question at hand, but a certain amount of extraneous dialogue must be accommodated. Allowing extra time between interviews is often helpful.

During the actual data collection process, the interviewer must follow the precise wording of instructions and questions on the interview schedule. If there are variations from this script, different respondents will have different understandings of what is being asked, and inconsistencies or inaccuracies can be a source of measurement error.

Variations in the way the interview schedule is presented may also bias the respondent toward giving a particular type of answer. This does not mean that the interviewer should adopt a robotic approach in conducting the interview.

SELF-ADMINISTERED SURVEYS: GROUP-ADMINISTERED QUESTIONNAIRES

The critical barrier to the use of face-to-face interviews is the expense involved in hiring, training, and transporting interviewers. The obvious solution to this problem is to devise means whereby respondents can complete the survey instrument by themselves without the necessity of having an interviewer present. Of the two most common types of self-administered surveys (i.e., group-administered questionnaires and mail surveys), the first is discussed in this section, and the following section is devoted to mail surveys.

Group-administered questionnaires are used in situations where respondents can be brought together for the purpose of completing a survey instrument. The questionnaire is distributed to a group of respondents who complete it individually, though a member of the research team is usually present to assist. A cover letter to explain the project and obtain the respondents' consent should be handed out with the questionnaire (see Figure 15.5). A more detailed discussion of cover letters for use with self-administered questionnaires is given in the section on mail surveys.

To assess client satisfaction with agency services, for example, we might begin by sampling clients by community areas and making arrangements for those living in each area to gather at a central location. The cost of securing a meeting place and transporting clients to and from the site is likely to be much less than the cost of sending interviewers to many locales to meet with individual respondents.

The arrangements for group administration are outlined in Figure 15.7. In addition, a checklist for introducing group-administered questionnaires to potential respondents is displayed in Figure 15.8.

Group administration is also used with groups who meet on a regular basis. An agency administrator examining social workers' reactions to revised state guidelines for assistance to low-income clients could use this approach, for example. At a regular meeting of workers for case staffings and training, questionnaires could be distributed to solicit workers' anonymous opinions on the change and their experiences in acquainting clients with the new regulations.

Group administration is less expensive than face-to-face interviews, and it usually yields a much higher response rate than mail surveys. Nevertheless, for numerous other reasons, mailed questionnaires are the type of self-administered survey that is used most frequently.

SELF-ADMINISTERED SURVEYS: MAIL SURVEYS

Until recently, when telephone surveys became commonplace, mail questionnaires were the method of data collection most commonly associated with survey research. In the United States, the most familiar example of a mail survey is the national population census conducted every 10 years by the Bureau of the Census, most recently in March 1990. Though the census still makes some use of face-to-face interviews, most of the data are collected from mail questionnaires.

Indeed, with a survey that attempts to collect data on the entire population of a country with some 260 million people, no other method of data collection currently used would be economically feasible. The U.S. census is unusual because it attempts to cover an entire population rather than a sample of its members, but it demonstrates the importance of mail surveys in allowing us to study a much larger number of respondents than is otherwise possible.

By far the most important advantage of mail surveys is their low unit cost. These savings are possible because recipients themselves complete the questionnaire, so there is no cost for interviewers' time, and the survey instrument is both delivered and returned by mail, which is substantially less expensive than transporting interviewers to and from respondents' locations. Mail surveys also usually are less expensive than telephone interviews, particularly where respondents are widely distributed geographically. The cost of mailing a questionnaire is the same whether it is mailed across town or across the country.

The fact that the questionnaire is self-administered, so no contact with another person is required, can be a disadvantage. Respondents who do not understand a question cannot readily obtain clarification, and more detailed verbal responses cannot be recorded. At the same time, there are no problems

	YES	NO
1. Are there enough questionnaires?	____	____
2. Have plans been developed for persons unable to attend the questionnaire completion session to complete and return the instrument at another time?	____	____
3. Have all staff been notified in writing and verbally at a staff meeting about the date and time of the group administration?	____	____
4. Has the physical environment been checked in advance to make sure there will be sufficient space and adequate lighting for writing?	____	____
5. Have efforts been made to anticipate and eliminate possible sources of noise or distraction during the questionnaire completion session?	____	____
6. Are there plans to read aloud the instructions on the face sheet at the questionnaire completion session?	____	____
7. Will specific instructions be given on how to mark the questionnaire or answer sheet?	____	____
8. Is sufficient time allowed for questions from respondents before beginning to complete the questionnaire?	____	____
9. Will clarification announcements based on respondents' questions about an item on the questionnaire be made slowly, in a clear voice that is loud enough for all to hear?	____	____
10. Are all questionnaires to be collected immediately after completion and checked for completed identification information and consent form signature?	____	____
11. Have all respondents been informed of a sign-up roster to receive copies of the results of the study?	____	____
12. Will each respondent be personally thanked when the questionnaire is returned?	____	____
13. Are follow-up letters to be sent to agency administrators and key staff members who facilitate the implementation of the group-administered questionnaire?	____	____

Figure 15.7   Checklist for Administration of Group-
                   Administered Questionnaires

with interviewer error or bias, either in asking for data or in recording the research participant's responses.

Reliance on written instruments can also be a liability. It is virtually impossible to write a questionnaire that does not contain at least a few potentially confusing questions. In the absence of an interviewer who can explain the questions, respondents must interpret each one as best they can, which increases the possibility of error in the data. Moreover, written questionnaires are useful only with respondents who have the reading comprehension, sight, and other physical capacities necessary to complete the forms. Surveys of populations that include illiterate or visually or physically disabled persons cannot make use of these instruments unless personnel are assigned to assist respondents who are unable to complete the questionnaires on their own.

Nevertheless, the ability of mail surveys to present questions in written form can greatly enhance both the clarity of the questions and the types of data that can be gathered. Interview schedules, for example, have a restricted range of response categories for a given question because respondents can keep only a limited number of options in mind. Written questionnaires can list a wide range of options for review and reference as necessary.

Graphic illustrations of response categories also can be provided to enhance respondents' understanding. One study that focused on children, for example, gave examples of pictorial scales, including one that offered response categories in the form of simple drawings of faces with expressions ranging from happy to sad (Alreck & Settle, 1985). Children who might not comprehend the numerical gradations on a typical rating scale can use this type of visual representation to express variations in their feelings.

Overcoming the Disadvantage of Low Response Rates

The primary disadvantage of a mail survey is its low response rate. A person who receives a questionnaire in the mail usually can opt not to participate by passive means such as setting it aside and forgetting it, deciding not to fill it

---

	YES	NO
1. Does the face sheet of the questionnaire include general information about the purpose of the study?	____	____
2. Is there an indication of how much time it should take to complete the questionnaire?	____	____
3. Is a separate consent form attached to the questionnaire for the respondent to sign?	____	____
4. Does the face sheet include all necessary instructions for completing all items (e.g., "Don't skip around," "Answer all items to the best of your ability.")?	____	____

Figure 15.8   Checklist for Introducing Group-
                    Administered Questionnaires

out, or throwing it away. Choosing not to participate in other types of surveys usually involves a more direct (and therefore more difficult) refusal.

Without careful efforts to increase returns, it is not uncommon for mail surveys to yield response rates of only 10 to 20 percent. Rates this low call into question the external validity of the data, which has its basis in the assumption that those who did return the questionnaire comprise a sample that is representative of the larger population. The measurement validity of a survey design, or the assumption that the survey measures what it is supposed to measure and does so accurately, also can be jeopardized by a low response rate.

To ensure the most accurate count in the 1990 national census of the U.S. population, massive information programs preceded the mailing of official survey forms to residential addresses, follow-ups were sent requesting compliance with instructions to complete the forms, and face-to-face interviews were conducted among the homeless, immigrants, and others who might be missed. Nevertheless, after a follow-up survey, including a random sample of racial, ethnic, and other groups, the Census Bureau reported in June 1991 that the 1990 census had missed 2.1 percent of the U.S. population overall, and 4.8 percent of African Americans and 5.2 percent of Hispanics had been undercounted. By the revised figures, the U.S. population was 253.9 million in 1990, 5.3 million people more than had originally been counted, and the percentages of African Americans and Hispanics missed were more than double the average.

There are no absolute standards for response rates in mail surveys used by social workers, and the question of what constitutes a minimally acceptable response rate can be a difficult one. Earl R. Babbie (1995) offers a rough guide of 50 percent as an "adequate" response rate, 60 percent as a "good" rate, and 70 percent as "very good." This is consistent with the views of most social work researchers, but the question still remains about what to do with studies that yield lower response rates.

This question is gaining greater immediacy as mail survey research becomes harder to carry out effectively. The proliferation of pseudosurveys, such as sales promotions or political tracts disguised as questionnaires, along with surveys that are poorly designed or executed, make the public less willing to participate. Because of this, those of us conducting legitimate, good-quality studies are struggling to obtain adequate response rates.

When initial response rates are low, we must be willing to make a dispassionate and open-minded assessment of whether our study is worth pursuing further. Among the questions to be considered in such an assessment are:

- Have procedures for maximizing response rates been fully employed (see below), and is it clear that further follow-up efforts would not be helpful?
- What are the potential sources of bias in the responses received (e.g., is it likely that certain types of sample members responded while others did

not)? What effect might these biases have had, and how substantial is that effect?

- Did the original sample include extra cases (an oversample) in anticipation of survey nonresponse? If so, was the number of extra cases appropriate to the actual number of nonresponses?
- What is the purpose of the study? Will the benefits of providing data on a previously little-studied topic outweigh the risks of reporting results that may be inaccurate due to low response rates? What data will be provided to readers to allow them to make their own judgments about this issue?

As the above questions suggest, determination of what constitutes a satisfactory response rate is more often a matter of reasoned judgment than the application of absolute standards. In general, the best way to deal with the problem is to minimize it through vigorous efforts to reduce nonresponses. The following sections of this chapter offer ways in which response rates can be optimized without sacrificing the cost effectiveness and other advantages of mail surveys.

Use a Good Cover Letter

A straightforward, easy-to-read cover letter may improve return rates and response accuracy more than any other single factor, while a vague or highly technical letter can have the opposite effect. A good cover letter for a mail survey should perform the following functions:

- Give the exact date of the mailing of the questionnaire.
- Identify the researcher and institutional affiliation, preferably on official, printed stationery that is unique to the project or organization.
- Explain the research project sufficiently to allow the respondent to understand its general purpose, but not in such detail as to be confusing or discouraging.
- Explain the significance of the study in terms of its potential benefit to policy or practice.
- Convey to the respondent the importance of participation in the study.
- Estimate how long the questionnaire will take to complete.
- Explain how the responses are to be used and how confidentiality will be maintained.
- Instruct the respondent how to return the completed form.
- Identify the person to contact with questions or concerns about the survey.

Some cover letters contain basic instructions on how to complete a questionnaire, but detailed directions should usually be reserved for the survey instrument. Some also specify a date by which the questionnaire is to be returned. This gives respondents a greater sense of urgency about the project, but the message must be carefully worded so they do not feel they are being pressured.

Before word processors made it easy to personalize letters, generic cover letters that were not addressed to any particular individual were used, or stick-on labels identical to those used to address the envelopes were added to the letters. Now most word processing and data management software programs for desktop computers can create individual labels and merge the names into the text of the letter. Personalized cover letters, which improve the likelihood of a response, then can be generated quickly and easily. The computerized label file also can produce address labels for the mailing envelopes, or, with some computer printers, envelopes can be fed in and addressed directly from the file.

Reduce Mailing Costs

Preparing a survey mailing becomes a balancing act between minimizing mailing costs and maximizing the appearance and readability of the questionnaire and the likelihood that it will be completed and returned. In an era of scarce funding for social programs in general and research projects in particular, the ability to cut costs is a critical factor in the successful completion of a study.

One problem is how to minimize the weight of the questionnaire in order to reduce the cost of both the initial mailing and the return postage. A comparatively easy option is to use both sides of the paper when printing the instrument, but this does not work when single sheets are stapled together.

The cover letter may appear on the front page of the booklet, with the questionnaire beginning on the first inside or first right-hand page. Using double-sided printing can cut as much as half the weight of the questionnaire. With lengthy instruments, it also reduces bulkiness, making them appear less formidable to respondents.

Other savings can be obtained in mailing survey instruments by using bulk mail rates or special discounts for nonprofit organizations. Bulk mail rates are based on volume—the larger the number of mailings, the cheaper the rate. The discount is higher still for nonprofit agencies.

Using bulk mail rates does have certain drawbacks. One is that the U.S. Postal Service requires all such mailings to be sorted by zip code before being delivered to the post office. This regulation can involve substantial expense in studies with a large number of mailings, and it has prompted many researchers to organize lists of survey recipients in zip-code order rather than alphabetical order. Another drawback is that bulk mail receives the lowest priority for handling, and slow delivery can cause problems if a timely response is needed.

Moreover, letters sent by bulk mail to incorrect or nonexistent addresses are usually discarded by the Postal Service rather than returned to the sender, and this makes the survey's nonresponse rate seem higher than it actually is. A comparatively new drawback of bulk mailings is their effect on recipients as mass mailings have proliferated. Many recipients have become skilled in spotting "junk" mail, usually by looking for the bulk mail classification on the postage stamp or meter mark, and envelopes bearing such marks are often discarded without being opened.

For any of these reasons, when a high return rate is important, we may choose to bear the added expense of first-class (or sometimes even special delivery) mail rates in order to improve the chances that the mail will be delivered on time, opened, and examined.

Enclose Suitable Return Envelopes

Another consideration in preparing mailings is to make it easy for respondents to return the completed questionnaire. Usually a return envelope is enclosed in the initial mailing, in most cases with return postage attached. The return envelope must fit easily inside the outgoing envelope but be large enough to accommodate the completed questionnaire.

Too little postage on the return envelope will cause the questionnaire to be sent back to the respondent, so the questionnaire should be weighed with the return envelope to determine the exact amount of postage needed. In the United States, an alternative is to use business reply envelopes. We are billed only for questionnaires that are returned, but business reply mail is billed at a higher rate than regular postage, so it might not be cost effective when high return rates are expected. Because bulk mail rates cannot be used on return envelopes, it is not unusual for the cost of returns to exceed that of outgoing mailings. A checklist for survey mailing procedures can be found in Figure 15.9.

Assure the Confidentiality of Respondents

Including some sort of identification of respondents on survey instruments is helpful in keeping track of those who have completed and returned them, so the number of follow-ups necessary is reduced. However, the use of any type of identifier (such as a number) can jeopardize the principle of confidentiality of participants. One way to deal with this is to inform respondents that identifying information included on the questionnaires in the form of a numerical code can only be interpreted from a master list retained by those

	YES	NO
1. Is the envelope an unusual size, shape, or color to attract attention, along with embellishments such as "Immediate reply requested"?	____	____
2. Has the size of the questionnaire and envelope been determined in relationship to using first-class postage and minimizing the appearance of bulky contents?	____	____
3. Has a mailing list been developed which includes the number of the questionnaire beside the name of the respondent?	____	____
4. Are the envelope contents folded together when inserted so that respondents will find all relevant materials on opening the envelope?	____	____
5. Is the mailing planned for early in the week in anticipation of time needed to forward mail to new addresses?	____	____
6. Will the mailing avoid a holiday period when respondents are likely to be away from home, and will it avoid December and the crush of holiday mail?	____	____

Figure 15.9   Checklist for Survey Mailing Procedures

administering the survey. Respondents also should be apprised of the measures that will be taken to maintain the security of this list and assured that it will be destroyed once the study has been completed.

Instead of identifying information on the questionnaire, each initial mailing could include a self-addressed, stamped postcard with coded information identifying the respondent. When respondents return these postcards separately at the same time they put the completed questionnaires in the mail, we can identify those who have returned the survey without being able to link them to a particular completed form. Follow-ups then need to be sent only to those who did not return the postcards and the completed questionnaires.

Follow Up on the Mailing

Procedures for following an initial mailing with subsequent reminders are often crucial to attaining a satisfactory return rate. The two major considerations in planning follow-ups are timing, or the intervals at which follow-ups should be sent, and format, or the types of follow-ups to be sent. Generally, for any survey there should be at least two follow-ups at roughly three-week intervals.

These intervals can be reduced if initial returns are slow, but postponing follow-ups for more than three weeks risks losing the impact of the mailings.

More than two follow-ups also may be appropriate, particularly if each is successful in bringing in a new wave of returns.

A variety of formats may be used for follow-ups, including postcards, letters, additional copies of the questionnaire, telephone calls, and face-to-face contacts. Donald A. Dillman (1978) argues for the use of a variety of these methods, with certain types of follow-ups occurring at specific intervals after the initial mailing. A postcard reminder is sent one week after the initial mailing; a follow-up letter, with an additional copy of the questionnaire and return envelope, two weeks later; and a final letter and another questionnaire copy and return envelope by certified mail on the seventh week following the initial mailing.

Some of us have added telephone contacts to this sequence. These can be extremely effective, because they convey our desire to obtain a response much more personally and directly than is possible in a letter, and they can produce immediate responses. A checklist for survey follow-up procedures is found in Figure 15.10.

TELEPHONE SURVEYS

Use of the telephone as a tool for conducting surveys has developed only within the past 25 years or so. Prior to this time, the proportion of households having telephones was too small to justify their use in data collection. As recently as 1960, only 78.5 percent of households in the United States had telephone service; excluding those who did not, those who tended to live in certain areas, or those who had certain other characteristics would lead to systematic bias in a study's findings (Lavrakas, 1987). In 1987, however, 92.5 percent of households had service, so the telephone became more viable as a research tool (U.S. Bureau of the Census, 1987).

Indeed, telephone surveys have become something of a modern phenomenon, assuming a place in the mind of the public that was once occupied by person-on-the-street interviewers or door-to-door census takers. These developments have been both favorable and unfavorable for surveys, as will be shown in this section.

One reason for the growth of telephone surveys is that they offer many of the merits of face-to-face interviews and mail survey techniques, without some of their drawbacks. Telephone interviews are relatively inexpensive, particularly compared to face-to-face interviews, because there are no transportation costs for either the interviewers or respondents.

Moreover, local telephone calls are often cheaper than first-class postage, and even if long-distance calls are necessary, WATS lines and other discounts for high-volume calling can keep unit costs comparatively low. Printing expenses also are generally lower for telephone surveys because interviewers need only one copy of an interview schedule. Nevertheless, telephone surveys

	YES	NO
1. Is there a preprinted follow-up postcard for mailing one week after mailing of cover letter?	____	____
2. Does the postcard include the respondent's name and address and the investigator's signature?	____	____
3. Does it thank the respondent if the questionnaire has already been returned?	____	____
4. Is a second follow-up letter ready for sending three weeks after mailing of the cover letter, with a replacement questionnaire and return envelope?	____	____
5. Is a third follow-up letter ready for certified mailing to remaining nonrespondents seven weeks after original mailing, with a replacement questionnaire and return envelope?	____	____

Figure 15.10   Checklist for Survey Follow-Up Procedures

are more expensive than mailings, falling about midway between mail surveys and face-to-face interviews.

Another reason telephone interviews are popular is that studies employing this technique can be completed much faster than those using other methods. Survey findings based on a representative sample of the U.S. population can be obtained by telephone interviewers in less than 24 hours, provided that a large and well-trained staff of interviewers, ample access to direct-dial long-distance telephone lines, and a prepared and tested interview schedule are all available.

Political pollsters and other public opinion research firms now employ telephone methods almost exclusively, for example. Opinion poll results and survey ratings of winners and losers in political debates can be announced quickly, because interviewers can enter responses directly into a computer file that can be analyzed immediately once the data collection has been completed.

As with face-to-face interviews, in telephone interviews an interviewer is present to offer assistance to respondents who need it. Thus it is possible to directly explain instructions, clarify questions, and deal with any other concern a respondent may have.

Limitations

The interaction of an interviewer with respondents is not always an advantage in telephone surveys. It can be a drawback, because it introduces opportunities for interviewer bias in data collection and coding. This source of error must be controlled for through the careful selection and training of the interviewers. At the same time, because telephone interviews do not allow visual contact between the interviewer and respondent, establishing rapport with respondents and gaining their trust and cooperation is more difficult. In addition, there is no opportunity to observe or record nonverbal communication.

Because the time respondents are willing to talk with an interviewer is usually much shorter on the telephone than in person, both the length of the survey instrument and the scope of respondents' answers are restricted. Telephone interview schedules also must be kept simple and direct because respondents cannot refer to written versions of the questions. To allow more latitude, a cover letter and questionnaire may be sent by mail in advance for respondents to use as a reference during the telephone interview. Of course, this appreciably increases costs.

Telephone surveys usually are not prearranged, however, and a common problem is an inability to reach intended respondents. The contact rate for telephone surveys in the United States (operationally defined as reaching a viable respondent on the first call) was about 56 percent in 1989. Thus for almost half of all respondents, at least two calls were required to reach them. Moreover, just 53 percent of individuals contacted in 1989 agreed to complete a telephone survey. Like the proliferation of junk mail, the rapid growth of telephone sales, solicitations, and pseudosurveys has saturated homes with unwanted calls, increasing the likelihood that people will decline to participate in legitimate research efforts presented by phone. Data indicate that only 30 percent of prospective respondents to a telephone survey can be expected to be reached on the first call and to agree to participate in the study. If contact and cooperation rates continue to drop, the traditional advantages of telephone surveys over mail surveys with respect to ease of use and high response rates can be expected to diminish.

Despite the fact that the great majority of households now have telephones, a disproportionate number of poor people are among those who do not. This is important for social work researchers because low-income families comprise a sizable share of social service clients, and underrepresentation of these individuals can lead to measurement error in survey results. A study in 1988 of the distribution of U.S. households having telephones showed that in regions such as the South, which has a high rate of rural poverty, more than 20 percent of households still lacked telephone service (Groves). Accordingly, telephone surveys are inappropriate for use with rural populations or in geographic areas that are known to have a large number of low-income residents.

Sampling Approaches for Telephone Surveys

Most sampling approaches used with face-to-face interviews or mail surveys can also be used in telephone surveys. It can be more difficult to obtain telephone numbers than addresses of potential respondents, however. Even if most people have telephones, some will have unlisted numbers, which are not available to researchers. In 1989, over 31 percent of all telephone customers in the United States had unlisted numbers, up from 22 percent in 1984 (Survey Sampling, 1990). In some parts of the country (California, for example), the proportion of households with unlisted numbers is almost one-half. Since such households may differ in some systematic way from those with listed numbers, a sample that excludes them can threaten the external validity of the data for making inferences about the population of interest.

One way to address this problem is with random-digit dialing (RDD), in which numbers that have been generated at random are dialed. In fact, RDD is not entirely random, since most research projects are targeted toward a particular geographic location, and telephone companies generally assign seven-digit numbers with different three-digit prefixes for various localities. Thus a researcher interested in households in a particular neighborhood who knows they all have telephone numbers beginning with 256, 257, 292, and 294 can restrict the selection of random numbers to the range of possible telephone numbers beginning with these four prefixes.

As a rule, the best use of RDD is for studies in which results from a sample will be generalized to the entire population of interest. The selection of potential sample members cannot be narrowed by any other criteria than three-digit prefixes or area codes that encompass an entire city or metropolitan area. In public opinion polls or practice applications such as needs assessments, this is not a major drawback. RDD, however, would clearly be inappropriate in cases such as an agency study to evaluate former clients' satisfaction with services. A telephone survey could be used, but it would be necessary to work from a list of former clients in order to identify the sample of potential respondents. If the list has a high percentage of missing, incorrect, or unlisted telephone numbers, the likelihood of obtaining a representative sample of former clients would be small.

A new type of telephone poll, promoted by newspapers, television stations, and special-interest groups, asks people to call a particular number to record their opinion about some topic or issue. Often a 900 area-code number is used and a charge is added to the caller's phone bill. Such polls do not constitute telephone survey research, because the sampling techniques do not produce generalizable data. The people who call in to register their opinions have strong feelings on the subject (especially if they are willing to pay the fee), and those who do not feel so strongly are not represented in the survey. As a consequence, the results of such surveys cannot be generalized to any larger population.

Telephone Interviewing Skills

The skills and attributes necessary for effective telephone interviewers vary in some respects from those required for face-to-face interviewers. The need to match characteristics of interviewers and respondents is not so great in telephone surveys, because personal differences are less apparent over the telephone. Other considerations such as voice quality, telephone manner, and ability to cope with the sometimes tedious aspects of telephone interviewing have a greater priority.

Of greatest importance in telephone surveys are the interviewer's verbal skills and familiarity with telephone etiquette—the conventions for considerate, polite behavior in telephone communications. A courteous attitude must be maintained, even if telephone customers decline to participate in ways that are not socially acceptable. Some may agree to complete the survey but change their minds or become uncooperative midway through the interview. In such situations, the interviewer must be able to avoid losing composure, be able to reassure respondents and encourage them to continue, and know when and how to end a session.

Since telephone interviews are rarely preceded by cover letters, interviewers must be able to establish their own legitimacy and that of the study to the satisfaction of the respondent. An interviewer's legitimacy can be undermined by unclear speech, a flippant or disinterested attitude, exaggerated mannerisms, or poor grammar. Sometimes it is best for the interviewer to strictly follow the text of the interview schedule, though this can create other problems, such as reading in a dull or halting manner.

Interviewers must also know how to mediate between the goals of the study and the needs of the respondent. While some contacts refuse to participate, others provide far more data than the interviewer can handle or indulge in conversation that has nothing to do with the study. The interviewer must be able to weigh the benefits of completing such an interview against the costs of taking too long to do so. If respondents are reticent, the interviewer must know how to probe for additional information without seeming to be too inquisitive or aggressive. If respondents have difficulty understanding or keeping track of questions, the interviewer must be prepared to repeat or clarify.

Perhaps the best way to develop the skills needed by telephone interviewers is through techniques such as role-playing, in which prospective interviewers take the roles of interviewers and respondents in hypothetical telephone surveys in a controlled setting. By participating in problematic situations, they learn how to deal with them and can practice appropriate responses until they become confident. Another training technique is to allow prospective interviewers to listen in on a second phone to interviews conducted by more experienced staff. Or the researcher or a supervisor might listen in on an interviewer's first few calls to prospective respondents and offer feedback on the exchange and suggestions for improvement. Calls also can be monitored throughout the data collection to ensure that the interviews are being conducted properly.

COMPUTERIZED DATA COLLECTION IN SURVEYS

Computers have become a basic tool in surveys, particularly for recording and analyzing data. In many cases, however, the process of translating data from respondents onto a form that can be read by a computer (called coding) still requires a number of laborious steps. In self-administered surveys, for example, responses to a questionnaire are usually reviewed and translated into numerical codes by a reader who writes them out in rows of numbers on a coding form. Data from these forms are then transferred by entering them into a computer file, using a keyboard and video display screen. Some of us have begun coding data from survey instruments onto optical scanning forms similar to those used with standardized tests. These forms can be read by a scanner, which then transfers the data to a computer, thus saving a step in the coding process.

The greater the number of steps between getting an answer from a respondent and recording it in a computer, the greater the number of coding errors the data are likely to contain. With telephone surveys, interviewers can enter data on responses directly into a computer. This process is known by the acronym CATI, for computer-assisted telephone interviewing. It is not possible with self-administered questionnaires, except in rare cases where skilled respondents can sit at a computer to answer questions. It also has not been feasible in face-to-face interviews, though the growing use of laptop computers is creating new possibilities.

CATI allows the elimination not only of coding forms but also of written interview schedules. Questions to be asked of respondents are displayed on the computer screen, along with prompts for recording the answer, gathering supplementary data, or proceeding to another part of the instrument.

Figure 15.11 provides an example of a computerized interview schedule in the form of a series of computer screens developed for a telephone interview. An interviewer sitting in front of the computer would see only one screen at a time. As each question is read and the required data are entered, the program automatically proceeds to the next screen. In cases where one type of response would lead to a certain question and a different response would lead to another, the program automatically takes the interviewer to the appropriate screen. In Screen 1, for example, when the interviewer enters a 9, indicating that the respondent has refused to participate, the program skips to a screen that provides a message for the interviewer to read, expressing regrets that the person has chosen not to participate. If the respondent agrees to complete the survey, the program skips to Screen 2, where the interviewer is instructed to enter the person's identifier, and so on.

With this approach, the interviewer is unlikely to lose the place or skip questions. The computer can be programmed to signal when invalid values are entered, thus reducing coding errors. Data entered on each screen are automatically entered in the computer in a form that can be directly extracted and analyzed. CATI systems require a personal computer for each interviewer or a network of keyboards and display screens linked to a single computer.

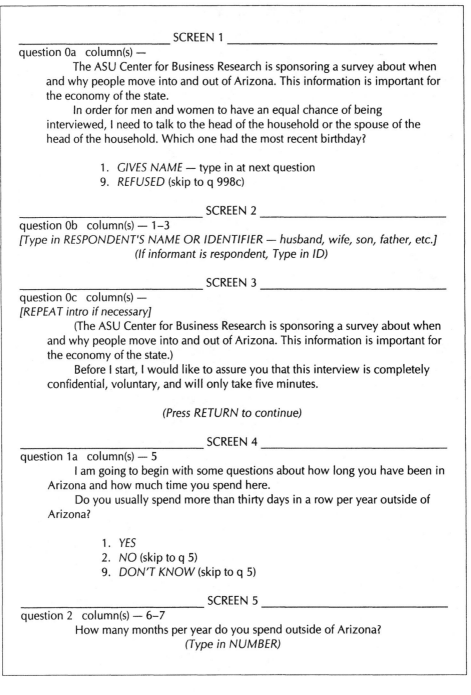

_____ SCREEN 1 _____
question 0a   column(s) —
        The ASU Center for Business Research is sponsoring a survey about when and why people move into and out of Arizona. This information is important for the economy of the state.
        In order for men and women to have an equal chance of being interviewed, I need to talk to the head of the household or the spouse of the head of the household. Which one had the most recent birthday?

        1. *GIVES NAME* — type in at next question
        9. *REFUSED* (skip to q 998c)

_____ SCREEN 2 _____
question 0b   column(s) — 1–3
[Type in RESPONDENT'S NAME OR IDENTIFIER — husband, wife, son, father, etc.]
        (If informant is respondent, Type in ID)

_____ SCREEN 3 _____
question 0c   column(s) —
[REPEAT intro if necessary]
        (The ASU Center for Business Research is sponsoring a survey about when and why people move into and out of Arizona. This information is important for the economy of the state.)
        Before I start, I would like to assure you that this interview is completely confidential, voluntary, and will only take five minutes.

        (Press RETURN to continue)

_____ SCREEN 4 _____
question 1a   column(s) — 5
        I am going to begin with some questions about how long you have been in Arizona and how much time you spend here.
        Do you usually spend more than thirty days in a row per year outside of Arizona?

        1. *YES*
        2. *NO* (skip to q 5)
        9. *DON'T KNOW* (skip to q 5)

_____ SCREEN 5 _____
question 2   column(s) — 6–7
        How many months per year do you spend outside of Arizona?
        (Type in NUMBER)

Figure 15.11   Example of a Computerized Telephone Interview Schedule

        Some types of telephones are better than others; a headset with earphones and microphone that fits into a standard-sized jack can be purchased or rented for moderate cost. Using a headset frees up the interviewer's hands to dial the telephone and record data. With personal computers, the interviewer's headset can be connected to a telephone modem in the computer, and the machine will automatically dial each number. Beyond a basic knowledge of the use of personal computers, special expertise is not required to create and use computerized interview schedules. With commercial software packages, users can devise their own CATI and other computer systems for recording and analyzing survey data.

EMERGING DATA COLLECTION APPROACHES

Approaches to data collection in survey research are tied to the means by which information may be exchanged, thus new modes of communication bring about fresh possibilities for conducting surveys. Face-to-face communication, for example, is as old as the human race, but reliable mail service has been around for a few hundred years at best, and the telephone came into wide use only in this century. Now, the pace of advancement in technology may soon bring about a variety of new methods of conducting surveys.

One example is electronic mail, in which people communicate through computers hooked to telephone lines, satellite relays, and other transmission media. This remains a very new technology, and the 13 percent of Americans who report having been "online" (Fineman, 1995) is about the same percentage as households in the U.S. that had telephones in 1910 (Fischer, 1992).

Roughly one-third of American households now have at least one computer, however, and the presence of both computers and online capabilities continues to grow rapidly. Also, virtually all American households have television sets, and the technology of interactive cable television is another source of two-way communication that will gradually become widespread. In fact, the mainstay of the coming "Information Superhighway" is likely to be a single, high-capacity, fiber optic cable carrying television, telephone, and other forms of communication to most households.

Still, many barriers need to be overcome before these technologies become broadly useful for survey research in social work. One problem is that computers, modems, and interactive cable links are expensive, thus there is a wide disparity in access to them between wealthy and poor families. Almost three-fourths of families with annual incomes greater than $75,000 own computers, but this is true of a mere fraction of poor families. Ownership is also distributed unequally across ethnic and racial groups, with three times as many white families owning computers as black or Hispanic families.

Finally, as noted earlier in the chapter, the proliferation of junk mail, telephone solicitations, and sales pitches disguised as surveys has made legitimate survey research much harder to conduct. The same is likely to be true of surveys using newer technologies, the difficulty increasing almost simultaneously with the growth of new communication technologies.

SUMMARY

As one of the most common forms of data collection methods, survey research is often chosen as the means for studying groups and social phenomena by collecting data on individuals, organizations, and communities. As with other types of data collection methods, the genesis of survey research is in the formulation of the research question; only by clearly defining what it is we wish to know can the means for obtaining an answer be selected.

If our research question can be addressed by survey methods, the choice is between cross-sectional designs, which gather data on a particular population at a given moment in time, and longitudinal designs, which examine changes in the population over time. The three main methods of data collection in surveys are face-to-face, mail, and telephone.

The following chapter continues our discussion of data collection by describing secondary analysis. Unlike surveys, which collect original data to address research questions, secondary analyses draw on data that already exist.

Judy L. Krysik

C h a p t e r 16

Secondary Analysis

THE PRACTICE OF ANALYZING an existing data set for a purpose other than the purpose for which it was originally collected is referred to as a *secondary analysis*—an unobtrusive data collection method. Thus, secondary analysis is any further analysis of an existing data set that presents interpretations, conclusions, or knowledge additional to, or different from, those presented in prior analyses of the data.

SECONDARY ANALYSIS: PAST AND PRESENT

Although gaining in popularity, the use of secondary data sets is not new. One of the earliest examples of a secondary analysis of existing data sets is Emile Durkheim's 1897 study on suicide. Durkheim and his associates collected data from existing hospital death records to understand the social factors associated with suicide (Pope, 1976). Thus, Durkheim used existing data for a purpose not intended by those who originally collected them. As should be very evident by now, analyzing existing data sets is an unobtrusive data collection strategy in that it does not collect original data from research participants.

Advanced computer technology and the widespread implementation of management information systems (MIS) have made the task of accessing and analyzing secondary data sets much easier than in Durkheim's era. In fact, a plethora of data sets are available on individuals, families, organizations, communities, and countries. The current state of secondary analyses was perhaps best captured by Hyman (1987) who stated, "Now, late in the twentieth century, social scientists can also be described as standing atop of a giant mountain of data, from which they might see farther back into the past, away into remoter regions of the world, and over a larger vista of problems than ever before."

Upon identifying a research problem area appropriate for a secondary analysis, we need to choose from a variety of data sets. Most of these secondary data sets can be accessed in a matter of a week or two, in computer-readable form, ready for analysis. Along with the data set we can expect to receive information on: (1) the name and affiliation of the data collector, (2) the data collection period, (3) the type of sampling method used, (4) the size of the sample, (5) the data collection method, including the survey instrument or interview schedule, (6) the data source, (7) notes on data coding procedures, and (8) suggestions for analyses. Most data sets are available at a fraction of what they cost to produce.

TYPES OF SECONDARY DATA

There are three principal types of secondary data that are available. They are (1) micro-level data, (2) aggregate-level data, and (3) qualitative-level data.

Micro-Level Data

The term *micro-level data* is used to describe data derived from individual units of analysis, whether these data sources are persons, households, or organizations. Number of children, for example, is a micro-level variable. For the past two centuries, the federal government has been the most important source of micro-level data by providing large national surveys of households through means such as the population census (Oyen, 1990).

Aggregate-Level Data

Aggregate-level data consist of statistics and/or tables derived from quantitative micro-level data, in which the characteristics of individual units of analysis are no longer identifiable. Unemployment rate, for example, is an aggregate-level variable. The calculation of an unemployment rate requires a number of individuals to respond to a question asking whether or not they are gainfully employed. The micro-level data from individual respondents are then aggregated to produce an aggregate measure of unemployment. Chapter 17 describes in detail how to use aggregate-level data to answer research questions or test hypotheses.

Qualitative-Level Data

Qualitative-level data are any kind of nonquantitative data. Secondary data sets that are qualitative in nature include descriptive narratives and records of personal communication such as diaries and letters. Understanding soldiers' experiences of war by examining letters they sent home would be an example of a secondary analysis using qualitative-level data.

Combining Types of Data for a Particular Analysis

As stressed throughout this book, most research problems are best understood and answered through the use of both qualitative-level data and quantitative data. Secondary analysis provides a means to this end by blending both research approaches. While many studies using secondary data are based on only one type of data (i.e., micro-, aggregate-, or qualitative-level), some studies combine all three types.

LOCATING SECONDARY DATA SETS

A major challenge in collecting primary data for a given research study is to locate and secure the participation of research participants. In contrast, for the secondary analyst, the challenge is to locate an appropriate existing data set. Thus we need to be aware of the many published guides, directories, and other resources available for identifying existing data sets. However, while books and articles that list existing data sets are available, such resources can become quickly obsolete (e.g., Dale, Arber, & Proctor, 1988; Kiecolt & Nathan, 1985).

Increased computer technology has prompted the development of numerous data archives throughout Europe and North America. They primarily hold micro-level data and have become an important source in secondary data analyses. The largest data archive in the world is the Inter-University Consortium for Political and Social Research (ICPSR). Currently, the ICPSR has more than 17,000 files of computer-readable data that span two centuries and more than 130 countries. The ICPSR, as do many data archives, has a system of university member affiliates that entitles faculty and students to use the data sets at a minimal cost (if any). Most data archives publish catalogues on an annual basis to inform the public of their holdings. Other less formal sources of micro-level data exist, however, such as government departments, social service agencies, private foundations, charitable organizations, and private industry, and usually require more effort to locate.

Aggregate data are available in standardized and unstandardized formats. The Congressional Information Services (CIS) publishes an index to the statistical publications of international, intergovernmental organizations on an annual basis. It is not the intent of CIS, however, to present data in a standardized format. As an alternative, the Organization for European Cooperation and Development (OECD), the International Labor Office (ILO), and the Euromonitor are three sources that publish data using standardized operational definitions of certain variables.

Data from publications that attempt standardization of variables are superior for secondary analyses. For instance, in Durkheim's era, official suicide rates varied by region according to whether secular or religious officials were responsible for recording the cause of death. We could argue, therefore, that the lack of a standardized operational definition of suicide was a limitation in Durkheim's study.

Secondary data sets are not always in the form of surveys and official records, however. Qualitative-level data may be gathered from a variety of sources such as books, unpublished manuscripts, articles, monographs, personal communication, and even audio tape and videotape recordings. Locating the best source (or sources) of data for a particular research study is often a trial-and-error process. Contacting a reference librarian at a university library for assistance is an excellent way to start.

EXAMPLE: THE WELFARE STATE AND WOMEN'S EMPLOYMENT

To demonstrate how a secondary analysis is done, an example is used throughout this chapter that involves the use of several existing data sets archived in the Luxembourg Income Study (LIS). The LIS is an international data cooperative that has available family and household micro-level data for over 21 countries from the late 1960s to early 1990s. The data sets for LIS are national income surveys administered by each member country. The U.S. Current Population Survey and the Canadian Survey of Consumer Finances are included in the LIS database.

Even though women in North America have entered the labor force in large numbers, they remain disadvantaged. This disadvantage has multiple forms—for instance, low employment participation rates, low pay, a predominance of part-time labor, and occupational segregation. For women, full integration into paid labor has implications that extend far beyond economic well-being. Employment may impact women's physical and emotional well-being, for example, as well as their participation in cultural, political, and social life.

Although women are increasingly involved in employment, they still carry the majority of responsibility for family care. The interface between employment and family creates significant tensions that may present barriers to women's participation in paid labor. Women's opportunities to enhance their employment careers rest on their access to income-generating work and on support for domestic responsibilities. For many women, such access may be reflected in welfare state policies and programs that address issues such as employment equity, parental leave, and child care.

Thus, to the extent that the modern welfare state intervenes to address tensions between employment and family and thereby attempts to influence gender equity, it would be expected that the welfare state would be more or less successful in decreasing women's labor force disadvantage. Examining the relationship between the welfare state and women's employment falls clearly in the domain of our profession.

STEPS IN SECONDARY ANALYSES

At a basic level, a secondary analysis follows seven steps: (1) selecting a problem area, (2) formulating a research question or hypothesis, (3) formulating a research design, (4) evaluating the data set, (5) constructing operational definitions, (6) analyzing the data, and (7) writing the research report.

Step 1: Selecting a Problem Area

The first task in conducting any research study is to decide on a problem area. It is important that we devote as much time and effort defining the research problem in a secondary analysis as we would in conducting a primary research study that requires original data. As can be expected, there is some temptation with a secondary analysis to formulate the research problem based on whatever data are available. This approach, however, will seldom lead to good results.

With regard to our example, a review of the literature indicated that the welfare state has been a major contributor in reducing poverty among demographic groups such as the elderly and the disabled. When observed cross-nationally, however, a great deal of variation in the redistributive capacities of various welfare states has been noted. In Scandinavian countries, for example, the redistributive effects of the welfare state are substantial, whereas the United States is often characterized as a welfare state laggard. This variation in welfare state performance has been explained in a typology of welfare state regimes (Esping-Andersen, 1990).

The research problem in our example is, "How might Esping-Andersen's typology of welfare state regimes apply to women's employment outcomes?" If three different types of welfare state regimes do exist, then it could be expected that women's employment outcomes would differ across countries according to the type of welfare state regime it had. Thus, if policy makers could identify countries based on their achievement of positive outcomes, then they could consider the transferability of the welfare state strategies employed in these countries.

Step 2: Formulating a Research Question or Hypothesis

In order for a problem area to be researched it must be formulated into more manageable questions or hypotheses. A review of the literature on women's employment suggested that inequities resulting from macroeconomic conditions such as unemployment, as well as social differences such as marital status, education, and number of children, could be reduced by policies and programs introduced by the welfare state.

Based on Esping-Andersen's typology of welfare state regimes we were able to hypothesize what employment outcomes each type of welfare state regime would produce. For instance, countries with social democratic welfare state regimes, because of their commitment to full employment and gender equity, should be characterized by high levels of female participation in employment, a predominance of full-time labor at relatively high wages, and low gender segregation within occupations.

The conservative welfare state regime, in contrast, supports the traditional roles of wife and mother. Women's employment participation in the conservative welfare state regime was therefore predicted to be low and characterized by part-time status in female-dominated occupations. Because the state monetarily supports nonemployment, the demand for labor in the conservative welfare state regime would be low.

Given that some participation in paid labor among women is necessary to meet the demands of capitalism, wages must be high enough to make women's employment worthwhile, and low enough to keep demand and supply in equilibrium, resulting in moderate wage rates. In the liberal welfare state, the inability to earn income outside of the market system will force women to accept whatever labor is available. Because women need paid labor to survive, the supply of female laborers will exceed the demand for labor, increasing competition and forcing wages downward. A lack of support for family responsibilities will constrain women's availability, leading to moderate rates of labor force participation and a predominance of part-time, gender-segregated labor.

Finally, if women's employment is systematically influenced by the welfare state, employment outcomes should be different across the various regime types and similar within each regime. Without a thorough understanding of the problem area, we might not have considered the multifaceted nature of employment inequity. For instance, we may have dealt only with women's employment participation, ignoring hours employed, pay, and occupational segregation.

Two research questions (derived from the research problem) were formulated to represent our study's general problem area: (1) What are the differences in women's labor force participation outcomes across western industrialized countries? and (2) Are differences in women's labor force participation outcomes related to the nature of the welfare state? At times, the only way to answer a certain research question is through secondary analysis. Imagine, for a moment, that we were interested in women's employment and attempted to collect nationally representative, original data from several countries. The scope of the data required and cost would be prohibitive, not to mention language barriers and time.

Step 3: Formulating a Research Design

Secondary analysis is extremely versatile in the sense that it can be used to examine the present or the past, understand change over time, examine phenomena comparatively, and replicate or expand on prior research studies. Each of these uses requires a different research design, developed according to the requirements of the research question or hypothesis. Three of the most common research designs that are easily facilitated through a secondary analysis are (1) comparative research designs, (2) temporal research designs, and (3) cross-sectional research designs.

Comparative Research Designs

The study of more than one group, event, or society in order to isolate factors that explain patterns is called *comparative research*. Designs that facilitate comparative studies can be divided into two basic strategies: (1) the study of elements that differ in many ways but that have some major factor in common, or (2) the study of elements that are highly similar but that differ in some important respect (Vogt, 1993).

Following the first strategy, if we were interested in gender we could examine the distribution of unpaid labor and educational attainment across many countries to explain the universal nature of women's disadvantaged economic status. To ascertain the impact of the welfare state on women's employment, however, we choose to study only western industrialized countries. Holding constant key variables that could influence employment, such as democratic political institutions, market economies, and cultural and religious traditions, was important to do in order to isolate their effects on the welfare state.

Temporal Research Designs

All temporal research designs include time as a major variable. Their purpose is to investigate change in the distribution of a variable (or in relationships among variables) for entire populations or subgroups. As discussed in Chapters 12 and 15, there are three types of temporal research designs: cohort, panel, and trend.

Cohort studies investigate characteristics of groups that have experienced some major life event, such as entry into the labor force at a particular interval. A temporal cohort study, for example, might compare the employment profiles of women born in three different decades: pre–World War II, baby boomers, and Generation X.

Panel studies utilize data to study the same persons or entities over time. We could, for example, analyze data to understand how employment careers change before, during, and after childbearing years. Cohort studies require data from only one point in time, whereas panel studies require data to be collected more than once from the same individuals.

Trend studies also look at change, but they do not require data from the same persons or entities. A trend study, for example, might look at attitudes toward women's employment over three different time periods, such as the 1930s, the 1970s, and the 1990s.

Cross-Sectional Research Designs

Cross-sectional designs examine a phenomenon at one point in time and can be used to address a wide range of research questions. Our study on women's employment, for example, was interested in only one period of data collection. We chose data from the mid 1980s because this period was characterized by slow economic growth, high unemployment rates, and rising deficits in social service budgets among all western nations. Thus, the period was considered appropriate for assessing welfare state performance under adverse economic conditions.

Step 4: Evaluating the Data Set

Not all secondary data sets are equally valid or reliable. We need to answer four questions prior to engaging in analyzing an existing data set.

Question 1: What Was the Original Purpose of the Data Set?

Data are not collected without a purpose. At times, they may be collected to support a particular point of view or to test a particular research hypothesis. If this is the case, the data set may be limited in scope and may not lend itself to testing an alternative explanatory model.

The degree of precision in data collection, the variable categories used, and the method of data collection are all influenced by the primary researcher's intent. Understanding the original purpose of the study, therefore, is mandatory.

Question 2: How Credible Are the Data Source and Data Set?

Credibility refers not only to potential biases the original researcher might have had, but to his or her knowledge of research methodology and level of access to physical and financial resources. Official surveys tend to have greater financial sponsorship, which generally results in larger samples and higher response rates than those obtained by nonofficial surveys. Sample size and representation have implications for those of us who are interested in studying small subgroups within a population.

Another advantage of using data from official sources is that the limitations of standard operational definitions are well documented by both the provider of the data set and by others who have used it. This provides some preliminary guidance for those of us who are embarking on a statistical analysis of the data.

Question 3: Are the Data Representative of the Population?

Knowledge of the sampling frame used provides an indication of the extent to which the study's sample is likely to correspond to the true population from which it was drawn. For instance, our interpretation of a finding that 80 percent of survey respondents did not support affirmative action might be very different if we were to learn that the sample was drawn from a list of Republicans in California. Knowledge of the sampling frame, rates of nonresponse, and the amount of missing data are important points to consider if generalizations from the data set's sample to the population are to be supported. If rates of nonresponse and/or missing data are high, we may want to obtain additional information from other sources and data sets to evaluate the extent of misrepresentation. The sampling method used also has implications for the kinds of statistical analyses that are appropriate.

Question 4: Are Weighting Procedures Needed?

When subgroups in the data set are over- or underrepresented, in comparison to their actual distribution within the population, we may need to employ a weighting procedure. Adjusting data to reflect differences in the number of population units that each case represents is referred to as weighting.

Some data sets, the LIS data in particular, provide the option of using weighted or nonweighted data. It is also possible to pool data from two or more data sets to create a larger data set that will facilitate the examination of underrepresented groups. This procedure is particularly helpful for studying ethnic minorities and never-married mothers, for example.

Step 5: Constructing Operational Definitions

As we know, operationalization is the process of defining variables so they can be measured. In primary research studies, a considerable amount of effort is invested in operationalizing variables before the data are actually collected. On the other hand, in secondary analysis, we create operational definitions after the data are in hand, making the most of whatever is available within the data set. A distinctive feature of a secondary analysis, therefore, is the derivation of new variables by combining a number of variables or by recoding existing ones.

In our study, for example, the LIS data sets did not include a variable to indicate whether or not women were employed. The absence of a variable to indicate employment participation prompted us to construct a new operational definition. In our new operational definition, women were considered to be employed if their income from annual wages (or salaries) was greater than zero. If income from annual wages or salary was equal to zero, a woman was classified as nonemployed. We made a decision to exclude "self-employed income" from the calculation of income because the LIS data sets did not differentiate between income from labor and income from capital, such as rental property. This process of redefining one variable, such as income, into a second variable, such as employment participation, is known as recoding.

At times we may want to create an index as an alternative to using a single indicator variable. An index is nothing more than a composite measure of a general concept that is constructed from multiple variables to produce a single variable (Vogt, 1993). Jodi Jacobson (1992), for instance, developed a single index of "human development" that included three variables: (1) the degree to which people have the option to lead a long and healthy life, (2) the degree to which people have the option to be become knowledgeable, and (3) the degree to which people have the option to find access to the assets, employment, and income needed for a decent standard of living.

It is our task when doing a secondary analysis to create operational definitions that are meaningful, valid, and reliable. If this is not possible given the existing data set, an alternative data set may have to be accessed or the objectives of our research study revised. If a secondary analysis will not permit us to adequately measure the variables required, it may not be the appropriate data collection method to use.

Step 6: Analyzing the Data

The statistical methods used to analyze secondary data sets are the same as those used to analyze original data sets. A common characteristic of secondary data sets, however, is the generally large number of cases and variables they contain. Thus, the statistical techniques employed often require advanced knowledge of statistical methods and competency in computer use. There is no single computerized statistical software program that is most appropriate for statistical analyses. Many are available, and the final choice is dictated by the requirements of the analysis, availability, familiarity, and personal preference.

The data sets used in our example present an anomaly. Whereas most secondary analysts access data sets from a computer-readable data tape that can be copied onto a personal or mainframe computer, direct access to our LIS data sets was not permitted. Researchers access the LIS data sets by electronic mail. Computerized statistical programs were developed in SPSS *(Statistical Package for the Social Sciences)* language and were sent to the Government of Luxembourg mainframe computer where the data sets are stored. Statistical results were returned by electronic mail. The rationale for limiting access to the LIS data sets is to protect the privacy and confidentiality of survey respondents.

We should always begin the statistical analysis of secondary data by investing time in becoming familiar with the data set. This means generating basic descriptive statistics for key variables and comparing them with existing sources to check for compatibility. When the data are congruent across multiple independent sources, we can have more confidence in our analysis.

When disagreement results, it may be necessary to identify potential reasons for such differences and to determine which data source is the more credible. When differences occur, however, we should be skeptical of the data. Some data sources provide basic descriptive statistics on key variables to facilitate comparison. Besides basic descriptive statistics, those people judged to be specialists in a particular area can assist in evaluating the validity of the results.

Step 7: Writing the Research Report

Research reports based on the analysis of a secondary data set are not readily distinguishable from those based on an original data set. The author may refer the reader to the original research report for details of the methodology used. Moreover, it is contingent upon the author to document the limitations of the data set being used. In addition, some suppliers of data sets have certain requirements regarding their use. The source for the LIS data sets, for example, requires that any paper published using the LIS data sets must be included in the *Luxembourg Income Study Working Paper Series.*

ADVANTAGES AND DISADVANTAGES

Weighing the advantages of secondary analysis against its limitations can help decide when to use a secondary data set versus gathering original data.

Advantages

Five of the most salient advantages of secondary data analyses are: (1) maximizing resources, (2) increasing accessibility, (3) avoiding intrusiveness, (4) developing knowledge, and (5) facilitating replication.

Maximizing Resources

One of the most important ways to maximize limited resources is to build on the work already done by others. The cost of conducting original research studies includes the development of survey instruments and interview schedules, and the hiring and training of data collectors, data coders, and data-entry personnel. By using secondary data, savings are incurred in money, time, and personnel. Often it is the only feasible means of obtaining representative data. Conducting a secondary data analysis is not, however, cost free. The cost of conducting a secondary analysis can vary depending on the cost of the data set(s) and the requirements of its use. Some data archives offer workshops to those interested in secondary analysis. With research dollars becoming increasingly scarce, it is important that resources be saved by using secondary data wherever possible so that money can be diverted to studies requiring original data.

Increasing Accessibility

The current state of secondary analyses means that the opportunity of conducting research studies is no longer in the hands of a privileged few. Affordable computer technology has made secondary data sets broadly accessible to the point that even a social work student can conduct a large-scale research project. The development of numerous data archives has both increased the likelihood that data will be discovered and facilitated their use.

Avoiding Intrusiveness

As we know from Chapter 15, studies have shown that survey response rates are declining in general (Groves & Cialdini, 1992). This decrease has been attributed in part to the large number of surveys that are now being conducted. The use of secondary data sets limits the reporting burden placed on the public. Also, there are occasions when the introduction of a survey would create tensions or intensify negative emotions. In these circumstances, secondary data can be particularly beneficial.

Developing Knowledge

Secondary data analyses are used to create knowledge at all three levels. At the exploratory level, secondary data are used to generate relevant research questions and tentative hypotheses. They are used at the descriptive level by describing a phenomenon or the characteristics of a population. Many descriptive demographic research studies are based on the analysis of secondary data. Secondary analysis is also useful in explanatory studies. By comparing Esping-Andersen's three theoretical welfare state regimes to actual situations, for example, knowledge development moves from comparative descriptions to explanatory statements.

Facilitating Replication

Because secondary data sets exist in the public domain, further research studies are easily replicable. Replication is a powerful tool for making research findings less vulnerable to error, as well as protecting them from the transient circumstances of respondents. Also, the same data set can be analyzed from different perspectives and theoretical frameworks, producing a more holistic understanding of the phenomena under study (Dale, Arber, & Procter, 1988).

Disadvantages

As secondary data analysis is not without limitations, before embarking on a secondary analysis we should avoid potential difficulties by becoming aware of the more common ones. Four of these are: (1) lack of standardization, (2) omission of relevant variables, (3) overabundance of data, and (4) complicated statistical analyses.

Lack of Standardization

Secondary data sets are commonly confronted with a lack of standardized operational definitions of their variables. In the LIS data sets used in our example, the education variable was coded as "years of schooling" in the United States and as "education level" in Canada, Australia, Germany, and the Netherlands. This required recoding of the education variable into the two dichotomous categories of high and low, where "high" represented some post-secondary education, and "low" represented no postsecondary education. The process of dichotomizing the variable was necessary to include "education" in the statistical analysis of more than one country, but resulted in decreased measurement precision. The lack of fit between concepts and the variables they contain is always a problem in analyzing secondary data sets.

Despite recoding, some variables are not sufficiently comparable to allow for their inclusion in a data analysis. In the LIS data, for example, the categories for the ethnicity variable were not comparable across country data sets. The United States differentiated ethnicity by the categories: White, Black, Spanish origin, and other races. In Australia, ethnicity was defined by country of birth and included Australia, the United Kingdom, Italy, Other Europe, Asia, North/South America, Africa, and Oceania. In Canada, ethnicity was defined as Canadian born or immigrant. In Germany, ethnicity was recorded as German, Turkish, Yugoslav, Greek, Italian, Spanish, or other nationality.

The data set for The Netherlands did not contain any information on ethnicity, and, surprisingly, aboriginal status was not recognized in any of the U.S., Australian, and Canadian data sets. Because of the variability in definition and the lack of validity in variable categories, ethnicity is not a valid variable to include in cross-national research studies using the LIS data sets. In our study on women's employment, the inability to include ethnicity may have masked important differences in employment participation and pay across all countries included in our study.

Omission of Relevant Variables

The omission of relevant variables in secondary data sets can also be a problem. Studies focusing on gender may be particularly difficult because many national census and surveys have not included social indicators meaningful to the experiences of women (Norris, 1987). Data on unpaid domestic labor, for instance, are not collected despite its impact on paid labor. In our example on women's employment, social characteristics such as the number of children, age of the youngest child, and marital status were used as proxies for domestic responsibility. A proxy is an indirect measure of a variable.

The use of proxies to represent domestic responsibility is somewhat problematic in that domestic responsibility associated with marriage and children is likely to be inversely related to class status. Households with higher overall income, for example, are more apt to purchase domestic services such as ready-made foods, child care, laundry, and cleaning, than are low-income households. The extent that women and men conform to traditional gender roles will also influence women's domestic responsibilities. The lack of a better measure of domestic responsibility contained in the LIS data sets represents a threat to the validity of our study's findings and implications.

Overabundance of Data

For many secondary data sets, the abundance of variables is so great that it sometimes gets difficult to decide which variables to include and which to exclude from any given data analysis. The decision on which variables to include is made easier when our study is guided by a thorough literature review. Without such advance preparation, we can be adrift in a sea of computer printouts, searching aimlessly for statistically significant results that will invariably occur but which are unlikely to have any substantive meaning. An overabundance of data is best confronted by having a thorough understanding of the research problem, and a well-designed and well-documented plan of data analysis.

Complicated Statistical Analyses

The degree of difficulty involved in analyzing secondary data sets depends to a large extent on the number of data sources required for a particular analysis. In general, the greater the number of sources, the more complex the data analysis. This is especially true if different units of analysis, (e.g., individual, family, community) must be considered. In the example we have been using on women's employment, one of the research questions we were interested in answering was: Are differences in women's employment participation rates affected by the welfare state, controlling for macroeconomic and social factors? Ideally, to answer this question, we should have included in our statistical analysis variables from each of the welfare states, macroeconomic, and social subsets.

Examining a small number of countries, however, limits the ways in which aggregate-level and micro-level data can be combined. Five countries are too few to represent sufficient variation on aggregate-level variables such as unemployment rate. When aggregate-level data are merged with micro-level data, each case in a specific country is assigned the category, or value, for unemployment rate. Unemployment rates for the five countries included in our study on women's employment ranged from a low of 6.9 percent to a high of 9.6 percent, a mere 2.7 percentage points difference. A lack of variability in the range of responses on this variable severely limited its utility to our research study.

SUMMARY

Secondary analyses in social work research are increasing. Much of this increase can be easily attributed to advanced computer technology that has made the analysis of secondary data sets more accessible and affordable. There are many data archives available, and the search for the most appropriate one is a process of trial and error.

There are many benefits in analyzing secondary data sets. They include savings in time, money, and personnel; increased access to research opportunities; decreased intrusiveness; and ease of replication. Certain limitations are also present, however. Data available through secondary sources are often not exactly what is desired. The lack of standardized operational definitions among variables and the omission of relevant variables within various existing data sets are common problems. We must be prepared to do the best we can with what is available. This may mean recoding variable values, using proxy variables, and developing indexes. If the data are not sufficient to represent the study's important concepts, using more than one data set may be necessary.

It is particularly important that we become fully aware of the nature of the data set to be used, its method of collection, and any limitations that this imposes on our study's findings and implications. Prerequisite skills that the secondary analyst should have are a good knowledge of research designs, statistical techniques, and facility with computers.

Jackie D. Sieppert
Steven L. McMurtry
Robert W. McClelland

C h a p t e r   17

Utilizing Existing Statistics

THE PREVIOUS CHAPTER PRESENTED how secondary data are used as an unobtrusive data collection method—a method that uses existing micro-level, aggregate-level, and qualitative-level data. This chapter continues our discussion of using existing data by concentrating on the use of aggregate-level data within a secondary analysis. In a nutshell, analyzing existing statistics is nothing more than performing a secondary analysis of aggregate-level data.

This unobtrusive data collection method requires our *utilizing existing statistics*, the title of this chapter. Like the chapter before (and after) this one, this unobtrusive data collection method does not collect primary, or firsthand data. Rather, we turn to existing statistical records as our data sources.

As explained in Chapter 16, an unobtrusive data collection method uses existing data sources located within government, private, and collaborative international organizations. It is technically correct to assume, however, that the "real data sources" are not those organizations that have the existing data, but are the individual units of analyses on which the statistics are based.

As we know from the chapters in Part V of this book, obtrusive data collection methods (i.e., structured observation, surveys, participant observation) collect firsthand data directly, in one way or another, from the research participants themselves (individual units of analyses). When using these obtrusive data collection methods, we are totally responsible for our study's internal and external validities, from selecting our research question to disseminating our results. This is not true when using existing statistics as a data collection method because we have no control over how the statistics were derived; they have been computed by other researchers.

Thus, research studies that use existing statistical records focus not on reexamining the *data* collected by others, but rather on examining the *data analyses* previously generated by others. Aggregated summaries and reports, not micro-level data, are the fuel that drive research studies using existing statistical records. This point represents a subtle but important difference that makes research studies using existing aggregated statistics sufficiently unique to warrant a closer examination. We will now turn our attention to locating these existing aggregated statistics.

LOCATING SOURCES OF EXISTING STATISTICS

The range of research topics that can be studied using existing statistical data is matched by the wide variety of organizations and groups that collect such data. Aggregated statistics are reported on almost all aspects of our personal and professional lives—by governments, by employers, by private marketing firms, by professional associations, and so on. For this reason, finding the right source of existing statistics to answer a particular research question can be a huge task.

The single most important piece of advice that can be given to a person using existing statistics as a data collection method is to seek help from information specialists found in local college and university libraries. These people are often very familiar with major sources of existing statistical data and are knowledgeable about the types of data (unit of analysis) contained in each source. If they do not know of a particular existing source appropriate to answer a specific research question, they have the knowledge and skills to track down sources that otherwise might never be discovered. Thus, we usually begin a search for an existing statistical data source at the local college or university library.

As we have said, sources of statistical data are generally classified into three broad categories: (1) government and other public agencies; (2) private, or proprietary organizations; and (3) collaborative, international organizations. Each offers aggregated-level data, in the form of statistics, suitable for answering different types of research questions. Thus, with relevant research questions and variables in mind, we can locate an appropriate source(s) of statistical data and then examine it in order to answer our research question. Let us now turn our attention to the first source of existing statistics—government and other public agencies.

Government and Other Public Agencies

Federal, state, and municipal governments are the most available and largest sources of existing statistics. Departments and agencies at most levels produce numerous books, reports, and computerized compilations of data acquired through various sources. The U.S. Bureau of the Census annually publishes a book called the *Statistical Abstract of the United States*, for example, which is a collection of statistics gathered from over 200 government and private agencies. Presented in a wide variety of statistical lists, charts, figures, and tables, the *Statistical Abstract of the United States* contains data about many of the topics relevant to our profession. It contains, for example, statistics about death rates within states, the percentage of families with children who live in poverty, spending on law enforcement and rehabilitation, changes in divorce rates, number of physicians by region of the country, trends in the population of elderly Americans, and hundreds of other social work–relevant topics.

In fact, the only way to grasp the scope and magnitude of the *Statistical Abstract* is to obtain a copy and explore its contents. Best of all, the book is available free of charge at most public libraries. Computerized versions are being developed for easy access through large-scale data networks such as the Internet. Also, most university and college libraries and larger municipal libraries have separate sections for government documents such as the *Statistical Abstract*.

Many other forms of federal, state, and municipal statistics also exist. Answers to research questions can be found in existing statistics published by public agencies such as the National Center for Health Statistics, the Department of Labor, and the Federal Bureau of Investigation. State agencies (such as each state's department of social services) provide statistics about social workers' caseloads in public social service agencies, changes in reporting of alleged child sexual abuse cases, recidivism rates among young offenders, patterns of physical and mental health care usage, and so on.

Municipal departments are obviously more limited in scope and resources, but they too compile statistics relevant to our profession. We must never overlook any of these public departments and organizations, as they are often a good starting point for any piece of social work research that uses existing statistics as a data collection method. Government agencies can be found in local telephone books (many of which have a "blue pages" section for governmental listings). We need to look through these listings and make note of those agencies that appear to be related to our research question. We can then call these agencies to find out whether they publish annual reports on our topic.

Private, or Proprietary Organizations

A second source of existing statistical data is the myriad of nonprofit or proprietary agencies and organizations. Statistics collected and/or reported by private sources are often harder to locate than those provided by governmental sources. They may be more expensive to access as well. However, such sources provide statistical data that may be unavailable in any other form. If we wanted to conduct a research study on attitudes about abortion in a particular state, for example, the best source of data might be existing statistics that were generated by a commercial polling firm in the region. Or, to find data about changes in housing availability and construction in a particular geographical area, we might turn to the local Chamber of Commerce.

Even private social service agencies increasingly collect and report statistical data as part of their emphasis on accountability. Finally, "watchdog" organizations and various advocacy groups make disseminating statistics a particular part of their work. Together these can provide data to examine an agency's effectiveness and efficiency, for example.

There are other nongovernmental organizations that can also provide useful statistics. Two private sources of existing statistical data most relevant to our profession are the National Association of Social Workers (NASW) and the Council on Social Work Education (CSWE). Like other professional accrediting organizations, they keep records regarding the characteristics and activities of their members. Both organizations produce numerous statistical reports about issues of interest to their members. We could turn to the NASW for data about the number of Americans with no or inadequate health insurance coverage, for example. The CSWE regularly publishes statistics on faculty and students within all accredited schools and departments of social work in the United States.

What about organizations that focus on specific substantive issues? In child welfare, for example, there are organizations such as the Child Welfare League of America, the American Association for Protecting Children, the American Public Welfare Association, and the Children's Defense Fund. Other fields have similar organizations and serve the same purpose as those in social work.

Collaborative International Organizations

The third, and final, source of existing statistical data is collaborative international organizations. These organizations operate on a cooperative basis to collect and distribute statistical data that allow for cross-cultural comparisons on issues of direct relevance to social policy. The United Nations, for example, publishes the *Demographic Yearbook* and the *United Nations Statistical Yearbook*. These two publications supply data from many countries regarding birth rates, death rates, literacy rates, the proportion of people living in urban areas, and numerous other variables.

With the rapid evolution of computers, and thus information technology, international compilations of existing statistics are increasing in both their scope and quality. Statistical databases are becoming more comprehensive, more timely, and more easily accessed. A good illustration of this is the *Luxembourg Income Study (LIS)*, mentioned in Chapter 16. The *LIS* is a financially independent division of the Center for the Study of Population, Poverty, and Public Policy/International Networks for Studies in Technology, Environment, Alternatives, & Development (CEPS/INSTEAD).

This lengthy acronym just means that the Luxembourg Government has created an independent organization whose mandate is to foster international comparative research on income and well-being. The organization maintains over 40 data sets that contain comprehensive measures of income and well-being for over 17 modern industrialized welfare states. Each country contributes a wide range of statistical data, such as population demographics, family structure, levels of income, and changes in industrial or agricultural output. Use of these statistical summaries is restricted to social science research purposes, however, and no private or commercial use is permitted. *LIS* is one example of a source for comparative and policy research in applied economics, sociology, and public policy. Existing statistical data sets on other topics are increasingly becoming available through improved computer technology.

Whether we turn to governmental agencies, private and proprietary channels, or international organizations, it is clear that existing statistical data *are* available to answer many research questions. Once we know what we want to study, and go to the library to talk with an information specialist, we will soon be immersed in statistical data that we might never have dreamed existed.

Let us take a simple example to illustrate how the forgoing data sources can be used to examine a simple research problem—the overrepresentation of ethnic minorities in foster care services. How might the named organizations, the data sources, be helpful in studying this issue? The example in Box 17.1 shows how we could turn to private and governmental child welfare organizations as a way of gathering data on this issue.

ADVANTAGES AND DISADVANTAGES

Like all data collection methods, analyzing existing statistics has its advantages and disadvantages.

Advantages

Analyzing existing statistics has many benefits. Among these are that existing statistics: (1) provide historical and conceptual contexts to a research study that uses primary, or firsthand, data (2) can be the only data collection method

Box 17.1_____

Using Governmental and Private-Agency Statistics

Fran is clinical director of a private, nonprofit agency that provides foster care, group-home care, and residential treatment for children in a small city in Arizona. She has noticed that there is a higher number of ethnic minority children in her agency's caseload than would be expected based on the proportion of ethnic minority children in the general population. She decides to do a study of this issue using existing statistics already gathered by various sources as her data collection method.

Fran first talks with the information specialist at the local library, asking for help to conduct a computer search through the library's existing data bases. The search reveals a series of reports, titled *Characteristics of Children in Substitute and Adoptive Care*, that were sponsored by the American Public Welfare Association and that provide several years of data reported by states on their populations of children in various kinds of foster and adoptive care. She also locates an annual publication produced by the Children's Defense Fund, and this provides a variety of background data on the well-being of children in the United States. Next, Fran checks in the library's government documents section. She locates recent census data on the distribution of persons under the age of 18 across different ethnic groups in her county.

Fran now turns to state-level resources, where a quick check of government listings in the telephone book reveals two agencies that appear likely to have relevant data. One is the Foster Care Review Board, which is comprised of citizen volunteers who assist juvenile courts by reviewing the progress of children in foster care statewide.

A quick call to the Board reveals that they produce an annual report that lists a variety of statistics. These include the number of foster children in the state, where they are placed, and how long they have been in care, and descriptive data such as their ethnicity, race, gender, age and so on.

Fran also learns that the Board's annual reports from previous years contain similar data, thus a visit to the Board's office provides her with the historical data needed to identify trends in the statistics she is using. Finally, she discovers that two years earlier the Board produced a special issue of its annual report that was dedicated to the topic of ethnic minority children in foster care, and this issue offers additional statistics not normally recorded in most annual reports.

Another state agency is the Administration for Children, Youth, and Families, a division of the state's social services department. A call to the division connects her with a staff member who informs her that a special review of foster children was conducted by the agency only a few months before. Data from this review confirm her perception that minority children are overrepresented in foster care in the state, and it provides a range of other data that may be helpful in determining the causes of this problem.

From these sources Fran now has the data she needs to paint a detailed picture of minority foster children at the national and state levels. She also has the ability to examine the problem in terms of both point-in-time circumstances and longitudinal trends, and the latter suggests that the problem of overrepresentation has grown worse. There is also evidence to indicate that the problem is more severe in her state than nationally. Finally, corollary data on related variables, together with the more intensive work done in the special studies by the Foster Care Review Board and the Administration for Children, Youth, and Families, gives Fran a basis for beginning to understand the causes of the problem and the type of research study that must be done to investigate solutions.

available; (3) save time, money, and labor; (4) facilitate the development and refinement of the research question; and (5) facilitate theory development.

Provides Historical and Conceptual Contexts

Utilizing existing statistics provides a historical or conceptual context to a research study that uses primary, or firsthand, data. If we wanted to study the effects of poverty among single-parent families, for example, we might first want to determine the nature of poverty in our society. Existing statistics are ideal for this purpose. Through official governmental reports we could determine overall poverty rates, poverty rates for different types of families, long-term changes in family incomes, and so on. We might even be able to tell what percentage of families live under the poverty line in a particular geographical region, and how many of these are single-parent families. These data alone would allow us to do a better job in conceptualizing and operationalizing our study.

Can Be the Only Data Collection Method Available

Existing statistical records are extremely useful in situations where our research questions are unanswerable by other data collection methods. Take, for example, the concepts of crime rates, health indicators, prevalence of child abuse, death rates, affirmative action, immigration trends, changes in unemployment, and so on. We cannot directly observe these concepts, and primary, firsthand, obtrusive data collection methods such as surveys, for example, are usually far beyond the resources available. However, the data (the statistics) we need may already exist, we just have to find them and make them work for us to answer our research question.

Much of what we know about our past, the current structures in society, and societal change is a direct product of analyzing existing statistics gathered by others. It is best, therefore, not to view the use of existing statistics as a limited, rarely employed data collection method. Instead, our ability to answer many important research questions may be limited only by our own research skills and the quality of available statistical data sources.

Saves Time, Money, and Labor

On a practical level, we can save a considerable investment in time, money, and labor by using existing statistics (Singleton, Straits, and Miller-Straits, 1993). These savings are realized because the cost of developing data collection instruments and the effort of actually collecting the data have already been borne by others. We do not have to find resources to design question-naires or interview schedules, train interviewers, devise sampling strategies, place telephone calls to research participants, and so on.

Similarly, the process of collecting, aggregating, and reporting the statistics has been done for us. This obviously saves time and money. Even when a fee is charged for using an existing statistical data set, the true cost of conducting the original study is almost always substantially higher than the fee. In a nutshell, using existing statistical data often allows us to answer research questions that we could not possibly answer on our own limited research budgets.

Facilitates the Development and Refinement of the Research Question

In addition to making a large-scale research study more feasible, existing statistics also facilitate the development and refinement of our research question. By first exploring statistical records, for example, we can often test the potential of future research efforts. This is usually accomplished by testing our preliminary hypothesis using existing statistics. If our hypothesis is not supported we can rethink the theoretical foundations underlying the hypothesis, reshape the conceptual and operational definitions of the concepts within it, or consider alternative measurement instruments.

Facilitates Theory Development

Using existing statistical records as a data collection method contributes to theory development. Most social work research studies, for example, are based on small sample sizes and often lack longitudinal time frames. This obviously limits their generalizability and thus their contributions to our profession's knowledge base. Statistical data are often compiled (via aggregation) from large randomly selected samples. The statistics provided by the U.S. Census Bureau, for example, are based on a wide range of data collection methods and data sources. They incorporate data about diverse respondents and social problems.

The unique nature of statistical data contributes to theory development in one more way. Many organizations that distribute statistical data have been collecting the same data for decades. This enables us to compare statistical data across different time periods in an attempt to understand social and cultural change. We can use statistics from the U.S. Census Bureau, for example, to trace changes in family structures in America, the aging of our population, the impact of Generation X on the labor force, and so on. The contribution of existing statistical records to this type of theory development cannot be overemphasized. Research studies using existing statistics as a data collection method is one of the few ways we can effectively conduct long-term longitudinal studies.

Disadvantages

Existing statistical records are usually intended to serve administrative and public policy uses. This creates a number of methodological concerns when they are employed for research purposes. In general, there are four broad concerns that apply to any given statistical record. They include: (1) the "ecological fallacy" issue, (2) reliability, (3) validity, and (4) missing data.

The "Ecological Fallacy"

We frequently want to learn something about single individuals (units of analysis). What do we know about individuals who live below the poverty line in a particular city or town, for example? What is their life like, and what problems do they face in trying to make a living? Existing statistics often cannot provide data that easily answer these questions. As we know, existing statistics are published in the form of aggregate-level data. They summarize and describe the characteristics of larger groups, but tell us nothing about individuals, or micro-level data. This represents a critical distinction in terms of our unit of analysis.

Published statistics provide estimates of how many people live below the poverty line in the whole nation, or in a particular state, for example. They may even provide the sources of income the poor rely on, what their average income is, or how that income is spent. All of these aggregated statistical estimates, though, tell us only about "groups" of the poor. We cannot make any inferences about the characteristics or experiences of any individual person from the aggregated statistics. To do so would be to commit an *ecological fallacy*, which is a serious threat in research studies using existing statistical records. An ecological fallacy occurs when the characteristics or properties of a group are used to draw conclusions about an individual.

Using our example, we might be tempted to make inferences about the poor who rely on a local food bank for assistance. Based on *group* data, or aggregated-level data, it would be all too easy to conclude that these people are mother-only families, work in unpaid or low-wage jobs, or have limited educational attainment. In reality, though, some individuals who visit the food bank may be very different than the aggregated-level data suggest. Some people may be comparatively well educated and members of intact family units that were unexpectedly caught in the decline of a vital local industry.

The lesson to be drawn from these examples is that when using existing statistical records for any research study, we must first identify our unit of analysis. It is then necessary to examine our data source to ensure that the data relate to the unit we wish to describe.

Assessing Reliability

As we know, reliability is essentially a matter of consistency. The reliability of existing statistical records refers to the same thing. That is, do the records reliably report the variables they claim to report? There are two common reliability problems that appear when using existing statistical records: changes, over time, in how variables are conceptually and operationally defined; and alternate definitions of those variables across multiple data sources.

Changes in Conceptual and Operational Definitions   The first reliability issue—changes in conceptual and operational definitions over time—is one that affects most existing statistical records. Changes occur in the official definitions of many variables targeted by social work researchers. The operational definitions of variables measuring poverty, unemployment, types of crime, child abuse, and so on often change as our own perspectives about the problem change. Child abuse is a good example. Thirty or forty years ago, views about what constitutes child abuse were very different than those now espoused by our society. A slight spanking was considered by many to be a routine part of parenting. Now, this once-sanctioned act might often be considered a form of child abuse. Thus, the findings from a longitudinal study on the rates of child abuse, using existing statistics, may be inconsistent and thus not reliable. The operational definition of the variable being measured has simply changed over time.

Temporal changes affect more than operational definitions, however. They also have subsequent impacts on the way the data are collected. Let us look again at child abuse as an illustration of this point. Twenty years ago all recording of alleged child abuse perpetrators was done on paper files. Today, most of our child welfare agencies rely on computerized management information systems. These changes allow for more timely and accurate record keeping regarding alleged perpetrators. In other words, computerized management information systems may have indirectly helped to increase the apparent rates of child abuse. Also, public awareness of child abuse may have made it much more likely to be reported, though the actual incidence may not have changed.

Alternate Operational Definitions of Variables   The second major issue surrounding reliability of existing statistics relates to the equivalence of the statistics across multiple data sources. There is always more than one way to measure any variable, and many are open to a variety of operational defini-tions. A good example of this can be found in crime statistics.

Most police departments maintain records about the incidence of domestic violence in their particular communities. Keeping statistics about domestic violence would appear to be a relatively routine and straightforward matter. The operational definition of domestic violence, however, more often than not differs from one department to another. In reports of domestic violence, some departments might include incidents of verbal abuse, or cases where official charges were not filed against the alleged offender.

On the other hand, other departments might record only those incidents in which official criminal charges were filed or some severe form of violence occurred. This makes discrepancies between police department records not only possible, but very likely. Reported incidence of domestic violence, therefore, may often be very different than the *actual* incidence of domestic violence in any particular geographical area. It would be high if a department chose to have a very loose and global operational definition of domestic violence, and it would be low if a department chose to have a narrow and strict operational definition of domestic violence.

The reliability of existing domestic violence statistics depends on more than operational definitions alone, however. Let us say that police statistics report the incidence of domestic violence to be much higher in California than in other states. Even if we have ruled out differences in operational definitions, there are other factors that could produce this result. The state's apparently higher incidence of domestic violence might simply reflect the results of a crackdown on domestic violence, which served to increases domestic violence arrest rates. The results might also reflect a broader societal awareness of domestic violence, or increased media coverage of the problem (remember the O.J. Simpson trial in California?). In any case, the reliability of these data would have to be examined closely.

Another reliability problem is that changes occur over time in both *how* statistics are reported and *which* statistics get reported. Suppose, for example, we are tracking physical and mental health records that report the incidence of alcoholism by age groups. For several years, data may be reported on age groups 15 to 25, 25 to 35, 35 to 45, and over 45. Suddenly, however, the age groups change to 10 to 20, 20 to 30, 30 to 40, and so on. Comparisons of alcoholism in age groups across time would thus be difficult to analyze because of the inconsistency in the way age groups were aggregated.

Changes in which statistics are reported are also problematic. We may be interested in tracking trends in binge drinking as one particular form of alcoholism, for example. Current statistical reports available from one key source may provide these data, breaking down alcoholism into statistics on binge drinking and other forms. We may find, however, that earlier reports from the same source do not separate various types of alcoholism in this way. Thus, we could be thwarted in our efforts to make comparisons over time, because we would have no reliable way of determining how many alcoholics were binge drinkers at the earlier date.

Assessing Validity

Some of the major benefits offered by existing statistical records can also lead to validity problems. As we know from Chapter 8, validity has to do with whether the variable we are measuring is being measured accurately. Problems can occur because we trade savings in time, money, and labor for our direct control over the entire research study. Such control is always maintained by the organization that originally collected and aggregated the data. This means that our research question, conceptual and operational definitions, research methods and procedures, and statistical reports were all previously chosen by the organization supplying the statistics. Any errors in these areas represent errors in measurement, and hence validity problems.

There are a few methods we can use to ensure that conceptual or data collection errors have been avoided in any given existing statistical data source. Most important of these is that we must carefully and critically examine how the data were collected in the first place, with an eye toward the study's "scientific rigor." Were understandable questions asked, and could they in fact be answered? Were respondents selected using appropriate random sampling techniques? Were data collection procedures rigorous, and were they closely followed? Were the variables measured correctly? Answering such questions provides a solid foundation from which to judge the validity of an existing statistical data record.

Deductive Versus Inductive Reasoning   Even if a critical review of the statistical data is positive, however, problems of validity still arise. One of the most common validity problems revolves around the issue of using existing data in an inductive research study (Monette, Sullivan, & DeJong, 1990). A research study using existing statistics as a data collection method can indeed be an deductive one, however. That is, a deductive study starts with a theoretical framework and has a hypothesis derived from the framework. The hypothesis is operationally defined, research measuring instruments are selected, and data collection is implemented. The data are analyzed, and based upon the data analysis, the hypothesis is rejected or accepted. Our study is conducted in a deductive manner, progressing from an abstract way of thinking to a concrete way of thinking.

As noted above, however, research studies using existing statistics as a data collection method do not have to rely on a deductive process. Instead, they can also use inductive processes where we move from a concrete way of thinking to an abstract way of thinking. Our inquiry begins not with a well-defined theoretical framework, as in deductive studies, but with micro-level data aggregated in a statistical report(s). These inductive studies start out by examining the existing statistics in relation to the general research questions. From this point, we focus on detecting patterns within the statistics themselves. Are there, for instance, employment, educational, and family characteristics that are typical of poor families in a particular state? If such patterns are found, our next step is to develop hypotheses and theories that might explain the findings. Over time these hypotheses might be supported by detecting the same patterns in other existing statistical records, thereby building upon or altering an existing theory.

There are two major ways that the inductive research process generates validity problems: (1) the lack of an original theoretical framework for collecting the data, and (2) the need to construct indirect measures of variables.

1. Lack of an original theoretical framework

The theoretical framework used to guide the original data collection strategy is often not made clear in subsequent statistical reports. This means that the rationale underlying such steps as the selection of and the operationalization of variables is unknown. Just as frequently, our own conceptualizations can differ from those of the persons who collected the original data. In either case, a common theoretical framework is lacking, meaning that the variables found in the existing statistical records may not be a valid measure of the concept we are trying to assess in our study.

Consider the work that women do in our society as an example. In studying the contributions made by women to the workforce, official government agencies tend to define women's labor only in terms of paid employment, and they tend to ignore work that does not earn cash for the family (Jacobson, 1992). When studying the same topic, using the statistics provided by those same government agencies, we would likely want to expand our operational definition of "work."

Along with paid labor, our new operational definition of work might include meal preparation, child care, and general housework. This new operational definition would not be measured by official statistics, however. It might be argued that our definition of "work" is more valid than that used in the government statistics. The problem is that by expanding our operational definition of work we might begin to address an entirely different concept than the one measured by "the official statistics." By relying on existing statistical records, therefore, we are constrained by the initial measures used in compiling the statistics, and our own study may be limited by the degree of validity of those initial measurements.

2. Indirect measurement of variables

The second validity issue directly relates to the first. It occurs when the variables of interest are not measured directly within the existing statistical records. This situation is common in social science research. Even though social service programs collect statistics on many aspects of their operations, few directly measure the achievement of their objectives, client change, or worker effectiveness.

In such situations, we are forced to construct proxy variables from the available statistics. In other words, we need to create an indirect measure of the concept we are studying. Unfortunately, the validity of this indirect measure or proxy variable is hard to establish.

A good example of constructing indirect measures is found in assessments of physical and mental health in the elderly. The U.S. Census Bureau might ask elderly citizens a series of questions about their physical and mental health. These questions might ask them to compare how "healthy" they are relative to others their age, whether they are physically active, whether they have had a major physical or mental problem over the last year, whether they received medical assistance over the last year, and whether they suffered an accidental injury over the last year.

Now, suppose we want to use these existing statistics to conduct a study of the elderly, and we need a measure of their *current* physical and mental health status. None of these variables directly measure what we want. However, we could construct a proxy variable—an index that uses all of these variables—to identify those seniors who are most likely to enjoy good health right now. If the seniors are physically active, feel healthy, and have been both accident and illness free for the last year, we could conclude that they are probably healthy right now. There are, however, no guarantees that such responses to these questions ensure current good health. Our proxy variable, physical and mental health, would have an unknown degree of error, or uncertain measurement validity.

Assessing the Extent of Missing Data

We all know some people who refuse to answer certain questions on any survey. It might be a question about their income, their age, or any other topic they might consider sensitive. Whenever an individual refuses to answer such questions, it creates gaps in the subsequent data set and any statistics computed from it. Such refusals are common in most studies. We are rarely able to ensure that all respondents answer every question asked of them. This means that missing data are inevitably an issue in any research study using existing statistical records.

Missing data cannot be blamed on respondents alone, however. Many other factors play a role in contributing to missing data. The original research team, for example, may have inadvertently neglected to interview all respondents from a preselected neighborhood. Or perhaps social workers delegated to collect data on particular variables found it very difficult to do so and thus did not provide data on those variables for many of their cases. One example is data on household income which, for a variety of reasons, is often very difficult to collect accurately.

Still other reasons for missing data include failure by the administrator, or researcher, to provide clear instructions on how line-level staff should record the data. A common example is written forms or computerized information systems that are sometimes so difficult to understand that data are frequently omitted. Finally, we may find that data are missing from statistical records simply because those who originally collected the data did not share our ideas about what was important and thus did not gather data on one or more variables we see as being critical.

Next to respondent refusals, the most common reason for missing data in existing statistical data sets is probably societal change itself. As society changes, questions that are deemed important also change. Statistics regarding liquor prohibition do not mean much in today's society, for example. Nor were questions about the growth of HIV/AIDS even known in past decades. As a reflection of these changes, organizations that collect data regularly start or stop gathering certain types of data. This practice inevitably generates missing data in statistical records.

Random and Systematic Errors   Regardless of the reason for missing data, it is a very serious issue. The occurrence of missing data introduces error into the statistics. As we know from Chapters 8 and 11, this error has two forms, random error and systematic error. Random error occurs when, for no particular reason, data are lacking on some cases in the data set from which the statistics were compiled. Because there is no pattern as to which cases are missing data and which cases are not, it is also unlikely that the presence of random error will bias the statistics in any particular direction.

Of greater concern is systematic error. This occurs when data are missing on specific types of cases from which statistics were compiled. For example, suppose statistics were gathered on employment in a particular region, but the people on which the statistics were based included only those with known residences. This would mean that homeless people would not be among those included in the statistics. Because homeless people have a much higher rate of joblessness, the effect of their omission would be to cause the statistics to underestimate the level of joblessness in the region, and this, in turn, would drastically limit the overall value of the data.

The only solution is to exercise caution when using statistical records. Before we commit to conducting a research study using a particular statistical record, we need to ensure that the data set is not missing an inordinate amount of data. In addition, we need to spend some time exploring the statistics provided. Not only should the data be generally complete, but the people who collected the original data should have reported the steps that were taken to minimize missing data.

STEPS IN ANALYZING EXISTING STATISTICS

We recently completed a study that utilized existing statistical records as a data collection method. We will use it as an example here because of our familiarity with how the study was conducted and because it addresses an issue of interest to social work students—faculty/student ratios within graduate schools of social work (McMurtry & McClelland, 1995). This section address four basic steps when using existing statistics as a data collection method: (1) formulating the research question, (2) finding existing statistical records, (3) assessing validity and reliability, and (4) analyzing the data.

Step 1: Formulating the Research Question

Our study began with personal experiences suggesting that the number of undergraduate and graduate social work students was increasing, but few corresponding increases were occurring in the number of social work faculty available to teach them. This raised a concern that there may be too few qualified faculty to meet the needs of social work students. From this assumption, two research questions were generated: (1) what are the trends in social work student enrollments, staffing patterns, and faculty/student ratios in schools and departments of social work in recent years? and (2) how do these trends compare to those in related disciplines?

Step 2: Finding Existing Statistical Records

As mentioned earlier, after developing the initial research questions, our next step in using existing statistical records as a data collection method was to identify an appropriate data source. In our case, we were aware that the accrediting body for social work programs in the United States, CSWE, publishes an annual report on accredited schools and departments. This report is titled *Statistics on Social Work Education in the United States*. Its primary unit of analysis is the social work programs themselves. These data are collected via cross-sectional surveys mailed to each social work program each year.

Schools and departments are asked to provide data on their students, their faculty, and other aspects of their program as of November 1 of the year being studied. Five standardized, self-administered survey instruments are used to collect data on: faculty, bachelors programs, masters programs, doctoral programs, and programs in candidacy. Each school or department receives only the instrument(s) that apply to its specific programs.

Our study's original intent was to examine faculty/student ratios in social work programs at all three degree levels. Standards recommended by the CSWE are for a 1:12 ratio of faculty to students at the masters level and a 1:25 ratio at the bachelors level (no specific standard is suggested for doctoral programs). As can be all too common when doing a research study using statistical records, we found we had to narrow our study's focus because of the lack of data in the CSWE's published statistics.

Specifically, the CSWE annual statistics did not record data on faculty/ student ratios at the bachelors level, and it was impossible to compute these ratios retroactively from the data available. General data on faculty/student ratios were available for doctoral programs, but other data (such as the number of faculty specifically assigned to doctoral education in each school or department) were not present, so our study had to be narrowed to masters programs alone, where a full range of necessary data was readily available.

Step 3: Assessing Validity and Reliability

Our next consideration was the validity and reliability of the statistics in the CSWE annual reports, our data sources. Copies of these reports were obtained for the years 1977 to 1993, which allowed us to review trends over the 17-year period. To do this reliably, however, data on key variables such as student enrollment and faculty numbers would have to have been collected in a consistent way over that entire 17-year period. Fortunately, we found that in gathering data from member schools and departments, the CSWE has used the same operational definition over time for each variable used in computing faculty/ student ratios in schools and departments of social work. All part-time students, for example, are assigned a value of one-half, and full-time students a value of one.

Faculty numbers are differentiated by whether they hold tenured or non-tenured positions and by the amount of time they spend teaching at the BSW, MSW, and doctoral levels. Also, data in the annual report show that response rates for the survey have remained high over the years. For masters programs, nonresponse rates averaged between 1 and 3 percent per year, meaning that missing data were not sufficiently frequent to cast doubt on the consistency of the data over time.

While these factors suggest that the CSWE data were reliable, determining validity is an equally important but often more difficult task. Low reliability is often a sign that validity is also low, but high reliability is not a guarantee of high validity. This is because the measure in question may be reliably measuring the wrong variable. In our study, for example, the reliability of the CSWE data appeared to be high, so our task in assessing the validity of these data was to examine whether ambiguity existed in the operational definitions of the variables that could lead to their being misunderstood and thus mismeasured. Fortunately, the CSWE data had four important strengths that, when combined, suggested that the validity of the statistics they presented was high. First, the variables being measured—student enrollments and faculty numbers—are relatively straightforward and unambiguous variables.

Second, these variables (and others, such as full-time-equivalency of faculty and students, distinctions between degree-seeking and nondegree-seeking students, etc.) are based on established measurement practices in higher education and are thus familiar to most respondents. Third, these variables were clearly explained and operationalized in the data collection instruments. Finally, the instruments used in the CSWE's data collection process remained similar and predictable over time, and response rates remained high over the 17-year period assessed in our study.

One issue regarding validity did arise, however. Despite ongoing high response rates to the CSWE surveys, there were usually some missing data. In a few cases all the data for a particular variable were missing; in others cases some but not all of the data for a variable were provided. No patterns in the missing data were evident, and the amount of missing data was small (seldom exceeding 1 to 2 percent of all cases). Still, as in other research studies using existing statistics as a data collection method, the issue of missing data should be considered a caution against overgeneralizing a study's findings.

To discover how trends in social work education compared with those in related disciplines, we then had to find the accrediting organization for each of those disciplines and determine whether the organization published data similar to that in the CSWE annual statistics.

An information specialist at our university library helped us find a publication titled *Accredited Institutions of Post Secondary Education*, which is published by the American Council on Education. This book lists all the accredited programs in various disciplines at U.S. universities and colleges, and it also lists the name, address, and telephone number of each accrediting organization. From this list, we identified 13 related disciplines with which social work might appropriately be compared.

Each organization was contacted by phone, given a description of the CSWE annual statistics, and asked whether it published a similar report. Unfortunately, only four disciplines—communication sciences and disorders, law, public affairs and administration, and psychology—were found to publish comparable statistics. Copies of relevant reports were obtained either directly from the accrediting bodies for these disciplines or, when available, in our university library. Data from these reports became the basis for comparing these fields with social work.

Step 4: Analyzing the Data

This brings us to the question of what our study found. After producing numerous statistics and graphs, we found that faculty/student ratios rose steadily, from a median of 1 faculty member to 9.9 students in 1981 to a median of 1 faculty member to 13.4 students in 1993. Remembering the 1 to 12 ratio recommended by CSWE, it is evident that faculty/student ratios have been higher than desirable since 1988, with the current ratio now being almost 12 percent above the maximum ratio set by the CSWE.

In 1981, for example, most schools had a faculty/student ratio in the range of eight to nine students per faculty member, and only about 10 percent of them reported faculty/student ratios over 1 to 14. In contrast, by 1993 the most frequently occurring level of faculty/student ratios was over 15 students per faculty member. Almost 40 percent of the schools and departments had faculty/student ratios at or above the level of 1 to 14.

The CSWE statistics were also used to examine other aspects of the issue of faculty/student ratios. We looked at trends in MSW student enrollment, for example. Results showed that MSW enrollment has grown markedly in recent years. Though the number of full-time MSW students declined during the early and middle 1980s, since 1986 enrollments have increased by 50 percent. As of late 1993, more than 21,000 full-time MSW students were enrolled in accredited U.S. schools and departments of social work, a higher number than ever before.

Growth has also occurred in the number of part-time MSW students. The CSWE statistics show that enrollment of part-time MSW students has increased steadily, almost tripling since 1977 to a total of more than 11,000. Together, part-time and full-time MSW students numbered more than 32,000 in late 1993.

We also found that the number of full-time, tenure-track faculty members in the CSWE-accredited schools and departments was about the same in 1993 as in 1977, with the 1993 number actually being slightly lower. This contrasts sharply with the high growth in student (undergraduate and graduate) enrollment of more than 50 percent over that same period. Clearly, schools and departments of social work in the United States have taken in many additional students without commensurately increasing tenure-track faculty.

With regard to whether similar trends have occurred in related disciplines, we were able to obtain suitable comparative data from the four fields noted earlier (communication sciences and disorders; law; public affairs and administration; psychology). In the process, though, we also encountered one of the major difficulties of using existing statistical records. This is, the CSWE statistics and those of the other four accrediting organizations were collected at different times, for different periods, and in different ways. Thus, we had to report separately the data gathered from each discipline, and it also made the process of comparing across disciplines more difficult.

Our research study could not have been done without the use of statistical records. With them, however, we were able to show some important changes that have affected how graduate social work education is provided. These changes are meaningful for social work graduate students, since they imply that each student now has a one-third smaller share of any faculty members' time than 11 years ago. Moreover, the faculty members whose time students now seek are more likely to be part-time instructors and other nontenure-track faculty than they are to be full-time faculty. Since part-time faculty usually do not remain on site, students are probably even more isolated from faculty than the overall faculty/student ratios suggest.

Of course many part-time and nontenure-track faculty are very capable instructors, and some are better than many tenure-track faculty. Still, data from the CSWE statistics show that as of 1993, full-time tenure-track faculty were four times more likely to have a doctoral degree than full-time nontenure-track faculty or part-time faculty. Assuming that doctoral-level training has value for social work educators, there are clearly qualitative issues raised by these trends.

One implication is that graduate social work education may be making a de facto return to a kind of apprentice model, where experienced practitioners (part-time faculty hired from field settings) teach those in the next generation. Meanwhile, workloads for full-time faculty may continue to increase as their numbers relative to part-time faculty drop and student enrollments rise. It should be no surprise to learn that full-time faculty report feeling less productive, while graduate students struggle with gaining access to their professors.

SUMMARY

The process of using existing statistical records as a data collection method is relatively straightforward and quite simple. We begin with a general research question or a specific hypothesis. A statistical data record(s) that might answer our question or hypothesis is then identified, often with the assistance of an information specialist located at a local library. Existing statistics are obtained and their quality is assessed by examining factors such as the conceptual framework used to shape the data collection process, the scientific rigor of data collection procedures, and the appropriateness of measures used to collect the data. If the reported statistics indeed seem to be empirically sound, we then conduct a quantitative data analysis of the statistics to answer our research question or to test our hypothesis.

As we know, using existing statistics as a form of data collection is unobtrusive, that is, we do not intrude into our research participants' lives in any way. The following chapter continues our discussion of unobtrusive data collection methods by presenting how a social work research study can use another unobtrusive data collection method, known as content analysis, for doing a research study.

Craig W. LeCroy
Gary Solomon

C h a p t e r   18

Content Analysis

ONTENT ANALYSIS is similar to secondary analysis, discussed in the
preceding two chapters, in that both use existing data sets. In content
analysis, however, the data are generated by quantifying units of analysis
in the content of recorded communications so they can be counted. Because
content analysis allows us to investigate research questions without needing to
collect original data, we can formulate research questions about anything that
has taken place and been recorded. Our research question may involve content
describing some historical situation or something that occurred a moment ago.
In either case, the content is defined, coded, and tallied to generate new data
that may be analyzed immediately or at some future date.

If our research question can be stated in terms that meet the criteria of
specificity, relevancy, researchability, feasibility, and ethical acceptability (see
Chapter 5), and if recorded communications on the question exist, a content
analysis could well be the best method of collecting data to investigate it.
Content analyses are well suited to the study of communications because they
address the questions of who says what to whom, why, how, and with what
effect. The "what" of a research study, or the defining aspect, is found in the
content of the text to be studied.

CHARACTERISTICS OF CONTENT ANALYSES

In content analyses, communications are examined in a systematic, objective, and quantitative manner (Holsti, 1969). To be systematic, a content analysis must follow specified procedures. If we want to compare the lyrics in the songs of three different rock groups, for example, we must systematically use the same procedures in examining the content for each group. As we know from Chapter 8 through 10, if the same measuring procedures are not used, our results will not be considered reliable; it could be argued that the difference in the way the criteria were applied to the groups is a source of bias or error in our results. This occurs when we structure our data collection procedures to confirm our own predictions or support our own theoretical positions.

Objectivity is another characteristic of content analyses that helps ensure validity and avoid bias. This characteristic is concerned with making the criteria or rules used to categorize the contents of the text impartial and objective. Clearly defining the criteria to be applied and making explicit the rules to be used in classifying the content of a communication help control any special interest or ideology that might influence our research study (Williamson et al., 1982).

In our study of rock lyrics, for example, the rules to be used in categorizing the lyrics must be specified. Otherwise a conclusion that rock lyrics consist of sexual and violent content, or a conclusion that they are harmless, could be considered invalid. While people interested in the results of our research study might not agree with the categories that we devised, the standards for deciding how to categorize the data and code them for recording would be clear, so others could evaluate how our conclusions had been reached. Objective procedures also allow others to replicate our study; even if they have different biases, if they follow the same rules for categorizing the content, the results should be the same.

A Quantitative Research Approach

Content analyses are ordinarily used in quantitative research approaches because they focus on the operational definitions and quantifications of the dependent variables (and sometimes the independent variables) in research questions or hypotheses. Before the content of any communication can be analyzed it must be possible to quantify it in some manner. In a study to examine the way women are portrayed in children's books, for example, the number of times women are portrayed as mothers and as workers outside the home could be counted. The unit of analysis is women. Each time a unit occurs in a particular category (mother or worker), it is "counted" and recorded in that category.

A common use of content analyses is recording the frequency with which certain symbols or themes appear in a communication. Dodd, Foerch, and Anderson (1988), for example, did a content analysis of women and racial and ethnic minorities as subjects of newsmagazine covers, an indication of their coverage in the content of a particular issue. The covers of *Time* and *Newsweek* from 1953 through 1987 were studied, and each appearance of a woman or minority member was counted. The researchers then could determine whether these variables were represented in relation to their proportions in the U.S. population and whether there had been changes in the subjects of the covers and cover stories over time.

When quantification is used in this manner, the results are usually presented in terms of simple proportions or percentages. A content analysis of a diary, for example, may reveal that the term "love" made up 5 percent of the total words used or that it appeared on 61 percent of the pages. Also, it could show an increase in use of the term between certain dates.

Quantification is not always that easy, however. We must often attempt to examine not just the frequency of a variable but also its intensity or deeper meaning. To compare how liberal two congressional candidates are, a content analysis of their speeches could be done. In addition to counting the number of "liberal" statements each one made, according to some specified criteria, there might be an attempt to evaluate how liberal each statement is. The task of devising adequate categories then would become much more complicated. Perhaps each statement could be rated as extremely liberal, moderately liberal, or minimally liberal. Because the concept of liberalism is becoming increasingly difficult to define in terms of political parties or ideologies, there would be limits to the possible options in using such a content analysis.

STEPS IN DOING A CONTENT ANALYSIS

To illustrate the process of conducting a content analysis, we will use an example involving a problem area of great social concern to social workers: suicide. While the steps in this process closely follow those in the quantitative research process described in Chapter 6, they are collapsed in this section to four distinctive steps that emphasize the nature and characteristics of content analyses: (1) developing a research question, (2) selecting a sample, (3) selecting the unit of analysis, and (4) coding, tallying, and analyzing the data.

Step 1: Developing a Research Question

As in all research studies, content analyses begin with a researcher's interest in a problem area and the development of a specific research question or hypothesis. In our example, we are interested in the problem area of suicide, and the purpose of our study is to contribute to an understanding of why people commit suicide. From this general perspective, a group of research questions could be advanced:

- Are there predictable patterns of behavior in people who commit suicide?
- Are the reasons for suicide different now than they were 20 years ago?
- Can we predict the act of suicide by examining the themes in suicide notes?
- Do people who leave suicide notes use similar words or describe common experiences and feelings?
- Do the suicide notes written by women and men differ?

For this example, our study will focus on the last two questions. The method will be a content analysis of suicide notes written in recent years.

Step 2: Selecting a Sample

Choosing the appropriate sampling strategy in a content analysis can be tedious. Suppose, for example, we are interested in how men and women are portrayed in children's books. Our population is all available children's books, and it is necessary to decide which parameters should be used to limit the sample. A sample from the population of writers might be selected, or the books published in a certain year might be chosen instead. Our sample could be limited to schoolbooks used for second- and third-graders, and if this universe is still too large, the books used by all elementary schools in a specific city might be sampled. Such options must be considered in an attempt to gather a representative sample. The sample selection process also can redefine the specific problem area.

The decisions that must be made in selecting a sample for a research study are discussed in Chapter 11. For our suicide note example, the sampling plan is relatively straightforward. The universe (or population) from which our sample is to be extracted is identified as the suicide notes in the files of the Suicide Prevention Center, which collects and records suicide notes written in various U.S. cities that agree to participate. Although the content analysis for this example will be limited to what is available at the Center, that universe is still large, and sampling considerations are necessary.

The Center has been in existence for over 30 years and has collected over 15,500 suicide notes. For our study, therefore, our universe is further limited to suicide notes written in a two-year period, and only the suicide notes of adult men and women (21 years of age and older) are included. Within these parameters, a total of 1,327 suicide notes is available. From this population, a random sample of 100 suicide notes is selected.

Random sampling thus is chosen as the sampling strategy, but other techniques could also be used. With stratified sampling, for example, the suicide notes would be grouped according to strata such as year written, age category, or gender. After grouping, equal-sized samples of notes would be generated for each stratum and sampled separately, using simple or systematic random sampling techniques.

The limitation of the population parameters to determine the composition of our sample often follows a three-part process: sampling of sources (which suicide notes?), sampling of dates (suicide notes from what years?), and sampling of units (which aspects of the notes are to be analyzed?). When sampling according to units analyzed, our decisions are often based on what characterizes the content best for purposes of our study.

Step 3: Selecting the Unit of Analysis

In all content analyses, the specific unit of analysis, that is, what is to be counted, must be specified. This step is dependent on the quantification, or operational definition, of the dependent variable(s) in our research question. Units of analysis vary considerably, depending on the complexity of the research question and the universe of communications to be sampled. In many studies, recording the unit of analysis is simple, such as counting the number of certain words; in others, recording involves the establishment of complex categorical systems and coding rules and procedures.

In our suicide note example, the word content of suicide notes is chosen as the unit to be counted. To begin, the choice of a single concept, death, as a unit of analysis keeps our coding simple and reliable. We do not have to struggle to make judgments about whether a particular unit fits in the category—all the units do. We simply count the number of words that refer to the variable, death. But because many different words refer to death, there must be coding rules to clarify what to code in the category of death. In our example, any reference to death—words such as dying, dead, ending, or terminating—is to be used as the unit of analysis and counted.

Step 4: Coding, Tallying, and Analyzing the Data

The coding of data has to do with the categories of the unit of analysis. With a single concept such as death, there is only one category, but the different words that refer to death are defined as belonging in that category. With a concept such as gender there are two obvious categories, male and female. Thus, coding data is dependent on the way the categories are operationally defined; they should reflect the concepts (the dependent and independent variables) represented in the research question.

To aid in the data collection process, a coding or tally sheet is developed. Figure 18.1 is an example of a coding sheet used to record the data we want to extract from the suicide notes sampled. Three references to death were counted in Note 1, written by a male, and five references to death in Note 2, written by a female. The coder continues to count and tally until all 100 randomly selected suicide notes have been tallied. Then the individual tallies are totaled and the frequencies of the tallies for men and women are compared.

If different units of analysis, other than the concepts of death and gender, were used, additional concepts and categories would be included in the tally sheet. For instance, the age of the writer, the city of residence, any reference to a friend, parent, spouse, or relevant other, or a mention of a plan for the suicide might be operationally defined, coded, and tallied.

Categorizing Latent Content

In our example, coding is limited to the tabulation of gender and the frequency of occurrence of words relating to death. This type of information is referred to as manifest content—the obvious, clearly evident, viable aspects of the communication. Examples of coding manifest content are counting certain types of words, coding whether men or women appear on the cover of a magazine, and counting the number of times violence occurs in a TV program.

Beyond the manifest content of communications, we often are interested in their latent content—content that is present but not evident or active. Latent content is an indicator of the underlying meaning of what is communicated. We may, for example, want to assess the political orientation of a newspaper editorial or the intensity of the violence portrayed on certain television shows. Manifest content is specific, is easy to code, and produces reliable data. Latent content is less specific and more difficult to code because it represents the meaning, depth, and intensity of a communication.

Suicide Notes	Death Concept Tally	Gender of Writer	
		Male	Female
Note 1	3	✔	
Note 2	5		✔
Note 3			
Note 4			
Note 5			
Note 6			

Figure 18.1   Recording Sheet for Two
Categories in Suicide Notes

In our example, we may want to understand what people considering suicide think and feel. Because it could be difficult to get these impressions via simple word counts, we attempt to characterize the meanings expressed in the suicide notes, which requires more judgment and interpretation.

As we study the various suicide notes in the sample, we recognize several recurrent themes. We may decide, for example, to code the notes according to four themes identified in suicide notes (Schneidman, 1985): unendurable psychological pain, searching for solutions, helplessness and hopelessness, and constriction of options. Obviously, these themes are difficult to code, but operational definitions could be formulated from types of statements found in the notes. For the first two concepts, for example, *unendurable psychological pain* could be coded from the statements: "I feel so desperate" and "This will all be over soon"; *searching for solutions* could be coded from the statements: "I can't face life, there's only one thing to do" and "I've done everything I can, there are no more options for me."

By uncovering such themes, we may develop an interest in discovering in what ways the themes differ in notes written by men and women, or we may want to examine the degree of intensity in each theme. Using such latent content results in a complex coding task because the themes must be identified in the content and then coded or placed in an assigned category, to indicate the intensity with which the theme is being expressed. Once the theme of helplessness and hopelessness has been defined in terms of certain types of statements found in suicide notes, for example, three ordinal categories might be set up to indicate the intensity of particular statements:

1 = Great feelings of helplessness and hopelessness

2 = Average feelings of helplessness and hopelessness

3 = Minimal feelings of helplessness and hopelessness

The coder must identify each statement according to theme and determine in which of the three categories of intensity it belongs.

When such judgments must be made in the coding of data, the reliability of the data produced by the coding system must be established. This is done in terms of interrater reliability, using a process whereby two or more independent coders or judges agree on how a unit of analysis should be categorized. While it is not necessary for them to agree completely on the categorization of every statement, if they can reach no agreement, the study's results will lack reliability and will seriously jeopardize the findings.

Coders, or judges, should agree on their coding results about 80 percent of the time. To achieve good reliability, coders often go through a training program to teach them how to compare and discuss their decisions about the coding and categorization of data. Code books are often developed with operational definitions and rules for how the data should be coded.

Content analysis thus can go beyond simple word counts and manifest content to examine communications more intensively. For some research questions, studies that have great specificity and reliability are required; for others, it is necessary to attempt to grapple with the meaning of the content in depth. When the research study uses latent content to elicit depth and meaning, several considerations emerge: the number of categories increases, the time required to do the coding increases, and the reliability of the coding decreases, because more interpretation by coders is necessary. Nevertheless, the research questions asked often determine the necessity of searching for depth and meaning in order to explore answers for them.

USES IN SOCIAL WORK RESEARCH

Despite the structured process of content analyses, they can be put to a variety of uses in social work research. They serve several distinct purposes and can be used in combination with other data gathering methods. Developments in methodology, such as the use of computers to analyze communications with both quantitative and qualitative content and the acceptance of less structured forms such as ethnographic analyses, are increasing the range of uses to which content analyses can be put.

Classification of Content Analyses by Purpose

Content analyses can be classified into four broad categories according to the purpose of the analysis: (1) to make inferences to the source of communications, (2) to make inferences to populations, (3) to evaluate the effects of communications, or (4) to make structured observations (Williamson et al., 1982).

Inferences to the Source of Communications

An example of how content analyses are used to make inferences about the source of communications is analysis of the content of messages in an effort to understand the motives, values, or intentions of those who wrote them. Content analyses also may be done in order to understand something about people or institutions through their symbolic communications, which can reveal attitudes or beliefs. To do this, such documents as diaries, speeches, newspapers, or transcriptions of interviews might be examined.

Diaries or personal documents were used in some of the first examples of content analyses. An example is an early study of the psychology of adolescence, for which a collection of over 100 diaries of adolescent girls was established at the Psychological Institute at the University of Vienna. This made possible a comparison of adolescents at two different time periods, 1873 and 1910, which would have been difficult with other methods of data collection. The results indicated that despite the significant cultural changes that took place between these years, many basic developmental issues such as the need for intimate personal relationships remained the same. Changes were observed, however, in such factors as the girls' relationships with their parents. Analysis of the diaries, particularly the girls' descriptions of rare or significant events, produced unique knowledge and provided a perspective on the inner aspects of life for adolescents in those times.

A much more recent content analysis was done to examine the experience of loneliness, using the accounts of people who were asked to describe in writing their loneliest experience (Rokach, 1988). Analysis of these descriptions enabled the researcher to build a conceptual model to help explain the phenomenon of loneliness.

Other content analyses attempt to build understanding of how political or social issues are reflected in the content of communications such as professional journals, laws, and existing policies (Williamson et al., 1982). To evaluate how social work practice had changed from 1960 to the 1980s, for example, one such study involved a content analysis of social work practice position vacancy descriptions (Billups & Julia, 1987). Job advertisements in the *Journal of Social Casework* and the *NASW News* were randomly sampled to determine how job titles and fields of practice had changed over three consecutive 10-year periods, the 1960s, 1970s, and 1980s. This study helped answer such research questions as: Have there been changes in the way social work practice is conceptualized? What jobs are being advertised most frequently?

In a similar manner, a content analysis of course outlines of social work practice courses was done to discover the extent to which the teaching of these courses reflected current theoretical and ideological issues in social work (LeCroy & Goodwin, 1988). Course units, required textbooks, required outside readings, and types of assignments were used as categories of practice courses (the unit of analysis), and the researchers attempted to make inferences about how these courses were being conceptualized. This study sought to answer such questions as: Is there any commonality among the course units? Do the courses include content on women and ethnic minorities? What textbooks are used most often? The results were used as a basis for characterizing the content and teaching methods currently being used in social work practice courses.

Inferences to Populations

By making inferences to populations, content analyses can be used to ascertain the values of the audiences that are reached by various communications. A well-known content analysis, for example, examined the relationship between economic development and the value a society places on achievement. David C. McClelland (1961) operationalized the definition of achievement as the presence of achievement themes in over 1000 children's stories from almost every country in the world and the definition of a society's economic development in terms of such factors as coal and electricity consumption. The results of this study indicated that countries with high achievement values were more likely to have higher rates of economic growth than countries with lower achievement values.

Other content analyses have attempted to make inferences about social change and cultural values. The portrayal of women and men in the content of television commercials (Bretl & Cantor, 1988) and the portrayal of violence on prime-time television (Cumberbatch, Jones, & Lee, 1988) have been analyzed, for example. Such studies must be understood in terms of the assumption that the content being analyzed represents society's values.

In the content analysis of the covers of two major newsmagazines described earlier in this chapter (Dodd, Foerch, & Anderson, 1988), it was concluded that society did not see women and minorities as more newsworthy in the 1980s than in the preceding decades, and values about how women and minorities are perceived had not changed. But would it be accurate to say that the covers of two magazines represent how society perceives women and minorities? Such conclusions point to the need for replications of the study using different printed media to see if similar conclusions are reached.

Evaluating the Effects of Communications

In addition to studying themes discerned in communications, content analyses can focus on the effects of items of analysis recorded in communications. One of the earliest uses of content analysis in social work research was in an attempt to measure the effectiveness of social work interventions, using clients' records. John Dollard and O. H. Mowrer (1947), for example, hypothesized that the effectiveness of social work intervention would be revealed in reduced tension in the clients. They evaluated the variable of tension according to a change in the relative proportions of verbal expressions of discomfort (or distress) and expressions of relief from distress recorded in the clients' case records. They then developed a complex coding system to classify emotional tone as a unit of analysis according to categories of distress clauses, relief clauses, or neither.

They also devised a distress quotient, the number of distress clauses divided by the sum of distress and relief clauses, to be used in measurement. Unfortunately, this complex method was found to have little relationship to client change. Later research studies in which similar methods were used to analyze client case records did establish the effectiveness of short-term interventions, however (Reid & Shyne, 1969).

A more recent application of an outcome-oriented content analysis was a single-case study with an emotionally disturbed child. The goal of this study was simply to evaluate the effects of the social worker's behavior (the intervention) on the client's acting-out behavior (Broxmeyer, 1979). Recorded and transcribed interviews were analyzed, and two behaviors the social worker used in working with the child—empathy and limit setting—were coded. These behaviors were then correlated with the child's acting-out behavior.

The results of the content analysis revealed that the social worker had responded to acting out with empathic responses eight times, and on six of those occasions the child stopped; therefore there was a 75 percent reduction in the behavior. When the social worker used limit setting, the child discontinued the behavior 45 percent of the time. When the worker displayed no response, there was only a 25 percent reduction in the child's acting out.

In these examples the focus of the research studies was to determine whether communications can indicate the cause of certain behaviors. Studies that make such inferences are experimental in nature, and measurement of the dependent and independent variables must be carefully controlled. If this is done, analysis of the relationships between variables indicated in recorded communications can contribute to the knowledge base of social work as much as other experimental studies can.

Making Structured Observations

Content analyses can also be used with other data collection methods. A content analysis of observational data can specify clearly what is being observed and what measurements are to be used. Typically, the frequency, duration, intensity, and effects of various verbal and nonverbal behaviors are coded in the analysis.

Robert F. Bales (1950) conducted numerous research studies on small-group behavior by developing a coding scheme for group behaviors. He divided small-group interactions into three classes:

1. Positive interactions in the social-emotional area
2. Negative interactions in the social-emotional area
3. Neutral interactions in the task area

Under each category the observational unit could represent various behaviors such as agrees, disagrees, gives suggestions, and asks for opinions. Observers also gathered qualitative data by taking notes on events not covered by the three categories. Much of what is known about small-group behavior is a result of these types of research studies.

By coding various units of verbal and nonverbal behavior observed in marital interactions, John Gottman (1979) developed an elaborate Couples Interaction Scoring System. The system involved transcribing videotaped interactions and breaking them down into thought units for analysis. Each thought unit received a verbal content code and a nonverbal content code. The verbal content code included categories such as agreement, disagreement, mind reading, summarizing self, and feelings about a problem.

In the nonverbal content code were such categories as positive, neutral, or negative ratings, based on nonverbal cues from face, voice, and body movements. It took approximately 28 hours to transcribe and code each hour of videotape—a time-consuming process. But the process made it possible to examine the effects of different interactions; for example, one partner who is mind reading is most likely to cause the other partner to disagree.

Developments in Procedures

A large part of a content analysis involves the tedious process of coding the data. Computers are proving invaluable in counting and synthesizing masses of data, not only from communications such as books and records in which the units of analysis can be easily defined in quantitative terms, but from communications such as speeches and interviews with extensive qualitative content. As we have seen in Chapters 6 and 7 , a less formal form of analysis that deals with qualitative data sources is ethnographic content analysis, another development that some researchers have found useful.

Computerized Content Analysis

Computer programs are increasingly being used in content analysis (Weber, 1984; Weitzman & Miles, 1995). Analyzing a large body of text very quickly is facilitated by computerized text coding, which requires unambiguous coding rules and classifications. Computerized content analyses are limited to the study of manifest content and typically are used for data reduction and analyses in which words or phrases are the units of analysis.

Two widely used computer software programs in content analyses are the *General Inquirer* and *Textpack*. These programs code the text according to word groupings, using electronic dictionaries in which specific words have been tagged. The computer is programmed to identify these tag words and put them in previously defined categories. The computerized analysis produces data such as a list of tag words, the frequency of tag words, the proportion of sentences in the text containing certain tag words, and so forth.

There are limitations to the use of electronic data processing in content analysis. Complex or abstract notions cannot be reduced to word groupings, and the communication as a whole may have to be considered. The meaning of a communication comes from sentences, phrases, and paragraphs—not single words. Therefore, computers cannot be used for content analysis when there is an interest in the abstract or thematic meaning of a communication (Weitzman & Miles, 1995). To understand such latent content, interpretive judgments about the meaning of the content must be made before assigning a unit of analysis to a category.

Ethnographic Content Analyses

As we know from Chapters 6 and 7, ethnographic content analysis, a form developed in the qualitative research approach, is used to document the communication of meaning as well as to verify theoretical relationships. Its distinctive characteristic is the highly reflexive and interactive nature of the relationships between the researcher and the study's concepts, data collection, and analysis.

In an ethnographic content analysis, the researcher is a central figure in evaluating the meaning of the content. It is less rigid in its research approach, compared to traditional content analyses. Categories and variables guide the study; however, as is the practice in the qualitative research approach, ethnographic content analysis allows for the emergence of new categories and variables during the study.

ADVANTAGES AND DISADVANTAGES

Like all the data collection and utilization methods considered in Part V of this text, a content analysis has its advantages and disadvantages. Perhaps the greatest advantage is its unobtrusive nature. Observations, interviews, self–report surveys, and other data collection methods used in social work research intrude into the research situation and may produce reactive effects that change or disturb the concepts under study in some way. Content analyses do not fall into this trap because what is being studied has already taken place. The measuring instrument is applied to an undisturbed system, allowing content analyses to uncover data without influencing the data collection process.

If we want to find out which candy is most popular at the state fair, for example, we could approach customers and ask, "What is your favorite candy?" We could stand by the candy counter and record the purchases. In either case, our presence may affect the outcome, and it may be difficult to approach each customer or to observe clearly what candy is being purchased in a crowd. So we could go to the trash cans, collect the wrappers, divide them into piles and draw conclusions from the findings. Or we could get the records of suppliers and determine how many boxes of each kind of candy were ordered and how many were unsold or returned at the end of the fair. These unobtrusive options are examples of content analyses.

These unobtrusive options also would be the least expensive and time-consuming, because observers and interviewers would not have to be trained and paid to be present for a specified period. For many research studies, a content analysis may be the most economical and time-efficient data collection method.

Another advantage is that a content analysis can be used in a historical research study to answer questions about the past that cannot be examined with other research methods (Woodrum, 1984). Communications from any time period can be used, as long as historical documents are available for study. A content analysis therefore allows for the examination of trends in both recent times and the distant past. An example was our study described earlier in this chapter that used the diaries of adolescent females written in 1873 and 1910 to examine how relationships with parents had changed between these periods. Thus, we can use content analyses to bridge the gap in time that separates us from our research participants or respondents.

Content analysis is not without disadvantages, however. By definition, the method is confined to the exploration and examination of previously recorded data. If the data are not part of a permanent record, they cannot be content-analyzed.

A distinct disadvantage is the questionable validity of the data provided by some content analyses. Whether what is being measured is really a valid measure of the unit of analysis must be determined, particularly when inferences about populations are to be made. Accurate operational definitions of the units and their categories are essential to ensure validity. The effects of reducing data to categories, as a result of which the true meaning of the data may be lost, must also be taken into account.

The quantification of the data that characterize content analyses can be both an advantage and a disadvantage. It allows for a systematic and objective approach to social work research studies, but the cost may be in terms of limits to the depth of understanding that the analysis can provide. Over time, social work researchers have increasingly become interested in studying the latent content of data in order to get at the underlying meaning.

SUMMARY

A content analysis is a versatile data collection method in which communications are examined in a systematic, objective, and quantitative manner. It can be applied to different types of content, including personal documents such as diaries and suicide notes; mass communications such as magazine covers and television programs; and interviews such as counseling sessions. It is often used to discover themes present in a communication—for example, themes that represent the inner aspects of an individual's life, the values of a society, or the effects of a communication.

The process of conducting a content analysis is straightforward, consisting of four steps. From a problem area, we formulate a research question, which leads to a consideration of how to sample the content of interest. The unit of analysis is operationally defined and categories are developed for the coding of the data. Findings and conclusions are then drawn from the data gathered.

Content analysis is an unobtrusive data collection method. As long as we develop reliable coding procedures and valid categories for the classification of the data, through content analyses we will be able to build new knowledge for social work practice.

Yvonne A. Unrau

C h a p t e r   19

Selecting a Data Collection Method and Data Source

DATA COLLECTION IS THE HEARTBEAT of a research project. The goal is to have a steady flow of data collected systematically and with the least amount of bias. When the flow of data becomes erratic or stops prematurely, a research study is in grave danger. When data collection goes well it is characterized by an even pulse and is rather uneventful. This chapter examines the data collection process from the vantage point of choosing the most appropriate data collection method and data source for any given research study.

DATA COLLECTION METHODS AND DATA SOURCES

There is a critical distinction between a data collection method and a data source that must be clearly understood before developing a viable data collection plan. A data collection method consists of a detailed plan of procedures that aims to gather data for a specific purpose—that is, to answer a research question or to test a hypothesis. As we know, the previous seven chapters in this book presented seven different data collection methods. Each one can be used with a variety of data sources, which are defined by who (or what) supplies the data. Data can be provided by a multitude of sources such as people, existing records, and existing databases.

When data are collected directly from people, data may be first- or secondhand. Firsthand data are obtained from people who are closest to the problem we are studying. Male inmates participating in an anger management group, for example, can provide firsthand data about their satisfaction with the program's treatment approach. Secondhand data may come from other people who are indirectly connected to our primary problem area. The anger management group facilitator or the prison social work director, for example, may be asked for a personal opinion about how satisfied inmates are with treatment. In other instances, secondhand data can be gained from existing reports written about inmates or inmate records that monitor their behavior or other important events.

DATA COLLECTION AND THE RESEARCH PROCESS

Data collection is a critical step in the research process because it is the link between theory and practice. Our research study always begins with an idea that is molded by a conceptual framework, which uses preexisting knowledge about our study's problem area. Once our research problem and question have been refined to a researchable level, data are sought from a selected source and gathered using a systematic collection method. The data collected are then used to support or supplant our original study's conceptions about our research problem under investigation. The role of data collection in connecting theory and practice is understood when looking at the entire research process.

As we have seen in Chapter 6, choosing a data collection method and data source follows the selection of a problem area, selecting a research question, and developing a sampling plan. It comes before the data analysis phase and writing the research report phase. Although data collection is presented in this text as a distinct phase of the research process, it cannot be tackled separately or in isolation. All phases of the research process must be considered if we hope to come up with the best strategy to gather the most relevant, reliable, and valid data to answer a research question or to test a hypothesis. This section discusses the role of data collection in relation to four steps of the research process: (1) selecting a problem area and research question, (2) formulating a research design, (3) analyzing data, and (4) writing the report.

Selecting a Problem Area and Research Question

The specific research question identifies the general problem area and the population to be studied. It tells us what we want to collect data about and alerts us to potential data sources. It does not necessarily specify the exact manner in which our data will be gathered, however. Suppose, for example, a school social worker proposes the following research question: How effective is our Students Against Violence Program (SAVP) within the Forest Lawn High School? One of the many objectives of our program is "To increase student's feelings of safety at school." This simple evaluative research question identifies our problem area of interest (school violence) and our population of focus (students). It does not state how the question will be answered.

Despite the apparent clarity of our research question, it could in fact be answered in numerous ways. One factor that affects how this question is answered depends upon how its variables are conceptualized and operationalized. Students' feelings of safety, for example, could be measured in a variety of ways. Another factor that affects how a research question is answered (or a hypothesis is tested) is the source of data; that is, who or what is providing them. If we want to get firsthand data about the student's school safety, for example, we could target the students as a potential data source.

If such firsthand data sources were not a viable option, secondhand data sources could be sought. Students' parents, for example, can be asked to speculate on whether their children feel safe at school. In other instances, secondhand data can be gained from existing reports written about students (or student records) that monitor any critical danger or safety incidents.

By listing all possible data collection methods and data sources that could provide sound data to answer a research question, we develop a fuller understanding of our initial research problem. It also encourages us to think about our research problem from different perspectives, via the data sources. Because social work problems are complex, data collection is strengthened when two or more data sources are used. If the students, teachers, and parents rate students' feelings of safety as similar, then we can be more confident that the data (from all these sources) accurately reflect the problem being investigated. Reliability of data can be assessed, or estimated, when collected from multiple sources.

The exercise of generating a list of possible data collection methods and sources can be overwhelming. With reasonably little effort, however, we can develop a long list of possibilities. We may also end up seeing the problem in a different light than what we had thought of previously. By considering parents as a source of secondhand data, for example, we open up a new dimension of the problem being studied. All of a sudden, family support factors may seem critical to how safe students feel at school.

We may then want to collect data about the family. This possibility should be considered within the context of our study's conceptual framework. Once we have exhausted all the different ways to collect data for any given study, we need to revisit our original research question. In doing so, we can refocus it by remembering the original purpose of the study.

Formulating a Research Design

As we know, the research design flows from the research question, which flows from the problem area. A research design organizes our research question into a framework that sets the parameters and conditions of the study. As mentioned, the research question directs *what* data are collected and *who* data could be collected from. The research design refines the *what* question by operationalizing variables and the *who* question by developing a sampling strategy. In addition, the research design also dictates *when, where,* and *how* data will be collected.

The research design states how many data collection points our study will have and specifies the data sources. Each discrete data gathering activity constitutes a data collection point and defines *when* data are to be collected. Thus, using an exploratory one-group, posttest-only design, we will collect data only once from a single group of research participants. On the other hand, if a classical experimental design is used, data will be collected at two separate times with two different groups of research participants—for a total of four discrete data collection points.

The number of times a research participant must be available for data collection is an important consideration when choosing a data collection method. The gathering of useful, valid, and reliable data is enhanced when the data collection activities do not occur too frequently, and are straightforward and brief. Consider the high school students targeted by our SAVP. Already, many of the students live with the fears of avoiding confrontations with hostile peers and *if* they should tell someone about being threatened or harmed. Asking students about their feelings of safety too often may inadvertently make them feel less safe, or alternatively they may tire of the whole process of inquiry and refuse to participate in our study.

Where the data are collected is also important to consider. If our research question is too narrow and begs for a broader issue that encompasses individuals living in various geographic locations, then mailed surveys would be more feasible than interviews. If our research question focuses on a specific population where all research participants live in the same geographic location, however, it may be possible to use direct observations or individual or group interviews.

Because most social work studies are applied, the setting of our study usually involves clients in their natural environments where there is little control over extraneous variables. If we want to measure the students' feelings toward school safety, for example, do we observe students as they walk the school halls, observe how they interact with their peer groups, or have them complete a survey form of some kind? In short, we must always consider which method of data collection will lead to the most valid and reliable data to answer a specific research question or to test a specific hypothesis.

The combination of potential data collection methods and potential data sources is another important consideration. A research study can have one data collection source and still use multiple data collection methods. High school students (one data source) in our study, for example, can fill out a standardized questionnaire that measures their feelings of safety (first data collection method) in addition to participating in face-to-face interviews (second data collection method).

In the same vein, another study can have multiple data sources and one data collection method. In this case, we can collect data about how safe a student feels through observation recordings by the students' parents, teachers, or social workers. The combination of data collection methods should not be too taxing on any research participant or any system, such as the school itself. That is, data collection should try not to interfere with the day-to-day activities of the persons providing (or responsible for collecting) the data.

In some studies, there is no research design *per se*. Instead we can use existing data to answer the research question. Such is the case when a secondary analysis is used. Content analysis may also be used on existing data, as when we gather data from existing client records. When the data already exist, we must then organize them using the best-case scenario, given the data at hand and the details of how they were originally gathered and recorded. In these situations, we give more consideration to the analysis of data.

Analyzing Data

Collecting data is a resource intensive endeavor that can be expensive and time consuming. The truth of this statement is realized in the data analysis phase of our research study. Without a great deal of forethought about what data to collect, data can be thrown out because they cannot be organized or analyzed in any meaningful way. In short, data analyses should always be considered when choosing a data collection method and data source because the analysis phase must summarize, synthesize, and ultimately organize the data in an effort to have as clear-cut an answer as possible to our research question. When too much (or too little) data have been collected, we can easily become bogged down or stalled by difficult decisions that could have been avoided with a little forethought.

After we have thought through our research problem and research question and have arrived at a few possible data collection methods and data sources, it is worthwhile to list out the details of how the dependent and independent variables will be measured by each data collection method and each data source. We must think about how they will be used in our data analysis. This exercise provides a clearer idea of the type of results we can expect.

One of the dependent variables in our example is the students' feelings of safety. Suppose the school social worker decides to collect data about this variable by giving students (data source) a brief standardized questionnaire (data collection method) about their feelings of safety. Many standardized questionnaires contain several subscales that, when combined, give a quantitative measure of a larger concept. A questionnaire measuring the concept of feelings of safety, for example, might include three subscales: problem awareness, assertiveness, and self-confidence. We need to decide if each subscale will be defined as three separate subvariables, or if only the total combined scale score will be used.

Alternatively, if data about feelings of safety were to be collected using two different data sources such as parent (Source 1) and teacher (Source 2) observations, we must think about how the two data types "fit" together. That is, will data from the two sources be treated as two separate variables? If so, will one variable be weighted more heavily in our analysis than the other? Thinking about how the data will be summarized helps us to expose any frivolous data—that is, data that are not suitable to answer our research question.

It is also important to be clear on how our independent variable(s) will be measured and what data collection method would be most appropriate. In our example, we want to know whether our SAVP is effective for helping students feel more safe in the school environment. Because a social service program is being evaluated, it is essential to know what specific intervention approach(es), procedures, and techniques are used within the program. What specific intervention activities are used? Is student participation in our SAVP voluntary? How often do our SAVP's intervention activities occur in the school? Anticipating the type of data analysis that will be used helps to determine which data collection method and data source provide the most meaningful and accurate data to gather.

Besides collecting data about the independent and dependent variables, we must also develop a strategy to collect demographic data about the people who participated in our study. Typical demographic variables include: age, gender, education level, and family income. These data are not necessarily used in the analysis of the research question. Rather, they provide a descriptive context for our study. Some data collection methods, such as standardized questionnaires, include these types of data. Often, however, we are responsible for obtaining them as part of the data collection process.

Writing the Report

It is useful to think about our final research report when choosing a data collection method and data source as it forces us to visualize how our study's findings will ultimately be presented. It identifies both who the audience of the study will be and the people interested in our findings. Knowing who will read our research report and how it will be disseminated helps us to take more of an objective stance toward our study.

In short, we can take a third-person look at what our study will finally look like. Such objectivity helps us to think about our data collection method and data source with a critical eye. Will consumers of our research study agree that the students in fact were the best data collection source? Were the data collection method and analysis sound? These are some of the practical questions that bring scrutiny to the data collection process.

CRITERIA FOR SELECTING A DATA COLLECTION METHOD

Thinking through the research process, from the vantage point of collecting data, permits us to refine the conceptualization of our study and the place of data collection within it. It also sets the context within which our data will be gathered. At this point, we should have a sense of what the ideal data collection method and data source would be. Clearly, there are many viable data collection methods and data sources that can be used to answer any research question. Nevertheless, there are many practical criteria that ultimately refine the final data collection method (and sources) to fit the conditions of any given research study. These criteria are: (1) size, (2) scope, (3) program participation, (4) worker cooperation, (5) intrusion into the lives of research participants, (6) resources, (7) time, and (8) previous research findings. They all interact with one another, but for the sake of clarity each one is presented separately.

Size

The size of our study reflects just how many people, places, or systems are represented in it. As with any planning activity, the more people involved, the more complicated the process and the more difficult it is to arrive at a mutual agreement. Decisions about which data collection method and which data source to use can be stalled when several people, levels, or systems are consulted. This is simply because individuals have different interests and opinions. Administrators, for example, may address issues such as accountability more than do line-level social workers.

Imagine if the effectiveness of our SAVP were examined on a larger scale such that all high schools in the city were included. Our study's complexity is dramatically increased because of such factors as the increased number of students, parents, school principals, teachers, and social workers involved. Individual biases will make it much more difficult to agree upon the best data collection method and data source for our study.

Our study's sample size is also a consideration. The goal of any research study is to have a meaningful sample of the population of interest. With respect to sample size, this means that we should strive for a reasonable representation of the sampling frame. When small-scale studies are conducted, such as a program evaluation in one school, the total sampling frame may be in the hundreds or fewer. Thus, dealing with the random selection of clients poses no particular problem.

On the other hand, when large-scale studies are conducted, such as when the federal government chooses to examine a social service program that involves hundreds of thousands of people, dealing with a percentage is more problematic. If our sample is in the hundreds, it is unlikely that we would be able to successfully observe all participants in a particular setting. Rather, a more efficient data collection method—say a survey—may be more appropriate.

Scope

The scope of our research study is another matter to consider. Scope refers to how much of our problem area will be covered. If in our SAVP, for example, we are interested in gathering data about students' academic standings, family supports, and peer relations, then three different aspects of our problem area will be covered. In short, we need to consider whether one method of data collection and one data source can be used to collect all the data. It could be that school records, for example, are used to collect data about students' academic achievements, interviews with students are conducted to collect data about students' family supports, and observation methods are used to gather data about students' peer relationships.

Program Participation

Many social work research efforts are conducted in actual real-life program settings. Thus, it is essential that we gain the support of program personnel to conduct our study. Program factors that can impact the choice of our data collection methods and data sources include variables such as the program's clarity in its mandate to serve clients, its philosophical stance toward clients, and its flexibility in client record keeping.

First, if a program is not able to clearly articulate a client service delivery plan, it will be difficult to separate out clinical activity from research activity, or to determine when the two overlap.

Second, agencies tend to base themselves on strong beliefs about a client population, which affect who can have access to their clients and in what manner. A child sexual abuse investigation program, for example, may be designed specifically to avoid the problem of using multiple interviewers and multiple interviews of children in the investigation of an allegation of sexual abuse. As a result, the program would be hesitant for us to conduct interviews with the children to gather data for "research purposes."

Third, to save time and energy there is often considerable overlap between program client records and research data collection. The degree of willingness of a program to change or adapt to new record-keeping techniques will affect how we might go about collecting certain types of data.

Worker Cooperation

On a general level, programs have few resources and an overabundance of clients. Such conditions naturally lead their administrators and social workers to place clinical activity as a top priority. When our research study requires social workers to collect data as a part of their day-to-day client service delivery, it is highly likely that they will view it as additional work. In short, they may not be likely to view these new data collection activities as a means to expedite their work, at least not in the short term.

Getting cooperation of social workers within a program is a priority in any research study that relies directly or indirectly on their meaningful participation. They will be affected by our study whether they are involved in the data collection process or not. Workers may be asked to schedule additional interviews with families or adjust their intervention plans to ensure that data collection occurs at the optimal time. Given the fiscal constraints faced by programs, the workers themselves often participate as data collectors. They may end up using new client recording forms or administer questionnaires. Whatever the level of their participation, it is important for us to strive to achieve a maximum level of their cooperation.

There are three factors to consider when trying to achieve maximum cooperation from workers. First, we should make every effort to work effectively and efficiently with the program's staff. Cooperation is more likely to be achieved when they participate in the development of our study plan from the beginning. Thus, it is worthwhile to take time to explain the purpose of our study and its intended outcomes at an early stage in the study. Furthermore, administrators and front-line workers can provide valuable information about what data collection method(s) may work best.

Second, we must be sensitive to the workloads of the program's staff. Data collection methods and sources should be designed to enhance the work of professionals. Client recording forms, for example, can be designed to provide focus for supervision meetings, as well as summarize facts and worker impressions about a case.

Third, a mechanism should be set up by which workers receive feedback based on the data they have collected. When data are reported back to the program's staff before the completion of our study, we must ensure that the data will not bias later measurements (if any).

Intrusion Into the Lives of Research Participants

When clients are used as a data source, client self-determination takes precedence over research activity. As we know, clients have every right to refuse participation in a research study and cannot be denied services because they are unwilling to participate. It is unethical, for example, when a member of a group-based treatment intervention has not consented to participate in the study, but participant observation (Chapter 14) is used as the data collection method. This is unethical because the group member ends up being observed as part of the group dynamic in the data collection process. The data collection method(s) we finally select must be flexible enough to allow our study to continue, even with the possibility that some clients will not participate.

Cultural consideration must also be given to the type of data collection method used. One-to-one interviewing with Cambodian refugees, for example, may be extremely terrifying for them, given the interrogation they may have experienced in their own country. If direct observational strategies are used in studies in which we are from a different cultural background than our research participants, it is important to ensure that interpretation of their behaviors, events, or expressions is accurate from their perspectives.

We must also recognize the cultural biases of standardized measuring instruments, since most are based on testing with Caucasian groups. The problems here are twofold. First, we cannot be sure if the concept that the instrument is measuring is expressed the same way in different cultures. For instance, a standardized self-report instrument that measures family functioning may include an item such as, "We have flexible rules in our household that account for individual differences," which would likely be viewed positively by North American cultures, but negatively by many Asian cultures. Second, because standardized measuring instruments are written in English, research participants must have a good grasp of English to ensure that the data collected from them are valid and reliable.

Another consideration comes into play when particular populations have been the subject of a considerable amount of research studies already. Many aboriginal people living on reserves, for example, have been subjected to government surveys, task force inquiries, independent research projects, and perhaps even to the curiosities of social work students learning in a practicum setting. When a population has been extensively researched, it is even more important that we consider how the data collection method will affect those people participating in the study. Has the data collection method been used previously? If so, what was the nature of the data collected? Could the data be collected in other ways, using less intrusive measures?

Resources

There are various costs associated with collecting data in any given research study. Materials and supplies, equipment rental, transportation costs, and training for data collectors are just a few things to consider when choosing a data collection method. In addition, once the data are collected, additional expenses can arise when they need to be entered into a computer or transcribed.

An effective and efficient data collection method is one that collects the most valid and reliable data to answer a research question or test a hypothesis while requiring the least amount of time and money. In our example, to ask students about their feelings of safety via an open-ended interview may offer rich data, but we take the risk that students will not fully answer our questions in the time allotted for the interview. On the other hand, having them complete a self-report questionnaire on feelings of safety is a quicker and less costly way to collect data, but it gives little sense about how well the students understood the questions being asked of them or whether the data obtained reflect their true feelings.

Time

Time is a consideration when our study has a fixed completion date. Time constraints may be self- or externally imposed. Self-imposed time constraints are personal matters we need to consider. Is our research project a part of a thesis or dissertation? What are our personal time commitments?

Externally imposed time restrictions are set by someone other than the one doing the study. For instance, our SAVP study is limited by the school year. Other external pressures may be political, such as an administrator who wants research results for a funding proposal or annual report.

Previous Research

Having reviewed the professional literature on our problem, we need to be well aware of other data collection methods that have been used in similar studies. We can evaluate earlier studies for the strengths and weaknesses of their data collection methods and thereby make a more informed decision as to the best data collection strategy to use in our specific situation. Further, we need to look for diversity when evaluating other data collection approaches. That is, we can triangulate results from separate studies that used different data collection methods and data sources to answer a research question or test a hypothesis.

SELECTION OF A DATA COLLECTION METHOD

As should be evident by now, choosing a data collection method and data source for a research study is not a simple task. There are numerous conceptual and practical factors that must be thought through if we hope to arrive at the best possible approach to gathering data. How do we appraise all the factors to be considered in picking the best one? The previous seven chapters in this book present seven different non–mutually exclusive data collection methods. Theoretically, all of them could be used to evaluate the effectiveness of our SAVP. Each one would offer a different perspective to our research question and would consider different data sources.

Table 19.1 is an example of a grid that can be used to assist us in making an informed decision about which data collection method is best. The grid includes both general and specific considerations for our study question. The first section of the grid highlights the eight criteria for selecting a data collection method discussed earlier. The bottom section of the grid identifies five additional considerations that are specific to our SAVP.

The grid can be used as a decision-making tool by subjectively rating how well each data collection method measures up to the criteria listed in the left-hand column of Table 19.1. We mark a " + " if the data collection method has a favorable rating and a "–" if it has an unfavorable one. When a particular criterion is neutral, in which case it has no positive or negative effect, then a zero is indicated.

Once each data collection method has been assessed on all eight criteria, we can simply add the number of + 's and –'s to arrive at a plus or minus total for each method. This information can be used to help us make an informed decision about the best data collection method, given all the issues raised. Based on Table 19.1, the survey research method of data collection is most appealing for our study if a single method of data collection is used.

TRYING OUT THE SELECTED DATA COLLECTION METHOD

Data collection is a particularly vulnerable time for a research study because it is the point where "talk" turns to "action." So far, all the considerations that have been weighed in the selection of a data collection method have been in theory. All people involved in our research endeavor have cast their suggestions and doubts on the entire process. Once general agreement has been reached about which data collection method and data source to use, it is time to test the waters.

Trying out a data collection method can occur informally by simply testing it out with available willing research participants or, at the very least, with anyone who has not been involved with the planning of the study. The purpose

Table 19.1   Decision-Making Grid for
Choosing a Data Collection Method

	Data Collection Methods				
	Survey Research (Chapter 15)	Participant Observation (Chapter 14)	Secondary Analysis (Chapter 16)	Content Analysis (Chapter 18)	Existing Statistics (Chapter 17)
General Criteria:					
1. Size	+	0	+	+	+
2. Scope	+	–	–	–	–
3. Program participation	+	0	+	+	+
4. Worker cooperation	+	+	–	+	+
5. Intrusion to clients	–	–	–	+	+
6. Resources	+	–	+	+	+
7. Time	+	–	+	+	+
8. Previous research	+	0	–	–	–
Specific Criteria:					
1. Student availability	+	+	0	0	0
2. Student reading level	+	0	0	0	0
3. School preference	+	–	–	–	–
4. School year end	–	–	+	+	+
5. Access to existing records	0	0	0	+	+
Totals...	–6	8	–6	5	5

of this trial run is to ensure that those who are going to provide data understand the questions and procedures in the way that they were intended. Data collection methods might also be tested more formally, such as when a pilot study is conducted.

A pilot study involves carrying out all aspects of the data collection plan on a miniscale. That is, a small portion of our study's actual sample is selected and run through all steps of the data collection process. In a pilot study, we are interested in the process of the data collection as well as the content. In short, we what to know whether our chosen data collection method produces the expected data. Are there any unanticipated barriers to gathering the desired data? How do research participants (data source) respond to our data collection procedures? Is there enough variability in research participants' responses?

IMPLEMENTATION AND EVALUATION

The data collection phase of a research study can go smoothly if we act proactively. That is, we should guide and monitor the entire data collection process according to the procedures and steps that were set out in the planning stage of our study and were tested in the pilot study.

Implementation

The main guiding principle to implementing the selected data collection method is that a systematic approach to data collection must be used. This means that the steps to gathering data should be methodically detailed so that there is no question about the tasks of the person(s) collecting the data—the data collector(s). This is true whether using a quantitative or qualitative research approach. As we know from Chapters 6 and 7, the difference between these two research approaches is that the structure of the data collection process within a qualitative research study is often documented as the study progresses. On the other hand, in a quantitative research study, the data collection process is decided at the study's outset and provides much less flexibility after the study is under way.

It must be very clear from the beginning who is responsible for collecting the data. When we take on the task, there is reasonable assurance that the data collection will remain objective and be guided by our research interests. Data collection left to only one person may be a formidable task. We must determine the amount of resources available to decide what data collection method is most realistic. Regardless of the study size, we must attempt to establish clear roles with those involved in the data collection process.

The clearer our research study is articulated, the less difficulty there will be in moving through all the phases of the study. In particular, it is critical to identify who will and will not be involved in the data collection process. To further avoid mix-up and complications, specific tasks must be spelled out for all persons involved in our study. Where will the data collection forms be stored? Who will administer them? How will their completion be monitored?

In many social work research studies, front-line social workers are involved in data collection activities as part of their day-to-day activities. They typically gather intake and referral data, write assessment notes, and even use standardized questionnaires as part of their assessments. Data collection in programs can easily be designed to serve the dual purposes of research *and* clinical inquiry. Thus, it is important to establish data collection protocols to avoid problems of biased data. As mentioned, everyone in a research study must agree *when* data will be collected, *where*, and in *what* manner. Agreement is more likely to occur when we have fully informed and involved everyone participating in our study.

Evaluation

The process of selecting a chosen data collection method is not complete without evaluating it. Evaluation occurs at two levels. First, the strengths and weakness of a data collection method and data source are evaluated, given the research context in which our study takes place. If, for example, data are gathered about clients' presenting problems by a referring social worker, it must be acknowledged that the obtained data offer a limited (or restricted) point of view about the clients' problems. The strength of this approach may be that it was the only means for collecting the data. Such strengths and weakness are summarized in the decision-making grid presented in Table 19.1.

A second level of evaluation is monitoring the implementation of the data collection process itself. When data are gathered using several methods (or from several sources), it is beneficial to develop a checklist of what data have been collected for each research participant. Developing a strategy for monitoring the data collection process is especially important when the data must be collected in a timely fashion. If pretest data are needed before a client enters a treatment program, for example, the data collection must be complete before admission occurs. Once the client has entered the program, opportunity to collect pretest data is lost forever.

Another strategy for monitoring evaluation is to keep a journal of the data collection process. The journal records any questions or queries that arise in the data gathering phase. We may find, for example, that several research participants completing a questionnaire have difficulty understanding one particular question. In addition, sometimes research participants have poor reading skills and require assistance with completion of some self-report standardized questionnaires. Documenting these idiosyncratic incidents accumulates important information by which to comment on our data's validity and reliability.

SUMMARY

There are many possible data collection methods and data sources that can be used in any given research situation. We must weigh the pros and cons of both within the context of a particular research study to arrive at the best data collection method and data source. This process involves both conceptual and practical considerations. On a conceptual level, we review the phases of the research process through a "data collection and data source lens." We think about how various data collection methods and data sources fit with each phase of the research process. At the same time, considering the different data collection methods and data sources helps us to gain a fuller understanding of our problem area and research question.

There are many considerations that need to be addressed when deciding upon the best data collection method(s) and data source(s) for a particular study. Factors such as worker cooperation, available resources, and consequences for the clients all influence our final choices. We can map out such decision-making criteria by using a grid system, by which all criteria to be considered are listed and evaluated for each potential data collection method and data source.

Part VI

Writing and Evaluating Proposals and Reports

C h a p t e r 20

Writing Research Proposals

BEFORE WE CAN UNDERTAKE a research study, we must first obtain both permission to conduct the study and the funds with which to conduct it. We therefore submit a request to a grant-awarding agency or to an academic committee in the form of a research proposal. The research proposal will contain information about *what* we propose to study, *why* we propose to study it, *how* we propose to study it, and *how much* the study will cost.

CHARACTERISTICS OF RESEARCH PROPOSALS

Before we begin to write the proposal, we must ask ourselves three questions: What is the purpose of writing this proposal? What format, or layout, would best serve our purpose? And, what writing style should we adopt?

Purpose

The primary purpose of writing a research proposal is to obtain the permission and the funds necessary to conduct our study. We want to show the reviewers who read our proposal that our study is grounded in theory, methodologically sound, and practically organized, and that it will make an essential contribution to the knowledge base of our profession. However, we also want to demonstrate that we, the authors of the study, are competent to conduct it. Our competence is reflected not only in what we include and what we choose to leave out, but in the way we commit our thoughts to paper—in our format and writing style.

The writing of a research proposal serves another purpose too. When we are forced to write down precisely what research question we wish to investigate or what specific hypothesis we wish to verify, we clarify the topic in our own minds. When we have to justify our choice of topic with respect to its theoretical basis and the potential relevance of its findings, we know more clearly why we wish to conduct this particular study. When we have to spell out what data we will collect, how we will collect them, and how we will analyze them, once they are collected, we may see difficulties that were not apparent in the first rush of enthusiasm. When we have to list the study's limitations, we understand more clearly what they are. When we have to itemize the cost of the study in terms of the necessary resources and personnel, we have a better idea of what is practically possible and what is not.

We write a research proposal, therefore, not only for the benefit of the reviewers but for ourselves. We need a plan to conduct a research study in the same way that a builder needs a plan to build a house.

Format

The way we organize a research proposal—what information we put under what headings—will vary according to the information we have to include. Sometimes, both the information and the format are decided for us by the organization for whom the proposal is prepared. In some simple cases, it is necessary only to fill out an application form. At other times, a "letter of intent" may be all that is required. Such a letter summarizes the major points that would be addressed in a full-length proposal. However, favorable reception by a funding source to a letter of intent does not mean that the potential study will be approved. Typically, the next step is a request by the funding organization for a full-length proposal.

The format of a proposal and the information contained in it vary according to whether the proposal is submitted to an academic committee or a funding organization. A proposal for an academic committee typically is more detailed and scholarly than one submitted to a funding organization. Similarly, different types of funding organizations have varying requirements. In some cases, funding organizations provide quite detailed instructions about the format and length of proposals they wish to receive. In other instances, *Requests for Proposals,* commonly termed *RFPs*, are sent to outside reviewers. RFPs usually supply instructions prepared by funding organizations; they specify research topics that will be funded along with the proposal's format requirements. Most commonly, however, funders usually allow a great deal of latitude, leaving the form of research proposals to the discretion of their authors.

Style

Despite their differences, research proposals have many similarities. One similarity is their style. There are basically three stylistic characteristics common to all research proposals. Proposals should be: (1) clearly worded, (2) written in a nonliterary style, and (3) clearly organized.

Clearly Worded

The wording of a research proposal should be simple, matter-of-fact, and unadorned. The content of a research proposal should also be matter-of-fact and unadorned, even if it is not necessarily simple. Research proposals that contain unrelated or nonessential information usually give the impression that the author will not be able to execute the research study logically and objectively. We should not explain in detail, for example, why we became interested in the topic we propose to study. Proposal review committees are never interested in autobiographical excursions by prospective authors. Rather, a well-written proposal is a straightforward document containing only the information that is absolutely necessary—not one detail more.

Nonliterary in Style

A research proposal is not the same thing as a gothic drama. We do not wish to convey to the reviewers a graphic vision of heavy breathing among the tombstones; we wish to convey instead a flavor of conservative and earnest competence. While we are being conservative and competent, we also wish to convey information about our study. The best way to do this is to avoid flowery flourishes and stylistic circumlocutions—get the message? All words, sentences, and paragraphs should be clear, precise, and brief.

Clearly Organized

Proposal reviewers usually have a difficult and time-consuming task. They are often faced with numerous proposals to evaluate at a given time. A majority of proposals submitted to funding agencies must be turned down due to the scarcity of funds. However, despite the number of proposals to be reviewed and the differences in their quality, most proposal reviewers read each proposal very carefully. The more clearly organized a proposal is, the easier it is to read. And the easier it is to read, the better the chance that the reviewers will react to it favorably.

Several factors facilitate clear organization. As noted above, a clear, unadorned prose style is absolutely essential. Short and simple paragraphs are required. Such paragraphs help proposal reviewers quickly assess whether the authors know what they are talking about. In contrast, rambling paragraphs can so obscure main points that they become difficult or even impossible to follow. Major and minor headings also enhance a proposal's organization. They highlight important points and allow proposal reviewers who may be more interested in one substantive (or methodological) issue than another to thumb back and forth through the proposal with ease.

The parts of the proposal should progress in an orderly sequence so that one part follows logically from the part before it and leads logically into the part after it. We can envisage a proposal as a linked chain in which each link supports and interacts with every other link, yet has a definite place in the whole.

COMPONENTS OF PROPOSALS

Most funding agencies and academic committees leave the structure of research proposals to the discretion of their authors. However, reviewers need, and thus obviously look for, certain basic types of information in assessing proposals. This basic information is usually broken into eleven general components, or parts, that parallel the actual working steps of the proposed research study. Although there is no one specific format to follow in writing research proposals, the ordering of the components in the following discussion is typical. Other approaches, however, may be chosen if they are more suitable to particular research areas.

To illustrate the sequential development of most proposals, we will take as our research topic: the adjustment of former residents of psychiatric institutions in community settings. Using this example, we will discuss in turn each of the common eleven parts of a research proposal. The parts are: (1) specifying the research topic, (2) creating a literature review, (3) providing a conceptual framework, (4) delineating the general research question to be answered or the specific hypothesis to be tested, (5) constructing the operational definitions of the independent and dependent variables, (6) describing the specific research design, (7) delineating the population and sample, (8) describing the method(s) of data collection, (9) describing the method(s) of data analysis, (10) detailing the study's limitations, and (11) describing the study's administrative procedures.

Part 1: Research Topic

When we use the term *research topic,* we are referring to the overall area of investigation, as distinguished from the general research question or specific hypothesis to be investigated. The term *topic statement* refers to a succinct description of the research topic.

On occasion, research topics are so complex that introductory information must be provided before the area of investigation can be identified. If possible, however, we use a topic statement to set forth the research topic at the outset of the proposal. For example, if we were proposing a study of why some former residents of psychiatric institutions adjust more successfully than others in community settings, our proposal might state at the beginning:

> The concern of the proposed study is the successful adjustment in community settings by former residents of psychiatric institutions.

The next part of the proposal usually discusses the significance of the proposed study to our profession. Reviewers may be familiar with the proposed area of investigation and its relative importance; facts, nonetheless, are marshaled for reviewers who do not have this background.

When we write a social work research proposal, we must usually address three areas of the study's significance: social policy significance, theoretical significance, and practice significance (or implications for social work practice).

- When we describe the policy-making significance of the study, we must provide specific ways in which the findings would facilitate some aspect of the policy-making process. A vaguely worded statement such as "An increased knowledge of factors contributing to the successful adjustment in communities by former psychiatric patients is important to social work" would be insufficient.
- When we discuss the theoretical significance of the study, we must delineate how it would either test existing theory or generate new theory of potential use by our profession.
- The implications for social work practice must include a discussion of how knowledge obtained from the proposed study might enhance the effectiveness of individual social workers in their everyday practices.

Sometimes the theoretical significance and implications for practice are treated as separate components and placed either immediately following the discussion on the social policy significance or at the end of the proposal. This is acceptable practice and is commonly followed (see the following chapter).

Although all three elements are usually fully explicated in proposals submitted to academic committees, funding organizations attach varying degrees of importance to these elements. It is important, therefore, to assess both formally and informally a funding organization's priorities and to emphasize the appropriate elements accordingly before submitting proposals. In the first part of our proposal, then, we state in succinct terms *what* we propose to study and the potential significance of our findings.

Part 2: Literature Review

The purpose of a literature review is to provide a basis and a background for the study. An effective literature review achieves five objectives:

1. It demonstrates that the author of the proposal has mastered the available and relevant literature.
2. It demonstrates the similarities between the proposed study and past research findings of similar studies.
3. It demonstrates the differences between the proposed study and past research findings of similar studies.
4. It discusses how the proposed investigation will contribute to the knowledge base of the social work profession.
5. It supports and interacts with the conceptual framework by introducing and conceptually defining the key variables that are the subject of the study.

One of our primary considerations in developing a literature review is *how much* literature to summarize. In general, literature reviews prepared for academic committees are far more comprehensive than those prepared for funding organizations. In either case, the literature review must be brief enough not to become tedious but extensive enough to inform proposal reviewers about the study's topic. If we provide too much information, we may end up with a literature review that is burdensome to read; if we do not provide enough information, we will have an inadequate background on which to base the conceptual framework and subsequent components of the study.

A second consideration is *what* information to present. Although the literature review usually discusses how the proposal will mesh with and differ from past studies, there are frequently too many related studies to allow a discussion of all pertinent past findings. In general, when there is an extensive body of related studies, we should concentrate on the most recent findings. If there are "classic" studies related to the proposed investigation, it is advisable to present them as well.

Conversely, the body of directly relevant studies may sometimes be too limited to provide adequate information on the research topic. In this case, we should include findings that are indirectly pertinent. If, for example, there were a scarcity of existing studies concerning the adjustment of former residents of psychiatric institutions in community settings, we might present research findings related to the adjustment of mentally retarded persons in community settings. As presented in Chapters 6 and 7, qualitative studies are also useful in the absence of related quantitative ones. Qualitative literature demonstrates in a persuasive manner the importance and background of the proposed study and may present alternative ways of conceptualizing it.

All independent and dependent variables are discussed in the literature review; these variables must also be *conceptually* defined. At this stage we do not *operationally* define our variables; that is, we do not define them in a way that will enable us to measure them. We merely draw semantic clarifications from the relevant literature. For example, for one person, the variable community adjustment may suggest comfortable living arrangements, a job, and recreation in a community setting. For another person, the variable community adjustment may also include a supportive family.

As we saw from Chapter 5, we must avoid such ambiguity through clear conceptual definitions. For example, we should make it clear in our proposal that our conceptualization of community adjustment includes not only comfortable living arrangements, a job, and recreation, but also meaningful interaction with family. Key independent and dependent variables that are not conceptually defined in the literature review are defined in the conceptual framework.

Part 3: Conceptual Framework

The third part of the proposal provides a conceptual framework—a frame of reference that serves to guide the study. It is developed from theories, quantitative and qualitative studies, and the author's personal experiences and values. It helps formulate the study's research problem or hypothesis; it defines what are and are not relevant data; and it provides a basis for interpreting those data.

As presented in the previous chapters of this book, when we construct a conceptual framework we identify independent and dependent variables, conceptually define them, and predict relationships between them. This process overlaps with that of reviewing the literature. Returning to our example—a study of the adjustment in community settings by former residents of psychiatric institutions—we might include in the conceptual framework a review of studies related to the adjustment of former residents of institutions so that we can use these studies as a basis from which to discuss our variables.

We might also include in this section our own experiences and value assumptions as a further basis from which to discuss our variables. However, it is obviously quite legitimate to place the review of previous studies and/or our own experiences in the literature review section, and we do not want to repeat ourselves. We must decide in which section to place them on the basis of logical and stylistic considerations. In some proposals, little attention is paid to the author's personal experiences and values, while in others these data will enhance understanding of why certain variables are emphasized and others omitted.

So far, in our conceptual framework, we have identified our variables, conceptually defined them, and predicted relationships between them on the basis of previous studies and our own experience. Now, we must identify our variables and predict relationships between them on the basis of *theory*. The theories we select (e.g., psychosocial theories, behavioral theories) may be directly related to our research topic; in our example, psychosocial variables suspected to affect the adjustment of former residents of psychiatric institutions would be presented. Sometimes, our selected theories may not be directly related to our research topic, but they must always help us to explain why we selected specific variables and why we predicted relationships between them in the way we did.

Part 4: Questions and Hypotheses

As we have seen already, the term *research topic* refers to an overall area of investigation. The terms *research question* and *research hypothesis* both refer to a specific aspect of this overall area. A general question may not always precisely identify the variables that are the subject of the study. A hypothesis, on the other hand, by definition, always contains specific independent and dependent variables (see Chapter 6). A general question about the topic of community adjustment might be:

A General Question:
What social and interpersonal factors are most important in explaining the successful adjustment of former residents of psychiatric institutions in community settings?

In contrast, a specific hypothesis related to this topic might be:

A Specific Hypothesis:
The more contact former residents of psychiatric institutions have with relatives and friends, the more successful will be their adjustment in community settings.

In this specific hypothesis, the independent variable is contact with relatives and friends, and the dependent variable is adjustment in community settings. The terms *contact, former residents, psychiatric settings, relatives, friends, adjustment,* and *community settings* would all be conceptually defined in the Conceptual Framework (Part 3) and operationally defined under Operational Definitions (Part 5).

The general research questions or specific hypotheses flow from prior components of the proposal. First, both are derived logically from the original topic. For example, suppose we have indicated in our topic statement that our study is concerned with the adjustment of former psychiatric patients in community settings. We are now committed to "former patients" and "community settings." We cannot go on to frame a question or hypothesis concerning the adjustment of new patients in psychiatric institutions.

Our questions or hypotheses must also follow logically from the perspective and definitions provided by the literature review and conceptual framework. Thus, for instance, we cannot include the independent variable "contact with relatives and friends" in our specific hypothesis unless we have first conceptually defined this variable in our literature review or conceptual framework.

Questions or hypotheses, then, flow *from* prior components of the research proposal. In the same way, they lead *to* subsequent components of the proposal. Specifically, if questions or hypotheses are introduced in this component, they are always considered in subsequent components. If they are not introduced in this component, they are usually not discussed in the following components.

For example, suppose we wish to state in the data collection and data analysis components (Parts 8 and 9) that our data will account for the effect of community psychiatric support services on the adjustment levels of former patients. In order to make such a statement, we must first have introduced in our question or hypothesis the idea that psychiatric support services available in the community will affect the adjustment levels of former psychiatric patients.

Some research proposals contain both general questions *and* specific hypotheses; others have only a question *or* a hypothesis. Frequently, when we conduct an exploratory or descriptive study, as presented in Chapters 2, 12, and 13, we do not have enough knowledge in the area prior to the study to generate a hypothesis; in fact, one of the purposes of an exploratory study is to generate data that may then lead to the formulation of a hypothesis. Our research proposal, in this case, would be based just upon a general question.

In contrast, when we use an explanatory research design, a great deal is known about the area prior to the study and we are able to formulate a specific hypothesis on the basis of this prior knowledge. In this case, it is common practice to omit a research question and to identify only the specific research hypothesis to be verified.

Part 5: Operational Definitions

This component sets forth operational definitions for each independent and dependent variable under investigation. When we *conceptually* defined our variables in the Conceptual Framework (Part 3), we were only interested in making sure that the meaning of each variable was clear and unambiguous. Now, when we *operationally* define our variables, we have to take two more steps. First, we have to define each variable in a way that will enable us to measure it. Next, we have to indicate what specific data will be collected for each variable during the measurement process. Thus, when scales are utilized to measure certain variables, the operational definitions identify the specific scales employed. When other data collection techniques are utilized, the operational definitions state precisely the nature of the data to be collected.

For example, suppose our hypothesis is: The more contact former residents of psychiatric institutions have with relatives and friends in community settings, the more successful will be their adjustment in community settings. The independent variable, contact with relatives and friends, leaves room for confusion, even after being conceptually defined. Exactly how much contact is meant? What constitutes contact? With which relatives and what types of friends is contact established? The dependent variable, successful adjustment, leaves equal room for confusion. What if the nature of one person's adjustment is substantially different from that of another person, but both have remained in community settings? Have both "successfully" adjusted or has one person's adjustment been more successful than the other's? If so, in what way and to what extent?

In fact, it is not uncommon for research proposals to omit the operational definitions component and instead to answer such questions in the data collections component (Part 8). Yet, we want proposal reviewers to visualize the precise meaning of each independent and dependent variable in terms of what will be observed and/or measured and how observations and/or measurements will occur. We can make it easier for reviewers to do this by providing a clear listing of operational definitions for each pertinent independent and dependent variable.

Part 6: Research Design

In this part of our proposal, we describe the research design we will use to obtain answers to the general question and/or to verify the specific hypothesis. As presented in Chapters 2, 12, and 13, there are three major classifications of research designs: exploratory, descriptive, and explanatory. When we describe the design we have selected, we must include information about *who* will be studied; *what* will be observed or measured; *when* the observations and/or measurements will occur; and *how* these data will be gathered.

For example, we might propose a descriptive survey design to examine the adjustment of former residents of psychiatric institutions in community settings. We would next briefly describe the sample for the survey (e.g., a stratified random sample of all former residents of the Greenwood State Hospital discharged to the community in the last year). Then we would describe what data are to be collected from the sample (e.g., data concerning contact with relatives and friends, residential circumstances, and vocational and social adjustment), when data collection will occur (e.g., between January and March of the next fiscal year), and the data gathering procedures to be used (e.g., mailed questionnaires, interviews, content analysis, existing statistics, participant observation).

The research design links the component just prior to it (operational definition) with the two components that follow it (population and sample; and data collection). For example, when we describe in the research design component what will be observed and/or measured, we must also summarize the operational definitions given in the previous component (Part 5). When we discuss in the research component who will be studied, when the observations or measurements will occur, and how these data will be gathered, we must give a brief preview of material to be presented in detail in the sample and data collection components (Parts 7 and 8).

Part 7: Population and Sample

As presented in Chapter 11, this part of a research proposal provides a description of the population to whom the study's findings will be generalized; the study's sample and sampling strategy; and the potential generalizability of the study's findings. Usually, the description of the population is not long or detailed. Armed with information from earlier parts of the proposal, reviewers have often determined what the population will be prior to reaching this section of the proposal.

Nevertheless, since research studies are usually undertaken in order to generalize to larger populations rather than to make statements about samples, a succinct statement describing the population is needed. Such a statement is typically included in this part, regardless of the extent to which the population has been described earlier in the proposal. In the community adjustment proposal, for example, we must identify the study's population as all former residents of a specific psychiatric institution discharged between January 1, 2002, through December 31, 2003, and presently living in community environments.

The population is also differentiated from the study's sample. In some instances, the population and sample are the same. When this is the case, the proposal makes this clear. Most of the time, however, we are not able to study an entire population due to limitations of time and cost, and we are obliged to draw a sample. This component describes in detail the nature of the sample and the strategy for selecting it.

Describing the study's sample and sampling strategy involves specifying the unit of analysis (the persons or things to be studied); the precise procedures to be used in selecting the sample; the reasons for choosing the procedures; and the actual, estimated, or minimum number of persons or things to be included in the sample. The description of a sample is usually a detailed discussion; it is a primary means by which proposal reviewers can determine the potential generalizability (external validity) of the study's findings.

We should also include our own assessment about the generalizability of the study's findings, the reasoning behind this assessment, and a discussion of limitations in generalizing from the sample back to the larger population from which the sample is drawn.

Part 8: Methods of Data Collection

A detailed description of the data gathering procedures for the planned investigation is needed. This description covers the specific techniques to be employed, the specific measuring instruments to be utilized, and the specific series of activities to be conducted in making the measurements. When original measuring instruments are to be constructed, as discussed in Part III of this text, we must give a detailed account of the procedures to be employed in constructing them and we must also discuss the validity and reliability of the completed instruments. When existing measuring instruments are to be utilized, their validity and reliability must also be discussed. Finally, we must detail ethical considerations or any other factors that may result in problems in obtaining access to data, and we must discuss the steps to be taken to overcome these potential problems.

Suppose, for example, that we intend to interview former residents of psychiatric institutions to assess their adjustment in community settings. The data collection component would then contain detailed information about the type of question to be asked; the procedures for constructing, administering, and ensuring the validity and reliability of the interview instruments; the sequence of activities to be undertaken in arranging and conducting the interviews; and the steps to be taken to ensure a high response rate (external validity) to the interviews, despite the probably sensitive nature of the questions.

Alternatively, if we intended to use participant observation to collect data on adjustment, the data collection component would describe the setting, individuals, behaviors, and interactions to be observed; whether people would be aware that they were being observed; whether the observer would observe as a participant, quasi-participant, or nonparticipant; how the observer would gain access to data; and the planned duration of the observation period.

Part 9: Methods of Data Analysis

In this component, we describe the procedures we will use to analyze these data. If we are employing statistical analyses, this involves detailing each specific procedure to be employed for each general research question to be answered or specific hypothesis to be tested. For example, we must identify the particular tests of significance and the correlational procedures to be employed in verifying the relationship between the independent and dependent variables. The majority of social work studies utilize statistical procedures to analyze data (Weinbach & Grinnell, 2001). However, there are many situations where the use of statistical analysis is not only impossible but also inappropriate.

Part 10: Limitations

Potential limitations are often numerous in even the most carefully planned research study, and it is important that we list them in the proposal. Generally, when identifying limitations, we must consider:

1. The validity and reliability of all data collection instruments.
2. The generalizability of the sample to the population from which it was drawn.
3. Access to data.
4. Ethical problems.
5. The ability to control for extraneous factors in the environment and in respondents.

For example, a limitation in the community adjustment proposal may be the inability to obtain access to a truly representative random sample of former residents of psychiatric institutions. This, in turn, would limit our ability to generalize to the larger population of such persons from whom the sample was drawn.

Although all problems are never completely eliminated from any social work research study, it is necessary that we spell out the various means by which we will try to reduce the problems. For example, we might specify, as one of our study's limitations, that a truly representative sample of former residents of psychiatric institutions cannot be obtained. We must then detail the specific steps we will take to try to ensure that the sample is as representative as possible of the population from which it is drawn.

Part 11: Administration

All proposals address the resources that are available and that are needed to carry out the study. All studies must develop organizational, work, and financial plans. A majority of funding organizations specify that these three plans be addressed as separate components in the proposal. Although it is useful to consider them separately in determining which resources are available and which are necessary to execute the study, all three areas involve consideration of basic resources and can be seen as one component.

We must address a number of questions in the development of the proposal's organizational plan. Which organization, department, or departmental subunit will assume the administrative responsibility for the study? Where will the project be physically housed? What personnel are needed to carry out the study? What are their specific responsibilities? What should their qualifications be? What will the chain of authority be? What is the procedure for access to specialized facilities? Answering these questions provides an organizational chart that illustrates the proposed study's organizational context, the personnel to be employed, and the flow of authority that connects them.

When we develop a work plan, we must identify the sequence of activities necessary to execute the study, the person(s) responsible for carrying out each activity, and the anticipated dates for beginning and completing each specific activity. Research projects usually have explicit time frames. Time periods for developing the research operation and for data analysis and report preparation are usually underestimated. Based on the principles of management planning, the work plan promotes efficient organization in the execution of the research project. In addition, the work plan aids proposal reviewers to judge the extent to which the study will be effectively organized.

Finally, the administration component translates the work plan into dollars by providing a detailed budget description. The budget identifies resources that are needed to accomplish the activities described in the work plan and estimates the cost of each activity. Line-item budgets show exactly what amount of money will be needed for each activity. Typically, the items included in a line-item budget in social work research proposals are: personnel (including secretarial, research assistant, etc.); consultants; travel; supplies and equipment; telephone expenses; computer service; facilities; and special categories. Institutional overhead costs may be a critical factor over which we have little control; nevertheless, we must take them into account in our budget.

SUMMARY

Many of us need to prepare research proposals in order to undertake research studies in the organizations for which we work, to seek funds from grant awarding agencies, or to fulfill the requirements of academic committees. Before we begin to write the proposal, we must ask ourselves general questions concerning the purpose of the proposal, and the writing style and format that would best serve that purpose. All proposals should be clearly worded and clearly organized so that reviewers are presented with a precise outline of our study and we, ourselves, know exactly what it is that we intend to do.

In general, research proposals contain certain basic types of information that is usually broken into general components. However, it is essential that there be a logical progression through the components of the proposal leading from *why* we want to do our study to *what* precisely we want to do to *how* we intend to do it, detailing the difficulties we expect to encounter along the way and the steps we will take to ameliorate those difficulties.

After a research proposal has been funded and the study has been executed, the next step in the research process is to write a research report derived from the study's data or findings. In the next chapter, we look at how to write and publish a research report.

William J. Reid

C h a p t e r   21

Writing Research Reports

RESEARCH REPORTS SERVE AN IMPORTANT FUNCTION in social work because they put new contributions to the knowledge base of the profession into a permanent written form. Without published research reports, the claim of a scientific knowledge base for social work might be difficult to substantiate.

The knowledge obtained from social work research can be reported in a variety of forms. These reports may vary in length from a brief note to a full-scale presentation several hundred pages long. They may stand by themselves or be embedded in larger works. They may be so technical that only readers with a high degree of research sophistication will understand them, or expressed in language that can be readily comprehended by any literate person. Reports can also be communicated in the form of films.

The audiences to whom reports are directed are an even more important source of variation. Reports may be read (or heard) by a handful of persons or may reach thousands. The scope of the audience reached depends largely on the medium of distribution. Reports may be circulated informally, read at a conference, distributed through mailing lists, or published as journal articles, monographs, or books, among other possibilities.

Some social work research reports are based on student projects, particularly doctoral dissertations. Both Ph.D. and MSW candidates are encouraged to try to get reports of their studies published, provided they are of sufficient merit and interest, and some social work instructors make an effort to help students achieve this goal (see the final section of this chapter). Most of the unpublished social work literature consists of such materials as conference papers, presentations of student projects, and shorter reports to sponsoring agencies.

RESEARCH REPORTS FOR PROFESSIONAL JOURNALS

The general type of report discussed in this chapter is suitable for publication as an article in a professional social work journal. Most such reports consist of from 10 to 25 typewritten pages, including tables, figures, and references. They are usually based on single research studies and are written for a potentially wide audience. This type of report is the most common means of sharing the results of studies with other social work professionals, and it is also probably the most important, because in any field of study, articles published in journals are the principal source of additions to or modifications of the knowledge base.

Purpose of a Research Report

The major purpose of a research report is to communicate to others the knowledge that has been derived from a particular study. The researcher, taking the role of author, customarily provides a rationale for conducting the study, reviews what is already known in the problem area under investigation, and states the research question. The researcher then explains the design and methods of the study and presents the findings and the conclusions drawn from the data.

In the report, all aspects of the study should be related to the purpose of communicating the knowledge derived from it. In particular, the distinction between what has been found out and the author's use of the findings must be made clear. If this is not done, and if the findings or the means of obtaining them are distorted to advance the author's point of view, the purpose of the report will be subverted.

Writing for an Audience

Since a research report is written to be understood and utilized by a particular audience, or those who will read it, assumptions regarding the intended audience are critical. In social work, readers vary considerably in their ability to comprehend research and evaluation concepts, in their interest in technical detail, and in the criteria they use for assessing findings and conclusions. Social workers who specialize in research may desire a range and depth of information about a study's methodology. This may be of secondary concern to social workers who specialize in direct practice and are more likely to be interested in the author's speculations concerning applications of the study's findings. Professional social workers minimize such differences in audience orientations.

Authors of research reports understandably would like to satisfy both interests. There are various ways of doing this, but none is completely satisfactory. A hard-line approach taken by some authors is to write for an audience of research specialists, without a great deal of concern for other readers. In another approach, sometimes referred to as spoon-feeding, the author glosses over technical aspects of the study and concentrates on delivering "useful" information. A more technical version of the same study may also be prepared for an audience of researchers.

There is a satisfactory solution that avoids both of these two extremes. The essential technical aspects of a study must be presented. It is impossible for readers to assess a study's findings properly with no understanding of the methods by which the findings were obtained. Researchers writing reports can help readers with the task of comprehension by providing explanations of technical procedures, and they can make an effort to enhance the relevance of a study's findings, implications, and conclusions to social work practice.

In terms of the development of the social work profession and the services it provides, the best long-run solution is to raise the level of research literacy among social workers. Professional education provides one means to this end. What students learn about research at schools of social work soon fades, however, if as professionals they are not continually exposed to research concepts by reading reports they find of interest.

ORGANIZATION AND CONTENT

This section is concerned with the "how to" of social work report writing. The best way to get a sense of how social work research is reported is to read articles that have been published in professional social work journals. Additional resources that are useful in learning to write reports include books, articles, and manuals on writing skills and report preparation.

The general format of the article-length report usually follows a standard sequence. Within this sequence, there may be a good deal of variation in how different parts of the report are labeled, in the attention given to each part, and in the nature and internal organization of the content.

Table 21.1   Organization of Parts in a Research Report

Parts	Contents
1. Problem	Background, rationale, and significance of the study; review of relevant research and theory; presentation and explanation of the research problem, research question, research hypothesis, and variables.
2. Method	Delineation of the strategy (design) and methods of the investigation, including a description of the setting and the sampling plan; description of data collection procedures, instruments, and measurement approach.
3. Findings	Presentation of findings, including data displays (tables, graphs, etc.); textual exposition of data; description of relevant analytic procedures.
4. Discussion	Discussion of findings, including interpretation of data, implications for theory, practice, education, and research; limitations of study; relationship to other research; summary and conclusions.

Organizational Framework

A commonly used framework for a research study report intended for publication in a professional journal consists of four parts: problem, method, findings, and discussion. The topics each part of this sequence is likely to contain are listed in Table 21.1 above.

This general progression of headings is followed in most reports of positivistic research studies. The example outlined in Table 21.2 on the next page shows the relation of the headings used in an actual published report to these four parts. In this example, the author elicited from hospital patients critical incidents (important examples) of helpful and nonhelpful staff behavior. These incidents were then classified and analyzed to present a picture of the patients' perception of their hospital care.

The basic structure of this report follows the four-part scheme presented in Table 21.1, but the actual headings used are dictated by the particulars of the study. "Method," for example, appears under two headings, "Plan of Study" and "Classifying the Incidents." The example also illustrates a point worth noting: The first few paragraphs of a report, which present some aspects of Part 1, often have no heading.

A useful way to outline a report prior to actually writing it is to generate the major headings from the four-part structure, and then break them down into subheadings applicable to the specific study. This outline is helpful in organizing divisions to be used in writing the report.

There is a significant deviation from this structure when a study is conducted in stages. For example, an evaluation of an intervention upon its termination may constitute the first stage of a study, and a follow-up of clients

Table 21.2   Headings in a Published Research Report

Parts	Headings in Report	Contents
1. Problem	Unheaded introduction	Review of previous research studies.
2. Method	Plan of Study	Study design; setting; sampling plan; critical incident technique.
	Classifying the Incidents	Method of classifying incidents; reliability of the classifications.
3. Findings	Major Findings	Frequency distribution of helpful and nonhelpful incidents; relation of patients' perceptions to different factors.
4. Discussion	Discussion	Reasons why findings may differ from those of previous research studies.
	Implications for Practice	Importance of patients' perceptions in shaping hospital services and staff behavior.
	Implications for Training	Use of patients' questionnaires in staff monitoring and training.

six months later may comprise the second stage. In such cases, the report could begin with a fairly standard Part 1 (statement of the problem), and then each stage could be presented as if it were a separate study, with description of the methods, presentation of findings, and discussion of findings for each stage. The report could conclude with an overall discussion and summary. This type of organization makes most sense when the different stages of the study are sufficiently distinct in methods and findings to warrant presentation as separate units.

Statement of the Problem

The introduction to a report often proves the most difficult section to write. Although the study must be placed in some perspective, any study is potentially connected to a wide range of topics, and it is difficult to know where to begin or end. If a study evaluates a method for helping marital partners with communication problems, for example, should something be said about marital conflict as a social problem? What about theories of family communication, or other methods of marital treatment?

A pragmatic way to approach the writing of Part 1 of a report is to begin with its most essential elements—the statement of the problem area and specification of specific research questions or hypotheses. The researcher then can ask: What do readers need to know in order to understand the problem, to place it in an appropriate context, to appreciate its significance, and to determine how its solution will contribute to existing knowledge?

The amount of attention given to these factors depends on the nature of the research question and the assumptions about the audience to whom the report is primarily directed. If the research question involves concepts or theoretical formulations that are likely to be unfamiliar to readers, some explanation of these ideas is in order. The significance of some research questions will be self-evident and need not be belabored; the importance of others has to be made clear. The relevance of the study's problem area (and resulting research questions) to social work practice should be articulated if it is not obvious.

The expected contribution of the report to existing knowledge can be stated through a review of literature directly related to the problem area. The review should not consist of a string of paragraphs, each presenting a capsule summary of a different study. Rather, it should organize findings pertinent to different aspects of the study, with emphasis on identifying gaps in knowledge that the report intends to fill. These preliminaries can be overdone, however. The introduction to a report is not the place for a lengthy review of the literature. It also should not be used as a vehicle for an incidental essay.

Explanation of the Research Method

Part 2 sets forth the methodology of the study, usually including descriptions of the research design, the sampling plan, data collection procedures, and measuring instruments. If an evaluation of a program or an experiment is being reported, this section should describe the setting, the nature of the program, and the independent and dependent variables.

Substantive findings (findings bearing directly on the research question or hypothesis) are not presented in this part but are deferred until Part 3. Data on the validity and reliability of the measuring instrument(s) and on characteristics of the setting may be included, however. Information concerning the sample may also be presented here rather than in Part 3, particularly if there is only a small amount of data to be reported. Aspects of methodology that may better be understood in conjunction with presentation of the findings also may be deferred until Part 3. Methods of data analysis or secondary measures obtained from manipulations of the data may best be discussed there, in the context of data presentation.

The most common shortcoming in Part 2 is insufficient or unclear presentation of the study's methods. The researcher's own intimate familiarity with these methods may breed insensitivity to the reader's ignorance of them. As a result, the study methodology may be presented in an indirect, cryptic manner. An excellent device whereby to avoid this is for researchers to put themselves in the position of unsophisticated readers.

It is particularly important to provide a clear picture of the connection between the research question and the data obtained. In order to accomplish this, some description of the study's measuring instrument, including a presentation of sample questions, is usually necessary. Ideally, the actual instrument or key portions of it should be included as an appendix, but this is usually not feasible for reports published in professional journals. In any case, the steps by which the data were obtained from the measuring instrument should be delineated. It may also be advisable to restate the research question or hypothesis in operational language, indicating the quantitative basis for measurement. For example, a hypothesis may be stated as a prediction that certain scores will be correlated or that statistically significant differences between sample groups will be found on the dependent variable.

Presentation of the Findings

The essential purpose of Part 3 is to present findings that have been anticipated by the statement of the research question or hypothesis and the explanation of the research method. While all the findings of a study need not be reported in an article-length report, all important results that bear on the research question should be shared with the audience. The two principal formats for presenting the findings are data displays and text descriptions.

Data Displays

In working on Part 3, a useful first step is to prepare the tables, graphs, figures, or other data displays that will form the core of the presentation. The narrative portion of the findings section can then be organized according to these displays, which may be in the form of tables, charts, or figures.

The first principle in displaying data is to present them in a manner that can be readily understood, given the information provided up to that point in the report. In tabular data displays, the most widely used form, this criterion is met by providing a descriptive title for the table and labels for columns and rows. In Table 21.3, hypothetical data on clients' ratings of satisfaction can be quickly grasped, even if nothing else were known about such a study. The data are reasonably complete. Percentages are given to facilitate comparisons between two groups of clients, according to whether the social workers assigned to them had MSW degrees or only BSW degrees. The number of clients giving each response to indicate their level of satisfaction—the data on which the percentages were based—is also given.

Information concerning the statistical test of significance used to test the hypothesis is given at the bottom of Table 21.3. A likely research hypothesis for this study would be that clients of social workers with MSW degrees will be

Table 21.3   Table Showing Client Satisfaction with Social
                   Work Services, by Educational Level of Workers

| | Educational Level of Workers | | | | Total | |
| | MSW | | BSW | | | |
Satisfaction	Number	Percent	Number	Percent	Number	Percent
Satisfied	23	57.5%	28	50.0%	51	53.1%
Neutral	16	40.0	13	23.2	29	30.2
Dissatisfied	1	2.5	15	26.8	16	16.7
Totals	40	100.0%	56	100.0%	96	100.0%

$X^2 = 10.7, \ df = 2, \ p < .01$

more satisfied with services than clients of workers whose educations include only BSW degrees. The statistic used to test this hypothesis (or the null hypothesis, that there is no difference in level of clients' satisfaction according to workers' level of education) is chi-square (X^2), which was found to be 10.7. The number of degrees of freedom (*df*) is needed to perform this test with a calculator or computer, or by hand computation and the use of a published statistical table. The *p* is the level of statistical significance found in the chi-square test, or the probability that the null hypothesis can be rejected and the research hypothesis supported.

As a matter of convention, routine statistical procedures such as these are not explained in a journal report, either as part of the graphic display or in the text. This creates obvious communication difficulties for readers who lack a knowledge of statistics. Without a course in statistics, the information on statistical significance in tables appearing in professional journals can only be understood in general terms.

The purpose of a data display is to communicate information to the reader in a graphic manner. If a display has achieved this purpose efficiently, there should be no need to repeat the information it contains in the text of the report. Textual commentary on data displays should be used to emphasize the main points of the data or to draw attention to characteristics of the data that might be overlooked.

Thus, in interpreting Table 21.3, the text should not plod through the obvious—"57.5 percent of the clients who had MSW social workers were satisfied; 40 percent were neutral," and so on. Rather, the text might observe that clients with MSW social workers were relatively more satisfied with service than clients with BSW social workers. In addition, it might note that dissatisfied clients accounted for the largest share of the difference.

In keeping with the purpose of data displays to enhance the reader's understanding, complex displays, such as a graph with half a dozen crisscrossing lines, should not be used. Indeed, displays should not be used at all to communicate basic information that can be expressed more simply in the text.

In the example, if satisfaction data had been obtained only for clients served by MSW social workers, Table 21.3 would not be necessary.

Description in Text

The text on the findings of the report should follow a logical sequence. Data describing characteristics of research participants or respondents (demographic data) often are presented first, as a means of defining the group to which the findings relate. A convenient way to proceed with the description of findings is in the order of the research questions or hypotheses formulated from the problem area. Other findings not anticipated in this formulation can then be introduced.

It may be necessary to describe additional measurement procedures as well as analytic methods. The amount of detail and explanation necessary to present the data analysis techniques varies. Routine data processing procedures that are of no consequence to the study's findings certainly do not need to be reported. For example, informing readers that the data were coded, entered into the computer, and analyzed adds nothing of value to the report.

Common statistical techniques, such as standard measures of association to measure the strength of a relationship between variables, are neither explained nor referenced. It is good practice, however, to clarify their function so the essential meaning of the statistical findings can be grasped. In describing a correlation between expenditures for social work services and the patient discharge rate in mental health facilities, for example, the report might state: "The correlation coefficient between expenditures and the discharge rate was .76, which suggests a relatively high degree of association between these two variables." Specialized methods that are not in common use should be fully explained, however.

Presentation or Discussion of Findings

The usual practice in writing Part 3 is to present the study's findings and clarify them if necessary, but not to discuss them at length. There may be reasons to deviate from this format, however. For instance, if a study produces a number of findings, some of them may be summarized, and Part 4, the discussion section, can focus on those that are to be emphasized. If the findings and their significance are immediately apparent, the description can be brief, and Part 4 can be devoted to recommendations based on the findings.

In reports of studies using the naturalistic research approach, the presentation and discussion of the findings are often combined, and the organization follows the themes that emerge in the analysis of the data. Brief examples from the researcher's text (the notes on observations or experiments that comprise the data in naturalistic research) may be presented, often in the form of quotes from participants or observers. These extracts, which provide both illustration and documentation, also can enliven the reports of positivistic studies.

Reports based on qualitative data are not likely to contain technical information that readers will find hard to comprehend. These studies can suffer, however, from needless imprecision caused by the author's reluctance to use quantitative measures or positivistic descriptions. In summarizing the results, selected behaviors or attitudes might be described as if they were characteristic of everyone in the sample. Although excessive discriminations (one person said this, a second said that, a third said something else) should be avoided, some quantification is useful to avoid overgeneralization.

Discussion of the Findings

Part 4 is primarily concerned with the meaning and importance of the findings reported in Part 3. The point for presenting data has passed; now, discussion of what the findings add up to and where they may lead is in order.

Researchers are liable to succumb to two shortcomings in writing this part. One is to turn the discussion into a mere repetition of findings already presented in the report, without much commentary on their practical or theoretical significance. While it may be useful to remind readers of results that will be the focus of discussion, if the findings were adequately presented in Part 3, Part 4 should focus on further implications, general conclusions, and so on.

The second shortcoming approaches the opposite extreme. This is to ignore the findings and concentrate on an exposition of the researcher's own point of view—perhaps because the findings did not meet the researcher's expectations for the study. The findings for any study, no matter how trivial, merit some discussion, even if only to give reasons why they were not more revealing.

Explanations and Implications

The content of the discussion section varies according to the nature of the findings and what has been previously said about them. In most studies, the findings are sufficiently complex (or ambiguous) to warrant some explanation of what was in fact learned about the sample studied. Causal connections found between variables should always be discussed. For example, the length of social work treatment may be found to be positively correlated with clients' outcomes. Does this mean that greater amounts of treatment played a causative role in the outcome, or does it mean that clients who were getting better on their own tended to remain in treatment longer? Tests of rival hypotheses or other evidence or argument that can be brought to bear on this point should be presented.

In examining such relationships and determining the meaning of descriptive findings, possible sources of bias or error in data collection and measurement should be pointed out. Were the interviewers' perceptions influenced by knowledge of the study's hypothesis? Is it possible that clients were giving socially desirable responses? Inconsistencies in the findings, such as discrepancies among measures of the same phenomenon, should be identified and accounted for. The author's speculations about the reasons for unanticipated findings may also be offered. In trying to understand and explain the meaning of a study's findings, however, researchers are limited to the persons, objects, or events they actually investigated.

A rather different point concerns the importance or meaningfulness of the study's findings to other persons or situations. This is the payoff for research studies; an understanding derived from persons, objects, or events actually studied should have a broader application. Because many social work studies are not based on representative samples, however, it is not always possible to generalize within known margins of error to larger populations. Nevertheless, if some kind of generalization or implications cannot be derived from the findings, there would be little point in conducting the study.

In stating the implications, obvious statements such as "Since the sample studied was not representative, generalizations of the findings are not possible" should be avoided. Claims that the findings necessarily reflect universal truth are also needless. For most studies, it can appropriately be assumed that the findings have some implications for the field of social work. Even findings based on small, nonrepresentative samples may provide some support for, or challenge to, existing hypotheses or social work practices. They might also be used as a basis for suggesting new hypotheses or practices.

While the findings may not "prove" or "establish" a great deal, they may "provide evidence for," "suggest the possibility that," or "raise questions about" a conclusion. With such qualified language, implications can be presented that readers will find useful but not misleading. Authors often do not push either their imaginations or their data far enough. Ultraconservative interpretations of findings may have the dubious advantage of avoiding criticism from other professionals, but they also may fail to extract useful ideas from the findings.

The conclusions of a study may be strengthened or qualified by references to related literature, using sources reviewed in Part 1 of the report or introduced in this part in order to connect the findings of the study to the results of other investigations. Introducing other authors' findings in Part 4 is also appropriate when the study's findings have been serendipitous or were not covered in the literature referred to in the introduction.

Limitations and Recommendations

The limitations of a research study, particularly major shortcomings that may affect how the findings are interpreted or applied, should be made explicit.

If this is not done in a separate subsection in which specific limitations are cited, it can be made clear in interpreting the findings or developing their implications for social work. For example, a study of the needs of older people in a community may have used a sample that overrepresented the younger, healthier members of the elderly population. In discussing implications of the findings for community planning, the limiting effects of the sample bias can be pointed out.

Some authors make recommendations for further study based on the findings. These recommendations should be informative; if nothing more specific can be said than, "It is important to do more research studies in this area," it is better to say nothing. To be helpful, a recommendation for further study should specify particular research questions, variables, or designs.

Recommendations for changes in policies, programs, practices, and so on are most likely to appear in reports addressed to particular decision makers (such as key agency staff members) who might be able to initiate them. In making these recommendations, the findings of the study should be synthesized with assumptions about desirable goals and some knowledge of the relevant policy or program.

SUMMARIES AND LONGER REPORTS

A final section of Part 4 sometimes is included, particularly with longer types of reports, to give a brief summary of the important findings and conclusions of the study. This may be needed if the discussion deals with a range of findings in a lengthy or discursive fashion but not if the discussion is brief, well focused, and in itself summarizes the major findings. A summary also may not be needed if an abstract of the study is furnished.

Longer reports such as master's theses, doctoral dissertations, and reports to sponsoring agencies are usually richer in detail and provide a more complete picture of the findings of a research study than article-length journal reports do. In fact, article-length reports may be based on only a portion of the findings presented in longer reports.

The length and comprehensiveness of students' course papers or reports to agencies usually make summaries necessary. A common way of studying such reports is to read only the summary and the portions that are of interest. Agency decision makers, particularly, require nontechnical summaries of studies, with emphasis on the major findings. Often such an "executive summary" is presented at the beginning of the report.

The use of footnotes and appendixes also helps unburden the text of longer reports. This suits readers who are not interested in ploughing through a great deal of technical detail. At the same time, it provides valuable information for those who wish to pursue the topic further.

PUBLICATION AND DISSEMINATION

All authors are interested in communicating their work to readers who will find it of interest or potential value. The general term for exposure of a research study to an audience is dissemination, and the most extensive dissemination is accomplished through publication. More limited forms include distribution of copies to the staff of an organization, mailing copies to a list of prospective readers, presentations at staff meetings and conferences, and interlibrary circulation of master's theses and doctoral dissertations.

Although a simple distinction between published and unpublished reports is commonly made, there is a considerable grey area between these categories. Many reports, particularly more lengthy ones, may be "quasi published" by schools, agencies, conferences, and so forth. For example, several hundred copies of a report may be duplicated (or even printed), advertised, and sold by an agency. Because such reports lack the imprimatur of established publishers, they are sometimes referred to as "near print."

The most common means of large-scale dissemination of a research report is publication in a professional journal. The importance of the other forms should not be overlooked, however. With a little imagination and initiative, an unpublished report of potential interest to others can be put into circulation. For example, a state department of mental health may be able to distribute a study to its field offices, or copies might be sent to a small number of interested parties who may cite it in their own publications.

Publication in Professional Journals

Professional journals provide ready access to studies, regardless of when they were published, because present and past issues can usually be found in libraries serving the field. Searches of the professional literature in journals or periodicals can be assisted by a variety of information-retrieval tools, such as publications that print abstracts, computerized abstract services, and citation indexes. A research study reported in a periodical thus becomes part of an information network and has a better chance of being located and utilized. Moreover, because most professional journals use some form of expert review for papers submitted, there is some assurance that the articles published meet certain standards.

The number of social work journals being published changes frequently. Over 60 such journals yield a combined annual harvest of over a thousand articles. Most of these are geared to special-interest groups, defined by field of practice, region, auspices, social work method, and so forth. With the exception of *Social Work*, the journals have limited numbers of subscribers, and a sizable proportion is likely to be libraries.

Unsolicited reports of research studies are not received with enthusiasm by some social work journals. For one reason, editors may be concerned that the content is too technical for their readers to comprehend. Other problems may be posed by the length of the report, the cost of reproducing data displays, or difficulties in securing experts to do prepublication reviews and technical editing. If a report is accepted, the editor may want the author to revise it and perhaps to tone down technical content, eliminate tables, or reduce the length.

Submitting a Report for Publication

The surest way to get an article published in a professional journal is to write a good report based on a good research study. In writing a report for possible publication, the first step is to identify the journal to which it will be initially submitted. The report can then be written to relate to the interests of the readers of that journal and to meet its requirements concerning length, footnote style, and so forth. Information on journal policy, usually published in each issue on the journal's masthead, includes a description of the types of reports the journal is interested in and submission procedures. Various issues should be consulted for models of reports the journal has published.

If the report is rejected by the journal originally selected, it may be submitted, with whatever revisions seem advisable, to other journals. Sending copies of a report to several journals simultaneously is considered unethical and can prove embarrassing if it is accepted by more than one.

The submission of a report is simple. It is sent with the number of required photocopies (usually three or four) to the journal's editorial office, together with a brief cover letter stating that the report is being submitted for possible publication by the journal. At the journal's editorial office, a decision-making process begins that will determine whether the report will appear in the journal's pages. Key persons in this process are the editor and reviewers (referees). The reviewers are in most instances experts in the field covered by the journal and contribute their time on a voluntary basis.

The report is read independently by two or more reviewers, who are usually not informed of the author's identity. They make recommendations regarding whether the report is suitable for publication and give reasons for their decisions. Disagreements among reviewers are common, and agreement to reject a report is more usual than agreement to publish one. When reviewers disagree, the editor often makes the final decision. The position of arbitrator gives the editor a good deal of influence over which reports are published. Journal contents therefore tend to reflect the standards and biases of their editors. An editor rarely has free rein, however. Few editors would refuse to publish a report that has been endorsed by all the journal's reviewers, regardless of their own biases.

The journal's decision about using a report frequently falls somewhere between total rejection and unqualified acceptance. If the report is rejected, the author may be encouraged to revise and resubmit it, but this does not commit the journal to accept the revised report for publication. Journals tend to reject more reports than they accept. Most reports are appropriate for several journals, however, including some outside the field of social work. Since acceptance criteria vary from journal to journal, it pays to be persistent. Journals also vary concerning the feedback they supply with rejected reports. Some send out only a form letter; others include the reviewers' comments, which may be painful to read but can be enormously helpful to an author who intends to submit the report elsewhere after revision.

The author's work does not end with acceptance for publication. A copy editor then goes over the manuscript, mainly to make the report fit the style and format of the journal, though in the process questions may arise about clarity, redundancy, omissions, and the like. The author normally reviews the edited copy and makes corrections or additional changes if necessary. The author usually sees proofs of the article after the manuscript has been typeset but is discouraged from making changes at that point.

The processes of review, editing, and production take time. For authors, the clock ticks most slowly between the submission of a report and a final decision by a journal. This period of uncertainty may vary from a few weeks to several months or a year, depending on the time absorbed by the review process. There is also a time lag between acceptance and actual publication that may range from a few weeks to two years or more. A delay of six to nine months is fairly typical for social work journals, due to such factors as the number of issues published a year, the time consumed by editing, printing, and distribution, and the backlog of accepted manuscripts.

Getting Student Work Published

For social work students who wish to submit for publication reports of studies they do in their academic work, a good first step is to consult with an instructor. If students are serious about publication, they should rewrite their course papers with that objective in mind after selecting a journal to which the finished product is to be submitted. As a rule, course papers should not be submitted as is. There is usually a great deal of distance between a first-class student paper and a report of publishable quality. In rewriting the paper, the student should be particularly sensitive to aspects of the study that may have been glossed over because of assumptions about the instructor's knowledge of those areas.

In some cases, the instructor may be willing to collaborate with the student in the rewriting and be listed as a coauthor. If the original work is a joint effort, senior authorship (the first author listed) is usually given to the one with the greatest responsibility for conducting the study and writing up the results. It is usually assumed that the senior author has made a greater contribution, but some coauthors determine the order randomly.

Students should not confine submissions to the better-known social work journals, which receive numerous reports of publishable quality. They may find greater receptivity and fewer delays with some of the less well-known journals, particularly those that are relatively new. And students should not be discouraged if their initial submissions are rejected. Even well-established authors must learn to live with the unpleasant reality that their work is not always welcome. If reviewers' comments are supplied, they can have considerable learning value.

SUMMARY

The purpose of conducting a social work research study is greatly enhanced by the communication of the results to others. Published reports, particularly, put new contributions to the knowledge base of the profession into a permanent, written form. The most common type of research report, and the most important in terms of dissemination of research findings, is represented by research articles published in professional social work journals.

The organization of reports published in journals follows a more-or-less standard format consisting of four parts: statement of the problem, explanation of the research method, presentation of the findings, and discussion of the findings. The findings are reported in the form of graphic displays such as tables and figures and in accompanying text descriptions. Explanations, implications, limitations, and recommendations of the findings are discussed in the final part of the study report.

A research report is usually written with a definite audience in mind; it may be a limited audience, such as the staff of an organization, or a more extensive audience, such as the readers of a social work journal. If the report is to be submitted to a particular journal, the author must keep in mind its requirements for such matters as article length and format. If the author is not successful with a first submission, the report can be revised, perhaps with the assistance of reviewers' comments, and submitted to another social work journal, an interdisciplinary journal, or a journal in an allied field.

The following chapter continues the discussion of social work research reports. It presents a framework for evaluating reports of quantitative research studies based on the four parts of a report discussed in this chapter—problem, method, findings, and discussion. An additional section is included on conclusions related to the utilization of knowledge from the study.

Joel Fischer

C h a p t e r   22

Evaluating Research Reports

THIS CHAPTER has two basic functions. It provides a framework for evaluating published research reports—specifically, reports of studies in which the quantitative approach has been used. It also undertakes to integrate and synthesize the content of the preceding chapters in this book as it pertains to the evaluation of such studies.

To some extent, the discussion and the criteria for evaluation are applicable to both quantitative and qualitative reports. Our focus, however, is on the quantitative approach that traditionally has been taken in following the steps of the social work research process, and around which the discussion in this text has been structured. As we know, this approach relies on quantitative methods in the collection and analysis of data for use in examining research questions or testing hypotheses. But this text supports a pluralistic methodology rather than a single approach, so the qualitative approach, in which qualitative methods are used to examine and describe problem situations or behaviors and then generalize about them, also is considered. Nevertheless, the emphasis in this chapter is on reports of quantitative studies.

Quantitative research reports are published articles based on studies designed to contribute to the social work knowledge base through rigorous, replicable, and empirical methods. This definition is based on the belief that the systematic, orderly procedures of social work research provide a productive means to organize, understand, test, and develop social work knowledge. Moreover, research studies should be applicable in social work practice situations, and the field of social work should not be dichotomized into separate practice and research orientations. The capacity to perform competently in the social work profession, therefore, is based in part on the ability to analyze and utilize the results of social work research studies.

Social work practice must be guided as much as possible by empirically validated principles and techniques. However, few, if any, quantitative studies of social work research are without limitations. Thus social workers must be able to analyze research findings from reports and make judgments as to their applicability to practice. Otherwise, even minimal effectiveness in applications of the results is unlikely, and the contributions of research studies to the knowledge base may go unrecognized or unused.

THE FRAMEWORK FOR EVALUATION

The framework presented in this chapter defines the key criteria for the evaluation of quantitative research reports in the field of social work. It should help social workers develop the basic skills for analyzing reports and evaluating research studies and alert them to how these skills can be applied in conducting and writing up their own studies. The key evaluative criteria suggested for each category of the analysis can be applied on a point-by-point basis in the evaluation of a single study or in comparing several studies.

The framework for evaluation given in Figures 22.1 through 22.5 is built around the four parts of a research report identified in Chapter 23—problem, method, findings, and discussion—with the addition of a separate section for conclusions as to utilization. Together, the criteria in these categories constitute a measurement instrument for rating quantitative research reports and the studies they represent. Each criterion is to some extent distinct, although there is a clear overlap among them. The criteria are to be rated on a four-point scale, with a rating of 1 meaning low, unclear, poor, or not addressed by the study, and a rating of 4 meaning high, clear, excellent, or well covered.

Analyzing a report criterion by criterion makes it easier to draw accurate conclusions about the study. The criteria listed are related to various dimensions of the social work research process, but they apply after the fact to the completed study, as reported in the publication. The criteria therefore ask for ratings of various components of the report according to such qualities as clarity, adequacy, and reasonableness. Thus in using the framework, the content of the research report is what is being evaluated, but the analysis can also be a vehicle for evaluating the research study reported. The final category of the analysis, conclusions, goes beyond the research study to evaluate how its findings can be applied in social work practice.

The framework was developed by abstracting and synthesizing criteria for analysis from a number of different sources, both from within the field of social work and outside it (Campbell & Stanley, 1963; Herzogg, 1959; Huck, Cormier, & Bounds, 1974; Tripodi, Fellin, & Meyer, 1983). The criteria in each category are described in the following sections.

PROBLEM CRITERIA

The problem category of the framework for evaluation is concerned with the problem area under investigation, out of which the research question or hypothesis is formulated for a study (see Chapters 6 and 7). It deals with the researcher's conceptualization of the phenomenon to be tested and can be used as an aid in understanding and evaluating the overall background and aims of the study. The criteria cover such components of the research process as formulation of the research question or hypothesis, operational definition of the independent and dependent variables, and statement of rival hypotheses. The 15 criteria to be ranked in evaluating the problem category of a research report are shown in Figure 22.1.

The Literature Review

Most social work research studies are based on previous research studies or established theoretical concepts. The report of a study must demonstrate an adequate knowledge of the relevant literature in the problem area under investigation and should include references citing existing studies of similar phenomena.

The evaluation of the author's use of the literature should examine how the study is related to the existing literature, conceptually and methodologically. It should also assess how the research question derived from the problem area is related to the literature. This facilitates comparison of similarities between the study and others that address the same research problem area.

The Research Hypothesis

The research hypothesis should clearly formulate a proposed answer to the research question in the form of a prediction. For example, a hypothesis derived from the research question "Are the social work services in a given agency effective?" might be restated as "Professional social work services in a given agency will produce significantly more positive changes in clients' self-images than will services provided by other professionals."

	Low		High	
1. Adequacy of the literature review	1	2	3	4
2. Clarity of the problem area and research question under investigation	1	2	3	4
3. Clarity of the statement of the hypothesis	1	2	3	4
4. Clarity of the specification of the independent variable	1	2	3	4
5. Clarity of the specification of the dependent variable	1	2	3	4
6. Clarity of the definitions for major concepts	1	2	3	4
7. Clarity of the operational definitions	1	2	3	4
8. Reasonableness of assumption of relationship between the independent and dependent variables	1	2	3	4
9. Number of independent variables tested	1	2	3	4
10. Specification of independent variables in rival hypotheses	1	2	3	4
11. Adequacy in the control of independent variables in rival hypotheses	1	2	3	4
12. Clarity of the researcher's orientation	1	2	3	4
13. Clarity of the study's purpose	1	2	3	4
14. Clarity of the study's auspices	1	2	3	4
15. Reasonableness of the author's assumptions	1	2	3	4

Figure 22.1   Criteria for Assessing Problem Category
of a Research Report

The hypothesis should serve as a guide for the design of the study and the selection of the methods for data collection and analysis. In the evaluation of the study report, it is the basis for rating many other criteria. The analyses of the next three framework categories (method, findings, and discussion) rest on the study's purpose, as indicated by the research hypothesis.

The Independent and Dependent Variables

As we have seen from Chapters 6 and 7, a hypothesis is stated in terms of a predicted effect of the independent variable on the dependent variable. Thus, a testable hypothesis requires a clear definition of these variables. The independent variable is the assumed or predicted causal variable, and the dependent variable is the outcome variable, or the one that the independent variable is assumed to affect.

The independent and dependent variables comprise the major concepts of the study. Since concepts are abstractions of ideas, the variables must have nominal definitions, or be defined in terms of the general meaning they are intended to convey. These concepts should also have operational definitions, that is, be defined in quantitative, concrete terms with regard to the procedures used to measure or observe the variables. The greater the extent to which the variables are operationalized, the better. A study that simply suggests that "casework services" affect clients' self-esteem provides much less information than one that defines the exact techniques comprising the casework services. Unless the variables are clearly operationalized, they cannot be measured, and application of the results to social work practice is difficult.

A study should be rated higher if it tests more than one kind of independent variable. This rating criterion (Number 9 in Figure 22.1) can be explained in terms of the type and amount of information that can be generated from studies that test one independent variable, as compared to studies that test more than one. For example, comparisons between several interventions can be made. Studies that have examined one social work intervention technique provide valuable information, but the information is increased tremendously if the effectiveness of the technique in interaction with other variables (such as the practitioner's level of interpersonal skills) can be simultaneously evaluated.

Evaluation of the report in terms of the independent and dependent variables therefore should address several issues. Is there a clear specification of these variables? Is the anticipated cause-effect relationship stated clearly in the hypothesis? Are the assumptions of the relationships between the two variables reasonable (i.e., is it reasonable to believe that the independent variable can affect the dependent variable)? Is more than one independent variable tested?

In addition to the independent and dependent variables in the research hypothesis, the independent variables in the rival hypotheses that the researcher has designated as possible explanations of the research question should be identified (see Chapters 6 and 12). These variables have the potential to qualify, modify, or explain any obtained relationship between the independent and dependent variables. Attempts to control for the possible effects of rival hypotheses through the study's design should be examined in the evaluation. If they are not controlled for, a variety of other variables, rather than those in the research hypothesis, may be the true cause of change in the dependent variable.

The Researcher's Orientation

The next part of the evaluation of the problem seeks to identify any biases of the researcher. What is the orientation (theoretical and otherwise) of the researcher? What is the stated purpose or goal of the study? Why was it undertaken? How is the researcher's conceptualization of the research question or hypothesis under investigation different from those in similar studies? What information was sought? How are the findings to be utilized, and who is to utilize them? The study's auspices should also be clarified. Who sponsored the study? Where was it conducted?

These questions are important in the identification of possible biasing effects. For example, an administrator may want (or need) to prove that a particular social service program is effective, or a researcher may hope to prove that a particular social work intervention is worthwhile. If either the administrator or the researcher becomes directly involved in the research process, intentionally or unintentionally, the supervision of the intervention or the collection of the data could influence or alter the study's results. Their presence in the intervention would emerge as a potential bias that would affect the independent-dependent variable relationship.

In addition, the reasonableness of the researcher's assumptions about the study—both methodological and conceptual—should be assessed. These assumptions are propositions that are taken for granted ("given") in a study and usually are not subject to investigation in that study. They can be evaluated by reviewing other knowledge concerning the study's problem area. An example is a study in which it was assumed that group therapy is a universal phenomenon, independent of profession, style of group therapist, and so on; thus group therapy was "whatever group therapists do." The reasonableness of this assumption is open to question on the basis of information provided in the report regarding the differential effects of the therapists' personality conditions.

The problem area thus should be evaluated in terms of the researcher's conceptualization of the study and possible biases. A study may be conceptualized very thoroughly and still be subject to question on theoretical or ideological grounds; in addition, researcher bias may help to explain or define methodological weaknesses or strengths of the methods.

METHOD CRITERIA

The method category of the framework for evaluation is concerned with the methodology of the study—the research design and data collection techniques that are at the heart of any study. The criteria in this category concern such research concepts as outcome measures, random assignment, and internal and external validity. The 35 criteria to be rated in evaluating the method category of a research report are given in Figure 22.2.

The Outcome Measures

Examination of the type of outcome (or criterion) measures adopted to indicate change in the dependent variable is one of the most important steps in the evaluation of the data collection techniques for a study. Statement of the research question and adoption of a research design should reflect the kind of change that has been hypothesized, or, at least, the kind of changes or outcomes to be examined. In the specification of the outcome measures, the

	Low		High	
1. Clarity of the specification of the kinds of changes desired	1	2	3	4
2. Appropriateness of the outcome measures in relation to the purpose of the study	1	2	3	4
3. Degree of validity of the outcome measures	1	2	3	4
4. Degree of reliability of the outcome measures	1	2	3	4
5. Degree of use of a variety of outcome measures (e.g., subjective and objective)	1	2	3	4
6. Clarity about how data were collected	1	2	3	4
7. Clarity about who collects data	1	2	3	4
8. Degree of avoidance of error in process of data collection	1	2	3	4
9. Clarity of the statement of the research design	1	2	3	4
10. Adequacy of the research design (re: purpose)	1	2	3	4
11. Clarity and adequacy of time between pretest and posttest	1	2	3	4
12. Appropriateness in the use of control group(s)	1	2	3	4
13. Appropriateness in the use of random assignment procedures	1	2	3	4
14. Appropriateness in the use of matching procedures	1	2	3	4
15. Experimental and control group equivalency at pretest	1	2	3	4
16. Degree of control for effects of history	1	2	3	4
17. Degree of control for effects of maturation	1	2	3	4
18. Degree of control for effects of testing	1	2	3	4
19. Degree of control for effects of instrumentation	1	2	3	4
20. Degree of control for statistical regression	1	2	3	4
21. Degree of control for differential selection of clients	1	2	3	4
22. Degree of control for differential mortality	1	2	3	4
23. Degree of control for temporal bias	1	2	3	4
24. Degree of control for integrity of treatment	1	2	3	4
25. Ability to distinguish causal variable	1	2	3	4
26. Degree of control for interaction effects	1	2	3	4
27. Overall degree of success in maximizing internal validity (16-26)	1	2	3	4
28. Adequacy of sample size	1	2	3	4
29. Degree of accuracy in defining the population	1	2	3	4
30. Degree of adequacy in the representativeness of the sample	1	2	3	4
31. Degree of control for reactive effects of testing (interaction with independent variable)	1	2	3	4
32. Degree of control for interaction between selection and experimental variable	1	2	3	4
33. Degree of control for special effects of experimental arrangements	1	2	3	4
34. Degree of control for multiple-treatment interference	1	2	3	4
35. Overall degree of success in maximizing external validity	1	2	3	4

Figure 22.2   Criteria for Assessing Method Category of a Research Report

conceptual or empirical basis for selecting the desired types of change should be identified.

For example, if a study of casework intervention focuses on positive changes in family functioning, this section of the research report should clarify how these changes are to be identified; that is, the outcome measures utilized should be specified. The evaluation is concerned with whether the outcome measures selected are clearly defined and described in regard to how they are to be applied and their potential limitations.

In addition, the measures (or measuring instruments) selected by the researcher should be appropriate to the study's purpose (see Part III). In a study to examine the effects of casework intervention on family interaction, for example, individual psychological tests might not be appropriate outcome measures. To verify the appropriateness of the measures, the validity and reliability for each outcome measure utilized should be clearly stated.

Measurement reliability has been defined in this text as the degree of consistency provided by the measuring instrument. Sufficient reliability must be established so the results of the study can be generalized from the sample to the population or to another research situation. The methods for establishing reliability described in Chapter 8 are the test-retest, alternate-forms, and split-half methods including coefficient alpha. The higher the reliability, the greater is the confidence that can be placed in the reliability of the measure. Measurement validity has been defined as the extent to which a measuring instrument actually measures what it is supposed to measure and does so accurately. The three major types of validity described in Chapter 8—content, criterion, and construct—are related to the purposes of measures.

Use of a variety of outcome measures is preferable because change tends to be multidimensional. Extensive examples in the literature examining the effects of social work interventions show that client change may surface in numerous, often unrelated, areas. A major client change demonstrated in a projective test may not be reflected in actual behavioral change, and clients' subjective self-reports of improvement frequently are not reflected in other, more objective measures. Outcome measures therefore should involve both objective measures, such as behavior ratings or physiological indicators, and subjective measures, such as self-report questionnaires, whenever possible.

The Data Collection

In reporting the data collection procedures for the study, it should be made clear who collects the data, how and when they are collected, and how errors are avoided (see Part V). Analysis of this aspect of the study's method is primarily directed toward author objectivity and data reliability. Specifically, the controls for interviewer, test, and judgment biases in data collection should be examined. In a study to assess casework effectiveness, for example, social workers were requested to provide basic data on their clients' progress in the experimental group, while a group of "trained researchers" provided data on the control group (Geismar & Krisberg, 1967). Such differential procedures present an obvious source of potential bias.

The Research Design

The method for collecting and analyzing data is usually specified in the research design. The design utilized, the methodological issues involved in using the design, and the methods specified for handling data collection and analysis should be clearly stated in the report. The general adequacy of the research design with regard to the purpose of the study should also be evaluated. If, for example, the purpose of the study is to evaluate the effectiveness of a specific casework technique, an exploratory research design would be inappropriate.

If the research design involves multiple measurements of the dependent variable, the adequacy of the time provided between the pretest and posttest should be examined. The question is whether the desired changes could logically be expected to have taken place over the length of time allowed. If the period is fairly brief, a judgment must be made of the likelihood that the posttest results were affected by the pretest. Participants may remember the answers from the pretest and answer the posttest accordingly, or they may be less interested, less motivated, or less anxious during the second testing.

The Use of Control Groups and Group Assignment

Another consideration in analyzing a research design is whether control or comparison groups are utilized. If one or more control groups is used, the author should identify the type of control. Types of control groups include untreated groups, waiting lists, terminations, attention/placebo groups, and groups receiving other treatment. Probably the most desirable control group situation represents some combination, such as an untreated group whose characteristics are comparable to those of the experimental group, plus a group that receives another form of social work treatment, plus an attention/placebo group. The strengths and weaknesses of the types of control groups selected must also be considered.

Because control or comparison groups are desirable in most social work studies to rule out the alternative explanations for the independent variables, it is important to evaluate how the members of the experimental and control groups are assigned (see Chapter 12). Group assignment is sometimes done on a haphazard, arbitrary, or post hoc basis, but methods such as random assignment or matching can be used to avoid sampling error.

Random assignment is the preferred method of group assignment. It should ensure that every individual has the same chance of being assigned to either group. Ideally and theoretically, the experimental and control groups should consist of individuals who differ only with regard to the group assignment; that is, some are assigned to the experimental group and others are assigned to the control group. In this sense, the term "random" is not synonymous with arbitrary. Rather, it refers to strict scientific procedures for the assignment of individuals to two or more groups.

In matching, group assignment is made on the basis of similarities among individuals on certain meaningful variables, particularly client characteristics that may be expected to affect the outcome of the study in some way. Matching may be done on the basis of pretest scores, age, gender, type of client problem, and so on. Matching is also initiated to ensure an equal distribution of any given variable in both groups, as opposed to a priori, individual-by-individual matching. The main problem with matching is that it does not control for differences between the groups on any other variables that could affect the outcome (i.e., that are not matched).

Another form of group assignment combines matching and randomization procedures. For example, individuals can be screened in advance and matched according to meaningful variables, and then randomly assigned to either the experimental or control group. This allows for equivalency between groups at the pretest occasion, although each individual still has an equal chance of being assigned to either the experimental or control group.

With any method of group assignment, it is important to determine whether the two groups are equivalent at the beginning of the study. Differences between the groups existing at the beginning could be responsible for differences in the results at the end. Within a certain probability level, pretest equivalence can be achieved through randomization. Group equivalency can also be determined following assignment by pretests of the groups.

Internal Validity of the Research Design

Random assignment and the appropriate use of control groups is the best method for handling problems of internal validity. Evaluation of the control of extraneous variables allows for conclusions that the introduction of the independent variable alone can be identified as the cause of change in the dependent variable.

Extraneous variables that must be controlled for are called threats to internal validity. Those discussed in Chapter 12 include the effects of history, maturation, testing, instrumentation, statistical regression, differential selection, mortality, and interaction effects. Others are temporal bias, integrity of treatment, and ability to distinguish the causal variable. A review of these threats is useful in evaluating the report's research methodology.

The effects of history occur when anything happening outside the study produces changes in the dependent variable. These effects are due to changes in the environment, such as a client getting a job or resolving family problems, that produce changes in the dependent variable that cannot be attributed to the introduction of the independent variable. They are the most plausible rival hypotheses for explaining changes when appropriate controls are not (or cannot be) used. A similar variable is the effects of maturation, which include physiological or psychological processes that may occur in individuals due to the passage of time. For example, maturation occurs as clients grow older or go through different developmental stages.

The pretest can contribute to poor internal validity by influencing scores on the posttest. These are the effects of testing. Testing can be controlled to some extent under one or both of the following conditions:

1. The time between the two tests is long enough to reduce memory of the first test.
2. Both experimental and control groups are subject to the same testing conditions.

Closely related to testing biases are the effects of instrumentation, or instrument error or decay. Instrument decay is due to a change in either the measuring instrument or the users of the instrument (e.g., observers may become more sensitive).

A particularly important threat to internal validity to control for is statistical regression, or regression to the mean. Especially within groups selected on the basis of their extreme high or low scores, the scores tend to change over time by moving toward the mean. Change of this type is predictable and is more likely to be due to statistical regression than to the independent variable. Statistical regression is controlled for by random assignment to control groups. For example, groups of clients who score poorly on certain psychological tests are often provided with treatment, but they tend to change whether or not they receive treatment. If there is no control group for comparison purposes, it is tempting to conclude that such groups receive treatment and then show improvement as a result.

Another threat to internal validity is differential selection, or bias in the selection of members of experimental and control groups so the potential for change differs. The principles of randomization aid in preventing this threat. A related threat is differential mortality, which occurs when one group loses more members than the other group during the study. For example, in a study that compared the effectiveness of groups of professional and nonprofessional practitioners, the author concluded that the nonprofessionals were favored on the outcome measures at the end of the treatment. But though the groups started with similar sample sizes, by the end of the study the nonprofessionals had lost 21 percent of their clients and the professionals had lost only 3.4 percent, so the groups were no longer comparable (Poser, 1966). Perhaps the only conclusion that could be drawn was that the professionals maintained a lower client dropout rate than the nonprofessionals.

To control for temporal bias, all groups involved in the study should be measured at precisely the same time. If, as in the example above, two groups of practitioners are being compared, the frequency and length of contacts with their respective clients also should be similar.

Integrity of treatment is a threat that could operate in several ways. Social workers may not use the treatment techniques they have agreed to provide for the study, for example, or they may vary their treatments from client to client, such as using behavior therapy with one client, insight therapy with another, and so on. This would make it difficult to conclude why any observed improvements took place.

Inability to distinguish the experimental or causal variable is a threat because even in a study with random assignment and a control group, it is not always possible to rule out a range of possible alternative explanations in addition to the standard threats to internal validity. Observed differences between groups may be due to attention; heightened expectations; the treatment itself; practitioner's style, enthusiasm, or interpersonal skills; a placebo effect; and so on. Such alternative explanations can be addressed by adding additional groups to the study (e.g., an attention/placebo group, alternative treatments), by using factorial designs that control for interpersonal skill differences, or by logical analysis by both the author and the evaluator as to the plausibility of explanations of observed changes.

A final threat to internal validity is a result of interaction between any of the other threats. This occurs, for example, when the selection of the experimental and control groups is not equivalent in terms of other possible threats such as maturation or regression. An example would be comparing "normal" with distressed clients, or clients with extremely negative pretest scores to clients in another group with far more positive pretest scores. Independent of the treatment, the group with more negative scores ("distressed") would be expected to change far more than the other group ("normal").

Once the study has been evaluated by these criteria, a summary judgment as to the overall success in maximizing internal validity is required.

External Validity of the Research Design

Another key concern in evaluating a study has to do with its external validity. This refers to limitations on the extent to which findings can be generalized to individuals, agencies, environmental conditions, or measures other than those involved in the study being evaluated. The main considerations in assessing external validity are the representativeness of the sample, internal validity of the design (without good internal validity, it would be unclear what could be generalized), and replication.

Sampling Considerations

In assessing generalizability, sampling plans and procedures (see Chapter 11) must be taken into account. The adequacy of the study's sample size is related to the description of the exact population for the study, an entire set or universe of all individuals or elements (objects or events) that conform to some designated set of specifications. The sample consists of elements or members drawn from the population in order to find out something about the population in general. If the study uses an extremely small sample as representative of a large population, the grounds for selecting such a sample should be clearly stated and justifiable. Few social work research studies can claim a representative random sample drawn from either clients or social workers, the principal populations used, because they usually are too large and complex. Nevertheless, every study must be evaluated in terms of the ways in which the author attempts to deal with sample selection.

The essence of external validity is the degree to which the sample is representative of the population from which it was drawn. The most obvious approach lies with the sampling procedure. The relevant populations to which the generalizations are to be made must be clearly defined, and, in the optimal study, samples must be randomly drawn from them. Usually this is very difficult, but without random selection, generalizability cannot be ensured.

Other limitations might be placed on the sample. For example, a study might have a limited sample in regard to size, time, place, type of problem, demographics, and so on. Such limitations must be reported so the adequacy of the sampling procedures can be evaluated. There may be genuine attempts to obtain representative samples of some client groups, for example, but attempts to obtain representative samples of practitioners are rare. A study may focus on social workers selected from a single agency, or graduate social work students may be used as substitutes for experienced social workers. Generalizations from such studies are constrained by failure to obtain a representative sample of practicing social workers.

Representativeness can also be addressed by testing or comparing the sample with other known samples from the same population or with data from the population as a whole. Tests or inventories may be administered to the sample group, or demographic data can be used. These data can then be compared with the known facts about the population of concern. For example, the age, gender, and socioeconomic status of social workers studied can be compared with the demographic characteristics of other social workers at one or more agencies or with social workers nationally, using NASW data. Or social workers might complete inventories of therapeutic attitudes and preferences, which could then be compared to similar inventories completed by other workers.

Threats to External Validity

The threats to external validity described in Chapter 12 include pre-test-treatment interaction, selection-treatment interaction, specificity of variables, reactive effects, multiple-treatment interference, and researcher bias. These threats are discussed here in terms of perhaps the most common research situation in social work, where the independent variable is the treatment or intervention provided to clients, and the dependent variable is the client's outcome.

The threat of pretest-treatment interaction has to do with the possibility of reactive or interactive effects between the testing and the independent or experimental variable. The pretest may have made clients more sensitized to the treatment, so that changes in treatment effectiveness occur. This may mean that results would be generalizable only to clients who had been pretested and thereby sensitized. The best method to control for such effects is to choose outcome measures that are not specifically related to the treatment, such as everyday performance or a behavioral criterion like the frequency of marital arguments during the month prior to treatment.

The threats of selection-treatment interaction and specificity of variables involve a possible interaction between selection of the sample (clients) and the independent experimental variable (treatment). In these circumstances, special characteristics of the sample selected for treatment could interact with the treatment and change its effects. For example, if a study shows that middle-class children respond well to verbal therapy, it cannot be assumed that all children, or children from low-income groups, will also respond well to this type of treatment. Rather, special characteristics of the sample such as socioeconomic status (rather than verbal therapy) could have produced the results. Generalizability would therefore be limited to groups similar to those in the study being evaluated.

The possibility of reactive effects due to experimental arrangements refers to the fact that knowledge of being in a study may have special meaning to some research participants, and their performance or reactions therefore may be atypical. An example would be an experimental group that becomes more productive as a result of knowing they were taking part in a study. Another example would be changes due to clients' expectations. The fact that the clients had sought and obtained services could lead to a change in the outcome which would be independent of (or sometimes prior to) treatment. There are examples of numerous other reactive effects in Huck, Cormier, and Bounds (1974).

Reactive effects can also be due to the perhaps unintentional communication of the researcher's orientation. This results in researcher bias, another threat based on the tendency of researchers to find the results they expect or want to find. The researcher's knowledge of which clients are in the experimental group and which clients are in the control group may be enough to alter the study's results.

With all of these effects, limits are placed on generalizability unless the groups to which the findings are to be generalized also are exposed to such effects. Thus reactions to experimental arrangements could preclude generalizations regarding the effects of the intervention to any client who was not exposed to the treatment in experimental situations.

Lack of control for multiple-treatment interference requires caution in making generalizations in order to avoid commingling results of successive treatments. Multiple-treatment interference occurs, for example, when clients in all groups receive other interventions, such as medication or an institutional regimen, in addition to the experimental intervention. The effects of the additional treatment may either not be erasable or may have some sort of enhancing or depressing effect on the intervention. Generalizations therefore would pertain only to those groups that receive all the same treatments.

Once the analysis of all these criteria has been completed, a judgment as to the overall degree of control for external validity can be made. At the least, both the independent and dependent variables should be described clearly enough to allow for replication.

FINDINGS CRITERIA

The findings section of the framework for evaluation concentrates on assessing the ways in which the data collected for a study are analyzed and conclusions are derived. The appropriateness of the statistical procedures and tests used is an important consideration in this category. Figure 22.3 summarizes the six criteria to be evaluated in assessing the findings category of a research report.

The first task in this evaluation is to determine whether or not manipulation of the independent variable was adequate to influence the dependent variable (see Chapter 12). In a sense, this is assessing the strength of the independent variable. It can be accomplished by examining the intensity of the independent variable, duration of time over which the variable was presented, frequency of treatment sessions, and so forth.

Related to this factor is the persistence of the outcome, or change, over time. Evaluation of appropriateness of the outcome measures (the second criterion for evaluating method) might include the suitability of the length of time chosen for the follow-up. This should be based, at least in part, on the rationale for this decision presented in the study.

Data Collection and Statistical Procedures

Overall, the data collected must be adequate to provide evidence for the testing of the hypothesis. They also should be of sufficient quantity and quality, in both the experimental and control groups, to allow further evaluation. Basic judgments about the statistics utilized in the study include the clarity of presentation of the statistics or statistical tests used and the appropriateness of the statistical controls. As noted in Chapter 12, statistical procedures are often used to control for the intervening variables in alternative hypotheses. For example, if it is not possible to match the experimental and control groups on potentially meaningful variables, they should be controlled by statistical means, using procedures such as analysis of covariance.

The Statistical Analysis

Analysis of the appropriateness of the statistics utilized in the study reported depends on the type of data collected and the type of conclusions derived from the data. This analysis requires a greater knowledge of statistics than can be provided in this text, though some general concepts have been discussed. The statistical concepts and tests referred to in this section are introduced to give an idea of the possible content of this part of the study report. The five topics included in this criterion cover different aspects of the statistical analysis.

Every statistic assumes a particular level of measurement; for example, interval and ratio measurement are necessary for the use of parametric tests such as analysis of variance. Information on the level of measurement should be the first step in determining whether the statistics used are appropriate for the conditions of the study.

Analysis of the use of between-groups procedures involves consideration of the type of conclusions the author attempts to draw from the data. If the conclusions are regarding cause and effect, a between-groups statistic designed to test hypotheses in which the independent variable is introduced to the experimental group and not to the comparison or control group should be used. The statistic should indicate a probability or significance level, which allows for a conclusion regarding whether or not observed differences between the groups are due to chance and are likely to reflect true differences in the populations from which the groups, or samples, were drawn. Statistically significant results provide a basis for drawing inferences about causality.

In an explanatory study, for example, a t-test between the groups or analysis of variance should be used rather than a correlational statistic such as Pearson's r, the correlation coefficient, because these statistical techniques provide information that allows an inference regarding cause and effect. However, use of a statistic provided by a particular test or procedure in itself cannot generate causal conclusions, since the nature of the design and the research question being studied are the critical factors in making this judgment.

Between-group measures are also needed for statistics used in inferring cause-effect relationships between or among variables. One of the most common statistical errors is to compute two separate correlated t-tests for the differences between pretest and posttest scores within the experimental group

	Low			High
1. Adequacy of the manipulation of the independent variable	1	2	3	4
2. Appropriateness in the use of follow-up measures	1	2	3	4
3. Adequacy of data to provide evidence for testing of hypotheses	1	2	3	4
4. Clarity in reporting statistics	1	2	3	4
5. Appropriateness in the use of statistical controls	1	2	3	4
6. Appropriateness of statistics utilized				
a. Statistics appropriate to level of measurement	1	2	3	4
b. Use of between-groups procedures	1	2	3	4
c. Multivariate statistics used appropriately	1	2	3	4
d. Post hoc tests used appropriately	1	2	3	4
e. Overall appropriateness of statistics	1	2	3	4

Figure 22.3 Criteria for Assessing Findings Category of a Research Report

and within the control group. If the differences are statistically significant for the experimental group but not for the control group, the researcher might conclude that the independent variable has had an effect, though no direct statistical comparison between the two groups was calculated. A study of nonprofessional social workers clearly demonstrates this effect (Fischer & Greenberg, 1972).

In a comparison of three groups to assess the effects of different methods of training, two groups showed statistically significant pretest-to-posttest mean changes within the groups on two different outcome variables. An overall analysis of variance between the groups, however, failed to show statistically significant differences among the three groups.

Analysis of the use of multivariate statistics involves an understanding of the number of outcome measures in the study. For a variety of reasons, discussed in detail in Glisson and Fischer (1982), when more than one outcome measure is involved in a study, and especially when those measures are correlated, repeated use of standard univariate statistics—such as t-tests, analyses of variance or covariance, and nonparametric statistics—are inappropriate.

Essentially, these statistics are likely to produce Type I errors (finding "statistically significant" results that actually are due to chance) or Type II errors (not finding statistical significance when, in fact, it is present). In such cases, more sophisticated multivariate statistics should be used. These include Hotelling's T^2 for two groups and multivariate analysis of variance and covariance for two or more groups.

The choice of univariate or multivariate statistics is complicated to assess. Multivariate statistics require a substantially larger sample than univariate statistics, if they are to be used with any degree of reliability. Both the use of univariate statistics with more than one outcome measure and the use of multivariate statistics with a small sample can be reasons for lack of confidence in the obtained results.

Another aspect of the statistical analysis is the appropriate use of post hoc tests. Whenever three or more groups are involved in one of the independent variables and a significant effect is found on the primary test (such as a statistically significant F-test), specialized post hoc, follow-up or multiple-comparison tests must be used to determine which group is significantly different from which other groups. The use of standard t-tests to examine these differences is inappropriate and likely to result in Type I error. Several post hoc tests are available for this task, including Fisher's LSD, Duncan's new multiple-range test, Newman-Keuls, Tukey's HSD, and Scheffei's test.

Once these four subcriteria have been evaluated, a judgment can be made as to the fifth criterion—overall appropriateness of the statistics utilized.

DISCUSSION CRITERIA

The discussion category of a study report gives the researcher's ideas about the meaning and implications of the findings. Among the 14 criteria to be evaluated in this category (see Figure 22.4), the first is the extent to which the data support the research hypothesis and the kinds of qualifications stated in the report. For example, it may be suggested that when additional variables were introduced (e.g., age, gender), the strength of the findings was diminished. In fact, the findings may have been weakened when such variables were introduced, or they may have been applicable in only certain select circumstances.

An example is a study in which casework effectiveness was assessed (Beck & Jones, 1973). The authors said "about seven of ten" clients and caseworkers reported global evaluations of "much better" or "somewhat better." They concluded, therefore, that the casework intervention was effective. However, when the clients were asked why they terminated (discontinued) treatment, only 30.6 percent said the "problem was solved or less stressful," and only 32 percent reported overall evaluations of "much better." These figures may more accurately depict client sentiments regarding treatment than the authors' 7:10 ratio for both clients and caseworkers.

Consistency in using the data should also be assessed. The conclusions should be consistent with the data, and there should be uniformity in the data presented in the tables and in the text. This calls for a careful review of the description of the data in the report. Researcher bias, a threat to external validity described in the method section, may show up in the design or data analyses, or in inadequate or erroneous interpretations or conclusions drawn from the data. Results that do not support the hypothesis also should be dealt with, to ensure that such data are not simply ignored.

		Low		High	
1.	Degree to which data support the hypothesis	1	2	3	4
2.	Extent to which the researcher's conclusions are consistent with data	1	2	3	4
3.	Degree of uniformity between tables and text	1	2	3	4
4.	Degree of researcher bias	1	2	3	4
5.	Clarity as to cause of changes in dependent variable	1	2	3	4
6.	Degree to which rival hypotheses were avoided in the design	1	2	3	4
7.	Degree to which potential rival hypotheses were dealt with in discussion	1	2	3	4
8.	Degree of control for threats to internal validity	1	2	3	4
9.	Reasonableness of opinions about implications	1	2	3	4
10.	Clarity as to meaning of change(s)	1	2	3	4
11.	Adequacy in relating findings to previous literature	1	2	3	4
12.	Adequacy of conclusions for generalizing beyond data	1	2	3	4
13.	Extent to which the research design accomplishes the purpose of the study	1	2	3	4
14.	Appropriateness in the handling of unexpected consequences	1	2	3	4

Figure 22.4   Criteria for Assessing Discussion Category of a Research Report

Conclusions About the Study

The other criteria in the discussion category address the results and implications of the study, in terms of both the researcher's conclusions and the evaluator's judgments. First to be assessed is the evidence presented regarding the degree to which change in the dependent variable is actually a function of the independent variable. A main consideration is the researcher's success in controlling threats to internal validity. If the threats to internal validity have not been successfully controlled and it still is argued that a cause-effect relationship exists, the basis and soundness of these judgments must be evaluated.

The reasonableness of the opinions stated about the implications of the study and judgments regarding the meaning of the changes found should also be assessed. The author should be clear as to the social, psychological, and professional meaning of the findings. The findings should be discussed in terms of existing norms or standards, cost effectiveness, efforts to obtain results, efficacy of the methods, and so on.

The findings and conclusions should be related to the literature, and changes in theory or methodology suggested by the results should be proposed. The adequacy of the conclusions regarding the generalizability of the findings should then be evaluated in terms of applicability of the data to different samples or populations.

Finally, the extent to which the study accomplishes its purpose as developed in the formulation of the research question or hypothesis should be evaluated. If there were unexpected consequences, the researcher should address these and attempt to determine whether they were produced by some aspect of the research design or by the research methods or treatment utilized.

UTILIZATION CONCLUSIONS CRITERIA

The final part of the evaluation of a quantitative research report consists of eight criteria for conclusions as to the utilization of knowledge gained from the study (see Figure 22.5). This calls for making judgments and decisions regarding the possible ways in which knowledge derived from the study can be applied in social work research or practice. Utilization is concerned with the relevance or meaningfulness of the study to the social work profession and the development of practical applications of the knowledge derived.

In a sense, this conclusions section of the analysis is a general summary of all the 70 previous criteria presented in the framework. Decisions regarding utilization are based on the information gathered from analyzing the problem, method, and findings, and the discussion is drawn from these analyses.

The meaningfulness of the study's findings for social work practice can be determined by assessing its major implications in terms of the dimensions of social work it addresses. These dimensions include clients, service delivery systems, methods and techniques of intervention, and qualities of social workers. Of course, a study need not be specifically conducted on social workers or their clients to be relevant to social work. Social work knowledge can be derived from numerous related fields such as anthropology, political science, clinical psychology, and sociology.

The next two criteria are concerned with the internal and external validity of the study's design and results. An overall evaluation of the soundness of the study is a summary judgment based on preceding sections of the framework. For the sake of convenience, this judgment can be based on the extent to which threats to internal validity have been avoided. It should consider the extent to which the independent variable clearly leads to the changes observed and whether it is specified clearly enough for replication. The generalizability of the study's findings, or the extent to which threats to external validity are avoided, must also be evaluated. Can similar methods be applied for different goals or purposes or with different individuals, groups, or problems? Is it reasonable to expect that positive results would ensue? The greater the internal and external validity (soundness and generalizability) of the study, the greater value it will have.

	Low		High	
1. Degree of relevance to social work practice	1	2	3	4
2. Overall soundness of the study (internal validity)	1	2	3	4
3. Degree of generalizability of the study's findings (external validity)	1	2	3	4
4. Degree to which the independent variables are accessible to control by social workers	1	2	3	4
5. Extent to which a meaningful difference would occur if the independent variable were utilized in actual social work practice situations	1	2	3	4
6. Degree of economic feasibility of the independent variable if utilized in actual social work practice situations	1	2	3	4
7. Degree of ethical suitability of the manipulation of the independent variable	1	2	3	4
8. Extent to which the research question has been addressed	1	2	3	4

Figure 22.5   Criteria for Assessing Utilization and Conclusions Categories of a Research Report

There are several additional criteria for assessing the potential utilization of reported research findings. One is the extent to which the independent variables in the study are actually accessible to control by social workers. They should be clearly identifiable (observable) and easy to manipulate (able to be affected by the social worker). If need be, as with reports of new techniques, they should also be teachable.

The difference a particular independent variable would make in social work practice if it were actually utilized also should be assessed. For example, a study might show that the use of an intervention technique successfully decreases the number of clients' eye blinks per minute. Could this technique be evaluated as involving an important goal for professional social work practice? Could the use of such a technique reasonably be expected to produce other more pervasive or more meaningful changes?

The economics of utilizing the independent variable must always be considered. Another criterion is whether it is ethically suitable to manipulate the independent variable. For example, as we have seen in Chapter 6, changes can be demonstrated under laboratory conditions that would be entirely unethical in practice with clients. An intervention technique may also appear unethical, either professionally or personally, to other social workers.

The final criterion is the extent to which the primary research question has been answered. In other words, in the typical social work research study, what kinds of social workers, working with what kinds of clients, with what kind of client problems, in what practice situations, using what techniques, derived from what theory, produced what kinds of results?

RATING THE CRITERIA

The framework for evaluation of quantitative research reports presented in Figures 22.1 through 22.5 includes a total of 78 criteria. Some are obviously far more important than others, and there is considerable overlap among them. Some criteria are actually subtopics, such as the various threats to internal and external validity listed in Figure 22.2 for the method category.

In social work as in other fields of knowledge, ideal research conditions are rarely possible, due to any number of economic, personal, political, or organizational constraints. Most researchers are forced to compromise on some of these conditions. Therefore, in the conclusions category, the overall impact of a study's deficiencies should be taken into account in judging the applicability of the knowledge derived from the study to social work research or practice. By themselves, low ratings on few if any criteria would not necessarily invalidate a study. No matter how inappropriate the statistics or how serious the design flaws, for example, the results of a study may still be useful enough to be applied. Serious flaws, however, do diminish the confidence with which such results can be viewed.

The rating of the criteria on a scale from 1 to 4 calls for careful observation and personal judgment. In some instances, the report indicates that the study either meets a criterion or it does not. For example, on Criterion 12 in Figure 22.2, a study that uses some type of control group would be rated with a 3 or 4; a study that does not would be rated with a 1 or 2. In other situations, it is necessary to decide whether or not the study "adequately" meets a given criterion. An example is deciding whether there is a sufficiently clear specification of the independent variable (Criterion 4 in Figure 22.1). In other circumstances, the relative rating will be less evaluative. For example, a study using three independent criterion measures would be rated higher on Criterion 5 in Figure 22.2 than a study using only one.

Because there are clear differences in the importance of the various criteria, the overall rating given a study may be less important than ensuring that certain criteria have been met. With an experimental or explanatory study, for example, it is more important to demonstrate appropriate use of a control group than to specify the theoretical orientation of the researcher. The implications for social work of research that meets the various criteria must always be considered.

In using this framework, one standard to consider is that if a study's results cannot be readily incorporated into the knowledge base of the social work profession, it is, for all intents and purposes, practically useless. A study may be designed and executed perfectly yet have only limited value to the profession because it does not address a meaningful problem area and the results cannot be put into practice by social workers. Utilization of results is the ultimate outcome in social work research and evaluation.

SUMMARY

In presenting a framework for the evaluation of quantitative research reports, this chapter has demonstrated how the same criteria can be used to evaluate the research studies on which the reports are based. It also has served as a summary of the main topics of the preceding 21 chapters in the text.

The framework for evaluation is built around the four parts of a research report discussed in Chapter 21—problem, method, findings, and discussion. An additional category on conclusions reflects a concern with the utilization of the knowledge derived from the study in social work practice. Criteria for evaluating each of these categories are presented in figures representing rating scales.

Part VII

From Research to Evaluation

Bruce A. Thyer

C h a p t e r   23

Single-System Designs

A TRADITIONAL RESEARCH DESIGN is a blueprint or detailed plan for how a research study is to be conducted–operationalizing variables so they can be measured, selecting a sample of interest to study, collecting data to be used as a basis for testing hypotheses, and analyzing the results. In social work research, there are two principal classifications of research designs— single-system designs, the topic of this chapter, and group designs, the topic of Chapter 12. One of the major virtues of single-system designs is that there may be no prospective blueprint, hence the designs can emerge retrospectively according to the clinical and logistical demands of the circumstances of social workers and clients. Unlike group designs (Chapter 12), single-system designs can be responsive and flexible.

CONCEPTS IN RESEARCH DESIGNS

Some multivariate research efforts try to establish causality; the relationship tested is whether one variable causes an effect in another. However, causality is not a foundation stone for the researcher, but quicksand. Theoretically, it is impossible—and it always will be impossible—to unequivocally state that X causes Y, whatever the nature of X and Y. Accordingly, some social work research studies try to produce statements such as: If X occurs, then Y will probably result. While absolute certainty about anything—let alone that X has an effect on Y—is not possible, the extent to which certainty can be approached in social work research depends on the research design used and the manner in which the study is conducted.

Before single-system and group designs can be examined separately, some further distinctions must be made in the two types of concepts on which research questions are based—variables and constants (see Chapter 6). Whereas variables are concepts that include differences in characteristics and so can vary, constants do not vary and neither cause change nor are affected by it. Therefore there cannot be a relationship between a constant and a variable.

The most important distinction among variables for research design purposes is the designation of the variables in a relationship as dependent or independent. Generally, the concept that produces the change or action is the independent variable; the concept that is affected is the dependent variable.

To make this distinction clear, consider how a social work researcher might go about examining the possibility of a relationship between X and Y. The study begins with the idea that, perhaps, if X occurs, Y will result. This idea is expressed in the form of a hypothesis that is written in such a way that it can be proven or disproven by the data collected in the course of the study. For example, the hypothesis might be that when a client enters treatment, the length of time in treatment will be related to the outcome for the client. More specifically, the hypothesis might state that the longer the client stays in treatment, the better the outcome for the client will be.

Since the intervention must occur before there can be a client outcome, the outcome is said to be dependent on the length of the intervention. In other words, the client's outcome is said to vary as the length of the intervention varies. Thus a variable whose variation is dependent on something else (in this example, the client's outcome) is called the dependent variable.

Because the intervention time can also vary, it too is a variable. However, since it is independent of any other variable, it is called the independent variable. A relationship between an independent and dependent variable is always expressed in terms of X to denote the independent variable, the active or causal concept, and Y to denote the dependent variable, the one that is affected. The hypothesis may be written in the general form: If X occurs, then Y will result. Here, X is the independent variable and Y is the dependent variable, since X must occur before Y can result.

PURPOSE OF SINGLE-SYSTEM DESIGNS

Single-system designs are used to find out what happens to a client system's situation—an individual client, a couple, a family, a group, an organization, or a community. Any of these client configurations can be studied with a single-system design. The problems social workers seek to solve for their clients are referred to as the client's target problem; the results of the intervention are called the client's outcome. These studies may also be described as single-subject designs, case-level evaluation, single-case experimentations, or idiographic research.

In short, social workers use single-system designs to monitor and evaluate clients' outcomes in the interventions with which they address clients' target problems. The strategy is to intensively study one client system, as opposed to a more cursory investigation of large numbers of participants.

The earliest reports of studies to evaluate social work practice with single-system designs appeared in the literature during the 1960s (e.g., Staats & Butterfield, 1965; R. Stuart, 1967). They are currently used by practitioners who hold a variety of theoretical orientations (see Thyer & Thyer, 1992), but the methodology is firmly grounded in the quantitative research method.

Evaluative and Experimental Questions

Depending on the level of sophistication of the research design and the validity and reliability of the data collected under it, studies of client systems based on single-system designs can be used to answer two different types of questions, evaluative and experimental. The evaluative question is: Did the client system improve during the course of social work intervention? The experimental question is: Did the client system improve because of social work intervention?

Only the second type of question can address problems in terms of causality, so it can be plausibly concluded whether X, a specific intervention, causes improvement in Y, the client's outcome. In such questions, outcome is the dependent variable, the variable being affected. The intervention is the independent variable, the variable that may bring about the improvement.

Obviously the experimental question is considerably more difficult to answer with confidence than the evaluative question. Nevertheless, it may be possible for a social worker to produce some evidence that it may have been the treatment intervention that brought about positive changes in the client's target problem. Such evidence is of obvious value in demonstrating the accountability of the practitioner and the agency. In addition, single-system designs provide help to social workers in conducting program evaluations (see following chapter) and applying for funding or research grants, as well as in clinical supervision and self-evaluation of practice.

REQUIREMENTS FOR SINGLE-SYSTEM DESIGNS

There are three general requirements for a single-system research design:

1. Objectives must be clearly stated and measurable.
2. Outcome measures used to evaluate accomplishment of the objectives must be capable of producing quantitative data that are both valid and reliable.
3. Data must be displayed appropriately.

Statement of Measurable Objectives

All interventive efforts by social workers, regardless of the level or scale of their practices, are undertaken to facilitate the achievement of measurable objectives. Often the purpose involves a change in the frequency, magnitude, or duration of a client system's target problem.

With individuals, the desired outcome may be the reduction or limitation of some aspect of the client's life, such as severity of depression or suicidal behaviors, or an improvement in other aspects, such as self-esteem or the use of contraceptives to ensure safe sex or avoid pregnancy. In marital, group, or family therapy, the goal may be to reduce the incidence of conflict or to improve communication skills. In community practice, it may be to lower the murder rate or increase the supply of adequate housing. A social policy goal may be to reduce unemployment, promote investment in inner cities, or increase college enrollments by minorities.

For research purposes, objectives at every level must be stated in terms of variables that have been operationally defined so the outcome of the intervention can be measured.

Selection of Outcome Measures

The expected outcome of a single-system design is improvement for the client system. The outcome measure, or the dependent variable, must have reliability (be able to measure the outcome accurately and consistently) and validity (be able to measure what it is supposed to). It must also be a measure that can be used consistently. The concepts of reliability and validity of measurement instruments were discussed more fully in Chapter 8, and the selection of outcome measures to assure validity and reliability in instrument design and construction were discussed in Chapters 9 and 10.

In selecting outcome measures, the social work researcher is limited to assessing one or more of only three possible domains: the actual observable behaviors of a client system, verbal reports obtained from clients or significant others, and physiological measures such as heart rate, the results of drug or alcohol screening tests, weight records, and blood sugar and blood pressure levels. All three can produce variables measured in quantitative terms.

The value of any single-system design depends almost exclusively on the appropriateness of the dependent variable selected (see Bloom, Fischer, & Orme, 1999).

Graphic Display of Data

The data obtained from studies conducted following single-system designs are almost always presented in a simple graphic format. This chapter presents 10 examples of such data displays in Figures 23.1 through 23.10.

Conventionally, the dimension of time (sessions, days, weeks) is shown on the horizontal axis, and the outcome measure is scaled along the vertical axis. If the design has various phases, they are separated on the graph by dashed vertical lines. Data points should stand out from the lines that connect them and should be connected only within phases, not between them. Each phase should have a label (e.g., "Baseline," "A Phase," "Treatment 1").

The *Journal of Applied Behavior Analysis* provides excellent examples of single-system designs in graphic format and, periodically, detailed instructions on the preparation of such graphs. Commercially available computer programs that provide graphic capabilities and can save much time also are available.

SINGLE-SYSTEM EVALUATIVE DESIGNS

The two types of questions addressed by single-system designs—evaluative and experimental—form the basis for categorizing these designs into two major types. This and the following section describe various single-system evaluative and experimental designs and illustrate them with examples and graphic displays.

Two of the principal single-system designs used to evaluate social work practice are the *B* design and the *AB* design. Both provide answers to the evaluative question, Did the client system improve during the course of social work intervention?

The *B* Design

In the *B* design, systematic assessment of the outcome measure(s) and implementation of the intervention begin simultaneously. Repeated measurements are taken while the treatment continues, and at the end of the treatment period the data are depicted on a simple graph. Visual inspection of this graph permits the social worker to make inferences as to whether or not the client's target problem has improved over the treatment period.

The *B* design indicates whether the level of the client's target problem is changing in the desired direction. This alone is an important piece of information; if the target problem is not changing in the way the social worker anticipated, other interventions can be considered. The *B* design also provides for the systematic collection of data in relatively simple form that can provide feedback to both social workers and clients regarding the achievement of treatment objectives. Graphs also can be used by agency supervisors to supplement or replace other methods of presenting clinical data.

Example 1: Treatment for Childhood Bedwetting

An example of a study to evaluate client outcomes with a *B* design included a treatment intervention package for enuretic (bedwetting) children. The package consisted of a bell and pad alarm device, in addition to family counseling (Sluckin, 1989).

The client was a six-year-old boy named Brian who lived with his mother, who was blind. Brian had never achieved nighttime urinary continence, although he had been dry during the day since he was three years old, and his bedwetting was having a negative impact on both him and his mother. A simple *B* design was used because a design requiring a prospective baseline (such as the *AB* design, to be discussed next) would have meant a delay in initiating treatment.

The mother was loaned a bell and pad alarm device to be used at home with Brian, and its operation was fully explained to her. The outcome measure was the number of episodes of nighttime bedwetting per week, recorded by the mother and turned in at the weekly family counseling sessions. Over the course of six weeks, bedwetting declined from about 30 times a week to no episodes at all. These results are depicted in the *B* design format in Figure 23.1.

From the data in this figure, it can be concluded that the client's target problem had indeed improved (been reduced) over the course of treatment. However, it could not be justifiably claimed that this improvement was caused by the treatment intervention package. Alternative explanations (rival hypotheses) for this outcome were possible, including the possibility of spontaneous remission, maturational factors, unknown biological variables, and other psychosocial factors.

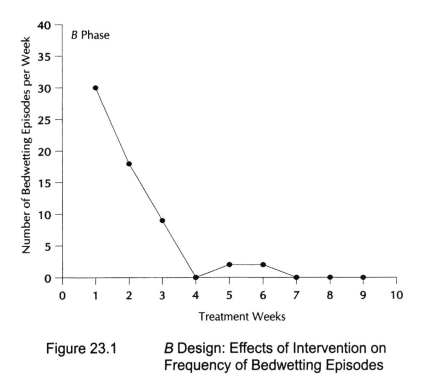

Figure 23.1   *B* Design: Effects of Intervention on
Frequency of Bedwetting Episodes

Thus the *B* design is usually incapable of producing causal knowledge; it cannot answer the experimental question of whether the client improved because of the treatment. It is, however, highly useful in answering the evaluative question of whether the client did improve over the course of treatment.

Example 2: Treatment for Anxiety Disorder

Another example of a *B* design involved the treatment of a client, Donald, who had a severe fear of enclosed spaces (Thyer, 1987). With a social worker, Donald agreed to a program of graduated exposure to anxiety-evoking situations as the initial treatment intervention.

Three outcome measures were selected: a measure of Donald's overt behavior (how many minutes he was willing to remain locked in a small closet), a physiological measure (maximum heart rate during each session in the closet), and a self-report measure (Donald's self-rating of anxiety on a scale from 0 to 100). The first treatment session was preceded by several assessment and relationship-building sessions.

Donald was asked to step into the closet, which contained a comfortable chair, and to specify the time period during which he was willing to have the social worker close and lock the door. The verbal contract between them was that the door would be unlocked after the agreed-upon time, but not before. A portable pulse monitor was used to record Donald's maximum heart rate for each such trial, and he was to rate the level of his anxiety (0 = calm, 100 = panic) after each trial.

The results of the first 14 trials of this treatment approach are depicted in Figure 23.2. For the first trial, Donald agreed to remain in the closet for only 30 seconds. He rated his anxiety level at 80 percent, and his highest heart rate, as recorded by the pulse monitor, was 128 beats per minute.

When Donald was praised for his bravery and asked if he was willing to try again, he agreed to another 30-second interval. For the third trial, however, he agreed to a full 60 seconds, and the remaining 11 trials proceeded without incident for increasingly longer periods.

At the end of the first 14 trials, the data in Figure 23.2 indicated that the treatment intervention seemed to be working. The client went from being willing to sit in the closet for only 30 seconds to remaining in it for 10 minutes. His self-rating for anxiety considerably decreased over the 14 trials; his heart rate, while declining somewhat, remained slightly elevated.

After each trial the data were recorded and shared with Donald, who was encouraged to continue the treatment by the systematic changes occurring literally before his eyes. The social worker also used the data during weekly supervision meetings to support the continued application of this treatment intervention. Treatment eventually was moved out of the office to locations of significance in Donald's life, such as elevators.

In this example of a *B* design, as in the first one, the intent was to determine if the client system (in this case, Donald) was improving, not if the social work intervention could be credited with bringing about the improvement.

The *AB* Design

The *AB* design to evaluate client system outcomes, like the *B* design, requires a valid and reliable outcome measure that is amenable to repeated assessment. This design, however, calls for assessing the client system's target problem several times before the intervention begins.

There are two phases in *AB* designs. In the baseline period, or *A* Phase, fluctuations in the client system's target problem are monitored but no attempt is made to effect any changes in the problem. The social worker is measuring only the target problem. Interventions are carried out in the *B* Phase, which follows the baseline period.

Sometimes it is possible to conduct an *AB* design study with a retrospective baseline, for which the data are obtained from historical records, memory, or some other source of information on past events. Use of a retrospective baseline avoids the main disadvantage of the *AB* design, which is delaying an intervention in order to obtain the baseline data. If the retrospective data are

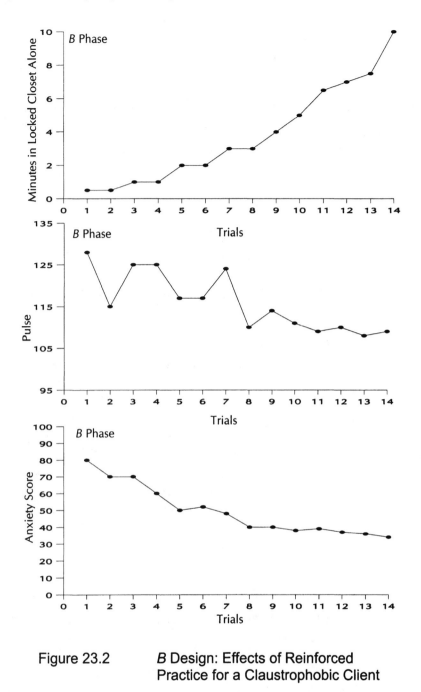

Figure 23.2   *B* Design: Effects of Reinforced
                       Practice for a Claustrophobic Client

known to be accurate, such an approach is scientifically credible. However, the reliability and validity of the data must be demonstrated, because some methods of collecting retrospective data, such as recollection, can produce inaccurate measurements (Green & Wright, 1979).

Example: Behavioral Treatment

An *AB* design was used in a study conducted by a social worker who had been employed as a program director at a large state psychiatric facility serving chronically disabled patients (Wong, Woolsey, & Gallegos, 1987). One of the patients, Priscilla, was mildly developmentally handicapped and also had an organic personality syndrome; she had been psychiatrically hospitalized over 15 times. In the words of the researchers:

> *Priscilla was utterly obnoxious and irritating to those near her. Her behavior consisted of incessant complaints, accusations, and demands, with tearful outbursts in which she would scream and cry. Actual disagreements with staff and/or imagined offenses by others could trigger these emotional scenes. Priscilla would claim that the staff and fellow patients were persecuting her, and say that her conflicts with other people would disappear if she were not locked in the unit all day long.*

The hospital staff knew that Priscilla's chances of long-term community placement were minimal as long as she engaged in such socially unacceptable behavior. An interdisciplinary treatment team was asked to implement and evaluate a treatment intervention to help improve her target problem—inappropriate social responses.

The first step was to develop a reliable and valid means of recording the client's inappropriate social responses on a daily basis. This plan was implemented for a nine-day baseline period before formal treatment was begun. Such a preliminary period of data recording permits a more objective appraisal of "where the client is at" before treatment begins than is available with the *B* design. The baseline data (Phase *A*) show if the client's target problem is stable, improving, or deteriorating at the outset of treatment. Often the graphic depiction of such data reveals subtle changes in the client's state that more informal assessments cannot ascertain.

The staff arranged for Priscilla to be allowed to move freely to and from the unit during the baseline period (the *A* Phase in Figure 23.3). After graphing the data on the number of inappropriate social responses, it was clear that Priscilla's behavior was remaining relatively stable and was not improving when she was allowed to come and go as she pleased, as she had claimed would happen. Accordingly, a treatment intervention was implemented. A graph of the daily frequency of her inappropriate social outbursts was publicly displayed, and she was restricted to the unit for a 24-hour period whenever the number of outbursts exceeded a given criterion that was gradually lowered. This treatment intervention is the *B* Phase in Figure 23.3.

The intervention continued for about two months, during which time Priscilla's social behavior dramatically improved. In the last 11 days, she had only four inappropriate outbursts (compare this to the number of outbursts recorded during the nine-day *A* Phase). It then was possible to transfer Priscilla

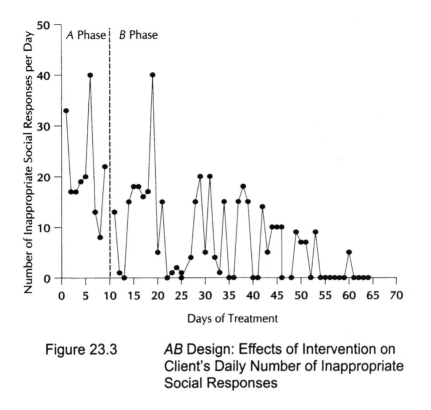

Figure 23.3   *AB* Design: Effects of Intervention on
                     Client's Daily Number of Inappropriate
                     Social Responses

to an open treatment unit, where the program was continued; she was discharged to the community two months later.

Clearly the staff was able to document substantial improvements in the client's target problem. These improvements would have been difficult to ascertain by relying on the narrative case notes usually found in such clients' charts. Graphically depicting the data produces a more "fine grain" analysis of a client's condition than the impressions of staff alone can provide.

Thus the evaluative question, "Did the client improve during the course of social work treatment?" was satisfactorily answered. The experimental question cannot be responded to. Certainly the treatment helped Priscilla acquire skills in self-control, but changes in her diet, health status, medication regimen, or ward milieu could account in part for these improvements. It is possible that she suffered from a cyclic type of disorder, and it was just a coincidence that she began to improve when the treatment intervention began. Where single-system designs are used for routine purposes in practice, such considerations may be left to research methodologists. The needs of most social workers can be satisfied by simply answering the evaluative question.

SINGLE-SYSTEM EXPERIMENTAL DESIGNS

A variety of single-system designs can be used to answer the experimental question in social work practice and research: Did the client system improve because of social work intervention? Four examples are discussed in this section: (1) the *ABAB* design, (2) the *BAB* design, (3) the *BCBC* design, and (4) the multiple-baseline design. These designs are called experimental because they may permit causal inferences to some degree.

Controlling the Threats to Internal Validity

The purpose of doing studies based on single-system experimental designs, as with "ideal" experiments, is to determine whether the researcher can appropriately draw the inference that the independent variable (the intervention) is the plausible cause of change in the dependent variable (the client system's outcome). This involves the concept of the internal validity of the design—the extent to which it can demonstrate that any changes in the dependent variable would result from the independent variable and from no other plausible factors (see Chapter 12).

The process of logical inference employed in experimental single-system designs follows what may be called "the principle of unlikely successive coincidences." With the evaluative designs described above, in most cases it cannot be clearly demonstrated that it was the treatment intervention that produced the improvement in the client system's target problem. Any number of other explanations (referred to as rival or alternative hypotheses) could account for the same improvement.

The possibilities include spontaneous improvement, maturation effects, or changes in other aspects of the client's life, such as medication or a new job. Such factors are known as threats to internal validity; the various types are identified and discussed in Chapter 12. These threats can be minimized in an *AB* design—which has a baseline (the *A* Phase) and which tracks a target problem that is known to be resistant to change—but they cannot be eliminated.

Experimental single-system designs attempt to control for rival hypotheses by demonstrating that there was more than one coincidence in which treatment began and then the client system improved or in which treatment was discontinued and the client deteriorated. One such relationship may plausibly be attributable to coincidence (as in the *B* and *AB* designs), but if the researcher is able to demonstrate that there were two or more times in which improvement in a target problem began only after a given treatment was initiated, the potential relevance of rival explanations is greatly reduced. This will be demonstrated by the designs described in this section.

The *ABAB* Design

The *ABAB* experimental single-system design is also called a withdrawal design. A study using this design is conducted by first employing the evaluative *AB* design described above (a baseline period followed by an intervention phase) and then temporarily halting treatment for a second baseline period before the intervention is resumed. In effect, the *ABAB* design represents two *AB* designs in succession.

Designs such as the *ABAB* format are appropriate only when the intervention employed has readily removable or temporary effects. If the treatment provided is one that produces rapid and durable change, as in teaching a client a new social skill such as assertiveness, the effects of the treatment may not be reversible, even temporarily. Moreover, removing treatment interventions in this manner is ethically acceptable only if the client will not be put at risk.

Example 1: Contingency Management in a Group Home

An *ABAB* design was used to determine the value of a contingency management procedure in promoting exercise for psychiatrically disabled persons living in a group home (Thyer, Irvine, & Santa, 1984). The activity therapist employed by the home approached the social work consultant regarding strategies she could employ to motivate the residents to participate in an aerobic exercise program. She was trying to get them out of bed at 7:00 a.m. to watch a televised exercise program and follow along as she demonstrated the exercises and provided verbal encouragement. The heavily sedated residents were not too enthusiastic about this approach, and they either stayed in bed or simply sat on the couch watching the therapist exercise along with the television program.

The therapist and the consultant devised an alternative exercise program. A stationary exercise bicycle was acquired and set up in front of the television set, and residents were encouraged to use it. Data were collected on each resident's use of the bike, with miles ridden per day serving as the dependent variable.

There was one week of baseline observations (the A_1 Phase). In week two, the intervention was initiated by offering residents several reinforcers for riding the bike, based on their individual daily mileage records (the B_1 Phase). The reinforcers were discontinued in week three (the second baseline period, or A_2 Phase), and then reinstated in week four (the second intervention period, or B_2 Phase).

The results for one resident, David, are depicted in Figure 23.4. In the A_1 Phase, during the first week, David barely rode the bike at all. When reinforcement was provided immediately after bike riding during the B_1 Phase, his exercise quickly and substantially increased. Thus far the design conforms to

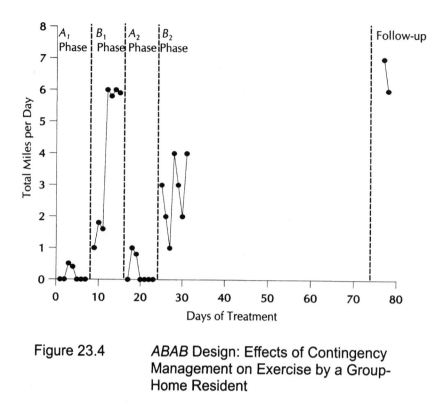

Figure 23.4   *ABAB* Design: Effects of Contingency
                     Management on Exercise by a Group-
                     Home Resident

the conventions of an *AB* design. This procedure was repeated in the A_2 Phase
and B_2 Phase. Removal of the intervention (reinforcing contingencies for riding
the bike) in the A_2 Phase and reinstatement of it in the B_2 Phase immediately
brought a corresponding change in bicycle riding.

   The "principle of unlikely successive coincidences" suggests that the only
plausible explanation for these changes was the treatment intervention. It is
unlikely that the spurts of exercise and bouts of lethargy seen in this client
coincidentally happened to occur just when the activity therapist introduced
or removed reinforcement for exercise. Likewise, these changes are unlikely to
be attributable to other changes such as diet, medications, mood, or family
visits. In other words, this example of an *ABAB* design possesses high internal
validity. Virtually all rival hypotheses that could have accounted for the positive
changes were ruled out. The hypothesis that it was the contingency management intervention that produced the changes remains.

Example 2: Effects of Treatment Lapse

   Unintended lapses in treatment can sometimes provide data that can be
retrospectively fit into an *ABAB* format. L.K. and O.L. Miller were social
workers who employed this strategy in their study of the effects of providing
prizes to participants in a citizens' self-help group (1970). The Millers were

working in a low-income community and were attempting to mobilize the residents into taking some grassroots action on certain community problems.

The citizens' group had been formed by a small number of committed community members, but attendance at the weekly meetings was low. The Millers kept accurate records of attendance and worked with the group organizers to award prizes to community members who attended meetings and participated in activities. Donated prizes of food, household goods, used appliances, toys, and clothing were provided to participants after each meeting. Group attendance and participation soared.

Then the program of prizes was inadvertently halted when one of the workers was unexpectedly hospitalized for several weeks. Attendance plummeted, and the group's activities stalled. After she resumed her duties and reinstated the prize program, the group's membership and activities quickly picked up again.

Weekly attendance figures were employed as the outcome measure, along with some qualitative data on the functioning of the self-help group. The attendance figures were retrospectively formatted into an *ABAB* design, with the second baseline (A_2 Phase) corresponding to the time the social worker was off the job. The results provided a clear experimental demonstration of the value of tangible incentives in promoting the formation and maintenance of a community-based self-help group.

Example 3: Effects of Reminders

An *ABAB* design was used to give graduate social work students some firsthand experience with single-system designs. The students were asked to unobtrusively record whether or not passengers in their automobiles buckled up their seat belts. They were given a standardized data recording form and instructed to use their own seat belts. The forms were to be turned in anonymously and tabulated on a weekly basis.

The dependent variable in this study (Thyer & Geller, 1987) was the daily percentage of passengers who were recorded as having buckled their seat belts. (Frequency data could not be used, since the numbers of passengers varied each day.) After 14 days to collect baseline data (A_1 Phase), the students were given printed stickers reading "Safety Belt Use Required in This Vehicle!" to place on the right-hand side of their dashboards. They continued to record their passengers' seat-belt use for 14 additional days while the stickers were in place (B_1 Phase). Then the stickers were removed for 14 days (A_2 Phase) and replaced for another 14 days (B_2 Phase).

The collective data reported by the class are displayed in Figure 23.5. A clear effect of the intervention (reminder stickers) is evident, with three immediate and substantial changes in reported seat-belt use following the introduction, removal, and reintroduction of the dashboard stickers. These

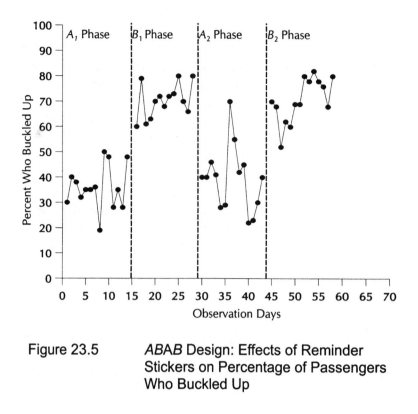

Figure 23.5   *ABAB* Design: Effects of Reminder
                     Stickers on Percentage of Passengers
                     Who Buckled Up

coincidental changes cannot reasonably be attributable to ongoing environmental events, such as media reports of automobile wrecks.

The *BAB* Design

Sometimes it is not feasible to use a baseline period (*A* Phase) for ethical
reasons; the client's target problem may be too severe or dangerous to
postpone an intervention, for example. There may also be pragmatic reasons
to avoid using a baseline period; a program to be evaluated may already be
operating. In such cases the *BAB* design is appropriate.

The *BAB* design records outcome measures repeatedly over time while an
existing program is in operation or treatment is being applied. In keeping with
the terminology used in single-system designs, this would be called the first *B*
Phase (B_1) of a *BAB* design. Then the existing program or treatment is
temporarily removed, and records are kept of the outcome measures. This
would correspond to the *A* Phase (or baseline) of a *BAB* design. In the B_2 Phase,
the program or treatment is reinstated and the effects are again observed.

Example: Evaluation of a Point System

A MSW student completing his field placement at a group home for physically handicapped and emotionally disturbed adults used a *BAB* design to evaluate the home's point system (Stocks, Thyer, & Kearsley, 1987). This system, a token economy, was being used to promote the residents' performance of adaptive living skills. For example, each day a client could earn points for engaging in functional tasks such as preparing a meal, doing laundry, or performing home chores. These points then could be exchanged for various privileges and rewards, such as tickets to local movies and extra snacks. The point system had been set up more than 10 years earlier when the group home was first established, but no efforts had been made to evaluate it systematically to determine whether it was actually serving a useful role in promoting the clients' functioning.

The average number of points earned per day by all residents of the home was used as the dependent variable. These data, graphed for seven days, formed the first *B* Phase (B_1) of a *BAB* design.

Then the residents were informed that they no longer would earn points for engaging in functional skills in daily living. Instead, they could have free access, on a noncontingent basis, to the privileges and rewards they previously had to earn. Over the next seven days, records were kept of their performance of the same functional skills and chores recorded earlier. Then the average number of points such behaviors would have earned if the point system had been in effect were totaled. This corresponds to the *A* Phase, or baseline period, of a *BAB* design.

When the manager of the group home reinstated the point system, the average number of points earned by the residents for seven days was again recorded. This final period comprised the second *B* Phase (B_2) of the *BAB* design.

The data depicted in Figure 23.6 suggest that the existing point system operating in the group home was indeed serving to motivate the residents' performance of adaptive living skills. Two changes in the data pattern support this conclusion: the decrease in points earned after the shift from the B_1 Phase to the *A* Phase, and the increase in points earned corresponding to the shift from the *A* Phase to the B_2 Phase. In a sense, the *BAB* design has twice the potential internal validity of an *AB* design alone, because two data shifts (or coincidental changes) are possible, as opposed to only one in the *AB* design.

The *BCBC* Design

Social workers sometimes need to compare the relative effectiveness of two different treatment interventions. The *BCBC* design, also referred to as the multiple-component design, can be creatively employed in such instances.

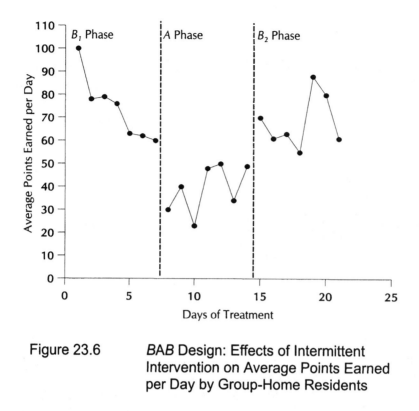

Figure 23.6   *BAB* Design: Effects of Intermittent
                     Intervention on Average Points Earned
                     per Day by Group-Home Residents

Example: Alternative Treatments for SIB

George, a patient at the Georgia Retardation Center, a 37-bed residential treatment facility for severely developmentally disabled youth, was profoundly developmentally disabled and autistic. He displayed serious levels of self-injurious behavior (SIB), which consisted of striking his head and face with his hand or fist.

An MSW student assigned to work with George as part of his field placement reviewed the literature on reducing severe SIB among developmentally disabled persons. He found two psychosocial treatment interventions that had promise. One intervention (*B*) was called "interruption alone, or I," and the other (*C*) was called "differential reinforcement plus interruption, or DRI + I." Arrangements were made for George to be treated in daily sessions of 15 minutes each in order to ascertain which approach would prove most effective in reducing his SIB. External observers objectively recorded the occurrence of George's SIB, while the MSW students provided either the *B* or *C* intervention.

Because of the dangerous nature of George's SIB, a baseline period (*A* Phase) was not appropriate. The treatment consisted of five sessions of Treatment *B* (*B₁* Phase), followed by 15 sessions of Treatment *C* (*C₁* Phase). Then Treatment *B* was reapplied (*B₂* Phase), followed by Treatment *C* (*C₂* Phase). The data on effects of Treatments *B* and *C* depicted in Figure 23.7 suggest that Treatment *C* (DRI + I) was slightly more effective in reducing George's SIB than Treatment *B* (I) was (Underwood et al., 1989).

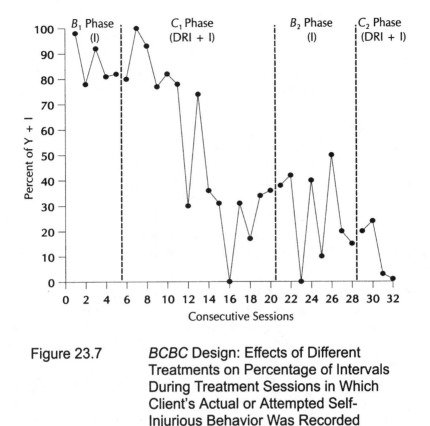

Figure 23.7   *BCBC* Design: Effects of Different
                     Treatments on Percentage of Intervals
                     During Treatment Sessions in Which
                     Client's Actual or Attempted Self-
                     Injurious Behavior Was Recorded

Treatment *C* was subsequently adopted as a regular part of George's treatment plan and implemented by the center's staff. This study illustrates another potential role of single-system designs: pilot testing several social work interventions with clients in order to determine which one is likely to be more effective.

The Multiple-Baseline Design

The multiple-baseline design enables researchers to draw causal inferences regarding the relationship between a specific treatment intervention and its effect on a client's target problem. The three types of multiple-baseline designs measure outcomes across clients, across settings, and across client's multiple target problems.

Outcomes Across Clients

The multiple-baseline across clients design measures the effects of an intervention as it is applied to two or more clients with the same client target problem. It is best used with clients whose target problems are not influenced by others with the same problem, as interrelation may cause all clients to change when one client changes.

An example of this design is reported in Maeser and Thyer (1990). An MSW student completing her field placement at the Georgia Retardation Center found that a significant problem for many of the developmentally disabled adolescents was that they had never acquired socially acceptable dining skills. They did not know how to use eating utensils; food was often scattered across the table and floor or on the residents' faces and clothing, and restaurant employees and patrons were often upset by their lack of social grace in the community.

The center's staff felt that if the residents could acquire acceptable dining skills, their potential for eventual community placement would be enhanced. The MSW student was asked to work intensively with several of the residents to help them accomplish this task. Three residents were selected to receive the training—Peter, Danny, and Michael.

Reviewing the literature, the student found a program for teaching dining skills to developmentally disabled individuals. This involved selecting a specific skill, constructing a detailed task analysis in which the steps comprising the skill were identified, and then using reinforcement procedures to teach these smaller, more manageable steps in their proper sequence. She chose the task of using a serving spoon to take an appropriate portion of food from a large dish and constructed a task analysis consisting of nine steps.

The requisites to evaluate the training program by using a multiple-baseline design across clients were now in place. These included three clients with the same target problem (lack of acceptable dining skills), an intervention to be sequentially applied with each client, and a reliable and valid dependent variable (the number of steps in the nine-level task analysis completed by each resident).

Baseline assessments, which began with all three clients at the same time (and on the same day), were individually conducted in a small training room. The clients were seated at a small table across from the MSW student and asked to use the serving spoon to place on their own plates a portion of food from a large bowl. Direct observations were taken of their individual success at this task, as defined by the number of steps of the task analysis that they completed in proper sequence.

After ten baseline trials (*A* Phase) with Peter, the teaching program (*B*₁ Phase) was begun with him. Assessment trials were repeated during the course of training. For Danny, the baseline period was extended for ten more days (a total of 20), and for Michael it was extended for a total of 30 days before their teaching programs were begun.

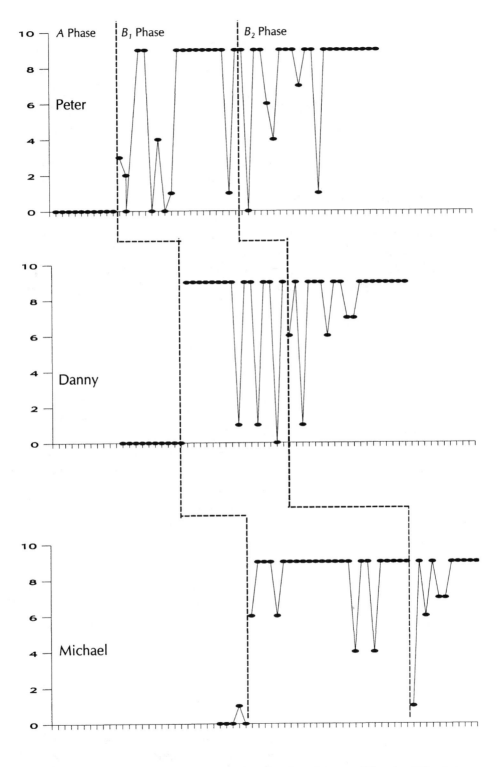

Figure 23.8   Multiple-Baseline Design Across Clients: Effects
of Intervention on Number of Successive Task
Analysis Steps Completed by Developmentally
Disabled Adolescents

In the B_2 Phase, the training sessions were moved from the small treatment room to the center's cafeteria during breakfast. The sessions were at first conducted individually and then with all three residents and the MSW student eating together, to promote the generalization and maintenance of the teenagers' dining skills.

Toward the end of data collection, her role in providing prompts, reinforcement, or manual guidance had gradually faded, and the teenagers were autonomously using the skill without staff assistance.

The results of the training program are depicted in Figure 23.8. During the baseline periods, all three teenagers displayed very little skill in properly using a large spoon to serve themselves a portion of food from a communal bowl. It was only after the teaching program intervention that Peter began to improve, eventually reaching and maintaining near-perfect performance. But the longer baseline periods for Danny and Michael meant their skills did not improve at the same time as Peter's. This lent credibility to the contention that the intervention, and few other factors, was responsible for Peter's improvement. Similar improvements were observed in Danny and Michael only after they were directly taught the dining skill.

These improvements, observed only following training and only following the sequential administration of the intervention, exclude most plausible threats to internal validity in this study. It is unlikely that factors such as maturation, history, diet or medication changes, nonspecific interpersonal relationship factors, or placebo influences could account for these improvements.

The data support two conclusions: that the teenagers' dining skills had improved over the course of time, and that it was the social work intervention that probably caused these improvements. It is this ability of multiple-baseline designs to examine causal effects that justifies labeling them as experimental research designs. The inferential logic in these designs is the same as in the ABAB and other experimental designs: repeatedly demonstrating that changes in the client's target problem occurred only following the introduction or removal of an intervention.

Outcomes Across Settings

The multiple-baseline across settings design is used to evaluate the effectiveness of a treatment intervention applied to a single client system's target problem in different environmental settings.

This design can be illustrated by a study of how to get drivers to buckle up their seat belts (Williams et al., 1989). The goal was to evaluate the relative effectiveness of two interventions: posting a standard black-and-white metal traffic sign that read "Fasten Safety Belt" at the exits of two parking lots, or having someone stand at the lot exits and display the sign to drivers. This study was an extension of an earlier experiment that also used signs to promote

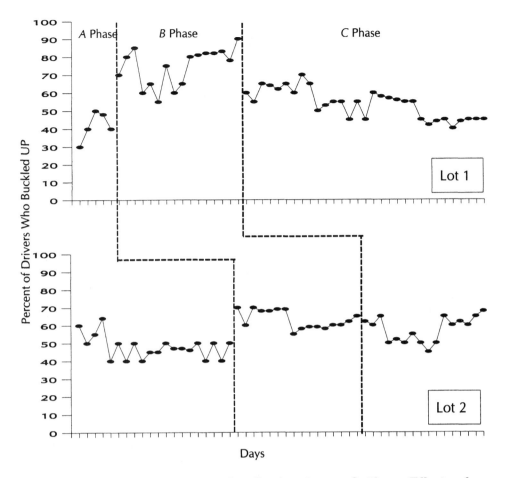

Figure 23.9   Multiple-Baseline Design Across Settings: Effects of
Interventions on Daily Percentage of Safety-Belt Use
by Drivers Exiting Two Parking Lots

safety-belt use and employed an *ABAB* design to evaluate the effects of the intervention (Thyer et al., 1987).

Two parking lots were chosen and a reliable and valid means of observing the use of over-the-shoulder safety belts by drivers exiting the lots was developed. The dependent variable was the percentage of drivers exiting on a given day of observation who used safety belts.

Baselines (*A* Phases) were begun at both lots (on the same day) with observations taken between 4:00 p.m. and 5:00 p.m. No prompting signs were used in the baseline phases. After five consecutive days of observations, a graduate social work student stood at the exit to Lot 1 holding the metal traffic sign (*B* Phase). After several weeks, the same sign was posted at the Lot 1 exit (*C* Phase), without a human prompter present. In the meantime, the baseline for Lot 2 was extended for over three weeks, and then the same two interventions were successively introduced (*B* and *C* Phases).

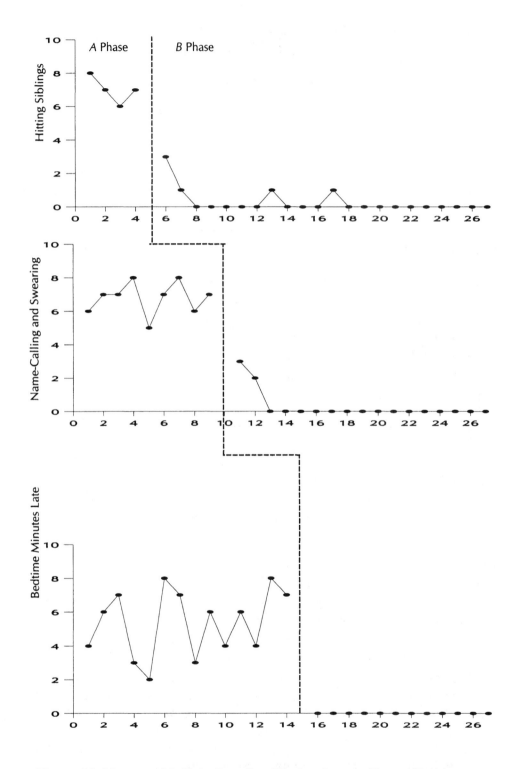

Figure 23.10   Multiple-Baseline Design Across Target Problems:
                       Effects of Intervention with Parents on Behaviors of a
                       Seven-Year-Old Girl

The results are depicted in Figure 23.9. It is clear that introducing a human prompter (*B* Phase) produced immediate increases in the safety-belt use of the exiting drivers. In the "sign alone" intervention that followed (*C* Phase), safety-belt use also was maintained above baseline levels, but the effect was somewhat smaller than when a human prompter was present.

The effects of the *B* Phase are immediate, but the data from Lot 2 do not shift at the same time the *B* Phase was implemented in Lot 1. This tends to rule out some concurrent historical events that might be responsible for the improvements in Lot 1 (such as a well-publicized accident). A number of other threats to internal validity were irrelevant (e.g., medication, maturation). Because the drivers did not know they were being observed, observational reactivity could be ruled out.

Outcomes Across Client Target Problems

The multiple-baseline design across client target problems can be applied to evaluate the effectiveness of a similar treatment program when applied to various problems experienced by the same client.

This design was used to measure intervention outcomes across three target problems experienced by a seven-year-old girl in her home: hitting siblings, name-calling and swearing, and minutes late to bed (Polster & Lynch, 1985). The intervention was introduced to the first target problem, hitting siblings, after a five-day baseline period (*A* Phase). This intervention included a parent training program in child management techniques, which the parents then systematically applied to each target problem in succession.

Figure 23.10 shows that the intervention affected the three target problems in a positive manner. The frequencies of all three behaviors went down after the introduction of the intervention—the techniques the parents learned in their training program.

SUMMARY

Single-system designs are ideally suited to evaluate social work practice. Social workers conduct studies based on these designs to monitor and evaluate the interventions they use to address the problems of clients—individuals, groups, or communities. These problems are referred to as the client system's target problem; the results of the intervention are called the client system's outcome.

Depending on the level of sophistication of the design employed and the validity and reliability of the data collected, single-system designs can be used to answer two different types of questions. The evaluative question is: Did the client system improve during the course of social work intervention? The experimental question is: Did my client improve because of my social work intervention?

The next chapter is a logical extension of this one, as it addresses the question: Is my social service agency effective?

Peter A. Gabor
Yvonne A. Unrau
Richard M. Grinnell, Jr.

C h a p t e r   24

Program-Level Evaluation

THE PROFESSION YOU HAVE CHOSEN to pursue has never been under greater pressure. Our public confidence is eroding, our funding is diminishing at astonishing rates, and the private and public calls for us to become more accountable are increasing more than we would like; the very rationale for our professional existence is being called into question. We have entered a new era in which only the best social service delivery programs—that can demonstrate they provide needed, useful, and competent services for our clients—will survive.

How do we go about providing these services? The answer is simple. We provide them utilizing the quality improvement process. This process is a philosophy; it is a commitment to continually look for and seek new ways to make the services we offer clients more responsive, more efficient, and more effective. Quality improvement means that we continually monitor and adjust (when necessary) our practices, both at a practitioner level and at a program level. Thus, evaluation simply provides the means to this end. In short, the goal of the quality improvement process is to deliver excellent client and program services. Evaluations provide the basic tools for us to engage in the quality improvement process.

QUALITY IMPROVEMENT AND THE DELIVERY OF SERVICES

The delivery of social services can be viewed at two levels: at the case level and at the program level. It is at the case level that we actually provide services to clients—individuals, couples, families, groups, organizations, and communities. With this point in mind, and at the simplest level, a program-level evaluation is nothing more than aggregations of case-level evaluations. To put it another way, case-level evaluations evaluate the effectiveness and efficiency of our individual services while program-level evaluations evaluate the effectiveness and efficiency of our programs where we work.

MYTHS ABOUT QUALITY IMPROVEMENT AND EVALUATION

There are a few reasons why social work practitioners and the programs in which they are employed should embrace the concepts of "the quality improvement process" and "evaluation." In today's current political environment it is a matter of survival. Moreover, we believe it is ethically and professionally the right thing to do. Nevertheless some social work students, practitioners, and administrators resist performing or participating in evaluations that can enhance the quality of the services they deliver.

Why is there such resistance when, presumably, most of us would agree that the pursuit of quality improvement, through the use of evaluations, is a highly desirable aspiration? This resistance is essentially founded upon two interrelated myths: That evaluations cannot properly and usefully be applied to the art of social work practice, and that evaluation, by its very nature, is to be feared. Both myths undercut the concept of evaluation when they are used to develop quality social service programs. The myths spring from two interrelated sources: philosophy and fear.

Philosophical Bias

Some of us maintain that the evaluation of social services—or the evaluation of anything for that matter—is impossible, never really "objective," politically incorrect, meaningless, and culture-biased. This belief is based purely on a philosophical bias. Our society tends to distinguish between "art" and "evaluation"— sometimes incorrectly thought of as "science." This is a socially constructed dichotomy that is peculiar to industrial society. It leads to the unspoken assumption that a person may be an "artist" or an "evaluator" but not both, and certainly not both at the same time.

Artists, as the myth has it, are sensitive and intuitive people who are hopeless at mathematics and largely incapable of logical thought. Evaluators, on the other hand, who use "scientific research and evaluation methods" are supposed to be cold and insensitive creatures whose ultimate aim, some believe, is to reduce humanity to a scientific nonhuman equation.

Both of the preceding statements are absurd, but a few of us may, at some deep level, continue to subscribe to them. Some of us may believe that social workers are artists who are warm, empathic, intuitive, and caring. Indeed, from such a perspective, the thought of evaluating a work of art does seem almost blasphemous.

Other social workers, more subtly influenced by the myth, argue that evaluations carried out using appropriate evaluation methods do not produce results that are relevant in human terms. It is true that the results of some evaluations that are done to improve the quality of our social service delivery system are not directly relevant to individual line-level practitioners and their clients. This usually happens when the evaluations were never intended to be relevant to those two groups of people in the first place. As we have seen in Chapters 1 and 2, perhaps the purpose of such an evaluation was to increase our knowledge base in a specific problem area—it was simply more "pure" than "applied."

Or perhaps the data were not interpreted and presented in a way that was helpful to the line-level practitioners who were employed by the program. Nevertheless, the relevance argument goes beyond saying that an evaluation produces irrelevant data that spawn inconsequential information to line-level workers. It makes a stronger claim: that evaluation methods *cannot* produce relevant information, because human problems have nothing to do with numbers and "objective" data. In other words, evaluation, as a concept, has nothing to do with social work practice.

The previous paragraph used the words *data* and *information*—two words that are often used interchangeably. The term *data* signifies isolated facts, in numerical or descriptive form, that are gathered in the course of an evaluation: for example, the number and demographic characteristics of people in a specific lower socioeconomic community or the number of clients referred by a particular referral source.

How we interpret data when they have all been collected, collated, and analyzed is called *information*. For example, *data* collected in reference to client referral sources gathered from a program's intake unit may indicate that the program accepts 90 percent of those who were referred by other social service programs but only 5 percent of people who are self-referred. One of the many pieces of *information* (or conclusions or findings drawn from the data) generated by these data may be that the program is somehow discriminating between clients who were referred by other social service programs and those who were self-referred.

The simple reporting of data, however, can also be a form of information. The distinction we would like to make between data and information is simple—data are obtained to provide information to help guide various decision-making processes in an effort to produce more effective and efficient services to clients. As we have previously mentioned, the idea that evaluation has no place in social work springs from society's perceptions of the nature of evaluation and the nature of art. Since one of the underlying assumptions of this book is that evaluation *does* belong in social work, it is necessary to explore these perceptions a bit more.

Perceptions of the Nature of Evaluation

It can be argued that the human soul is captured most accurately not in painting or in literature, but in advertisements. Marketers of cars are very conscious that they are selling not transportation, but power, prestige, and social status; their ads reflect this knowledge. In the same way, the role of evaluation is reflected in ads that begin, "Evaluators say. . . ." Evaluation has the status of a minor deity. It does not just represent power and authority; it *is* power and authority. It is worshiped by many and denigrated with equal fervor by those who see in it the source of every human ill.

Faith in the evaluation process can of course have unfortunate effects on the quality improvement process within our profession. It may lead us to assume, for example, that evaluators reveal "truth" and that conclusions (backed by "scientific and objective" research and evaluation methods) have an unchallengeable validity. Those of us who do social work evaluations sometimes do reveal "objective truth," but we also spew "objective gibberish" at alarming rates.

Conclusions arrived at by well-accepted evaluative methods are often valid and reliable, but if the initial conceptualization of the problem to be evaluated is fuzzy, biased, or faulty, the conclusions (or findings) drawn from such an evaluation are unproductive and worthless. Our point is that the evaluation process is not infallible; it is only one way of attaining the "truth." It is a tool, or sometimes a weapon, that we can use to increase the effectiveness and efficiency of the services we offer to clients.

The denigration of evaluation can have equally unfortunate results. If it is perceived as the incarnation of all that is materialistic, in possible opposition to common social work values, then either evaluative methods will not be applied or their results will not be believed and hence not incorporated into day-to-day practice activities. In other words, practitioners will have deprived themselves and their clients of an important source of knowledge. A great deal will be said in this chapter about what evaluation can do for our profession. We will also show what it cannot do, because evaluation, like everything else in life, has its drawbacks.

Evaluations are only as "objective" and "bias-free" as the evaluators who do them. For example, people employed by the tobacco industry who do "objective" evaluations to determine (1) if smoking causes lung cancer, or (2) whether the advertisement of tobacco products around school yards influences children's using tobacco products in the future, may come up with very different conclusions than will people employed by the American Medical Association to do the same studies. Get the point?

Perceptions of the Nature of Art

Art, in our society, has a lesser status than evaluation, but it too has its shrines. Those who produce art are thought to dwell on an elevated spiritual plane that is inaccessible to lesser souls. The forces of artistic creation—intuition and inspiration—are held to be somehow "higher" than the mundane, plodding reasoning of evaluative methods. Such forces are also thought to be delicate, to be readily destroyed or polluted by the opposing forces of reason, and to yield conclusions that may not (or cannot) be challenged.

Art is worshiped by many who are not artists and defamed by others who consider it to be pretentious, frivolous, or divorced from the "real world." Again, both the worship and the denigration can lead to unfortunate results. Intuition, for example, is a valuable asset for social workers. It should neither be dismissed as unscientific or silly, nor regarded as a superior form of "knowing" that can never lead us astray.

The art of social work practice and the use of concrete and well-established evaluative methods to help us in the quality improvement process can easily coexist. Social workers can, in the best sense and at the same time, be both "caring and sensitive artists" *and* "hard-nosed evaluators." Evaluation and art are interdependent and interlocked. They are both essential to social work practice.

Fear (Evaluation Phobia)

The second myth that fuels resistance to the quality improvement process via evaluations is that an evaluation is a horrific event whose consequences should be feared. Social workers, for instance, may be afraid of an evaluation because it is they who may be evaluated; it is their programs that are being judged. They may be afraid for their jobs, their reputations, and their clients, or they may be afraid that their programs will be curtailed, abandoned, or modified in some unacceptable way. They may also be afraid that the data an evaluation obtains about them and their clients will be misused. They may believe that they no longer control these data and that the client confidentiality they have so very carefully preserved may be breached.

In fact, these fears have some basis. Programs *are* sometimes curtailed or modified as a result of an evaluation. In our view, however, it is rare for a social service program to be abandoned because of a negative evaluation. They are usually shut down because they are not doing what the funders intended, or they are not keeping up with the current needs of the community and continue to deliver an antiquated service that the funding sources no longer wish to support. They can also be terminated because of the current political climate.

On the other side of the coin, a positive evaluation may mean that a social service program will be expanded or similar programs put into place. And those who do evaluations are seldom guilty of revealing data about a client or using data about a staff member to retard career advancement. Since the actual outcome of an evaluation is so far removed from the mythical one, it cannot be just the results and consequences of an evaluation that generate fear: It is the idea of being judged.

It is helpful to illustrate the nature of this fear using the analogy of the academic examination. Colleges and universities offering social work programs are obliged to evaluate their students so that they do not release unqualified practitioners upon an unsuspecting public. Sometimes, this is accomplished through a single examination set at the end of a course. More often, however, students are evaluated in an ongoing way, through regular assignments and frequent small quizzes. There may or may not be a final examination, but if there is one, it is worth less and feared less.

Most students prefer the second, ongoing course of evaluation. A single examination on which the final course grade depends is a traumatic event; a mid-term, worth 40 percent, is less dreadful; and a weekly, 10-minute quiz marked by a fellow student may hardly raise the pulse rate. So it is with the evaluation of anything, from social service programs to the practitioners employed by them.

An evaluation of a social service program conducted once every five years by an outside evaluator is traumatic. On the other hand, an ongoing evaluation conducted by the practitioners themselves as a normal part of day-to-day program operations becomes a routine part of service delivery. The point is that "evaluation phobia" stems from a false view of what an evaluation necessarily involves.

Of course, one of the disadvantages of an ongoing evaluation of a social service program is that the workers have to carry it out. Some may fear it because they do not know how to do it: They may never have been taught the quality improvement process during their studies, and they may fear both the unknown and the specter of the "scientific." One of the purposes of this book is to alleviate the fear and misunderstanding that presently shroud the quality improvement process, and to show that some forms of evaluations can be conducted in ways that are beneficial and lead to the improvement of the services we offer clients.

WHY SHOULD WE DO EVALUATIONS?

We have discussed two major reasons why social workers may resist the concept of evaluation—philosophical biases and fear. The next question is: Why should evaluations *not* be resisted? Why are they needed? What are they *for*? We have noted that the fundamental reason for conducting evaluations is to improve the quality of services. More specifically, evaluations also: (1) increase our knowledge base, (2) help guide decision making, (3) help demonstrate accountability, and (4) help assure that our clients are getting what they need.

Increase Our Knowledge Base

One of the basic prerequisites of helping people to help themselves is knowing what to do. Knowing how to help involves practitioners possessing both practice skills and relevant knowledge. Child sexual abuse, for example, has come to prominence as a social problem only during the past few decades, and many questions still remain to be answered. Is the sexual abuse of children usually due to the individual pathology in the perpetrators, to dysfunctions in the family systems, or to a combination of the two?

If individual pathology is the underlying issue, can the perpetrator be treated in a community-based program or would institutionalization be more effective? If familial dysfunction is the issue, should clients go immediately into family services or should some other form of help be offered? In order to answer these and other questions, we need to acquire general knowledge from a variety of sources in an effort to increase our knowledge base in the area of sexual abuse.

One of the most fruitful sources of this knowledge is from the practitioners who are active in the field. What do they look for? What do they do? Which of their interventions are most effective? For example, it may have been found from experience that family therapy offered immediately is effective only when the abuse by the perpetrator was affection-based, intended as a way of showing love. When the abuse is aggression-based, designed to fulfil the power needs of the perpetrator, individual therapy may be more beneficial. If similar data are gathered from a number of evaluation studies, theories may be formulated about the different kinds of treatment interventions most likely to be effective with different types of perpetrators who abuse their children.

Once formulated, a theory has to be tested. This, too, can be achieved by means of the evaluations using simple evaluation designs. It should be noted that in our profession, however, very few evaluations test theories because the controlled conditions required for theory-testing are more readily obtained in an artificial setting.

The data gathered to increase general knowledge are sometimes presented in the form of statistics. The conclusions drawn from the data apply to groups of clients (program-level evaluation) rather than to individual clients (case-level evaluation), and thus will probably not be helpful to a particular practitioner or client in the short term. However, many workers and their future clients will benefit in the long term, when evaluation findings have been synthesized into theories, those theories have been tested, and effective treatment interventions have been derived.

Knowledge-based evaluations, then, can be used in the quality improvement process in four ways:

- To gather data from social work professionals in order to develop theories about social problems
- To test developed theories in actual practice conditions
- To develop treatment interventions on the basis of actual program operations
- To test treatment interventions in actual practice settings

Guide Decision Making

A second reason for doing evaluations to improve the quality of our services is to gather data in an effort to provide information that will help decision makers at all levels. The people who make decisions from evaluation studies are called *stakeholders*. Many kinds of decisions have to be made in social service programs, from administrative decisions about funding to a practitioner's decision about the best way to serve a particular client (e.g., individual, couple, family, group, community, organization).

Six stakeholder groups benefit from evaluations: (1) state and federal policy makers, (2) administrators of the programs, (3) practitioners who work within the programs, (4) funders of the programs, (5) the general public, and (6) the clients served by the programs.

Policy Makers

To policy makers in governmental or other administrative bodies, any particular social service program is only one among many. Policy makers are concerned with broad issues: How effective and efficient are programs serving women who have been battered, youth who are unemployed, or children who have been sexually abused? If one type of program is more effective than another but also costs more, does the additional service to clients justify the increased cost? Should certain types of programs be continued, expanded, cut, abandoned, or modified? How should money be allocated among competing similar programs? In sum, policy makers want comparative data about the effectiveness of different social service programs serving similar clients.

Administrators

An administrator is mostly concerned with his or her own program. Administrators want to know how well the program operates as a whole, in addition to how well its components operate. Is the assessment process at intake (a specific component) successful in selecting only those referred persons who are likely to benefit from the program's services? Does treatment planning (a second component) provide for the integration of individual, dyadic, group, and family services in an order and time that consider the client's particular demographic characteristics? Does the discharge process (a third component) provide adequate consultation with other involved professionals? Like the policy makers mentioned above, a director may also want to know which interventions are effective and which are less so, which are economical, which must be retained, and which could be modified or dropped.

Practitioners

Practitioners who deal directly with clients are most often interested in practical, day-to-day issues: Is it wise to include adolescent male sexual abuse survivors in the same group with adolescent female survivors, or should the males be referred to another service if separate groups cannot be run? What mix of role playing, educational films, discussion, and other activities best facilitates client learning? Will parent education strengthen families? Is nutrition counseling for parents an effective way to improve school performance of children from impoverished homes?

Of greatest importance to a practitioner is the question: Is my particular treatment intervention with this particular client working? A periodic evaluation of an entire social service program (or part of the program) cannot answer questions about individual clients. However, as we have seen in the last chapter, case-level evaluations can be carried out by workers as a way of determining the degree to which their clients are reaching their practice objectives.

Funders

The public and private funding organizations who provide money to run social service programs want to know that their money is being spent wisely. If funds have been allocated to combat family violence, is family violence declining? And, if so, by how much? Is there any way in which the money could be put to better use? Often, the funder will insist that some kind of an evaluation of the program it is funding must take place. Administrators are thus made *accountable* for the funds they receive. They must demonstrate that their programs are achieving the best results for the least cost.

General Public

Increasingly, taxpayers are demanding that state and federal government departments in turn be accountable to them. Lay groups concerned with the care of the elderly, support for families, or drug rehabilitation or child abuse are demanding to know what is being done about these problems: How much money is being spent and where is it being spent? Are taxpayers' dollars effectively serving *current* social needs? In the same way, charitable organizations are accountable to donors, school boards are accountable to parents, and so forth. These bodies require evidence that they are making wise use of the money entrusted to them. An appropriate evaluation can provide such evidence through evaluation data.

An evaluation can also be used as an element in a public relations campaign. Programs want to look good in the eyes of the general public or other parties. Data showing that a program is helping to resolve a social problem may, for example, silence opposing interest groups and encourage potential funders to give money. On occasion, an evaluation can help highlight a program's strengths in an effort to improve its public image. In other cases, however, administrators may merely wish to generate support for what they believe to be a good and beneficial program.

Clients

Only recently have the people who use social service programs begun to ask whether the program's services meet their needs. Does the program's intent (goal) reflect the needs of the people it serves? Are ethnic and religious issues being sensitively considered? Do clients *want* what program administrators and funding sources think they ought to want? In short, is the social service program actually in tune with what the clients really need?

A factor relevant to serving client needs is whether the program is administered, to some degree, by the clients' social group. If a community is predominantly African American or Asian or Mormon, is the program operated, to some extent, by people from these respective groups? If it is not, how much input does the community have in setting the program's objectives and suggesting appropriate intervention strategies for achieving them? An evaluation study might look not only at how well the program's objectives are being achieved, but also at whether they are appropriate to the clients being served.

Demonstrate Accountability

A third purpose of how evaluations are used in the quality improvement process is to demonstrate accountability. As mentioned, administrators are accountable to their funders for the way in which money is spent, and the funders are similarly accountable to the public. Usually, accountability will involve deciding whether money should be devoted to this or that activity and then *justifying* the decision by producing data to support it.

Demonstrating accountability, or providing justification of a program, is a legitimate purpose of an evaluation insofar as it involves a genuine attempt to identify a program's strengths and weaknesses. Sometimes, however, an evaluation of a demonstration project may be undertaken solely because the terms of the grant demand it. For example, a majority of state and federally funded social work projects are forced to have periodic evaluations or their funds will be taken away. In such cases, a program's staff, who are busy delivering services to clients, may inappropriately view the required evaluation as simply a data gathering ritual that is necessary for continued funding. Accountability in our profession can take four forms:

- Coverage Accountability — Are the persons served those who have been designated as targets? Are there beneficiaries who should not be served?
- Service Delivery Accountability — Are proper amounts of services being delivered?
- Fiscal Accountability — Are funds being used properly? Are expenditures properly documented? Are funds used within the limits set by the budget?
- Legal Accountability — Is the program observing relevant laws, including those concerning affirmative action, occupational safety and health, and privacy of individual records?

Assure That Client Objectives Are Being Achieved

The last purpose of evaluations in the quality improvement process is to determine if clients are getting what they need from a social service program.

Responsible practitioners are interested in knowing to what degree each of their individual client's practice objectives, and those of their caseloads as well, are being achieved; That is, they are interested in evaluating their individual practices.

Clients want to know if the services they are receiving are worth their time, effort, and sometimes money. Usually, these data are required while treatment is still in progress, as it is scarcely useful to conclude that services were ineffective after the client has left the program. A measure of effectiveness is needed while there may still be time to try a different intervention.

On a general level, our profession has the responsibility to continually improve our social service programs. On a more specific level, the ethical obligation to evaluate our programs is addressed in the *Specialty Guidelines for the Delivery of Services by Counseling Psychologists* (APA, 1981) which states:

> *Evaluation of the counseling psychological service delivery system is conducted internally, and when possible, under independent auspices as well. This evaluation includes an assessment of effectiveness (to determine what the service unit accomplished), efficiency (to determine the total costs of providing services), availability (to determine appropriate levels and distribution of services and personnel), accessibility (to ensure that the services are barrier free to users), and adequacy (to determine whether the services meet the identified needs for such services).*

FIVE TYPES OF EVALUATIONS TO IMPROVE CLIENT SERVICES

As can be expected by now, there are many types of evaluations that can be done to improve the delivery of our services. We will briefly present the five that are most relevant to our profession: (1) establishing need, (2) assessing evaluability, (3) assessing outcome, (4) determining efficiency, and (5) specifying the process of the service delivery.

Needs Assessment

The first type of evaluation is needs assessment. These evaluations must take place *before* a program is conceptualized, funded, staffed, and implemented. In short, a needs assessment assesses the feasibility of (or need for) a given social service. A needs assessment is intended to verify that a social problem exists within a specific client population to an extent that warrants the implementation of a program.

To do this, a needs assessment must produce fairly precise estimates of the demographic characteristics of individuals exhibiting the problem believed to exist. A needs assessment seeks to answer such questions as:

- What is the socioeconomic profile of the community?
- What are the particular needs of this community with respect to the type of program being considered (e.g., physical health, mental health, employment, education, crime prevention)?
- What kinds of service are likely to be attractive to this particular community?
- Is the program meeting the needs of the people it believes it is serving?
- Is the program meeting the needs of people in the best possible way?
- Are there any other needs that the program could be meeting?

Social service programs should never gather data to justify their own maintenance needs. They must collect data to ascertain the *real* needs of the people they hope to serve and then tailor the structure of their service delivery to meet these needs.

As mentioned, an evaluation does not necessarily assess a whole program; particular parts of a program may be the focus, as in a needs assessment. For example, there may be some doubt that the program is currently addressing a specific community's needs. The composition of the community may have changed since the program was first established, and there may now be a high proportion of African American children being referred for service whereas, before, the majority of referrals were Caucasian.

The goal of a needs assessment may be to determine to what degree the program is responsive to the special needs of African American children and to the present concerns of the African American community. This may involve conducting a needs assessment within the community and comparing the community's *current* perceived needs with the program's *original* intent.

Experienced program directors and their funding sources know that the demographic characteristics of communities tend to change over time. Perhaps there is now a higher proportion of senior citizens than formerly, or perhaps the closure of a large manufacturing plant has meant high unemployment and an increase in all of the problems associated with job loss. Changes may also have occurred in the community's social service delivery network.

Perhaps a program for pregnant teens has had to close its doors or a meals-on-wheels service has recently been instituted for disabled seniors. Perceptive program directors try to keep abreast of changes like these by becoming members on interagency committees, consulting with local advisory boards and funding sources, establishing contact with community organizations, talking with social work professors, and taking other like action.

Despite all such preemptive measures, however, there is occasionally some doubt that a program is meeting the *current* needs of the people it was funded to serve. On these occasions, a needs assessment may be an appropriate type of evaluation to conduct, as it can ascertain what the community currently needs (if any) in the way of social services.

It is possible to avoid periodic and disruptive evaluative efforts if a program's responsiveness to its community needs is continually monitored. Indications that a target population is changing can be seen in changing referral patterns, novel problem situations presented by clients, and unusual requests from other programs. We believe all social service programs should have monitoring systems through which such data are routinely collected and analyzed, and any lack of responsiveness to a community's needs can be easily picked up and dealt with immediately.

Evaluability Assessment

After a needs assessment has determined that a social service program is required to solve a perceived social need, we can do another type of evaluation—evaluability assessment. It is nothing more than the development of a specific program model(s) that is presumed to solve the social problem believed to exist as evidenced by the needs assessment. A program model is a diagram of the way in which the program itself is run and is intended to illuminate such questions as:

- What is the program's *goal*?
- What program *objectives* does the program hope to achieve in relation to its goal?
- What *practice activities* do line-level workers undertake in order to achieve practice and program objectives?

Since most social service programs are complex, with a number of interlinking parts, a program model can be developed only through careful study of a program's operations; once developed, of course, it has to be tested to ensure its accuracy. So far, it should be evident that evaluations can be used to increase our knowledge both about the existence of social problems (via needs assessments) and about the ways in which social service programs can address these problems (via evaluability assessments).

Another task of an evaluability assessment is to determine whether a program's objectives are conceptualized and operationalized in a way that would permit a meaningful evaluation. This is not, however, a black and white matter. Often, an evaluability assessment indicates areas of the program's conceptualization and/or organization that interfere both with the delivery of its services and with the program evaluation effort itself.

Many social service programs really cannot be evaluated as they are currently organized. Many do not have the objectives of their programs written in such a way that makes common sense, or they are written in a form whereby they cannot be evaluated—circumstances that apply not only to the evaluators but to their funding sources as well. These programs are not necessarily ineffective or inefficient. They just have a great degree of difficulty proving otherwise.

Since it is the program's objectives that are always evaluated, it only follows that if a program's objectives are not clearly defined it is impossible to determine whether or not they are being achieved. In such situations, evaluators need to work closely with the program's staff to clarify the program's objectives so that the program can be properly evaluated.

Outcome Assessment

A third type of evaluation is outcome assessment. It is an evaluation that determines to what degree the program is meeting its overall objectives. In a treatment program, this usually means the degree to which treatment interventions are effective. For example, a program in which a high proportion of clients achieve their individual practice objectives (sometimes referred to as treatment objectives, or client objectives) can be considered a successful program. If the majority of clients terminate unilaterally without reaching their practice objectives, the program can be considered less than successful.

An outcome evaluation indicates *whether* the program is working, but it says nothing about *why* it is working (or failing to work). Nor is there any mention of efficiency; that is, the time and dollar cost of client success. After all, if a program achieves what it is supposed to achieve, via the attainment of its program objectives, what does it matter how it achieves it? If the program is to be replicated or even improved, it does matter; nevertheless, client outcome alone is the focus of many outcome assessments. Questions related to outcome generally fall into four categories:

- First, the evaluator wants to know to what degree the program is achieving its program objectives: For example, do people who participate in a vocational training program have improved job skills, and by how much have their job skills improved (a program objective)?
- Second, the evaluator wants to know whether people who have been through the program have better job skills than similar people who have been through similar programs.
- Third, and highly related to the point directly above, there is the question of causality. Is there any evidence that the program caused the improved job skills?
- Fourth, how long does the improvement last? Many clients who are discharged from social service programs return to the environment that was at least partially responsible for the problem in the first place. Often, client gains are not maintained, and equally often, programs have no follow-up procedures to find out if they in fact have been maintained.

Questions about how well the program achieves its objectives can be answered by aggregating, or bringing together, the data that individual social workers collect about their individual clients. Questions about how well client success is maintained can be answered in a similar way. However, comparisons between those who have and those who have not been through the program, as well as questions about causality, require a different sort of data, collected via descriptive and explanatory evaluation designs involving two or more groups of clients.

Efficiency Assessment

The fourth type of evaluation is efficiency assessment. These types of evaluations address such questions as:

- How many hours of therapy are generally required before clients reach their practice objectives?
- What do these hours cost in clinical and administrative time, facilities, equipment, and other resources?
- Is there any way in which cost could be reduced without loss of effectiveness, perhaps by offering group therapy instead of individual therapy?
- Is a particular program process—intake, say—conducted in the shortest possible time, at minimum cost?

If an outcome evaluation has shown the program to be effective in achieving its program objectives, the efficiency questions become:

- Does the program achieve its success at a reasonable cost?
- Can dollar values be assigned to the outcomes it achieves?
- Does the program cost less or more than other programs obtaining similar results?

Efficiency assessments are particularly difficult to carry out in social work because so many of our client outcomes cannot be realistically (socially and professionally) measured in terms of dollars. In fact, it would be unthinkable to measure some client outcomes in terms of efficiency—such as counseling terminally ill cancer patients. Efficiency in terms of what?

The benefits of a job-training program that removes its clients from welfare rolls can be more easily quantified in terms of efficiency (cost savings) than a program that is designed to reduce the feeling of hopelessness in terminal cancer patients. Nevertheless, there is only so much money available for social service programs, and decisions regarding which ones to fund, no matter how difficult, have to be made—especially if funding decisions are made on efficiency criteria. We do not need to put a price on program results in order to use costs in decision making, but it is necessary to be able to describe in detail what results have been achieved via the expenditure of what resources.

Note that the four focuses of evaluation listed so far are linked in an ordered sequence: Without a determination of need, programs to meet the need cannot be planned; without implementation of the planned program, there can be no meaningful outcome; and without a valued outcome, there is no point in asking about efficiency.

Process Analysis

A fifth type of evaluation that is highly related to evaluability assessment is process analysis. Process analysis is the monitoring and measurement of treatment interventions—the assumed cause of client success or failure. As mentioned previously, an evaluation of efficiency determines the ratio of effectiveness or outcome to cost, but says nothing about *why* the program is or is not efficient, either overall or in certain areas. To answer that question, we need to consider program *process*: the entire sequence of activities that a program undertakes to achieve its objectives, including all the decisions made, who made them, and on what criteria they were based.

An evaluation of process might include the sequence of events throughout the entire program or it might focus on a particular program component: intervention, say, or follow-up. A careful examination of *how* something is done may indicate *why* it is more or less effective or efficient. To state the point another way: When a program is planned, via an evaluability assessment, it should have included a definition of the population the program serves, a specification of the client needs it will meet, and a description of the specific social work interventions it will undertake to meet the client needs within the population.

If client needs are not being met, or the population is not being adequately served, it may be that the practitioner activities are not being carried out as originally planned. A process evaluation can ascertain whether this is so. Sometimes, a needs assessment will have determined that the program is serving a sufficient number of the people it is meant to serve. If not, a process evaluation will determine this, and will also determine exactly what treatment interventions (activities) are being undertaken by its social workers with their clients. It addresses such questions as:

- What procedures are in place for assessment?
- Are staff members who do assessments thoroughly trained for the job?
- What modes of therapy are offered?

- What criteria are used to decide when a client should move from individual to family therapy, or into group therapy, or should be discharged or referred elsewhere?
- What follow-up procedures are in place?
- How much and what type of staff training is available?
- How are client records kept?
- What do staff do compared with what they are supposed to do?

In order for a process analysis to occur, however, the program has to be specifically delineated in a written form that makes it extremely clear how a client goes through the entire program. In short, a client path flow must be established that depicts the key activities, decision points, and client flow through the program in a graphic format. We need to present a detailed diagram, called a *client path flow chart*, of the chronological order of how a client comes into and goes through our program.

The data necessary for a process evaluation will generally be available within the program itself, but rarely in usable form. Client demographic and assessment data may be on file but will probably not be summarized. Services provided to clients are typically recorded by social workers in handwritten notes deposited in client files. Training courses taken by staff may be included in staff files, or general training files or may not be recorded at all.

Where no systematic management data system (sometimes incorrectly referred to as Management Information System) is in place, gathering, summarizing, and analyzing data are extremely time-consuming endeavors. As a result, of course, it is rarely done until someone outside the program insists on it. Again, the use of routine monitoring procedures will avoid the need for intrusive evaluations initiated by outside sources.

We have assumed that both outcome and process evaluations are necessary components of any comprehensive program evaluation. If, however, we are concerned only with the client outcome of a specific program, it might be asked why we need to monitor the program's implementation. The answer is simple: An outcome analysis investigates any changes that are believed to be brought about by an orderly set of program activities. We cannot be certain, however, that any change was caused by the program's activities unless we know precisely what these activities were. Therefore, we need to study the program operations via process evaluations.

INTERNAL AND EXTERNAL EVALUATORS

Each one of the five types of evaluations mentioned in the previous section can be done by an internal and/or external evaluator. In short, any evaluation may be *internally driven*, that is, initiated and conducted by staff members who work within a program. In other cases, the evaluation may be *externally driven*—initiated by someone outside the program to be evaluated, often a funding source.

The main motive behind internal evaluations is usually to improve the quality of services to clients immediately. A distinct advantage of internal evaluations is that the evaluation questions framed are likely to be highly relevant to staff members' interests. This is hardly surprising; staff members are responsible for conducting the evaluation and, with their firsthand knowledge of the program, they are in a position to ensure that the evaluation addresses relevant issues. Thus, feedback from an evaluation nurtures the quality improvement process. Moreover, a practitioner (or organization) who evaluates his or her practice is in a position to demonstrate accountability to funders and other stakeholders.

A drawback to internal evaluations is that they may be viewed as lacking the credibility that comes with independent, outside evaluations. Sometimes, therefore, funding bodies are not content with data from internal evaluations and request external ones. Because they are carried out independent of the programs to be evaluated, external evaluations are often perceived to be more credible. Because they are commissioned by people outside social service programs, however, they tend to reflect those interests and may not address questions that are most relevant to program staff. As well, outside evaluations often impose an onerous data collection burden on staff and tend to be disruptive to normal program operations.

When externally driven evaluations are to occur, organizations that conduct internal evaluations are in an advantageous position. A priori, internal evaluations may identify some things that need to be improved before the outside evaluators appear. They may also identify programs' strengths, which can be displayed. As well, staff members are likely to be conversant with evaluation matters, allowing them to engage in knowledgeable discussions with outside evaluators and thus help ensure that the evaluation process will deal fairly with the programs' interests.

SCOPE OF EVALUATIONS

The word *program* can refer to many different things. It may refer to something small, specific, and short term, such as a film developed for use during a training session on AIDS. It may refer to a nationwide effort to combat family violence, and include all the diverse endeavors in that field, with different practice objectives and their corresponding intervention strategies. Or, it may refer to a specific treatment intervention used with a specific social worker and undertaken with a specific client.

Obviously, these different types of programs need to be evaluated using different evaluative methods. Thus, we need to know what the characteristics of the program are. The scope of any evaluation has to be sensitive to the following program characteristics:

- **Boundary** — The program may extend across a nation, region, state, province, city, parish, county, or community; or it may be extremely limited—for example, a course presented in an individual agency or school.

- **Size** — The program may serve individual clients, such as people seeking individual therapy, or many clients, such as people infected with the HIV virus.

- **Duration** — The program may be designed to last for half an hour—a training film, for example—or it may be an orientation course on child safety lasting for two days, a group therapy cycle lasting for 10 weeks, or a pilot project designed to help the homeless being evaluated after two years. Or, as in the case of a child protection agency, it may be intended to continue indefinitely.

- **Complexity** — Some programs offer integrated components, combining, for instance, child protection services, individual therapy, family therapy, and educational services under one common umbrella. Such a program is obviously more complex than one with a simpler, singular focus—for example, providing nutrition counseling to pregnant adolescents.

- **Clarity and Time Span of Program Objectives** — Some programs have objectives that can readily be evaluated: for example, to increase the number of unemployed adolescents who find full-time jobs two months after a six-week training course (the intervention). Others have objectives that will not become evident for some time: for example, to increase the utilization by seniors of a meals-on-wheels program.

- **Innovativeness** — Some social service programs follow long-established treatment interventions, such as individual treatment; others are experimenting with new ones designed for use with current social problems, such as AIDS.

TWO APPROACHES TO QUALITY IMPROVEMENT

As we have seen, there are many types of evaluations that can be done to improve the quality of the services we offer to clients. Each type can be classified under the project approach or the monitoring approach to quality improvement. Sometimes, a particular type of evaluation can be classified under both approaches, depending on how often it is done within a social service program.

An evaluation whose purpose is to assess a completed social service program (or project) has a *project* approach to quality improvement. Complementary to the project approach, an evaluation whose purpose is to provide feedback while a program is still under way has a *monitoring* approach to quality improvement; that is, it is designed to contribute to the ongoing development and improvement of the program as it goes along. In addition, the data generated by both approaches must be utilization-focused. That is, the data must be useful to one or more of the stakeholders, or the evaluation effort is a waste of time and money and is really unethical! Let us now turn our attention to the first approach to quality improvement—the project approach.

The Project Approach to Quality Improvement

As we have seen, evaluations that enhance the quality improvement process in our profession may be carried out daily or they may not be initiated until the program has been in operation for a number of years. A substantial evaluation carried out periodically, at long intervals, illustrates the *project approach* to quality improvement. This approach tends to give rise to evaluations with the following eight characteristics:

- **Externally Driven** — The evaluation will almost certainly be externally driven, that is, it will be initiated by someone outside the program who more often than not will decide on the evaluation questions to be answered and the data to be collected that will presumably answer the questions.
- **Resistant Staff** — Program staff may react badly to the idea of an evaluation that is externally driven and may see it as unnecessary, intrusive, irrelevant, and judgmental.
- **Intrusive** — Evaluation procedures are very likely to be intrusive, no matter how hard the person doing the evaluation works to avoid this. Because the procedures are not a part of a program's normal day-to-day routine but must be introduced as additional tasks to be performed, staff usually have less time to spend on normal, client-related activities. This diversion of attention may be resented when workers prefer to spend more time with clients rather than participating in an evaluation process that was mandated "from above," or "from outside the program."
- **Periodic or No Feedback to Staff** — The evaluation data obtained from a project-type approach to quality improvement, even if shared with the practitioners, is usually not directly or immediately relevant to them or to their current clients. This is particularly the case if an evaluation is designed to answer questions posed by administrators or funders, and workers' practice concerns cannot be addressed using the same evaluation methods.

    If, as sometimes happens, the project-type approach does yield useful information (via the data collected) for the staff, and changes are made on the basis of this information, the next evaluation may not take place for a long time, perhaps for years. If the evaluator is not on hand to analyze the benefits resulting from the changes, staff members may not be sure that there *were* any benefits.

- **Resistant to Implementation** — When an evaluation is externally driven, staff may resist implementation of an evaluator's recommendations, even if the program's administration insists that changes be made. By the time that a project approach is initiated, day-to-day program procedures, both good and bad, may have become set. It is virtually a law of nature that the longer a routine has been in operation, the more difficult it is to change.

- **Large Recommended Changes** — The changes recommended as a result of a project approach to quality improvement can be enormous. Administrators and evaluators may feel that since an evaluation occurs only once in a number of years, it is a major event that requires drastic findings and recommendations to justify it. When a program is monitored continually, errors can be caught at once and can be corrected with minimal effort. Periodic evaluations, on the other hand, often result in more sweeping recommendations.

- **Not Practical in Applied Settings** — All evaluations must be based on well-established evaluation principles and methods. However, the rigorous techniques necessary to obtain cause-and-effect knowledge may not be practical in a normal program setting. Chapter 14 discussed the basic types of evaluation designs that can be used to obtain knowledge at different levels. For now, it is enough to point out that evaluation designs used to obtain higher levels of quality improvement recommendations may require that clients be randomly assigned to experimental or control groups without regard for their special needs. Similarly, evaluation designs to measure client change may require that measurement be carried out both before and after the treatment intervention, without regard to clinical time restraints or the client's emotional condition.

Usually, rigorous experiments for the purpose of increasing knowledge are carried out in laboratories, not in applied practice settings. However, the same rigorous conditions may be suggested if the purpose is, for example, to evaluate the effectiveness and efficiency of a therapy group. The worker might argue that more time will be spent administering measuring instruments than conducting therapeutic work; the evaluator can easily reply that results will be valid only if experimental conditions are observed. The issue here is: Whose interests is the evaluation intended to serve? Who is it *for*—the social work practitioner or the external evaluator?

In a project approach to quality improvement the answer is that it is sometimes for the evaluator, or for the administrative, academic, or funding body that has employed the evaluator. It should be stressed that this is not always the case. Many project approaches use unobtrusive evaluation techniques geared to actual practice situations. If, however, the evaluation is undertaken only once in a number of years, intrusion can be considered warranted in order to obtain reliable and valid results.

- **Difficult to Incorporate in Practice Settings** — A final characteristic of a project approach to quality improvement is that the methods used by the evaluator are difficult for staff to learn and almost impossible for them to incorporate into their normal day-to-day practices. In fact, staff are not expected to learn anything about evaluation procedures as a result of the program being evaluated. Nor is it expected that the evaluation methods employed will be used again before the next major periodic evaluation. The project approach is carried out by the evaluator and, essentially, until the next time, that is that.

The reader may have noticed that all the preceding characteristics we listed for the project approach to quality improvement can be viewed as negative; without a doubt, the project approach is intrusive and traumatic, fails to meet the immediate needs of the workers, and may engender resentment and fear. Nevertheless, this approach must be periodically performed in order to improve the quality of services that clients receive. We now turn to a second approach to quality improvement that complements the project approach—the monitoring approach.

The Monitoring Approach to Quality Improvement

The monitoring approach to quality improvement is based on reliable and valid evaluation methods that can be integrated into a social service program as a part of its normal operating routine. This approach measures the extent that a social service program is reaching its intended population and the extent to which its services match those that were intended to be delivered. In addition, this approach provides immediate and continual feedback on client progress to practitioners.

The monitoring approach is nothing more than the continual collection, analysis, reporting, and use of program data. This ongoing and dynamic approach to evaluation within a program contrasts with the periodic approach, in which evaluations are conducted on an infrequent, interval basis.

A program's administrator, for example, might decide to have a day-care program evaluated, receive the results, and then not have any further evaluations conducted for several years, if ever again. The program can be said to have been evaluated, if only on a one-time basis. But it is likely to change over time; years after the original evaluation was done, there are likely to be important new data needs that go unattended.

The alternative is to implement an ongoing monitoring system that provides continuous program data. Ideally, such a system would be integrated with the program's records system so as to avoid duplication and enhance efficiency.

For example, demographic data on clients referred to the program can be collected at intake. Data on the services provided to clients can also be collected throughout their involvement with the program.

Finally, data on the changes the program aims to effect can be collected at intake, at specified times during treatment, at termination, and at follow-up. In this way, a constant stream of systematic data is collected, analyzed, and reported in an effort to help the program focus client-orientated interventions as they come into (intake), go through (treatment), and leave (termination) the program, and go on with their lives (follow-up).

Evaluations resulting from a monitoring approach to quality improvement tend to have the seven characteristics described below:

- **Internally Driven** — Continuous routine use of evaluation methods may have been initially suggested by an administrator or an outside consultant or funder. However, the evaluation methods are put into place and used by practitioners for their own and their clients' benefit without the request (or demand) from any outside source. The evaluation may thus be said to be internally driven.

- **Cooperative Staff** — When evaluation is a process instead of an event, practitioners generally do not resent it because it is an accepted part of the daily routine of delivering high-quality services to clients.

- **Nonintrusive** — By definition, an intrusion is something unrelated to the task at hand that interferes with that task. Evaluation methods that are routinely used to improve services to clients are certainly relevant to our profession. Such methods do not interfere with the task at hand because they are an integral part of that task.

- **Ongoing Continuous Feedback** — There are some activities in a social service program that need to be monitored on a continuing basis. For example, client referrals are received daily and must be processed quickly. In order to estimate remaining program space, intake workers need a list of how many clients are presently being served, how many clients will be discharged shortly, and how many clients have recently been accepted into the program. This continually changing list is an example of a simple evaluative tool that provides useful data. The resulting information can be used to compare the actual number of clients in the program with the number the program was originally designed (and usually funded) to serve.

  In other words, the list can be used to fulfill a basic evaluative purpose: comparison of what is with what should be, of the actual with the ideal. It might be found, in some programs, that the arithmetic of intake is not quite right. For example, suppose that a program has space for 100 clients. At the moment, 70 are being served on a regular basis. In theory, then, the program can accept 30 more clients. Suppose also that the program has five social workers; each will then theoretically carry a maximum caseload of 20.

In the caseloads of these five workers there ought to be just 30 spaces. But for some reason, there are more than 30. The supervisor, who is trying to assign new clients to workers, discovers that the workers can muster 40 spaces between them. In other words, there are 10 clients on the computer who are theoretically being served, but who are not in any of the five workers' caseloads. What has happened to these 10 clients?

Investigation brings to light the fact that the workers and the intake computer keep their records in different ways. The computer assumes that every client accepted will continue to be served until formally discharged. However, the practitioner who has not seen Ms. Smith for six months, and has failed to locate her after repeated tries, has placed Ms. Smith in the "inactive" file and accepted another client in her place. The result of this disparity in record keeping is that the program seems to have fewer available spaces, and clients who might be served are being turned away.

The problem might be solved simply by discussing inactive files at a staff meeting. What steps will be taken to locate a client who does not appear for therapy? How long should attempts at contact continue before the client is formally discharged? Which other involved professionals need to be informed about the client's nonappearance and the discharge? When and how should they be informed? Is it worth modifying the intake computer's terminal display to include inactive files, with the dates they became inactive and the dates they were reactivated or discharged? Once decisions have been made on these points, a straightforward procedure can be put in place to deal with the ongoing problem of inactive files.

Other problems may also come to light. It may be found, for example, that a continual source of inappropriate referrals is the result of inaccurate information about the program's eligibility criteria. Neither the problem nor the solution can be identified unless data are routinely collected about the characteristics of clients referred by various sources. This sort of continuous feedback is obtained through the monitoring approach; problems that would otherwise continue to trouble staff can be immediately identified and solved.

Many social service programs routinely go through similar processes in order to identify and solve operational problems. They do not dignify them with the term "evaluations," but that is nevertheless what they are.

• Accepting of Changes — Necessary client-centered changes for solving problems are usually agreed upon by line-level practitioners and are usually accepted without difficulty. Resistance arises only when practitioners are not consulted about the changes or cannot see that they solve any specific problem. This is a fairly common occurrence in the project approach to quality improvement. A monitoring approach, on the other hand, usually allows the workers themselves to identify the problems and suggest tentative solutions.

- Minor Recommended Changes — When changes occur constantly as a result of an ongoing monitoring process, they tend to be small. Of course, continual monitoring can suggest that fundamental changes are needed in the way that the program is conceptualized or structured, but such large changes are rare. Most often, monitoring gives rise to continual minor adjustments instead of the larger, more traumatic changes that may result from the project approach.

- Easy to Incorporate in Practice Settings — The monitoring approach, like the project approach to quality improvement, is based on well-established evaluation methods. The difference between them can lie in whom the evaluation is intended to serve: the line-level worker or the evaluator. When evaluation is undertaken by the workers themselves for their own and their clients' benefit, there is no doubt about whom the evaluation is intended to serve.

Advantages of the Monitoring Approach

Social workers who are interested in improving the quality of the services they offer via evaluations are well on their way to becoming self-evaluating professionals, or members of a self-evaluating organization. In other words, they are taking responsibility for providing the best possible service to clients through systematic examinations of their strengths and weaknesses via the quality improvement process. Becoming a self-evaluating social work professional (or program) has definite advantages not only for clients, but also for workers. Some of these advantages are:

Increased Understanding of Programs   A social service program is often a complex entity with a large number of interlinked components. Practitioners' main concerns usually have to do with the effectiveness of their treatment interventions. How can the confused sexual identity of an adolescent who has been sexually abused best be addressed? What teaching technique is most effective with children who have learning disabilities? Is an open-door policy appropriate for group homes housing adolescents who are mentally challenged? Answers come slowly through study, intuition, hunches, and past experience, but often the issues are so complex that practitioners cannot be sure if the answers obtained are correct.

Many social workers stumble onward, hoping their interventions are right, using intuition to assess the effectiveness of their particular interventions (or package of interventions) with a particular client. Chapter 23, on single-system designs (case-level evaluation), showed how the use of simple evaluation designs can complement a worker's intuition so that an inspired guess more closely approaches knowledge. However, no amount of knowledge about how well an intervention worked will tell the worker *why* it worked or failed to work. *Why* do apparently similar clients, treated similarly, achieve different results? Is it something about the client? About the worker? About the type of intervention?

It is always difficult to pinpoint a reason for unsatisfactory achievement of program objectives because there are so many possible overlapping and intertwined reasons. However, some reasons may be identified by a careful look at the program stages leading up to the interventions. For example, one reason for not attaining a client's practice objective may be that the client was unsuited for the program and ought never have been admitted in the first place. Or, perhaps the program's assessment procedures are inadequate; perhaps unsuitable clients are accepted if the referral comes from a major funding body. In other words, perhaps the lack of client success at the intervention stage derives from problems at intake.

Social workers who have been involved with a do-it-yourself evaluation may become familiar with the program's intake procedures, both in theory and in reality. They may also become familiar with the planning procedures, discharge procedures, follow-up procedures, staff recruitment and training procedures, recording procedures, and so on. The worker will begin to see a link between poor client outcomes at one program stage and inadequacies at another, between a success here and an innovation somewhere else. In sum, practitioners may be able to perform their own tasks more effectively if they understand how the program functions as a living organism. One way to gain this understanding is to participate in a hands-on, do-it-yourself evaluation.

Relevant Feedback   A second advantage of internally driven evaluations is that meaningful and relevant questions can be formulated by the workers within the program. They can use evaluation procedures to find out what they want to know, not what the administrator, the funder, or a university professor wants to know. If the data to be gathered are perceived as relevant, staff are usually willing to cooperate in the evaluation. And if the information resulting from that data *is* relevant, it is likely to be used by the practitioners.

It is our belief that all evaluative efforts conducted in our profession provide feedback loops that improve the delivery of services. Feedback provides data about the extent to which a program's goal is achieved or approximated. Based on these data, services may be adjusted or changed to improve goal achievement.

Timely Feedback   A third advantage is that the workers can decide when the evaluation is to be carried out. Evaluation procedures can be carried out daily, weekly, monthly, or only once in five years. The point here is that data are most useful when they help to solve a current problem, less useful when the problem has not yet occurred, and least useful after the event.

Self-Protection   Most social service programs are evaluated eventually, often by outside evaluators. If staff have already familiarized themselves with evaluation procedures and with the program's strengths and weaknesses, they are in a better position to defend the program when an externally driven evaluation occurs. In addition, because improvements have already been made as a result of their self-evaluations, the program will be more defensible. In addition, the staff will indirectly learn about evaluation designs and methodology by monitoring their practices on a regular basis. Modifications recommended by an outside evaluator are hence likely to be less far-reaching and less traumatic.

An additional consideration is that staff members themselves are likely to be less traumatized by the idea of being evaluated: Evaluation is no longer a new and frightening experience, but simply a part of the routine—a routine that tries to improve the quality of services for clients.

Practitioner and Client Satisfaction   A case-level evaluation can satisfy the worker that an intervention is appropriate and successful, and it can improve a client's morale by demonstrating the progress that has been made toward his or her practice objective. Moreover, data gathered at the case level can always be used at the program level. Improvement of the program as a whole can follow from an improvement in one worker's practice.

SUMMARY

This chapter introduced the concept of quality improvement and explained how evaluation provides tools for the quality improvement process. We presented a brief introduction to why our profession needs evaluations: to increase our knowledge base; to guide decision making for policy makers, administrators, practitioners, funders, the general public, and clients; to demonstrate accountability; and to assure that clients' practice objectives are being met.

We have presented five non–mutually exclusive types of evaluations that can be used to improve the quality of our services: needs assessment, evaluability assessment, outcome assessment, efficiency assessment, and process analysis. We did not attempt to classify the various types of evaluations into a project approach to quality improvement or into a monitoring approach to quality improvement. The types of evaluations cannot be meaningfully classified by approach. The needs assessment project-type of evaluation, for example, can be used in a monitoring fashion if it is undertaken on a regular and systematic basis.

The point we want to make is simply that there are advantages and disadvantages to each quality improvement approach and one is not inherently better than the other; they complement one another, and each has its place in the evaluative process. That is, they are both used to improve the quality of services delivered by social work professionals.

External and internal evaluations were introduced with the notion that internally driven evaluations are usually concerned with the improvement of services and external evaluations are usually required by funding sources who want to know about effectiveness and/or efficiency issues.

Yvonne A. Unrau
Peter A. Gabor

C h a p t e r   25

Evaluation in Action

THIS CHAPTER FOCUSES on the implementation of the two complimentary evaluation approaches, case level (Chapter 23) and program level (Chapter 24), presented in the two preceding chapters. Our emphasis is on creating case- and program-level data systems that are integrated within a typical social service delivery system. These systems provide data on which to base decisions about individual client cases and specific social service programs.

As we know, numerous evaluation methods exist that evaluate social work practice at both the case and program levels. Although evaluation principles are applied, the evaluation process is not the same as the process of conducting a pure research study or an individual assessment (Posavac & Carey, 1994). Because evaluations are carried out in the context of ongoing service delivery, it is difficult to apply single-case or group designs with the same level of rigor expected in "pure" research studies.

Random assignment is usually not possible, some variables are not controllable, withdrawal designs may be precluded by ethical considerations, and the overall evaluation process is affected by the unique context of the setting in which it takes place. Evaluations are usually less rigorous then would be desirable from a purely research perspective. Thus, some people who misunderstand the evaluation process tend to dismiss its findings. In reality, truly airtight methodological designs are rare even in "pure" research studies; in evaluation research, however, they are almost never seen. Nevertheless, well-designed and well-implemented evaluations provide valuable data upon which to base practice and program decisions.

PRINCIPLES UNDERLYING THE DESIGN OF EVALUATIONS

Three important principles affect the design and implementation of evaluations: (1) feedback, (2) development, and (3) integration.

Feedback

Feedback is the major purpose of an evaluation, whether at the case or program level; that is, feedback generates data upon which further practice and program decisions are based. All social systems are feedback directed and function better when data are available about the degree to which they are moving toward (or away) from their formally stated objectives. This is similar to a child, named Ben, who is playing the game of "blind person's bluff." As long as Ben is receiving accurate data about whether he is getting "warmer" or "colder" he will find the object fairly quickly. In the absence of these meaningful feedback cues, however, Ben's search may be lengthy and unsuccessful. Likewise, feedback is indispensable to the achievement of practice and program objectives.

Expanding on the content above, the more frequent the feedback, the more efficient the achievement of objectives. Returning to our example, if Ben receives continuous data about how warm or cold he is getting, he will find the hidden object much more quickly than if he received infrequent or occasional feedback. Therefore, in the absence of continuous feedback, numerous wrong turns and directions can be taken. Thus, practice and program evaluations provide continuous ongoing feedback and make the achievement of their objectives much more efficient by reducing the amount of time spent "off task."

Development

A second principle underlying evaluations is that they are conducted primarily for developmental purposes. In other words, feedback obtained from the data is most helpful when the feedback is used to guide continued practice and program development. This concept is more applicable to a program-level evaluation than a case-level evaluation, however. In this approach, sometimes referred to as *formative* evaluation, various aspects of a program's performance are continually monitored and the resulting data are used to make incremental changes to the program's services. On the other hand, a *summative* evaluation is used for the purpose of making judgments about a program's performance. Summative evaluations lead to major decisions about a program's expansion, replication, downsizing, or termination.

It goes without saying that formative evaluations are more likely than summative evaluations to create less stress and anxiety within a program. They are likely to be seen as a constructive means for improving the program's services rather than judging them. When an evaluation's purpose is developmental, methodological rigor becomes less critical; the key issue is to generate the best possible data upon which to base further developmental decisions.

Integration

The third principle underlying evaluations relates to the integration of evaluation activities with normal day-to-day practice activities. In social service agencies, evaluations are too often conceived of as something separate from service provision as they utilize a different set of activities. In such situations, many staff members may view data collection as additional chores that yield little immediate relevant utility. A more constructive approach, however, is one that fits with the concepts of continuous feedback, program development, and integration of evaluative activities with normal day-to-day service delivery. Using this approach, "practice" data that also can be used for "evaluation" data are collected at each step of service delivery .

STAKEHOLDERS

The starting point in designing any evaluation is to know the stakeholder groups for whom it is intended. Each stakeholder group has a different set of questions regarding the program's overall operations and subsequent outcomes. Thus, in designing a built-in evaluation system in any social service organization, it is important to be clear about each stakeholder's data needs. On a general level, there are five non–mutually exclusive groups of stakeholders for any given program: (1) clients, (2) social work practitioners, (3) policy makers and funders, (4) managers and administrators, and (5) the general public.

- *Clients* are obviously concerned with their personal and immediate problems. Prior to entering a social service program as consumers, they want to know if a particular program is the best one to address their specific problems. Sometimes they even want to know how the program operates. Whom does it serve? What types of services does it provide?

What treatment interventions are used? Does it consider ethnic and religious differences? Do clients have input into treatment interventions?

Once receiving services, clients become primarily interested in data that relate to their overall progress. It is useful to provide clients with objective feedback related to how their identified needs and problems are changing, and the rate at which they are changing. This provides both the workers and the clients additional data to decide whether they are going to reach their practice objectives that were established at the beginning of the intervention.

- *Social work practitioners* are also interested in questions that relate to their clients' needs and their day-to-day practice problems. A summative evaluation of an entire social service program (or part of the program), however, does not answer questions about individual clients. We can carry out formative case-level evaluations to determine the degree to which our clients' practice objectives are being met. Is a particular treatment intervention with this particular client working? What mix of treatment activities best facilitates a client's progress?

- *Policy makers and funders* focus their interests on expenditures. In other words: Is the money they provide being spent wisely? Is a program cost-efficient and cost-effective? How many clients are being served given the amount of funds? What proportion of funds is allotted to client services versus administrative costs? How could money be put to better use? Are services being responsibly managed? How should money be allocated among competing similar programs?

    Policy makers and funders are concerned with very broad issues. They often want data in relation to a program's effectiveness and efficiency. They are interested in knowing: Is the program fulfilling its formal mandate? Does the program's goal reflect the needs of the clients it purports to serve? Is the program achieving desirable client outcomes? How does a specific program compare to similar programs? If one type of program is more effective than another but also costs more, are the higher costs justified? Should certain types of programs be modified, expanded, or abandoned?

- *Managers and administrators* are aware of accountability questions that are often asked by the policy makers and funders mentioned above. As well, they focus on questions specific to client needs, program operations, and client outcomes. Managers need to know: What is the typical client profile? Are the program's objectives being met? What interventions are most efficient and effective? What staffing is needed? Are clients satisfied with the services they received?

- The *general public* is a lay citizen group and their evaluation questions reflect the concerns raised by political leaders and the media. What is being done about a specific social problem? How much money is being spent and where is it being spent?

CASE AND PROGRAM DECISION MAKING

Given the various stakeholder groups briefly mentioned above, and the many types of evaluation questions that can be asked of any social service program, the purpose for which an evaluation is designed can vary tremendously. An evaluation can yield important data about client needs, program operations, service outcomes, cost-benefits, and cost-effectiveness. The common thread among these different functions, however, is the type and kind of data that are collected, which in turn are used for decision making.

The result of an evaluation is the analysis of the collected data. The data should help us better understand some aspect of delivering services within a program. In turn, this understanding helps us to assess the results of our previous decisions and to provide a sound base for making further decisions. In general, decision making occurs at two non–mutually exclusive levels: (1) at the case level, in relation to individual clients, or groups of clients; and (2) at the program level, in relation to the program as a whole and the relationship between the program and the local community, including policy makers, funders, and the general public. We will now turn our attention to case-level decision making.

Case-Level Decision Making

Evaluation activities provide important data that can enhance our decision making at all phases of intervention, from intake to follow-up. As we know, these decisions must be made on useful, valid, and reliable data. Often, these decisions are made quickly, and it is important that we always have at hand current and accurate data about a client's situation.

Data collected at regular intervals (or at predetermined times) provide information on which to base client-related decisions. Each decision in turn leads to the collection of more data that, once properly analyzed and synthesized, yield further data to form the basis of future client-related decisions. Data gained in this way are never a substitute for our professional judgment, but they can guide our client-related decisions and provide a method whereby decisions, once made, can be evaluated.

The use of data for case-level decision making also serves to empower our clients because the clients can take an active role in the measurement process, particularly when standardized self-administered measuring instruments are used. Being actively involved in data collection, clients are likely to develop a better understanding of their own needs and progress. They can then take a more active role in interpreting evaluation data to make informed decisions about the amount of time, energy, effort, and money going into specific interventions.

In summary, the benefits of using evaluation data to make case-level decisions are: (1) it yields current, comprehensive, and accurate data to guide decision making; (2) it allows us to retrace our steps and evaluate our client-related decisions in a timely fashion so that our interventions can be continued, discontinued, or changed where indicated; (3) it permits us to continually evaluate the effectiveness of our own practices; and (4) measurement results can be readily shared with our clients, enabling them to see their progress (if any).

Program-Level Decision Making

A social service program is a coordinated set of objectives that seeks to fulfil its formal goal. Decisions made at the program level focus on the program's functioning so that it can be further developed and improved. "Functioning" includes all aspects of the program: how well the program is meeting community needs; whom it is serving; how well the program's activities are designed and implemented; how well it is managed; and, how effectively and efficiently it is achieving its objectives. Access to data can help in choosing between various interventive options and also provides the means of monitoring how the chosen alternative works out. In short, an evaluation allows links to be established between community needs, program process, and program results (or client outcomes) so that all facets of the program can be considered as a whole.

Administrators often are faced with problems of restructuring or reorganizing their program's services. In times of economic cutbacks, the "do more with less" scenario is now an administrative motto. What should be changed, both administratively and programmatically, and how? In other situations, administrators want to know which programs are most effective. Based on evaluations results, decisions can be taken to increase funding for successful programs and to reduce or terminate funding for less effective ones. It is more likely, however, that administrators will make incremental changes to programs in an effort to improve existing social services. In this way, program decisions are based, at least partly, on evaluation results.

Policy makers and funders, who have little direct contact with a program, are often provided an annual report that presents the program's results. Program successes are highlighted to justify current funding or proposed expansion. In instances where a program's results do not show great promise, data are used to identify areas for its further development. This allows policy makers to ensure that funds are spent on effective services.

Program results are also used to build public support for a social service program. Data help to educate the community about social needs that exist as well as about the efforts undertaken by the program to meet these needs. In addition, program outcomes are used to educate other helping professionals about a program's intervention options and their effectiveness.

THE MONITORING APPROACH TO EVALUATION

Approaches to evaluation are continually changing. The traditional, "project" approach, usually associated with summative evaluations, is slowly giving way to the monitoring approach, usually associated with formative evaluations. The monitoring approach is more congruent with the principles of feedback, development, and integration than the project approach. This approach uses data that are continuously collected, synthesized, and analyzed to provide solid data on which practice and program decisions are based.

The monitoring approach to evaluation provides ongoing feedback so that a program can be improved as it continues to operate. It differs from the project approach in which a program (or some component of a program) is assessed on a one-shot basis, a summative method of evaluation. The monitoring approach is integrated into the program's operations where evaluation and clinical activity are jointly designed. It provides data about the extent to which a program is reaching its intended population, how well its services measure up to what were intended to be delivered, and the extent to which it is meeting its program objectives. In addition, this approach provides immediate and continuous feedback on client progress. There are several benefits to using a monitoring approach to evaluation:

- This type of evaluation is internally driven by program staff. Evaluation methods are put into place and used by practitioners for their own benefit (and their clients' as well) without the request from any outside source.
- When evaluation is a process instead of an event, practitioners generally are more cooperative because it is an accepted part of the daily routine of delivering high-quality services to clients.
- Because evaluation methods are routinely used to improve services to clients, they do not interfere with the task at hand because they are an integral part of that task.
- Data are made available to all social workers for ongoing feedback.
- A monitoring approach allows workers themselves to identify practice and program problems and suggest tentative solutions. It avoids problems of top-down solution strategies, in which practitioners are not consulted about the changes or cannot see that they solve any specific problem.
- A monitoring approach gives rise to continual minor adjustments instead of the larger, more traumatic changes that may result from a project evaluation. When changes occur regularly as a result of an ongoing monitoring process, they tend to be small. In short, the monitoring approach engages a program in its continuous pursuit of quality improvement.

ETHICAL CONSIDERATIONS

Data obtained through an evaluation are a powerful means for improving a program's services. The evaluation process and its results, like any powerful tool, can be misused and abused, however. Potential misuses include justifying decisions already made, using results for public relations or performance appraisal purposes, and fulfilling funding requirements. The two most appropriate uses of an evaluation are for decision making and for meeting accountability demands. Thus, evaluations must not be misused but must be conducted in accordance with ethical and professional standards.

Ethical Standards

In general, all research-related ethical guidelines (Chapter 4) are applicable to evaluations. The most important ones are discussed in this section.

As in any ethical research project, informed consent is obtained from all those involved. This means that clients understand the purpose of the evaluation, know what is going to happen in the course of it, understand its possible consequences, and have voluntarily agreed to participate. Needless to say, clients are informed that they can decline to participate or may withdraw from the evaluation process at any time, without penalty.

When evaluation activities are integrated as a normal part of service provision, the process of informing a client about an evaluation is part and parcel of explaining the program. Clients usually do not object to an evaluation when they understand that it is used to ensure that they receive the best possible service. We should never presume that our clients are not willing to participate in an evaluation or that it will have negative effects on them. The principle of self-determinism applies to all aspects of the helping relationship, including evaluation activities. Thus, clients ought to be informed about the evaluation process in the same way as they are told about other aspects of service delivery.

Confidentiality issues apply in the same way as they do in normal service delivery. Those conducting evaluation activities are responsible for ensuring that only authorized persons have access to data and that individual clients cannot be identified or connected to any data presented in written program evaluation reports.

The selection of an evaluation design also involves ethical considerations. At both the case and program levels, the use of inferentially powerful designs is likely to create ethical problems. In the case of withdrawal designs, for example, such as the *ABAB* design, it is not ethical to withdraw a successful intervention simply to build an explanatory single-case design. In the case of group explanatory designs, withholding service to randomly selected clients for the purpose of creating a control group is similarly unethical if withholding of the targeted service will, in any way, be harmful to clients. Given the many ethical issues that can arise, the use of any explanatory design must be justifiable on practice grounds. Such clearance is usually provided by an independent ethics review board.

Finally, evaluations should be conducted in an atmosphere of openness and honesty. This should characterize all evaluation phases, from initial conceptualization and operationalization to report writing. Initially, the purpose of an evaluation should be spelled out with clarity and frankness. Those who are asked to participate in any aspect of an evaluation, as well as those who may be affected by its results, have a right to know what the true purpose of the evaluation is and what decisions are likely to be based on its results.

Hidden agendas regarding its purpose serve to deceive clients, staff members, and others involved and are, therefore, incompatible with social work ethics. In the same vein, early and wide dissemination of an evaluation's results should be the normal practice. Withholding or delaying results is an inequality of power between those who have the results and those who do not and creates the possibility that its results will be used in a manipulative manner.

Professional Standards

In addition to carrying out evaluations in an ethical manner, it is important that they be competently conducted in accordance with accepted professional standards. The Joint Committee on Standards for Educational Evaluation has identified several general guidelines, three of which will be briefly discussed.

First, if the results of an evaluation are to be relied on, it is obviously important that they be based on valid, reliable, and accurate data. Second, in addition to accuracy, the results are affected by such methodological choices as the definition of the population or sample, the timing of data collection, and the selection of data that are reported. Competing interests can influence the people conducting the evaluation. The requirement of fairness implies that a well-balanced, representative, accurate picture of the program is presented.

Finally, evaluations are more practical than theoretical; they have practical utility to those who are responsible for decision making. Obviously, their results are presented in a clear and understandable manner. Moreover, evaluators establish links between evaluation results and the decisions to be based on those results; all recommendations must be feasible in the circumstances of a specific program.

EVALUATION IN ACTION

Although there is no single strategy for designing and implementing case- and program-level evaluations, it is advisable to base an evaluation design on the principles of feedback, development, and integration. As well, knowing the intended audience for an evaluation effort helps to frame relevant questions. Beyond these general guidelines, however, every evaluation situation is unique; if an evaluation is to be successful, it must be planned to meet the specific needs and fit into the specific context of the given situation.

In the remaining part of this chapter, the evaluation process is discussed using an example. We focus on the question of whether or not a Teen Parenting Program (TPP) is effective in attaining one of its many program objectives—to increase positive physical contact between teen parents and their infants.

Operationalizing Service Delivery

The first step in implementing an evaluation is to clearly operationalize the program. This step must never be underestimated. Operationalizing a program means that its goal, objectives, and activities are articulated so that all staff have a common understanding of the general nature of the services it provides, as well as of the specific operations involved in client service delivery. The program's goal is a statement that flows logically from its mandate and announces the expected general outcomes dealing with the social problem that it is attempting to prevent, eradicate, or ameliorate.

Our TPP's goal is: *to build healthy parent-child relationships by developing a home environment that is nurturing and safe.* The stated goal is broad, and thus, is not directly evaluated. Rather, the program's objectives are articulated, which gives the flavor of its service delivery structure. Program objectives are statements that clearly and exactly specify the expected change, or intended result, for clients receiving its services. Three objectives of our TPP are:

- To increase positive physical contact between teen parents and their infants
- To increase teen parents' abilities to cope with stressful situations
- To increase teen parents' knowledge levels about infant and child development

Meaningful evaluation questions cannot be developed without clear program objectives. The first objective stated above acts as a guide to developing case-level questions (e.g., What interventions will increase teen parents' positive physical contact with their infants? Do different parents respond better or worse to different interventions?), and program-level questions (e.g., What proportion of parents increase the amount of positive physical contact given to their infants at program completion? What alternative parenting skills are taught to parents in the program?).

Design Selection at the Case Level

Given the problem-solving nature of our profession, we engage in a constant process of evaluation. In our TPP, for example, we can assess client needs, estimate levels of client problems, appraise client strengths, and gauge client progress. As such, we can participate in informal processes of evaluation through supervisory meetings, case consultation, and case conferences. We can then generate tentative hypotheses about client concerns. In most cases, such data provides us with a starting place when working with clients.

The primary purpose of case-level evaluation designs is to objectively examine client strengths, client problems, and client needs. Data obtained in the assessment phase are examined to confirm any clinical hunches. Ideally, an explanatory case level is used to evaluate a treatment intervention for each client. Like life itself, however, evaluation designs need to be flexible. The contextual variables of the client situation often dictate the most viable evaluation design. We have the choice to initiate, remove, or reinstate observation or intervention periods within a case-level design; however, the contextual variables of a client's situation greatly influence the nature of such choice. In planned interventions, we may have more opportunity to select a design, but in crisis interventions, the evaluation or practice design is established by the circumstances of the client's unique situation.

Planned Interventions

Social workers in our TPP can use case-level designs as a method of monitoring clients' individualized treatment objectives. Factors that influence the choice of design and measurement tools include the clients' abilities to measure their own progresses, their involvement with other family members, and the opportunity to manipulate a single intervention. Furthermore, we must orient our client to the terminology and procedures of evaluative practice. By stating our first program objective—to increase positive physical contact between teen parents and their infants—we help our clients to understand that the services they receive are specifically intended to help them learn new ways to nurture and show physical affection toward their infants.

We simply explain to teen parents how important it is that they understand our intervention process and participate in monitoring their own results. The data collected from this evaluation procedure are presented at case conferences at the end of the intervention, where the social worker, the program's administrator, Sharon, and the teen parent assess progress and the need, if any, for further services.

The complex nature of problems faced by teen parents compels us to initiate several different intervention strategies concurrently. We could, for example, address problems related to the teen parents' lack of supports, as well as work with teens to develop plans to improve their parenting abilities. Given that several important clinical activities can be occurring at once, it is even more important that we be clear about the specific interventions used. In most cases, we rely on a simple *AB* design, in which Phase *A* reflects the initial assessment and observation period of family members and Phase *B* launches the intervention process.

The *B* phase, however is more typically a package of interventions rather than a discrete intervention technique. Consider Brandy, for example, a 17-year old mother, who is referred to our TPP one month after giving birth to her daughter, Angie. Brandy, who understandably is anxious about her new parenting role, wants to be a good parent for Angie; but rather than express this desire in terms such as, "I want to build a healthy relationship with my child" (i.e., our program's goal), Brandy is more likely to say, "I want to give my daughter the love I never got from my parents."

Further conversation reveals that Brandy views her own childhood negatively. She explains that her parents argued all the time, they did not pay her much attention, and when they did she was usually being yelled at or hit. Brandy's admits that her parents were poor role models and that she is uncertain of how to deal with Angie, especially when Angie cries. Often, Brandy is afraid to hold Angie because of Angie's small size.

As Brandy explains her situation, we can reflect on several of our program's objectives as an anchor in determining how to tackle her most pressing problem(s). We decide together to formulate a treatment plan that targets one of Brandy's parenting abilities—her worries about what to do when Angie cries. This plan fits nicely with our first program objective to increase positive physical contact between teen parents and their infants.

To help Brandy achieve our first program objective, for example, it is necessary to determine the various types of positive physical contact possible and to work with Brandy to ensure she fully understands them. Together with Brandy, we operationalize "positive physical contact" when Brandy:

- Lightly strokes Angie's cheek with her finger
- Gently holds Angie in her arms when she is crying
- Carries Angie in a "baby knapsack" when going on an outing
- Lays Angie on her lap while supporting her head

Once we have outlined clear-cut examples of positive physical contact, Brandy can easily count and record the number of times each positive physical contact occurs each day.

The limitation of using an *AB* design is that we cannot determine what factors directly contribute to the change in Brandy's behaviors. Such data could be obtained if we used a more methodical approach to the onset of intervention techniques. After the initial baseline period, for example, we could use a teaching approach where we provide Brandy with basic reading materials about the importance of positive physical contact between parents and their infants.

If the amount of positive physical contact between Brandy and Angie, as measured by a simple counting form, shows no change, then we can introduce a second intervention phase, such as actively showing Brandy, by example and coaching, a variety of ways in which she can give positive physical contact to Angie. By delaying the onset of the second intervention, we have effectively developed an *ABC* design. No matter what design is used, however, we have developed a structure for continuous feedback that contributes to our client's understanding of the situation and our decisions about treatment.

Crisis Interventions

When a client's situation involves a crisis, we need to intervene immediately, thus forming a *B* design. Such a design, exploratory in nature, generates data about whether or not our client shows change over time, but it does not tell us whether the change was caused by our intervention, due to the fact that no initial measurements occurred.

Suppose that on the same day that Brandy was referred to our TPP, for example, she has a hostile argument with her parents, who have reluctantly agreed to let Brandy and Angie continue living with them. When we arrive at her parent's home, we witness an argument where Brandy's parents threaten to kick her out of their house. As we enter the home, Brandy's parents leave the house with Brandy crying and screaming after them. Angie is left unattended and crying out from another room.

Clearly, it is neither appropriate to begin recording any baseline data (*A*) of positive physical contact between parent and child, nor appropriate to launch into a full explanation of our TPP's goal and objectives. We immediately shift to a plan to get Brandy into a state of security and stabilization. First, we need to calm Brandy and make sure Angie is attended to so that we can assess the seriousness of her living situation. Without a plan for her immediate problem, Brandy is not able to concentrate on her parenting role with Angie.

Once a satisfactory plan for the immediate problem is developed (e.g., we have identified some steps to take with Brandy's living situation), we are then in a position to explain the services of our TPP. At this point, the time for collecting pretest measures or establishing a true baseline phase (*A*) has past. By necessity, our initial contact with Brandy has been primarily reactive. That is, we have relied on previous practice experience, in addition to general practice knowledge and intuition to help Brandy through her period of crisis.

Although formal measuring instruments (e.g., planned observation or standardized self-report measuring instruments) were not used, this initial period of contact gave us a chance to assess contextual variables, such as Brandy's willingness to accept help and patterns of interaction between her and Angie under stressful circumstances. Because we have already intervened in the situation, any baseline measures are contaminated by our previous interactions. Consequently, work with Brandy and Angie begins with an intervention phase (*B*).

Throughout the crisis period, we informally collect observational data by which to generate tentative hypotheses about how Brandy and Angie function together and with Brandy's parents. After the crisis period, we can gather other relevant data using more formal assessment approaches. A period of baseline data could be collected, and then an intervention such as the one discussed in the planned situation could be implemented, thus forming a *BAB* design.

Design Selection at the Program Level

Whereas case-level evaluations produce data that are largely used to direct treatment planning, program-level data are concerned more with the overall effectiveness of a program's services. Data obtained from program-level evaluations make a more generalizable contribution to our knowledge base as they offer measurements on a group of clients rather than on a single client.

Nevertheless, the options for selecting a design at either the case or program level are similar. A program evaluation may begin with an exploratory design and later move to descriptive or explanatory design. In our TPP, for example, we can apply: (1) aggregated case-level evaluation designs, and (2) group evaluation designs.

Aggregated Case-Level Evaluation Designs

A number of single-case evaluations with clients who have common treatment objectives can be aggregated, or combined, to examine treatment outcome across a group of clients. Suppose, for example that Sharon, our TPP's administrator, observes that in the past several months 10 teen parents referred to our program had problems with being afraid to physically handle their babies. Furthermore, all of them used a recording form that counted the number of times they gave positive physical contact to their infants. In reviewing client files, Sharon notes that in all 10 cases, workers primarily used teaching and counseling techniques as interventive activities. By grouping individual client outcome scores, she can assess the general change across the 10 clients.

The results are presented in Table 25.1, which shows a self-rating score for the first and last week of intervention. The data show that there was a general trend toward improvement for nine clients and no improvement for one client (i.e., #133). Sharon can also get a sense of the overall improvement for the clients by computing an average score.

By comparing the average score for the first week with the average score for the last week, she can get a sense of how much clients improved after receiving services. A quick glance at the actual measurements used by clients will tell her the clinical significance of the observed change.

Aggregated case-level designs provide only a rough estimate as to how a similar group of clients are progressing within a program. Because measurements are developed according to the idiosyncratic needs of each client (they are not standardized instruments), they provide a crude indication of change.

Nevertheless, the aggregated data offer valuable feedback for Sharon and her coworkers to consider. First, workers can assess whether the reported changes are clinically significant. Are the items contained within the measurement too easy or too difficult to attain? Second, by comparing the client scores in the last week, the program can develop a profile that reflects the level of parenting skill that clients have achieved when exiting the program. Third,

Table 25.1   Aggregated Case-Level
                     Data: Frequency of
                     Positive Physical Contact

Client #	First Week	Last Week	Difference
121	12	20	08
122	11	19	08
124	13	14	01
126	13	25	12
127	13	16	03
129	14	24	10
130	12	22	10
131	13	17	04
133	11	10	–01
134	12	25	13
Mean	12.4	19.2	6.8

attention may be given to the client who did not show improvement (i.e., #133). Were the client's circumstances unique? Are there reasons as to why the client did not improve? If so, what are they?

Questions that arise from aggregated case-level evaluations are relevant, as they can be introduced at case review sessions to help stimulate ideas for program development. The feedback gained from the evaluation process helps all of us to more fully understand the problems faced by our clients.

Group Evaluation Designs

Group evaluations differ from aggregated case-level evaluations in that they are preplanned and are directly aimed to answer a specific evaluation question, such as, "Is the program effective?" To measure a program's effectiveness, for example, pretest and posttest scores on the program's objectives can be gathered using an appropriate, valid, and reliable measuring instrument(s).

To examine trends that appear to arise from the grouped case-level data, descriptive group designs (see Chapter 12) can be employed. Suppose, for example, Sharon learns from her coworkers that they favor a particular intervention, a self-help support group. In reviewing files of the past six months, she notices that about one third of the clients participated in the program's self-help support group.

Further, single-case evaluations suggest that clients who participated in weekly support group meetings displayed higher rates of improvement than those who did not. Sharon has a hunch that participation in the support group is related to improvement, but she would like to support the hunch by using an explanatory-level group design known as the classical experimental design.

This design can be implemented by randomly assigning start dates to clients. Random assignment is possible because there happen to be 16 clients eligible for support group services but the group only has eight spots. Because the support group is not considered a critical service, Sharon chooses to randomly assign half of the teen parents to the next round of support group sessions (the experimental group). The remaining eight teen parents are placed on a waiting list for the support group. They receive all other program services, however. Clients with delayed starting dates form the control group, as they do not receive support group treatment for a six-week period.

After six weeks, pretest and posttest scores of the two groups are compared to determine if there are clinically or statistically significant differences in client outcome. If clients who participate in the support group consistently show improvement on a specified program objective over those who do not, then more confidence can be placed in the support group intervention.

Group evaluations incorporate many more research principles, such as sampling, manipulation of an independent variable, and careful measuring of the dependent variable. As such, the data generated by group-level evaluations are more valid and reliable, as compared to aggregate case-level evaluations. The results are useful because we can assess client change using data from standardized measuring instruments. These data not only give us a measure of client change, but they also give us a sense as to how an individual client's score compares to the scores of other clients with similar problems.

The results of a grouped evaluation also provide data that are useful to our profession. Program data can be summarized and carefully compared with results from other similar programs. Are outcome results comparable for programs with similar client profiles? Are there unique features of one program that appear to have a great impact on client change?

SUMMARY

The focus of this chapter has been on integrating evaluation activity with client service delivery. The primary purpose of implementing a monitoring evaluation system is to provide ongoing, accurate, and useful feedback. These data are then used to fine-tune the service delivery of a social service program. The specific nature of evaluation activities is influenced by the targeted evaluation consumers. Policy makers and funders are interested in program data that are more general, while program administrators and workers are interested in data that offer a richer understanding of a program's service delivery structure and client outcomes.

There are several steps to take prior to implementing evaluations. Most important are ethical considerations. By adapting ethical and professional standards to evaluation activity within a program, clients are ensured a quality service and we can account for our actions.

As with pure research studies, applied research studies (i.e., evaluations), are always easier to read about then they are to implement. This chapter provided examples of evaluation in action using a single program. A Teen Parenting Program was used to demonstrate how evaluation is implemented to assist with case-level and program-level decision making. At the case-level evaluation, efforts can be used in planned or crisis situations. Using an evaluation framework helps a worker structure and direct the course of client interventions. At the program level, program administrators can gain important evaluation data using aggregate or group designs. The implementation of evaluation is a critical aspect of service provision that can enhance decision making and ensure that all clients have a rich understanding of the services a program offers.

Yvonne A. Unrau
Judy L. Krysik
Richard M. Grinnell, Jr.

Glossary

Abstracting indexing services Providers of specialized reference tools that make it possible to find information quickly and easily, usually through subject headings and/or author approaches.

Abstracts Reference materials consisting of citations and brief descriptive summaries from quantitative and qualitative research studies.

Accountability A system of responsibility in which program administrators account for all program activities by answering to the demands of a program's stakeholders and by justifying the program's expenditures to the satisfaction of its stakeholders.

Aggregated case-level evaluation designs The collection of a number of case-level evaluations to determine the degree to which a program objective has been met.

Aggregate-level data Derived from micro-level data, aggregate-level data are grouped so that the characteristics of individual units of analysis are no longer identifiable; for example, the variable, "gross national income," is an aggregation of data about individual incomes.

Alternate-forms method A method for establishing reliability of a measuring instrument by administering, in succession, equivalent forms of the same instrument to the same group of research participants.

Alternative hypothesis See Rival hypothesis.

Analytical memos Notes made by the researcher in reference to qualitative data that raise questions or make comments about meaning units and categories identified in a transcript.

Analytic generalization   The type of generalizability associated with case studies; the research findings of case studies are not assumed to fit another case no matter how apparently similar; rather, research findings are tested to see if they do in fact fit; used as working hypotheses to test practice principles.

Annual report   A detailed account or statement describing a program's processes and results over a given year; usually produced at the end of a fiscal year.

Antecedent variable   A variable that precedes the introduction of one or more dependent variables.

Antiquarianism   An interest in past events without reference to their importance or significance for the present; the reverse of presentism.

A Phase   In case-level evaluation designs, a phase (*A* Phase) in which the baseline measurement of the target problem is established before the intervention (*B* Phase) is implemented.

Applied research approach   A search for practical and applied research results that can be utilized in   actual social work practice situations; complementry to the pure research approach.

Area probability sampling   A form of cluster sampling that uses a three-stage process to provide the means to carry out a research study when no comprehensive list of the population can be compiled.

Assessment-related case study   A type of case study that generates knowledge about specific clients and their situations; focuses on the perspectives of the study's participants.

Audit trail   The documentation of critical steps in a qualitative research study that allows for an independent reviewer to examine and verify the steps in the research process and the conclusions of the research study.

Authority   The reliance on authority figures to tell us what is true; one of the six ways of knowing.

Availability sampling   See Convenience sampling.

Axes   Straight horizontal and vertical lines in a graph upon which values of a measurement, or the corresponding frequencies, are plotted.

Back-translation   The process of translating an original document into a second language, then having an independent translator conduct a subsequent translation of the first translation back into the language of origin; the second translation is then compared with the original document for equivalency.

Baseline   A period of time, usually three or four data collection periods, in which the level of the client's target problem is measured while no intervention is carried out; designated as the *A* Phase in single-system designs (case-level designs).

Between research methods approach   Triangulation by using different research methods available in *both* the qualitative and the quantitative research approaches in a single research study.

Bias   Not neutral; an inclination to some form of prejudice or preconceived position.

Biased sample   A sample unintentionally selected in such a way that some members of the population are more likely than others to be picked for sample membership.

Binomial effect size display (BESD)   A technique for interpreting the *r* value in a meta-analysis by converting it into a 2 by 2 table displaying magnitude of effect.

Biography   Tells the story of one individual's life, often suggesting what the person's influence was on social, political, or intellectual developments of the times.

B Phase   In case-level evaluation designs, the intervention phase, which may, or may not, include simultaneous measurements.

Case The basic unit of social work practice, whether it be an individual, a couple, a family, an agency, a community, a county, a state, or a country.

Case-level evaluation designs Designs in which data are collected about a single client system—an individual, group, or community—in order to evaluate the outcome of an intervention for the client system; a form of appraisal that monitors change for individual clients; designs in which data are collected about a single client system—an individual, group, or community—in order to evaluate the outcome of an intervention for the client system; also called single-system research designs.

Case study Using research approaches to investigate a research question or hypothesis relating to a specific case; used to develop theory and test hypotheses; an in-depth form of research in which data are gathered and analyzed about an individual unit of analysis, person, city, event, society, etc.; it allows more intensive analysis of specific details; the disadvantage is that it is hard to use the results to generalize to other cases.

Categories Groupings of related meaning units that are given one name; used to organize, summarize, and interpret qualitative data; categories in a qualitative study can change throughout the data analysis process, and the number of categories in a given study depends upon the breadth and depth the researcher aims for in the analysis.

Category In a qualitative data analysis, an aggregate of meaning units that share a common feature.

Category saturation The point in qualitative data analysis when all identified meaning units fit easily into the existing categorization scheme and no new categories emerge; the point at which first-level coding ends.

Causality A relationship of cause and effect; the effect will invariably occur when the cause is present.

Causal relationship A relationship between two variables for which we can state that the presence of, or absence of, one variable determines the presence of, or absence of, the other variable.

CD-ROM sources Computerized retrieval systems that allow searching for indexes and abstracts stored on compact computer discs (CDs).

Census data Data from the survey of an entire population in contrast to a survey of a sample.

Citation A brief identification of a reference that includes name of author(s), title, source, page numbers, and year of publication.

Classical experimental design An explanatory research design with randomly assigned experimental and control groups in which the dependent variable is measured before and after the treatment (the independent variable) for both groups, but only the experimental group receives the treatment (the dependent variable).

Client system *An* individual client, *a* couple, *a* family, *a* group, *an* organization, or *a* community that can be studied with case- and program-level evaluation designs and with quantitative and qualitative research approaches.

Closed-ended questions Items in a measuring instrument that require respondents to select one of several response categories provided; also known as fixed-alternative questions.

Cluster diagram An illustration of a conceptual classification scheme in which the researcher draws and labels circles for each theme that emerges from the data; the circles are organized in a way to depict the relationships between themes.

Cluster sampling A multistage probability sampling procedure in which the population is divided into groups (or clusters) and the groups, rather than the individuals, are selected for inclusion in the sample.

Code The label assigned to a category or theme in a qualitative data analysis; shortened versions of the actual category or theme label; used as markers in a qualitative data analysis; usually no longer than eight characters in length and can use a combination of letters, symbols, and numbers.

Codebook   A device used to organize qualitative data by applying labels and descriptions that draw distinctions between different parts of the data that have been collected.

Coding   (1) In data analysis, translating data from respondents onto a form that can be read by a computer; (2) In qualitative research, marking the text with codes for content categories.

Coding frame   A specific framework that delineates what data are to be coded and how they are to be coded in order to prepare them for analyses.

Coding sheets   In a literature review, a sheet used to record for each research study the complete reference, research design, measuring instrument(s), population and sample, outcomes, and other significant features of the study.

Cohort study   A longitudinal survey design that uses successive random samples to monitor how the characteristics of a specific group of people, who share certain characteristics or experiences (cohorts), change over time.

Collaterals   Professionals or staff members who serve as indigenous observers in the data collection process.

Collective biographies   Studies of the characteristics of groups of people who lived during a past period and had some major factor in common.

Collectivist culture   Societies that stress interdependence and seek the welfare and survival of the group above that of the individual; collectivist cultures are characterized by a readiness to be influenced by others, preference for conformity, and cooperation in relationships.

Comparative rating scale   A rating scale in which respondents are asked to compare an individual person, concept, or situation, to others.

Comparative research design   The study of more than one event, group, or society to isolate explanatory factors; there are two basic strategies in comparative research: (1) the study of elements that differ in many ways but that have some major factor in common, and (2) the study of elements that are highly similar but different in some important aspect, such as modern industrialized nations that have different health insurance systems.

Comparison group   A nonexperimental group to which research participants have not been randomly assigned for purposes of comparison with the experimental group. Not to be confused with control group.

Comparison group posttest-only design   A descriptive research design with two groups, experimental and comparison, in which the dependent variable is measured once for both groups, and only the experimental group receives the treatment (the independent variable).

Comparison group pretest-posttest design   A descriptive research design with two groups, experimental and comparison, in which the dependent variable is measured before and after the treatment for both groups, but only the experimental group receives the treatment.

Compensation   Attempts by researchers to compensate for the lack of treatment for control group members by administering it to them; a threat to internal validity.

Compensatory rivalry   Motivation of control group members to compete with experimental group members; a threat to internal validity.

Completeness   One of the four criteria for evaluating research hypotheses.

Complete observer   A term describing one of four possible research roles on a continuum of participant observation research; the complete observer acts simply as an observer and does not participate in the events at hand.

Complete participant   The complete participant is at the far end of the continuum from the complete observer in participant observation research; this research role is characterized by total involvement.

Comprehensive qualitative review   A nonstatistical synthesis of representative research studies relevant to a research problem, question, or hypothesis.

Computerized retrieval systems   Systems in which abstracts, indexes, and subject bibliographies are incorporated in computerized data bases to facilitate information retrieval.

Concept An understanding, an idea, or a mental image; a way of viewing and categorizing objects, processes, relations, and events.

Conceptual classification system The strategy for conceiving how units of qualitative data relate to each other; the method used to depict patterns that emerge from the various coding levels in qualitative data.

Conceptual framework A frame of reference that serves to guide a research study and is developed from theories, findings from a variety of other research studies, and the author's personal experiences and values.

Conceptualization The process of selecting the specific concepts to include in quantitative and qualitative research studies.

Conceptual validity See Construct validity.

Concurrent validity A form of criterion validity that is concerned with the ability of a measuring instrument to predict accurately an individual's status by comparing concurrent ratings (or scores) on one or more measuring instruments.

Confidentiality An ethical consideration in research whereby anonymity of research participants is safeguarded by ensuring that raw data are not seen by anyone other than the research team and that data presented have no identifying marks.

Confounding variable A variable operating in a specific situation in such a way that its effects cannot be separated; the effects of an extraneous variable thus confound the interpretation of a research study's findings.

Consistency Holding steadfast to the same principles and procedures in the qualitative data analysis process.

Constant A concept that does not vary and does not change; a characteristic that has the same value for all research participants or events in a research study.

Constant comparison A technique used to categorize qualitative data; it begins after the complete set of data has been examined and meaning units identified; each unit is classified as similar or different from the others; similar meaning units are lumped into the same category and classified by the same code.

Constant error Systematic error in measurement; error due to factors that consistently or systematically affect the variable being measured and that are concerned with the relatively stable qualities of respondents to a measuring instrument.

Construct See Concept.

Construct validity The degree to which a measuring instrument successfully measures a theoretical construct; the degree to which explanatory concepts account for variance in the scores of an instrument; also referred to as conceptual validity in meta-analyses.

Content analysis A data collection method in which communications are analyzed in a systematic, objective, and quantitative manner to produce new data.

Content validity The extent to which the content of a measuring instrument reflects the concept that is being measured and in fact measures that concept and not another.

Contextual detail The particulars of the environment in which the case (or unit of analysis) is embedded; provides a basis for understanding and interpreting case study data and results.

Contradictory evidence Identifying themes and categories that raise questions about the conclusions reached at the end of qualitative data analysis; outliers or extreme cases that are inconsistent or contradict the conclusions drawn from qualitative data; also called negative evidence.

Contributing partner A social work role in which the social worker joins forces with others who perform different roles in quantitative and qualitative research studies.

Control group A group of randomly assigned research participants in a research study who do not receive the experimental treatment and are used for comparison purposes. Not to be confused with comparison group.

Control variable   A variable, other than the independent variable(s) of primary interest, whose effects we can determine; an intervening variable that has been controlled for in the study's research design.

Convenience sampling   A nonprobability sampling procedure that relies on the closest and most available research participants to constitute a sample.

Convergent validity   The degree to which different measures of a construct yield similar results, or converge.

Correlated variables   Variables whose values are associated; values of one variable tend to be associated in a systematic way with values in the others.

Cost-benefit analysis   An analytical procedure that not only determines the costs of the program itself but also considers the monetary benefits of the program's effects.

Cost-effectiveness analysis   An analytical procedure that assesses the costs of the program itself; the monetary benefits of the program's effects are not assessed.

Cover letter   A letter to respondents or research participants that is written under the official letterhead of the sponsoring organization and describes the research study and its purpose.

Credibility   The trustworthiness of both the steps taken in qualitative data analysis and the conclusions reached.

Criterion validity   The degree to which the scores obtained on a measuring instrument are comparable to scores from an external criterion believed to measure the same concept.

Criterion variable   The variable whose values are predicted from measurements of the predictor variable.

Cross-cultural comparisons   Research studies that include culture as a major variable; studies that compare two or more diverse cultural groups.

Cross-sectional research design   A survey research design in which data are collected to indicate characteristics of a sample or population at a particular moment in time.

Cross-tabulation table   A simple table showing the joint frequency distribution of two or more nominal level variables.

Cultural encapsulation   The assumption that differences between groups represent some deficit or pathology.

Culturally equivalent   Similarity in the meaning of a construct between two cultures.

Cultural relativity   The belief that human thought and action can be judged only from the perspective of the culture out of which they have grown.

Cut-and-paste method   A method of analyzing qualitative data whereby the researcher cuts segments of the typed transcript and sorts these cuttings into relevant groupings; it can be done manually or with computer assistance.

Data   The numbers, words, or scores, generated by quantitative and qualitative research studies; the word *data* is plural.

Data analyses   The process of turning data into information; the process of reviewing, summarizing, and organizing isolated facts (data) such that they formulate a meaningful response to a research question.

Data archive   A place where many data sets are stored and from which data can be accessed.

Data coding   Translating data from one language or format into another, usually to make it readable for a computer.

Data collection method   Procedures specifying techniques to be employed, measuring instruments to be utilized, and activities to be conducted in implementing a quantitative or qualitative research study.

Data set A collection of related data items, such as the answers given by respondents to all the questions in a survey.

Data source The provider of the data, whether it be primary—the original source—or secondary—an intermediary between the research participant and the researcher analyzing the data.

Datum Singular of data.

Decision-making rule A statement that we use (in testing a hypothesis) to choose between the null hypothesis; indicates the range(s) of values of the observed statistic that leads to the rejection of the null hypothesis.

Deduction A conclusion about a specific case(s) based on the assumption that it shares a characteristic with an entire class of similar cases.

Deductive reasoning Forming a theory, making a deduction from the theory, and testing this deduction, or hypothesis, against reality; in research, applied to theory in order to arrive at a hypothesis that can be tested; a method of reasoning whereby a conclusion about specific cases is reached based on the assumption that they share characteristics with an entire class of similar cases.

Demand needs When needs are defined by only those individuals who indicate that they feel or perceive the need themselves.

Demographic data Vital and social facts that describe a sample or a population.

Demoralization Feelings of deprivation among control group members that may cause them to drop out of a research study; a threat to internal validity.

Dependability The soundness of both the steps taken in a qualitative data analysis and the conclusions reached.

Dependent events Events that influence the probability of occurrence of each other.

Dependent variable A variable that is dependent on, or caused by, another variable; an outcome variable, which is not manipulated directly but is measured to determine if the independent variable has had an effect.

Derived scores Raw scores of research participants, or groups, converted in such a way that meaningful comparisons with other individuals, or groups, are possible.

Descriptive research Research studies undertaken to increase precision in the definition of knowledge in a problem area where less is known than at the explanatory level; situated in the middle of the knowledge continuum.

Descriptive statistics Methods used for summarizing and describing data in a clear and precise manner.

Design bias Any effect that systematically distorts the outcome of a research study so that the study's results are not representative of the phenomenon under investigation.

Determinism A contention in quantitative research studies that only an event that is true over time and place and that will occur independent of beliefs about it (a predetermined event) permits the generalization of a study's findings; one of the four main limitations of the quantitative research approach.

Deterministic causation When a particular effect appears, the associated cause is always present; no other variables influence the relationship between cause and effect; the link between an independent variable that brings about the occurrence of the dependent variable every time.

Dichotomous variable A variable that can take on only one of two values.

Differential scale A questionnaire-type scale in which respondents are asked to consider questions representing different positions along a continuum and to select those with which they agree.

Differential selection A potential lack of equivalency among preformed groups of research participants; a threat to internal validity.

Diffusion of treatments Problems that may occur when experimental and control group members talk to each other about a research study; a threat to internal validity.

d index A measure of effect size in a meta-analysis.

Directional hypothesis See One-tailed hypotheses.

Directional test See One-tailed hypotheses.

Direct observation An obtrusive data collection method in which the focus is entirely on the behaviors of a group, or persons, being observed.

Direct observation notes These are the first level of field notes, usually chronologically organized, and they contain a detailed description of what was seen and heard; they may also include summary notes made after an interview.

Direct relationship A relationship between two variables such that high values of one variable are found with high values of the second variable, and vice versa.

Discriminant validity The degree to which a construct can be empirically differentiated, or discriminated from, other constructs.

Divergent validity The extent to which a measuring instrument differs from other instruments that measure unrelated constructs.

Dominant–less dominant research model A model combining qualitative and quantitative research approaches in a single study where one approach stands out as having the major role in the research design; the other approach has a minor or complementary role.

Double-barreled question A question in a measuring instrument that contains two questions in one, usually joined by an *and* or an *or*.

Duration recording A method of data collection that includes direct observation of the target problem and recording of the length of time each occurrence lasts within a specified observation period.

Ecological fallacy An error of reasoning committed by coming to conclusions about individuals based only on data about groups.

Edge coding Adding a series of blank lines on the right side of the response category in a measuring instrument to aid in processing the data.

Effect size In meta-analysis, the most widely used measure of the dependent variable; the effect size statistic provides a measure of the magnitude of the relationship found between the variables of interest and allows for the computation of summary statistics that apply to the analysis of all the studies considered as a whole.

Empirical Knowledge derived from the six ways of knowing.

Error of central tendency A measurement error due to the tendency of observers to rate respondents in the middle of a variable's value range, rather than consistently too high or too low.

Error of measurement See Measurement error.

Ethical research project The systematic inquiry into a problem area in an effort to discover new knowledge or test existing ideas; the research study is conducted in accordance with professional standards.

Ethics in research Quantitative and qualitative data that are collected and analyzed with careful attention to their accuracy, fidelity to logic, and respect for the feelings and rights of research participants; one of the four criteria for evaluating research problem areas *and* formulating research questions out of the problem areas.

Ethnicity A term that implies a common ancestry and cultural heritage and encompasses customs, values, beliefs, and behaviors.

Ethnocentricity Assumptions about normal behavior that are based on one's own cultural framework without taking cultural relativity into account; the failure to acknowledge alternative world views.

Ethnograph A computer software program that is designed for qualitative data analysis.

Ethnographic A form of content analysis used to document and explain the communication of meaning, as well as to verify theoretical relationships; any of several methods of describing social or cultural life based on direct, systematic observation, such as becoming a participant in a social system.

Ethnography The systematic study of human cultures and the similarities and dissimilarities between them.

Ethnomethodology Pioneered by Harold Garfinkel, this method of research focuses on the common-sense understanding of social life held by ordinary people (the ethos), usually as discovered through participant observation; often the observer's own methods of making sense of the situation become the object of investigation.

Evaluation A form of appraisal using valid and reliable research methods; there are numerous types of evaluations geared to produce data that in turn produce information that helps in the decision-making process; data from evaluations are used to develop quality programs and services.

Evaluative research designs Case- and program-level research designs that apply various research designs and data collection methods to find out if an intervention (or treatment) worked at the case level and if the social work program worked at the program level.

Existing documents Physical records left over from the past.

Existing statistics Previously calculated numerical summaries of data that exist in the public domain.

Experience and intuition Learning what is true through personal past experiences and intuition; two of the six ways of knowing.

Experiment A research study in which we have control over the levels of the independent variable and over the assignment of research participants, or objects, to different experimental conditions.

Experimental designs (1) Explanatory research designs or "ideal experiments"; (2) Case-level research designs that examine the question, "Did the client system improve because of social work intervention?"

Experimental group In an experimental research design, the group of research participants exposed to the manipulation of the independent variable; also referred to as a treatment group.

Explanatory research "Ideal" research studies undertaken to infer cause-effect and directional relationships in areas where a number of substantial research findings are already in place; situated at the top end of the knowledge continuum.

Exploratory research Research studies undertaken to gather data in areas of inquiry where very little is already known; situated at the lowest end of the knowledge continuum. See Non-experimental design.

External evaluation An evaluation that is conducted by someone who does not have any connection with the program; usually an evaluation that is requested by the agency's funding sources; this type of evaluation complements an in-house evaluation.

External validity The extent to which the findings of a research study can be generalized outside the specific research situation.

Extraneous variables See Rival hypothesis.

Face validity   The degree to which a measurement has self-evident meaning and measures what it appears to measure.

Feasibility   One of the four criteria for evaluating research problem areas *and* formulating research questions out of the problem areas.

Feedback   When data and information are returned to the persons who originally provided or collected them; used for informed decision making at the case and program levels; a basic principle underlying the design of evaluations.

Field notes   A record, usually written, of events observed by a researcher; the notes are taken as the study proceeds, and later they are used for analyses.

Field research   Research conducted in a real-life setting, not in a laboratory; the researcher neither creates nor manipulates anything within the study, but observes it.

Field-tested   The pilot of an instrument or research method in conditions equivalent to those that will be encountered in the research study.

File drawer problem   (1) In literature searches or reviews, the difficulty in locating studies that have not been published or are not easily retrievable; (2) In meta-analyses, errors in effect size due to reliance on published articles showing statistical significance.

Firsthand data   Data obtained from people who directly experience the problem being studied.

First-level coding   A process of identifying meaning units in a transcript, organizing the meaning units into categories, and assigning names to the categories.

Flexibility   The degree to which the design and procedures of a research study can be changed to adapt to contextual demands of the research setting.

Focus group interview   A group of people brought together to talk about their lives and experiences in free-flowing, open-ended discussions that usually focus on a single topic.

Formative evaluation   A type of evaluation that focuses on obtaining data that are helpful in planning the program and in improving its implementation and performance.

Frequency recording   A method of data collection by direct observations in which each occurrence of the target problem is recorded during a specified observation period.

Fugitive data   Informal information found outside regular publishing channels.

Gaining access   A term used in qualitative research to describe the process of engagement and relationship development between the researcher and the research participants.

Generalizable explanation evaluation model   An evaluation model whose proponents believe that many solutions are possible for any one social problem and that the effects of programs will differ under different conditions.

Generalizing results   Extending or applying the findings of a research study to individuals or situations not directly involved in the original research study; the ability to extend or apply the findings of a research study to subjects or situations that were not directly investigated.

Goal Attainment Scale (GAS)   A modified measurement scale used to evaluate case or program outcomes.

Government documents   Printed documents issued by local, state, and federal governments; such documents include reports of legislative committee hearings and investigations, studies commissioned by legislative commissions and executive agencies, statistical compilations such as the census, the regular and special reports of executive agencies, and much more.

Grand tour questions   Queries in which research participants are asked to provide wide-ranging background information; mainly used in qualitative research studies.

Graphic rating scale   A rating scale that describes an attribute on a continuum from one extreme to the other, with points of the continuum ordered in equal intervals and then assigned values.

Grounded theory   A final outcome of the qualitative research process that is reached when the insights are grounded on observations and the conclusions seem to be firm.

Group evaluation designs   Evaluation designs that are conducted with groups of cases for the purpose of assessing to what degree program objectives have been achieved.

Group research designs   Research designs conducted with two or more groups of cases, or research participants, for the purpose of answering research questions or testing hypotheses.

Halo effect   A measurement error due to the tendency of an observer to be influenced by a favorable trait(s) of a research participant(s).

Hawthorne effect   Effects on research participants' behaviors or attitudes attributable to their knowledge that they are taking part in a research study; a reactive effect; a threat to external validity.

Heterogeneity of respondents   The extent to which a research participant differs from other research participants.

Heuristic   A theory used to stimulate creative thought and scientific activity.

Historical research   The process by which we study the past; a method of inquiry that attempts to explain past events based on surviving artifacts.

History in research design   The possibility that events not accounted for in a research design may alter the second and subsequent measurements of the dependent variable; a threat to internal validity.

Homogeneity of respondents   The extent to which a research participant is similar to other research participants.

Hypothesis   A theory-based prediction of the expected results of a research study; a tentative explanation that a relationship between or among variables exists.

Hypothetico-deductive method   A hypothesis-testing approach that a hypothesis is derived on the deductions based from a theory.

Ideographic research   Research studies that focus on unique individuals or situations.

Implementation of a program   The action of carrying out a program in the way that it was designed.

Independent variable   A variable that is not dependent on another variable but is believed to cause or determine changes in the dependent variable; an antecedent variable that is directly manipulated in order to assess its effect on the dependent variable.

Index   A group of individual measures that, when combined, are meant to indicate some more general characteristic.

Indigenous observers   People who are naturally a part of the research participants' environment and who perform the data collection function; includes relevant others (e.g., family members, peers) and collaterals (e.g., social workers, staff members).

Indirect measures   A substitute variable, or a collection of representative variables, used when there is no direct measurement of the variable of interest; also called a proxy variable.

Individualism   A way of living that stresses independence, personal rather than group objectives, competition, and power in relationships; achievement measured through success of the individual as opposed to the group.

Individual synthesis   Analysis of published studies related to the subject under study.

Inductive reasoning   Building on specific observations of events, things, or processes to make inferences or more general statements; in research studies, applied to data collection and research results to make generalizations to see if they fit a theory; a method of reasoning whereby a conclusion is reached by building on specific observations of events, things, or processes to make inferences or more general statements.

Inferential statistics   Statistical methods that make it possible to draw tentative conclusions about the population based on observations of a sample selected from that population and, furthermore, to make a probability statement about those conclusions to aid in their evaluation.

Information anxiety   A feeling attributable to a lack of understanding of information, being overwhelmed by the amount of information to be accessed and understood, or not knowing if certain information exists.

Informed consent   Signed statements obtained from research participants prior to the initiation of the research study to inform them what their participation entails and that they are free to decline participation.

In-house evaluation   An evaluation that is conducted by someone who works within a program; usually an evaluation for the purpose of promoting better client services; also known as an internal evaluation; this type of evaluation complements an external evaluation.

Institutional review boards (IRBs)   Boards set up by institutions in order to protect research participants and to ensure that ethical issues are recognized and responded to in the a study's research design.

Instrumentation   Weaknesses of a measuring instrument, such as invalidity, unreliability, improper administrations, or mechanical breakdowns; a threat to internal validity.

Integration   Combining evaluation and day-to-day practice activities to develop a complete approach to client service delivery; a basic principle underlying the design of evaluations.

Interaction effects   Effects produced by the combination of two or more threats to internal validity.

Internal consistency   The extent to which the scores on two comparable halves of the same measuring instrument are similar; inter-item consistency.

Internal validity   The extent to which it can be demonstrated that the independent variable within a research study is the only cause of change in the dependent variable; overall soundness of the experimental procedures and measuring instruments.

Interobserver reliability   The stability or consistency of observations made by two or more observers at one point in time.

Interpretive notes   Notes on the researcher's interpretations of events that are kept separate from the record of the facts noted as direct observations.

Interquartile range   A number that measures the variability of a data set; the distance between the 75th and 25th percentiles.

Interrater reliability   The degree to which two or more independent observers, coders, or judges produce consistent results.

Interrupted time-series design   An explanatory research design in which there is only one group of research participants and the dependent variable is measured repeatedly before and after treatment; used in case- and program-evaluation designs.

Interval level of measurement   The level of measurement with an arbitrarily chosen zero point that classifies its values on an equally spaced continuum.

Interval recording   A method of data collection that involves a continuous direct observation of an individual during specified observation periods divided into equal time intervals.

Intervening variable   See Rival hypothesis.

Interview data   Isolated facts that are gathered when research participants respond to carefully constructed research questions; data, which are in the form of words, are recorded by transcription.

Interviewing   A conversation with a purpose.

Interview schedule   A measuring instrument used to collect data in face-to-face and telephone interviews.

Intraobserver reliability   The stability of observations made by a single observer at several points in time.

Intrusion into lives of research participants   The understanding that specific data collection methods can have negative consequences for research participants; a criterion for selecting a data collection method.

Itemized rating scales   A measuring instrument that presents a series of statements that respondents or observers rank in different positions on a specific attribute.

Journal   A written record of the process of a qualitative research study. Journal entries are made on an ongoing basis throughout the study and include study procedures as well as the researcher's reactions to emerging issues and concerns during the data analysis process.

Key informants   A subpopulation of research participants who seem to know much more about "the situation" than other research participants.

Knowledge base   A body of knowledge and skills specific to a certain discipline.

Knowledge creator and disseminator   A social work role in which the social worker actually carries out and disseminates the results of a quantitative and/or qualitative research study to generate knowledge for our profession.

Knowledge level continuum   The range of knowledge levels, from exploratory to descriptive to explanatory, at which research studies can be conducted.

Latent content   In a content analysis, the true meaning, depth, or intensity of a variable, or concept, under study.

Levels of measurement   The degree to which characteristics of a data set can be modeled mathematically; the higher the level of measurement, the more statistical methods that are applicable.

Limited review   An existing literature synthesis that summarizes in narrative form the findings and implications of a few research studies.

Literature review   See Literature search and Review of the literature.

Literature search   In a meta-analysis, scanning books and journals for basic, up-to-date research articles on studies relevant to a research question or hypothesis; sufficiently thorough to maximize the chance of including all relevant sources. See Review of the literature.

Logical consistency   The requirement that all the steps within a quantitative research study must be logically related to one another.

Logical positivism   A philosophy of science holding that the scientific method of inquiry is the only source of certain knowledge; in research, focuses on testing hypotheses deduced from theory.

Logistics   In evaluation, refers to getting research participants to do what they are supposed to do, getting research instruments distributed and returned; in general, the activities that ensure that procedural tasks of a research or evaluation study are carried out.

Longitudinal case study   An exploratory research design in which there is only one group of research participants and the dependent variable is measured more than once.

Longitudinal design A survey research design in which a measuring instrument(s) is administered to a sample of research participants repeatedly over time; used to detect dynamic processes such as opinion change.

Magnitude recording A direct-observation method of soliciting and recording data on amount, level, or degree of the target problem during each occurrence.

Management information system (MIS) System in which computer technology is used to process, store, retrieve, and analyze data collected routinely in such processes as social service delivery.

Manifest content Content of a communication that is obvious and clearly evident.

Manipulable solution evaluation model An evaluation model whose proponents believe that the greatest priority is to serve the public interest, not the interests of stakeholders, who have vested interests in the program being evaluated; closely resembles an outcome evaluation.

Matching A random assignment technique that assigns research participants to two or more groups so that the experimental and control groups are approximately equivalent in pretest scores or other characteristics, or so that all differences except the experimental condition are eliminated.

Maturation Unplanned change in research participants due to mental, physical, or other processes operating over time; a threat to internal validity.

Meaning units In a qualitative data analysis, a discrete segment of a transcript that can stand alone as a single idea; can consist of a single word, a partial or complete sentence, a paragraph, or more; used as the basic building blocks for developing categories.

Measurement The assignment of labels or numerals to the properties or attributes of observations, events, or objects according to specific rules.

Measurement error Any variation in measurement that cannot be attributed to the variable being measured; variability in responses produced by individual differences and other extraneous variables.

Measuring instrument Any instrument used to measure a variable(s).

Media myths The content of television shows, movies, and newspaper and magazine articles; one of the six ways of knowing.

Member checking A process of obtaining feedback and comments from research participants on interpretations and conclusions made from the qualitative data they provided; asking research participants to confirm or refute the conclusions made.

Meta-analysis A research method in which mathematical procedures are applied to the quantitative findings of studies located in a literature search to produce new summary statistics and to describe the findings for a meta-analysis.

Methodology The procedures and rules that detail how a single research study is conducted.

Micro-level data Data derived from individual units of analysis, whether these data sources are individuals, families, corporations, etc.; for example, age and years of formal schooling are two variables requiring micro-level data.

Missing data Data not available for a research participant about whom other data are available, such as when a respondent fails to answer one of the questions in a survey.

Missing links When two categories or themes seem to be related, but not directly so, it may be that a third variable connects the two.

Mixed research model A model combining aspects of qualitative and quantitative research approaches within all (or many) of the methodological steps contained within a single research study.

Monitoring approach to evaluation   Evaluation that aims to provide ongoing feedback so that a program can be improved while it is still underway; it contributes to the continuous development and improvement of a human service program; this approach complements the project approach to evaluation.

Mortality   Loss of research participants through normal attrition over time in an experimental design that requires retesting; a threat to internal validity.

Multicultural research   Representation of diverse cultural factors in the subjects of study; such diversity variables may include religion, race, ethnicity, language preference, gender, etc.

Multigroup posttest-only design   An exploratory research design in which there is more than one group of research participants and the dependent variable is measured only once for each group.

Multiple-baseline design   A case-level evaluation design with more than one baseline period and intervention phase, which allows the causal inferences regarding the relationship between a treatment intervention and its effect on clients' target problems and which helps control for extraneous variables. See Interrupted time-series design.

Multiple-group design   An experimental research design with one control group and several experimental groups.

Multiple-treatment interference   Effects of the results of a first treatment on the results of second and subsequent treatments; a threat to external validity.

Multistage probability sampling   Probability sampling procedures used when a comprehensive list of the population does not exist and it is not possible to construct one.

Multivariate   (1) A relationship involving two or more variables; (2) A hypothesis stating an assertion about two or more variables and how they relate to one another.

Multivariate analysis   A statistical analysis of the relationship among three or more variables.

Narrowband measuring instrument   Measuring instruments that focus on a single, or a few, variables.

Nationality   A term that refers to country of origin.

Naturalist   A person who studies the facts of nature as they occur under natural conditions.

Needs assessment   Program-level evaluation activities that aim to assess the feasibility for establishing or continuing a particular social service program; an evaluation that aims to assess the need for a human service by verifying that a social problem exists within a specific client population to an extent that warrants services.

Negative case sampling   Purposefully selecting research participants based on the fact that they have different characteristics than previous cases.

Nominal level of measurement   The level of measurement that classifies variables by assigning names or categories that are mutually exclusive and exhaustive.

Nondirectional test   See Two-tailed hypotheses.

Nonexperimental design   A research design at the exploratory, or lowest, level of the knowledge continuum; also called preexperimental.

Nonoccurrence data   In the structured-observation method of data collection, a recording of only those time intervals in which the target problem did not occur.

Nonparametric tests   Refers to statistical tests of hypotheses about population probability distributions, but not about specific parameters of the distributions.

Nonprobability sampling   Sampling procedures in which all of the persons, events, or objects in the sampling frame have an unknown, and usually different, probability of being included in a sample.

Nonreactive   Methods of research that do not allow the research participants to know that they are being studied; thus, they do not alter their responses for the benefit of the researcher.

Nonresponse The rate of nonresponse in survey research is calculated by dividing the total number of respondents by the total number in the sample, minus any units verified as ineligible.

Nonsampling errors Errors in a research study's results that are not due to the sampling procedures.

Norm In measurement, an average or set group standard of achievement that can be used to interpret individual scores; normative data describing statistical properties of a measuring instrument such as means and standard deviations.

Normalization group The population sample to which a measuring instrument under development is administered in order to establish norms; also called the norm group.

Normative needs When needs are defined by comparing the objective living conditions of a target population with what society—or, at least, that segment of society concerned with helping the target population—deems acceptable or desirable from a humanitarian standpoint.

Null hypothesis A statement concerning one or more parameters that is subjected to a statistical test; a statement that there is no relationship between the two variables of interest.

Numbers The basic data unit of analysis used in quantitative research studies.

Objectivity A research stance in which a study is carried out and its data are examined and interpreted without distortion by personal feelings or biases.

Observer One of four roles on a continuum of participation in participant observation research; the level of involvement of the observer participant is lower than of the complete participant and higher than of the participant observer.

Obtrusive data collection methods Direct data collection methods that can influence the variables under study or the responses of research participants; data collection methods that produce reactive effects.

Occurrence data In the structured-observation method of data collection, a recording of the first occurrence of the target problem during each time interval.

One-group posttest-only design An exploratory research design in which the dependent variable is measured only once.

One-group pretest-posttest design A descriptive research design in which the dependent variable is measured twice—before and after treatment.

One-stage probability sampling Probability sampling procedures in which the selection of a sample that is drawn from a specific population is completed in a single process.

One-tailed hypotheses Statements that predict specific relationships between independent and dependent variables.

On-line sources Computerized literary retrieval systems that provide printouts of indexes and abstracts.

Open-ended questions Unstructured questions in which the response categories are not specified or detailed.

Operational definition Explicit specification of a variable in such a way that its measurement is possible.

Operationalization The process of developing operational definitions of the variables that are contained within the concepts of a quantitative and/or qualitative research study.

Ordinal level of measurement The level of measurement that classifies variables by rank-ordering them from high to low or from most to least.

Outcome The effect of the manipulation of the independent variable on the dependent variable; the end product of a treatment intervention.

Outcome measure   The criterion or basis for measuring effects of the independent variable or change in the dependent variable.

Outcome-oriented case study   A type of case study that investigates whether client outcomes were in fact achieved.

Outside observers   Trained observers who are not a part of the research participants' environment and who are brought in to record data.

Paired observations   An observation on two variables, where the intent is to examine the relationship between them.

Panel research study   A longitudinal survey design in which the same group of research participants (the panel) is followed over time by surveying them on successive occasions.

Parametric tests   Statistical methods for estimating parameters or testing hypotheses about population parameters.

Participant observation   An obtrusive data collection method in which the researcher, or the observer, participates in the life of those being observed; both an obtrusive data collection method and a research approach, this method is characterized by the one doing the study undertaking roles that involve establishing and maintaining ongoing relationships with research participants who are often in the field settings, and observing and participating with the research participants over time.

Participant observer   The participant observer is one of four roles on a continuum of participation in participant observation research; the level of involvement of the participant observer is higher than of the complete observer and lower than of the observer participant.

Permanent product recording   A method of data collection in which the occurrence of the target problem is determined by observing the permanent product or record of the target problem.

Pilot study   See Pretest (2).

Population   An entire set, or universe, of people, objects, or events of concern to a research study, from which a sample is drawn.

Positivism   See Logical positivism.

Posttest   Measurement of the dependent variable after the introduction of the independent variable.

Potential for testing   One of the four criteria for evaluating research hypotheses.

Practitioner/researcher   A social worker who guides practice through the use of research findings; collects data throughout an intervention using research methods, skills, and tools; disseminates practice findings.

Pragmatists   Researchers who believe that both qualitative and quantitative research approaches can be integrated in a single research study.

Predictive validity   A form of criterion validity that is concerned with the ability of a measuring instrument to predict future performance or status on the basis of present performance or status.

Predictor variable   The variable that, it is believed, allows us to improve our ability to predict values of the criterion variable.

Preexposure   Tasks to be carried out in advance of a research study to sensitize the researcher to the culture of interest; these tasks may include participation in cultural experiences, intercultural sharing, case studies, ethnic literature reviews, value statement exercises, etc.

Preliminary plan for data analysis   A strategy for analyzing qualitative data that is outlined in the beginning stages of a qualitative research study; the plan has two general steps: (1) previewing the data, and (2) outlining what to record in the researcher's journal.

Presentism Applying current thinking and concepts to interpretations of past events or intentions.

Pretest (1) Measurement of the dependent variable prior to the introduction of the independent variable; (2) Administration of a measuring instrument to a group of people who will not be included in the study to determine difficulties the research participants may have in answering questions and the general impression given by the instrument; also called a pilot study.

Pretest-treatment interaction Effects that a pretest has on the responses of research participants to the introduction of the independent variable or the experimental treatment; a threat to external validity.

Previous research Research studies that have already been completed and published; they provide information about data collection methods used to investigate research questions that are similar to our own; a criterion for selecting a data collection method.

Primary data Data in its original form, as collected from the research participants; a primary data source is one that puts as few intermediaries as possible between the production and the study of the data.

Primary language The preferred language of the research participants.

Primary reference source A report of a research study by the person who conducted the study; usually an article in a professional journal.

Probability sampling Sampling procedures in which every member of the designated population has a known probability of being selected for the sample.

Problem area In social work research, a general expressed difficulty about which something researchable is unknown; not to be confused with research question.

Problem-solving process A generic method with specified phases for solving problems; also described as the scientific method.

Process-oriented case study A type of case study that illuminates the micro-steps of intervention that lead to client outcomes; describes how programs and interventions work and gives insight to the "black box" of intervention.

Professional standards Rules for making judgments about evaluation activity that are established by a group of persons who have advanced education and usually have the same occupation.

Program An organized set of political, administrative, and clinical activities that function to fulfill some social purpose.

Program development The constant effort to improve program services to better achieve outcomes; a basic principle underlying the design of evaluations.

Program efficiency Assessment of a program's outcome in relation to the costs of obtaining the outcome.

Program evaluation A form of appraisal, using valid and reliable research methods, that examines the processes or outcomes of an organization that exists to fulfill some social purpose.

Program goal A statement defining the intent of a program that cannot be directly evaluated; it can, however, be evaluated indirectly by the program's objectives, which are derived from the program goal; not to be confused with program objectives.

Program-level evaluation A form of appraisal that monitors change for groups of clients and organizational performance.

Program objectives A statement that clearly and exactly specifies the expected change, or intended result, for individuals receiving program services; qualities of well-chosen objectives are meaningfulness, specificity, measurability, and directionality; not to be confused with program goal.

Program participation   The philosophy and structure of a program that will support or supplant the successful implementation of a research study within an existing social service program; a criterion for selecting a data collection method.

Program process   The coordination of administrative and clinical activities that are designed to achieve a program's goal.

Program results   A report on how effective a program is at meeting its stated objectives.

Project approach to evaluation   Evaluation that aims to assess a completed or finished program; this approach complements the monitoring approach.

Proxy   An indirect measure of a variable that a researcher wants to study; it is often used when the variable of inquiry is difficult to measure or observe directly.

Pure research approach   A search for theoretical results that can be utilized to develop theory and expand our profession's knowledge bases; complementary to the applied research approach.

Purists   Researchers who believe that qualitative and quantitative research approaches should never be mixed.

Purpose statement   A declaration of words that clearly describes a research study's intent.

Purposive sampling   A nonprobability sampling procedure in which research participants with particular characteristics are purposely selected for inclusion in a research sample; also known as judgmental or theoretical sampling.

Qualitative data   Data that measure a quality or kind; when referring to variables, qualitative is another term for categorical or nominal variable values; when speaking of kinds of research, qualitative refers to studies of subjects that are hard to quantify; qualitative research produces descriptive data based on spoken or written words and observable behaviors.

Qualitative research approach   Research studies that focus on the facts of nature as they occur under natural conditions and emphasize qualitative description and generalization; a process of discovery sensitive to holistic and ecological issues; a research approach that is complementry to the quantitative research approach.

Quantification   In measurement, the reduction of data to numerical form in order to analyze them by way of mathematical or statistical techniques.

Quantitative data   Data that measure a quantity or amount.

Quantitative research approach   A research approach to discover relationships and facts that are generalizable; research that is "independent" of subjective beliefs, feelings, wishes, and values; a research approach that is complementry to the qualitative research approach.

Quasi-experiment   A research design at the descriptive level of the knowledge continuum that resembles an "ideal" experiment but does not allow for random selection or assignment of research participants to groups and often does not control for rival hypotheses.

Questionnaire-type scale   A type of measuring instrument in which multiple responses are usually combined to form a single overall score for a respondent.

Quota sampling   A nonprobability sampling procedure in which the relevant characteristics of the sample are identified, the proportion of these characteristics in the population is determined, and research participants are selected from each category until the predetermined proportion (quota) has been achieved.

Race   A variable based on physical attributes that can be subdivided into the Caucasoid, Negroid, and Mongoloid races.

Random assignment   The process of assigning individuals to experimental or control groups so that the groups are equivalent; also referred to as randomization.

Random error   Variable error in measurement; error due to unknown or uncontrolled factors that affect the variable being measured and the process of measurement in an inconsistent fashion.

Randomized cross-sectional survey design   A descriptive research design in which there is only one group, the dependent variable is measured only once, the research participants are randomly selected from the population, and there is no independent variable.

Randomized longitudinal survey design   A descriptive research design in which there is only one group, the dependent variable is measured more than once, and research participants are randomly selected from the population before each treatment.

Randomized one-group posttest-only design   A descriptive research design in which there is only one group, the dependent variable is measured only once, and research participants are randomly selected from the population.

Randomized posttest-only control group design   An explanatory research design in which there are two or more randomly assigned groups, the control group does not receive treatment, and the experimental groups receive different treatments.

Random numbers table   A computer-generated or published table of numbers in which each number has an equal chance of appearing in each position in the table.

Random sampling   An unbiased selection process conducted so that all members of a population have an equal chance of being selected to participate in a research study.

Rank-order scale   A comparative rating scale in which the rater is asked to rank specific individuals in relation to one another on some characteristic.

Rating scale   A type of measuring instrument in which responses are rated on a continuum or in an ordered set of categories, with numerical values assigned to each point or category.

Ratio level of measurement   The level of measurement that has a nonarbitrary, fixed zero point and classifies the values of a variable on an equally spaced continuum.

Raw scores   Scores derived from administration of a measuring instrument to research participants or groups.

Reactive effect   (1) An effect on outcome measures due to the research participants' awareness that they are being observed or interviewed; a threat to external and internal validity; (2) Alteration of the variables being measured or the respondents' performance on the measuring instrument due to administration of the instrument.

Reactivity   The belief that things being observed or measured are affected by the fact that they are being observed or measured; one of the four main limitations of the quantitative research approach.

Reassessment   A step in qualitative data analysis in which the researcher interrupts the data analysis process to reaffirm the rules used to decide which meaning units are placed within different categories.

Recoding   Developing and applying new variable value labels to a variable that has previously been coded; usually, recoding is done to make variables from one or more data sets comparable.

Reductionism   In the quantitative research approach, the operationalization of concepts by reducing them to common measurable variables; one of the four main limitations of the quantitative research approach.

Relevancy   One of the four criteria for evaluating research problem areas *and* formulating research questions out of the problem areas.

Reliability (1) The degree of accuracy, precision, or consistency in results of a measuring instrument, including the ability to produce the same results when the same variable is measured more than once or repeated applications of the same test on the same individual produce the same measurement; (2) The degree to which individual differences on scores or in data are due either to true differences or to errors in measurement.

Replication Repetition of the same research procedures by a second researcher for the purpose of determining if earlier results can be confirmed.

Researchability The extent to which a research problem is in fact researchable and the problem can be resolved through the consideration of data derived from a research study; one of the four criteria for evaluating research problem areas *and* formulating research questions out of the problem areas.

Research attitude A way that we view the world. It is an attitude that highly values craftsmanship, with pride in creativity, high-quality standards, and hard work.

Research consumer A social work role reflecting the ethical obligation to base interventions on the most up-to-date research knowledge available.

Research design The entire plan of a quantitative and/or qualitative research study from problem conceptualization to the dissemination of findings.

Researcher bias The tendency of researchers to find results they expect to find; a threat to external validity.

Research hypothesis A statement about a study's research question that predicts the existence of a particular relationship between the independent and dependent variables; can be used in both the quantitative and qualitative approaches to research.

Research method The use of quantitative and qualitative research approaches to find out what is true; one of the six ways of knowing.

Research participants People utilized in research studies; also called subjects or cases.

Research question A specific research question that is formulated directly out of the general research problem area; answered by the qualitative and/or quantitative research approach; not to be confused with problem area.

Resources The costs associated with collecting data in any given research study; includes materials and supplies, equipment rental, transportation, training staff, and staff time; a criterion for selecting a data collection method.

Response categories Possible responses assigned to each question in a standardized measuring instrument, with a lower value generally indicating a low level of the variable being measured and a larger value indicating a higher level.

Response rate The total number of responses obtained from potential research participants to a measuring instrument divided by the total number of responses requested, usually expressed in the form of a percentage.

Response set Personal style; the tendency of research participants to respond to a measuring instrument in a particular way, regardless of the questions asked, or the tendency of observers or interviewers to react in certain ways; a source of constant error.

Review of the literature (1) A search of the professional literature to provide background knowledge of what has already been examined or tested in a specific problem area; (2) Use of any information source, such as a computerized data base, to locate existing data or information on a research problem, question, or hypothesis.

Rival hypothesis A hypothesis that is a plausible alternative to the research hypothesis and might explain the results as well or better; a hypothesis involving extraneous or intervening variables other than the independent variable in the research hypothesis; also referred to as an alternative hypothesis.

Rules of correspondence A characteristic of measurement stipulating that numerals or symbols are assigned to properties of individuals, objects, or events according to specified rules.

Sample   A subset of a population of individuals, objects, or events chosen to participate in or to be considered in a research study.

Sampling error   (1) The degree of difference that can be expected between the sample and the population from which it was drawn; (2) A mistake in a research study's results that is due to sampling procedures.

Sampling frame   A listing of units (people, objects, or events) in a population from which a sample is drawn.

Sampling plan   A method of selecting members of a population for inclusion in a research study, using procedures that make it possible to draw inferences about the population from the sample statistics.

Sampling theory   The logic of using methods to ensure that a sample and a population are similar in all relevant characteristics.

Scale   A measuring instrument composed of several items that are logically or empirically structured to measure a construct.

Scattergram   A graphic representation of the relationship between two interval- or ratio-level variables.

Science   Knowledge that has been obtained and tested through use of quantitative and qualitative research studies.

Scientific community   A group that shares the same general norms for both research activity and acceptance of scientific findings and explanations.

Scientific determinism   See Determinism.

Scientific method   A generic method with specified steps for solving problems; the principles and procedures used in the systematic pursuit of knowledge.

Scope of a study   The extent to which a problem area is covered in a single research study; a criterion for selecting a data collection method.

Score   A numerical value assigned to an observation; also called data.

Search statement   A preliminary search statement developed by the researcher prior to a literature search and which contains terms that can be combined to elicit specific data.

Secondary analysis   An unobtrusive data collection method in which available data that predate the formulation of a research study are used to answer the research question or test the hypothesis.

Secondary data   Data that predate the formulation of the research study and which are used to answer the research question or test the hypothesis.

Secondary data sources   A data source that provides nonoriginal, secondhand data.

Secondary reference source   A source related to a primary source or sources, such as a critique of a particular source item or a literature review, bibliography, or commentary on several items.

Secondhand data   Data obtained from people who are indirectly connected to the problem being studied.

Selection-treatment interaction   The relationship between the manner of selecting research participants and their response to the independent variable; a threat to external validity.

Self-anchored scales   A rating scale in which research participants rate themselves on a continuum of values, according to their own referents for each point.

Self-disclosure   Shared communication about oneself, including one's behaviors, beliefs, and attitudes.

Semantic differential scale   A modified measurement scale in which research participants rate their perceptions of the variable under study along three dimensions—evaluation, potency, and activity.

Sequential triangulation When two distinct and separate phases of a research study are conducted and the results of the first phase are considered essential for planning the second phase; research questions in Phase 1 are answered before research questions in Phase 2 are formulated.

Service recipients People who use human services—individuals, couples, families, groups, organizations, and communities; also known as clients or consumers; a stakeholder group in evaluation.

Simple random sampling A one-stage probability sampling procedure in which members of a population are selected one at a time, without a chance of being selected again, until the desired sample size is obtained.

Simultaneous triangulation When the results of a quantitative and qualitative research question are answered at the same time; results to the qualitative research questions, for example, are reported separately and do not necessarily relate to, or confirm, the results from the quantitative phase.

Situationalists Researchers who assert that certain research approaches (qualitative or quantitative) are appropriate for specific situations.

Situation-specific variable A variable that may be observable only in certain environments and under certain circumstances, or with particular people.

Size of a study The number of people, places, or systems that are included in a single research study; a criterion for selecting a data collection method.

Snowball sampling A nonprobability sampling procedure in which individuals selected for inclusion in a sample are asked to identify other individuals from the population who might be included; useful to locate people with divergent points of view.

Social desirability (1) A response set in which research participants tend to answer questions in a way that they perceive as giving favorable impressions of themselves; (2) The inclination of data providers to report data that present a socially desirable impression of themselves or their reference groups. Also referred to as impression management.

Socially acceptable response Bias in an answer that comes from research participants trying to answer questions as they think a "good" person should, rather than in a way that reveals what they actually believe or feel.

Social work research Scientific inquiry in which qualitative and quantitative research approaches are used to answer research questions and create new, generally applicable knowledge in the field of social work.

Socioeconomic variables Any one of several measures of social rank, usually including income, education, and occupational prestige; abbreviated "SES."

Solomon four-group design An explanatory research design with four randomly assigned groups, two experimental and two control; the dependent variable is measured before and after treatment for one experimental and one control group, but only after treatment for the other two groups, and only experimental groups receive the treatment.

Specificity One of the four criteria for evaluating research hypotheses.

Split-half method A method for establishing the reliability of a measuring instrument by dividing it into comparable halves and comparing the scores between the two halves.

Spot-check recording A method of data collection that involves direct observation of the target problem at specified intervals rather than continuously.

Stakeholder A person or group of people having a direct or indirect interest in the results of an evaluation.

Stakeholder service evaluation model Proponents of this evaluation model believe that program evaluations will be more likely to be utilized, and thus have a greater impact on social problems, when they are tailored to the needs of stakeholders; in this model, the purpose of program evaluation is not to generalize findings to other sites, but rather to restrict the evaluation effort to a particular program.

Standardized measuring instrument A professionally developed measuring instrument that provides for uniform administration and scoring and generates normative data against which later results can be evaluated.

Statistics The branch of mathematics concerned with the collection and analysis of data using statistical techniques.

Stratified random sampling A one-stage probability sampling procedure in which a population is divided into two or more strata to be sampled separately, using simple random or systematic random sampling techniques.

Structured interview schedule A complete list of questions to be asked and spaces for recording the answers; the interview schedule is used by interviewers when questioning respondents.

Structured observation A data collection method in which people are observed in their natural environments using specified methods and measurement procedures. See Direct observation.

Subscale A component of a scale that measures some part or aspect of a major construct; also composed of several items that are logically or empirically structured.

Summated scale A questionnaire-type scale in which research participants are asked to indicate the degree of their agreement or disagreement with a series of questions.

Summative evaluation A type of evaluation that examines the ultimate success of a program and assists with decisions about whether a program should be continued or chosen in the first place among alternative program options.

Survey research A data collection method that uses survey-type data collection measuring instruments to obtain opinions or answers from a population or sample of research participants in order to describe or study them as a group.

Synthesis Undertaking the search for meaning in our sources of information at every step of the research process; combining parts such as data, concepts, and theories to arrive at a higher level of understanding.

Systematic To arrange the steps of a research study in a methodical way.

Systematic random sampling A one-stage probability sampling procedure in which every person at a designated interval in a specific population is selected to be included in a research study's sample.

Systematic error Measurement error that is consistent, not random.

Target population The group about which a researcher wants to draw conclusions; another term for a population about which one aims to make inferences.

Target problem (1) In case-level evaluation designs, the problems social workers seek to solve for their clients; (2) A measurable behavior, feeling, or cognition that is either a problem in itself or symptomatic of some other problem.

Temporal research design A research study that includes time as a major variable; the purpose of this design is to investigate change in the distribution of a variable or in relationships among variables over time; there are three types of temporal research designs: cohort, panel, and trend.

Temporal stability Consistency of responses to a measuring instrument over time; reliability of an instrument across forms and across administrations.

Testing effect The effect that taking a pretest might have on posttest scores; a threat to internal validity.

Test-retest reliability Reliability of a measuring instrument established through repeated administration to the same group of individuals.

Thematic notes   In observational research, thematic notes are a record of emerging ideas, hypotheses, theories, and conjectures; thematic notes provide a place for the researcher to speculate and identify themes, make linkages between ideas and events, and articulate thoughts as they emerge in the field setting.

Theme   In qualitative data analysis, a concept or idea that describes a single category or a grouping of categories; an abstract interpretation of qualitative data.

Theoretical framework   A frame of reference that serves to guide a research study and is developed from theories, findings from a variety of other studies, and the researcher's personal experiences.

Theoretical sampling   See Purposive sampling.

Theory   A reasoned set of propositions, derived from and supported by established data, which serves to explain a group of phenomena; a conjectural explanation that may, or may not, be supported by data generated from qualitative and quantitative research studies.

Time orientation   An important cultural factor that considers whether one is future-, present-, or past-oriented; for instance, individuals who are "present-oriented" would not be as preoccupied with advance planning as those who are "future-oriented."

Time-series design   See Interrupted time-series design.

Tradition   Traditional cultural beliefs that we accept—without question—as true; one of the six ways of knowing.

Transcript   A written, printed, or typed copy of interview data or any other written material that have been gathered for a qualitative research study.

Transition statements   Sentences used to indicate a change in direction or focus of questions in a measuring instrument.

Treatment group   See Experimental group.

Trend study   A longitudinal study design in which data from surveys carried out at periodic intervals on samples drawn from a particular population are used to reveal trends over time.

Triangulation   The idea of combining different research methods in all steps associated with a single research study; assumes that any bias inherent in one particular method will be neutralized when used in conjunction with other research methods; seeks convergence of a study's results; using more than one research method and source of data to study the same phenomena and to enhance validity; there are several types of triangulation, but the essence of the term is that multiple perspectives are compared; it can involve multiple data sources or multiple data analyzers; the hope is that the different perspectives will confirm each other, adding weight to the credibility and dependability of qualitative data analysis.

Triangulation of analysts   Using multiple data analyzers to code a single segment of transcript and comparing the amount of agreement between analyzers; a method used to verify coding of qualitative data.

Two-phase research model   A model combining qualitative and quantitative research approaches in a single study where each approach is conducted as a separate and distinct phase of the study.

Two-tailed hypotheses   Statements that *do not* predict specific relationships between independent and dependent variables.

Unit of analysis   A specific research participant (person, object, or event) or the sample or population relevant to the research question; the persons or things being studied; units of analysis in research are often persons, but may be groups, political parties, newspaper editorials, unions, hospitals, schools, etc.; a particular unit of analysis from which data are gathered is called a case.

Univariate   A hypothesis or research design involving a single variable.

Universe   See Population.

Unobtrusive methods Data collection methods that do not influence the variable under study or the responses of research participants; methods that avoid reactive effects.

Unstructured interviews A series of questions that allow flexibility for both the research participant and the interviewer to make changes during the process.

Validity (1) The extent to which a measuring instrument measures the variable it is supposed to measure and measures it accurately; (2) The degree to which an instrument is able to do what it is intended to do, in terms of both experimental procedures and measuring instruments (internal validity) and generalizability of results (external validity); (3) The degree to which scores on a measuring instrument correlate with measures of performance on some other criterion.

Variable A concept with characteristics that can take on different values.

Verbatim recording Recording interview data word-for-word and including significant gestures, pauses, and expressions of persons in the interview.

Wideband measuring instrument An instrument that measures more than one variable.

Within-methods research approach Triangulation by using different research methods available in *either* the qualitative *or* the quantitative research approaches in a single research study.

Words The basic data unit of analysis used in qualitative research studies.

Worker cooperation The actions and attitudes of program personnel when carrying out a research study within an existing social service program; a criterion for selecting a data collection method.

Working hypothesis An assertion about a relationship between two or more variables that may not be true but is plausible and worth examining.

References and
Further Readings

Allen, M.J. (1995). *Introduction to psychological research.* Itasca, IL: F.E. Peacock.

Allen, M. J., & Yen, W. M. (1979). *Introduction to measurement theory.* Monterey, CA: Brooks/Cole.

Alreck, P.L., & Settle, R.B. (1985). *The survey research handbook.* Homewood, IL: Irwin.

Altheide, D. (1987). Ethnographic content analysis. *Qualitative Sociology, 10,* 62-77.

American Association on Mental Deficiency (1977). *Consent handbook* (No. 3). Washington, DC: Author.

American Psychological Association. (1971). *Ethical principles in the conduct of research with human participants.* Washington, DC: Author.

American Psychological Association. (1973). *Ethical principles in the conduct of research with human participants.* Washington, DC: Author.

American Psychological Association. (1981). *Ethical principles in the conduct of research with human participants.* Washington, DC: Author.

American Psychological Association. (1981). *Specialty guidelines for the delivery of services by counseling psychologists.* Washington, DC: Author.

Anastasi, A. (1988). *Psychological testing* (6th ed.). New York: Macmillan.

Atherton, C., & Klemmack, D. (1982). *Research methods in social work.* Lexington, MA: Heath.

Atkinson, D.R., Morten, G., & Sue, D.W. (1983). *Counseling American minorities: A cross-cultural perspective.* Dubuque, IA: Brown.

Atkinson, J. (1987). Gender roles in marriage and the family: A critique and some proposals. *Journal of Family Issues, 8,* 5-41.

Attneave, C. (1982). American Indians and Alaska Native families: Emigrants in their own homeland. In M. McGoldrick, J.K. Pearce, & J. Giordano (Eds.), *Ethnicity and family therapy* (pp. 55-83). New York: Guilford Press.

Austin, M.J., & Crowell, J. (1985). Survey research. In R.M. Grinnell, Jr. (Ed.), *Social work research and evaluation* (2nd ed., pp. 275-305). Itasca, IL: F.E. Peacock.

Axelson, J.A. (1985). *Counseling and development in a multicultural society.* Belmont, CA: Wadsworth.

Babbie, E.R. (1992). *The practice of social research* (6th ed.). Pacific Grove, CA: Wadsworth.

Babbie, E.R. (1995). *The practice of social research* (7th ed.). Pacific Grove, CA: Wadsworth.

Badgley, R. (Chairman). (1984). *Sexual offenses against children. Volume 1: Report of the committee on sexual offenses against children and youths.* Ottawa, Canada: Ministry of Supply and Services.

Bailey, K.D. (1994). *Methods of social research* (4th ed.). New York: Free Press.

Balassone, M.L. (1994). Does emphasizing accountability and evidence dilute service delivery and the helping role? No! In W.W. Hudson & P.S. Nurius (Eds.), *Controversial issues in social work research* (pp. 15-19). Needham Heights, MA: Allyn & Bacon.

Bales, R.F. (1950). *Interaction process analysis.* Reading, MA: Addison-Wesley.

Bane, M.J. (1986). Household composition and poverty. In S.H. Danziger & D.H. Weinberg (Eds.), *Fighting poverty: What works and what doesn't* (pp. 209-231). Cambridge, MA: Harvard University Press.

Barlow, D.H., Hayes, S.C., & Nelson, R.O. (1984). *The scientist-practitioner: Research and accountability in applied settings.* Elmsford, NY: Pergamon.

Barlow, D.H., & Hersen, M. (1984). *Single-case experimental designs: Strategies for studying behavior change* (2nd ed.). Elmsford, NY: Pergamon.

Baumeister, R.F. (1988). Should we stop studiying sex differences altogether? *American Psychologist, 43,* 1092-1095.

Beck, D.F., & Jones, M.A. (1973). *Progress on family problems.* New York: Family Service Association of America.

Bellack, A.S., & Hersen, M. (1977). Self-report inventories in behavioral assessment. In J.D. Cone & R. P. Hawkins (Eds.), *Behavioral assessment: New directions in clinical psychology* (pp. 52- 76). New York: Brunner/Mazel.

Benner, P. (Ed.). (1994). *Interpretive phenomenology.* Newbury Park, CA: Sage.

Bennet, M.J. (1986). A developmental approach to training for intercultural sensitivity. *International Journal of Intercultural Relations, 10,* 179-196.

Berg, B.L. (1994). *Qualitative research methods for the social sciences* (2nd ed.). Boston: Allyn & Bacon.

Berlin, S.B, Mann, K.B., & Grossman, S.F. (1991). Task analysis of cognitive therapy for depression. *Social Work Research and Abstracts, 27,* 3-11.

Bettleheim, B. (March 1, 1982). Reflections: Freud and the sole. *New Yorker, 52.*

Beveridge, W.I.B. (1957). *The art of scientific investigation* (3rd ed.). London: Heinemann.

Billups, J.O., & Julia, M.C. (1987). Changing profile of social work practice: A content analysis. *Social Work Research and Abstracts, 23,* 17-22.

Bisno, H., & Borowski, A. (1985). The social and psychological contexts of research. In R.M. Grinnell, Jr. (Ed.), *Social work research and evaluation* (2nd ed., pp. 83-100). Itasca, IL: F.E. Peacock.

Blase, K., Fixsen, D., & Phillips, E. (1984). Residential treatment for troubled children: Developing service delivery systems. In S.C. Paine, G.T. Bellamy, & B. Wilcox (Eds.), *Human services that work: From innovation to standard practice.* Baltimore: Paul H. Brookes.

Bloom, M., Fischer, J., & Orme, J. (1999). *Evaluating practice: Guidelines for the accountable professional* (3rd ed.). Englewood Cliffs, NJ: Prentice-Hall.

Blythe, B.J., & Tripodi, T. (1989). *Measurement in direct practice.* Newbury Park, CA: Sage.

Bogdan, R., & Biklen, S.K. (1992). *Qualitative research for education* (2nd ed.). Needham Heights, MA: Allyn & Bacon.

Bogdan, R., Brown, M.A., & Foster, S.B. (1984). Ecology of the family as a context for human development. *Human Organization, 41,* 6-16.

Bogdan, R., & Taylor, R. (1990). Looking at the bright side: A positive approach to qualitative policy and evaluation research. *Qualitative Sociology, 13,* 183-192.

Borden, W. (1992). Narrative perspectives in psychosocial intervention following adverse life events. *Social Work, 37,* 135-141.

Borg, W.R., & Gall, M.D. (1989). *Educational research.* White Plains, NY: Longman.

Borowski, A. (1988). Social dimensions of research. In R.M. Grinnell, Jr. (Ed.), *Social work research and evaluation* (3rd ed., pp. 42-64). Itasca, IL: F.E. Peacock.

Bossert, S.T. (1979). *Tasks and social relationships in classrooms.* New York: Cambridge University Press.

Bostwick, G.J., Jr., & Kyte, N.S. (1993). Measurement in research. In R.M. Grinnell, Jr. (Ed.), *Social work research and evaluation* (4th ed., pp. 174-197). Itasca, IL: F.E. Peacock.

Bouey, E., & Rogers, G. (1993). Retrieving information. In R.M. Grinnell, Jr. (Ed.), *Social work research and evaluation* (4th ed., pp. 388-401). Itasca, IL: F.E. Peacock.

Bowman, P.J. (1993). The impact of economic marginality among African American husbands and fathers. In H.P. McAdoo (Ed.), *Family ethnicity: Strength in diversity* (pp. 120-140). Newbury Park, CA: Sage.

Bretl, D., & Cantor, J. (1988). The portrayal of men and women in U.S. television commercials: A recent content analysis and trends over 15 years. *Sex Roles, 18,* 595-609.

Bronson, D.E. (1994). Is a scientist-practitioner model appropriate for direct social work practice? No! In W.W. Hudson & P.S. Nurius (Eds.), *Controversial issues in social work research* (pp. 81-86). Needham Heights, MA: Allyn & Bacon.

Broxmeyer, N. (1979). Practitioner-researcher in treating a borderline child. *Social Work Research and Abstracts, 14,* 5-10.

Buros, O.K. (Ed.). (1978). *The eighth mental measurements yearbook* (2 vols.). Highland Park, NJ: Gryphon Press.

Campbell, D., & Stanley, J. (1963). *Experimental and quasi-experimental designs for research.* Chicago: Rand McNally.

Campbell, P.B. (1983). The impact of societal biases on research methods. In B.L. Richardson & J. Wirtenberg (Eds.), *Sex role research* (pp. 197-213). New York: Praeger Publishers.

Carley, M. (1981). *Social measurement and social indicators.* London: Allen & Unwin.

Ceci, S.J., Peters, D., & Plotkin, J. (1985). Human subjects review, personal values, and the regulation of social science research. *American Psychologist, 40,* 994-1002.

Chandler, S.M. (1994). Is there an ethical responsibility to use practice methods with the best empirical evidence of effectiveness? No! In W.W. Hudson & P.S. Nurius (Eds.), *Controversial issues in social work research* (pp. 106-111). Needham Heights, MA: Allyn & Bacon.

Charmaz, K. (1990). "Discovering" chronic illness: Using grounded theory. *Social Science in Medicine, 30,* 1161-1172.

Cheetham, J. (1992). Evaluating social work effectiveness. *Research on Social Work Practice, 2,* 265-287.

Chronicle of Higher Education: "Scholar who submitted bogus article to journals may be disciplined," November 2, 1988, pp. A1, A7.

Cialdini, R.B. (1980). Full-cycle social psychology. In L. Bickman (Ed.), *Applied social psychology annual* (vol 1, pp. 21-47). Beverly Hills, CA: Sage.

Coleman, H., Collins, D., & Polster, R.A. (1997). Structured observation. In R.M. Grinnell, Jr. (Ed.), *Social work research and evaluation: Quantitative and qualitative approaches* (5th ed., pp. 315-332). Itasca, IL: F.E. Peacock.

Coleman, H., & Unrau, Y. (1996). Phase three: Analyzing your data. In L.M. Tutty, M.A. Rothery, & R.M. Grinnell, Jr. (Eds.), *Qualitative research for social workers: Phases, steps, and tasks* (pp. 88-119). Needham Heights, MA: Allyn & Bacon.

Committee on the Status of Women in Sociology (1985-86). *The status of women in sociology.* New York: American Sociological Association.

Cook, T.D., & Campbell, D. (1979). Quasi-experimentation: Design and analysis for field settings. Boston: Houghton Mifflin.

Cooper, M. (1990). Treatment of a client with obsessive-compulsive disorder. *Social Work Research & Abstracts, 26,* 26-35.

Copeland, A.P., & White, K.M. (1991). *Studying families.* Newbury Park, CA: Sage.

Corcoran, K.J. (1988). Selecting a measuring instrument. In R.M. Grinnell, Jr. (Ed.), *Social work research and evaluation* (3rd ed., pp. 137-155). Itasca, IL: F.E. Peacock.

Council on Social Work Education (2000). *Baccalaureate and masters curriculum policy statements.* Alexandria, VA. Author.

Cowen, E.L., Hauser, J., Beach, D.R., & Rappaport, J. (1970). Parental perception of young children and their relation to indexes of adjustment. *Journal of Consulting and Clinical Psychology, 34,* 97-103.

Crabtree, B.F., & Miller, W.L. (Eds.). (1992). *Doing qualitative research.* Newbury Park, CA: Sage.

Crawford, K., Thomas, E.D., & Fink, J.J. (1980). Pygmalion at sea: Improving the work effectiveness of low performers. *The Journal of Applied Behavioral Science, 23,* 482-505.

Cresswell, J.W. (1997). Using both research approaches in a single study. In R.M. Grinnell, Jr. (Ed.), *Social work research and evaluation: Quantitative and qualitative approaches* (5th ed., pp. 141-158). Itasca, IL: F.E. Peacock.

Creswell, J.W. (1994). *Research design: Qualitative & quantitative approaches.* Newbury Park, CA: Sage.

Cromwell, R.E., & Ruiz, R.A. (1979). The myth of macho dominance in decision making within Mexican and Chicano families. *Hispanic Journal of Behavioral Sciences, 1,* 355-373.

Cronbach, L., & Meehl, P.E. (1955). Construct validity in psychological tests. *Psychological Bulletin, 52,* 281-302.

Cronbach, L.J. (1970). *Essentials of psychological testing* (3rd ed.). New York: Harper & Row.

Crowne, D.P., & Marlow, D. (1960). A new scale of social desirability independent of psychopathology. *Journal of Consulting Psychology, 24,* 349-354.

Cumberbatch, G., Jones, I., & Lee, M. (1988). Measuring violence on television. *Current Psychological Research and Review, 7,* 10-25.

Dale, A., Arber, S., & Proctor, M. (1988). *Doing secondary analysis.* Boston: Allen & Unwin

Dallas Morning News: "Welfare study withholds benefits from 800 Texans," February 11, 1990, p. 1.

Dangel, R.F. (1994). Is a scientist-practitioner model appropriate for direct social work practice? Yes! In W.W. Hudson & P.S. Nurius (Eds.), *Controversial issues in social work research* (pp. 75-79). Needham Heights, MA: Allyn & Bacon.

Darley, J.M., & Latane, B. (1968). Bystander intervention in emergencies: Diffusion of responsibility. *Journal of Personality and Social Psychology, 8,* 377-383.

DeMaria, W. (1981). Empiricism: An impoverished philosophy for social work research. *Australian Social Work, 34,* 3-8.

Denmark, R., Russo, N.F., Frieze, I.H., & Sechzer, J.A. (1988). Guidelines for avoiding sexism in research: A report of the Ad Hoc Committee on Nonsexist Research. *American Pyschologist, 43,* 582-585.

Denzin, N.K. (1978). *The research act: A theoretical introduction to sociological methods* (2nd ed.). New York: McGraw-Hill.

Denzin, N.K. (1989). *The research act: A theoretical introduction to sociological methods* (3rd ed.). Englewood Cliffs, NJ: Prentice-Hall.

Denzin, N.K., & Lincoln, Y.S. (Eds.). (1994). *Handbook of qualitative research.* Newbury Park, CA: Sage.

Department of Health, Education, and Welfare. (1978). *Code of federal regulations, title 45: Public welfare.* Washington, DC: U.S. Government Printing Office.

DePoy, E., & Gitlin, L.N. (1994). *Introduction to research: Multiple strategies for health and human services* (pp. 3-14, 28-39). St. Louis: Mosby.

Derogates, L.R., Rickles, K., & Rock, A.F. (1976). The SCL-90 and the MMPI: A step in the validation of a new self-report scale. *British Journal of Psychiatry, 128,* 280-289.

Diamond, J. (1987). Soft sciences are harder than hard sciences. *Discover, 8* (August), 34-39.

Diaz, J.O.P. (1988). Assessment of Puerto Rican children in bilingual education programs in the United States: A critique of Lloyd M. Dunn's monograph. *Hispanic Journal of Behavioral Sciences, 10,* 237-252.

Dillman, D.A. (1978). *Mail and telephone surveys: The total design method.* New York: Wiley.

Dodd, D.K., Foerch, B.J., & Anderson, H.T. (1988). Content analysis of women and racial minorities as newsmagazine cover persons. *Journal of Social Behavior and Personality, 3,* 231-236.

Dollard, J., & Mowrer, O.H. (1947). A method of measuring tension in written documents. *Journal of Abnormal and Social Psychology, 42,* 3-22.

Doyle, C. (1901/1955). *A treasury of Sherlock Holmes.* Garden City, NY: Hanover House.

Duehn, W.D. (1985). Practice and research. In R.M. Grinnell, Jr. (Ed.), *Social work research and evaluation* (2nd ed., pp. 19-48). Itasca, IL: F.E. Peacock.

Eagly, A.H. (1987). Reporting sex differences. *American Psychologist, 42,* 756-757.

Eichler, M. (1988). *Nonsexist research methods.* Boston: Allen & Unwin.

Emerson, R.M. (1983). Introduction. In R.M. Emerson (Ed.), *Contemporary field research* (pp. 1-16). Boston: Little Brown.

Epstein, I. (1988). Quantitative and qualitative methods. In R.M. Grinnell, Jr. (Ed.), *Social work research and evaluation* (3rd ed., pp. 185-198). Itasca, IL: F.E. Peacock.

Erlandson, D.A., Harris, E.L., Skipper, B.L., & Allen, S.D. (1993). *Doing naturalistic inquiry: A guide to methods.* Newbury Park, CA: Sage.

Esping-Andersen, C. (1990). Three post-industrial employment regimes. In J.E. Kolberg (Ed.), *The welfare state as employer* (pp. 148-188). Armonk, NY: M.E. Sharpe.

Fabricant, M. (1982). *Juveniles in the family courts.* Lexington, MA: Lexington.

Fairweather, G., & Tornatsky, L. (1977). *Experimental methods for social policy research.* Elmsford, NY: Pergamon.

Federal Register. (1978, May 4). Washington, DC: Government Printing Office.

Fetterman, D.M. (1989). *Ethnography: Step by step*. Newbury Park CA: Sage.

Fielding, R., & Lee, R. (Eds.). (1991). *Using computers in qualitative analysis*. Newbury Park, CA: Sage.

Fineman, H. (1995, February 27). The brave new world of cybertribes. *Newsweek, 125*, 30-33.

Finkelhor, D. (1984). *Child sexual abuse: New theory and research*. New York: Free Press.

Fischer, C.S. (1992). *America calling: A social history of the telephone to 1940*. Berkeley, CA: University of California Press.

Fischer, J. (1993). Evaluating positivistic research reports. In R.M. Grinnell, Jr. (Ed.), *Social work research and evaluation* (4th ed., pp. 347-366). Itasca, IL: F.E. Peacock.

Fischer, J., & Greenberg, J. (1972). *An investigation of different training methods on indigenous nonprofessionals from diverse minority groups*. Paper presented at the National Association of Social Workers Conference on Social Justice, New Orleans.

Frankfort-Nachmias, C., & Nachmias, D. (1992). *Research methods in the social sciences* (4th ed.). New York: St. Martin's Press.

Franklin, C., & Jordan, C. (1995). Qualitative assessment: A methodological review. *Families in Society, 76*, 281-295.

Franklin, C., & Jordan, C. (1997). Qualitative approaches to the generation of knowledge. In R.M. Grinnell, Jr. (Ed.), *Social work research and evaluation: Quantitative and qualitative approaches* (5th ed., pp. 106-140). Itasca, IL: F.E. Peacock.

Freedman, D.A. (1991). Statistical models and shoe leather. In P.V. Marsden (Ed.), *Sociological methodology* (pp. 291-313). Oxford: Basil Blackwell.

Gabor, P.A., & Grinnell, R.M., Jr. (1994). *Evaluation and quality improvement in the human services*. Boston: Allyn & Bacon.

Gabor, P.A., & Ing, C. (1997). Sampling. In R.M. Grinnell, Jr. (Ed.), *Social work research and evaluation: Quantitative and qualitative approaches* (5th ed., pp. 237-258). Itasca, IL: F.E. Peacock.

Gabor, P.A., Unrau, Y.A., & Grinnell, R.M., Jr. (1998). *Evaluation for social workers: A quality improvement approach for the social services* (2nd ed.). Boston: Allyn & Bacon.

Garmezy, N. (1982). The case for the single case in research. In A.E. Kazdin & A.H. Tuma (Eds.), *New directions for methodology of social and behavioral sciences* (pp. 517-546). San Francisco: Jossey-Bass.

Garvin, C.D. (1981). Research-related roles for social workers. In R.M. Grinnell, Jr. (Ed.), *Social work research and evaluation* (pp. 547-552). Itasca, IL: F.E. Peacock.

Geismar, L., & Krisberg, J. (1967). *The forgotten neighborhood*. Metuchen, NJ: Scarecrow Press.

Geismar, L.L., & Wood, K.M. (1982). Evaluating practice: Science as faith. *Social Casework, 63*, 266-272.

Gilbert, K.R., & Schmid, K. (1994). Bringing our emotions out of the closet: Acknowledging the place of emotion in qualitative research. *Qualitative Family Research, 8*, 1-3.

Gilgun, J.F. (1988). Decision-making in interdisciplinary treatment teams. *Child Abuse and Neglect, 12*, 231-239.

Gilgun, J.F. (1992a). Definitions, methodologies, and methods in qualitative family research. In J.F. Gilgun, K. Daly, & G. Handel. (Eds.), *Qualitative methods in family research* (pp. 22-40). Newbury Park, CA: Sage.

Gilgun, J.F. (1992b). Observations in a clinical setting: Team decision-making in family incest treatment. In J.F. Gilgun, K. Daly, & G. Handel (Eds.), *Qualitative methods in family research* (pp. 236-259). Newbury Park, CA: Sage.

Gilgun, J.F. (1994a). A case for case studies in social work research. *Social Work, 39*, 371-380.

Gilgun, J.F. (1994b). Avengers, conquerors, playmates, and lovers: Roles played by child sexual abuse perpetrators. *Families in Society, 75*, 467-480.

Gilgun, J.F. (1994c). Hand into glove: The grounded theory approach and social work practice research. In E. Sherman & W.J. Reid (Eds.), *Qualitative research in social work* (pp. 115-125). New York: Columbia University Press.

Gilgun, J.F. (1995). The moral discourse of incest perpetrators. *Journal of Marriage and the Family, 57,* 265-282.

Gilgun, J.F. (1997). Case designs. In R.M. Grinnell, Jr. (Ed.), *Social work research and evaluation: Quantitative and qualitative approaches* (5th ed., pp. 298-312). Itasca, IL: F.E. Peacock.

Gilgun, J.F., & Connor, T.M. (1989). How perpetrators view child sexual abuse. *Social Work, 34,* 349-351.

Gilgun, J. F., Daly, K., & Handel, G. (Eds.). (1992). *Qualitative methods in family research.* Newbury Park, CA: Sage.

Glaser, B.G., & Strauss, A.L. (1967). *The discovery of grounded theory: Strategies for qualitative research.* Chicago: Aldine.

Glisson, C.A., & Fischer, J. (1982). Use and non-use of multivariate statistics. *Social Work Research and Abstracts, 18,* 42-44.

Gochros, H.L. (1970). The caseworker-adoptive parent relationships in post-placement services. In A. Kadushin (Ed.), *Child welfare services.* New York: Macmillan.

Gochros, H.L. (1988). Research interviewing. In R.M. Grinnell, Jr. (Ed.), *Social work research and evaluation* (3rd ed., pp. 267-299). Itasca, IL: F.E. Peacock.

Gogolin, L, & Swartz, F. (1992). A quantitative and qualitative inquiry into the attitudes toward science of nonscience college students. *Journal of Research in Science Teaching, 29,* 487-504.

Goldfinger, S.M., Schutt, R.K., Tolomicenko, G.S., Turner, W.M., Ware, N., & Penk, W.E., et al. (1997). Housing persons who are homeless and mentally ill: Independent living or evolving consumer households? In W. Breakey, & J.W. Thompson (Eds.), *Mentally ill and homeless: Special programs for special needs* (pp. 29-49). The Netherlands: Harwood Academic Publishers.

Goldman, J., Stein, C.L., & Guerry, S. (1983). *Psychological methods of clinical assessment.* New York: Brunner.

Goldstein, H. (1983). Starting where the client is. *Social Casework, 65,* 267-275.

Goleman, D. (1995). *Emotional intelligence.* New York: Bantam Books.

Gottman, J.M. (1979). *Marital interaction.* New York: Academic Press.

Gouldner, A.W. (1970). *The coming crisis of western sociology.* New York: Basic Books.

Graham, J.R., & Lilly, R.S. (1984). *Psychological testing.* Englewood Cliffs, NJ: Prentice-Hall.

Green, G.R., & Wright, J.E. (1979). The retrospective approach to collecting baseline data. *Social Work Research and Abstracts, 15,* 25-30.

Greene, J.C., Caracelli, V.J., & Graham, W.E. (1989). Toward a conceptual framework for mixed-method evaluation designs. *Educational Evaluation and Policy Analysis, 11,* 255-274.

Greenwald, R.A., Ryan, M.K., & Mulvihill, J.E. (1982). *Human subjects research.* New York: Plenum Press.

Grinnell, F. (1987). *The scientific attitude.* Boulder, CO: Westview.

Grinnell, R.M., Jr. (1981a). Becoming a knowledge-based social worker. In R.M. Grinnell, Jr. (Ed.), *Social work research and evaluation* (pp. 1-8). Itasca, IL: F.E. Peacock.

Grinnell, R.M., Jr. (Ed.). (1981b). *Social work research and evaluation.* Itasca, IL: F.E. Peacock.

Grinnell, R.M., Jr. (1985a). Becoming a practitioner/researcher. In R.M. Grinnell, Jr. (Ed.), *Social work research and evaluation* (2nd ed., pp. 1-15). Itasca, IL: F.E. Peacock.

Grinnell, R.M., Jr. (Ed.). (1985b). *Social work research and evaluation* (2nd ed.). Itasca, IL: F.E. Peacock.

Grinnell, R.M., Jr. (Ed.). (1988). *Social work research and evaluation* (3rd ed.). Itasca, IL: F.E. Peacock.

Grinnell, R.M., Jr. (1993a). Group research designs. In R.M. Grinnell, Jr. (Ed.), *Social work research and evaluation* (4th ed., pp. 118-153). Itasca, IL: F.E. Peacock.

Grinnell, R.M., Jr. (Ed.). (1993b). *Social work research and evaluation* (4th ed.). Itasca, IL: F.E. Peacock.

Grinnell, R.M., Jr. (1997a). The generation of knowledge. In R.M. Grinnell, Jr. (Ed.), *Social work research and evaluation: Quantitative and qualitative approaches* (5th ed., pp. 3-24). Itasca, IL: F.E. Peacock.

Grinnell, R.M., Jr. (1997b). Preface. In R.M. Grinnell, Jr. (Ed.), *Social work research and evaluation: Quantitative and qualitative approaches* (5th ed., pp. xvii-xxvi). Itasca, IL: F.E. Peacock.

Grinnell, R.M., Jr. (Ed.). (1997c). *Social work research and evaluation: Quantitative and qualitative approaches* (5th ed.). Itasca, IL: F.E. Peacock.

Grinnell, R.M., Jr., Rothery, M., & Thomlison, R.J. (1993). Research in social work. In R.M. Grinnell, Jr. (Ed.), *Social work research and evaluation* (4th ed., pp. 2-16). Itasca, IL: F.E. Peacock.

Grinnell, R.M., Jr., & Siegel, D.H. (1988). The place of research in social work. In R.M. Grinnell, Jr. (Ed.), *Social work research and evaluation* (3rd ed., pp. 9-24). Itasca, IL: F.E. Peacock.

Grinnell, R.M., Jr., & Stothers, M. (1988). Research designs. In R.M. Grinnell, Jr. (Ed.), *Social work research and evaluation* (3rd ed., pp. 199-239). Itasca, IL: F.E. Peacock.

Grinnell, R.M., Jr., & Unrau, Y. (1997). Group designs. In R.M. Grinnell, Jr. (Ed.), *Social work research and evaluation: Quantitative and qualitative approaches* (5th ed., pp. 259-297). Itasca, IL: F.E. Peacock.

Grinnell, R.M., Jr., & Williams, M. (1990). *Research in social work: A primer*. Itasca, IL: F.E. Peacock.

Grinnell, R.M., Jr., Williams, M., & Tutty, L.M. (1997). Case-level evaluation. In R.M. Grinnell, Jr. (Ed.), *Social work research and evaluation: Quantitative and qualitative approaches* (5th ed., pp. 529-559). Itasca, IL: F.E. Peacock.

Grob, G.N. (1973). *Mental institutions in America*. New York: Free Press.

Groves, R.M. (1988). *Telephone survey methodology*. New York: Wiley.

Groves, R.M., & Cialdini, R.B. (1992). Understanding the decision to participate in a survey. *Public Opinion Quarterly, 56,* 475-496.

Guba, E.G. (1990). *The paradigm dialog*. Newbury Park, CA: Sage.

Guba, E.G., & Lincoln, Y.S. (1981). *Effective evaluation*. San Francisco: Jossey-Bass.

Hakim, C. (1982). *Secondary analysis in social research: A guide to data sources and methods with examples*. London: Allen & Unwin.

Hanson, J. (1989). *The experience of families of people with a severe mental illness: An ethnographic view*. Unpublished doctoral dissertation, University of Kansas.

Hartman, A. (1978). Diagrammatic assessment of family relationships. *Social Casework, 59,* 465-476.

Haynes, S.N. (1983). Behavioral assessment. In M. Hersen, A.E. Kazdin, & A.S. Bellack (Eds.), *The clinical psychology handbook* (pp. 397-425). Elmsford, NY: Pergamon.

Heineman, M.B. (1981). The obsolete scientific imperative in social work research. *Social Service Review, 55,* 371-397.

Hempel, C.G. (1966). *Philosophy of natural science*. Englewood Cliffs, NJ: Prentice-Hall.

Herek, G.M., Kimmel, D.C., Amaro, H., & Melton, G.G. (1991). Avoiding heterosexist bias in psychological research. *American Psychologist, 31,* 858-867.

Herzogg, E. (1959). *Some guidelines for evaluative research*. Washington, DC: U.S. Department of Health, Education, and Welfare.

Hewitt, S.K. (1994). Preverbal sexual abuse: What two children report in later years. *Child Abuse and Neglect, 18,* 821-826.

Hoffart, I., & Krysik, J. (1993). Glossary. In R.M. Grinnell, Jr. (Ed.), *Social work research and evaluation* (4th ed., pp. 439-450). Itasca, IL: F.E. Peacock.

Hofstede, G., Neuijen, B., Ohayv, D.D., & Sanders, G. (1990). Measuring organizational cultures: A qualitative and quantitative study across twenty cases. *Administrative Science Quarterly, 35,* 286-316.

Hogerty, G.F., & Ulrich, R. (1972). The discharge readiness inventory. *Archives of General Psychiatry, 26,* 419-426.

Holsti, O. (1969). *Content analysis for the social sciences and humanities.* Reading, MA: Addison-Wesley.

Hops, H., & Greenwood, C.R. (1981). Social skills deficits. In E.J. Mash & L.G. Terdal (Eds.), *Behavioral assessment of childhood disorders* (pp. 347-394). New York: Guilford.

Hornick, J.P., & Burrows, B. (1988). Program evaluation. In R.M. Grinnell, Jr. (Ed.), *Social work research and evaluation* (3rd ed., pp. 400-420). Itasca, IL: F.E. Peacock.

Hoshino, G., & Lynch, M.M. (1985). Secondary analyses. In R.M. Grinnell, Jr. (Ed.), *Social work research and evaluation* (2nd ed., pp. 370-380). Itasca, IL: F.E. Peacock.

Huck, S.W., Cormier, W.H., & Bounds, W.G. (1974). *Reading statistics and research.* New York: Harper & Row.

Huck, S.W., & Sandler, H.M. (1979). *Rival hypotheses: Alternative interpretations of data-based conclusions.* New York: Harper & Row.

Hudson, J., & Grinnell, R.M., Jr. (1989). Program evaluation. In B. Compton & B. Galaway (Eds.), *Social work processes* (4th ed., pp. 691-711). Belmont, CA: Wadsworth.

Hudson, W.W. (1981). Development and use of indexes and scales. In R.M. Grinnell, Jr. (Ed.), *Social work research and evaluation* (pp. 130-155). Itasca, IL: F.E. Peacock.

Humphrey, N. (1992). *A history of the mind: Evolution and the birth of consciousness.* New York: Simon & Schuster.

Hyde, J.S. (1991). *Half the human experience: The psychology of women* (4th ed.). Lexington, MA: Heath.

Hyden, M. (1994). Woman battering as a marital act: Interviewing and analysis in context. In C.K. Reissman (Ed.), *Qualitative studies in social work research* (pp. 95-112). Newbury Park, CA: Sage.

Hyman, H.H. (1987). *Secondary analysis of sample surveys: With a new introduction.* New York: Harper & Row.

Ihilevich, D., & Gleser, G.C. (1982). *Evaluating mental health programs.* Lexington, MA: Lexington Books.

Jackson, G.B. (1980). Methods for integrative reviews. *Review of Educational Research, 50,* 438-460.

Jacob, E. (1987). Qualitative research traditions: A review. *Review of Educational Research, 57,* 150.

Jacobson, J.L. (1992). *Gender bias: Roadblock to sustainable development.* ISBN 1-87071-10-6. Paper 110. Washington, DC: Worldwatch Institute.

Jenkins, S., & Norman, E. (1972). *Filial deprivation and foster care.* New York: Columbia University Press.

Jick, T. D. (1979). Mixing qualitative and quantitative methods: Triangulation in action. *Administrative Science Quarterly, 24,* 602-611.

Johnson, J.M. (1975). *Doing field research.* New York: Free Press.

Jordan, C., & Franklin, C. (1995). *Clinical assessment for social workers: Quantitative and qualitative methods*. Chicago: Lyceum Books, Inc.

Jordan, C., Franklin, C., & Corcoran, K. (1993). Standardized measuring instruments. In R.M. Grinnell, Jr. (Ed.), *Social work research and evaluation* (4th ed., pp. 198-220). Itasca, IL: F.E. Peacock.

Jordan, C., Franklin, C., & Corcoran, K. (1997). Measuring instruments. In R.M. Grinnell, Jr. (Ed.), *Social work research and evaluation: Quantitative and qualitative approaches* (5th ed., pp. 184-211). Itasca, IL: F.E. Peacock.

Jorgensen, D.L. (1989). *Participant observation: A methodology for human studies*. Newbury Park, CA: Sage.

Judd, C.M., Smith, E.R., & Kidder, I.H. (1991). *Research methods in social relations* (6th ed.). Fort Worth, TX: Harcourt Brace.

Junker, B.H. (1960). *Field work*. Chicago: University of Chicago Press.

Kahn, R. (1997). "A last drink on New Year's." *The Boston Globe*, January 3, pp. B1-B2.

Kaplan, A. (1964). *The conduct of inquiry: Methodology for behavioral science*. New York: Harper & Row.

Kazdin, A.E. (1981). Drawing valid inferences from case studies. *Journal of Consulting and Clinical Psychology, 49*, 183-192.

Kerlinger, F. (1986). *Foundations of behavioral research* (3rd ed.). New York: Holt.

Kiecolt, K.J., & Nathan, L.E. (1985). *Secondary analysis of survey data*. Newbury Park, CA: Sage.

Kogel, P., & Burnam, A. (1992). Problems in the assessment of mental illness among the homeless: An empirical approach. In M.J. Robertson, & M. Greenblatt (Eds.), *Homelessness: A national perspective* (pp. 77-99). New York: Plenum.

Krueger, R.A. (1997). *Focus groups: A practical guide for applied research*. Newbury Park, CA: Sage.

Krysik, J. (1997). Secondary analysis. In R.M. Grinnell, Jr. (Ed.), *Social work research and evaluation: Quantitative and qualitative approaches* (5th ed., pp. 391-406). Itasca, IL: F.E. Peacock.

Krysik, J., & Grinnell, R.M., Jr. (1997). Quantitative approaches to the generation of knowledge. In R.M. Grinnell, Jr. (Ed.), *Social work research and evaluation: Quantitative and qualitative approaches* (5th ed., pp. 67-105). Itasca, IL: F.E. Peacock.

Krysik, J.L., Hoffart, I., & Grinnell, R.M., Jr. (1993). *Student study guide for the fourth edition of Social Work Research and Evaluation*. Itasca, IL: F.E. Peacock.

Kuhn, T. (1970). *The structure of scientific revolutions* (2nd ed.). Chicago: University of Chicago Press.

Kushman, J.W. (1992). The organizational dynamics of teacher workplace. *Educational Administration Quarterly, 28*, 5-42.

Kyte, N.S., & Bostwick, G.J., Jr. (1997). Measuring variables. In R.M. Grinnell, Jr. (Ed.), *Social work research and evaluation: Quantitative and qualitative approaches* (5th ed., pp. 161-183). Itasca, IL: F.E. Peacock.

LaGory, M., Ferris, J., & Mullis, J. (1990). Depression among the homeless. *Journal of Health and Social Behavior, 31*, 87-101.

Lavrakas, P.J. (1987). *Telephone survey methods: Sampling, selection, and supervision*. Newbury Park, CA: Sage.

Lancy, D.F. (1993). *Qualitative research in education: An introduction to the major traditions.* White Plains, NY: Longman.

LaPiere, R. (1934). Attitudes and actions. *Social Forces, 13,* 230-237.

Larossa R., & Wolf, J.H. (1985). On qualitative family research. *Journal of Marriage and the Family, 47,* 531-541.

Lavrakas, P.J. (1987). *Telephone survey methods: Sampling, selection, and supervision.* Newbury Park, CA: Sage.

LeCroy, C.W., & Goodwin, C. (1988). New directions in teaching social work methods: A content analysis of course outlines. *Journal of Social Work Education, 19,* 43-49.

LeCroy, C.W., & Solomon, G. (1997). Content analysis. In R.M. Grinnell, Jr. (Ed.), *Social work research and evaluation: Quantitative and qualitative approaches* (5th ed., pp. 427-441). Itasca, IL: F.E. Peacock.

Lee, B.A., Jones, S.H., & Lewis, D.W. (1990). Public beliefs about the causes of homelessness. *Social Forces, 69,* 253-265.

Leedy, P.D. (1993). *Practical research: Planning and design* (3rd ed., pp. 128-131). New York: Macmillan.

Lewis, O. (1966). *LaVida: A Puerto Rican family in the culture of poverty.* New York: Random House.

Lincoln, Y., & Guba, E. (1985). *Naturalistic inquiry.* Newbury Park, CA: Sage.

Mackey, R.A, & Mackey, E.F. (1994). Personal psychotherapy and the development of a professional self. *Families in Society, 75,* 490-498.

Maeser, N., & Thyer, B.A. (1990). Teaching boys with severe retardation to serve themselves during family-style meals. *Behavioral Residential Treatment, 5,* 239-246.

Maloney, D.M. (1984). *Protection of human research subjects: A practical guide to federal laws and regulations.* New York: Plenum.

Maluccio, A.N. (1979). *Learning from clients.* New York: Free Press.

Mandell, N. (1984). Children's negotiation of meaning. *Symbolic Interaction, 7,* 191-211.

Marsh, J.C. (1983). Research and innovation in social work practice: Avoiding the headless machine. *Social Service Review, 57,* 584-598.

Marshall, C., & Rossman, G.B. (1995). *Designing qualitative research* (2nd ed.). Newbury Park, CA: Sage.

Mathison, S. (1988). Why triangulate? *Educational Researcher, 17,* 13-17.

Matsumoto, D. (1994). *People: Psychology from a cultural perspective.* Pacific Grove, Brooks/Cole.

McClelland, D.C. (1961). *The achieving society.* New York: Free Press.

McClelland, R.W., & Austin, C.D. (1996). Phase four: Writing your report. In L.M. Tutty, M.A. Rothery, & R.M. Grinnell, Jr. (Eds.), *Qualitative research for social workers: Phases, steps, and tasks* (pp. 120-150). Boston: Allyn & Bacon.

McMurtry, S.L. (1997). Survey research. In R.M. Grinnell, Jr. (Ed.), *Social work research and evaluation: Quantitative and qualitative approaches* (5th ed., pp. 333-367). Itasca, IL: F.E. Peacock.

McMurtry, S.L., & McClelland, R.W. (1995, March). *Alarming trends in faculty/student ratios in MSW programs.* Paper presented at the meeting of the Council on Social Work Education, San Diego, CA.

Meyer, C. (1983). *Clinical social work in the eco-systems perspective.* New York: Columbia University Press.

Meyer, C. (1993). *Assessment in social work.* New York: Columbia University Press.

Miles, M., & Huberman, M. (1994). *Qualitative data analysis: A sourcebook of new methods.* Newbury Park, CA: Sage.

Miles, M., & Weitzman, E. (1995). *Computer programs for qualitative data analysis.* Newbury Park, CA: Sage.

Milgram, S. (1963). Behavioral study of obedience. *Journal of Abnormal and Applied Social Psychology, 67,* 371-378.

Milgram, S. (1974). *Obedience to authority: An experimental view.* New York: Harper & Row.

Miller, L.K., & Miller, O.L. (1970). Reinforcing self-help group activities of welfare recipients. *Journal of Applied Behavior Analysis, 3,* 57-64.

Mindel, C.H. (1997). Designing measuring instruments. In R.M. Grinnell, Jr. (Ed.), *Social work research and evaluation: Quantitative and qualitative approaches* (5th ed., pp. 212-234). Itasca, IL: F.E. Peacock.

Mindel, C.H., & McDonald, L. (1988). Survey research. In R.M. Grinnell, Jr. (Ed.), *Social work research and evaluation* (3rd ed., pp. 300-322). Itasca, IL: F.E. Peacock.

Mischel, W. (1968). *Personality and assessment.* New York: Wiley.

Monette, D., Sullivan, T., & DeJong, C. (1990). *Applied social research: Tools for the human services* (2nd ed.). Fort Worth, TX: Holt, Rinehart, Winston.

Monette, D., Sullivan, T., & DeJong, C. (1994). *Applied social research: Tools for the human services* (3rd ed). Fort Worth, TX: Harcourt Brace.

Mook, D.G. (1983). In defense of external invalidity. *American Psychologist, 38,* 379-387.

Moon, S.M., Dillon, D.R., & Sprenkle, D.H. (1990). Family therapy and qualitative research. *Journal of Marital and Family Therapy, 16,* 357-373.

Morgan, D. (1988). *Focus groups as qualitative research.* Newbury Park, CA: Sage.

Morse, J.M. (1991). Approaches to qualitative-quantitative methodological triangulation. *Nursing Research, 40,* 120-123.

Morse, J.M., & Field, P.A. (1995). *Qualitative research methods for health professionals* (2nd ed.). Newbury Park, CA: Sage.

Murguia, E., Padilla, R.V., & Pavel, M. (1991). Ethnicity and the concept of social integration in Tinto's model of institutional departure. *Journal of College Student Development, 32,* 433-439.

Myers, D.G. (1983). *Social psychology.* New York: McGraw-Hill.

National Association of Social Workers (1999). *National Association of Social Workers code of ethics.* Silver Spring, MD: Author.

Neimeyer, R.A. (1993). An appraisal of constructivist psychotherapies. *Journal of Consulting and Clinical Psychology, 61,* 221-234.

Nelson, R., & Barlow, D.H. (1981). Behavioral assessment: Basic strategies and initial procedures. In D. Barlow (Ed.), *Behavior assessment of adult disorders* (pp. 13-43). New York: Guilford.

Neuman, W.L. (1991). *Social research methods: Qualitative and quantitative approaches.* Needham Heights, MA: Allyn & Bacon.

Neuman, W.L. (1994). *Social research methods: Qualitative and quantitative approaches* (2nd ed.). Needham Heights, MA: Allyn & Bacon.

Neuman, W.L. (1997). *Social research methods: Qualitative and quantitative approaches* (3rd ed.). Boston: Allyn & Bacon.

New York Times: "Charges dropped on bogus work," April 4, 1989, p. 21.

New York Times: "Test of journals is criticized as unethical," September 27, 1988, pp. 21, 25.

Norris, P. (1987). *Politics and sexual equality: The comparative position of women in western democracies.* Boulder, CO: Lynne Rienner.

Nunnally, J.C. (1975). *Introduction to statistics for psychology and education.* New York: McGraw-Hill.

Nunnally, J.C. (1978). *Psychometric theory* (2nd ed.). New York: McGraw-Hill.

Nurius, P.S., & Hudson, W.W. (1993). *Human services: Practice, evaluation, and computers.* Pacific Grove, CA: Brooks/Cole.

Oyen, E. (1990). *Comparative methodology: Theory and practice in international social research.* Newbury Park, CA: Sage.

Palys, T. (1997). *Research decisions: Quantitative and qualitative perspectives.* Toronto: Harcourt Brace.

Papell, C.P., & Skolnik, L. (1992). The reflective practitioner: A contemporary paradigm's relevance for social work education. *Journal of Social Work Education, 28,* 18-26.

Patton, M.Q. (1990). *Qualitative evaluation and research methods* (2nd ed.). Newbury Park, CA: Sage.

Pedersen, P. (1988). *A handbook for developing multicultural awareness.* Alexandria, VA: American Association for Counseling and Development.

Pedersen, P. (1991). Multiculturalism as a generic approach to counseling. *Journal of Counseling and Development, 19,* 6-12.

Pivin, F.F., & Cloward, R.A. (1971). *Regulating the poor: The functions of public welfare.* New York: Vintage Books.

Polkinghorne, D.E. (1991). Two conflicting calls for methodological reform. *The Counseling Psychologist, 19,* 103-114.

Polster, R.A., & Lynch, M.A. (1985). Single-subject designs. In R.M. Grinnell, Jr. (Ed.), *Social work research and evaluation* (2nd ed., pp. 381-431). Itasca, IL: F.E. Peacock.

Pope, W. (1976). *Durkheim's suicide: A classic analyzed.* Chicago: University of Chicago Press.

Posavac, E.J., & Carey, R.G. (1994). *Program evaluation: Methods and case studies* (3rd ed.). Englewood Cliffs, NJ: Prentice-Hall.

Poser, E.G. (1966). The effects of therapists' training on group therapeutic outcome. *Journal of Consulting Psychotherapy, 30,* 283-289.

Reid, P.N., & Gundlach, J.H. (1983). A scale for the measurement of consumer satisfaction with social services. *Journal of Social Service Research, 7,* 37-54.

Reid, W.J. (1990). Change process research: A new paradigm? In L. Videka-Sherman & W.J. Reid (Eds.), *Advances in clinical social work research* (pp. 130-148). Silver Spring, MD: National Association of Social Workers.

Reid, W.J. (1993). Writing research reports. In R.M. Grinnell, Jr. (Ed.), *Social work research and evaluation* (4th ed., pp. 332-346). Itasca, IL: F.E. Peacock.

Reid, W.J., & Shyne, A. (1969). *Brief and extended casework.* New York: Columbia University Press.

Reid, W.J., & Smith, A.D. (1989). *Research in social work* (2nd ed.). New York: Columbia University Press.

Reinharz, S. (1992). Feminist survey research and other statistical research formats. In S. Reinharz (Ed.), *Feminist methods in social research* (pp. 76-94). New York: Oxford University Press.

Riessman, C.K. (1994). *Qualitative studies in social work research.* Newbury Park: CA: Sage.

Roethlisberger, F.J., & Dickson, W.J. (1939). *Management and the worker: An account of a research program conducted by the Western Electric Co. Hawthorne Works, Chicago.* Cambridge, MA: Harvard University Press.

Rogers, G., & Bouey, E. (1993). Reviewing the literature. In R.M. Grinnell, Jr. (Ed.), *Social work research and evaluation* (4th ed., pp. 388-401). Itasca, IL: F.E. Peacock.

Rogers, G., & Bouey, E. (1996). Phase two: Collecting your data. In L.M. Tutty, M.A. Rothery, & R.M. Grinnell, Jr. (Eds.), *Qualitative research for social workers: Phases, steps, and tasks* (pp. 50-87). Boston: Allyn & Bacon.

Rogers, G., & Bouey, E. (1997). Participant observation. In R.M. Grinnell, Jr. (Ed.), *Social work research and evaluation: Quantitative and qualitative approaches* (5th ed., pp. 368-387). Itasca, IL: F.E. Peacock.

Rokach, A. (1988). The experience of loneliness: A tri-level model. *Journal of Psychology, 122,* 531-544.

Rosenhan, D. (1973). On being sane in insane places. *Science, 179,* 250-258.

Rossi, P.H. (1989). *Down and out in America: The origins of homelessness.* Chicago: University of Chicago Press.

Rossi, P.H., & Freeman, H.E. (1993). *Evaluation: A systematic approach* (5th ed.). Newbury Park, CA: Sage.

Roth, D., Bean, J., Lust, N., & Saveanu, T. (1985). *Homelessness in Ohio: A study of people in Need.* Columbus, OH: Department of Mental Health.

Rothery, M.A., Tutty, L.M., Grinnell, R.M., Jr. (1996). Introduction. In L.M. Tutty, M.A. Rothery, & R.M. Grinnell, Jr. (Eds.), *Qualitative research for social workers: Phases, steps, and tasks* (pp. 2-22). Needham Heights, MA: Allyn & Bacon.

Rubin, A. (1993). Secondary analysis. In R.M. Grinnell, Jr. (Ed.), *Social work research and evaluation* (4th ed., pp. 290-303). Itasca, IL: F.E. Peacock.

Rubin, A., & Babbie, E. (1993). *Research methods for social work* (2nd ed.). Pacific Grove, CA: Wadsworth.

Rubin, A., & Babbie, E. (1997a). Program-level evaluation. In R.M. Grinnell, Jr. (Ed.), *Social work research and evaluation: Quantitative and qualitative approaches* (5th ed., pp. 560-587). Itasca, IL: F.E. Peacock.

Rubin, A., & Babbie, E. (1997b). *Research methods for social work* (3rd ed.). Pacific Grove, CA: Wadsworth.

Ruckdeschel, R. (1994). Does emphasizing accountability and evidence dilute service delivery and the helping role? Yes! In W.W. Hudson & P.S. Nurius (Eds.), *Controversial issues in social work research* (pp. 9-14). Needham Heights, MA: Allyn & Bacon.

Russell, D. (1984). *Sexual exploitation: Rape, child sexual abuse, and workplace harassment.* Newbury Park, CA: Sage.

Sanders, J.R. (1994). (Ed.). *The program evaluation standards* (2nd ed.). (The joint Committee on Standards for Educational Evaluation.) Newbury Park, CA: Sage

Sattler, J.M. (Ed.). (1988). *Assessment of children* (3rd ed.). San Diego, CA: Jerome M. Sattler Publications.

Scarr, S. (1988). Race and gender as psychological variables: Social and ethical issues. *American Psychologist, 43,* 56-59.

Schinke, S.P., & Gilchrist, L.D. (1993). Ethics in research. In R.M. Grinnell, Jr. (Ed.), *Social work research and evaluation* (4th ed., pp. 79-90). Itasca, IL: F.E. Peacock.

Schneidman, E. (1985). At the point of no return. *Psychology Today, 19,* 55-58.

Schön, D.A. (1983). *The reflective practitioner: How professionals think in action.* New York: Basic Books.

Schuman, H. (1972). Two sources of antiwar sentiment in America. *American Journal of Sociology, 78,* 513-536.

Schuman, H., & Converse, J.M. (1971). The effects of black and white interviewers on black responses. *Public Opinion Quarterly, 35,* 44-68.

Schutt, R.K., & Garrett, G.R. (1992). *Responding to the homeless: Policy and practice.* New York: Plenum.

Schutt, R.K., & Goldfinger, S.M., & Peck, E. (1997). Satisfaction with residence and with life: When homeless mentally ill persons are housed. *Evaluation and Program Planning, 20,* 185-194.

Schutt, R.K., Meschede, T., & Rierdan, J. (1994). Distress, suicidality, and social support among homeless adults. *Journal of Health and Social Behavior, 35,* 134-142.

Seaberg, J.R. (1988). Utilizing sampling procedures. In R.M. Grinnell, Jr. (Ed.), *Social work research and evaluation* (3rd ed., pp. 240-257). Itasca, IL: F.E. Peacock.

Seidman, I.E. (1991). *Interviewing as qualitative research.* New York: Teachers College Press.

Seidman, L.J. (1997). Neuropsychological testing. In A.Tasman, J. Kay, & J. Lieberman (Eds.), *Psychiatry* (pp. 498-508). Philadelphia: W.B. Saunders.

Sells, S.P., Smith, T. E., Coe, M.J., Yoshioka, M., & Robbins, J. (1994). An ethnography of couple and therapist experiences in reflecting team practice. *Journal of Marital and Family Therapy, 20,* 247-266.

Sherman, E. (1994). Discourse analysis in the framework of change process research. In E. Sherman & W.J. Reid (Eds.), *Qualitative research in social work* (pp. 228-241). New York: Columbia University Press.

Siegel, D.H. (1988). Integrating data-gathering techniques and practice activities. In R.M. Grinnell, Jr. (Ed.), *Social work research and evaluation* (3rd ed., pp. 465-482). Itasca, IL: F.E. Peacock.

Siegel, D.H., & Reamer, F.G. (1988). Integrating research findings, concepts, and logic into practice. In R.M. Grinnell, Jr. (Ed.), *Social work research and evaluation* (3rd ed., pp. 483-502). Itasca, IL: F.E. Peacock.

Sieppert, J.D., McMurtry, S.L., & McClelland, R.W. (1997). Utilizing existing statistics. In R.M. Grinnell, Jr. (Ed.), *Social work research and evaluation: Quantitative and qualitative approaches* (5th ed., pp. 407-426). Itasca, IL: F.E. Peacock.

Simon, J. (1969). *Basic research methods in social science.* New York: Random House.

Singer, E., Frankel, M.R., & Glassman, M.B. (1983). The effect of interviewer characteristics and expectations on response. *Public Opinion Quarterly, 47,* 68-83.

Singleton, R.A., Jr., Straits, B.C., & Miller-Straits, M. (1993). *Approaches to social research* (2nd ed.). New York: Oxford.

Sluckin, A. (1989). Behavioral social work treatment of childhood nocturnal enuresis. *Behavior Modification, 13,* 482-497.

Smith, N.J. (1988). Formulating research goals and problems. In R.M. Grinnell, Jr. (Ed.), *Social work research and evaluation* (3rd ed., pp. 89-110). Itasca, IL: F.E. Peacock.

Snow, D., & Anderson, L. (1987). Identity work among the homeless: The verbal construction and avowal of personal identities. *American Journal of Sociology, 92,* 1336-1371.

Snyder, T.D. (1994). *Digest of education statistics.* (NCES Publication No. 94-115). Washington, DC: US Department of Education, Office of Education Research and Improvement.

Sperry, R.W. (1968). Hemisphere deconnection and unity in conscious awareness. *American Psychologist, 23,* 723-733.

Spradley, J.P. (1979). *The ethnographic interview.* New York: Holt, Rinehart, and Winston.

Spradley, J.P. (1980). *Participant observation.* New York: Holt, Rinehart, & Winston.

Staats, A.W., & Butterfield, W. (1965). Treatment of nonreading in a culturally deprived juvenile delinquent: An application of reinforcement principles. *Child Development, 36,* 925-942.

Stake, R.E. (1995). *The art of case study research.* Newbury Park, CA: Sage.

Stocks, J.T., Thyer, B.A., & Kearsley, M. (1987). Using a token economy in a community-based residential program for disabled adults: An empirical evaluation leads to program modification. *Behavioral Residential Treatment, 1,* 173-185.

Straus, M.A. (1987). *Qualitative analysis for social scientists.* New York: Cambridge University Press.

Straus, M.A. (1991). *Beating the devil out of them: Corporal punishment in American families.* New York: Macmillan.

Straus, M.A., & Corbin, J. (1990). *Basics of qualitative research: Grounded theory procedures and techniques.* Newbury Park, CA: Sage.

Straus, M.A., & Gelles, R. (1986). Societal change and change in family violence from 1975 to 1985 as revealed by two national surveys. *Journal of Marriage and the Family, 48,* 465-479.

Straus, M.A., Gelles, R., & Steinmetz, S. (1980). *Behind closed doors: Violence in the American family.* Garden City, NY: Anchor Books.

Straus, M.A., & Hafez, H. (1981). Clinical questions and "real research." *American Journal of Psychiatry, 138,* 1592-1597.

Stuart, P. (1997). Historical research. In R.M. Grinnell, Jr. (Ed.), *Social work research and evaluation: Quantitative and qualitative approaches* (5th ed., pp. 442-457). Itasca, IL: F.E. Peacock.

Stuart, R. (1967). Behavioral control of overeating. *Behavior Research and Therapy, 5,* 357-365.

Sunberg, N.D. (1977). *Assessment of persons.* Englewood Cliffs, NJ: Prentice-Hall.

Survey Sampling, Inc. (1990). *A survey researcher's view of the U.S.* Fairfield, CT: Author.

Survey Research Center. (1976). *Interviewer's manual* (revised edition). Survey Research Center, Institute of Social Research, University of Michigan.

Swigonski, M.E. (1994). The logic of feminist standpoint theory for social work research. *Social Work, 39,* 737-741.

Taylor, J. (1977). Toward alternative forms of social work research: The case for naturalistic methods. *Journal of Social Welfare, 4,* 119-126.

Taylor, J. (1993). The naturalistic research approach. In R.M. Grinnell, Jr. (Ed.), *Social work research and evaluation* (4th ed., pp. 53-78). Itasca, IL: F.E. Peacock.

Taylor, S., & Bogdan, R. (1984). *Introduction to qualitative research methods: The search for meanings.* New York: Wiley.

Tesch, R. (1990). *Qualitative research: Analysis types and software tools.* New York: Falmer.

Thomas, E.J. (1975). Uses of research methods in interpersonal practice. In N.A. Polansky (Ed.), *Social work research: Methods for the helping professionals* (rev. ed., pp. 254-283). Chicago: University of Chicago Press.

Thorndike, R.L., & Hagen, E. (1969). *Measurement and evaluation in psychology and education* (3rd ed.). New York: Wiley.

Thyer, B.A. (1987). *Treating anxiety disorders: A guide for human service professionals.* Newbury Park, CA: Sage.

Thyer, B.A., & Curtis, G.C. (1983). The repeated pretest-posttest single-subject experiment: A new design for empirical clinical practice. *Journal of Behavior Therapy and Experimental Psychiatry, 14,* 311-315.

Thyer, B.A. (1993). Single-system research designs. In R.M. Grinnell, Jr. (Ed.), *Social work research and evaluation* (4th ed., pp. 94-117). Itasca, IL: F.E. Peacock.

Thyer, B.A., & Geller, E.S. (1987). The "buckle-up" dashboard sticker: An effective environmental intervention for safety belt promotion. *Environment and Behavior, 19,* 484-494.

Thyer, B.A., Geller, E.S., Williams, M., & Purcell, E. (1987). Community-based "flashing" to increase safety belt use. *Journal of Experimental Education, 55,* 155-159.

Thyer, B.A., Irvine, S., & Santa, C. (1984). Contingency management of exercise by chronic schizophrenics. *Perceptual and Motor Skills, 58,* 419-425.

Thyer, B.A., & Thyer, K.B. (1992). Single-system research designs in social work practice: A bibliography from 1965 to 1990. *Research on Social Work Practice, 2,* 99-116.

Todd, T.A., Joanning, H., Enders, L., Mutchler, L., & Thomas, F. N. (1990). Using ethnographic interviews to create a more cooperative client-therapist relationship. *Journal of Family Psychotherapy, 1,* 51-63.

Toseland, R.W. (1993). Choosing a data collection method. In R.M. Grinnell, Jr. (Ed.), *Social work research and evaluation* (4th ed., pp. 317-328). Itasca, IL: F.E. Peacock.

Tripodi, T. (1981). The logic of research design. In R.M. Grinnell, Jr. (Ed.), *Social work research and evaluation* (pp. 198-225). Itasca, IL: F.E. Peacock.

Tripodi, T. (1985). Research designs. In R.M. Grinnell, Jr. (Ed.), *Social work research and evaluation* (2nd ed., pp. 231-259). Itasca, IL: F.E. Peacock.

Tripodi, T., & Epstein, I. (1978). Incorporating knowledge of research methodology into social work practice. *Journal of Social Service Research, 2,* 11-23.

Tripodi, T., Fellin, P.A., & Meyer. H.J. (1983). *The assessment of social research* (2nd ed.). Itasca, IL: F.E. Peacock.

Tutty, L.M., Grinnell, R.M., Jr., & Williams, M. (1997). Research problems and questions. In R.M. Grinnell, Jr. (Ed.), *Social work research and evaluation: Quantitative and qualitative approaches* (5th ed., pp. 49-66). Itasca, IL: F.E. Peacock.

Tutty, L.M., Rothery, M.L., & Grinnell, R.M., Jr. (Eds.). (1996). *Qualitative research for social workers: Phases, steps, and tasks.* Boston: Allyn & Bacon.

Underwood, L., Figueroa, R.G., Thyer, B.A., & Nzeocha, A. (1989). Interruption and DRI in the treatment of self-injurious behavior among mentally retarded and autistic self-restrainers. *Behavior Modification, 13,* 471-481.

Unrau, Y.A. (1993). A program logic model approach to conceptualizing social service programs. *The Canadian Journal of Program Evaluation, 8,* 33-42.

Unrau, Y.A. (1994). Glossary. In P.A. Gabor & R.M. Grinnell, Jr. *Evaluation and quality improvement in the human services* (pp. 399-406). Boston: Allyn & Bacon.

Unrau, Y.A. (1997a). Implementing evaluations. In R.M. Grinnell, Jr. (Ed.), *Social work research and evaluation: Quantitative and qualitative approaches* (5th ed., pp. 588-604). Itasca, IL: F.E. Peacock.

Unrau, Y.A. (1997b). Selecting a data collection method and data source. In R.M. Grinnell, Jr. (Ed.), *Social work research and evaluation: Quantitative and qualitative approaches* (5th ed., pp. 458-472). Itasca, IL: F.E. Peacock.

Unrau, Y.A., & Coleman, H. (1997). Qualitative data analysis. In R.M. Grinnell, Jr. (Ed.), *Social work research and evaluation: Quantitative and qualitative approaches* (5th ed., pp. 501-472). Itasca, IL: F.E. Peacock.

Unrau, Y.A., & Gabor, P.A. (1997). Implementing evaluations. In R.M. Grinnell, Jr. (Ed.), *Social work research and evaluation: Quantitative and qualitative approaches* (5th ed., pp. 588-604). Itasca, IL: F.E. Peacock.

Unrau, Y.A., Gabor, P.A., & Grinnell, R.M., Jr. (2001). *Evaluation for social social workers: An introduction.* Itasca, IL: F.E. Peacock.

U.S. Bureau of the Census. (1987). *Statistical abstract of the United States, 1988.* Washington, DC: Author.

Valentine, C.A. (1971). The culture of poverty: Its scientific significance and its implications for action. In E.B. Leacock (Ed.). *The culture of poverty: A critique* (pp. 193-225). New York: Simon & Schuster.

Van Maanen, J. (1988). *Tales of the field: On writing ethnography.* Chicago: University of Chicago Press.

Van Maanen, J., Dabbs, J.M., Jr., & Faulkner, R.R. (Eds.). (1982). *Varieties of qualitative research.* Newbury Park, CA: Sage.

Vogt, W.P. (1993). *Dictionary of statistics and methodology: A nontechnical guide for the social sciences.* Newbury Park, CA: Sage.

Walker, L. (1979). *The battered woman.* New York: Harper & Row.

Warwick, D., & Lininger, C. (1975). *The sample survey: Theory and practice.* New York: McGraw-Hill.

Watts, T.D. (1985). Ethnomethodology. In R.M. Grinnell, Jr. (Ed.), *Social work research and evaluation* (2nd ed., pp. 357-369). Itasca, IL: F.E. Peacock.

Webb, E., Campbell, D., Schwartz, R., & Sechrest, L. (1966). *Unobtrusive measures: Nonreactive research in the social sciences.* Chicago: Rand McNally.

Weber, R.P. (1984). Computer-aided content analysis: A short primer. *Qualitative Sociology, 7,* 126-147.

Weinbach, R.W., & Grinnell, R.M., Jr. (1987). *Statistics for social workers.* White Plains, NY: Longman.

Weinbach, R.W., & Grinnell, R.M., Jr. (1991). *Statistics for social workers* (2nd ed.). White Plains, NY: Longman.

Weinbach, R.W., & Grinnell, R.M., Jr. (1995a). *Applying research knowledge: A workbook for social work students.* Boston: Allyn & Bacon.

Weinbach, R.W., & Grinnell, R.M., Jr. (1995b). *Statistics for social workers* (3rd ed.). White Plains, NY: Longman.

Weinbach, R.W., & Grinnell, R.M., Jr. (1996). Applying research knowledge: A workbook for social work students (2nd ed.). Boston: Allyn & Bacon.

Weinbach, R.W., & Grinnell, R.M., Jr. (2001). *Statistics for social workers* (5th ed.). Boston: Allyn & Bacon.

Weinbach, R.W., Grinnell, R.M., Jr., Unrau, Y.A., & Taylor, L. (1999). *Applying research knowledge: A workbook for social work students* (3rd ed.). Boston: Allyn & Bacon.

Weingarten, H.R. (1988). Late life divorce and the life review. *Journal of Gerontological Social Work, 12,* 83-97.

Weitzman, E.A., & Miles, M.B. (1995). *Computer programs for qualitative data analysis: A software sourcebook.* Newbury Park, CA: Sage.

White, K. (1988). Cost analyses in family support programs. In H.B. Weiss & F.H. Jacobs (Eds.), *Evaluating family programs* (pp. 429-443). New York: Aldine de Gruyter.

Wicker, A.W. (1981). Nature and assessment of behavior settings: Recent contributions from the ecological perspective. In P. McReynolds (Ed.), *Advances in psychological assessment* (Vol. 5, pp. 22-61). San Francisco: Jossey-Bass.

Wilkinson, W.K., & McNeil, K. (1997). Cultural factors related to research. In R.M. Grinnell, Jr. (Ed.), *Social work research and evaluation: Quantitative and qualitative approaches* (5th ed., pp. 605-630). Itasca, IL: F.E. Peacock.

Williams, M., Grinnell, R.M., Jr., & Tutty, L.M. (1997). Research contexts. In R.M. Grinnell, Jr. (Ed.), *Social work research and evaluation: Quantitative and qualitative approaches* (5th ed., pp. 25-46). Itasca, IL: F.E. Peacock.

Williams, M., Thyer, B.A., Bailey, J.S., & Harrison, D.F. (1989). Promoting safetybelt use with traffic signs and prompters. *Journal of Applied Behavior Analysis, 22,* 71-76.

Williams, M., Tutty, L.M., & Grinnell, R.M., Jr. (1995). *Research in social work: An introduction* (2nd ed.). Itasca, IL: F.E. Peacock.

Williams, M., Unrau, Y.A., & Grinnell, R.M., Jr. (1998). *Introduction to social work research.* Itasca, IL: F.E. Peacock.

Williamson, J.B., Karp, D.A., Dalphin, J.R., & Gray, P.S. (1982). *The research craft.* Boston: Little Brown.

Wong, S.E., Woolsey, J.E., & Gallegos, E. (1987). Behavioral treatment of chronic schizophrenic patients. *Journal of Social Service Research, 4,* 4-35.

Woodrum, E. (1984). Mainstreaming content analysis in social science: Methodological advantages, obstacles, and solutions. *Social Science Research, 13,* 1-19.

Yllo, K. (1988). Political and methodological debates in wife abuse research. In K. Yllo & M. Bograd (Eds.), *Feminist perspectives on wife abuse* (pp. 28-49). Newbury Park, CA: Sage.

Zook, A., Jr., & Sipps, G.J. (1985). Cross-validation of a short form of the Marlowe-Crowne social desirability scale. *Journal of Clinical Psychology, 41,* 236-238.

Zuckerman, M. (1990). Some dubious premises in research and theory on racial differences. *American Psychologist, 45,* 1297-1303.

Credits

Figure 15.3: Adapted from: Shirley Jenkins and Elaine Norman, *Filial deprivation and foster care.* Copyright © 1972. Reprinted by permission of the publisher, Columbia University Press.

Figure 15.4: Adapted from: Harvey H. Gochros, "Research Interviewing." In Richard .M. Grinnell, Jr. (Ed.), *Social work research and evaluation* (3rd ed). Itasca, IL: F.E. Peacock.

Figures 15.5-15.8: Adapted from: Michael J. Austin and Jill Crowell, "Survey Research," in Richard M. Grinnell, Jr. (Ed.), *Social work research and evaluation* (2nd ed.). Copyright © 1985 by F.E. Peacock Publishers.

Figures 15.9 & 15.10: Adapted from: Don A. Dillman, *Mail and telephone surveys: The total design method.* Copyright © 1978 by John Wiley & Sons, Inc. Reprinted by permission of John Wiley & Sons, Inc.

Figure 23.1: Adapted from: A. Sluckin, "Behavioral Social Work Treatment of Childhood Nocturnal Enuresis," *Behavior Modification, vol. 13* (1989), pp. 482-497. Used with permission.

Figure 23.2: Adapted from: Bruce A. Thyer, *Treating Anxiety Disorders: A Guide for Human Service Professionals* (Newbury Park, CA: Sage, 1987), p. 49. Used with permission.

Figure 23.3: Adapted from: S.E. Wong, J.E. Woolsey, and E. Gallegos, "Behavioral Treatment of Chronic Schizophrenic Patients," *Journal of Social Service Research, vol. 10* (2/3/4), (1987), pp. 7-35. Used with permission.

Figure 23.4: Adapted from: Bruce A. Thyer, "Single-Subject Designs in Clinical Social Work: A Practitioner's Perspective," in H.R. Johnson and J.R. Tropman (Eds.), *Social Work Policy and Practice: A Knowledge-Driven Approach* (Ann Arbor, MI: The University of Michigan School of Social Work, 1987), pp. 292-310. Used with permission.

Figure 23.5: Adapted from: B.A. Thyer and E. S. Geller, "The "Buckle-up" Dashboard Sitcker: An Effective Environmental Intervention for Safety Belt Promotion," *Environment and Behavior, vol. 19* (1987), pp. 484-494. Used with permission.

Figure 23.6: Adapted from: J.T. Stocks, B.A. Thyer, and M.A. Kearsley, "Using a Token Economy in a Community-Based Residential Program for Disabled Adults: An Empirical Evaluation Leads to Program Modification," *Behavioral Residential Treatment, vol. 1* (1987), pp. 173-185. Used with permission.

Figure 23.7: Adapted from: L. Underwood, R.G. Figueroa, B.A. Thyer, and A. Nzeocha, "Interruption and DRI in the Treatment of Self-Injurious Behavior among Mentally Retarded and Autistic Self-Restrainers," *Behavior Modification, vol. 13* (1989), pp. 471-481. Used with permission.

Figure 23.8: Adapted from: Nell Maeser and Bruce A. Thyer, "Teaching Boys with Severe Retardation to Serve Themselves during Family-Style Meals," *Behavioral Residential Treatment, vol. 5* (1990), pp. 239-246. Used with permission.

Figure 23.9: Adapted from: Melvin Williams, B.A. Thyer, J.S. Bailey, and D.F. Harrison, "Promoting Safety Belt Use with Traffic Signs and Prompters," *Journal of Applied Behavior Analysis, vol. 22* (1989), pp. 71-76. Used with permission.

Figure 23.10: Richard A. Polster and Mary Ann Lynch, "Single-Subject Designs," in R. M. Grinnell, Jr. (Ed.), *Social Work Research and Evaluation* (Itasca, IL: F E. Peacock Publishers, 1981), p. 410.

Chapter 1: Adapted and modified from: "Becoming a knowledge-based social worker," by Richard M. Grinnell, Jr, in Richard M. Grinnell, Jr. (Ed.), *Social work research and evaluation.* Copyright © 1981 by F.E. Peacock Publishers; "Becoming a practitioner/ researcher," by Richard M. Grinnell, Jr., in Richard M. Grinnell, Jr. (Ed.), *Social work research and evaluation* (2nd ed.). Copyright © 1985 by F.E. Peacock Publishers; "The generation of knowledge," by Richard M. Grinnell, Jr., in Richard M. Grinnell, Jr. (Ed.), *Social work research and evaluation: Quantitative and qualitative approaches* (5th ed.). Copyright © 1997 by F.E. Peacock Publishers; "Research in social work," by Richard M. Grinnell, Jr., Michael A. Rothery, and Ray J. Thomlison, in Richard M. Grinnell, Jr. (Ed.), *Social work research and evaluation* (4th ed.). Copyright © 1993 by F.E. Peacock Publishers; *Research in social work: A primer*, by Richard M. Grinnell, Jr. and Margaret Williams. Copyright © 1990 by F.E. Peacock Publishers; *Research in social work: An introduction* (2nd ed.), by Margaret Williams, Leslie M. Tutty, and Richard M. Grinnell, Jr. Copyright © 1995 by F.E. Peacock Publishers; and *Introduction to social work research*, by Margaret Williams, Yvonne A. Unrau, and Richard M. Grinnell, Jr. Copyright © 1998 by F.E. Peacock Publishers.

Chapter 2: Adapted from: Russell H. Schutt, *Investigating the social world* (2nd ed.). Copyright © 2000 by Pine Forge Press. Used with permission.

Chapter 5: Adapted from: David E. Cournoyer and Waldo C. Klein, *Research methods for social work.* Copyright © 2000 by Allyn & Bacon. Used with permission.

Chapter 6: Adapted from: *Introduction to social work research*, by Margaret Williams, Yvonne A. Unrau, and Richard M. Grinnell, Jr. Copyright © 1998 by F.E. Peacock Publishers.

Chapter 12: Adapted from: "Utilizing research designs," by Richard M. Grinnell, Jr. and Margaret Stothers, in *Social work research and evaluation* (3rd ed.). Copyright © 1988 by F.E. Peacock Publishers; "Group research designs," by Richard M. Grinnell, Jr., in Richard M. Grinnell, Jr. (Ed.), *Social work research and*

Index

SOCIAL WORK RESEARCH AND EVALUATION:

QUANTITATIVE AND QUALITATIVE APPROACHES

Sixth Edition

Edited by John Beasley

Production supervision by Kim Vander Steen

Cover design by Cynthia Crampton, Park Ridge, Illinois

Internal design and composition by Grinnell, Inc., Dallas, Texas

Printed and bound by McNaughton & Gunn, Saline, Michigan